Writing New Identities

Writing New Identities

Gender, Nation, and Immigration in Contemporary Europe

Gisela Brinker-Gabler and
Sidonie Smith, editors

University of Minnesota Press
Minneapolis
London

Published by the University of Minnesota Press
111 Third Avenue South, Suite 290, Minneapolis, MN 55401-2520
Printed in the United States of America on acid-free paper

Library of Congress Cataloging-in-Publication Data

Writing new identities : gender, nation, and immigration in contemporary
Europe / Gisela Brinker-Gabler and Sidonie Smith, editors.
    p.   cm.
    Includes bibliographical references (p.   ) and index.
    ISBN 0-8166-2460-7 (hard : alk. paper). —ISBN 0-8166-2461-5
(pbk. : alk. paper)
    1. Europe—Emigration and immigration. 2. Migration, Internal—
Europe. 3. Nationalism—Europe. 4. Ethnicity—Europe. 5. Europe—
Social conditions—20th century. 6. Emigration and immigration in
literature. 7. Nationalism in literature. 8. Women in literature.
I. Brinker-Gabler, Gisela. II. Smith, Sidonie.
JV7590.W75   1997
304.8'2'094—dc20   96-26047

The University of Minnesota is an equal-opportunity educator and employer.

To Charlotte and Kathryn

Contents

Acknowledgments   xi

Introduction
Gender, Nation, and Immigration in the New Europe
Sidonie Smith and Gisela Brinker-Gabler   1

Part I.   **Post/Coloniality in the New Europe**

1 / Ethnicity on the French Frontier
Winifred Woodhull   31

2 / Narrative Strategies and Postcolonial
Identity in Contemporary France:
Leïla Sebbar's *Les Carnets de Shérazade*
Françoise Lionnet   62

3 / (Con)figuring Identity:
Cultural Space of the Indo-British Border Intellectual
Gita Rajan   78

4 / Black British Women Writing the
Anti-Imperialist Critique
Carole Boyce Davies   100

5 / Looking through Non-Western Eyes:
Immigrant Women's Autobiographical Narratives in Italian
Graziella Parati   118

6 / Exile in the Promised Land: Self-Decolonization
and Bodily Re-Membering in Ken Bugul's *The Abandoned Baobab*
Julia Watson   143

Part II. **The New Europe and Its Old Margins**

7 / Reclaiming Space: Jewish Women in Germany Today
Karen Remmler   171

8 / Hidden Subjects, Secret Identities: Figuring Jews, Gypsies,
and Gender in 1990s Cinema of Eastern Europe
Catherine Portuges   196

9 / Migrants' Literature or German Literature?
Torkan's *Tufan: Brief an einen islamischen Bruder*
Leslie A. Adelson   216

10 / Scheherazade's Daughters: The Thousand and
One Tales of Turkish-German Women Writers
Azade Seyhan   230

11 / "Life from Its Very Beginning at Its End":
The Unhomely Boundaries in the Works of
Bulgarian Author Blaga Dimitrova
Hannelore Scholz   249

12 / Exile, Immigrant, Re/Unified:
Writing (East) Postunification Identity in Germany
Gisela Brinker-Gabler   264

Part III. Nationalisms, Gender, and Sexualities

13 / EU-phoria? Irish National Identity, European Union,
and *The Crying Game*
Katrina Irving   295

14 / Maternal Abject, Fascist Apocalypse, and Daughter
Separation in Contemporary Swedish Novels
Ebba Witt-Brattström   315

15 / *Ona:* The New *Elle*-Literacy and the Post-Soviet Woman
Greta N. Slobin   337

16 / What Are Women Made Of? Inventing
Women in the Yugoslav Area
Svetlana Slapšak   358

Contributors   375

Index   379

Acknowledgments

In 1991, Gisela Brinker-Gabler organized a conference, "The Question of the Other," that drew scholars from various global locations together to explore experiences of otherness and cultural contact, the consequences of the homogenizing force of cultural domination, and possibilities for transformative resistance. After that conference we started thinking about a collaborative project that would respond to the dramatic changes taking place in "the New Europe." Gradually the idea took shape to seek essays that would consider how the languages of nationalism inform gendered self-representations in a variety of cultural forms—in autobiography, film, magazines, and novels.

We wanted from the first to find scholars working in Europe as well as in the United States and to include essays on cultural practices not only in the old Western Europe but also the newly reconfigured Eastern Europe and the former Soviet Union. Thus we have depended for guidance upon several colleagues and reviewers to whom we would like to offer our thanks. Sander Gilman read the incomplete early draft of this project and helped us broaden our net of contacts. He directed us to Karen Remmler. Toril Moi directed us to scholars in Denmark and Sweden and helped us find Ebba Witt-Brattström. Petar Ramadanovic recommended that we contact Svetlana Slapšak, with whom he had studied in the former Yugoslavia before coming to the graduate program in comparative literature at Binghamton University.

Our very special thanks go to Biodun Iginla, former senior acquisitions editor at the University of Minnesota Press, for his unqualified commitment to this project and for his intelligence, breadth of knowledge, and commitment to global theoretical studies. And we owe thanks to his assistant, Elizabeth Knoll Stomberg, for her assiduous attention to detail and her patience.

Introduction

Gender, Nation, and Immigration in the New Europe

Sidonie Smith and Gisela Brinker-Gabler

In this last decade of the twentieth century, large-scale political realignments have accelerated the pace of changes across Europe. In 1989 the Iron Curtain opened and the Berlin Wall came down. Six months later Eastern European countries had extracted themselves from the Soviet sphere. Fifteen months later Germany reunified. Twenty-four months later the Warsaw Pact dissolved. Thirty months later the Soviet Union became a federation. All during this period Western Europeans debated vigorously and then voted, if not by large majorities, for the new transnational European Union.

As they continue to debate the advantages and the threats of European federation, peoples of different nations address changing notions of community, renegotiate borders and territory, imagine new markets, and adjust to the transformations wrought by the dissolution of the Communist bloc. Through these debates people revive and refashion the various bases upon which community has been imagined. Across Europe there are calls for traditional national identities, proposals for new forms of transnational community, and assertions of regionalized corporate identities.

These debates take place in an increasingly multicultural environment. For in the last two decades large numbers of immigrants, migrant workers, and

1

asylum seekers have sought safety, economic opportunity, and refuge in the nations of Europe. Algerians, Moroccans, and Ethiopians have migrated to France and Italy. Peoples from the Caribbean Islands nations have migrated to Britain and to France, former colonial centers. Earlier on people from Italy, Greece, Spain, and Yugoslavia and more recently people from Turkey have traveled north to Germany to become "guest workers." In addition, over one million refugees from the former Yugoslavia and migrants from Eastern and Central Europe continue to search for new homes in Western Europe.

The collapse of Eastern European state socialism, the massive immigration into Western Europe, and the emergence of a federated Europe with a common market all focus renewed attention on issues of national histories and transnational futures. This volume of essays attends to this critical moment at the end of the twentieth century. And it does so by assaying the mutually constitutive nature of nationalism, multiculturalism, and gender in the writing of new European subjects.

The History of Nationalism

"Germany for Germans, foreigners out!"
—Rostock demonstrators, August 1992

"I will only accept a united Europe like that of Charlemagne—one ruled by France."   —French doctor, quoted in Alan Riding,
New York Times, September 13, 1992

As relatively recent phenomena, "nations" are implicated in the history of modernity itself (Smith, 73).[1] They are, as Bill Schwarz suggests, "one form in which modern cultures have been articulated" (202). In a provocative analysis of this phenomenon, Benedict Anderson teases out the preconditions of modern nation-building in the West: the demise of Latin as a universal language, the emergence of a new sense of time, and the rise of print capitalism and its efficient reproduction of vernacular texts. According to Anderson, "The lexicographic revolution . . . created, and gradually spread, the conviction that languages (in Europe at least) were, so to speak, the personal property of quite specific groups—their daily speakers and readers—and moreover that these groups, imagined as communities, were entitled to their autonomous place in a fraternity of equals" (84). As they consumed the outpourings of print capitalism, the literate middle classes began to understand themselves as communities of individuals, unknown to one another, yet held together "by vernacular legibilities" (77). In the first half of the nineteenth century European vernacular communities, communities forged through legibilities, had available to them certain "blueprints" for nation-building, blueprints imported from the Americas, blueprints ready for "pirating" (80–82).[2]

Now, some two hundred years after the emergence of the modern nation, many and diverse strands of identification combine to sustain the imagined community. Since not all nationalisms are founded upon the same discourses of identity and difference, the ways in which groups of people construct national identities and understand themselves as national subjects are complex, various, and differentially intersected with other understandings of identity. They are, as well, imbricated in different histories.[3] So it is important to look at what is included in a specific iteration of nationalism's identity contents (such contents as language, ethnicity, territory, history, religion, values, traditions, and so on) and what is excluded.

Friedrich Heckmann delineates three concepts of nationalism specific to Western Europe. "Ethnic nationalism" is founded on what Heckmann calls "ethnicity," that is, common language, customs, and history. As political ideology it seeks congruence of national borders with ethnic borders. This imagining of nationalism developed in eighteenth-century Germany as an intellectual movement directed against the "Frenchness" of an oppressive feudal culture. Only later in the nineteenth century did it become a political ideology and a mass social movement (63). Once institutionalized as a state nationalism, ethnic nationalism establishes citizenship on the basis of ethnicity. Thus national subjects share a common descent and a collective memory that binds them into an indissoluble whole. In this ethnocentric ideology, national identity is originary.

Heckmann differentiates two kinds of political nationalisms from ethnic nationalism. While both are founded upon common values, institutions, and political ideology rather than common descent, one promotes a demotic-unitarian concept of community and the other an ethnic-plural concept. The demotic-unitarian nation emerged out of the upheavals of bourgeois revolutions, such as the one that occurred in France. Citizenship in France, for instance, is not based on ethnic origin. Rather it is based on the individual's acceptance of the progressive, rationalist, and universalistic values of the enlightened nation-state. Any individual can become a citizen of the state by becoming *like,* that is, by assimilating as one and the same. However, in the demotic-unitarian state a national language is central (71). "One is French," according to D. Schnapper (whom Heckmann cites), "since one speaks the language, since one has interiorized the culture, since one wants to participate in the political and economical life" (23; quoted in Heckmann, 72).

In contrast, the polyethnic state, like Switzerland, is a political community imaginatively forged not through common descent or through common language but through common political traditions, institutions, and an invented corporate history. As Anderson points out, "The appearance of Swiss nationalism on the eve of the communications revolution of the twentieth century made it possible and practical to 'represent' the imagined community in ways that did not require linguistic uniformity" (139). Ethnic differences are embraced. Yet only certain ethnicities constitute this polyethnic state. There has been no invitation to multiply ethnicities.

To these three nationalisms characterizing many states in Western Europe we would add another, the coerced polyethnic nationalism forged out of revolution, war, and "realpolitik." The Soviet Union, Yugoslavia, and Czechoslovakia were formerly states joined by political exigency and/or external domination in service to an ideological call for socialist revolution. Throughout the last half-century authoritarian control maintained national stability in service to a common future by suppressing differences (differences in histories, languages, ethnicities, religious affiliations, and traditions) that threatened to fracture solidarity and socialist union.

If the practical result of the call for a socialist revolution was the Russification of disparate peoples under the sign of a Soviet Union or the joining of disparate peoples under the sign of Yugoslavia, the ideological call remained a utopian gesture of "internationalism," a call for socialist community beyond national borders and identities. Schwarz traces this call for internationalism to the generation of cosmopolitan political revolutionaries coming of age in the early twentieth century. These leaders promoted "a more generous internationalism," founded upon a global community of workers undivided by their "regional, ethnic, national" identifications (201). In fact, nationalism was considered retrograde, bourgeois, and detrimental to the betterment of the lives of workers. Greater social and economic good would flow from the expansion of community to a transnational union of workers.

In the East this discursive promotion of an international working class and the dream of internationalism sustained rhetorically the imagined community of the discrete socialist state. Yet now various peoples are rejecting an expedient polyethnic nationalism in pursuit of localized dreams of ethnic and cultural nationalisms. Nations forged together for forty to seventy years have split apart, sometimes peacefully, as happened in the former Czechoslovakia and parts of the Commonwealth of Independent States, and sometimes violently, as has happened in Chechnya. The large Hungarian and Turkish populations in Romania consider the formation of separatist movements or press for a redrawing of national boundaries along ethnic lines. Kosovo has been claimed by Albania on geographic grounds and on historic grounds by Serbian nationalists. Europe (along with the world) watches as the former Yugoslavia struggles with peace after a war waged by new nationalists who suppressed the recent history of peaceful cohabitation in ethnically mixed areas in service to the mythology of an ethnically pure, or "natural" (Schwarz, 204), history of the land.[4]

If in the East this dream of international "brotherhood" has faded, in the West the impetus to forge a European "family of nations," a notion embedded in early Enlightenment thinking about "nation,"[5] has intensified in the last decades. Since World War II, politicians and financiers in European countries have been busy assembling the blueprint for a "United States of Europe." The earliest plans focused on the need for a united front against an aggressive Communist bloc and the containment of a destructive German nationalism. But with the easy movement of information, goods, and capital around the globe and the recognition that, in this global environment, nations can benefit from alliances with other nations that share common concerns or common commodities, the focus now centers on the promise of greater competitive clout in the economic struggle with the United States and Japan as well as the containment of German economic power. This promise of economic superpower status, evidenced in the enthusiasm of economists such as Lester Thurow—"With judicious expansion, there is no reason why the house of Europe could not be by far the largest and most prosperous economic region in the world" (76)—drives discourses of familial transnationalism.

Interestingly, national interests encourage the imagining of transnational union. Yet the closer European union looms, the more fragile the sense of national identity becomes, even as union is meant to strengthen constituent nations. Bit by bit the forging of a federated Europe erodes the sovereignty of participant nations (to level taxes, establish border controls, mint currency, regulate trade, and determine citizenship status)[6] and erodes the sense of a specifically national identity. This threat to national identity permeated debates in France in anticipation of the referendum on the Maastricht Treaty. Opponents of Maastricht argued vigorously that a common currency and a federated Europe would effectively render the life of rural France a thing of the past. The implication in such arguments is that the "essence" of Frenchness (rural French life) would be lost in union. "Behind the debates on Europe," Schwarz concludes, "lurks a more fundamental question about the conditions of existence of national cultures" (206–7).

Nationalism and Immigration

We don't want to see the multiracial nightmare come to Britain.
—Representative of the National Party in Britain

On the eve of the vote in France on the Maastricht Treaty, both sides, those supporting the treaty and those arguing vigorously against it, invoked the Rostock riots in Germany in support of their case. In the outbreak of violence against immigrants the French saw the return of earlier twentieth-century German aggression and national xenophobia. And so those who supported the treaty described a federated Europe as a means to contain German nationalism. If the price was some loss of French sovereignty, the price was worth paying. For others, renewed German xenophobia could only be countered by a fortified French nationalism. Maastricht had to be defeated. As this debate reveals, the arguments of nationalists and transnationalists are inflected in complex and often contradictory ways with the history of national figurings of the "foreigner" in Europe.

In the nineteenth century and the first half of the twentieth century Europe was an exporting country in terms of immigration. People left Europe to escape poverty, famine, lack of opportunities, religious persecution, or enforced conscription. Many moved to European colonies in Africa, India, and South America. Many sought new lives in the United States, Canada, Australia, and New Zealand. With the current prosperity of Europe and its colonialist legacies, that direction has now reversed. In the last decade of the twentieth century Europe is the destination for increasing numbers of immigrants and migrant workers. For Umberto Eco, the massive migration of Africans toward Europe, for example, is a phenomenon far more significant than the "crisis of communism" in Eastern Europe.

Peoples from former colonies make the journey to metropolitan centers, to Italy, France, England, and the Netherlands. Migrants from the south join the temporary workers already resident in many countries. Political refugees from the former Yugoslavia and Romania seek asylum in the West. Eastern and Central Europeans migrate westward in search of "the better life." These new immigrants join other groups of immigrants, among them an earlier generation, the avant-garde intellectuals who relocated in Europe, but most specifically in France and England, in the 1950s and 1960s. Now in the mid-1990s there are upwards of 15 million foreign nationals resident in European countries. In France, the figure is 3 million immigrants in a population of 55 million; in England 3 million in a population of 60 million; and in Germany 7 million in a population of 79 million.

In response to the social unrest attending the increase in immigrant and migrant worker populations, European Community nations have strictly limited the bases for legal immigration. In the 1980s France and Britain tightened immigration laws in response to increased immigration from former colonies. Recently, in Germany, the Netherlands, and France, asylum laws have been modified and broader questions of citizenship reopened. The Martelli Law in Italy has put severe restrictions on immigration from North and West Africa through the regulation of visas. "As internal borders become lower, the external borders become higher," reflects Jan Nederveen Pieterse, to which he adds: "Fortress Europe is becoming a reality" (5).

Official explanations for the increase in restrictions emphasize the escalation of violence directed at immigrants and migrant workers. Restrictions are seen as means to curb such violent outbreaks. But the containment of violence functions also as a screen for the containment of the "foreign" within, since restrictions establish categories of the included and the excluded. The very metanarrative of national identity depends upon the representation of the foreign. "Implying 'some element of alterity for its definition,' " suggest the editors of *Nationalisms and Sexualities,* "a nation is ineluctably 'shaped by what it opposes.' . . . Hence, on the one hand, the nation's insatiable need to administer difference through violent acts of segregation, censorship, economic coercion, physical torture, police brutality. And hence, on the other, the nation's insatiable need for representational labor to supplement its founding ambivalence, the lack of self-presence at its origin or in its essence" (Parker et al., 5). Because European nations have not understood themselves as countries of immigration, immigrants are represented as "foreigners." In "Fortress Europe," the immanent "foreign" has become the immigrant/migrant within the borders of the nation.

In bureaucratic and legalistic arenas, the proliferation of laws and regulations function to differentiate the "citizen" from the "noncitizen" and to contain the "foreign" in a clear and efficient hierarchy of categories of people. But there are many other means of containment, not least of which is the way in which "citizens" create the "foreigner within" as a scapegoat for disaffection, instability, poverty—all that is wrong with the imagined community. In relatively wealthy Sweden, young people who do not have access to housing resent the state's willingness to allocate scarce housing stock to new immigrants. Those who relocate in Germany confront there the hostility of former East Germans, for whom the dream of unification, driven by the founding assumptions of cultural nationalism, has faded with the insistent realities of economic dislocation. In Rostock and other "East" German cities, disaffected youths joined skinheads and right-wing organizers in burning projects housing immigrants. Others watched passively as the violence unfolded to the sound of the refrain, "Germany for Germans, foreigners out!"[7] Resentment toward foreigners in Germany has turned into murderous xenophobia, as the deaths of Turkish women and children in housing torched by neo-Nazis in Moelln and Solingen demonstrate.

But the violence is not limited to Germany. In France, as in Germany, new waves of anti-Semitism mark the renewal of a millennial figuring of the foreign. Often the violence is directed at Jewish cemeteries, where the desecration of the place of the dead strikes at the core of the sacred (and the site of religious difference). In France racial violence is directed at immigrants from North Africa, who are charged with "the Islamization of France." Such threats of an "unnatural" transformation of national character screen the everyday uncertainties attending the transformation to a postindustrial Europe (Lloyd and Waters, 62–63). In England racially motivated murders are on the increase. Of course, there is always the solution of Finland. Admit no immigrants; remain a monoculture.

But that has not been the choice, or a real possibility, for other countries, especially those whose histories include colonial rule. Now post/colonial encounters take place "at home" in the metropolitan centers, with profound effects for the imagining of national identity. "This re-enactment of the primal colonial encounter between black and white on the territory of the metropolitan homeland itself," observes Schwarz, "force[s] the members of the declining nation to imagine themselves, in a new way, as white" (205). Not only have the "ends" of the empire been brought home, in several senses of the term, but, in addition, the legacies of colonial rule have profoundly destabilized "older, more global imperial identities" (Schwarz, 206) and have made "visible" the racial nature of the old national identity and the multicultural ruptures of the new.

Inevitably, discursive constructions of the immigrant and of multiculturalism inflect discourses of nationalism, but differentially and incommensurably. Let us consider, then, what kinds of attitudes toward immigration and multiculturalism play through the various nationalisms we sketched in the first section.

If the basis of national identity is linked to common descent and culture, then the introduction of large numbers of immigrants into the imagined community threatens to destabilize national identity by disrupting cultural homogeneity. If citizenship in the "ethnic national state" is assigned to people on the basis of an originary ethnicity, then certain immigrants might be awarded citizenship (for example, the ethnic Germans from Eastern European countries in the case of Germany), but others would always be identified in their difference as an ethnic minority within the ethnic nation (for instance, Turkish guest workers in Germany). Conversely, the awarding of citizenship to large numbers of immigrants would signal a new notion of nation and would call for an act of reimagining. In response to this threat to an originary national identity, officials can close borders to immigrants. Or they can, as Germany did, develop a system of "demand-oriented recruitment" through which workers from other countries enter as "guests," who must then, as Heidrun Suhr points out, "accept and adapt to the conditions of the moment" (77).[8] Or they can, again as Germany has done, pay for the deportation of "foreigners" to their "homelands."[9]

If the debates about immigration proceed from the liberal Enlightenment notion of nation as a community imagined on the basis of common values, institutions, and political convictions rather than common descent, then the debates about immigration come to focus on the process and the practices of "assimilation" (the term current in France) or "integration" (the term current in Germany). Supposedly, anyone (an immigrant from anywhere) can become a citizen, so long as he or she accepts the common values and lives "by the standards and basic codes of the national community ('France,' say) with which [persons], by choosing to live there, have signalled affiliation" (Bammer, 58).[10]

But this notion of assimilation is a problematic one. Grounded on the discourse of universalism, it operates always unidirectionally. It assumes the resolvability of difference, its erasure in the becoming like, becoming the same. A stable, essential, unified national identity absorbs, refines, and neutralizes difference, but remains itself unchanged by those differences. Yet in the cultural imaginary differences may never be fully resolvable. Immigrants—first-generation immigrants especially but also second-generation immigrants—make differences everywhere manifest, differences in behaviors, in foods, and in music and cultural forms, as well as in physiology. Since some immigrants and their descendants might display an identity distinct from the imagined national identity, there is always something—some behavior, some activity, some linguistic inflection, some mark of difference—that can be defined as the not-assimilated. The marks of a visible difference are taken to figure an essential, nonassimilable difference. So differences are ultimately irresolvable. And immigrants themselves, and their descendants, may choose not to assimilate but to maintain their cultural specificity, their languages, customs, practices, and religions.

In a polyethnic state such as Switzerland, the stability of the nation is posited upon the stability of the polyethnic balance. Here the multiculturalism matrix is strictly delimited and immigration policy is designed to maintain the balance. And in the coerced polyethnic communities now breaking apart in Eastern Europe, the very boundaries of the nation are redrawn through violence in order to fit geography to ethnicity and to secure ethnicity in geography. These are arenas in which nationalist discourses materialize in violence, violence that leads to the making of refugees rather than the taking in of refugees or immigrants. The "foreigner" within, and thus multiculturalism itself, is forced out. This violent expulsion of the other within is the outcome of what Etienne Balibar has called nationalism's inevitable relationship with racism, a relationship grounded on a fictive concept of ethnicity. "Racism," he argues, "is not an 'expression' of nationalism, but a supplement of nationalism or more precisely a supplement internal to nationalism, always in excess of it, but always indispensable to its constitution" (54).

But let us consider as well how "the immigrant" troubles the discourses of transnational European community. For opponents to transnationalism, European union will invite increased immigration of peoples from North Africa and from Eastern Europe as people flee to the economically more stable and richer countries. Increased numbers of immigrants will increase pressure on national resources, and the promise of the federation's added prosperity will remain unrealized. For those who imagine the new transnational community positively, only a united Europe will be able to help stabilize other countries and thereby interrupt the flow of immigration. "Until people can live well in their own countries, we'll never stop them from coming here," argued a supporter of the Maastricht Treaty (Riding). From both sides, the immigrant becomes the sign of foreign disruption threatening on the one hand a national and on the other a familial transnational identity and destiny. For both, it is desirable to keep "the foreign" out, if by different means.

Gender and Nationalism

Poles are cheaper than Asians both in terms of capital investment and in mainte-nance: what is a cheap train ticket in comparison to a 5,000 DM air ticket from Bangkok or Manila? And, whereas a Thai is unprepared for cold German win-ters—one has to buy her clothes—a Pole brings her own boots and a fur coat. And she is as good in bed and industrious in the kitchen.

    —Bild-Zeitung, January 9, 1991 (Quoted in Morokvasic, 69)

In *Nationalism and Sexuality: Middle-Class Morality and Sexual Norms in Mod-ern Europe,* George L. Mosse tracks the coterminous rise of a concept of nation-alism in Europe and the cultural construction of a bourgeois morality founded on normative gender identities and essentialized sexual differences. He explores how during the eighteenth century the middle classes legitimized and defined themselves against the aristocracy and lower classes through a code of morality based on "virtuous" men and "pure" women. These gender "characters" became increasingly polarized through the subsequent division of labor, dissociation of private and public spheres, and emergence of the modern family. Around 1800, manliness (that is, activity, rationality) and femininity (passivity, emotionality) were "adopted" by nationalism as a foundation around which "to build its na-tional stereotypes" (10).[11]

    Other scholars have turned their attention as well to the systems of cultural representations through which nationalism and gender become mutually constitutive locations of social construction (Hausen; Janssen-Jurreit; Riley; Yuval-Davis and Anthias). As Anne McClintock emphasizes, "nationalism is . . . constituted from the very beginning as a gendered discourse, and cannot be understood without a theory of gender power" (63). Various forms of na-tionalism secure and in turn depend upon specific constructions of femininity, masculinity, and normative sexuality. But as the editors of the more recent *Na-tionalisms and Sexualities* remind us, different forms of nationalism promote and depend upon different forms of sexuality, and the discourses of nationalism invoke various, sometimes contradictory, discourses of gender.

    We can rehearse here only briefly some ways in which national identities are gendered and sexualities collectivized. Take, for instance, those discourses of nationalism that name and allegorize the nation as female: Germania, Britan-nia, Marianne/La France. (In France the specificities of gender-marked lan-guage collude in feminization.) In this way the nation is constituted as the ideal feminine in what becomes a chivalric romance of national identity, and na-tional citizens assume the role of adoring man. Or consider the discourses of conquest that have often assigned an inviting yet passive femininity to the land. The land is there to be penetrated, explored and mapped, subdued, and then domesticated in service to nation. In this discourse, the making of the nation becomes a masculine activity, and the land upon which nation is constituted is feminized, first under the sign of the seductive virgin and then under the sign of the nurturing mother. Once the nation is founded and the land domesticated, the nation becomes "motherland." Metaphorizing geography in such a way posits a primal, essential, universal, and emotional linkage of individuals to "the mother," to "the motherland" (see, for instance, Koontz), and thus to national identity.

In this context, the national language becomes the mother tongue. As mother tongue, language is identified with infancy, early memory, and the very sound of the mother's voice. Additionally, as Anderson notes, since "no one can give the date for the birth of any language," the basis of a national identity secured in a mother tongue seems ahistorical, natural, primordial, or, as he notes, "horizonless." Linking memory to nationalism thus reinforces the concept of nation as an essentialized, indistinct, horizonless remembered past, an antique concept secured by the long umbilical cord of linguistic signs. Linkages to motherland and mother tongue emphasize the primal dimension of national identity over other kinds of identities. National identity is thereby "naturalized." Without attention to the way in which he glosses the centrality of ideologies of gender, Anderson concludes his discussion of patriotism thus: "Through that language, encountered at the mother's knee and parted with only at the grave, pasts are restored, fellowships are imagined, and futures dreamed" (154).

In other discourses of nationalism, the family works as trope for the nation. One iteration of the family trope operates to naturalize what McClintock describes as "social *hierarchy* within a putative *organic unity* of interests" (64). That is, the traditional hierarchical relationship of children to parents and wife to husband provides a familial metaphor through which to legitimate sociopolitical hierarchies, or differences, within the nation. Another iteration of the trope works to emphasize the homogeneity of citizens: they are one in blood, or one family sharing a common history or inheritance, or siblings sharing the mother tongue, or the like. In times of trouble, as Anderson notes, the "vocabulary of kinship" (143) and the resonance of "home" calls people to risible patriotism. Both vocabularies of kinship and of home "denote something to which one is naturally tied" (143). In the latter case there can be no nation without "home,"

home both as consciousness of secure locatedness and as material site. In the former instance, the ties of nation, like the ties of kinship, are unchosen. Thus, according to Anderson, there is a sense of fatality about national identity as there is a fatality about the ties of kinship. Neither is chosen; both are inherited. Since fatality lies outside the realm of choice and agency, national identity seems "natural." And this kind of fatality lies close to the fatality of a "femininity" and "motherhood" aligned almost exclusively with the natural world.

Recourse to the trope of kinship generates another set of metaphorical relationships between nationalism and gender, that is, the relationship of the "family" to the state. If familial and national identity mutually attest one another in certain discourses of nationalism, then the right or wrong workings of families and the proper relationships among family members variously signify the stabilities and instabilities of the nation-state. The calls for a potent nation-state are often metaphorized as the call for stable bourgeois families, families in which individuals fill their proper roles for the good of the state. If the nation is the enshrined "mother" sanctioning this fellowship, then the stability of its "proper" functioning depends upon the degree to which the nation's real women embrace the identity and enact the destiny of the idealized "mother" (Parker et al., 6). Homology begets national identity.

This relationship between a stabilized national context and the proper mother is particularly prominent in postrevolutionary moments. The restoration of order in the body politic and the consolidation of the bourgeois state after the American revolution, for instance, glorified what Betsy Erkkila calls the "virtuous republican mother" (219).[12] And oppositional nationalist discourses, forged in the history of colonialism, invoke the priority and purity of traditional familial relationships as constitutive of the postcolonial nation. The power of the new nation is the power to recover the old traditions, those put under erasure or destabilized during the Westernization forced through colonial policies. Traditional families, made up of people who assume appropriately feminine and masculine roles, become the stabilizing bedrock of the new nation.[13]

If the family is set in homologous relationship to the state in certain nationalist discourses, it is also set in opposition to the state in other discourses, particularly those of citizenship. In the liberal ideology through which the notion of nation was forged in the late eighteenth and early nineteenth centuries, the notion of the public sphere as the sphere of contractual "fellowship" or kinship was set over against the private sphere of the family identified as the "natural" rather than contractual sphere. The assignment of the family to nature reinforced the assignment of women to nature and of women's work to the nonwage sector. "In this discourse," notes Wendy Brown, "women are 'naturally' suited for the family, the reproductive work women do is 'natural,' the family is a 'natural' entity—everywhere nature greets nature and the historical constructedness and plasticity of both women and the family is nowhere in sight" (17). Women are, as well, represented as "the atavistic and authentic 'body' of national tradition (inert, backward-looking, and natural), embodying nationalism's conservative principle of continuity" (McClintock, 66), while men, agents in the public sphere, are identified with progress, revolution, and national destiny.

The opposition of the domestic to the public sphere secures the historical identification of the citizen with the white male subject. "The liberal subject," argues Brown, "is a man who moves freely between family and civil society, bearing prerogatives in the former and rights in the latter. This person is male rather than generic because his enjoyment of his civil rights is buttressed rather than limited by his relations in the private sphere while the opposite is the case for women" (18). Or as Ursula Vogel argues, citizenship is conferred not upon "individuals as such, but upon men in their capacity as members and representatives of a family (i.e., a group of non-citizens)" (2, quoted in Yuval-Davis, 63). Thus, in what Mosse calls the homosocial bonding that secured new nationalisms, the citizen, as a universalistic conception, was gendered male, and to women was assigned the status of the nonperson, the nonsubject, the noncitizen who inhabits the extralegal domain of the household. Even when citizenship rights were won for women through the suffrage campaigns, the notion of citizenship remained a liberal notion.

For Brown this means that "not merely the structure and discourse but the ethos of the liberal state appears to be socially masculine: its discursive currencies are rights rather than needs, individuals rather than relations, autogenesis rather than interdependence, interests rather than shared circumstances" (20). And the prerogative powers of the nation-state are "masculine" prerogatives, the powers to protect but also the institutionalized powers of violence. All these forms of prerogative power "construct and reinforce male dominance across the social order—and not only through overtly masculinist displays of power by the Pentagon or the police" (24). The bureaucracy of the state operates on masculinist principles since, as Brown suggests, "the instrumental rationality comprising both the foundation of bureaucratic order and the process of bureaucratic rationalization is grounded in the social valorization of maximized power through maximized technocratic control" (27)—in other words, the masculinist will to control that feminizes the subjects whom it administers.

Finally, in times of national instability, nationalist discourses turn history and destiny into sexualized scenarios. If the right working of the nation is the right working of masculinity enforced, threats to the nation are represented as emasculating. In times of war nationalist fervor is fanned and sustained by the rhetoric of masculinity under siege. The warrior is symbolically recast as the romantic hero saving the vulnerable heroine from the foul seducer. In this scenario the nation becomes the female body subject to ravishment. A defeated nation lies prostrate before its conqueror, the body impregnated by and with the enemy. A victorious nation celebrates safety from defilement. Or in times of national trauma, the nation is a masculine body sapped of its lifeblood, corrupted by contaminating influences, weakened, stripped of its independence and autonomy, emasculated. In such times, threats to healthiness and purity of the body politic are identified with the "foreign" or "alien" within.

This brief survey is meant to suggest the variety of ways in which discourses of nationalism take up and deploy gender ideologies, figures of "woman," family likenesses, and sexualized scenarios, if sometimes contradictorily. There are many nationalisms. And the discourses are specific to each nation; to specific groups within the nation; and to specific locations, institutions, and practices within the nation, and are emergent in specific historical circumstances.

This survey is also meant to map out the ideological and material environment that affects the everyday lives of the millions of immigrants in Europe who are women. These women are variously subjects within discourses of nationalism, rights, and citizenship, discourses through which their otherness within comes to signify and to materialize in the allocation of rights, privileges, and resources in their new nation. For instance, their sexual, racial, ethnic, and class positioning conjoin in the assignment of a particular status. They may be migrant or immigrant, foreign national, ethnic or racial minority, guest worker, or resident alien. These assignments of identities have material and cultural effects.

Mirjana Morokvasic argues that "women are those who suffer most from this treatment by the state, whether directly or indirectly" (71). Patriarchal gender arrangements in countries of origin differentially affect the decision about, reasons for, and timing of women's migration and thus "the differing patterns of migratory movement of women and men" (72). At the border women are often subject to bodily invasion. For instance, since pregnant women are not allowed to enter certain countries as guest workers, women are subjected to pregnancy testing. They enter a new nation where masculinist state policies define them as dependents and capitalist labor conditions differentially affect their access to specific kinds of jobs (very often "domestic" jobs that isolate them from other workers and earn them extremely low wages) and the informal rather than contractual arrangements governing their work. They are subjected to strict controls on their reproductive capacities and rules that enforce family dislocations. They are exploited through the sex industry and the marriage bureau. Furthermore, they are, as Morokvasic notes, often blamed for their own victimization. For the assertion that immigrant women accept their subordinate position is based on "the assumption that this subordinate position is a result of migrant women's own cultural heritage," an assumption that "contributes to their victimization but also defines them as partly responsible for their situation" (79).

In the practices of everyday life, immigrant women confront and grapple with their status as an "other" within the imagined community as well as their multicultural identifications. They struggle with the very real material circumstances of their differential treatment and experiences as migrant and immigrant women as well as the differential impacts of racial, ethnic, and class differences. In the process of doing so, some immigrant women take up writing as a means of constituting and changing themselves as subjects.

New Subjectivities, Representations, and National Identities

At the end of the twentieth century, some peoples in the nation-states of Europe imagine a transnational Europe, and with it a common market, a common currency, and the drift toward a common "future" history. Others imagine more discrete, and ethnically defined, corporate identities. Still others rethink nationalism as a complex, multiethnic horizon in response to the presence of millions of immigrants and the reconfiguration of national borders. These imaginings have profound effects upon debates about national literatures. For some, national literature may be superseded by a transnational European literature. And certainly *Europe* has been used by literary historians, for example, Ernst Robert Curtius, as a conceptual frame of reference. "European literature," he writes, "is coextensive in time with European culture" (12). For some, national literature remains a form of cultural and ethnic nation-building. For others, national literature becomes a multiethnic and multinational literature.

However imagined, debates will turn upon the problematic notion of the "purity" or "integrity" of national literature, and of readings of that literature, just as debates have turned upon the purity and integrity of national identity. For literary forms are part of the system of cultural representations through which national identities and national subjects come into being, through which communities are more and more fully and explicitly imagined and consolidated (see Hohendahl; Bhabha). Nations require narratives through which individuals imagine themselves as national subjects and align themselves in the national narrative.

Contributors to this volume are particularly interested in the ways in which women in the New Europe negotiate representational practices, and sometimes more particularly self-representational practices, and in doing so participate in the production, interpretation, and adjustment of discourses of gendered nationalisms. What Keya Ganguly says of postcolonial identity we would apply to transnational multicultural identity as well. It is not "a self-fulfilling prophecy"; rather it is "articulated in the related but discontinuous sites of representation—of the representation of experience, its inscription in (literary) writing and its interrogation in theory. . . . It is an artifice of representation and is, therefore, never a finished product or an authorized totality" (46). The writing of/toward new identities is a writing driven by memory and amnesia (see Anderson). Memory is founded upon forgetting. An insistent coherence of memory and narrative implies forgetfulness. Yet incoherences and discontinuities make spaces for lost memory traces, with the result that the relationship of memories to amnesias is ever adjustable, fluid, and productive of new meanings and new narratives.

Thus the essays that follow engage, from a variety of theoretical and critical standpoints, the following questions: What are the interrelationships of nationalism, gender, and representational practices? How are women writing new identities into and against the old national (meta)narratives? Through what means are they interrogating the grounds of corporate identity? What experimentations with form characterize this unstable context? How do multicultural subjects transform national forms and subjectivities? What do they make of the irresolvabilities of differences, the horizons of what Bhabha calls incommensurabilities ("Third Space," 209), in subjects and communities? Finally, what impact might new forms of subjectivity have upon the construction and deconstruction of national identities in the New Europe?

The Essays

While the essays in this volume take up diverse cultural practices across the breadth of the New Europe—from Ireland to Russia, from Sweden to Italy—for us they can be grouped into three sections based on the motivating questions driving the theoretical and critical analyses. Issues of borders and crossings, of placements and displacements, and of remembered colonialisms and vexed post/colonialities weave through the essays in Part I, "Post/Coloniality in the New Europe."

In "Ethnicity on the French Frontier" Winifred Woodhull points out that in the French political arena today the discourse of "immigration" depends upon a particular binarism, referring as it does to the influx into France of non-Europeans, some of whom are not immigrants at all. (The Beurs, for example, are descendants of Maghrebian immigrants who either were born in France or have lived there since childhood.) Following Etienne Balibar's and Maxim Silverman's critiques of binary discourses of difference, Woodhull argues that as long as such binary conceptions of ethnic and national identity ignore the constitutive role of colonialism in the formation of national identity during the Enlightenment, conflictual relations of race and ethnicity in France cannot be seen as a *national* problem but only as a problem of assimilation. In her reading of Farida Belghoul's *Georgette!* Woodhull shows how Belghoul's text eludes binarism through its exploration of the complexity, ambiguity, and instability of ethnic identities and its depiction of the shifting frontiers of national belonging.

Over the past decade Leïla Sebbar, the daughter of a French woman and an Algerian man, has become well known for her writing about Beurs and other minority groups in France. Her *Shérazade* trilogy is the focus of Françoise Lionnet's contribution. Lionnet reads Shérazade's journey as a cultural itinerary that succeeds in establishing a set of seductive relations between a mythic France and an equally mythic Orient. Shérazade constructs her "diffracted, yet recomposed" world through her storytelling, using a hybrid language borrowed from the speech of others. Mapping out a new geography, not on the margins of the colonial empire but within the very territory of the former colonial power, she destabilizes the distinction between "French" and "francophone" literature, between colony and metropole.

The politics of bicultural identity in an Indo-British context is the topic of Gita Rajan's essay on the writings of Kamala Markandaya, Ruth Prawer Jhabvala, and Suniti Namjoshi. Rajan draws upon Abdul JanMohamed's concept of the border intellectual to frame her analyses. For JanMohamed the border represents an interstitial cultural space, a location from which the syncretic intellectual combines elements of both cultures in order to articulate new forms and experiences. For the specular intellectual the border becomes a vantage point from which to define other utopian possibilities. Rajan reads both Markandaya and Jhabvala as syncretic intellectuals whose novels deal with the constructed identity of India as a new nation-state and the de/colonized subjectivities of Indian and British citizens. Namjoshi she reads as the specular border intellectual who focuses on cultural and sexual issues in the context of a more stable nation-state and citizen identity.

The renegotiation of identities is fundamental to Black women's writing in cross-cultural contexts, Carole Boyce Davies argues. In "Black British Women Writing the Anti-Imperialist Critique," Boyce Davies explores women's voices and life stories that assertively critique empire building and its displacements from within the seat of the British Empire. Among other works, Boyce Davies looks at Joan Riley's novel *The Unbelonging,* a text highlighting the unbelonging produced by migration as it critiques false constructions of "belonging"; Vernella Fuller's *Going Back Home,* a reflection on the multiple locations and politics of Black women who are "strangers" in Britain and "stranger-outsiders" returning home; and various other poetic and narrative writings that dismantle, through what she calls "uprising textualities," colonial boundaries, establish journeys across difference, and create new worlds.

In "Looking through Non-Western Eyes: Immigrant Women's Autobiographical Narratives in Italian," Graziella Parati considers the recent production of personal narratives by women who have immigrated to Italy. Such women's testimonies are often documented only through interviews organized and transcribed by Italian academics and students, so the first part of Parati's essay explores the relationship between a "white interviewer" and, in most cases, a "black interviewee." The second part of the essay focuses on two narratives, one by an Italian Ethiopian woman, the second by an Algerian woman from a nomadic group in the Saharan desert. The narrative structures reflect the hybrid identities that Maria Viarengo and Nassera Chohra aim to create in order to define themselves as daughters of both Western and North African traditions.

After migrating from Senegal to Brussels, where she went to university, and then returning to Senegal, the West African writer Marietou M'baye published an autobiographical narrative, *The Abandoned Baobab,* in French under the pseudonym Ken Bugul. (It has recently been translated into English.) This post/

colonial text is the subject of Julia Watson's "Exile in the Promised Land." Watson looks to the mixture of voices and languages and the thematics of sexuality, de/colonization, and memory in order to understand how Bugul's text frames a series of negotiations between Western literary culture and the oral, communal culture of rural Senegal. As Bugul's narrator journeys from the traditional Muslim world of Senegalese village life through the decadent world of contemporary Brussels, she discovers her ambivalence about the conflicting and contradictory values of her two cultures and her marginalization within both of them.

The essays in Part II explore contemporary refigurations of the "new" Europe's "old" margins, for the designation of "other" has not only been directed at the immigrants from former colonies now living in countries throughout Europe. It has been applied as well to those people who are not Christian and not identified as "white" who have been living on the margins of Europe for centuries. Among them have been Jews, Turks, and Gypsies.

In "Reclaiming Space," Karen Remmler explores how Jewish women who have immigrated to Germany or who are the daughters of Jewish immigrants define themselves and view their experience in light of the commemoration of the Shoah and the formation of German national identity after unification. Reading *Nach der Shoah geboren,* a collection of interviews and essays by Jewish women, Remmler considers the heterogeneous and fluid meanings of Jewish identity. In these essays "Jewishness" and "Germanness" represent shifting positionalities rather than fixed common denominators. Among the women included in this collection are a woman rabbi, who was born in South Africa and lived in Germany for about twenty years before she left for London to become a rabbi (not possible for her in Germany) and who since then has lived in many countries, and a woman born in Istanbul who comes to Germany only to learn that as a Jew and a Turk she must live at the "nonwhite" margins.

Jews and Gypsies (or Sinti and Roma) are among the "hidden subjects" Catherine Portuges writes about in her essay on 1990s Hungarian cinema. Exploring the intersection of nationality and sexuality within the context of post-Communist cinematic practices, Portuges foregrounds the inscription of "minority" populations, including women as well as Jews and Sinti or Roma, in contemporary documentary and feature films by such directors as Ildiko Szabo, Robert Koltai, Judit Elek, and Gyula Gazdag. She does so in order to understand the ways in which the multicultural subjects of a "new Europe" become sites for the negotiation of a politics of location and dislocation in an era of increasingly transnational cinematic practice.

The growing body of literature written in German by authors of non-German origin who live in Germany has stimulated a debate in that country on how to categorize and name this literature. Leslie A. Adelson argues that the debate about correct terminology obscures the point that what is at stake is not the appropriate category for a foreign "addendum" but the fundamental need to reconceptualize the understanding of an identifiably German core of German national literature. In Germany, migrant literature is very often identified by a single signifier, Turkish, reducing Turkish writers to a national stereotype and displacing non-Turkish writers. Adelson looks at the first novel of such a displaced non-Turkish writer, who because of her name—Torkan—is often categorized as Turkish but who is actually Iranian. Her novel *Tufan* is an imagined dialogue between a first-person narrator and her younger brother, imprisoned and tortured by the Khomeini regime. A fanatic child and adolescent, this brother had violently controlled his older sister back in Iran in accordance with his belief in Muslim tenets. In telling her (*their*) story, the first-person narrator ceases to be her brother's victim as she establishes herself as subject of a narrative that is not just a story of the oppression of Muslim women but that raises questions as to how we choose to understand, theorize, and narrate relations of power and oppression under changing historical and political circumstances.

In "Scheherazade's Daughters: The Thousand and One Tales of Turkish-German Women Writers," Azade Seyhan explores writings by the contemporary Turkish writers Aysel Özakin, Alev Tekinay, and Emine Sevgi Özdamar. Multicultural texts, their works draw on the literary culture of writing by and about women in their native country as they question the ideologies implicated in certain representations of women both in their own cultural traditions and in the popular culture of their host country. Subverting, fragmenting, and reconfiguring these images in liberating ways, their texts become a site of social intervention in the oppressive practices against women in their home and host cultures. Their tales highlight both the constitution of selfhood as the interlinkage of personal experience and historical process and the coextensivity of language and cultural space.

Looking at "unhomely boundaries," Hannelore Scholz focuses on one of the greatest Balkan poets and writers, Blaga Dimitrova, who served her country as vice president after the democratic revolution of 1989 until 1993. Prior to 1989 Dimitrova had been publicly attacked as a "national traitor" because she had defended the human rights of the Bulgarian Turks during "Bulgarization." While Dimitrova has backed the development of national specificity, she has always taken a stance for the inclusion of the foreign and against "ethnic cleansing" as a means for her country to become a multicultural part of Europe. Dimitrova emerges as an intellectual claiming European identity, as opposed to the narrow Bulgarian, nationalistic identification that has led people to develop a hatred against everything foreign in the country. In her story "Elmaz," a narrative about an elderly woman writer who receives a letter from a young Turkish woman who calls herself Blaga, Dimitrova explores the painful process of becoming "Elmaz," becoming the "other" of Bulgarian socialist society.

Although the unification of the Federal Republic of Germany (FRG) with the former socialist German Democratic Republic (GDR) has often been represented as a "familiar reunion," in practical terms it has been a very complicated process. East Germans have experienced a specific form of displacement, being at the same time familiar and foreign, central and marginal, participating in *one* (West) German nation but deprived of the history and tradition of their former nation-state. Gisela Brinker-Gabler explores the specifics of what she calls the dis(re)placement of East German subjects with reference to the theories of Edward Said and Abdul JanMohamed, among others. Dis(re)placement, she argues, involves a rupture of the collective GDR subject and the individual subject—a rupture that is also a rupture of language—and a replacement in a reunited Germany with new conditions of experience. Recent works by the two East German writers Christa Wolf and Helga Königsdorf negotiate rupture and come to terms with differing communities, creating new sites like that of the resistant or ambivalent re/united subject with de- or reterritorializing visions of the new nation.

The essays in Part III think through the ways in which sexualities and genders are mobilized in the imaginings and the practices of national identity formation.

European integration and with it a newly emerging concept of "Europe of the Regions" have led to calls for the refashioning of Irish national identity in a more pluralist direction. In "EU-phoria? Irish National Identity, European Union, and *The Crying Game*," Katrina Irving shows how critiques of nationalist discourse in the Irish context reproduce the logic of that discourse, which elides indigenous differences in order to promulgate the myth of the "pure," undivided nation space. Neil Jordan's film *The Crying Game*, released in 1992, combines two narrative strands, the public and the private, the work of IRA terrorists in Ireland and Britain and a romance between a Black British male cross-dresser and a white Irish terrorist. In her analysis Irving unsettles the "obvious" reading, the film's problematization of normative sex/gender relations, arguing that it is a displacement of the film's major preoccupation: the need to overcome essentialist formulations of (Irish) national identities. While the film rejects the homogenizing imperative of nationalist rhetoric by demonizing and exterminating the "Mother Eire" incarnation in the film, it rejoins nationalist discourse in evading the issue of Ireland's marginal population, a complicity with nationalist ideology that is reproduced across a range of contemporary Irish historical and critical texts.

Ebba Witt-Brattström, in "Maternal Abject, Fascist Apocalypse, and Daughter Separation in Contemporary Swedish Novels," investigates the way that immigration to Sweden after World Wars I and II has provided a metaphor that has now become one of the generic means through which contemporary Swedish women writers explore issues of nationalism and xenophobia. The essay opens with a discussion of Julia Kristeva's theory of abjection and goes on to apply this concept to the works of two Swedish authors. Witt-Brattström turns first to the work of Birgitta Trotzig, which explores the instinctual bases for fascism in the cruel and therefore failed separation of mother and child. Then she investigates the works of the younger author Mare Kandre (born in 1962 in Sweden of Estonian parents). Kandre's texts explore the conflict between fascism and Communism within the Baltic states through the theme of biological motherhood as trauma. Inscribing themselves in a tradition little explored by female authors—that of apocalypse, nausea, the grotesque—these writers posit a deeply repressed truth about our civilization, the instinctual origin of racism and xenophobia in the separation between mother and child, a bloody event that can only be conveyed in metaphors of destruction.

As new ethnic and cultural nationalisms have emerged in Central and Eastern Europe, discourses of gender, very often contradictory, are (re)produced and representations of the female body are (re)promoted. The conjunction of gender and national redefinition is starkly revealed in post-Communist Russia, at this stage in its transition from empire and centralized economy to democratic nationhood and a market economy modeled on Western capitalism. In "*Ona:* The New *Elle*-literacy and the Post-Soviet Woman," Greta Slobin focuses on the period from perestroika to the present as she describes changes in women's status from worker-producer to woman-consumer. Concentrating on the 1990 issue of an expensive glossy magazine, *Ona* (She), or the new Russian *Elle,* Slobin tracks the variety of ways this magazine imagines the identity of the post-Soviet woman as inseparable from Russia's struggle to reinvent itself as a nation. While a plurality of new voices is evident, *Ona* is very specific about its politics of forgetting and remembering femininity. The new woman is called upon to remember the "origin," the prerevolutionary village community based on nature qua "human ecology"—and her traditional role as creator of the cosmic hearth and the spiritual charm that creates beauty. At the same time, the sexual revolution of the twenties reappears and with it the image of the unconventional woman living out her sexual freedom—suggesting a variety of choices for Russian women, whose basic economic security is now under threat. As Slobin points out, the emphasis on biological sex differences links national identity with sexual identity, implying that clearly defined sexuality will have a positive effect on the new state.

The volume concludes with Svetlana Slapšak's urgent inventory of the ways in which contemporary inventions of "woman" in the Yugoslav area invoke even as they revise earlier inventions of "woman" in the popular traditions of Balkan societies. The oral tradition consolidated in the early nineteenth century she describes as "the panoply of patriarchal social values and ideals." She finds as well that the discourse of the socialist woman did not change the inventories of gender in any radical way, since that discourse was eventually abandoned by the Party and by dissidents. Slapšak then considers the ways in which women have invented "woman," concentrating on three generic sites: the women's lamentation, oral poetry about the Battle of Kosovo, and memoirs of incarceration from the Communist era. Here she finds strategies of intervention in patriarchal and nationalist inventions of woman. She concludes by arguing that "the present war . . . has offered feminists and women writers new narratives, new politics of writing and publishing, and new patterns of self-definition."

Chantal Mouffe argues that every articulation of the "we" of the corporate nation "implies the delimitation of a 'frontier' and the designation of a 'them.' " Consequently, in the social imaginary difference and diversity within become the horizon of otherness that is "the very condition of [the community's] existence" (379). Yet there are heterogeneous horizons of otherness, and horizons shift continually. We hope this volume contributes to the surveying of some of these horizons in recent cultural productions in Europe.

Notes

1. As Anthony D. Smith argues, there are historians who do not subscribe to the theory of nation as a construct of modernity and seek to explore cultural models of premodern corporate identities. Smith suggests that such models "may afford a better point of departure for the study of

the transformations and revivals involved in the formation of modern nations and the role played by nationalism in those processes" ("Nationalism and the Historians," 74).

2. Anderson differentiates creole and vernacular nationalisms, the latter a nationalism of print culture, the former a nationalism of bureaucratic units administered by creole colonists. To these two forms of national consciousness Anderson adds "official" nationalism, what he calls the "willed merger of nation and dynastic empire" (86) that evolved out of the European imperial centers of the nineteenth century.

3. Scholarly interest in the emergence of nationalisms has increased over the last two decades, as evidenced by a procession of studies. See Anderson, Armstrong, Breuilley, Chatterjee, Gellner, Hobsbawm, Hroch, Seton-Watson, and Smith.

4. In his recent study of nationalisms and civil society, Seligman calls what is going on in the former Yugoslavia the "new tribalism."

5. See, for instance, Montesquieu's *Mes Pensées*. Herder already in "Auch eine Philosophie" (1774) pointed out possible problems with such a concept insofar as one perspective on nation becomes universalized and subjugates other notions. For a critique of Western concepts of nation that have been imposed on non-Western nations, see Partha Chatterjee, *Nationalist Thought*. He states that Western theories, with their emphasis on the power of reason, the primacy of the hard sciences, and the dominance of the empirical method, are understood as universally valid and have contributed to the destruction of non-Western peoples' own views on community.

6. Such activities secure national sovereignty. With union, the prerogatives of the nation are eroded. For instance, the nation's authority to mint its own money, to set its own customs laws, to set prices for its own commodities, and so on, is eliminated. The European Exchange Rate System having become a necessity to a federated Europe, so too will a European Monetary System, a common currency. Eventually a European Bank will emerge. The decision making will move from national capitals to Brussels as the headquarters of the European Community.

7. Recent surveys indicate that 51 percent of the German population agree with this slogan.

8. Under this policy, beginning in 1955, workers first from Italy and then from other south European and North African countries were given only temporary residence in the Federal Republic of Germany. This recruitment was discontinued in 1973, at which time the German government provided financial assistance for "guest workers" to relocate in their home countries.

9. Interestingly enough, the policy of relocation was reactivated in 1992 as a response to the large numbers of Romanians, but particularly Gypsies, in Germany. The German government offered $20 million "to pay for their deportation and job training programs in Romania" (*New York Times,* September 25, 1992, A7). As the *Times* concludes, "Critics contend that the accord is a capitulation to growing xenophobia." There are also accords with Poland, Czechoslovakia, and Bulgaria.

10. Angelika Bammer is here paraphrasing the argument made by Julia Kristeva in "Lettre ouverte à Harlem Desir," in *Nations without Nationalisms.*

11. See also Hausen on the polarization of gender identities at the turn of the nineteenth century; Janssen-Jurreit on "Nationalismus und Frauenkult" (esp. chap. 5); and Riley on the post-Enlightenment sexualization of the soul of woman.

12. Of course, specific women have played significant roles in struggles of national liberation, and large numbers of women have participated in revolutionary struggles and national movements in Europe, America, and formerly colonized nations. Through the struggles, different feminisms have emerged that have occasioned specific histories of gender adjustments in nations.

13. Katrak has specifically discussed this identification of women with tradition in nationalist movements. "The dangers of reifying 'traditions,' of ahistoricizing them as the transcendent emblems of a culture, are felt most negatively by women, particularly after independence when the rationale of justifying tradition against the enemy is no longer needed. Gandhi's exaltation of women's role in protecting tradition colluded with British debates about tradition where, as Lata Mani has pointed out, women were simply the *ground* on which debates about tradition were

threshed out; women themselves were not significant as human beings; tradition was" (168). Since the arena of sexuality—"fertility/infertility, motherhood, the sexual division of labor"—is the primary arena of oppression for women, and since traditions are identified with this arena, "the key issue of the control of female sexuality is legitimized, even effectively mystified, under the name of 'tradition' " (168). For a materialist analysis of the economic reasons for the return after revolutionary movements to traditional gender role alignments, see Mies (194–99).

Works Cited

Anderson, Benedict. *Imagined Communities*. London: Verso, 1991.

Armstrong, J. A. *Nations before Nationalism*. Chapel Hill: University of North Carolina Press, 1982.

Balibar, Etienne. "Racism and Nationalism." In *Race, Nation, Class,* edited by Etienne Balibar and Immanuel Wallerstein. London: Verso, 1991.

Bammer, Angelika. "Xenophobia, Xenophilia, and No Place to Rest." In *Encountering the Other/s: Studies in Literature, History, and Culture,* edited by Gisela Brinker-Gabler, 45–62. Albany: State University of New York Press, 1995.

Bhabha, Homi K., ed. *Nation and Narration*. New York: Routledge, 1990.

———. "The Third Space." In *The Location of Culture,* 207–21. London: Routledge, 1994.

Breuilly, John. *Nationalism and the State*. Manchester: Manchester University Press, 1982.

Brown, Wendy. "Finding the Man in the State." *Feminist Studies* 18 (Spring 1992): 7–34.

Chatterjee, Partha. *Nationalist Thought and the Colonial World: A Derivative Discourse?* London: Zed Books, 1986.

Curtius, Ernst Robert. *European Literature and the Latin Middle Ages*. Translated by W. R. Task. Princeton, N.J.: Princeton University Press, 1973.

Eco, Umberto. "L'Africa e l'est: Migrazione e liberazione." *L'Espresso,* April 15, 1990.

Erkkila, Betsy. "Revolutionary Women." *Tulsa Studies in Women's Literature* 6 (Fall 1987): 189–223.

Ganguly, Keya. "Migrant Identities: Personal Memory and the Construction of Selfhood." *Cultural Studies* 6 (January 1992): 27–50.

Gellner, Ernest. *Nations and Nationalism*. Oxford: Blackwell, 1983.

"Germany and Romania in Deportation Pact." *New York Times,* September 25, 1992, A7.

Hausen, Karin. "Die Polarisierung der Geschlechtscharaktere—eine Spiegelung der Dissoziation von Erwerbs- und Familienleben." In *Sozialgeschichte der Familie in der Neuzeit Europas,* edited by Werner Conze. Stuttgart: Klett, 1977.

Heckmann, Friedrich. "Ethnos, Demos und Nation, oder: Woher stammt die Intoleranz des Nationalstaats gegenüber ethnischen Minderheiten?" In *Das Eigene und das Fremde: Neuer Rassismus in der Alten Welt?* edited by Uli Bielefeld, 51–78. Hamburg: Junius Verlag, 1991.

Herder, Johann Gottfried. "Auch eine Philosophie der Geschichte zur Bildung der Menschheit." In *Werke,* vol. 1, 589–683. Munich: Carl Hanser, 1984.

Hobsbawm, Eric. *Nations and Nationalism since 1788*. Cambridge: Cambridge University Press, 1990.

Hohendahl, Peter Uwe. *Building a National Literature*. Translated by Renate Baron Franciscono. Ithaca: Cornell University Press, 1989.

Hroch, Miroslav. *Social Preconditions of National Revival in Europe*. Cambridge: Cambridge University Press, 1985.

Janssen-Jurreit, Marielouise. *Sexismus/Über die Abtreibung der Frauenfrage*. Munich: Carl Hanser, 1976.

Katrak, Ketu H. "Decolonizing Culture: Toward a Theory for Postcolonial Women's Texts." *mfs* 35 (Spring 1989): 157–79.

Koontz, Claudia. *Mothers in the Fatherland: Women, the Family, and Nazi Politics.* London: Jonathan Cape, 1987.

Kristeva, Julia. "Open Letter to Harlem Desir." In *Nations without Nationalisms,* translated by Leon S. Roudiez, 49–64. New York: Columbia University Press, 1993.

Lloyd, Cathie, and Hazel Waters. "France: One Culture, One People?" *Race and Class* 32 (January 1991): 49–65.

McClintock, Anne. "Family Feuds: Gender, Nationalism, and the Family." *Feminist Review* 44 (Summer 1993): 61–80.

Mies, Maria. *Patriarchy and Accumulation on a World Scale: Women in the International Division of Labour.* London: Zed Books, 1986.

Montesquieu, Charles-Louis de Secondat, Baron de. *Mes Pensées.* Vol. 1 of *Œuvres Complètes.* Paris: Gallimard, 1985.

Morokvasic, Mirjana. "Fortress Europe and Migrant Women." *Feminist Review* 39 (Winter 1991): 69–84.

Mosse, George L. *Nationalism and Sexuality: Middle-Class Morality and Sexual Norms in Modern Europe.* New York: Howard Fertig, 1985.

Mouffe, Chantal. "Feminism, Citizenship, and Radical Democratic Politics." In *Feminists Theorize the Political,* edited by Judith Butler and Joan W. Scott, 369–84. New York: Routledge, 1992.

Nederveen Pieterse, Jan. "Fictions of Europe." *Race and Class* 32 (January 1991): 3–10.

Parker, Andrew, Mary Russo, Doris Sommer, and Patricia Yaeger. Introduction to *Nationalisms and Sexualities,* edited by Parker et al. New York: Routledge, 1992.

Riding, Alan. "In French Town, Unity Is Secondary." *New York Times,* September 13, 1992, E5.

Riley, Denise. *"Am I That Name?" Feminism and the Category of "Women" in History.* Minneapolis: University of Minnesota Press, 1988.

Schnapper, D. "La Nation, les Droits de la Nationalité et l'Europe." *Revue Européenne des Migrations Internationales,* 1989, 21–31.

Schwarz, Bill. "England in Europe: Reflections on National Identity and Cultural Theory." *Cultural Studies* 6, no. 2 (May 1992): 198–206.

Seligman, Adam B. *The Idea of Civil Society.* New York: Free Press, 1992.

Seton-Watson, Hugh. *Nations and States.* Boulder, Colo.: Westview Press, 1977.

Smith, Anthony D. *The Ethnic Origins of Nations.* Oxford: Blackwell, 1986.

———. "Nationalism and the Historians." *International Journal of Comparative Sociology* 33, nos. 1–2 (1992): 58–80.

Suhr, Heidrun. *"Ausländerliteratur:* Minority Literature in the Federal Republic of Germany." *New German Critique* 46 (1989): 71–103.

Thurow, Lester. *Head to Head: The Coming Economic Battle among Japan, Europe, and America.* New York: Morrow, 1992.

Vogel, Ursula. "Is Citizenship Gender Specific?" Paper presented at the Political Science Association Annual Conference, April 1989.

Yuval-Davis, Nira. "The Citizenship Debate: Women, Ethnic Processes and the State." *Feminist Review* 39 (Winter 1991): 58–68.

Yuval-Davis, Nira, and Floya Anthias, eds. *Women-Nation-State.* New York: St. Martin's Press, 1989.

Part I

Post/Coloniality in the New Europe

1 / Ethnicity on the French Frontier

Winifred Woodhull

In an age of cultural diversity and transnational economies, when immigration and racial and ethnic conflict are key political issues in all industrialized Western societies, the writing of minorities is an important reflection of and engagement in cultural-political struggles. Some of the most exciting literary scholarship in the United States today looks at the ways the texts of minority writers dislocate fixed identities not only of race, ethnicity, and nationality, but also of gender, sexuality, class, and language. Their exploration of the intersection of these identities and their figurations of subjective and social hybridity engage the most trying, but also the most promising, dimensions of social experience in our time.

In Europe, as in the United States, the most compelling literary and critical texts by and about racial and ethnic minorities call attention to the fact that immigration is not the problem that governments, political parties, and the media often make it out to be. That is, it is not a matter of industrialized countries whose populations are mainly of European descent being invaded by aliens who take jobs from deserving nationals, drain the countries' resources in the domains of education and health services, and threaten the national culture by clinging to religious beliefs and cultural practices that are fundamentally incompatible with Western values and modern life. Rather, these texts suggest that the highly charged notion of immigration figures the unsettling transformation of national landscapes in industrialized countries in the past fifty years. They show how the term is used to stigmatize certain minority groups, notably

Latinos and Asian Americans in the United States and peoples of non-European descent in Europe—North African Arabs and Berbers, sub-Saharan Africans, Middle Easterners (notably Turks), and Asians. In many of its current usages, the term "immigration" enables various political factions to hold these minority groups accountable not only for the hardships brought on by the recessions of the past two decades, but also for the social dislocations and cultural fragmentation that have accompanied economic globalization since World War II and that have now reached a crisis point because industrialized countries cannot make good their claim to stand for political and social equality for all.

In the French political arena today, the term "immigration" does not refer to the settlement of Italians in the early twentieth century or to the later settlement of Portuguese, who are presently the largest immigrant group in France. Rather, it refers to the influx of non-Europeans, some of whom are not immigrants at all. These include people from France's overseas departments in the Caribbean (Martinique and Guadeloupe), as well as from former French colonies such as Vietnam, Senegal, Cameroon, and the Maghreb (Algeria, Morocco, and Tunisia). The latter group includes the Beurs, descendants of Maghrebian immigrants who either were born in France or have lived there since childhood.[1] Of all these non-European groups, Maghrebians and Beurs are by far the most numerous and have had the most political visibility, whether in 1970s struggles for equal rights in the workplace or in the 1980s explosion of alternative cultural forms in rock music, theater, film, video, radio, magazines, newspapers, and fiction.

Beur writing of the 1980s will be my focus in this chapter.[2] Given the context in which it emerged, one characterized by cultural mixing on an unprecedented scale, it may seem surprising that most Beur texts are organized by a binary opposition between France and the Maghreb, as are the advertising, press coverage, and prefaces to Beur texts, usually written by European French people. An entry from Sakinna Boukhedenna's *Journal* illustrates this tendency with particular clarity: "C'est en France que j'ai appris à être Arabe. C'est en Algérie que j'ai appris à être l'Immigrée" (It's in France that I learned to be Arab. It's in Algeria that I learned to be the Immigrant) (5). By and large, Beurs see themselves, and are seen by other French people, as being caught between two separate and incompatible cultures, with little chance of being fully integrated into either one. As a result, they are subject not only to an unsettling and sometimes debilitating crisis of personal identity, but to rejection by two national groups, exclusion from two homelands.

A reading of texts by Aïcha Benaïssa and Ferrudja Kessas will illustrate my point about the binarism of this writing. What will follow is a discussion of some reasons for this binarism, a discussion that will consider, in particular, some of the dominant political discourses in contemporary France, which are themselves structured by an oppositional logic. I will then examine the theoretical critiques of those discourses developed by Etienne Balibar and Maxim Silverman, who show that binarist conceptions of ethnic and national identity ignore both the constitutive role of colonialism in the formation of French national identity during the Enlightenment and the transformation of the French nation-state since World War II. As formerly colonized peoples have emigrated to metropolitan France in large numbers in the 1950s, '60s, and '70s, the most oppressive social differences, notably those of class, have become increasingly ethnicized. And as clear distinctions between cultural identities begin to fade in urban centers, racism intensifies because the blurring of cultural differences produces anxiety and hostility. Balibar and Silverman argue convincingly that current attempts to further Europeanize French national identity are symptomatic of the legacy of colonialism, which continues to shape European politics today by positing essential, nonnegotiable differences between Europeans and the peoples they colonized.

I will suggest that Balibar and Silverman's work is important for the interpretation of recent texts by writers of African and Asian descent in France. Rather than accepting the tendency to view ethnic groups as bounded entities with separate, unique histories and cultures, I will argue that it is crucial to see how various ethnic identities interlock. In the last part of my essay, I will analyze in detail Farida Belghoul's *Georgette!*, which compellingly discloses the intersection of French, Maghrebian, and other ethnic identities, while also indicating how ethnicity is overdetermined by other dimensions of social experience such as gender, class, and language.[3] Belghoul's novel eludes binarism, critically and productively exploring the complexity, ambiguity, and instability of ethnic identities while keeping in view the institutionalized inequalities between ethnic groups. In a nuanced and compelling manner, *Georgette!* figures the shifting frontiers of national belonging.

I begin with a testimonial, *Née en France* (*Born in France*), published by a Beur woman under the pseudonym Aïcha Benaïssa. One of the first things that strikes the reader is that the title page gives the impression that the book has been coauthored by a French woman, Sophie Ponchelet, since the latter's name appears beneath the author's in the same font. Ponchelet's afterword (which takes up only 5 of the text's 139 pages) explains that in conducting a survey on the forced marriage of young Beur women, she met Aïcha in the Paris suburbs and, with much difficulty, persuaded her "to tell her story, to tell all, to break [the] law of silence" (136). Ponchelet points to the urgency of revealing "the amplitude of the threat weighing on hundreds of girls [who may be subject to] forced marriage, sequestrations, flight, abduction, suicide" (137), and tells us that "this is the first time a young Beur has related, almost day by day, hour by hour, the conquest of her freedom" (136).

The prominence of Ponchelet's name on the title page undoubtedly reflects her role in prompting the writing (and probably facilitating the publication) of Benaïssa's testimonial. But it is Ponchelet's role in presenting the text that is most significant. First, it discloses an underlying assumption that the text is addressed to a French audience that will have trouble interpreting it, since the experience related is presumed to be quite foreign. (In "Writing for Others," Alec Hargreaves shows that this assumption is evident in the publication of most texts by Beurs and immigrants, and that, in some cases, the explanatory material is so voluminous as to overwhelm the testimony itself.) Second, the afterword suggests that Benaïssa has recently won a kind of freedom that Ponchelet and other European French women already have and that, on the grand scale of historical and social development, the Beur woman has progressed from a backward position to a modern one. Having escaped the "almost medieval" drama of sequestration and forced marriage (137), she now enjoys the freedom to be an autonomous human subject in an enlightened society. Finally, Ponchelet's sponsorship of Benaïssa suggests that the Beur's testimony is being introduced into a particular discursive field that has the power to shape the testimony itself. If the testimony that is being given for "the first time" has an audience, it is because it meets certain of the audience's expectations. Indeed, the discursive field has determined, to a considerable extent, the terms in which Benaïssa interprets her experience and tells her story.

In order to be heard in the French mainstream, in order to see herself as a potential participant in mainstream culture, Benaïssa must speak in terms of an opposition between French and Algerian identity that positions her main characters in one camp or the other, or relegates those who fit neatly into neither camp to a no-man's-land of despair or madness. It is true that Benaïssa's advocate, Ponchelet, exhorts her compatriots to recognize the Beurs, many of whom were born in France, as French people in their own right. A young woman like Benaïssa, she says, must be allowed "to be herself," "to be French without completely renouncing her roots" (136). But at the same time Ponchelet says that the "true integration" of Beurs into French society will "erase differences" (139). True integration, according to this logic, will situate Benaïssa firmly in the category of the same, delivering her from that of the other, whereas what is needed is a deconstruction of the binary oppositions between same and other, French and Algerian.

Née en France relates the frustrations of a Beur adolescent trying to reconcile the conflicting demands of the different cultural spaces in which she lives. Like many Beur girls of her age, Aïcha Benaïssa is profoundly disturbed by her parents' and brothers' obsession with preserving her virginity as a way of safeguarding the family honor. Her attraction to boys and their attraction to her become fearsome or shameful experiences. Once Aïcha reaches puberty, she is never allowed to leave the house except to attend school. And when her younger sisters childishly tease her about having a crush on a male classmate, her mother beats her furiously. Moreover, like many of her peers, she resents the power of the men in her family who "behave like kings, expecting to be waited on" (43). As a result of their unquestioned privilege (and of her mother's exhaustion from numerous closely spaced births), the responsibility for housework and the care of her younger brothers and sisters falls to her, preventing her from devoting enough time and effort to her studies to pass the baccalaureate examinations. It is at the point where these constraints become unbearable that Aïcha runs away from home.

When she returns to her family after running away, Aïcha believes that she has reconciled with her parents. However, she soon discovers that they have devised a terrible punishment for her. Aïcha is tricked into going to Algeria with her family for vacation, then forced to stay there while her grandmother tries to arrange her marriage to an Algerian Muslim who will keep her in her place. During her eight-month sequestration, Aïcha comes to identify Algeria in terms of its oppressive family traditions, its "authoritarian and archaic" political regime (95), and its "omnipresent" religion that is "always a form of subjection and alienation for women" (132). In short, she sees Algeria as a backward country: "J'avais parfois l'impression de me trouver en France, à une époque ancienne" (I sometimes had the impression that I was in France in the distant past) (98). An idealized France appears as the realm of "normal relations" (37), while Algeria appears as a realm of depravity that can appear "normal" only to a casual vacationer (95). It is this polarity between archaic Algeria and enlightened France that structures the entire narrative.

Algeria is a prison for Aïcha not only because she is under the tutelage of Algerian family members there, but because the Algerian government has the power to force her to stay in the country. Under Algerian law, Aïcha is an Algerian citizen because her parents are Algerian. Once she has been in Algeria for six months, she is considered a resident and can be required to remain there under certain conditions, for example, if she has worked for wages. The fact that she also has French citizenship does nothing to change this. (Because her parents are Algerian, and because she was born in France before 1962, that is, while Algeria was still officially a department of France, Aïcha has had French citizenship from birth.) So the problem goes well beyond the hostile surveillance of her grandmother, which her Italian boyfriend, Antonio, has great trouble eluding. Nor is the problem merely one of convincing her parents, as she eventually manages to do, that she has embraced their values and can be trusted to live in France again. For even if her father requests that she be allowed to return to France with him, the Algerian government has the power to detain her. And even if Antonio manages to get her the money she needs to make her way to the haven of the French embassy, anyone can stop her in the street and have her arrested if she is seen moving about alone or in the company of a suspicious stranger; a young Algerian woman does not have the prerogative to move about as she pleases. Aïcha's Algerian national identity thus threatens to condemn her to a life of confinement against her will. From the standpoint of the sequestered young woman, France appears to be a place of freedom, solid ground that promises security: "Tant que je n'aurais pas les deux pieds sur le sol français, je ne serais sûre de rien" (Until I had both feet firmly planted on French soil, I would be sure of nothing) (122).

Eventually, Aïcha is allowed to return to France with her father, but it should be noted that, when she does return, nothing is normal. The stark opposition between France (normality) and Algeria (abnormality) no longer makes sense, yet it continues to structure the narrative. For example, for some time after her return, Aïcha remains in the "état second," or "trance" (127), that she had been in in Algeria. In fact, despite her ultimate success in negotiating her anxiety and depression in a three-year course of psychotherapy, despite her marriage to Antonio, who proves a loyal friend and lover, Aïcha is never able to lead the "normal" life that France seemed to symbolize during her sequestration in Algeria. Shortly after returning to Paris, she runs away from her family again for fear of being abducted a second time. She never carries her papers with her on the rare occasions when she visits them, lest they confiscate them and destroy the proof of her French citizenship. (Ponchelet notes that the author publishes under a pseudonym not only as a way of protecting her family from embarrassment, but out of fear of reprisals from her family.) Because her family could never accept Antonio unless, perhaps, he converted to Islam, Aïcha's eventual marriage to him is kept secret for some time. Her brother, who has joined the extremely conservative Muslim Brotherhood, is now like a "stranger" (132), and her sister's marriage to a practicing Muslim is cause for worry. Finally, her father is weak and seems at times to be on the verge of death; Aïcha cannot help feeling responsible for his affliction. In short, where her family relations are concerned, nothing is going well, and the proposition that normality reigns in France becomes increasingly difficult for the reader to accept.

This is so despite the fact that *Née en France* invites readers to view Aïcha's troubled family relations as an Algerian problem playing itself out within France's borders, rather than a French problem per se. Nothing is said to differentiate the brother's Islamic conservatism from that of young men in Algeria or to distinguish the sister's marriage to a practicing Muslim from the marriages of her female cousins in Algeria. There is no discussion of the relationship between the Algerianness of Aïcha's immediate family members and the social context within and against which it is being articulated. Rather, it is suggested that Aïcha's problems stem from dysfunctional relationships that are peculiarly Algerian. Significantly, though, there is trouble in other parts of the young woman's life as well. Particularly in the first years after her return to Paris, Aïcha's life with Antonio is difficult because he has no job and has slim prospects of finding one, even though he is European and has had some postsecondary education. During this time, the couple's financial constraints are so great that they lack the means to rent their own apartment and so must rely on the generosity of friends. This situation contributes to Aïcha's anxiety, which often manifests itself in the form of nightmares. We must conclude that Aïcha's distress stems from economic hardship—that is, from inequality that is a structural feature of French society—as well as from her oppressive family relations.

Moreover, as Ponchelet emphasizes in her afterword, the fact that Aïcha faces sequestration at all is not only an Algerian problem, it is very much a French problem as well. Under present conditions, it often happens that French social workers, judges, and politicians can do nothing to help citizens like Aïcha, even if they are inclined to do so. They cannot prevent a girl's parents from imposing a husband she doesn't choose, or even prevent her being taken against her will to Algeria. Yet in Benaïssa's testimonial, the Beur girl's vulnerability to abduction and forced marriage seems to arise solely from Algerian cultural practices. There is no interrogation of France's failure to protect her from such abuses.

Née en France suggests that the incompatible demands of French and Algerian culture require that the Beur girl lead a double life. It suggests that the opposition between Frenchness and Algerianness structures the girl's very subjectivity. Aïcha says she is simultaneously "the person [I am] at home, the one my parents want me to be . . . and the other one, the one who was really me, that I would unveil one day, but somewhere else" (27). To be sure, Aïcha Benaïssa, like other young Beur writers, draws attention to the difficulty of being either Algerian or French; her identity is "somewhere else." Yet it is important to see that Aïcha's main goal is to be self-identical. Her will to be who she "really" is (that is, to be an independent young woman, a unique individual who enjoys the right to self-determination—to be, in short, a Beur incarnation of Man, as defined by Enlightenment ideals) obeys the same logic as her father's will to make her conform to the identity of the "good" Algerian woman, the woman whose virtue embodies the communitarian ideals associated with the homeland. In both cases, the Beur subject assumes, or is made to assume, a fixed, essential identity rather than coming to terms with the inherent ambiguity and instability of every identity. The implicit demand that the unique identity of the individual (or, in Ponchelet's terms, the distinct identity that is supposedly proper to Beurs) be granted the same coherence and legitimacy as French and Algerian national identities follows the identitarian logic of the dominant political discourses in France, rather than attempting to think in radically different terms.[4]

Ferrudja Kessas's novel *Beur's Story* also deploys an identitarian logic in its account of a girl's painful experience of leading a double life. Unlike the protagonist of *Née en France,* however, the main characters of *Beur's Story,* Malika and her best friend, Farida, fail to establish an identity of their own "somewhere else"; Farida kills herself, while Malika succumbs to madness. Their failure to establish a full, stable identity is presented as a tragic feature of Beur existence; it is not seen as a general condition of modern life. However, unlike Benaïssa's testimonial, which maps the tension between Frenchness and Algerianness in terms of an opposition between two nations separated by the Mediterranean Sea, Kessas's novel locates that tension squarely within France's borders, in the northern port city of Le Havre. The urban setting is organized around the polarity between the European French district of Sainte-Claire (symbolizing celestial light, enlightenment) and the immigrant district of Les Marais Noirs (The black swamps) near the seaport. In Malika's imagination, the open sea that lies beyond the constraining urban spaces briefly figures the freedom that Farida had dared to claim for herself: "Son amie ne s'était jamais gênée pour aller à la plage, elle y allait comme bon lui semblait, jetait ses scrupules au gré des vagues, projetant ses phantasmes au vent cajoleur et froid qui les emportait vers l'horizon" (Her friend never deprived herself of a trip to the beach; she went there whenever she pleased, letting her scruples be cast about by the waves, projecting her fantasies onto the cold, inviting wind that carried them toward the horizon) (218). But in the wake of Farida's suicide, provoked by her inability ultimately to escape parental control, the sea comes to embody the fear and discouragement that overwhelm Malika, thwarting her effort to escape Les Marais Noirs: "Il semblait à Malika que toute la mer déferlait sur elle" (It seemed to Malika that the entire sea was unfurling upon her) (218).

In their daily lives, Malika and Farida face many of the same problems as the narrator of *Née en France,* including subordination to their father and brothers, responsibility for housework and for the care of their younger siblings, confinement to the home except when attending school, and physical abuse. Theirs is a narrowly circumscribed existence, imposed not only by Algerian (Kabyl) culture but by poverty. The protagonists of *Beur's Story* see education as a means of escape. In fact, during the school day, the experience of camaraderie with other Beur girls who want to escape is already an experience of freedom. At school, these girls are temporarily freed from the constraints imposed by their families. And during recess, when they laugh and talk among themselves, the burden of appearing "francisées," or "Frenchified," is lifted as well (32). Sensing—and resenting—the liberating potential of education for a Beur girl, Malika's older brother, Mohamed, a factory worker and the family breadwinner, disparages her for preparing for exams late into the night and for wasting electricity in the process: "Ça fait mine de travailler, pour se donner une réputation d'intellectuelle, alors que c'est des petites merdes! Allez, fous-moi le camp!" (She pretends to be studying so people will think she's an intellectual, when she's nothing but a little piece of shit! Go on, get the hell out of here!) (174).

In the face of Mohamed's contempt and abuse, in the face of general indifference to her fate, Malika is said to wonder whether she "really exists" (90). Farida, on the other hand, is said to assert herself through acts of rebellion, such as a morning trip to a café with European French friends who have no idea of the transgression she is committing. "L'escapade du matin m'avait donné l'impression d'exister vraiment" (The morning's escapade had given me the impression that I really existed) (111). Yet Farida does not escape the asphyxiating control of her family. By virtue of straddling the cultures of France and Algeria, which are presented as distinct and irreconcilable, she succumbs to anxiety about falling into a "vide," or void (215), and ends by jumping out of the window of a tall apartment building. After Farida's suicide, Malika is afraid of being "anéantie," annihilated, in turn (215), as she in fact is at the end, when her distress leads to madness and reduces her to silence.

If Beur writing such as Kessas's and Benaïssa's generally organizes itself around an opposition between France and the Maghreb, it may well be because, for the past twenty years, Maghrebians have been effectively represented as a homogeneous ethnic and religious-cultural group residing in the territory of an equally homogeneous French nation (de Benoist, Girard, Le Gallou). This representation has gained such legitimacy in recent years that it is difficult for anyone—including European French and Maghrebian French intellectuals and writers on the left—to cast debates about national identity, cultural belonging, citizenship, and political and civil rights in other terms. Liberals, including minority activitists in groups such as S.O.S. Racisme, do not alter the terms of debate by defending minorities' "right to difference," not only because their slogan echoes right extremists' designation of minorities as "different" (and thus deserving of expulsion), but because they uncritically accept the view that, historically, in keeping with Revolutionary ideals, the French nation has assimilated and guaranteed equal rights to individuals irrespective of their national, racial, ethnic, and class origins, and that it has only to do the same today with members of minority groups who are generically referred to as "immigrants."

In taking this view, liberals ignore the inequalities that the modern nation-state has produced and institutionalized in the process of constituting and maintaining itself as such. They ignore they fact that exclusions grounded in racism are not accidental, are not external to national ideals. On the contrary, as Etienne Balibar has shown, national ideals are themselves based on universalist ideals whose history reveals a highly ambivalent process by which the ideals and their internal excess (in Bataille's sense), or their supplement (in Derrida's sense), are produced at one and the same time. In particular, Balibar points to

the "internal link" that has been established between [idealized] notions of humanity, the human species, the cultural progress of humanity, and anthropological "prejudices" concerning races, or the natural bases of slavery. This has to do with the very notion of race, whose modern meaning begins to be sketched out in the Enlightenment—that grand flowering of universalism—and affects it in turn, not accidentally, externally to its "essence," but intrinsically. ("Racisme," 11)

Balibar goes on to say that the ambivalence inherent in the production of ideals, which is a key aspect of the relation between racism and nationalism, accounts for the difficulty in distinguishing healthy patriotism, or "clean" nationalism, from "dirty" nationalism, that is, a nationalism "linked to imperialism and the oppression of ethnic minorities" ("Racisme," 17). Moreover, he argues, "what is at stake in nationalism is the constant (re)constitution of national unity, threatened by class struggles and by the fact that nation-states have absorbed human groups whose history and traditions are different, if not irreducible" ("Racisme," 17–18). National unity is fostered by institutions such as the army and schools, which may well function differently in different regions and contexts, yet do not fail to produce "a fictive ethnicity that allows the population of a nation-state, the people par excellence, to represent itself as a community" ("Racisme," 18). This ethnicity is necessarily fictive because modern nation-states' emergence coincides with a rapid acceleration in the mixing of peoples from various parts of the world. Today, core national identity—Englishness, Germanness, Frenchness—tends to be defined "in terms of racial and/or cultural purity, whether it be a matter of imposing its domination or 'only' of preserving it from miscegenation, from degeneracy" ("Racisme," 19).

The liberal view that the French nation has historically assimilated individuals irrespective of race, ethnicity, and national origin thus misses a basic feature of modern nation formation, namely, that inequalities based on race and ethnicity are intrinsic to it. It also misses the fact that French national identity is inseparable from French colonialism. Balibar argues convincingly that colonialism is not merely an episode in French history. Rather, it is constitutive of the modern French nation and lies at the root of France's current political crises. Economic and cultural domination by the United States, for example, is widely viewed as a form of colonization from which a former colonial power such as France should be exempt. Hence the recent move by Jacques Toubon, the French minister of culture, to prohibit the use of English in contracts and in the advertising of French products. France's colonial history also explains recent claims that European immigrants are assimilable whereas non-European immigrants are not, and should thus be expelled. Such claims are based on a retrospective view of national history that effaces the hostility and even the violence directed, for example, at Italians who came to France in the early twentieth century and at Spanish republicans who were interned in France in the 1930s after fleeing their country's civil war. Balibar writes: "The European immigrants of the prewar period and of today are said to be 'close' because they came or come from 'equal' countries that have never been colonized by France, unlike Maghrebians, Blacks, and Asians" (*Frontières*, 58). He points out that the myth of other Europeans' easy integration into French society is part of a larger myth of assimilation that not only shaped relations with foreigners who aspired to become French nationals, but also centrally informed French colonialism in the nineteenth century. Unlike the British, who trained native elites and set a date by which their protectorates would function independently, the French never envisaged a degree of independence for their protectorates, precisely because of the assimilationist ideal (Brunschwig, 58).[5]

French colonialism is part and parcel of the modern nation-state in another respect as well: it determines the conditions under which different groups of foreigners may become French nationals. Maxim Silverman has demonstrated, for example, that under article 23 of the French Code of Nationality

> the child born of foreign parents at least one of whom was born in France is French at birth (known as "the double jus soli" [loi du sol]). This article therefore covers those whose parents are from Algeria or French West Africa and who were born in their country of origin before independence (that is, when these countries were French territory). The proposed change to the Code [by the government in 1986] would have meant that these children would have lost their automatic right to French nationality at birth. This would have affected 23–24,000 children each year, of whom 16–17,000 have Algerian parents and about 7,500 are from West Africa. For those other countries not made part of French territory under colonial rule, article 44 of the Code stipulates that any child born in France of foreign parents born abroad acquires French nationality automatically at the age of majority, providing their country of residence for at least five years prior to the age of majority has been France. The proposed change to article 44 [requiring a voluntary request for French nationality] would have affected about 17,000 children of whom a large proportion have either Moroccan or Tunisian parents. (*Deconstructing the Nation*, 142–43)

Silverman notes that the government dropped the proposal to change article 23 for pragmatic rather than ideological reasons, and that

> the "jus soli" became a major site of struggle because, as with legal immigrant status, it is no guarantee of (cultural/ethnic) legitimacy. In other words, at the heart of the proposal is the idea that the link between the juridical and the cultural definition of nationality should be reformed so as to institutionalize more firmly the contemporary "Europeanized" framework for considerations of French national identity. (*Deconstructing the Nation*, 143)

The ideological and institutional links between "cultural/ethnic legitimacy" and French national identity exemplify a modern form of racism based not on biological theories of racial types but on a notion of irreducible cultural differences. In Balibar 's terms, this is a "racism without races" (Balibar and Wallerstein, *Race, nation, classe*, 32–33).

Conservative projects such as the proposal to change the French Code of Nationality have been opposed by various liberal and left groups calling for equal rights for all citizens and an end to racism. Yet, as Silverman suggests, antiracist discourses are largely ineffective insofar as they follow the same oppositional logic as their racist counterparts. Antiracists who view racism as a disease infecting a potentially pure social body think in the same terms as racists who point to immigrants as offending foreign bodies that could be expelled (*Deconstructing the Nation*, 121). The point is that there can be no pure body, no social order that does not produce difference within itself in the very process of constituting itself. This is particularly evident today, when France harbors within itself cultural differences that were once kept at a distance by the geographical, administrative, and symbolic distinctions between the metropolitan country and its colonies. As large numbers of formerly colonized peoples settled in France after World War II and these cultural differences were literally brought home, many French people became anxious—not so much because they were confronted by cultural differences, but because it was becoming difficult to *tell the difference* between themselves and the "others" who lived in proximity to them in their urban world. In the years that followed, class differences were gradually ethnicized and racialized, while at the same time racism was increasingly disavowed and recast as a legitimate concern with cultural difference as an obstacle to national cohesion.

The racism that fuels conservative attempts to further Europeanize considerations of French national identity is perhaps most effectively challenged by social movements that question the necessity of linking nationality and citizenship, as France has done for the past two centuries. Not only in France but elsewhere in Europe, there are calls for a "new citizenship" based on one's country of residence rather than on nationality. Today's disenfranchised immigrants would be recognized as legitimate inhabitants and would enjoy full political and civil rights in their country of residence. Despite these hopeful calls, however, most discussions of citizenship and of national and cultural identity in France still turn on an opposition between France and its former colonies in Africa or Asia, an opposition that cannot begin to account for the fragmentation and dislocation that characterize modern life.

The fact that this same opposition organizes most Beur literary texts seems to be a source of embarrassment for academic critics who are committed to deconstructionist methods and to theories that acknowledge the complexity, instability, and ambiguity of all individual and collective identities. Rather than come to terms with the binarist character of much Beur writing, critics have generally avoided discussion of it altogether. One avoidance tactic (I include myself in the group that has resorted to it) has been to sidestep the issue of binarism by focusing not on Beur writing per se, but on the more writerly texts of Leïla Sebbar, who is not Beur (Woodhull, 88–133). Born in Algeria to an Algerian man and a French woman, Sebbar has lived in Paris since she began her university education several decades ago and, for the past decade and a half, has been writing about Beurs and other minority groups in France. Another means of avoiding discussion of the binarism of Beur writing has been to develop elaborate formal analyses whose only real purpose seems to be to assure the analysts themselves, as well as their readers, that they have chosen a worthy object of postmodern literary study (Laronde).

I see this second tendency as an outgrowth of French literary critics' resistance, in the 1960s and 1970s, to the habit of reading Maghrebian texts as ethnographic documents that unproblematically reflect a preexisting social reality, rather than as innovative literary texts in their own right. However much liberal and leftist French readers of that period may have sympathized with Maghrebian anticolonial struggles of the 1950s, however much they may have wanted to familiarize themselves with the cultures of peoples who had overthrown French rule, they were complicit with colonial ideologies insofar as they regarded Maghrebian texts primarily as sources of information about a foreign culture rather than as works of art on a par with those produced in Europe. By contrast, literary scholars who insisted on the importance of reading Maghrebian writing as postmodern literature granted it artistic status and critical agency for the first time. A preoccupation with the postmodern "literariness" of texts by the Beur descendants of Maghrebians poses its own problems, however. For in France today, "literariness" is widely assumed to be critical of existing political discourses and social practices; a preoccupation with it often impels readers to pass over certain uncritical dimensions of Beur writing.

The fact is that, with the exception of Farida Belghoul's *Georgette!,* Beur texts, whether written by women or by men, are not particularly concerned with postmodern issues such as the degree to which *all* individuals and collectivities are inevitably at odds with themselves in today's world. Nor do they explore the Beur experience of the postmodern condition in an especially forward-looking way. Rather, they express a yearning to belong to one culture, as "normal" people are presumed to do. They give voice to the pain of not belonging wholly to any one culture, showing that it often results in despair, madness, or suicide, when it does not explode in acts of externalized violence. They point to young women's temptation to enter into traditional marriage in a necessarily futile attempt to identity fully as Arabs, as Muslims, and as "women" (as women are thought to be defined by Muslim Arabs of the Maghreb), or simply in an attempt to escape parental control. In these texts, there is no happy embrace of ambivalence and ambiguity. For brief moments, to be sure, the impossibility of belonging to one culture may be treated with good humor, or at least with salutary irony. But the predominant tone, particularly in women's writing, is one of sadness and sober protest against a divided existence to which they alone seem to be condemned.

The binarism of much Beur writing and its expression of a tenacious desire for coherence indicate the degree to which the notion of bounded cultural identities has shaped political debates and personal experience in contemporary France, to the detriment of that country's non-European inhabitants. Beur writing shows that French national discourses of assimilation remain very powerful, the more so for having been revitalized by the bicentennial celebration of the French Revolution in 1989 and by recent discussions of "immigration." Yet because assimilation is more a national myth than a social reality for the inhabitants of France, because cultural identities are not bounded and coherent, but rather are fragmented and heterogeneous, we see in Beur writing as well elements that point to the limits and failures of these notions. In particular, we discern the need to assess differences of gender, generation, and political orientation within ethnic groups, and to consider how these differences shape the cultural politics of those groups.

We have already seen how the writing of Beur women deals with differences of gender and generation regarding female sexuality, marriage, and education. In a less sustained and focused way, it also deals with differences in Maghrebians' and Beurs' relation to Islam. Many members of the older generation were raised as Muslims and continue to identify as Muslims after they settle in France, whether or not they actively practice their religion. Their religious conviction contrasts with the more secular outlook of the younger generation, although some young people—notably young men—have been Islamicized by fundamentalist factions whose understanding of Islam, and of the cultural-political function of religion, is vastly different from that of the parental figures portrayed in Beur novels. Beur women writers often regard young men's embrace of Islam as little more than a cynical means of preserving male privilege. As for political differences within the Maghrebian/Beur community, let us note the most basic one evoked in Beur writing, that between the Algerians who fought for independence in the Algerian War and those who fought with the French forces, the Harkis. In sum, Beur writers' attention to the differences within the Maghrebian/Beur community suggests that ethnicity does not determine identity in any simple way.

The Beurs are not alone in emphasizing the heterogeneity of ethnic groups in France. Le Huu Khoa, Gisèle Bousquet, and others who have studied the Vietnamese living in France have pointed to differences in the circumstances of their departure from Vietnam, in their political orientation, and in their relation to the French. Here are some of the groups discussed in recent work on these questions:

1. The Vietnamese who settled in France after World War I, after serving voluntarily or involuntarily in the colonial forces of the French army or working as unskilled laborers in France during the war.

2. Young people who came to France to study in the interwar years, became active in Communist politics, and helped to organize a national resistance movement—a group that includes Nguyen Ai Quo (Ho Chi Minh).

3. Those who settled in France after World War II, after serving in the French army or working as laborers during the war. The German occupation of France and above all the Vietnamese revolt of August 1945, which resulted in Ho Chi Minh taking power, distinguish the experience of this

group from that of the World War I–era immigrants: France had suffered a major defeat at the hands of a European power, and the experience of immigration was now inseparable from the struggle for national liberation, not only for the Vietnamese, but for the Algerians and other groups as well.

4. The students, merchants, and workers who fled the French War between 1945 and 1954.

5. The Vietnamese who went to France after the decisive defeat of the French forces at Dien Bien Phu in 1954, particularly those who had worked in the French colonial administration and had French citizenship. It was said that these people, many of whom had never been to France, were being "repatriated" from Indochina. After 1954 many Eurasians were "repatriated" as well, that is, the children of French women or, more often, French men, whose marriages with Vietnamese partners were legitimate in the eyes of the French government.

6. Those who fled the war against the United States between 1954 and 1975. This group included Vietnamese students, merchants, and workers, as well as Chinese merchants whose families had lived in Vietnam for over a century while maintaining their Chinese passports, their own schools, and so on.

7. Those who left Vietnam after the socialist victory of April 30, 1975, and entered France not as immigrants but as refugees.

8. The children of the groups listed above, who were born in France and whose relation both to France and to Vietnam is very different from that of their parents.

Le Huu Khoa underscores the fact that since 1975, the already existing division of France's Vietnamese community into pro- and anti-Communist camps has been accentuated and institutionalized in political and cultural associations. He points to the lethal physical attacks of anti-Communists on progovernment figures in France, in the aftermath of 1975, as evidence that the Vietnamese do not necessarily conform to France's mythic representations of them as a model minority whose diligence and tranquility contrast sharply with the violence and laziness attributed to Africans. He also points out that the arrival of large numbers of Vietnamese refugees in a period of economic recession has sparked fears in the established Vietnamese community that it will become a target of the more virulent forms of French racism once the "threshold of tolerance" is exceeded. The largely anti-Communist refugees arrive with little or no capital; their skills do not necessarily win them gainful employment; and their diplomas have no validity in France. They often meet with hostility for both political and economic reasons, not only from certain sectors of the French working class and from French veterans of Dien Bien Phu, who were outraged by the late President Mitterand's recent visit there, but from Vietnamese socialists who were radicalized in the 1950s and 1960s and from middle-class Vietnamese restaurateurs with whom they are forced to compete in an increasingly tight market. Moreover, the refugees have only the most tenuous links with the young people of Vietnamese descent in France, because the refugees are Vietnamese in a way the young people never have been and do not aspire to be, and also because they often do not speak French.

As the foregoing discussion suggests, minority literature and scholarship in France have devoted considerable attention to the divisions *within* ethnic groups and have thus called into question essentialist notions of ethnic identity. So far, however, they have not explored the relations *between* ethnic groups in a critical, productive way. Most texts leave unchallenged the pluralist view that various ethnic groups can live side by side in harmony merely by respecting and learning to appreciate each other's "difference." This view shapes the writing, publication, marketing, and reading of texts by ethnic minorities—so much so that an established author like Calixthe Beyala, a Cameroonian French woman, can now make a living selling Paris's "communauté nègre" (her phrase) to the general public in novels such as *Le petit prince de Belleville* (The little prince of Belleville) and *Maman a un amant* (Mama has a lover).[6] Granted, these books have the merit of being good-humored and avoiding what the French call *misérabilisme,* the sentimental portrayal and moralistic denunciation of poverty and oppression. Beyala's novels also have an admirable feminist dimension. For example, *Maman a un amant* sympathetically explores the life of a fifty-year-old Malian woman, M'ammaryam, whose economic independence as a maker and seller of jewelry enables her to establish a more egalitarian relationship with her domineering husband after moving in with, and then leaving, her European French lover, who gives her much sexual pleasure but no real respect. During her time away, she comes to see her husband not as her "maître" (master) but as a "soleil déchu" (fallen idol); she learns to read and, above all, learns to "lire le Blanc" (read the white man) (292). M'ammaryam's account of her experience, addressed to an imaginary female "Friend," is said to have been translated into French from her native Bambara by Loukoum, a boy born to one of her husband's other wives and raised by M'ammaryam.

Unfortunately, however, the salient feature of *Maman* is not its feminism, but rather its intention to address people who want to do some light reading on the subject of multiculturalism in France. M'ammaryam's sober, reflective narrative alternates with Loukoum's cheerful account of the family's first summer vacation in the French countryside. In Loukoum's narrative, an economically strapped African family from the Paris neighborhood of Belleville ventures into darkest Lozère, communing with the French (or having comical miscommunications with them) in pastoral bliss. The publisher of *Maman* seems to have banked on the entertainment value of the novel, which places the European French in the position of natives visited by African tourists from Paris, tourists whose own manners are displayed with gentle irony. The text invites readers to engage in cultural tourism and to be edified by virtue of coming to understand M'ammaryam, her family, and her community better than they did before. Unfortunately, the text leaves undone the work of exploring the intricate ways in which Africanness and Frenchness intersect, displacing and reconfiguring a range of identities in the Parisian context.[7]

Beyala's novel presents a society in which self-contained ethnic groups simply mirror each other. Its "I'm OK, you're OK" approach to social relations banishes any thought of real ethnic conflict (although its treatment of gender conflict is quite persuasive). In Beur texts, ethnic groups are similarly self-contained and unrelated except by mirroring. But instead of a sunny world where there is no real conflict, we find a gloomy one where there is no real connection between ethnic groups. This lack of connection partially explains the feeling of personal isolation that figures as a central theme in Beur novels, as well as the perception that young women who move in both French and Maghrebian cultural spheres must lead a double life. In Beur texts, the European French are usually distant figures whose way of life is inaccessible, either because it requires money that Beurs do not have or because it requires a freedom of movement denied to most Beur women. Other ethnic minorities are no less distant than the European French. While Beur writers do mention groups such as the Portuguese and the Africans who live in the same neighborhoods and work in the same types of jobs as Maghrebians do, they generally regard them with detachment, despite occasional expressions of sympathy or disdain for the young African and Portuguese men who have the same reputation for delinquency as young Maghrebian men.

On the other hand, Beur writers frequently link their plight to that of African Americans. Why should this be? At first sight, the linkage seems understandable enough. Is it not the case that Beurs, like African Americans (and American Indians, who also figure in many Beur texts), have been dispossessed and banished to the ghetto, if not the reservation? Certainly, in the past several years, the term "ghetto" has been used by writers and commentators across the political spectrum to refer to the urban and suburban housing projects and slums occupied by racial and ethnic minority groups in France. Whether they are viewed as unassimilable aliens or as an underclass produced by the globalization of capital and the racialization of social differences, these groups are considered to have little chance of being successfully integrated into middle-class French society as things stand now.

It is only recently, however, that the marginal social space occupied by France's minorities has been termed a ghetto. Only in the past few years have the French expressed alarm that their society may be subject to the cultural fragmentation and racial violence that have historically characterized Britain and the United States. Indeed, these unfortunate developments are often seen as signs of the Americanization of French society. Silverman has argued that, unlike Britain and the United States, which have officially recognized racial and ethnic communities within the national group (negatively through segregation practices, positively through affirmative action), France has deliberately avoided identifying individual citizens as members of particular racial or ethnic groups, just as it has avoided instituting social policies based explicitly on race relations (*Deconstructing the Nation*, 4–5). As we have already seen, there is a widespread conviction that no distinctions are made among French nationals on the basis of race or ethnicity, and that official recognition of such distinctions would necessarily do citizens an injustice; it is the distinction between the national and the foreigner that is considered to be significant where political and civil rights are concerned.

It is perhaps the power of this conviction that explains the frequent references in Beur fiction to race relations in the United States. Conflictual relations of race or ethnicity in France, particularly among French nationals, often cannot be seen as a *national* problem. The same is true of the perceived lack of connection between racial and ethnic groups. Social problems such as these can only be seen as a failure of assimilation or as an indicator of intolerance for cultural difference, both of which are understood as a failure of French nationalism, rather than an inevitable effect of that nationalism. As a result, both the conflicts and the lack of connection between ethnic and racial groups in France find expression in Beur novels as *American* problems.[8] Indeed, it might be said that the effectiveness of the association of Beurs with African Americans lies precisely in its wryness, its *outlandish* quality in the eyes of French readers. What is more, the conviction that there is no indigenous, institutionally sanctioned ethnic conflict in France sometimes leads writers to suggest that Beurs must have brought their problems on themselves. Witness Malika's observation, in *Beur's Story*, that "if we were in the United States, I'm sure *we would have found a way* to be black Americans" (114, my emphasis).

Despite real historical differences in the ways that France and the United States have dealt with race and ethnicity, the lack of conflict and lack of connection between ethnic groups in texts by minority writers in France suggest a need to think differently about social relations in that national context. One way to begin is to recognize that the European French are an ethnic group. Their identity should not be allowed to pass as an unmarked norm against which marked subjects, such as Beurs, are to measure themselves. Another is to recognize that Frenchness, like any other ethnic identity, is a "fictive ethnicity" that is necessarily unstable; it is fraught with conflict and ambiguity and has the burden of constantly reproducing itself. (Judith Butler would say that, like gender identity, it must continually be performed, and is therefore inevitably subject to change.)[9] A third is to consider how Beur identities intersect not only with those of the European French but also with those of other minority groups in France. This would involve an analysis of the histories various ethnic groups share, keeping in mind the power differences between them and the particularities of each one's position within those histories.[10]

Farida Belghoul's *Georgette!* is unique in dealing with all these issues in a compelling way, although its themes of poverty, cultural alienation, and madness are similar to those treated by other Beur women writers. The novel's first-person narrator and protagonist is an unnamed seven-year-old Beur girl whose experience in school is quite grim. Her teacher never calls upon her to recite the lesson she has prepared for the day, and never gives her any other kind of positive recognition. In fact, in the girl's perception, she is visible to the teacher only when she is singled out for punishment or when she fears punishment for a phantasmal act of aggression against the teacher—for example, when she associates the real transgression of putting her finger in the blue ink of the inkwell with the imaginary one of using that same finger to put out the teacher's blue eye. At recess, the girl shuffles around the playground in complete isolation. By walking stoop-shouldered and pretending to be an aged person, she is able to avoid seeing herself as a Beur child who has been left out of the other children's games. And by pretending that a mouth-watering snack awaits her, she finds an imaginary solution to the perpetual problem of hunger.

The girl's hunger for food and for recognition are emblems of her poverty and her marginalization in French society. And like many other characters in the novels of Beur women, she is faced with the irreconcilable demands of the French educational system on the one hand and her family on the other. The girl, like her mother, brother, and father, has values, beliefs, and an understanding of French-Maghrebian relations that conflict with those transmitted in the schools, the army, the workplace, children's "colonies de vacances," or "summer camps," and other institutions where the legacy of colonialism is shown to be in evidence. The impossibility of translating effectively between the two cultural systems causes the girl incommunicable distress that leads to madness, madness that is projected onto the key figures of her father and her teacher.

Caught between "un fou . . . et une cinglée," between "a madman . . . and a crazy woman" (136), the girl runs away from school one day, taking refuge in a city park where she meets an elderly Frenchwoman, another "folle," or "crazy" (146), who tries to enlist her to stand in for the three sons who have abandoned her—hence the Beur girl's imaginary baptism as "Georgette." Unwilling to throw in her lot with "une vieille toute nouvelle" (a new old lady) (147), unable to find her way home, and fearful of her father's violent response should she do so, the girl darts into the street where she is run over by a car. In the last line of the text the girl says to herself as she lies bleeding, "J'étouffe au fond d'un encrier" (I'm suffocating at the bottom of an inkwell) (163). It is as if she were about to die not only as a result of physical injury and the crushing material reality of poverty and racism, but also because of an inability to give voice to the ambiguities of her existence and to find readers or listeners who are able to take in what she has to say.

Despite its familiar theme of incommunicable distress arising from conflicts between the French and Maghrebian cultures, *Georgette!* is quite different from other Beur texts; it does something other than posit the irreconcilability of two discrete social spheres. In Belghoul's text, the unfortunate protagonist does not succumb to madness or commit suicide by virtue of falling into a gap that is presumed to separate these two spheres, as was the case with Malika and Farida in Kessas's *Beur's Story.* Rather, her stream-of-consciousness account of her predicament, comprising two interdependent narrative strands dealing with school and with family, shows how the identities associated with each sphere in fact overlap and interlock within a hierarchized but mutable network of power relations. The complex play of language within and between the two narrative strands, the interweaving of present reality with memory and fantasy, body forth the instability of all the subjective and social identities figured in the text and the ambivalence they necessarily generate.

The girl is painfully aware that both her father and her teacher are highly ambiguous figures whose stance toward her is at once protective and oppressive. The teacher who smiles kindly at her also raps her fingers with a ruler to impose discipline. And in the very act of expressing her wish to protect the girl from her father's blows, the teacher simultaneously threatens to inform the father of the girl's idiosyncratic work habits, thereby providing grounds for a beating. The teacher's references to the problem of physical abuse are double-edged as well. On the one hand, they divulge her contempt for Maghrebian men who "frappent leurs femmes et leurs enfants comme des animaux" (hit their wives and children like animals) (121), contempt that extends to the women and children who live with such men. On the other hand, the teacher's comments make the girl conscious of paternal violence not only as a source of fear and shame, but as an unacceptable practice that can and should be stopped.

Partly because her brief experience in school has altered her understanding of her relationship to her father, the narrator harbors great ambivalence toward him. She loves her father and admires his beautiful singing voice, saying that "même un lion . . . s'endormirait au paradis à l'entendre" (even a lion . . . would slumber in paradise at the sound of it) (34). She loves her father even though he is an angry, violent man who often speaks "avec du feu dans la gorge" (with flames in his mouth) (34). Once she has run away, though, she is no longer able to declare with confidence that while her father may be violent, he is also "gentil et généreux" (kind and generous); in conversation with a doll she finds in the park, she is forced to concede that "il chante faux" (he sings off key) (154) and that "il chante des horreurs comme: je te tue!" (he sings atrocious things like, "I'm going to kill you!") (155).

Although the key authority figures in the girl's life are equally ambiguous, they are not equally powerful. The teacher is presented as a higher authority whose interpretation of everyday reality prevails not only in the mind of the Beur girl, but in French society at large. This comes across most clearly in the teacher's comments on the girl's school notebook, in which the girl's first attempts at writing are recorded alongside the "écriture de môme" (childlike handwriting) (109) of her father. In order to teach his daughter to write, the father inscribes in her notebook, in Arabic, some words of the Prophet that he had learned to write as a youth in Algeria. From a European standpoint, which the girl adopts, the father's notations are written backwards, that is, from right to left, starting from the back of the book. When the teacher discovers the pages written by the girl's father, she assigns a double meaning to them in a conference with the girl. First, she interprets them as a course in Arabic that her father is giving his daughter so that when she returns to Algeria to be a doctor, she can communicate with the natives. The girl is dumbfounded by this, since she has never considered either becoming a doctor or returning to Algeria. Second, the teacher declares the father's notations to be out of place in the girl's school notebook. "Prends un autre cahier et laisse-le à la maison" (Get another notebook and leave it at home) (124), she tells the girl. The teacher is determined to assign the narrator to an Algerian homeland and to establish a clear boundary between French and Algerian education, one that could never exist for a pupil such as the Beur girl. Given the power play that has just taken place, given the girl's stunned silence and her confusion about all that the teacher has said, the teacher's final remark is particularly ironic: "Nous parviendrons à nous comprendre. La langue n'a jamais empêché de communiquer. Ça veut dire se parler" (We will manage to understand each other. Language has never prevented anyone from communicating. That means talking to each other) (124).

In Belghoul's novel, written and spoken language never figure as transparent means of communication. On the contrary, writing is shown to be a site of struggle over cultural meanings, one that is unavailable to some people, such as the protagonist's illiterate mother, who cleans houses for a living. And speaking often acquires an opacity that draws attention to the role of language in the performance of one's identity. For example, the protagonist's father's speech is often rendered in such a way as to underscore his rudimentary knowledge of French, which makes his authoritarian outbursts appear ludicrous. In the dispute over the type of pencil the teacher has required students to buy for school, the girl protests that she must have HB pencils, not the 2H pencils her mother has bought for her. Her father dismisses her concern in terms that comically disclose his ignorance in the matter. Misinterpreting the French term 2H, he says, "Zache c'est la marque . . . y'a d'autres marques" (Zache is the brand name . . . there are other brands) (17).

But it is not only the garbled French of underclass foreigners that acquires opacity in Belghoul's novel. By various other means, the text draws attention to the French language and, by extension, to Frenchness, as cultural constructs that should not be taken for granted. For instance, the only classmate with whom the protagonist seems to have any relationship is Mireille, who speaks with a lisp that renders her speech strange and repellent, as if she had an "asticot," or "maggot" (85), in her mouth. And the protagonist's remark in the first line of the novel, "La sonne cloche. . . . Non, la cloche sonne" (The ring is belling. . . . No, the bell is ringing) (9), is not just childish play with language. Her inversion of subject and verb in the expression "la sonne cloche" indicates that something is wrong, as in the expression "ça cloche," not only in the girl's school where "la cloche sonne" (the bell is ringing), but in all social institutions that take for granted the naturalness of French and of Frenchness.

If *Georgette!* renders the French language opaque, it also challenges the naturalness of Frenchness by emphasizing the link between Frenchness and whiteness or blankness, and by drawing attention to the very invisibility of this link. In Richard Dyer's words, it shows how "white power secures its dominance by seeming not to be anything in particular" ("White," 44).[11] For example, the narrator says of her teacher:

> Elle me surveille toujours avec ses deux trous vides. Les yeux de la maîtresse sont creux. Elle a aucune couleur à l'intérieur. . . . Je plonge, comme dans une piscine vide, au fond des yeux de la maîtresse. Je me fracasse la tête. (24)

> She watches me with her two empty holes. The teacher's eyes are hollow. She has no color inside. . . . I dive, as if into an empty swimming pool, deep into the teacher's eyes. I smash my head to pieces.

The emptiness of the teacher's gaze is far from innocuous. It is the mark of her power to withhold the recognition that is vital to the Beur girl striving to be a good student and a respected member of society in France. The teacher's unseeing gaze is twice linked to the girl's impulse to do violence to herself: first, when she tries in vain to get the teacher to notice her, phantasmally "smashing her head to pieces," as we saw above; and second, when the unseeing gaze turns into a persecuting gaze, fueling the girl's fear that her teacher is driving around town looking for her after she runs away from school. In the latter instance, the girl is haunted by the nightmarish image of her teacher as a "boule d'ogre" (140), in which the Maghrebian figure of a child-devouring "ogre" (94) merges with that of a "bouledogue" (bulldog), reminiscent of the deadly hound that accompanies Lautréamont's Maldoror (*Chants,* 176–79). The teacher's power of annihilation is a key factor in the girl's suicidal dash into the street, where she will be hit by a car.

It is precisely the devastating power of the teacher's blank stare that prompts the narrator's fantasy of putting out the teacher's eye. Similarly, the teacher's power to silence her Beur pupil—"elle [m']a coupé la voix" (she cut me off) (70)—provokes vengeful fantasies in which the narrator's father strangles the teacher (52), or in which the narrator herself is a doctor announcing to the teacher, "Je te coupe la langue" (I'm going to cut out your tongue) (132). These fantasies stage the power of Frenchness, of blankness, of whiteness that seems to be nothing in particular. The violence it provokes, whether phantasmal or real, mirrors the violence it inflicts. Equally important, the text shows how the identities of teacher and pupil interlock: "la respiration de la maîtresse m'é-touffe" (the teacher's breathing stifles me) (48); "je m'arrache la peau avec ses ongles rouges" (I tear at my skin with her red fingernails) (55). And insofar as it attributes some version of American Indian identity to every major character—the teacher, Mireille, the narrator, and every member of the narrator's family—Belghoul's novel emphasizes the fact that every ethnicity is, in a sense, fictive. It shows us that the meaning of Indianness changes constantly, that ethnicity is always bound up with other aspects of identity, and that it is subject to historical change.

In *Georgette!*, the figure of the Indian initially serves to illustrate how social institutions such as the education system press people to conform to a certain model of French identity. For example, the narrator's teacher requires that all her students line up "en file indienne," or "Indian file" (13), in order that she see "une seule tête" (12)—one head, one face, a single incarnation of the French schoolchild. Subsequently, however, Belghoul's novel puts into play an array of "Indian" identities that diffracts this unitary notion of Frenchness while keeping in view the institutional forces that constrain the play of identity. Indians appear, for instance, as characters in the American westerns that are broadcast on French television in the late 1950s and early 1960s, when the narrator is growing up. The presence of cowboys and Indians on the French airwaves poses a two-pronged challenge to the centrality of Frenchness. On the one hand, it signals the power of the U.S. culture industry to invade and colonize French cultural space, and on the other, it provides an occasion for marginalized TV viewers such as the Maghrebian narrator and her family to respond to Western popular cultural forms from a critical, non-Western standpoint: they side with the Indians rather than the cowboys.

The figure of the Indian also calls attention to the racialization of class differences in France and to the economic and cultural inequalities that generate conflict at various levels of society—in the workplace, the family, the public schools, and the subjective experience of individuals. Seeing her father in the fluorescent headband he wears while sweeping streets, for example, the narrator identifies him as a "chef indien," an "Indian chief" (82). She is soon unde-ceived, however, for her father tells her that the headband is not a prestigious ornament or even a protective device that alerts drivers of cars to the presence of streetsweepers, but an emblem of the streetsweepers' subjection: it allows the superviser to keep tabs on them at all times. In the father's eyes, the headband is a sign of the city's contempt for and abuse of minority employees who have little choice but to perform the menial, degrading tasks that are considered to be beneath the dignity of most European French people. At home, the narra-tor's father vents his rage by heaping abuse on the members of his family, nota-bly by attacking his disobedient son with a knife that the narrator dubs a "hache de guerre," or "war hatchet" (115).

In the eyes of the narrator's brother, the father's "Indian" headband is nothing but a mark of low status that brings shame upon the whole family. The same is true of the mother's gaudy clothing and the flash of her gold teeth; she is a "Cheyenne" (97) who causes the narrator and her brother boundless embar-rassment. If the narrator sometimes voluntarily assumes an Indian identity, it is the nobler one of an Indian princess who can lord it over Mireille (87) or of a young "Indian chief" (29) who is smitten with the teacher in her idealized as-pect as a gentle beauty. In the presence of the revered teacher, whose elegant fin-gernails are "rouges comme des fleurs" (red as flowers) (29), the narrator assumes the pose of a gracious creature with "peau rouge" (red skin) (77). But behind this facade, the narrator tells us, there lurks "un petit affreux avec des griffes pleines de sang comme les ongles de la maîtresse" (a horrid little thing with claws full of blood, like the teacher's fingernails) (77).

The "horrid little thing" in question is the narrator in her guise as a "chat sauvage" (wild cat) (76), which the teacher thinks she can tame. But the narra-tor is not the only wild thing in the novel; Mireille also qualifies as one. When she horrifies her mother by spitting, Mireille gets a scolding, which she reports to the narrator in her lispy speech: "Elle m'explique que ze suis pas une çauvaze [sauvage] tout de même" (she explained that I am not a savage, after all) (79). In Belghoul's text, adults often regard children as savages, but only in the sense that they do not yet conform to the only acceptable model of the civilized adult—the adult Frenchman. The possibility that "savages" who radically differ from that model may live within France's borders is flatly denied by those in authority. For example, Mireille's mother readily admits, upon being questioned by her daughter, that an Indian is an example of a savage, but fiercely disputes Mireille's claim to know an Indian, saying that Indians do not live in France (79). The Indian that Mireille refers to is, of course, the narrator, whose foreignness is equated with Indianness.

Significantly, Mireille's pejorative identification of the narrator as a "peau rouge," or "redskin" (69), is conflated, by means of a pun, with the teacher's refusal to recognize her as the holder of the "pot rouge" (69), or "red cup," which supposedly ensures that she will be asked to recite the lesson. Precisely because she is seen as a primitive, the narrator, in her guise as a "peau rouge," cannot reap the benefit of holding the "pot rouge." Rather than allowing her to recite, the teacher cuts her off and summarizes the day's lesson herself. Even if the narrator had been allowed to recite, she could only have parroted a lesson about little Rémi, the archetypal French boy depicted in the reader, whose experience stands in for her own. Belghoul's text suggests that as long as the identities of ethnic minorities are seen as utterly separate from and inferior to French identity, as long as French identity is presumed to be unitary and unchanging, minorities will likely be viewed as unassimilable aliens, as wild animals who can be tamed and kept as pets, or as cultural orphans who can be adopted by the European family of man, provided that they shed their gendered, racialized otherness, as far as possible, and take the family name ("Georgette"). Some members of minority groups will be driven to attempt to obliterate their supposedly irreducible difference through suicidal acts, as Belghoul's protagonist does, while others will continue to live on the margins of society. Their marginalization will likely be regarded as the fate they deserve, or as sheer bad luck ("manque de pot" [163]).

Although it presents a bleak view of the Beur girl's existence, *Georgette!* shows that the problem is not that Beurs cannot be clearly identified as either Maghrebian or French. Instead, it suggests that there is insufficient recognition of the fact that Maghrebian and French identities are always diffracted, that they always intersect with each other and with other identities—notably those of gender and class—and are organized by institutionally sanctioned hierarchies that are often disavowed: "peau rouge," "pot rouge," "manque de pot." Belghoul's novel signals the devastating effects of current social arrangements on girls like her protagonist while leaving open the possibility of meaningful change. On the one hand, the protagonist is situated within a set of social relations in which readers of various genders, ethnicities, and nationalities are subtly but surely implicated; the protagonist's debilitating isolation is identified as a social problem. And on the other hand, Belghoul's protagonist draws attention to her suffocation in a sentence that is not closed with a period; it is with this unfinished sentence that the novel ends. The account of the girl's predicament does not definitively end in madness or death, but potentially opens onto another life.

The importance of taking in what writers like Belghoul have to say is especially great now that notions of national identity are being increasingly Europeanized within the European Community: international agreements and rights based on former colonial relations are being rethought, and Europe's borders and cultural identities are being policed more strictly than ever. As Maxim Silverman points out, a two-tier Europe of nationals and nonnationals is emerging, in which even nationals, such as Beurs, face abuses in the 1990s (*Deconstructing the Nation*, 152–70). In an age of racism without races, the cultural work of reconfiguring ethnicity is crucial, and it is inseparable from struggles for equal rights and economic justice.

Notes

1. The term "Beur" comes from the slang of Parisian youths, which involves inverting the syllables of words, in this case, the word "Arabe." (The name for this slang, *verlan*, is itself a product of the process of inversion. The expression *à l'envers*, meaning "inverted" or "backwards," becomes *verlan*.) Some young people of Maghrebian descent have appropriated the term "Beur" for their own purposes; others revile it. In any case, it has passed into general usage thanks to the mass media.

2. For an overview of the background, themes, and forms of Beur writing as well as interviews with Beur writers, see Alec Hargreaves, *Voices from the North African Immigrant Community in France.*

3. All translations of fictional and critical texts are mine if no published translation is cited.

4. Leïla Houari's *Zeida de nulle part* (Zeida from nowhere) can usefully be compared to Benaïssa's testimonial because, despite significant differences between the two texts, they have the same oppositional structure. Houari was born in Morocco in 1957 and emigrated with her family to Belgium in 1965, where she has lived ever since. Her text, which is lyrical rather than plaintive, stages a young girl's voluntary return to her homeland in search of her roots: she hopes to escape the feeling of dislocation inspired by life in Europe by immersing herself in the Moroccan society where she was born. However, despite the affection of her relatives and an agreeable flirtation with a male friend of her cousin's, the author's persona, Zeida, realizes that she will never fit in in sunny Casablanca and returns, somewhat regretfully, to the gray skies of Brussels. As in Benaïssa's testimonial, a central issue is the protagonist's refusal to accept an arranged marriage, although unlike Benaïssa and most other Beur women writers, Houari opposes to it an idealized view of heterosexual romance. Houari's narrator assumes an affirmative stance toward her cultural predicament, saying that she must make the most of the unresolvable "contradictions" of her life (83). However, she deals only with contradictions, that is, with differences that are seen as extrinsic. Rather than exploring the differences and the ambivalence that are intrinsic to her identity, she vacillates, like Benaïssa, between the two poles organizing the contradictions of her life—Europe and the Maghreb.

5. Cited by Balibar, *Frontières,* 59.

6. Beyala's phrase "communauté nègre" appears in *Maman,* 249.

7. Beyala's *Tu t'appelleras Tanga* (You will be called Tanga), which deals with the relation between a white woman and a black woman who share a prison cell, is a more substantive text than *Maman a un amant.* Yet it deploys the same humanist vision, demonstrating that people of vastly different backgrounds and experience—people whose identities remain external to each other rather than being internally linked—can come to understand and empathize with each other.

8. Interestingly, the English title of Kessas's novel *Beur's Story* recalls the Broadway musical *West Side Story,* which stages conflicts between Latino and European American working-class youths.

9. For a discussion of both sexuality and race as performance, see the essay on Nella Larsen's *Passing* in Butler's *Bodies That Matter,* 167–85.

10. In this connection, however, one should be wary of texts that pretend to scrutinize the inherent instability of Frenchness while in fact reinforcing some of its more oppressive configurations. I'm thinking, for example, of Dominique Bona's *Malika,* which mobilizes a number of well-known Orientalist fantasies in order to suggest that Malika, an enchanting Moroccan au pair girl, profoundly disturbs and transforms the professional and personal lives of David Paul-Martin and his wife Marie-Hélène, the wealthy French couple who employ her while they are vacationing near Saint-Tropez in a fabulous villa overlooking the Mediterranean. Malika's powers of enchantment include the stereotypical ones of arousing carnal lust in David (a Pied-Noir whose instinctual urges are associated with his North African roots) and, correspondingly, provoking jealousy in Marie-Hélène (who at one point dresses as an Oriental vamp in order to heighten her attractiveness to her husband and to other men). Another of Malika's stereotypical powers is that of the muse who inspires Westerners—in this case, Marie-Hélène—to find and express their authentic self through creative activity, notably painting. Far from exposing the instability of Frenchness, Bona's novel merely recycles clichés about French culture (with a capital C), including its long-standing enthrallment with exotic femininity.

11. See also George Lipsitz, "The Possessive Investment in Whiteness," and Ruth Frankenberg, *White Women, Race Matters.*

Works Cited

Balibar, Etienne. *Les frontières de la démocratie.* Paris: La Découverte, 1992.
———. "Le racisme: Encore un universalisme." *MOTS* 18 (March 1989), "Racisme et antiracisme: Frontières et recouvrements." Published in English as "Racism as Universalism," *New Political Science* 16/17 (Fall/Winter 1989), special issue, "Racism in Europe" (not cited in my essay).
Balibar, Etienne, and Immanuel Wallerstein. *Race, nation, classe: Les identités ambigües.* Paris: La Découverte, 1988. Published in English as *Race, Nation, Class: Ambiguous Identities,* translated by Chris Turner. New York: Verso, 1991.
Belghoul, Farida. *Georgette!* Paris: Bernard Barrault, 1986.
Benaïssa, Aïcha. *Née en France: Histoire d'une jeune beur.* Paris: Payot, 1990.
de Benoist, A. *Europe, tiers monde, même combat.* Paris: Laffont, 1986.
Beyala, Calixthe. *Maman a un amant.* Paris: Albin Michel, 1993.
———. *Le petit prince de Belleville.* Paris: Albin Michel, 1992.
———. *Tu t'appelleras Tanga.* Paris: Stock, 1988.
Bona, Dominique. *Malika.* Paris: Mercure de France, 1992.
Boukhedenna, Sakinna. *Journal. Nationalité: Immigré(e).* Paris: L'Harmattan, 1987.

Bousquet, Gisèle L. *Behind the Bamboo Hedge: The Impact of Homeland Politics in the Parisian Vietnamese Community.* Ann Arbor: University of Michigan Press, 1991.

Brunschwig, H. *Mythes et réalités de l'impérialisme colonial français.* Paris: Colin, 1960.

Butler, Judith. *Bodies That Matter: On the Discursive Limits of Sex.* New York: Routledge, 1993.

———. *Gender Trouble: Feminism and the Subversion of Identity.* New York: Routledge, 1990.

Dyer, Richard. "White." *Screen* 4 (Fall 1988): 44–64.

Frankenberg, Ruth. *White Women, Race Matters: The Social Construction of Whiteness.* Minneapolis: University of Minnesota Press, 1993.

Girard, A. "Opinion publique, immigration et immigrés." *Ethnologie Française* 3 (1977): 219–28.

Hargreaves, Alec. *Voices from the North African Immigrant Community in France.* New York: Berg, 1991.

———. "Writing for Others." In *Race, Discourse and Power in France,* edited by Maxim Silverman, 111–19. Aldershot, U.K.: Avebury, 1991.

Houari, Leïla . *Zeida de nulle part.* Paris: L'Harmattan, 1985.

Kessas, Ferrudja. *Beur's Story.* Paris: L'Harmattan, 1990.

Laronde, Michel. *Autour du roman beur: Immigration et identité.* Paris: L'Harmattan, 1993.

Lautréamont, Comte de. *Les chants de Maldoror.* Paris: Librairie Générale Française (Livre de Poche), 1963.

Le Gallou, J.-Y. *La Préférence nationale: Réponse à l'immigration.* Paris: Albin Michel, 1985.

Le Huu Khoa. *Les Jeunes Vietnamiens de la deuxième génération: La semi-rupture au quotidien.* Paris: CIEMI et L'Harmattan, 1987.

———. *Les Vietnamiens en France: Insertion et identité.* Paris: CIEMI et L'Harmattan, 1985.

Lipsitz, George. "The Possessive Investment in Whiteness: Racialized Social Democracy and the 'White' Problem in American Studies." *American Quarterly* 3 (September 1995): 369–87.

Silverman, Maxim. *Deconstructing the Nation: Immigration, Racism and Citizenship in Modern France.* New York: Routledge, 1992.

———, ed. *Race, Discourse and Power in France.* Aldershot, U.K.: Avebury, 1991.

Woodhull, Winifred. *Transfigurations of the Maghreb: Feminism, Decolonization, and Literatures.* Minneapolis: University of Minnesota Press, 1993.

2 / Narrative Strategies and Postcolonial Identity in Contemporary France

Leïla Sebbar's Les Carnets de Shérazade

Françoise Lionnet

Exoticism . . . shows well its fundamental justification,
which is to deny any identification by History.
—Roland Barthes, *Mythologies*

Our history (or more precisely our histories)
is shipwrecked in colonial history.
—Jean Bernabé, Patrick Chamoiseau,
Raphaël Confiant, *In Praise of Creoleness*

Leïla Sebbar's novels, published in France since the late 1970s, stage the diversity of contemporary French society and the survival strategies deployed by immigrants in search of a cultural place to call their own. In her *Shérazade* trilogy, Sebbar explores the fascination that exoticism and Orientalism exert upon the imagination of a young *beure* who works her way across France and through its museums, discovering there for the first time a representation of her own cultural heritage. Shérazade's journey is a cultural itinerary that succeeds in establishing a set of seductive relations between a mythic France and an equally mythic Orient at the crossroads of which the young woman engages in self-discovery through self-displacement.[1]

Shérazade, who insists on this nontraditional spelling of her name, is the paradigmatic postcolonial subject who constructs her *monde diffracté mais re-composé*, her "diffracted, yet recomposed" world and identity, through her work of storytelling, which gives an oral character to the written text of the novel. The narrative becomes a site of mediation and subversion that allows the heroine to question the history of Orientalist painting, to unravel the myths they have created, and to use the threads that remain in order to weave a new tale, one better suited to her own discoveries as she travels through France.

Like Manon Lescaut, the eighteenth-century heroine, Shérazade is an itinerant, fugitive, and picaresque character who is somewhat of a social parasite and whose role is indispensable to the cultural redescriptions performed by the text.[2] The classic novel by Abbé Prévost is often linked to the origins of the French novel; it is also a story about the origins of French colonialism. The adventures of the Chevalier Des Grieux and his lover Manon are inscribed in one of the "grand narratives" of the Enlightenment, the great migrations of settlement and conquest of the New World by Europeans. Manon's transatlantic passage to America, however, ends in failure. Like many Romantic heroines, Manon is defeated and dies in Louisiana.[3] Unlike her, as we shall see, Shérazade succeeds in mapping out a new geography, not on the margins of the colonial empire, but on the very territory of the former colonial power. This new geography destabilizes the distinction between "French" and "francophone" literature, between colony and metropole.

Let me begin by situating Sebbar in relation to current controversies (in the U.S. academy) concerning the critical domain covered by the expression "francophone literature." There has long been talk of replacing the term "francophone" by one that would better reflect the diverse and heterogeneous realities of this field. The term "national literatures of French expression" has been used; others prefer "emergent literatures," especially since the University of Minnesota Press launched a new series under that title containing translations of various contemporary novels, including that of Moroccan writer Abdelkebir Khatibi, *Love in Two Languages*.[4] The attempt to redefine an increasingly protean discipline in light of the diverse geographic areas it covers, all of them marginal in relation to a center, "franco-French" literature, has certainly become necessary. It is in the wake of deconstructive theoretical reflections upon what is the "center" with respect to the "margins" that this redefinition continues.

The point, simply put, is to reject any simplistic opposition between French literature and so-called "francophone" literature, and to rethink the very idea of literature. After all, as Khatibi puts it, "who still appeals to . . . the unity of the French language?" (*FE,* 15). There has always been a network of influences and relations, since Montaigne even, between the systems of representation of the "metropole" and the subjects/objects it represented, whether it be in the sixteenth-century texts on the "Cannibals," in the eighteenth-century literature on the Persians, or in the Africanist discourse of poets and novelists in the nineteenth century.[5] If these real or imaginary cultural contacts gave Montaigne the material for some of his *Essays,* today they provide Khatibi and Sebbar a language in which to narrate and reconstruct their *histoire raturée,* or "wiped out" history.[6] As a number of critics and anthropologists have noted, cultural exchanges on a global scale, far from creating strongly homogenized societies, tend to facilitate the evolution of a system of interdependencies and relations, a *métis* lifeworld where disparate traditions cross over and dialogue with one another.[7]

The conflict that opposes the center to the margin is, according to Michel Foucault, the same ideological conflict that separates those who believe in History conceived of as an uninterrupted continuity and those who understand contemporary societies through models of heterogeneity and heterotopy.[8] As Foucault explains in his *Archaeology of Knowledge,* this vision of history is tied to a certain conception of the subject:

> Continuous history is the indispensable correlative of the founding function of the subject: the guarantee that everything that has eluded him may be restored to him; the certainty that time will dispense nothing without restoring it in a reconstituted unity; the promise that one day the subject—in the form of historical consciousness—will once again be able to appropriate, to bring back under his sway, all those things that are kept at a distance by difference, and find in them what might be called his abode. Making historical analysis the discourse of the continuous and making human consciousness the original subject of historical development and all action are the two sides of the same system of thought.[9]

Against this totalizing and teleological vision of time, Foucault opposes a continuously changing network of nodes, a system of relations binding together a diversity of sites and conflicting subjects. For the postcolonial writer, caught in this process of change despite herself, subjected to a system of thought that consigns her to the margins while necessarily implicating her in the system whose language she uses, the question of historical change has become a primordial one. After all, how does one reconcile a vision of history whose "function is to ensure the infinite continuity of discourse" (*AK,* 25) with the linguistic, spatial, and temporal dispersion of a once colonized subject? How does this subject reconcile "le rêve d'habiter,"[10] or the quest for a home, and the fate of being constantly torn between the metropole and its satellites, between the center that defines her, that she carries within, and the margin where she must try to live and work, with her only tools being the same representational system that can paralyze her by negating her? This subject must try to conceive her relation to the other in a way that rejects the binary opposition between the societies "without history" and the European societies that claim to manifest *une destinée historiale,* or a "historical destiny."[11] The massive displacement of population from the former colonies to the metropoles of the center has today reversed the patterns that began in the Renaissance and became increasingly visible during the eighteenth century, as, for example, in *Manon Lescaut.* This reversal has transformed the entire ideological situation, along with the concepts of tradition, linearity, and referential illusion, concepts that Western critics have learned to suspect through the works of Foucault and Derrida and that postcolonial writers have also been deconstructing for two generations.

As Khatibi has noted, "*Deconstruction,* as an overcoming of Western metaphysics, and as it has been developed in Derrida's singular style, has accompanied *decolonization* as an historical event. . . . This coincidence is not accidental" (*MP,* 47–48). Khatibi also adds:

> That is why, as we converse with Western reflections on difference (those of Nietzsche, Heidegger, and among our close contemporaries, Maurice Blanchot and Jacques Derrida), we take into account not only their style of thinking, but also their strategy and their weapons, in order to press them into the service of our struggle, which is necessarily another exorcism of the mind, demanding an effective decolonization, a concrete thinking of difference [*une pensée concrète de la différence*]. (*MP,* 20)

If it is true that we find this "thinking of difference" put into practice in the project of demystification launched by various contemporary authors, from Samuel Beckett to V. S. Naipaul, Maurice Blanchot, or Thomas Pynchon, with them this project remains negative. It is a vehicle of nihilism; it highlights the failure of every form of transcendence, the conceptual impasse reached by all belief in absolute truth (whether it be political or humanitarian, religious or philosophical), and the concomitant fragmentation of the postmodern subject. But for Leïla Sebbar, this fragmentation does not necessarily need to be conceived as the fatal breakdown and dispersion of the subject. For her, the attempt to deconstruct tradition is oriented toward a moment of insight or *prise de conscience* that leads to renewal and affirmation. The objective is a practice of difference that is not limited to the fictional domain (the telling of a story and the narration of history—what Todorov calls "l'histoire racontante" and Linda Hutcheon "historiographic metafiction") but includes the cultural context of the narrative, the broad domain of everyday practices in our pluralistic, polyphonic, and intertwined societies. Sebbar and Khatibi, like Salman Rushdie, Toni Morrison, or Assia Djebar, create dispersed images that reflect the contingencies of a multicultural world, with its social relations constantly in a state of renegotiation. It is therefore not surprising that these postcolonial texts find resonance with contemporary readers who are themselves marginalized or exiled subjects and cultural nomads. Although they must invest themselves in the work in order to make sense of it, they can also discover in it eclectic linguistic forms that resonate with their daily experiences.

Sebbar's novels belong to what has been called the "Maghrebian literature from France." She allows us to hear the voices and expressions of Maghrebian immigrants, and her narrative integrates these oral patterns, thus flaunting its own dispossession, since it knows itself to be, in Derrida's phrase, "parole soufflée"—hybrid speech, impure speech, always already borrowed from the speech of others and retransmitted by textual means.[12]

Sebbar invents a new France, tailored to the migrants working their way across it. Her novels are examples of texts that are "unclassifiable" according to the traditional criteria that oppose "French" and "francophone" literatures, since the standard opposition between the center and the margin is rendered inoperable. Neither "francophone" nor exactly French, Leïla Sebbar herself is the type of postcolonial writer whose "French" works published in Paris force us to rethink our pedagogical and ideological categories.[13] Through her use of the themes of exile, deracination, loss of memory, silence, and revolt, Sebbar belongs to the lineage of "francophone" writers who have risen up against the "civilizing mission" of France in Africa and elsewhere. But her original contribution is to have made immigrant women—doubly marginalized by their womanhood and their Arab background—the very center of a work that problematizes the entire visual and discursive tradition of European Orientalism.

Born in Algeria of an Algerian father and French mother, Leïla Sebbar chooses to write about what Michel Laronde calls "the *beur* indenture" while distancing herself from her fictional subjects.[14] Often denounced by Maghrebian intellectuals who consider her work suspect, given that she does not speak Arabic and is not herself an immigrant, Sebbar has explained her position in an exchange of letters with Nancy Huston:

> Every time I have to talk about my writing I must situate myself in my *métissage,* repeat that French is my mother tongue, and explain in what way I am neither an immigrant nor a *beur,* but simply an exile. Although I am certainly a gilded exile, I am from a land that is the land of my father and that haunts my memory, and I am living in a land that is the land of my mother, my language, my work, my children, but where I do not really find my home. . . .
>
> I am not an immigrant, nor the child of immigrants. I am not a Maghrebian writer "of French expression." . . . Now I know that I must find a way to speak, declare, affirm without ambiguity, without guilt, while saving myself the time to develop the subtleties of this singular position of mine: I am French, a French writer born of a French mother and Algerian father . . . and the subject matter of my books is not my identity. . . .
>
> My books . . . are the sign, the signs of my history, the history of a *croisée* [mixed-race person], of a *métis* obsessed by her path and the intersecting roads, obsessed by the surrealist encounter of the Other and the Same, by the unnatural but lyrical crossing of the country and the city, . . . of tradition and modernity, of East and West. . . .
>
> I am there, at the crossing . . . in my place, after all, since I am a *croisée,* one who searches for a filiation, who writes in a lineage, always the same, tied to history, memory, identity, tradition, transmission— I mean to the quest for an ascendance and a descendance, a place in the history of a family, a community, a people, with respect to History and the universe. It is in fiction that I feel like a free subject (free from father, mother, clan, dogma . . .) and strengthened by the responsibility and the burden of exile [*la charge de l'exil*]. Only there do I pull myself together, body and soul, and build a bridge between the two shores, upstream and down.[15]

Sebbar writes fiction in order to build herself a past *and* a future. She plays on the historical foundations of discourse in order to transform reality, putting into practice a "*pensée nomade*"[16] characterized by a play of overlapping and intertwining narrative voices. In *Les Carnets,* we move from Shérazade's interior monologue to free direct and indirect discourses that disregard the passage of time, moving upstream to blend stories from sixteenth-century Arab Spain with the contemporary adventures of characters such as Jeanne and Saïd. Representing the cultural itineraries and models of fiction that develop according to a *logique métisse*, Sebbar's narrative progresses through a set of relations that always postpone and defer the moment of conclusion. The activities of writing and reading come to mirror each other, and a *mise en abyme* of the reading process is activated from the very beginning, since Shérazade is writing in a notebook with the same title as that of the book, *Les Carnets de Shérazade*. The notebook also carries the number seven, a symbolic number for both Shérazade and the author, who uses it in the organization of the book, since Shérazade's journey through France lasts seven days. Narrators and narratees interact in ways that also mirror the writer-reader relation. It is not always easy to identify the exact moment when the narrative perspective changes. The continual movement from the thoughts of one character to those of another obscures the trail. As the free direct or indirect discourse floats from one person to the other to communicate different points of view, the interest seems to lie not in the distinct individuality of each one, but in the imperceptible slide from one identity to the other. While Shérazade is the nomadic fugitive, she also becomes all of the historical and fictional characters whose adventures she recounts. Instead of erecting an artificial partition between the self and the other, the narrative shows how the narrator is transformed, step by step, with every story told, at every new stage of the voyage. She is at once the subject who speaks and the one whose story is reconstituted and absorbed in the text. Intertextuality thereby points toward a nomadism that is, in the end, only a problematization or *mise en abyme* of the very process of interpretation and decoding of cultural ideologies. Reading thereby becomes a cultural itinerary that forces us to transpose the familiar and the foreign: the center-margin hierarchy is replaced by a more complex network or grid of interconnections.

The narrative creates a space in which Sebbar can begin to rebuild an entire cultural memory, a mythic core into which she can then braid images of ancient traditions as well as new explorations undertaken in the course of her textual and visual journey, a journey that becomes essential to her act of *appropriation* of time and space, history and geography. Shérazade brings along with her Flora Tristan's *Le Tour de France* and Rimbaud's letters, using these as constant frames of reference, traveling with other literary travelers and borrowing their journeys, their crossroads, their wanderings, and their return to what Khatibi has called a paradoxical France.[17] This "paradoxical France" Sebbar calls "la mythologie FRANCE" (*LP,* 40). She does so in order to demystify the very concept of "francité." Her purpose, however, is to piece together a new symbolic space, hybrid and *métis,* where difference and paradox show up precisely where one might have thought to find the *France profonde* of quiet pastures and "images d'Epinal." Under the guise of a simple linear narrative unfolding over a seven-day period, Sebbar completely destabilizes the cultural reality of the Hexagon.[18]

A picaresque heroine, she is in motion. But this movement does not lead her from the margins to the center, as with the heroes of Balzac and Stendhal, who come to Paris from the provinces in search of happiness and fortune. As she looks for images, in museums and libraries, Shérazade discovers herself through the Orientalist painters and their representation of odalisques. Her relation to the past, as to herself, passes through the medium of these historical associations. Because Shérazade is made aware of the way she is viewed by the dominant culture, her self-image is inscribed within the framework supplied by this culture. But because the text presents and dismantles the mechanisms through which she became aware of the conventions that surround the representation of odalisques, she can engage this dominant culture in a dialogue and take an active role in the decoding of these images. She thereby introduces another discourse into the very heart of the cultural conventions that only *described* her as a passively *watched* woman. As she invests herself in this code, it is with the goal of *reinscribing* the images of odalisques in the context of immigrant culture. As readers, we are therefore forced to superimpose the two contexts, the two traditions, both of which turn out to be plurivocal. Thus, when Gilles discovers Shérazade asleep in his truck, we see him watch her as if she were a sleeping odalisque:

> Dans son camion, à Marseille dans les docks, il y a une fille endormie, une inconnue. . . . On voit mal sa bouche renflée à cause de la position du visage sur le skaï du siège molletonné. Elle a de longues paupières bistres, orientales. . . . Il a regardé une moitié de fille, un demi-visage, un corps . . . coupé en deux, exposé du côté droit. Il s'arrête à nouveau aux mains nues croisées sur l'extrême bord du siège, dans la même position, offertes et fragiles. (*CS,* 13–15)

> [In his truck, on the docks in Marseille, there is a woman asleep, a stranger. . . . Her mouth is barely visible, bulging from the position of her face against the stuffed vinyl seat. She has long eyelids, bister, Oriental. . . . He watched half of a girl, a half face, a body . . . cut in two, exposed on the right side. His glance stops anew at the bare hands crossed at the far end of the seat, in the same position, open and fragile.]

One need only think of Ingres's *Odalisque endormie* or *Odalisque à l'esclave* to recognize these artistic figures in the above description of the young fugitive stretched out in the front seat, her face and body half concealed, half offered to the gaze of the observer. Here, Gilles's male gaze creates a *lieu commun*, a topos, of Orientalist paintings, situating the woman inside a specific cultural matrix, one that defines her as "strange" and "exotic." But Shérazade resists this static image of passive womanhood. Although touched by the image of the odalisque, she uses this topos to develop her own relation to colonial history, to construct her own ties to Algeria *and* France: Matisse's *L'Odalisque à la culotte rouge* hypnotizes her and invites her to leave and return to Algeria (*S*, 245).

No longer a spectator, but a reader—in the way Tournier understands this in *La Goutte d'or:* one must learn to read in order to free oneself from the enslaving power of the image—Shérazade gradually frees herself from both the weight of this tradition and the need for origins. The return to Algeria is never realized; it is constantly postponed as Shérazade continues to explore the paths of immigrants across France. All in all, we see her choosing a *beur*—therefore *métisse*—identity, and not a univocal point of origin. It is the voyage that defines her, not the origin or destination.

When Shérazade discovers Delacroix's *Femmes d'Alger dans leur appartement,* at the Louvre with her friend Julien, a dialogue is established (*S*, 98, 158). The canvas gives Julien an image of the Arab woman that influences the way he perceives and examines Shérazade. But for her, Delacroix's representation of this patriarchal imprisonment is the key that allows her to enter a previously unknown historical dimension: this canvas is the first visual contact she has with harem women. These women are "moins sultanes soudain que prisonnières. N'entretenant avec nous, spectateurs, aucun rapport. Ne s'abandonnant ni ne se refusant au regard. Etrangères mais présentes terriblement dans cette atmosphère raréfiée de la claustration" (suddenly less sultanas than prisoners. They have no relationship with us, the spectators. They neither abandon nor refuse themselves to our gaze. Foreign but terribly present in this rarefied atmosphere of confinement). Putting in parallel the past and the present, Shérazade compares them with the North African women living in small apartments in the French suburbs like the one she had fled. She learns to read the current reality of Arabs in France in the light of this artistic context and compares the idealized nineteenth-century figures with the neglected contemporary immigrant women:[19]

Le garçon la laissa à la porte de l'appartement 76. . . . Elle sonna. . . .
Le couloir était sombre, l'entrée minuscule. Shérazade restait debout à
la porte. . . . Elle avait hésité, seule sur le palier . . . comme si elle allait voir sa mère, sa soeur, les grandes et les petites. (*CS,* 150–51)
    [Ici], chez la mère de Farid, Shérazade se rappelait . . . les femmes
orientales de la peinture française, les esclaves blanches des harems,
oisives et belles, dans le luxe des parfums et de la soie, languides et
comme endormies. . . . On les aimait. Et les femmes d'Orient en
France, dans les cités au bord des capitales, sa mère, la mère de
Farid . . . dans le froid et la brique grise et noire. (*CS,* 152)

[The boy left her at the door of the apartment. . . . She rang. . . . The
hallway was dark, the entrance minuscule. Shérazade remained standing at the door. . . . She had hesitated, alone on the landing, as if she
were going to see her mother, her sister, the grown ones and little ones.
    [Here], with Farid's mother, Shérazade remembered . . . the Ori-
ental women of French painting, the white harem slaves, beautiful
and idle among luxurious perfumes and silks, languid, as if
asleep. . . . They were loved. But what about the Oriental women in
France, in the districts at the outskirts of capitals, her mother, Farid's
mother, . . . all of them cold among the gray and black bricks?]

These images build up a contrast between the small, dark apartments in
the cold suburbs and the interiors depicted by Delacroix. Shérazade's position
at the entrance of the apartment is the same as that of the painter, whose gaze
invades the closed space of the harem. She takes over the painter's position, but
does so in order to denounce the stifling world of Arab women, their status as
"Oriental women," displaced, dislocated, and shipwrecked in France; in other
words, she undermines the system of representation that imprisons women
within both patriarchal and neocolonial spaces.

If, as Michel Foucault has argued, "we are in the epoch of simultaneity . . .
of juxtaposition . . . of the near and far, of the side-by-side, of the dispersed
. . . [an] epoch . . . in which space takes for us the form of relations among
sites," then Sebbar's narratives are exemplary of a condition of hybridity that allows different historical and spatial configurations to coexist.[20] By reading texts
and images of the past in order to understand her own situation as a postcolonial nomad, Shérazade uses whatever means are at her disposal in order to survive and contest the negative representations of Oriental women that are
embedded in the dominant culture. Sebbar gives her character the opportunity

to refuse to be made into an "other": although subjected to the male gaze of Julien or Gilles, who can only perceive her through Orientalist codes, Shérazade is able to manipulate those codes, to historicize them, and to point to the historical Arab or Saracen influences on southern France, to the always already hybrid nature of French culture. As she says: "Do you know that Muslim warriors would arrive in Gaul with their families? They came from far away, from Arabia, via Egypt, Africa, the Atlas mountains. There were Mozarabs, Jews, Christian prisoners who had become allies of Islam, and Islamized Berbers" (*CS*, 264).

Contrary to popular views that hold that "la France profonde" of the provinces is the purer, more authentic France (unlike cosmopolitan urban centers), Sebbar stages heterogeneity among rural people as well. There, regional patois reinforce difference and plurality. As her friend Marie emphasizes: "Alsatian is a language; my father always tells me this, and he forbids me from saying that peasants speak patois; he says that it is a language, and that they should not be despised" (*CS*, 168). Sebbar's emphasis on regional minorities mirrors the postcolonial thematics of diversity. Here, as in Antillean novels such as Maryse Condé's *Traversée de la mangrove*, peasant culture is represented in all of its complexity, while it is implicitly contrasted to the appropriative gestures of the young urban *beurs* whose dress code reflects their postcoloniality:

> —Bon, alors ils disent que c'est leur look à eux, leur style, que personne peut leur piquer parce qu'ils sont les seuls à oser mettre en même temps une chéchia, tu sais ce que c'est? comme leurs ancêtres de là-bas et un jean comme tous les jeunes de partout, ou un battle dress des stocks américains ou une veste de smoking qu'ils trouvent aux Puces, ou un boléro brodé. . . . Tu comprends . . . les habits traditionnels de leurs grand-pères turcs, arabes, berbères, africains sont à eux et les habits européens sont à tout le monde et eux, leur look, c'est de tout mélanger, mais pas n'importe comment, c'est très étudié. (*CS*, 159)

> [Well, they say that this look is theirs alone. It is a unique style, and nobody can steal it from them because they are the only ones who dare to wear a *chéchia*, you know what that is? like their ancestors from over there, along with a pair of blue jeans like young people everywhere, or American army clothing, or a smoking jacket found at the flea market, and an embroidered bolero. . . . You see . . . the traditional clothes of their Turkish, Arab, Berber, African grandfathers are theirs, and European clothes belong to everybody, and their look, well, it is to mix everything, but not just any old way, it is a very carefully studied way.]

Dress is a signifying system that denotes not just the global process of neo-colonialism and assimilation ("un jean comme tous les jeunes de partout"), but the *beurs'* own rich construction of their lives and transcultural identities, their sense of how the past and the present, the near and the far come together in the material things that they use, in the practices that they adopt. Their control over their sense of personal identity is evident in this creative use of the means of self-representation, in the *logique métisse* of their sense of self.

Sebbar's fictional text reveals a similarly conscious control of the means of (self-)representation. *Les Carnets* draws a new geography of France from Marseille to the Ile de Ré, from Narbonne to Nantes. In its formal organization, the narrative integrates the voices and the idioms of regional or immigrant minorities and numerous intertextual references to eighteenth- and nineteenth-century travel narratives, as well as to traditional and classical Arabic texts and to film, operatic music, and popular culture, represented both by Carte de séjour ("un groupe rockarabe, rockmétèque" [*CS*, 148]) and by a group of female rappers ("rap arabe" [*CS*, 253]) who perform at a Moroccan country wedding near the southern town of Castres. Like the *beurs*, Sebbar weaves her own tapestry, using an esthetics of bricolage that carries over into her style of writing and into the way she actually puts words on paper, since she often writes in cafés, using bits and pieces of paper, "un morceau de nappe, des papiers-sucre, le dos de la note" (a piece of paper tablecloth, sugar cube wrappings, the back of the bill).[21] This image of the unassuming nomad or bohemian writer is nonetheless constructed from a studied ("C'est très étudié") appropriation of such objects and of techniques that can transform the relations of inequality, power, and domination that saturate the social and cultural field but cannot succeed in preventing intercultural exchanges.

Wandering across France, Shérazade discovers that diversion and diversity have always already been present in the Hexagon. From one library to the other (one of them recalling Montaigne's famous library), she forges a new vision of history, her purpose being to attempt a *re*construction of the past by using the disparate elements that are at her disposal:

> Un soir, tard dans la nuit, Shérazade lisait dans la bibliothèque. Comme si on avait su que Shérazade viendrait dans cette maison, les rayons portaient, serrés, les livres qu'elle cherchait. . . . Elle trouvait là, disponibles, nuit et jour, des livres qu'elle lisait avec la passion d'une folle, parce qu'ils racontaient une vieille histoire, l'histoire de sa mémoire en miettes, et une histoire nouvelle, moderne où se

croisent les continents et les civilisations, *une histoire qui serait la si-enne.* (*CS,* 129, my emphasis)

[One evening, late at night, Shérazade was reading in the library. As if it were known that Shérazade would come to this house, there were rows upon rows of the books she sought. . . . There she found, available day and night, books that she read with the passion of one possessed. They told an ancient story, the story of her fragmented memory, and a new story, modern, where continents and civilizations crossed, *a history that would be her own.*]

One of the postulates of Orientalist discourse is to make the woman and the "exote" into the very figure of absence.[22] Here the variables of the equation are transformed by a narrative that presents us with a revision of both the genre of the eighteenth-century novel and the nineteenth-century pictorial tradition. If at the end of her journey Manon Lescaut found silence and death in a desert in the New World, Shérazade, by contrast, acquires the right to move freely across a land that she appropriates through the spoken and written word. The history she reconstructs allows her to plant new stakes about her territory, a territory that expands in the course of a *récit* whose narrative economy is founded on the principle of exchange and barter—a principle as ancient as the one that was used by "the real Scheherazade" (*CS,* 141) in *The Thousand and One Nights.*

Like her namesake from *The Thousand and One Nights,* Shérazade is a storyteller and a narrator who exchanges words for the possibility of going on. Shérazade trades her stories for Gilles's offer of transportation. She is the typical parasite, since according to Michel Serres, "the parasite evades . . . and dodges mere exchange. It does not make an even trade, but makes change. It tries to exchange words for material substance, air for solid."[23] Through her mastery of speech, Shérazade succeeds in "making an exchange," thus transforming the symbolic economies of the culture. She constructs a parallel, inverted universe for herself and subjects it to continuous reorganization through the tactics and strategies of resistance that force her reader to rethink history, art, and literature in light of new paradigms. As Michel de Certeau noted, "immigrants are the pioneers of a civilization based on the blending of cultures."[24]

Sebbar shares with many postcolonial writers the goal of deconstructing European history and the cultural stereotypes it has served to transmit since the beginning of the colonial era. In *Les Carnets,* this deconstruction of the representations and clichés of the dominant culture is accomplished through travel and the use of orality, which infuses the narrative with the everydayness of the spoken, thus mapping out a narrative strategy that establishes a dialogue between "high" and "low" culture, between the written record and popular experiences, bringing together disparate and often antagonistic traditions, thus proposing a creative alternative to the polarizing approaches of dialectical thinking.

Translated by Joseph Heath

Notes

This chapter is an adapted and revised version of chapter 8 in Françoise Lionnet, *Postcolonial Representations: Women, Literature, Identity* (Ithaca, N.Y.: Cornell University Press, 1995). A French-language version appeared as "Parcours narratif, itinéraire culturel," in *Modernité, Fiction, déconstruction,* ed. Jean Bessière (Paris: Lettres Modernes, Etudes romanesques 2, 1994), and is translated here by permission of Lettres Modernes-Minard.

1. Leïla Sebbar, *Shérazade, Les Carnets de Shérazade,* and *Le Fou de Shérazade.* All further reference to the first two volumes will be cited in the text as *S* and *CS.* [A *beur* is a young Arab born in France of immigrant parents. Trans.]

2. I use the term "parasite" in the sense made familiar by Michel Serres, *Le Parasite.*

3. In using the term "defeat" I am alluding to Catherine Clément's *L'Opéra ou la défaite des femmes,* which deals with neither Prévost nor Massenet's opera *Manon,* but its argument applies perfectly to Manon.

4. Abdelkebir Khatibi, *Love in Two Languages.* See also Khatibi's *Figures de l'étranger dans la littérature française,* and *Maghreb pluriel.* Hereafter cited in the text as *FE* and *MP,* respectively. I am not promoting the "emergent literatures" expression here, since it strikes me as ideologically suspect, suggesting as it does an implicit opposition between a set of canonical works and a series of texts that innovate in opposition to this tradition. I simply want to contextualize the debate. My own view would be that there has always been an interdependence between traditions, but that this relation has often been obscured in the interests of rigid nationalism.

5. On this subject, see Edward Said, *Orientalism;* Christopher Miller, *Blank Darkness: Africanist Discourse in French;* V. Y. Mudimbe, *The Invention of Africa: Gnosis, Philosophy and the Order of Knowledge;* and Tzvetan Todorov, *Nous et les Autres.*

6. To use Edouard Glissant's expression, *Caribbean Discourse,* 64. This is an abridged translation of Glissant's *Le Discours antillais.*

7. See, for example, Jean-Loup Amselle, *Logiques métisses: Anthropologie de l'identité en Afrique et ailleurs;* and Ulf Hannerz, "The World System of Culture: The International Flow of Meaning and Its Local Management."

8. Michel Foucault, "Of Other Spaces," 22–23.

9. Michel Foucault, *Archaeology of Knowledge,* 12. Hereafter cited as *AK.*

10. See the excellent special issue of the Haitian journal, *Chemins Critiques* 1, no. 3 (December 1989), entitled *Le Rêve d'habiter,* especially the articles by Maryse Condé, "Habiter ce pays, la Guadeloupe"; Michèle D. Pierre-Louis, "La Quête de l'ailleurs"; Laënnec Hurbon, "Le Rêve d'habiter"; and Yanick Lahens, "L'Exil: Entre écrire et habiter."

11. Consider, for example, G. W. F. Hegel's comments on Africa: "Africa . . . [is] the land of childhood, which lying beyond the day of self-conscious history, is enveloped in the dark mantle of Night" (*The Philosophy of History,* 91). I would like to thank Jean-François Fourny for having drawn my attention to the Heideggerian expression "historical destiny." See Martin Heidegger, "The Question Concerning Technology," and "Über 'die Linie.' "

12. See Jacques Derrida, "La parole soufflée," 253–92.

13. Michel Laronde, "Leïla Sebbar et le roman 'croisé': Histoire, mémoire et identité"; Mildred Mortimer, *Journeys through the French African Novel;* Winifred Woodhull, "Exile."

14. Laronde, "La 'Mouvance beure': Emergence médiatique."

15. Nancy Huston and Leïla Sebbar, *Lettres parisiennes: Autopsie de l'exil,* 125, 126, 138. Hereafter cited as *LP.*

16. In Gilles Deleuze's sense, in "La Pensée nomade."

17. Khatibi, *Figures,* 13.

18. [The "Hexagon" refers to mainland France (the geographic region can be inscribed in a hexagon). Trans.]

19. Assia Djebar, "Regard interdit, son coupé," 171; Djebar, *Women of Algiers in Their Apartment,* 136.

20. Foucault, "Of Other Spaces," 22–23.

21. Huston and Sebbar, *Lettres parisiennes,* 9.

22. I use the term "exote" following Victor Segalen in *Essai sur l'exotisme: Une esthétique du divers.*

23. Serres, *Le Parasite,* 50.

24. Michel de Certeau, "Idéologie et diversité culturelle," 232; see also de Certeau, *The Practice of Everyday Life,* for the distinction de Certeau draws between a tactic and a strategy. See also Winifred Woodhull's careful reinterpretation of de Certeau's position in *Transfigurations of the Maghreb,* 101–2. Woodhull is uneasy with the ambiguities of Sebbar's statements about identity; I prefer to see this ambiguity as a source of both lucidity and agency. In light of current political and religious issues in Algeria, it seems to me that Sebbar's position is the only choice she can make as a woman and an intellectual who is truly committed to social change and justice. To suggest otherwise may be downright condescending.

Works Cited

Amselle, Jean-Loup. *Logiques métisses: Anthropologie de l'identité en Afrique et ailleurs.* Paris: Payot, 1990.

de Certeau, Michel. "Idéologie et diversité culturelle." In *Diversité culturelle, société industrielle, état national.* Paris: L'Harmattan, 1984.

———. *The Practice of Everyday Life.* Berkeley: University of California Press, 1984.

Clément, Catherine. *L'Opéra ou la défaite des femmes.* Paris: Grasset, 1979.

Condé, Maryse. "Habiter ce pays, la Guadeloupe." *Chemins Critiques* 1, no. 3 (1989).

———. *Traversée de la mangrove.* Paris: Mercure de France, 1989.

Deleuze, Gilles. "La Pensée nomade." In *Nietzsche aujourd'hui.* Paris: UGE, 1973.

Derrida, Jacques. "La Parole soufflée." In *L'Ecriture et la différence.* Paris: Seuil, 1967.

Djebar, Assia. "Regard interdit, son coupé." In *Femmes d'Alger dans leur appartement.* Paris: des femmes, 1980. Published in English as *Women of Algiers in Their Apartment,* translated by Marjolijn de Jager. Charlottesville: University Press of Virginia, 1992.

Foucault, Michel. *Archaeology of Knowledge.* Translated by A. M. Sheridan Smith. London: Routledge, 1972.

———. "Of Other Spaces." *Diacritics* 16 (1986): 22–27.

Glissant, Edouard. *Caribbean Discourse.* Translated by J. Michael Dash. Charlottesville: University Press of Virginia, 1989.

———. *Le Discours antillais.* Paris: Seuil, 1984.

Hannerz, Ulf. "The World System of Culture: The International Flow of Meaning and Its Local Management." Cited by James Clifford in *The Predicament of Culture: Twentieth Century Ethnography, Literature and Art,* 17n. Cambridge: Harvard University Press, 1988.

Hegel, G. W. F. *The Philosophy of History.* Translated by J. Sibree. New York: Dover, 1956.

Heidegger, Martin. "The Question Concerning Technology." In *Basic Writings,* translated by William Lovitt. New York: Harper and Row, 1977.

———. "Über 'die Linie.' " In *The Question of Being,* translated by William Kluback and Jean T. Wilde. New Haven, Conn.: College and University Press, 1958.

Hurbon, Laënnec. "Le Rêve d'habiter." *Chemins Critiques* 1, no. 3 (1989).

Huston, Nancy, and Leïla Sebbar. *Lettres parisiennes: Autopsie de l'exil.* Paris: Barrault, 1986.

Khatibi, Abdelkebir. *Figures de l'étranger dans la littérature française.* Paris: Denoël, 1987.

———. *Love in Two Languages.* Translated by Richard Howard. Minneapolis: University of Minnesota Press, 1990.

———. *Maghreb pluriel.* Paris: Denoël, 1983.

Lahens, Yanick. "L'Exil: Entre écrire et habiter." *Chemins Critiques* 1, no. 3 (1989).

Laronde, Michel. "Leïla Sebbar et le roman 'croisé': Histoire, mémoire et identité." *Celfan* 7 (1987–88).

———. "La 'Mouvance beure': Emergence médiatique." *French Review* 161 (1988).

Miller, Christopher. *Blank Darkness: Africanist Discourse in French.* Chicago: University of Chicago Press, 1985.

Mortimer, Mildred. *Journeys through the French African Novel.* Portsmouth, N.H.: Heinemann Educational Books, 1990.

Mudimbe, V. Y. *The Invention of Africa: Gnosis, Philosophy and the Order of Knowledge.* Bloomington: Indiana University Press, 1988.

Pierre-Louis, Michèle D. "La Quête de l'ailleurs." *Chemins Critiques* 1, no. 3 (1989).

Le Rêve d'habiter. Special issue of *Chemins Critiques* 1, no. 3 (1989).

Said, Edward. *Orientalism.* New York: Vintage, 1979.

Sebbar, Leïla. *Les Carnets de Shérazade.* Paris: Stock, 1985.

———. *Le Fou de Shérazade.* Paris: Stock, 1991.

———. *Shérazade.* Paris: Stock, 1982.

Segalen, Victor. *Essai sur l'exotisme: Une esthétique du divers.* Paris: Fata Morgana, 1978.

Serres, Michel. *Le Parasite.* Paris: Grasset, 1980.

Todorov, Tzvetan. *Nous et les autres.* Paris: Seuil, 1989.

Tournier, Michel. *La Goutte d'or.* Paris: Gallimard, 1986.

Woodhull, Winifred. "Exile." *Yale French Studies* 82 (1993): 7–24.

———. *Transfigurations of the Maghreb: Feminism, Decolonization, and Literatures.* Minneapolis: University of Minnesota Press, 1993.

3 / (Con)figuring Identity

Cultural Space of the
Indo-British Border Intellectual

Gita Rajan

Introduction

In an anthology that discusses the problematics of new European subjects, exploring the nuances of the textual identities of Kamala Markandaya, Ruth Prawer Jhabvala, and Suniti Namjoshi is an exciting venture.[1] Jhabvala, perhaps the most familiar name in the trio, has written scripts for such Merchant-Ivory ventures as E. M. Forster's *A Room with a View* and *Howards End* (the former won three Academy Awards in 1986). Vibrant, vivid, and experimental, the fictions of Markandaya and Jhabvala focus largely upon issues of the new nation-space, modernity, tradition, and decolonization in Indo-British contexts.[2] And they take as their protagonists the colonial subject inhabiting and traversing bicultural borders. Introducing Suniti Namjoshi's work into a discussion of colonial presences constructed by Markandaya and Jhabvala within the current location of a federated Europe provides the opportunity to move beyond what Homi K. Bhabha calls the postcolonial predicament of "nation and narration" to the radical nature of a lesbian identity in postcolonial fiction.

Some critics might find the inclusion of Namjoshi in the neat binarism of Markandaya and Jhabvala to be a forced reading. There are other postcolonial authors in the Indo-British contexts who would, perhaps, provide a third perspective or another dimension to my critique, such as Salman Rushdie (*Midnight's Children*, 1981) or V. S. Naipaul (*India: A Wounded Civilization*, 1977, and *India: A Million Mutinies Now*, 1990) or Shashi Tharoor (*The Great Indian Novel*, 1989) or Gita Mehta (*Karma Cola*, 1979, and *Raj*, 1989). But Suniti Namjoshi's work, situated in the nexus of acculturation, desire, and authority, calls attention to theoretical and methodological paradigms that are pertinent to the present debates in postcolonial, cultural, and feminist studies. Sara Suleri, speaking in a different context and in response to Henry Louis Gates's call for an ethical definition of race, says that critical "attention . . . is not simply an attempt to whitewash colonial and neocolonial history but an effort to complicate the precarious cultural crossings that mark the close of this century. As the identity formation of the nation-state becomes problematic, the question of diverse cultural locations self-evidently gains in critical significance" ("Multiculturalism and Its Discontents," 16).

"Precarious cultural crossings" and the "formation of new the nation-state" serve as a starting point for locating and situating a federated Europe within the colonial scene. Such a ploy reverses the usual arguments of postcolonial critics who have sought to structure the decolonized nation through geographic, nationalistic, social, and psychological metaphors. In other words, it is not the problematics of the newly decolonized nations that serves as a site for these writers and their fictions in my argument; it is instead their traversing of Indo-European borders that I wish to reexamine. Then, I will show that the politics of bicultural identity configured along essentialist/constructionist lines provides a whole range of vocabularies to discuss the works of Markandaya, Jhabvala, and Namjoshi as border intellectuals. In a general sense, an essentialist notion of identity is one that defines subjects via biological factors and natural essences and confines representation to a normative range. A constructionist approach to identity, in contrast, is one that profiles subjects based upon social and cultural preformations and allows or forces one to represent oneself according to learned behavior. Markandaya, Jhabvala, and Namjoshi engage differing essentialist and constructionist models of identity formation. In doing so they function as "syncretic" and "specular" border intellectuals (JanMohamed, 97). The opposition between essentialism and constructionism has been rehearsed on innumerable occasions by feminist and postcolonial scholars to show how limiting either category is, but critiques attentive to the locations of "border intellectuals" are relatively new.

Kamala Markandaya crosses over into her husband's English body and land to situate her discourses of empire, nation, and progress. Contrapuntally (to borrow Edward Said's word), Jhabvala crosses into her Indian husband's land (although not necessarily his body) and claims the right to speak about neocolonization and modernity as a European. She consequently reveals two border crossings. Both women write about India, but from different borders. Using her husband's body, Markandaya becomes an Indian writing in English, whereas Jhabvala, by not using her husband's body, remains a foreigner writing about India. This distinction is important in relation to their precise border crossings. Jhabvala and Markandaya belong to the "syncretic border intellectual" category that Abdul JanMohamed outlines. Suniti Namjoshi, odd (wo)man out in this sequence, uses her lesbian body to tell *Feminist Fables*, crossing and recrossing, without warning, East-West, individual-collective, creative-critical, and real-surreal borders. She would function as JanMohamed's "specular border intellectual."

In "Worldliness-without-World, Homelessness-as-Home: Toward a Definition of the Specular Border Intellectual," JanMohamed marks the difference between the "syncretic and specular border intellectuals" as the "*intentionality of their intellectual orientation*" (97; original emphasis). JanMohamed's definition of the two categories is brilliant and powerful. The "syncretic intellectual," he suggests, is

> more "at home" in both cultures than his or her specular counterpart, is able to combine elements of the two cultures in order to articulate new syncretic forms and experiences. . . . By contrast, the specular border intellectual, while perhaps equally familiar with two cultures, finds himself or herself unable or unwilling to be "at home" in these societies. Caught between several cultures or groups, none of which are deemed sufficiently enabling or productive, the specular intellectual subjects the cultures to analytic scrutiny rather than combining them; he or she utilizes his or her interstitial cultural space as a vantage point from which to define, explicitly or implicitly, other utopian possibilities of group formation. (97)

JanMohamed's clear way of demarcating different kinds of intellectuals (and, more important, their textual perspectives) helps me to veer away from the trope of "diaspora."[3] Although it has been an excellent critical tool in postcolonial discourse, diaspora as a trope does not have the same incisiveness that is attached to the *trajectories* of the border intellectual. Arjun Appadurai, discussing the nature of the diasporic subject, shows that even though diaspora signals the crossing of national (and cultural) borders, the subject herself erases that trajectory by fastening on to other members of the diasporic community, in effect activating a nationalist impulse to remain local and provincial. JanMohamed's concept of the border intellectual acknowledges the itinerary of the subject, but uses the bar of the border in a very different manner. He notes that the distinction between the two types of intellectuals is not based upon "categorical epistemic differentiation" (97). Displaced intellectuals cannot be distinguished merely as self/other, center/periphery, provincial/metropol, homo/heterosexual, and so on, but can be examined through their trails as border crossers.

Ultimately, Markandaya's, Jhabvala's, and Namjoshi's identities as border-crossing intellectuals (actual, textual, racial, cultural, national, and sexual) keep their individual projects alive. Their motives are intimate. Body, desire, marriage, passport, land, heritage, memory, and mythology serve as loci for these women to structure their fictions. My essay, then, grapples with strands of body-nation-text, as skin rubs against skin at the borders. I do so without resorting either to a neat symmetry of oppositions or to the attractive quilting of pluralist positions. Henry Louis Gates Jr., in "Beyond the Culture Wars: Identities in Dialogue," asks, "Gender identity, sexual identity, racial identity; if all these things are socially inflected and produced, rather than unmediatedly natural, why won't they fit into the culturalist model?" Then he answers, "[Because] gender identity and sexual identity are hard to reduce to the model of cultural difference, even though the meaning of these categories is culturally specific" (6). I want to examine the polemics of the term "mediated" (between the natural and cultural and the essential and constructed), which is part of establishing difference rather than just unraveling the oppositionality of difference as self and other. This is one of the strategies behind yoking and analyzing the works of Markandaya, Jhabvala, and Namjoshi.

A Federated Europe:
The Essentialist/Constructionist Model

*Like a frontier of civilization [the skin] is a bastion, a place at which skirmishes
are fought and invaders are resisted . . . our first and final defense.*
                                                              —Ashley Montagu

The concept of a federated Europe operates as the starting point in the reversal of colony-empire-nation formation, where federated means "united in an alliance" (*Oxford English Dictionary*). The term "federated" banks upon the stability of an *essence* of Europe, while building upon the constructed nature of the merger of countries such as Britain, Germany, France, and others. The premise of the essentialist/constructionist controversy that is at the center of contemporary critical debates can be used to underline and undermine the notion of a federated Europe. Here, Benedict Anderson's thesis of "imagined communities" as a substrata for nation formation serves to turn the gaze back on Europe.[4] Postcolonial critics have constructed the notion of "imagined communities" to talk about third world nationalistic impulses. Now, it seems, Europe naturally assumes this posture of an "imagined community." In other words, what was gradually shaped as "Europe" culminated in the Enlightenment moment of the sovereign subject, secure in its cultural, spiritual, and modern identity. This tendency, in turn, led to an othering impulse and to colonial expansion from the eighteenth century onward. However, with the ill-fitting sutures between modernism/postmodernism, structuralism/poststructuralism, and colonialism/postcoloniality, European nations and their citizen-subjects have not been able to rely upon their myth of a stable identity. European subjects have had to celebrate instead the "shifting boundary that alienates the frontiers of the modern nation" (Bhabha, 315), thereby calling attention to the phenomenon of borders vis-à-vis identity politics. With the present move to federation, it is apparent that it is not old-world religion and traditional culture but the European Currency Unit that is going to reseal the borders of Europe. This moment then shows how the construction and deconstruction of "Europe" and its subjects allow the mirror to be turned upon the imperial face. At a time when theoretical debates are focused upon dismantling generalizations and rejecting universalizations as models of cultural critique and postcolonial analyses, it is ironic that market forces (one of the primary motors of the first colonial engine) are working to rejoin and reuniversalize the different nations of present-day Europe.

The concept of federated Europe, then, manifests itself as an attempt to dissolve the borders between certain nations within Europe. Thus, the bar separating the essentialists and constructionist projects of a federated Europe can be legitimately animated in the relationship of authors to their works and, more important in this case, to critical responses to their works. Anderson points out in *Imagined Communities* that

> it is doubtful whether either social change or transformed consciousness, in themselves, do much to explain the attachment that peoples feel for the inventions of their imaginations. . . . In an age when it is

so common for progressive, cosmopolitan intellectuals (particularly in Europe?) to insist on the near-pathological character of nationalism, its roots in fear and hatred of the Other, and its affinities with racism, it is useful to remind ourselves that nations inspire love. . . . The cultural products of nationalism—poetry, prose, fiction, music, plastic arts—show this love very clearly in thousands of different forms and styles. (141)

In analyzing Markandaya's and Jhabvala's works, it is important to remember that India was a federated land before the British granted her "independence." Whereas the term "federated" may have been coined for contemporary use in Europe (as a political and economic convenience), it has always been part of the historical and national identity of India. In fact, India before August 14, 1947, was the sum total of India, Pakistan, and Bangladesh; it was dotted with numerous regions, princely states, and tribal zones; it had various languages and dialects; it had different sociocultural norms and religious groups (Hindus, Muslims, Christians, Jains, and so on). This variegated India, burgeoning with a nascent fervor of decolonization, is the backdrop for Markandaya's and Jhabvala's fictions. These women deal with the constructed identity of India as a new nation-state and the essential/constructed decolonized subjectivities of Indian and British citizens in their novels. Namjoshi, on the other hand, deals with cultural and sexual issues in the context of a more stable nation-state and citizen identity (albeit a heterosexual one).

Diana Fuss argues in *Essentially Speaking* that in some specifically feminist analyses, the opposition between essentialism and constructionism is situated at the blind spot of essentialism itself, because the "impasse in feminism is in the difficulty in theorizing the social in relation to the natural, or the theoretical in relation to the political" (2). She explains:

Essentialism is . . . a belief in true essences—that which is irreducible, unchanging, and therefore constitutive of a given person or thing. . . . Constructionism, articulated in opposition to essentialism and concerned with its philosophical refutation, insists that essence is itself a historical construction. . . . What is at stake for constructionists are systems of representations, social and material practices, laws of discourses, and ideological effects. In short, constructionists are above all concerned with the *production and organization* of differences, and they therefore reject the idea that any essential or natural givens precede the process of social determination. Essentialist arguments frequently make recourse to an ontology which stands outside the sphere of cultural and historical change. In this case, "man" and "woman" are taken to be ontologically stable objects, coherent signs which derive their coherency from their unchangeability and predictability.(2)

Fuss's definition can be employed to explain how Markandaya, Jhabvala, and Namjoshi position themselves as gendered intellectuals. Her framework can also explain how Markandaya's works are read along essentialist lines, how Jhabvala's are read along both constructionist and essentialist lines (in that order), and how Namjoshi's are balanced on the ephemeral border between essentialist and constructionist lines. The kinds of readings these women get lock them into essentialized categories as to who they are as citizen-subjects. In the case of Markandaya and Jhabvala, critiques of their positions as intellectuals become supplementary to their citizen-subject status, and in Namjoshi's case, criticism of both kinds is poor.

Markandaya: Indian Writing in English

Kamala Markandaya's major novels, *Nectar in a Sieve* (1954), *Some Inner Fury* (1955), *A Silence of Desire* (1960), *Possession* (1963), *A Handful of Rice* (1966), *The Coffer Dams* (1969), *The Nowhere Man* (1972), *Two Virgins* (1973), *The Golden Honeycomb* (1977), and *Pleasure City* (1982), are usually cataloged under "Indian Writing in English." (I list the dates of her novels to indicate the proximity of her work to the nationalist-independence struggle in India.) Markandaya writes about Indo-British relations around the time of India's decolonization (1947), showcasing impossible passions between her characters, problematizing their identity, locating them in and dislocating them from home and country and from the modern metropolis and superstitious villages. Interestingly, Markandaya is consistently and securely situated inside her skin by her critics and read as essentially, "irreducibly" Indian.

 Nectar in a Sieve, for example, a title that signals its intertextual alliances to Coleridge, is rendered transparent, and the subtitle *A Novel of Rural India* is made to bear the burden of plot, theme, and substance. It is praised as a "simple unaffected story of human suffering, which more than a shelf of books on history and economics explains the people of India" (*Fiction Catalogue,* 1961). The fascinating characters, who are Hindu, Muslim, and Christian (Anglo-Indian) and who are coping with the nightmare of forced (and ineffective) British industrialization (in the guise of a tannery in the middle of the village), are not granted the status of multiracial voices taut with ethnic tension. Instead, *Nectar* is often analyzed as a prototypical document of imperial intrusion, and Markandaya is lauded for her nationalist overtones. The characters are read as stereotypes of their socioreligious group, much like the colonized subjects/objects paradigm theorized by Albert Memmi and Frantz Fanon. Is George Eliot's *Middlemarch* (with its subtitle) just a study of English provincial life? Are Eliot's characters just stereotypes of simple peasants caught in the struggle of the First and Second Reform Bills in England? No, Eliot's novel is treated as a work of exemplary realism, radical feminism, startling agnosticism, cultural criticism, and so on. Markandaya, like many other "Indian writers in English," has not yet received the critical attention of many postcolonial scholars, so her work is circumscribed within essentialist, colonialist parameters.

It is perhaps useful to rephrase Fredric Jameson's (in)famous remark and say that third world literatures are often *read* as allegories of nationhood and simplistic propaganda.[5] *Some Inner Fury* is read through a reductionist framework that focuses on the incompatibility of the lovers, Mira and Richard. Their unconsummated relationship is seen as symptomatic of the aborted Indo-British encounter. The rich, textured readings of Brontë's ill-fated lovers in *Wuthering Heights* come to mind as an apt comparison. That couple is read as a refined metaphor of the horrific merger of the self with the other. Yet Markandaya's lovers are not read in the same way. In *Silence of Desire,* itself a literary borrowing from Longfellow's poem "The Three Silences of Molinos," the structural oppositions between Dandekar and Sarojini are highlighted by critics as the poles between husband/wife, westernized/orthodox, medicine/magic, science/superstition, and so on. Sarojini's radical politics as a woman expressing her unspeakable desire for her husband is brushed aside to create overarching explanations for India's *inherent* inability to live in a modern world. Markandaya's technique of metaphorizing desire as a cancer in Sarojini's womb is erased in a reading that looks only at a bipolar equation of the two men as guru/magic/provincial and husband/medicine/modern, respectively. The feminist politics of Markandaya's character is robbed of its force by making the heroine the object of contention between two men caught up in struggles of tradition and progress—the guru and the husband. So, too, her *Handful of Rice* is a poignant depiction of poverty, hunger, and defeat, comparable perhaps to Hardy's bitter *Jude the Obscure.* Yet, the Indian author is read as treating the damaging effects of modernity on the traditional, rural, or pastoral landscape of a neocolonial India. Finally, her *Two Virgins* flirts with the daring idea of homoerotic desires between two sisters who live independently (among other things). But critics have ignored this aspect, highlighting instead Markandaya's weakness in not engaging in any East-West conflict or rural-metropolis tensions.

Markandaya's skin becomes her essentializing border. She cannot transcend it in the eyes of her critics. Her potential as a border-crossing intellectual is glossed over so easily in part because she herself accepts the impasse of racial borders. She does not position herself as a self-critical, self-aware intellectual. Even though her works seem to meld seamlessly into the nineteenth-century British canon, she herself does not make the self-conscious effort to speak from within this arena. She becomes an exemplary case of the syncretic intellectual, and that is her problem. Since she does not position herself on the other side of the border (England), her critics push her back into her skin (India). Judie Newman points out, in "The Colonial Voice in the Motherland," that "origins, both historical and literary, . . . become the focus for the postcolonial writer who employs intertextual devices to re-write the past, to restore a silenced story and to 'write in' the postcolonial subject as neither Anglocentered nor Other. Self-invention involves the scrutinizing and remodelling of past inventions, of rehistoricizing the space and identity of the subject." My point thus far is not to argue for a total rewriting of criticism of Markandaya's fictions, but to suggest an added dimension to her work in view of the postcolonial debates over the last two decades.

In Markandaya's case, the category of "Indian Writing in English" allows for only a partial identity formation, because her politics of self are locked into a secondary relation to "English" rather than "Indian." This is very much like the master trope of colonizer and colonized. It is not my intention to suggest that all of Markandaya's critics have fallen short of the mark. Instead, I wish to point out that she has been judged by her so-called "true essences—that which is irreducible, unchanging, and therefore constitutive of a given person or thing" (Fuss, 2). In her case, it is an instance of the critical border encasing the creative one. As Gates points out, effective multiculturalism demands the "shift from race to ethnicity . . . [which is] a necessary move away from the essentialist biologizing of a previous era" (7). How Markandaya functions as an intellectual is dictated by critics who substitute their reading of her text for the text itself.

Jhabvala: Writing about India

In contrast, Ruth Prawer Jhabvala self-consciously constructs herself as the diasporic German intellectual, writing novels with Indian characters. She locates herself in a layered, constructed space in the literary canon (albeit an-other canon) and moves in a translucent, essentialist space of Europe. Thus, she is usually perceived as an author with imperial sensibilities. Jhabvala's major works written in and about India are *To Whom She Will* (1955; published in the United States as *Amrita,* 1956), *The Nature of Passion* (1956), *Esmond in India* (1958), *The Householder* (1960; film, 1963), *Get Ready for Battle* (1962), *A Backward Place* (1965), *An Experience of India* (1971; television film, 1980), *A New Dominion* (1972; published in the United States as *Travelers,* 1973), *Heat and Dust* (1975; film, 1976), and her powerful autobiographical essay, "Myself in India" (1976). Her publication dates are similar to those of Markandaya, but her fictive India is still the India of the raj. Categorized broadly as an Anglo-Indian writer, Jhabvala is treated as the daughter of E. M. Forster, Rudyard Kipling, and Paul Scott. In her case, the identity formation is more clearly demarcated. "Anglo" takes not only syntactical but semiotic precedence over "Indian." Her constructed intellectual position as writer is treated as complementary to her essential position as European. It is not surprising, then, that her critics have compared *To Whom She Will* and *The Nature of Passion* to Jane Austen's novels of manners, which are replete with instances of youthful flirtations and naive passions that culminate in happy endings and in evenly balanced class mergers—the well-known "brilliant matches" of *Pride and Prejudice, Sense and Sensibility,* and *Emma.* When Jhabvala writes about complacent middle-class Indians in the aftermath of an independence struggle, critics highlight the shared heritage of the Indo-British literary traditions. The stench and filth that are part of her later work are absent in the earlier novels, allowing these first works to fit seamlessly into the British country manor mode.

Jhabvala's position as a border intellectual (speaking from India but thinking as a European) seems to lend authority to her technique of scripting modern India as historically poised to get the better of tradition. Consequently, *A Backward Place, A New Dominion,* and *Heat and Dust* are often read as experiments with and extensions of Forster's *A Passage to India.* Critics are also quick to associate Jhabvala's vision with Paul Scott's epic view in *The Raj Quartet.* She herself alludes to this trend in critical responses in *An Experience of India,* in which she writes that "there is a cycle that Europeans—by Europeans I mean all

Westerners, including Americans—tend to pass through. It goes like this: first stage, tremendous enthusiasm—everything Indian is marvelous; second stage, everything Indian not so marvelous; third stage, everything Indian is abominable" (9). While this candid sentiment, so overtly imperial, does not endear her to the Indians about whom she writes, it is nonetheless quoted repeatedly by Western critics to talk of her "diasporic" sensibilities. Ralph Crane, one of Jhabvala's more meticulous and benevolent critics, treats her statement as her crossing of the Rubicon—another border. In language that mimics the author's own, he writes: "Jhabvala is 'strapped to a wheel' ("Myself in India" 9) that will control her responses to India. The Indian beast is an animal that appears to stop thrashing beneath Ruth Prawer Jhabvala only when she leaves India and moves to New York" (104). In contrast, Nissim Ezekiel, an Indian critic, remarks, "Her fiction [is] a monstrous distorting mirror."[6]

The initial opposition between Markandaya and Jhabvala grants us the opportunity to make quick comparisons based upon East versus West and Indian writer in English versus Anglo-Indian writing about India, and makes it possible for us to locate them as syncretic border intellectuals. But examining the critical responses to their fiction reveals how the bar between essentialism and constructionism operates along color lines. At this point, an examination of the polemics of the term "mediated" (between the natural and cultural and the essential and constructed), which is part of establishing difference rather than just unraveling the oppositionality of difference as self and other, can be useful. If critical presupposition is based upon the fact that race acts as locus of crisis in Markandaya's fiction because of her essentialist Indian identity, then class should serve the same purpose in Jhabvala's work, because of her essentially constructed European identity. Would it be legitimate to argue that if Markandaya (and her work) emblematize cultural border crossings as a way of mediating racial ones, then Jhabvala (and her work) brokers class as a way of assigning bourgeois values? Bourgeois, class-bound notions, for example, of family, religion, and property mediate Jhabvala's crossing the border into a modern India. If Markandaya is the inheritor of the motifs of India's nationalist struggles, then Jhabvala bears the European legacy of Marx's *Theses* on class struggles. It is well known that "race" serves as the overarching metaphor in critiques of the colony and "class" serves the same purpose in analyses of empire. In the comparison of Markandaya and Jhabvala (Indian and European), the claim to essentialism works in a particularly strange way because it reveals the scandal in the (objective) new-critical lens trained on these authors. To expose this bar (and bias) I made explicit comparisons between Markandaya's work and nineteenth-century British literature and restated Jhabvala's nestling inside twentieth-century British literature. In other words, an exposé of critical biases shows that there is no essential way to read a text, only a constructed one. And if these constructed reading positions are challenged, then the so-called objective or normal or essential meanings are shaken loose.

Fuss's point that constructionism is built upon the fault line in essentialism is proved in the way that Markandaya and Jhabvala have been read. Fuss writes that "the danger (and the usefulness) of 'always already' [the arch Derridean antiessentialist mechanism] is that it *implies* essence, it hints at the irreducible core that requires no further investigation. In so doing, it frequently puts a stop to analysis, often at an argument's most critical point" (17, original emphasis). Thus, in an attempt to tease out the "irreducible core," I have shown Jhabvala's intertextual heritage and gestured toward Markandaya's coaxial alliances with British literature, and have shown how both writers are "always already" read along essential lines. Some readers may find my situating Markandaya alongside nineteenth-century authors (instead of valorizing an indigenous canon) puzzling, imperial, and even demeaning. My focus, however, is on deconstructing the essentialism/constructionism myth by showing how clearly the two women are kept inside their cultural borders by critics.[7] Ironically, my reading also shows how Markandaya, through her lack of self-critical positioning, authorizes her critics to treat her as an "Indian writing in English."

Namjoshi: The Strategy of Essence

Recently, Gayatri Chakravorty Spivak argued for the renewed examination and usefulness of an essentialist space. In her dialogue with Ellen Rooney in "In a Word: Interview," Spivak encourages women, much as Stephen Heath, Diana Fuss and others do, to take the "risk of essence" as a master strategy, because "strategy works through a persistent (de)constructive critique of the theoretical. Strategy is an embattled concept-metaphor, and unlike 'theory' its antecedents are not disinterested" (3). Spivak's point regarding the political endeavor of "mobilizing" essentialism to work in favor of the writer/reader, instead of against her through charges of nativism, are vital, and can be applied very effectively in situating Suniti Namjoshi in this essay. While some theorists treat the lesbian subject as inherently subversive, I am more interested in Namjoshi's role as a border intellectual who deliberately polemicizes the essentialism/constructionism divide.[8] By deliberately constructing her lesbian identity in the text, Namjoshi practices what Fuss has called a kind of strategic essentialism. She deploys her sexual identity within the borders of her text (or stages her essence dramatically) to dislodge the reader's preconceived notions of the bar between homo- and heterosexuality.

Some important works by Suniti Namjoshi are *Poems* (1967), *Feminist Fables* (1981), *The Authentic Lie* (1982), *From the Bedside Book of Nightmares* (1984), *The Conversations of Cow* (1984), *Flesh and Paper* (coauthored with Gillian Hanscombe, 1986; film with Pratibha Parmar, 1989), *Because of India* (1989), and *The Mothers of Maya Dilip* (1989). The list of dates here is more an attempt to contextualize Namjoshi's radical, feminist perspective vis-à-vis the poetics of Kate Millett and Adrienne Rich than to document a chronology of her responses to Indo-British tensions and contentions. Namjoshi is exploring "desires" as the "beginning of an Asian perspective, an alien perspective, later a lesbian perspective" (*Because of India*, 22).[9] Not simply bicultural or nationalist, her work is often seductive, common, mythical, traumatized, and charged with surreal, homosexual desires, always colored with the broad brush strokes of her own, named identity. In a fascinating pirouette she reveals her essential lesbian body and then deliberately constructs it through her textual inferences, such that the reader is suspended in the interstitial spaces of realism, surrealism, and magical realism, much as in Laura Esquivel's *Like Water for Chocolate*. Namjoshi, it seems, is "concerned with the production and organization of differences" (Fuss, 2), yet she never quite lets the reader ignore her autobiographical presence in the text.[10] By including ironic visual matter to illustrate her punchline, Suniti Namjoshi's fiction emphasizes her doubled perspective. *Feminist Fables* and *The Conversations of Cow*, the clearest examples of this strategy, wed word to image and critique the very essence of the fabliaux tradition by constantly calling attention to her Indian, lesbian body. In these works, the author challenges the patriarchs of Western humanism with her fabulously entertaining, provocatively feminist, and stunningly multicultural perspective.

The Conversations of Cow, an imaginary, almost hallucinatory text, is about "Suniti," who is "down on [her] knees, waiting for the goddess to manifest herself . . . The Cow of a Thousand Wishes" (13). The much-joked-about Hindu holy cow is her conversation companion, her lesbian lover, and her bar-hopping "Buddy, Bhadravati." Similarly, in a chapter called "Conjuring Cow," Namjoshi presents the reader with the self doubled over in the character of "S2," who looks, thinks, and speaks like "Suniti." In this instance, Namjoshi goes beyond the doppelgänger metaphor to signal the *essential* premise of lesbian identity, the *desire for the same*. Yet, critical attention is nonexistent for Namjoshi's work, her strategy of constructing essentialism, and her method of storytelling, as older, oral, safer spaces of the fabliaux have not yet caught the imagination of critics. Is Namjoshi perhaps not "Indian" enough for essentializing critics? Have they not constructed a place for her yet because she speaks of implausible desires instead of invoking race, or class, or nationalism? Judith Butler remarks in another context, "To speak *as a lesbian* is a paradoxical appearance of this 'I,' one which feels neither true nor false. For it is a production, usually in response to a request, to come out or write in the name of an identity which, once produced, sometimes functions as a politically efficacious phantasm" (13).[11] Namjoshi does not fit into categories of essentialism or constructionism, and that could account, in part, for the lack of critical attention.

Border Intellectuals and Identity Politics

Markandaya and Jhabvala are syncretic border intellectuals. They borrow cultural ideas and mythologies from their host country and buttress their identity against the new country in order to remake it. Namjoshi is a specular intellectual, reshaping and reinventing possibilities of the real through her feminist gaze. Mixing genres of the novel with fantasy and fable, poems with nursery rhymes, signaling the horrific yet awesome side of lesbian emotions, moving from magical realism to science fiction, Namjoshi stresses the need for new feminist forms of expression. In his discussion of the border intellectual, Jan-Mohamed outlines four positions that the intellectual can occupy: an exile's, an immigrant's, a colonialist's, and/or a scholar's. More interesting than this taxonomy is the *agency* that JanMohamed invests in the intellectual. He emphasizes that borders do not inherently carry any concreteness in themselves because they are merely points that mark the separation of the inside from the outside. He says:

> They [borders] are not really spaces at all; as sites of differences between interiority and exteriority, they are points of infinite regression. Thus, intellectuals located in this site are not, so to speak, "sitting" on the border; rather, they are forced to *constitute themselves as the border*, to coalesce around it as a point of infinite regression. In consciously or unconsciously constituting themselves in this manner, they have to guard themselves against the trap of specularity, for the border only

functions as a mirror, as a site of defining the "identity" and "homogeneity" of the group that has constructed it. (103, original emphasis)

Abdul JanMohamed, Bruce Robbins, Homi Bhabha, Stanley Aronowitz, Gloria Anzaldúa, and Henry Giroux, among others, have all separately discussed borders and the politics of home (either fixed or transitory) as locations of enunciation. But, for the purpose of examining the locus of Markandaya's, Jhabvala's, and Namjoshi's identities vis-à-vis their works, JanMohamed's subtle, Yeatsian question of knowing the *dancer for the dance* is indeed useful. In this paradigm, borders and identities are constantly shuttling spaces, making up and making over each other—the moment one factor becomes stable, the intellectual becomes less effective.

Going back to Markandaya's role as a syncretic border intellectual, let us examine *Possession, The Nowhere Man, The Golden Honeycomb,* and *Pleasure City.* (These novels have not been critiqued in the earlier section.) The first two are set in England and India and deal with the nuances of intercultural/interracial interaction. *Possession* is a novel about the rite of passage of an artist, Valmiki from rural India, who is himself literally exhibited standing alongside his art in London by Caroline Bell. Valmiki, who was "discovered" by Caroline while he painted magnificent, larger-than-life gods and goddesses in caves in India, is alternately ecstatic and miserable in London. Markandaya scripts Caroline's avarice and her need to manipulate Valmiki so fully that the title of the novel takes on a sinister life of its own. Most critics have taken Markandaya's cue and read Caroline as a symbol of colonial oppression and imperial greed. The weakness of the novel lies less in its unidimensional depiction of character and more in Markandaya's carelessness with her role as a border intellectual. Read through JanMohamed's definition, she is no longer "at home in both cultures" (97), and she becomes censorious of her host. More important, she emphasizes the interior/exterior or host/guest opposition of *space as a static place* instead of balancing on the border. Ironically, she allows herself to be placed under the slogan of essentialism. Her exilic sensibilities take over, and she becomes nativist, provincial.

The Nowhere Man mirrors the problems of *Possession* in a slightly different way. Srinivas, the hero of this novel, is "the nowhere man looking for a nowhere city" (70) when he decides to move to London with his wife and two sons. Even though Markandaya carefully sketches the role of the immigrant for Srinivas, she smudges the canvas with crude marks of diaspora, so that Srinivas is never quite "at home," revealing his angst (and that of his author) in the statement,

"One does not realise when one leaves one's country how much is chopped off" (70). If in *Possession* she is too overtly nationalistic, in *The Nowhere Man* she tries too much to be an assimilationist. Yet, this role does not quite suit Markandaya, and with a vicious swipe (yet with the corrosive irony of Hardy), she kills off Srinivas with leprosy, an archaic, stereotypically colonial, Asian affliction. Here Markandaya exposes the border as an insurmountable barrier, not a utopian space revealing the "intentionality of [her] intellectual orientation" (JanMohamed, 97).

The *Golden Honeycomb* and *Pleasure City* (also called *Shalimar*) are two puzzling creations by Markandaya. Definitely Orientalist projects, these novels attempt to present India as exotic, alluring, and mystical, and in a sense, they mediate between the colonialist and scholar modes that JanMohamed outlines for the border intellectual. The comparison of *The Golden Honeycomb* (with its episodic structure) to Scott's *Raj Quartet* (with its epic quality) should have been possible, but Markandaya's syncretic aspect falls short. *Pleasure City* is an intertextual reply to her own *The Nowhere Man,* but here Indo-British relationships are cordial and pleasant. Yet *Pleasure City* reifies borders in a manner that serves as a reminder of Kipling's hegemonic remark, "East is East and West is West and never the twain shall meet." Markandaya's story reflects Kipling's sentiment and underscores her own role as a syncretic border intellectual who is only an Indian writing in English.

In contrast, Jhabvala's *Esmond in India, A Backward Place,* and *A New Dominion* are good examples of the successful manipulation of border spaces, and she functions as a more efficient syncretic intellectual. These novels are examples of Jhabvala's conscious positioning of her role as an intellectual. She belongs to the colonial, scholar (anthropologist) category that JanMohamed speaks about. And even though she is clearly an outsider who records and represents the culture and history of India, she makes it plausible by speaking about India as an insider, by using names of towns and people with easy familiarity. These works are peopled with gurus, Europeans and Indians, all seeking the "meaning of life," a phrase made popular by the hippie movement. Even though Jhabvala takes India to a new level of Orientalism, as a syncretic, she learns to be at home in the host country. By staying on the border and staging "infinite regression[s]" (JanMohamed, 103), Jhabvala makes India her own, without actually embracing Indian culture. In "Myself to India" she writes that to "live in India and be at peace one must to a very considerable extent become Indian and adopt Indian attitudes, habits, beliefs, assume if possible an Indian personality. But how is this possible? And even if it were possible—without cheating oneself—would it be desirable?" (16). She is thus very aware of her position as a border intellectual. *Heat and Dust,* more familiar in the film version, fills the gaps left over by Forster's *A Passage to India,* reiterating the imperial views of India. (Salman Rushdie virulently attacked this visual showcasing of empire in his essay "Outside the Whale.")

Her critics notwithstanding, Jhabvala aligns herself with her host culture on the border with ease, because it is a rational move rather than an emotional engagement for her. It is not one fraught with the nightmare of colonization, as it is for Markandaya. *Thus, the border itself has an imperial dimension that Jan-Mohamed has not touched upon.* It allows class as a trope to function efficiently for Jhabvala, but blocks race from serving the same function, as it does in Markandaya's case. Here, Benita Parry's comment from "Overlapping Territories and Intertwined Histories" adds to our understanding of Jhabvala's role as a border intellectual. She writes that "a critique of culture and imperialism that situates itself on the borders and boundaries of knowable communities, intellectual systems, and critical practices, celebrating unhoused and decentered counter-energies generated by the displaced critical consciousness, enacts a theoretical mode symptomatic of a postcolonial cosmopolitanism which proclaims its multiple detachments and occupancy of a hybrid discursive space" (19). Jhabvala has been able to occupy this "hybrid discursive space" because she has made an intellectual decision, she has been self-conscious about the borders between self/other, empire/colony. Markandaya, partly by choice and partly because of impositions of race, has blurred the boundaries between self/empire and other/colony.

Suniti Namjoshi's role as a specular border intellectual needs to be explored by a different route—through the use of her body in her works. In this context, Adrienne Rich's words from "Notes Towards A Politics of Location" are appropriate. Rich writes "when I write 'the body,' I see nothing in particular. To write 'my body' plunges me in into lived experience, particularity: I see scars, disfigurements, discolorations, damages, losses, as well as what pleases me" (215). While Namjoshi does not always call attention to her immediate, material body, she nonetheless forces us to look at her scars. For example, she writes in *Because of India:*

> Once, in one of the seminars, someone made a remark about what would have happened if the Germans had won the war. I shrugged and said that as far as I was concerned, all it would have meant was that I'd

have been a student of German Literature rather than British Literature. I hadn't meant to shock at all, but it was evident I had succeeded. "If a small island hadn't conquered the world . . . " I found myself thinking. It was the beginning of the notion of cultural clout. (45)

Here, Namjoshi speaks from her complicated border position, as an Indian student in America, as an ex-colonial subject of Britain for whom Europe is the other, who uses her "interstitial cultural space as a vantage point from which to define, implicitly or explicitly," other perspectives (JanMohamed, 97). She is never fully an exile, or immigrant, or anthropologist, yet she always voices the unthought-of possibility.

Namjoshi not only ironizes Western humanism (and its corollary, patriarchy) but she uses her Western perspective against the grain to challenge Indian cultural traditions as well. For example, in "From the Panchatantra"[12] in *Feminist Fables,* she tells a story of a brahmin who asked Lord Vishnu for a son, but got a daughter instead. Although terribly disappointed, both father and daughter meditated and Vishnu appeared again. Again the brahmin asked for a son, and Namjoshi continues, "In his next incarnation the brahmin was a woman and bore eight sons. 'And what do you want?' he asked the girl. 'I want human status.' 'Ah, that is much harder,' and the god hedged and appointed a commission" (1). This exchange between the brahmin and Vishnu shows that Namjoshi is "unwilling" to be complacent enough to be "at home" in any culture because she cannot find a site of stasis on the border. The shuttling spaces between border and identity are a lived-in reality for her, and she is always vigilant. The mirror/specular image is always shifting angles, such that the intellectual's mind must reflect the varying degrees of hegemonies. And finally, the prose poem "For Adrienne Rich—If She Would Like It" shows Namjoshi's emergent lesbian politics. (*The Conversations of Cow* is more explicit.) In an imaginary conversation in the poem, the Caliph asks Sheherazade what she would like for her reward. Turning to her younger sister, "Dinarzade smiled. And it was then that Sheherazade answered, 'I have my reward, I have been given it' " (70). Rich acts as sister, mentor, and friend, and as the line illustrates, Namjoshi effortlessly signals a moment of solidarity on the borders of lesbian identity.

Conclusion

Part of the agenda in this essay has been to engage feminist politics with multicultural and multiracial issues in Indo-British contexts in an attempt to move away from neat binarisms. Politics of identity formation based upon essentialism/con-structionism or arguments of us and them in locations of colony and empire, or even polarizations of hetero- and homosexuality can be avoided by looking at intellectuals at the borders. Richard G. Fox's general comments about Indo-British attitudes that are repeatedly validated in postcolonial fiction help refocus the specific differences between Markandaya's and Jhabvala's works. Fox notes:

> Gandhian cultural resistance depended on an Orientalist image of India as inherently spiritual, consensual, and corporate. This image had a complex authorship and a contradictory character. Pejorative stereotypes of India, mainly portrayed by European detractors, led to one aspect of it. . . . Affirmative stereotypes of India created another, although contradictory, aspect of this Orientalist image. These stereotypes butted up against the negative image of India and reversed it. What appeared in pejorative Orientalism as India's ugliness now became India's beauty; her so-called weakness turned out to be her strengths. (151–52)

I have attempted to expose stereotypes (both affirmative and pejorative) of the essentialized/constructed subject. And, by inserting a third category through Suniti Namjoshi and making an illogical inclusion, I have stressed the border instead of the territory on either side, hoping that the startling juxtapositions will force us to be scrupulously attentive in the analysis of us-them. By illogical, I mean the deliberate ploy to make the argument dense with the problematic sites of the border intellectual. And as the trope of the border gains significance over the works themselves, symmetrical opposition between empire/colony or interiority/exteriority and gender differences will give way to more revealing analyses of the intersections and discontinuities between these terms. Numerous feminist scholars have insisted that "woman" must be the agent of her own transformation, and a postcolonial woman has a more arduous task. In this essay I have attempted to focus critical attention on a progression of borders, beginning with skin and nationality and leading to desire and textuality.

Notes

1. My grateful thanks to Gurudev, Sidonie Smith, Gisela Brinker-Gabler, P. S. Chauhan, Radhika Mohanram, R. C. Davis, and Susan Davis for their support and scrupulous readings of the earlier drafts of this essay.
2. It is difficult to treat the works of these two writers as fully autobiographical. Markandaya, an intensely private person, is resistant to critical responses that treat her fiction as autobiography. She married an Englishman and lived in London for close to three decades, and has claimed

in her rare interviews that she is writing fiction. Jhabvala is of Jewish German origin, has British citizenship, resided in India for close to two decades, and now lives in the United States. She said in a *Washington Post* article that "being a displaced person . . . I've often felt I'm in between . . . not quite one thing or another" (Bernard D. Nossiter, "Enjoying the Fruits of Detachment," *Washington Post,* December 9, 1975, C2).

3. For different critical views comparing Markandaya and Jhabvala as diasporic, see the following: Meera Bai, "From Adolescence to Womanhood: Kamala Markandaya's *Two Virgins,* Ruth Jhabvala's *To Whom She Will,* and Santha Rama Rao's *Remember the House,*" in *Indian Literature since Independence,* ed. K. Ayyappa Paniker (New Delhi: Indian Association for English Studies, 1991), 91–97; Bharatalakshmi and Krishna Sarma, "The Brown British: A Study of Recent Immigrant Novels," *Literary Half-Yearly* 18, no. 2 (1976): 53–70; Ramesh Chandra, *Cross-Cultural Interaction in Indian-English Fiction: An Analysis of the Novels of Ruth Jhabvala and Kamala Markandaya* (New Delhi: National Book Organization, 1988) and "*Heat and Dust* and *The Coffer Dams:* A Comparative Study," in *Comparative Literature,* ed. R. K. Dhawan (New Delhi: Bahri, 1987), 146–52; Rekha Jha, *The Novels of Kamala Markandaya and Ruth Jhabvala* (New Delhi: Prestige Books, 1990); Yasmin Gooneratne, "Traditional Elements in the fiction of Kamala Markandaya, R. K. Narayan, and Ruth Prawer Jhabvala," *World Literature Written in English* 15, no. 1 (1976): 121–34; and Elena Kalinnikova, "The Hindu Woman from London: Kamala Markandaya," in *Indian English Literature: A Perspective* (Ghaziabad: Vimal Prakashan, 1982), 146–62. For a detailed study of Markandaya's works, see Shyam Asnani's "East-West Encounter in Kamala Markandaya's Later Novels," *Triveni* 48, no. 4 (1980): 22–28, and Margaret Joseph's *Kamala Markandaya* (New Delhi: Arnold-Heinemann, 1980). For a detailed study of Jhabvala's works, see Ralph Crane's *Ruth Prawer Jhabvala* and Crane, ed., *Passage to Ruth Prawer Jhabvala* (New Delhi: Sterling, 1991).

4. Benedict Anderson's powerful thesis in *Imagined Communities: Reflections on the Origin and Spread of Nationalism* (London: Verso, 1991) is based upon the concept that nations are more than geographic entities or contiguous locations. He says that a nation is constructed as much with the energies of people who share a sense of community and kinship as it is by physical realities of land and government. Therefore, diasporic peoples, too, participate in a free-floating terrain of "imagined communities." The first part of Anderson's argument has been used consistently by cultural anthropologists, postcolonial historians and literary critics such as Arjun Appadurai, Gyan Pandey, Aloka Parasher, and Homi K. Bhabha to trace the impetus behind insurgence in nationalist struggles in previously colonized nations and to locate a national consciousness for these people. The latter part of Anderson's thesis has been used by scholars to prove a sense of belonging that is felt by people who have no actual personal contacts, but share a common bond in their heritage, language, and culture. Even though Anderson's argument uses Europe as an example, it is mostly postcolonial scholars who appropriate it to discuss nation formation for so-called third world countries. For a detailed explanation, see his chapters "Cultural Roots," "The Origin of National Consciousness," and "Official Nationalism and Imperialism." Anderson's deconstructive critique shows how clearly colonizers relied upon educational policies and ideological programs to hierarchize the colonizers over the natives and to create formal governments with resident imperial agents usurping complete power. This logic has added force to postcolonial analyses of the decolonized nation-space.

5. See Fredric Jameson, "Third World Literature in the Era of Multinational Capitalism," in *Social Text* 15 (Fall 1986): 65–88. This essay unleashed a huge (negative) response from postcolonial scholars who felt that Jameson had been prejudiced and careless in his analysis of third world literature. However, when Aijaz Ahmad took Jameson to task in *In Theory,* critics soon closed ranks against Ahmad. For more, see Ahmad's *In Theory: Classes, Nations, Literatures* (London: Verso, 1992). For some summaries of this debate and other critical comments, see the essays in *Postcolonial Discourse and Changing Cultural Contexts,* ed. Gita Rajan and Radhika Mohanram, (Westport, Conn.: Greenwood Press, 1995).

6. For a full account, see Nissim Ezekiel, "A Distorting Mirror?" *Times of India,* January 4, 1976, 10. Ezekiel also says, "I found *Heat and Dust* worthless as literature, contrived in its narrative structure, obtrusive in its authorial point of view, weak in style, stereotyped in its characters and viciously prejudiced in its vision of the Indian scene" (quoted in Crane, *Ruth Prawer Jhabvala,* 123). Feroza Jussawalla's essay "On Three Continents: The 'Inside' is the 'Outside' " (in *Passages to Ruth Prawer Jhabvala,* ed. Crane) and Rekha Jha's *The Novels of Kamala Markandaya and Ruth Jhabvala* present rather positive readings of Jhabvala by Indian women.

7. Vicky Kirby's essay "Corporeographies" is an innovative way of looking at the inside/outside and self/same dichotomies with "skin" as the border of corporeality (in this case, subjectivity). Although it does not directly apply to my argument here, her thesis that binary logic has been first constructed, then deconstructed, while leaving the logic of a Eurocentric premise intact is presented in a very persuasive manner. For more, see her essay in *Traveling Theories, Traveling Theorists,* ed. James Clifford and Dhareshwar, *Inscriptions* 5 (1989): 103–20.

8. The role of essence in lesbian identity formation is pivotal because "woman" and thus "woman's sexuality" have featured prominently in feminist debates since Simone de Beauvoir's startling statement four decades ago that a woman is made, not born. Diana Fuss asks a series of interesting questions: "Exactly who is lesbian? Is there such a thing as a lesbian essence? Does 'woman' include 'lesbian'? Can we speak of a 'lesbian mind' as distinct from what Wittig calls 'a straight mind'?" (44). For more, see her chapters on Monique Wittig and Luce Irigaray in *Essentially Speaking.*

9. Namjoshi writes, "Christine [her lover in England] started me out on an elementary work of feminism, then Millett's *Sexual Politics,* then Adrienne Rich's work, and so on. When I returned to Toronto in August 1979, I began writing *Feminist Fables.* They were done by December 1980 and published in 1981" (*Because of India,* 79).

10. Sidonie Smith, in *Subjectivity, Identity, and the Body,* details various kinds of autobiographical stances as "manifestos" to situate the "pronominal I." According to her, authors use it "to appropriate/to contest sovereignty, and/or to announce publicly, and/or to perform publicly, and/or to speak as one of a group, to speak for a group, and/or to speak to the future." I will borrow one of Smith's categories to explain the kind of indulgent, autobiographical technique in Namjoshi. Namjoshi fits best into the "to perform publicly" space because, "expressly a public performance, this manifesto engages directly the cultural constructions of identities and their sanctioned and legitimated performances, engaging the ideological systems pressing specific identities on specific persons. It takes a public stand on behalf of purposeful deflections, intervening in oppressive identity performances, troubling culturally authorized fictions" (161).

11. Gates, in "Beyond the Culture Wars," writes, "The point is that identity politics cannot be understood as a politics in the harness of a pregiven identity. The identity half of the catchall phrase 'identity politics' must be conceived as being just as labile and dynamic as the politics half is. The two terms must be in dialogue . . . or we should be prepared for the phrase to be revealed as an oxymoron" (9). Taken in conjunction with Butler's quotation, this gives a glimpse into Namjoshi's nonrecognition in academic circles. There might also be some truth to a very well-known postcolonial critic's remark, "Namjoshi is just not good enough!"

12. Namjoshi explains, "The *Panchatantra* is a Sanskrit book of fables. Unlike Aesop's it contains both brahmins and beasts" (1).

Works Cited

Bhabha, Homi K. "DissemiNation: Time, Narrative, and the Margins of the Modern Nation. In *Nation and Narration,* 291–322. London: Routledge, 1990.

Butler, Judith. "Imitation and Gender Insubordination." In *Inside/Out: Lesbian Theories, Gay Theories,* edited by Diana Fuss. London and New York: Routledge, 1991.

Crane, Ralph J. *Ruth Prawer Jhabvala.* New York: Twayne, 1992.

Fox, Richard. "East of Said." In *Edward Said: A Critical Reader,* edited by Michael Sprinker, 151–75. Cambridge, Mass.: Blackwell, 1992.

Fuss, Diana. *Essentially Speaking.* London and New York: Routledge, 1989.

Gates, Henry Louis, Jr. "Beyond the Culture Wars: Identities in Dialogue." *Professions* 93 (1993): 6–11.

JanMohamed, Abdul J. "Worldliness-without-World, Homelessness-as Home: Toward a Definition of the Specular Border Intellectual." In *Edward Said: A Critical Reader,* edited by Michael Sprinker, 96–120. Cambridge, Mass.: Blackwell, 1992.

Jhabvala, Ruth Prawer. *To Whom She Will.* London: Allen and Unwin, 1955.

———. *The Nature of Passion.* London: Allen and Unwin, 1956.

———. *Esmond in India.* London: Allen and Unwin, 1958.

———. *A Backward Place.* London: John Murray, 1965.

———. *An Experience of India.* London: John Murray, 1971.

———. *A New Dominion.* London: John Murray, 1972.

———. *Heat and Dust.* London: John Murray, 1975.

Markandaya, Kamala. *Nectar in a Sieve.* Bombay: Jaico, 1954.

———. *Some Inner Fury.* London: Putnam, 1955.

———. *A Silence of Desire.* London: Putnam, 1955.

———. *Possession.* Bombay: Jaico, 1963.

———. *A Handful of Rice.* New Delhi: Hind Pocket Books, 1966.

———. *The Coffer Dams.* New Delhi: Hind Pocket Books, 1969.

———. *The Nowhere Man.* New Delhi: Orient Longman, 1972.

———. *Two Virgins.* New York: Signet, 1973.

———. *The Golden Honeycomb.* London: Chatto and Windus, 1977.

———. *Pleasure City.* London: Chatto and Windus, 1982.

Parry, Benita. "Overlapping Territories and Intertwined Histories: Edward Said's Postcolonial Cosmopolitanism." In *Edward Said: A Critical Reader,* edited by Michael Sprinker, 19–47. Cambridge, Mass.: Blackwell, 1992.

Namjoshi, Suniti. *Poems.* Calcutta: Writers Workshop, 1967.

———. *Feminist Fables.* London: Sheba Feminist, 1981.

———. *The Authentic Lie.* Fredericton: University of New Brunswick, Fiddlehead, Goose Lane Press, 1982.

———. *From the Bedside Book of Nightmares.* Fredericton: University of New Brunswick, Fiddlehead, Goose Lane Press, 1984.

———. *The Conversations of Cow.* London: Women's Press, 1985.

———. *Flesh and Paper.* With Gillian Hanscombe. Seaton, England: Jezebel Tapes and Books, 1986.

———. *Because of India: Selected Poems and Fables.* London: Onlywoman Press, 1989.

———. *The Mothers of Maya Dilip.* London: Women's Press, 1989.

Newman, Judie. "Colonial Voices in the Motherland." In *Postcolonial Discourses and Changing Cultural Contexts,* edited by Gita Rajan and Radhika Mohanram. Westport, Conn.: Greenwood Press, 1995.

Rushdie, Salman. "Outside the Whale." *Granta* 11 (1983): 123–41.

Rich, Adrienne. *Blood, Bread, and Poetry: Selected Prose, 1979–1985.* New York and London: Norton, 1986.

Smith, Sidonie. *Subjectivity, Identity, and the Body: Women's Autobiographical Practices in the Twentieth Century.* Bloomington: Indiana University Press, 1993.

Spivak, Gayatri Chakravorty. "In a Word: *Interview.*" In *Outside in the Teaching Machine,* 1–24. New York: Routledge, 1993.

Suleri, Sara. "Multiculturalism and Its Discontents," *Professions* 93 (1993): 16–17.

4 / Black British Women Writing the Anti-Imperialist Critique

Carole Boyce Davies

Living now within the administrative center of what was/is left of the British Empire, Black women writers in England are able to launch an internal/external critique that challenges simultaneously the history and meanings of imperialism, the projects of postcoloniality, the implications of the various nationalistic identifications of home, and the ways in which masculinity interacts with these various systems of domination. The result, then, is a complex decentering of both home and exile as master discourses. The dismantling of the categories that have been constituted to identify the various colonial subjects and thus keep them in their place is central to this process. Additionally, the various displacements that imperialist enterprises have produced is put on record. Through writing their experience, then, Black women redefine for themselves the contours of given discourses such as family, identity, location, and creativity. The work of Black British women writers becomes, in my view, crucial in any analysis of the critique of imperialism and the dismantling of imperialist constructs. Thus, even European feminist discourses, when they replay some of the formulae of imperialism, are brought in for the same scrutiny as Valerie Amos and Pratibha Parmar have given in "Challenging Imperialist Feminism." Black women's writing in England seems positioned to maintain a kind of literary activism, a practical/political project that also asserts the desire to develop new and creative possibilities.

A variety of redefinitions begin this process. This study, therefore, starts by asserting their relevance to larger understandings of anti-imperialist discourses. A collection edited by Shabnam Grewal, Jackie Kay, Liliane Landor, Gail Lewis, and Pratibha Parmar, *Charting the Journey,* is very strong in its identification of the idea of new journeys, new identifications, and multiple locations of home.[1] The opening section, entitled "Alien-Nation: Strangers at Home," begins with lines from June Jordan's poem "Notes towards Home," using it as a riff to engage the shifting meanings of home for Black women. In their poetic opening statement, home is foregrounded as a series of contradictory statements: for example, "home is where you live—home is where you can't live." In the rest of the introduction, the contradictory meanings of home are expressed as a reality:

> For black women, there is an inherent contradiction in the very word "home." . . . Where is home for starters? Can you call a country which has systematically colonized your countries of origin, one which refuses through a thorough racism in its institutions, media and culture to even recognize your existence and your rights to that existence—can you call this country "home" without having your tongue inside your cheek? (10)

They move from there to talk about a variety of homeless conditions in South Africa, India, and the Caribbean. Questions of deportation from Britain make a mockery of the safety of home. Attacks on Black people in their own homes challenge the myth of security that accompanies home. The dreaming of a nostalgic home back in the old country is beset with problems, for "back home" sometimes becomes an idealized, romanticized place of origins that often turns out to be not so beautiful when the "migrant" returns. They conclude therefore that "until we can be both visible and belong the word 'home' will remain for us ambiguous, ironic, and even sarcastic. We will still be 'Strangers at Home' " (Grewal et al., 11).

The introduction to *Charting the Journey* identifies well the terms for most of the deliberations on home and exile, the colonized and empire that one finds in Black British women's literature. Much of the empirical grounding for their assertions comes through Valerie Amos and Pratibha Parmar's important work in this area, which addressed the issues of gender and migration and significantly linked "patriarchal immigration legislation" to the ways in which the exploitation of women's labor benefits racist, patriarchal, and class structures, across boundaries, without neglecting the agency embedded in resistance. For

example, "Many Voices, One Chant: Black Feminist Perspectives," a special issue of *Feminist Review,* documents Black women's organizing in London and
opens with the essay by Valerie Amos and Pratibha Parmar, "Challenging Imperial Feminism," which says, "True feminist theory and practice entails an understanding of imperialism and a critical engagement with challenging
racism—elements which the current women's movement significantly lacks,
but which are intrinsic to Black feminism. We are creating our own forms and
content" (17). The creative work in *Charting the Journey,* then, is grounded in
the practical examinations of migration. Thus the section "Frontiers" engages
some of the issues of constructed boundaries and borders that have to be challenged (118). Still it leaves room for the personal and political, as "The Whole
of Me" talks about the many identities that have to be accounted for and
"Turning the World Upside Down" speaks to necessary resistance. In each section, the contributing writers engage, in a variety of modes, the various issues
that have to do with the Black women's experience in Britain. Similarly, the
Black Womantalk Collective's *Black Women Talk Poetry* is organized into sections like "England, this land that had been no mother to her . . . ," "Ask me
where home is . . . ," "Where do I go who do I turn to . . . ," "Being a lesbian . . . ," and so on.[2]

Black women's contemporary experience in England is the product of slavery and British colonialism. The disruptions that followed British involvement
in the forced migration, indenturing, and enslavement of African and Asian
peoples created the subsequent migrations to England for economic, political,
and other well-documented reasons. Black women's existence in England has
been produced through displacement. The creative response has been documented in a variety of places, such as Paul Gilroy's *There Ain't No Black in the
Union Jack* and Amon Saba Saakana's *The Colonial Legacy in Caribbean Literature.* These, however, do not account in any significant way for Black British
women. David Dabydeen and Nana Wilson Tagoe's *A Reader's Guide to West Indian and Black British Literature* offers a detailed identification of some of the
principal texts and writers in the Black British experience.[3] In the section on
"Women Writers," they comment that although Black women have been in
England from at least the sixteenth century, "the overwhelming experience of
black women in Britain has been less glamorous than that of courtly entertainment. In the seventeenth and eighteenth centuries, the records point to employment as domestic servants, seamstresses, laundrymaids, children's nurses,
fairground performers and so on. Many were forced into street prostitution"

(134). Dilip Hiro's *Black British, White British* examines a range of communities and conditions in the categories of "West Indians," "Asians," and "White Britons," looking at history, migration, social and economic conditions, consciousness, urban conditions, resistance, organization, policing, and so on. In that context, the state has been known to be overt in its hostility to the developing Black community, as expressed in a book by the Institute of Race Relations, *Policing against Black People,* which contains numerous cases of police brutality and repression. On its cover is a revealing photograph of a mature Black woman on the ground, recoiling in a position of submission, as a white policeman stands over her with his baton raised. The evidence compiled by the Institute of Race Relations paints a grim picture of sustained police harassment and miscarriages of justice.

More developed discussion, specific to women, can be found in *The Heart of the Race: Black Women's Lives in Britain,* edited by Beverley Bryan, Stella Dadzie, and Suzanne Scafe, which goes into detail on issues of labor; the relationship to state systems of education, welfare, health; and the ways that Black women had to organize. *Strangers and Sisters: Women, Race, and Immigration,* edited by Selma James, contains the proceedings of a 1982 conference in London on race and immigration titled "Black and Immigrant Women Speak Out and Claim Our Rights." It is a practical product including the voices of the many women who participated and the themes, concerns, and strategies for claiming those rights. Another helpful work for me was Marsha Prescod's *Black Women: Bringing It All Back Home,* organized as it is around women seeking empowerment, identifying why and how they got to Britain and how they plan to negotiate and demand more from the system. It is a text that carries a great deal more agency for Black women than do many of the other works that speak for Black women. Here Black women speak for themselves.

A more recent work, Heidi Safia Mirza's *Young, Female, and Black,* looks at how Black girls make the transition to adulthood in Britain. "Young black women," Mirza concludes, "bear all the hallmarks of a fundamentally inegalitarian society. They do well at school, contribute to society, are good efficient workers, yet, as a group, they consistently fail to secure the economic status and occupational prestige they deserve" (189). In other words, for Mirza nothing much has changed.

The articulation of the women's voices themselves, which is central to *Strangers and Sisters,* is echoed in Amrit Wilson's *Finding a Voice: Asian Women in Britain.* This book is organized around women's responses to migration, their family and community relations, education, marriage, and struggle. In each case the women's voices are privileged and their life stories together create the larger story of migration and living conditions in the seat of empire. It is a project that within the context of the life story genre gives a variety of women a chance to tell their stories.[4]

In the context of telling one's story, one's self, Beryl Gilroy's *Black Teacher* had earlier recorded autobiographically the experience of a Black woman immigrant from Guyana, trying to make her way with integrity and efficiency as a teacher in the British school system of the 1950s. It documents the journeys of a Black woman who experienced, then, the entrenched prejudice, racism, sexism, and foreign bias that subsequent generations of Black professional women have had to face. Beryl Gilroy calls it "a fight for survival and dignity" (10). Steeped in the culture of 1950s colonialism, Beryl Gilroy struggles through jobs such as filing clerk, uniformed maid to a Lady Anne, and so on. Looking on with the consciousness and eyes of the 1990s, it is easy to feel impatient at the postures of servility that Black women had to adopt at that time in order to survive and even, in the end, to find some benefit from the experience. Beryl Gilroy explains it as at least an opportunity to study upper-class British culture but, even more so, as a chance to define herself over and beyond their expectations: "Above all, during the months spent with her I found my own identity— learning how important to the development of my personality and my future purpose was a knowledge of both family and country" (43).

Beryl Gilroy, of course, became a successful teacher, headmistress of a North London School, reading specialist at the University of London Institute of Education, writer of children's stories, novelist, poet, psychologist, and all-around creative writer with an impressive record of work in a variety of genres. In my view, it is necessary to understand Black women writers like Beryl Gilroy in order to put into some historical context the creative achievements of younger writers. It also allows us to see some of the generational dynamics in the anti-imperialist critique. For it is against this background that a number of Black British women write today and assertively critique empire building and the displacements it produces.

The interrelations of home and exile, personal history and location in their multiple meanings operate as necessary conditions for the problematizing of these easily conflated, flattened, or homogenized categories. A collection of essays entitled *Let It Be Told: Black Women Writers in Britain* has an introduction by Lauretta Ngcobo, its editor, which outlines well the many issues, the writers, their texts, and their range. It also includes discussion on a variety of women writers (Amryl Johnson, Maud Sulter, Agnes Sam, Valerie Bloom, Grace Nichols, Marsha Prescod, Lauretta Ngcobo, and a collective of Beverley Bryan, Stella Dadzie, and Suzanne Scafe), with commentary on their work by other writers. In general, much of the work on Black British women's writing has emphasized creative production, and the scholarly inquiry into their work is beginning.[5]

Unbelongingness

A central theme that runs through the works of Black women in Britain is the notion of not ever belonging even as one makes one's home in the "mother country." This notion of unbelonging becomes a central and repeated experience of the colonized subject, and an experience that contrasts directly with, as it clarifies, the discourses of the colonizers, which assert to the subject that she or he indeed belongs in the Empire. But belongs how? It is similarly the experience, because of racism, for those who were born in England and are literally "at home" as it is a denial of the long history of Black presence in England. An additional lever is added once the question of gender or sexuality is included, thus creating a multilayered series of displacements.

Joan Riley's novel, *The Unbelonging,* best captures the issue of displacement, which is its central theme. It is perhaps the best known of the writings that engage the question of home and identity. Her character is a young girl, Hyacinth, who makes the journey from her Jamaican home to London to live with her father after living with her Aunt Joyce in the Caribbean. Her childhood becomes a series of traumas, which include physical and sexual abuse by her father and the British school system. She becomes a displaced figure caught between a family that cannot organize itself to love and protect her and an outside system that does not seem to care and even turns against her in violent ways.[6] Between the cold and the dinginess of London, her bed-wetting, and struggles to grow up are her idyllic dreams of "back home." Her dismay is expressed at her initial encounter in the airport in London:

> She had been feeling lonely and small, and wishing for Aunt Joyce, for Jamaica and her friends, hating the father who had insisted on sending for her. Well, she had thought she hated him then, but boy, had she been wrong. There had been a sea of white faces everywhere, all hostile. She had known they hated her, and she had felt small, lost and afraid. (13)

Significantly, her father learned to utilize this double fear and need against her (the fear of white racism and her desire for home) in order to maintain his control of her. Paralleling this fear was her own growing self-hatred, which located beauty always in European features and physical characteristics:

> She often wished that she had nice hair, that her skin was lighter. She was sure they would not pick on her then. The more she suffered, the more she clung to thoughts of Jamaica, sinking further into her world of dreams. (74)

Hyacinth's entire life becomes, then, a manifestation of this sense of "unbelonging," a sense of feeling "unwanted" that parallels the dream of going back home to Aunt Joyce. Images of homelessness, desire, dreaming, and strangeness permeate the entire text. Her escape at one point becomes reading cheap romance books, which further distance her from her practical experiences. Finally, running for her life from her father's house (he himself is victimized by British racism) because of his unrelenting abuse, she enters the system, and while it holds her at arm's length, she is able to make her way, develop her own interests, and claim some things for herself. A series of small, drab, and lonely rooms in foster homes, reception homes, institutional homes, and dormitories help make the statement of displacement come alive. A similar mood and condition is created by Maureen Ismay's "The Bed-Sitting Room," where the character "had lived in tiny rooms, it seemed forever," rooms whose walls began to close in on her (48) in a mood of greyness, isolation, and imprisonment. The young Black woman in this story never leaves, seems to have no home to go to. The landscape outside similarly does not embrace her as she negotiates between inside and outside.

Rooms in this context become metonymic references for reduced space, and the references to homes are therefore often within the context of alienation and outsideness. Homes here are contrasted with "home," as in back home for Hyacinth. At university, she resists the demystification of her dreams of home that she encounters through the progressive politics of the university students whom she meets.

All her movements therefore lead to returning to the flat, stereotypic, and overromanticized "home" as the culmination of all the desires she has carried over the years. When she returns, however, predictably, the reality and dream converge in a nightmarish sequence with the dying old aunt to whom she had not really written, a run-down housing situation, neglect and poverty and people hostile to "foreigners" and particularly those like Hyacinth, who, with all her dreams, had never written or sent anything to help. The importance of "writing home" (140) is thus foregrounded over the flat constructions of "dreaming of homeland." "She could not remember living in this hovel, could not recall this decay and neglect" (138). The refrain that she hears, "Go back whe yu come fram" (142), highlights her sense of unbelonging and identifies the critique of the false constructions of "belonging."

Migration thus produces a sense of this "unbelonging," which then triggers memories of England, with its own pain and the identical cries of "Go back where you belong" (140). Hyacinth's sense of displacement is juxtaposed with the tourists who seem to be more located and, because of whiteness, seem to her to be always "at home" wherever they go. In the end Hyacinth thinks of her friend Perlene and misses the fact she has not identified with her sense of a need to construct new worlds borne of resistance. Still, she returns to the world of her childhood, but it is no longer a romanticized dream of home, rather one of a childhood of powerlessness and loneliness from which she has to recuperate.

Joan Riley has written a number of other works that engage the Black British experience. *Waiting in the Twilight* begins with a disabled, middle-aged Black woman who mops public spaces with one good arm and revels in the lies of England that were sold to her and caused her to exchange her life in the Caribbean for one in the "Motherland," where she struggled to provide for her children.[7] It also speaks to the generation of Black British born in England who did not really know "back home" (10). For her England is still a grim place in which she struggles with an irresponsible husband, Staunton, buys a run-down house, and works to claim something of her own, but dies in the end with her dreams intact. The author indicates that this book was written to put "a small part of the record straight where the West Indian woman in Britain is concerned. To show that the tremendous act of Bravery in leaving their home countries and stepping into a society of alien values will not readily be forgotten."[8]

The theme of returning home is further explored in Vernella Fuller's *Going Back Home,* and it also runs through work such as Claudette Williams, "Gal . . . You Come from Foreign" (in Grewal et al., 145–56), which deals reflectively with migration, affirming that it will not "silence our voices and kill our spirit" (145). Williams reflects on the difficulties and pleasures of life both at home in the Caribbean and in London: "I still possess a strong emotional attachment to the concept of 'back home'; England has never emotionally become my home, even though I've lived here some twenty years now" (151). Life in Britain made itself clear to her through the educational system, the Eurocentric and paternalistic racist systems, and finally through Black consciousness groups and Black women's organizations.[9] The result, similar to what African American women have experienced, is an understanding of the multiple locations and politics of Black female identities. Still, her sense of being a "stranger" in Britain does not mask the fact that on returning home she is also a "stranger-outsider," but nevertheless one who brings a history and knowledge that extends beyond the limited identifications with which she began her journey.

In this context of deconstructing home, Beryl Gilroy's longer vision ends *Boy-Sandwich* with a final decision to return home. This novel, which charts the lives of an aging couple in London, living with difficulty in retirement homes, and their relationship to their grandson, has a narrative voice that sees coming home, not as a situation of joy, but rather as a "service for old folk seeking a familiar graveyard" (122).

"She Lives between Back Home and Home" is how Sindamani Bridglal sees the contradiction, identifying how the shifting meanings of "home," its nowhereness and everywhereness, capture the mood of migratory subjectivities (88).

Black British writing experience deals in interesting ways, poetically and narratively, with concepts of Empire and self-articulation in the midst of Empire. In a variety of poetic expressions, the anti-imperialist critique is articulated. The poetic texts in many ways carry the direct urgency of the critical response along with the desire to create in spite of the existence of stifling experiences. In a poem titled "Birth Certificate," Maya Chowdhry locates her birth in Edinburgh in 1964, and continues: "but I was born in the world / and the year doesn't matter" (23). In "Diary of Home," she explores many of the meanings surrounding her identity as a Black British woman and her origins, relation to home place, parentage, colonialism, and boundaries. It is a simultaneous telling of her father's story and hers—his of migration to the colonial center, hers of the need to return—and it is also a remapping of her identities.

A special issue of *Feminist Art News* (London, vol. 3, no. 10 [1991]: 1) says it was organized after "countless conversations which took place in the course of daily living—especially with many different Blackwomen, unpicking the nuances of how imperialism and patriarchy hold hands to bulldoze their borderlines through our homes" (1). The link between patriarchy and imperialism is central to the antiauthority discourses of Black and third world women's feminisms. So in "Ethnic Monitoring, or a Geography Lesson," Kamila Zahno begins: "Black, Asian, White, FAR EASTERN, Other!" (24). And Lesley Saket adds in an emotive dismantling of colonizing boundaries: "life affirming beyond the power of any passport / . . . that I live outside the boundaries of the nation into which I was born" (26).

Another poem, by Shahida Janjua, entitled "Will You," affirms the need for women to love each other beyond the boundaries that societies impose, beyond patriarchal games:

> Women loving women
> Is the hardest place to be. (22)

A clear recognition of all the colonizations, both externally and internally imposed, is communicated, along with the desire to dismantle the untruths and create new worlds. Many of these works have begun the intellectual task of dismantling colonial boundaries and establishing journeys across difference. They therefore move even beyond Gloria Anzaldúa's formulations of borderlands, searching for reconnections beyond the boundaries imposed by colonialism and imperialism.

Merle Collins is similarly conscious of the colonial boundaries in "The Sheep and the Goats," which talks of various immigration posts as places where the sheep and the goats of her mother's cryptic folk sayings are manifested. In fact the entire collection *Rotten Pomerack* is a series of meditations on home and exile and the meanings of displacement and dislocation.[10] Snatches of remembered colonial verses are mixed with folk songs in the consciousness of a London domestic as she rides the train. A woman ponders where home is in the poem "Seduction": "Twenty years, she said, / in this cold confinement / and every winter I am packing / to leave. . . . But that's changing / this place is the home of my children / so the picture is shifting again" (14–15). The title poem, "Rotten Pomerack," uses the formulaic "Crick Crack" to pursue the myth and history, truth and lie of Columbian/Western discoveries (60–63).

The directions these works take are revolutionary in the sense of renewed struggles rather than poststruggles. Narratives such as Leena Dhingra's "Breaking out of Labels" eschew patronizing labels of various kinds and instead articulate resistance. Meiling Jin's "Strangers in a Hostile Landscape" offers a story to explain the often-asked question about her presence in England.[11] It is a historical narrative in poetic form that breaks down key words like "indentured labourers," "colonial-ization," "in-Dee-pendence," "imperial-Ization," "Invisible-Ness." It is a poem that tracks similar historical ground as Merle Collins's "No Dialects Please," which challenges the British on their convenient acceptance—

"African Slaves Please!"—and rejection—"No African languages please!"—all the while missing the fact that the formerly colonized and enslaved are mastering the language of the master as they redefine their own. This, I would assert, moves us beyond the uneasiness or hesitancy of naming at the theoretical level. For it necessitates a move to a new kind of optimism and struggle for change rather than a pessimism and postness or belatedness. Black British women writers have already moved beyond the "posts."

Uprising Textualities

The inability to unequivocally name current conditions is a central feature of our current theoretical/academic discourses, such as postcoloniality. This need not be read as a lack, but as space for doing important work without the constraints of circumscribing definitions. Kumkum Sangari speaks of "The Politics of the Possible" and Stuart Hall, in *The Road to Renewal*, speaks of the difficult work of "rethinking" everything, including the ways to rethink (271–82). Paula Gunn Allen in *The Sacred Hoop* frames it as "recovery." The institutions in which academics work demand theories and theorizing. Feminist criticism was similarly pushed (and pushed itself) to develop a theoretical respectability. The new Western-trained, Western-academy-bound intellectual, outside "uprising textualities," can "get stuck" in this mandate to theorize. The "what are you saying now to us?," as a questioner of Gayatri Spivak had concluded (Harasym, 69–70), is that open question which begs the response of a reversal, a listening by the Western intellectual to some of the movements among the various dispersed populations.

Uprisings, in the many meanings of the word, represent one of those discourses that link reasoning to action: as in no justice, no peace. In 1992 the Los Angeles riots, as the press dubbed the incident, were called by grassroots activists internationally an "uprising," in the sense of the people rising up from oppression. I propose to identify the meaning implicit in "uprising" to reformulate a host of textualities that seek to destabilize the established knowledge/authoritarian bases. It is a new resistance to imperialism that eschews colonial borders, systems, separations, ideologies, and structures of domination. In that context, then, the intellectuals who stay behind the "posts" reveal an unwillingness to look at these new movements for social change and their specific naming of imperialism. We are clearly operating within hegemonic U.S. imperialist time, which imposes its agenda as synonymous with world time. Resisting colonialities, in this context, means resisting dominations of discourse and a parallel advancing of anti-imperialist discourses. I would therefore want to re-engage the spirit of a number of resistant articulations as expressed by a range of theorists and writers within the context of formulating some understanding of "uprising textualities."

The "uprising textualities" of Black women writing in England capture some of the creative movement upward and outward from constricted and sub-merged spaces.[12] It signifies resistance, reassertion, renewal, and rethinking. This energy allows a movement outside the pessimism of Western intellectuals. It addresses that condition of "unheardness" to which dominant discourses (pa-triarchal and imperialistic) relegate a range of voices. It allows some movement toward the unnamed, unmarked "elsewhere" of rearticulated worlds, operating on the same poles as "maroon societies," "slave rebellions," and "underground railroads." "Uprising textualities" similarly respond to the language, innova-tion, and energy of Rastafari, which identifies action and meaning with a cer-tain poetic intent, on the one hand, and a literalization structured in words, on the other.[13] The ideology implicit in "uprising textuality" is also available in cer-tain streams of "rap music," as in Sister Souljah's lyrics or those of Fugees (short for "refugees") and certain forms of urban popular culture. Finally "uprisings" in this context resist theorizing and cannot really be "read" or defined in total-ity, for while they come across as spontaneous, they are the products of mount-ing resentment to oppression and are always "to be continued." Since Black writing in England deals in interesting ways with concepts of self-articulation in the midst of empire, the voice of creative "uprising textualities," which also voices the anti-imperialist critique, comes in this context from Black women. In a poem titled "Black Women Uprising," Stephanie George captures the movement with active verbs like "rising," "leaving," "running," coming," and "fighting back."

Thus, these uprising discourses of Black women writers in England carry some of the energy with which I think we need to address the questions raised by postcoloniality. An uprising consciousness moves us out of postcoloniality and the state of "postness" or "afterness" and into a more radical consciousness of our creativity. Grace Nichols, in her poem "The Return," invokes the mem-ory of legendary Black women freedom fighters like Nanny of the Maroons, as she listens and questions her ability to hear the "Abeng voice echoing its warcry through the valleys" (65). But resistance for Black women can be the determi-nation to be lazy in the context of expropriated domestic labor, as Nichols affirms in her *Lazy Thoughts of a Lazy Woman,* which revels in "Grease" and "Dust" having their existence independently of her compulsion to "not clean" them. In "The Body Reclining," she says, "Those who dust and dust / incessantly / also corrupt the body / And are caught in the asylum / Of their own making / Therefore I sing the body reclining" (4–5). In the same collection, though, is the poem "Spell against Too Much Male White Power" (18): "How can I remove the 'Big Chiefs' / from the helm / How can I put them to sit on beaches / quiet, seagazing, retired old men" (19). Her *Fat Black Woman's Poems* similarly critique, by the oppositional existence of the fat Black woman persona against the socially embedded norm, what constitutes appropriateness, beauty, location, and identity. Nichols's work in general is a celebration of body, magic, sexuality, power, and resistance. It is the kind of self-celebratory poetry that is bold enough to say, on the question of home and exile, "Wherever I hang me knickers—that's my home" (10). Still, it is a conclusion that is arrived at after charting the journey from home to England and the many adjustments to her new world-self along the way: "I get accustom to de English life / But I still miss backhome side / To tell the truth / I don't know really where I belaang" (10). The deliberate fracturing of the English word disrupts from outside the contained identity of Englishness as expressed in its language.

A number of writers make the transition from the poetic page to other media—photography, film, art, performance. Grace Nichols's collection *I Is a Long Memoried Woman,* for example, has been reinterpreted as a filmic piece with the same title, produced by Frances Anne Solomon. Similarly, Maud Sulter, a photographer, has a collection, *As a Blackwoman,* that speaks to all the things about her that she loves—her passion, work, creativity, and politics—but also her pains. Her artistic installation booklets, such as "Hysteria" (installation, 1992), carry the poetic texts as well as the photographic. Sulter has also edited *Passion: Discourses on Blackwomen's Creativity,* which is a wonderful collection of photography, art, poetry, reflections, essays, and stories. It is a sense-challenging, norm-breaking work that moves outside the boundaries established for the written and the visual.

But "uprising textualities" can also refer to the growing body of creativity by Black lesbian writers, or Zamimass, in London, who take their name from Audre Lorde's reidentification of the Caribbean creole term and who creatively and politically assert a presence and leadership in a variety of contexts. Many of the poets in the collections I have identified speak to this identity, in overt and subtle ways, as one of their many identities. The context of women loving one another, for example in the earlier identified poem by Zahno, then articulates itself both in resistance and in affirmation, as Carmen Tunde's "Dreadlocks Lesbian" asserts: "Have you seen dreadlocks lesbian / I tell you / she is one powerful woman / she no bother 'bout no man / inna heartache fashion." Shabnam similarly says in "The Women Loving Women": "They are / Everywhere / Bearing no names / wearing no badges / an underground army / with no uniforms / and no weapons / except love / for women / Beware" (Black Womantalk, 111). Barbara Burford, who had earlier published the Black lesbian novel *The Threshing Floor*, has also jointly edited a collection of love poems by women called *Dancing the Tightrope.*

The performative/activist basis of much of the creativity of Black British women writers frees the creative to exist outside of the academy and instead in the practical, pedagogic, and experiential community contexts. Thus a great deal of the work is produced in workshops, small groups, and community organizations,[14] and as such constantly escapes institutional and publication-oriented identifications. In a more directly assertive stance, Rasta/dub/ performance poet Sister Netifa, in "We Are Revolting,"[15] takes an intended insult in London and hurls it back in the lines:

> riots, mobs, uprising, rebellion
> we are revolting! (16)

For me, therein lies the response to one of the guiding questions that informs this chapter: where are the women in the theorizing of postcoloniality? How are they voicing the anti-imperialist critique?

Critical responses to this work have been slow in coming.[16] A great deal has been written about Buchi Emecheta's work within the context of African women's writing. Her two early works, *In the Ditch* and *Second Class Citizen*,[17] are well recognized for engaging the British welfare system as they critique the cultural/familial practices that attempt to subordinate women.

The Black women who are writing out of their experience of Britain articulate temporalities and locations outside the paradigms set by men, white society, and British literary establishments. In the middle of the former colonial heartland, they create different spaces for women's work or for women speaking outside the given boundaries, standing outside some of the dominant discourses. Creative activity therefore takes place within and outside contexts of publishing and sometimes more as an affirmation of creativity and existence as

Black women in Britain. Thus, much of what exists may never see the published forum or have any desire to be thus exposed. Black women writers in England are therefore articulating assertive presences, rather than belatedness —they are voicing creative uprisings.

Notes

This chapter is a shortened version of "Decentering Home and Exile: Black Women Writing the Critique of Empire," in Carole Boyce Davies, *Black Women, Writing, and Identity: Migrations of the Subject* (London: Routledge, 1994), and is reprinted with permission of Routledge Press.

1. See also Parmar, 236–75.

2. See also the Black Womantalk Collective's *Don't Ask Me Why: An Anthology of Short Stories by Black Women.*

3. This volume offers an annotated bibliography with introductory discussions of a variety of texts of Black British literature.

4. See my "Collaboration and the Ordering Imperative in Life Story Production," 3–19, for further discussion of this mode.

5. This has its benefit but may relate to the marked absence of Black women at the university level, where the production of intellectual analysis often takes place. Susheila Nasta, who is employed at the university level, has produced a great deal of work, such as is represented in *Motherlands,* and her editing of the journal *Wasafiri* has given scholarly attention to a variety of literary works.

6. See Janice Liddell's review, "Pain and Pathology."

7. Another Riley novel, *Romance,* was also published in 1988, and *A Kindness to the Children,* her most recent novel, was published in 1992.

8. See frontispiece of Riley, *Waiting in the Twilight.*

9. Interview with Claudette Williams in London, April 1993.

10. Collins is also author of *Angel* and *Because the Dawn Breaks.*

11. See also Jin's collection, *Gifts from My Grandmother.*

12. There is some debate about the designation Black British, with suggestions that these two conjoined are contradictions in terms. A number of these writers may not refer to themselves as Black British but as Afro-Caribbean, Guyanese, Trinidadian, Black Scottish, Asian, and so on. Some feel they have no particular sets of identifications they need to claim. Dorothea Smartt would suggest that "Black British" often refers to the generation born in England as opposed to the ones who migrate. What many of these writers have in common, however, is that they define themselves as Black women writers (discussion with Dorothea Smartt, in London, May, 1993). Janice Shinebourne and other writers I talked to on several occasions helped clarify this point, particularly about making distinctions and not approaching this group as monolithic, but there are, of course, a variety of perspectives on this issue of naming.

13. See Velma Pollard's work, such as "Innovation in Jamaican Creole: The Speech of Rastafari."

14. Some of the creative energy is expressed in Centerprise Black Women's Poetry Space and in Apples and Snakes, *The Popular Front of Contemporary Poetry Anthology,* which allows some space for Black women poets. There are a number of collections, poets, and other writers that I could not identify here because of space and the nature of this present undertaking. There is room for a much more extended examination of this literature, which is still in process and still "to be continued."

15. Netifa has two recorded albums of poetry and a new collection of poetry forthcoming.

16. Much of the energy has been directed toward producing collections. See, for example,

the recent *Daughters of Africa,* edited by Margaret Busby. It seems that it is more important for the women to document their creativity and their presence in as many ways as possible. But see the recent Gina Wisker, *Black Women's Writing,* which brings Black British women writers under the same critical attention as Black American women writers. A more recent collection is Delia Jarrett-Macauley, ed., *Reconstructing Womanhood, Deconstructing Feminism: Writings on Black Women.*

17. Published jointly as *Adah's Story.* See also Emecheta's *Gwendolen,* also published as *The Family,* which attempts to deal with incest in a migrant Caribbean family in a manner similar to that in Joan Riley's earlier work. My review, "You Big 'Oman Nuh, June-June," discusses this further. See also the recently published *Emerging Perspectives on Buchi Emecheta,* ed. Marie Umeh.

Works Cited

Allen, Paula Gunn. *The Sacred Hoop.* Boston: Beacon Press, 1986.

Amos, Valerie, and Pratibha Parmar. "Challenging Imperial Feminism." *Feminist Review* 17 (1984): 3–19.

Apples and Snakes. *The Popular Front of Contemporary Poetry Anthology.* London: Apples and Snakes/Angel Press, 1992.

Black Womantalk Collective. Da Choong, Olivette Wilson Cole, Bernardine Evaristo, and Gabriela Pearse, eds. *Black Women Talk Poetry.* London: Black Womantalk, 1987.

———. *Don't Ask Me Why: An Anthology of Short Stories by Black Women.* London: Black Womantalk, 1991.

Boyce Davies, Carole. "Collaboration and the Ordering Imperative in Life Story Production." In *De/Colonizing the Subject: The Politics of Gender in Women's Autobiography,* edited by Julia Watson and Sidonie Smith, 3–19. Minneapolis: University of Minnesota Press, 1992.

———. "You Big 'Oman Nuh, June-June." *Belles Lettres* 6, no. 1 (1990): 20–21.

Bridglal, Sindamani. "She Lives between Back Home and Home." In *Watchers and Seekers,* edited by Rhonda Cobham and Merle Collins, 88. London: Women's Press, 1987.

Bryan, Beverley, Stella Dadzie, and Suzanne Scafe, eds. *The Heart of the Race: Black Women's Lives in Britain.* London: Virago, 1985.

Burford, Barbara. *The Threshing Floor.* London: Sheba Feminist, 1986.

Burford, Barbara, Lindsay MacRae, and Sylvia Paskin, eds. *Dancing the Tightrope.* London: Women's Press, 1987.

Busby, Margaret, ed. *Daughters of Africa.* London: Jonathan Cape; New York: Pantheon, 1992.

Chowdhry, Maya. "Birth Certificate." *Feminist Art News* 3, no. 10 (1992): 23.

———. "Diary of Home." In *Inside Ant's Belly,* edited by Merle Collins, 79–90. London: National Association for the Teaching of English, 1994.

Collins, Merle. *Angel.* Seattle, Wash.: Seal Press, 1987.

———. *Because the Dawn Breaks.* London: Karia Press, 1985.

———. "No Dialects Please." In *Watchers and Seekers,* edited by Rhonda Cobham and Merle Collins, 118–19. London: Women's Press, 1987.

———. *Rotten Pomerack.* London: Women's Press, 1992.

Dabydeen, David, and Nana Wilson Tagoe. *A Reader's Guide to West Indian and Black British Literature.* London: Hansib, 1988.

Dhingra, Leena. "Breaking Out of Labels." In *Watchers and Seekers,* edited by Rhonda Cobham and Merle Collins, 103–7. London: Women's Press, 1987.

Emecheta, Buchi. *Adah's Story.* London: Allison and Busby, 1983; New York: Fontana, 1988.

———. *The Family.* London: Collins, 1989; New York: Braziller, 1990.

Feminist Art News (London) 3, no. 10 (1991).

Fuller, Vernella. *Going Back Home.* London: Women's Press, 1992.

Gilroy, Beryl. *Black Teacher.* London: Cassell, 1976.

————. *Boy-Sandwich*. London: Heinemann, 1989.

Gilroy, Paul. *There Ain't No Black in the Union Jack*. London: Hutchinson, 1987.

Grewal, Shabnam, Jackie Kay, Liliane Landor, Gail Lewis, and Pratibha Parmar. *Charting the Journey*. London: Sheba Feminist, 1988.

Hall, Stuart. *The Road to Renewal*. London: Verso, 1988.

Harasym, Sarah, ed. *The Post-Colonial Critic: Interviews, Strategies, Dialogues*. New York: Routledge, 1990.

Hiro, Dilip. *Black British, White British*. London: Paladin, 1992.

Institute of Race Relations. *Policing against Black People*. London: Institute of Race Relations, 1987.

Ismay, Maureen. "The Bed-Sitting Room." In *Watchers and Seekers*, edited by Rhonda Cobham and Merle Collins, 40–49. London: Women's Press, 1987.

James, Selma, ed. *Strangers and Sisters: Women, Race, and Immigration*. Bristol: Falling Wall Press, 1985.

Janjua, Shahida. "Will You." *Feminist Art News* (London) 3, no. 10 (1991): 26.

Jarrett-Macauley, Delia, ed. *Reconstructing Womanhood, Deconstructing Feminism: Writings on Black Women*. London: Routledge, 1996.

Jin, Meiling. *Gifts from My Grandmother*. London: Sheba Feminist, n.d.

————. "Strangers in a Hostile Landscape." In *Watchers and Seekers*, edited by Rhonda Cobham and Merle Collins, 123–26. London: Women's Press, 1987.

Liddel, Janice. "Pain and Pathology." *Caribbean Commentary* 1, no. 3 (1990): 33–34.

Mirza, Heidi Safia. *Young, Female, and Black*. London: Routledge, 1992.

Nasta, Susheila. *Motherlands*. London: Women's Press, 1991; New Brunswick, N.J.: Rutgers University Press, 1992.

Netifa, Sister. "We Are Revolting." In *A Woman Determined*. London: Research Associates, 1987.

Ngcobo, Lauretta, ed. *Let It Be Told: Black Women Writers in Britain*. London: Virago, 1988.

Nichols, Grace. *Fat Black Woman's Poems*. London: Virago, 1984.

————. *Lazy Thoughts of a Lazy Woman*. London: Virago, 1989.

————. "The Return." In *I Is a Long Memoried Woman*, 65. London: Karnak House, 1983/1990.

Parmar, Pratibha. "Gender, Race and Class: Asian Women in Resistance." In *The Empire Strikes Back: Race and Racism in 70's Britain*, Centre for Contemporary Cultural Studies, 236–75. London: Hutchison, 1982.

Pollard, Velma. "Innovation in Jamaican Creole: The Speech of Rastafari." In *Varieties of English around the World*, vol. 8, edited by Manfred Gorlach and John A. Holm, 157–66. Amsterdam and Philadelphia: Benjamins, 1986.

Prescod, Marsha. *Black Women: Bringing It All Back Home*. Bristol: Falling Wall Press, 1980/1986.

Riley, Joan. *A Kindness to the Children*. London: Women's Press, 1992.

————. *Romance*. London: Women's Press, 1988.

————. *The Unbelonging*. London: Women's Press, 1985.

————. *Waiting in the Twilight*. London: Women's Press, 1987.

Saakana, Amon Saba. *The Colonial Legacy in Caribbean Literature*. London: Karnak House, 1987.

Sangari, Kumkum. "The Politics of the Possible." *Cultural Critique* 7 (Fall 1987): 157–86.

Solomon, Frances Anne. *I Is a Long Memoried Woman*. London: Leda Serene/YOD video, 1990. Available from Women Make Movies, New York.

Sulter, Maud. *As a Blackwoman: Poems, 1982–1985*. Hebden Bridge, West Yorkshire: Urban Fox Press, 1985.

————. Installation booklet, Foyer Galleries, Royal Festival Hall, London, April 7 to May 10, 1992.

Sulter, Maud, ed. *Passion: Discourses on Blackwomen's Creativity.* Hebden Bridge, West Yorkshire: Urban Fox Press, 1990.

Tunde, Carmen. "Dreadlocks Lesbian." In *Charting the Journey,* edited by Shabnam Grewal et al., 205. London: Sheba Feminist, 1988.

Umeh, Marie, ed. *Emerging Perspectives on Buchi Emecheta.* Trenton, N.J.: Africa World Press, 1996.

Wilson, Amrit. *Finding a Voice: Asian Women in Britain.* London: Virago, 1978.

Wisker, Gina. *Black Women's Writing.* New York: St. Martin's Press, 1993.

Zahno, Kamila. "Ethnic Monitoring, or a Geography Lesson." *Feminist Art News* (London) 3, no. 10 (1991): 24.

5 / Looking through Non-Western Eyes

Immigrant Women's
Autobiographical Narratives in Italian[1]

Graziella Parati

The limited Italian colonial experience in Africa (Somalia, Eritrea, Ethiopia, and Libya) did not eventuate in mass emigration of people to the colonial motherland. Groups of people from Eritrea, an Italian colony between 1890 and 1941, did arrive in Italy at the time of the annexation of their country to Ethiopia, but they did not acquire the visibility of the more recent immigrants. In the past ten years Italy has changed from a country of emigration to a site of immigration from Africa, Asia, and Eastern Europe. Consequently, Italian society is now being modified in its public and private structures. Italian restaurants now have to compete with African ones; people can buy "Egyptian" bread in the same bakeries where the traditional Italian breads are made, and Youssou N'Dour's music is becoming very popular. While these superficial expressions of multiculturalism, what Stanley Fish calls "boutique multi-culturalism," have become part of everyday life, they do not signify an acceptance of the "others" and their difference.[2] The new multicultural Italy is far from being a peaceful cultural melting pot of the nineties; racism, violence, and fear have often been the response of Italians to the changes taking place in their country.[3]

New immigration laws had to be created, especially given the way in which the *emergenza immigrazione* (immigration emergency) has often been blamed as the all-encompassing motive for Italy's declining economy. The immigration laws of the 1990s, attempting to find a solution to the problematic presence in Italy of large numbers of illegal immigrants, aimed to regularize the position of immigrants who entered Italy before December 1989. Tellingly, the laws' translation into practice was named *sanatoria*. *Sanare* actually means to restore someone's health; in this case, implementation of the new law was intended to heal the country. This terminology, borrowed from the rhetoric of sickness, is in this context based on the assumption that becoming a country of immigration involves a contamination of the body of the country. By calling the law a *sanatoria* (that is, the means to heal), the nation is characterized, and in the legal text it is narrated, as a diseased body—a metaphor that, in the age of AIDS, does not fail to attract people's attention. The legislation aims to heal the country and to prevent other people from immigrating illegally into the country. It deals with both the cure and prevention, as it contains "the migrants, the minorities, the diasporic [who] come to change the history of the nation."[4] Narrating the multiracial nation through the legal text, Italy has attempted, and failed, to "practice safe text."

Immigrants have appropriated the narratives created on and about them and have made their voices heard. African immigrants, for instance, have published novels, autobiographies, and diaries. Mohamed Bouchane from Morocco, Salah Methnani from Tunisia, and Saidou Moussa Ba and Pap Khouma from Senegal have written texts in Italian, often with the collaboration of an Italian writer. Few women, however, are included in this list; their narratives have for the most part not yet appeared on the Italian literary scene. In her article entitled "Migrant Women and Gender Role Redefinitions in the Italian Context," Jaqueline Andall explains the reasons for immigrant women's invisibility and unspeakability in the public sphere of literary publications.[5] "Women migrants in Italy invariably fulfill a paid work function as domestic workers," writes Andall, who describes the isolation and marginalization of migrant women enclosed in domestic spaces where their free time is limited, as are the contacts with their ethnic communities.

There are two women, however, Maria Viarengo and Nassera Chohra, who have recently published autobiographical texts that describe their experiences as immigrants in Italy. Maria Viarengo's Italian-Ethiopian autobiographical writings, "Scirscir n'demna" (published as "Andiamo a spasso" [Let's go for a walk] in 1990), and Nassera Chohra's French-Algerian-Italian autobiography, *Volevo diventare bianca* (I wanted to become white, 1993), cannot be considered representations of the "universal" experience of migrant women. On the contrary, they narrate two privileged women's stories of migration that have very little in common with most migrant women's experience as domestic laborers. Chohra first came to Italy as a tourist and later became an "accidental immigrant" when she met and married an Italian man. She grew up in Marseilles, France, but she never wrote in the language of her education. Viarengo spent the first twenty years of her life in Ethiopia. She is the daughter of a wealthy Italian man and of an Ethiopian woman. She was "sent" to Italy by her father, who wanted her to acquire an Italian college education. Viarengo's and Chohra's autobiographies are the objects of this critical investigation that looks at two women's constructions of their present and past diasporic selves and hybrid identities. In order to explore their texts I have felt the need to create a dialogue between my own critical voice and Viarengo's and Chohra's texts. Therefore, I complement and guide my close reading of their retrospective narratives with comments and observations made by both authors in interviews. These interviews became occasions during which both Viarengo and Chohra commented and directed my approach to their autobiographies.

In *Black Women Writing Autobiography* (1989), Joanne M. Braxton affirms that "the critic who is not a black woman must *simply* work harder to see the black woman at the center of her own (written) experience" (6, my emphasis). This *reductio ad unum* of the problematic relationship between white critic and black writer becomes too essentialistic in the context of this article that attempts to bring migrant women's creativity to the center of the discussion on the recently created concept of italophone literature. However, it is the ambiguity of "her own experience" (as it could refer to both the black woman's and the white critic's texts) that draws my attention to the importance of its double interpretation. To approach the black woman as center of her own narrative and at the same time as center of my own critical narrative requires the construction of an active dialogue. It is by using interviews with both Viarengo and Chohra that I have attempted not to drown their diasporic and hybrid experiences by writing them into my white critical position.[6] In *The Post-Colonial Critic* (1990), Gayatri Spivak comments that "the moment you say, 'this is a white position', again you are homogenizing. I think there is safety in specificity rather than in those labels" (60). If I personalize Spivak's assertion and inscribe it within this critical context, I need to consider the construction of my position as an ongoing process that is often defined by the "other's" interpretation of my role as reader of her life. In fact, Maria Viarengo only agreed to see me and grant me an interview after discovering my own experience as an immigrant to the United States. It is only on this shared ground that Viarengo decided to meet and construct a dialogue, which was influenced by her interpretation of my diasporic identity.

Viarengo resisted my intention to use the interview as a one-way process in which my investigation of her oral narrative could complement my critical reading of her autobiography. The distance created by my questions directed to her was destroyed by Viarengo's demand for a dialogue in which the privileged position of the "questioner" could be exchanged. She wanted to create an oral text of my life parallel to the testimonies of her own experience (she wanted to know if I was married, if I had children, and where and how I lived in America). Similarly, my interview with Nassera Chohra developed into her interview of me and consequently destroyed the hierarchical separation between interviewer and interviewee. To talk about Chohra's life in Marseilles meant to discuss her dream of coming to the United States. She demanded to know what it is like to live in the States, a question that I found an unpleasant interruption to my own questioning but that echoed, in the interview, my own investigations of Chohra's past. In *Ho trovato l'Occidente: Storie di donne immigrate a Palermo* (I have found the West: Stories of women who have immigrated to Palermo, 1992), Amelia Crisantino, a sociologist who lives and works in Palermo, encountered this response in one of her interviews:

> White people always want to know things, they think that they understand. In my country it is bad manners to ask a person about his life. If you write a book, then will you give us the money that you earn? Rather, what do you do, what is your job, how much do you earn? (174)[7]

After refusing to be read as a text, this woman attempts to change her role from interviewee to interviewer and to transform Crisantino into the text to be explored. She resisted the "process that objectifies the interviewee and renders her as a source, constructs her as passive."[8] To weaken the privileged position of the interviewer means to displace such a position into "a text" that becomes complementary to the immigrant author's narration of her life and that contributes to the multiple definitions of otherness.

In her book on oral history entitled *Storia e soggettività* (History and subjectivity, 1988), Luisa Passerini defines the concept of anybody's "right to autobiography" as a means to contribute to multiple and "weaker" interpretations of history. According to Passerini, personal narratives represent "the attempt to create a historical subject starting from a person's everyday condition, moving from sub-jection to sub-jectivity" (7). Such an attempt also involves "the affirmation of a double right: to be in history, and to have a history" (7). Immigrants' autobiographies contribute to the creation of their history of immigration, which Italian sociologists and historians are beginning to trace. Their oral and written life stories are the voices that create the historical narratives of their own migrations. In the context of this article, the creation of an oral autobiographical text is added to the written work and problematized by the creation of a critical text that draws from both the oral and the written. What is created is the "right to multiple autobiographical acts" that do not involve the presence of a historian, but rather of a literary critic. The oral text, therefore, facilitates the interpretation and limits the critic's intervention in the written texts. "Life stories," writes Carole Boyce Davies, "are boundary-breaking texts." She also adds:

> Collaboratively told and written by women . . . they present a multi-leveled relationship to discourse. . . . Black women's texts often contest established boundaries, offer alternative interpretations, create new public discourses, challenge hegemonic definitions of discourse. There is, necessarily, as well for black women an oppositional relationship to those in power: the range of experts, including feminist theorists and "interpreters." (17)

My interviews with both Viarengo and Chohra contained both writers' testimonies of their struggles against boundaries imposed by editors and publishers and created a context in which their complaints about external interventions in their autobiographies became published and, therefore, public. At the same time, the narrative of their disappointing experiences with people in positions of power described in this article directly weakens my own position in my analysis of their works and warns the readers of the limitations of my discourse that, ironically, attempts to define the limitations of other discourses on "other" women's texts.

To translate the interviewer, the facilitator and interpreter, into a text also means to attempt to control his or her interpretation of the interviewee's life. Nassera Chohra's resistance to the interview led to her request to turn off the tape recorder when she found herself in the position of commenting on the role of the editor of her book (Alessandra Atti di Sarro) to an interviewer, who had more in common with the editor than with Chohra herself. Chohra lamented the editor's constant intervention in the construction of the book. Chohra wanted a collaboration based on her need to "have her grammar corrected." The editor appropriated a more active role in creating the book. In an interview, Alessandra Atti di Sarro confirmed that their collaboration was marred by frequent disagreements. For her part, di Sarro wanted to create a text constructed on the model of a journalistic narrative; consequently, she intervened in Chohra's text. She revealed that she gave *Volevo diventare bianca* a diachronic structure because Chohra had written both past and present events in the present tense.[9] The "tidying" of Chohra's retrospective narrative has probably facilitated the process of finding a publisher, but it has changed the text itself. Many immigrant writers have collaborated with an Italian author or journalist in order to write their diasporic identities in Italian. In a few cases, the Italian author and the African writer appear as coauthors.[10] In other cases the italophone texts are edited by an Italian. After interviewing most of these writers, I concluded that Chohra and di Sarro's text remains the only collaborative project defined as problematic by both the author and the editor.

In "The Margin at the Center: On *Testimonio*," John Beverley describes the collaborative project that lies at the center of the creation of *testimonio*, testimonial narratives. He analyzes various texts and concludes that "the author has been replaced in testimonio by the function of a 'compiler' or 'activator' "; and that represents a loss of authority, a "relief from the figure of 'the great writer' or writer as cultural hero" (97). However, in this close relationship between the oral narrative recounted and the translation into written text by the "compiler," the risk is a "smothering of a genuine popular voice by well intentioned but repressive (Stalinist, feminist, humanist, and so on) notions of political 'correctness' or pertinence" (Beverley, 98). In the context of this article the concept of "genuine popular voice" or of "genuine voice" in itself cannot be discussed, as Chohra reveals in the complexity of her own life narrative. She wants to tell her story and to construct her fragmented identity without attempting to create an essentializing portrayal of herself as representative of "migrant women." The collaborative project with the editor, di Sarro, develops from an already typed version of the autobiography, which is created as the result of a collaborative project between Chohra and her husband, who helped type the text and was consulted while Chohra was creating the narrative in Italian (her husband is bilingual; the son of Italian immigrants in Belgium, he returned to Italy, where he has lived since). Such a collaboration, which cannot be described in detail but which Chohra mentioned in the interview, creates the first level of elaboration of a text that is further modified by di Sarro's contributions. Di Sarro is not, therefore, the sole compiler who listened to the narrator's story and translated it into a text, but she added to an autobiography in which more than one voice was already present. The "transnational" links created by this plurality of collaborations connect racial, cultural, and linguistic differences. Chohra appears as the only protagonist of a narrative that describes the journey of a woman in search of a community that is neither black nor white, that is neither Western nor African. The collective authorial entity that, as Caren Kaplan states, is "one form of subversion [because it] can be identified as the deconstruction of the individual bourgeois author (the sacred subject of autobiographical narrative)" is hidden by Chohra, who does not accept the "community" created by this collaboration (121). She searches for a still nonexistent community of which she can be part. Chohra's resistance is, therefore, not against any ideological agenda that she finds restrictive, but against the imposition of a collaborative relationship in which the other woman does not develop "new strategies of reading cultural production as transnational activity" (Kaplan, 122).

Displacing the analysis of difference into the hybrid space between cultures underlines a rejection of the concept of an "authentic voice" that can represent the immigrant as a universal entity. In The *Post-Colonial Critic,* Gayatri Spivak remarks:

> For the person who does the "speaking as" something, it is a problem of distancing from one's self, whatever that self might be. But when the cardcarrying listeners, the hegemonic people, the dominant people, talk about listening to someone "speaking as" something or other, I think *there* one encounters a problem. When *they* want to hear an Indian speaking as an Indian, a Third World woman speaking as a Third World woman, they cover over the fact of the ignorance that they are allowed to possess, into a kind of homogenization. (60)

Nassera Chohra weakens my role as interviewer and representative of hegemonic people and at the same time refuses to assume the identity of the writer who "speaks as" something definable. In our interview, Chohra adamantly rejected any models as inspiration for her work. She stated that she never read novels, and, when questioned about her high school readings, she asserted that she could not remember. Then she added that only after the publication of her book did she begin exploring francophone women writers' texts.

Nassera Chohra and Maria Viarengo can be defined as privileged immigrants in Italy. Chohra came to Italy as a tourist, attracted by the "myth of the beautiful country," and here met the man whom she later married. Maria

Viarengo, born in Ethiopia, obeyed her father and moved to Italy in order to study in a European university. Consequently, both Chohra's and Viarengo's life stories differ from those narrated by Methnani, Khouma, Bouchane, and Saidou Moussa Ba, who migrated from Tunisia, Morocco, and Senegal in order to improve their economic status. However, there is a common denominator among italophone authors: the italophone writer emerges in acts of mediation through multilayered cultural and linguistic levels. At present, most italophone authors come from a francophone background and acquire Italian as a third (or sometimes fourth) language. The French literary tradition and language, to which most immigrants in Italy are exposed throughout their school years, become intermediate passages that facilitate the immigrant authors' appropriation of another romance language and a new cultural context. The stratification of cultural and linguistic plains is not here intended to create a hierarchical structure of influences. In writing about the italophone context, my emphasis is not on assimilation into Western culture and, consequently, on the subordination of the non-Western traditions. What I want to focus on is migration—a concept that emphasizes two-way mobility, not either immigration or "emigration," which involve one-way movements from or to a new national context. The "center" is not to be found in any specific and self-contained cultural context. It is in the transnational hybrid space in-between that the concepts of nations, cultures, and traditions are redefined. For authors like the Senegalese Pap Khouma, choosing Italy as his new land and Italian as a literary language involves a rejection of France as the "natural" place of emigration and the acquisition of a new "voice." Interestingly, he learns Italian through a French grammar book. In this way, French is subordinated to the role of tool and intermediary between past and present. The colonizer's language and literature are therefore displaced from their usual privileged position and become secondary to the appropriation and personalization of another culture. This "articulation of cultural differences and identifications" is developed through a "dissemination of texts and discourses across cultures" (Bhabha, "DissemiNation," 292–93). The result is not only a redefinition of one's own diasporic and hybrid identity, but also a parallel intervention in Italian culture into which the immigrant writer is inscribing his or her own voice.

Chohra's French-Algerian-Italian identity is constructed in her autobiography, *Volevo diventare bianca*. Her narrative recounts Chohra's life in Marseilles, her childhood desire to become white (which she tried to accomplish by literally bleaching her skin), and her experiences in the French capital. Talking about her own and her family's diasporic identities, Chohra combines different cultural contexts of immigration. Her family comes from the Algerian Sahara Desert and her parents, Chohra stated in our interview, transgressed the unwritten rules that prohibited marriage between people of different tribes. Her dark-skinned mother and her lighter-skinned father represent for Chohra a culturally and ethnically mixed background that, translated into the French environment in which Chohra was born, becomes part of Chohra's hybrid identity. In addition, because of her choice of another country of residence, francophone and italophone spaces are linked in the realm in-between that is described in Chohra's autobiographical act.

The first chapter, entitled "To Be Black," describes the discovery of her blackness through the eyes of her little white friends. Naci is the protagonist of the chapters that describe Chohra's childhood in Marseilles. Naci and not Nassera is here the name of the character because age and choices separate the adult Nassera and the child Naci. Naci is the girl who "wanted to become white." According to Naci, to be defined as black means that she becomes the object of the white people's gaze, that she sees herself through that gaze and perceives the negative connotations attached to "blackness." When Corinne, Naci's white friend, refuses to give her an old doll because Naci is black, Naci runs home to find a mirror, a cracked looking glass, and sees herself as she is seen by Corinne. Like Pecola, the character in Toni Morrison's *The Bluest Eye,* Naci wants to become a mirror image of the white models, those dolls that she is not even allowed to touch. Once she "sees" her own color, she can compare her newly discovered identity with her mother's and sister's: "Corinne was right: they are black and . . . even more than I am!" (11). After recognizing degrees of otherness, Naci discovers the signifying system of "coloredness" and her difference from the models offered on television in her favorite programs. Determined to "become white," as if her blackness could be cured, Naci asks her teacher to tell her how to change her skin color. The teacher transforms Naci's request into an opportunity to teach the class that "being black is not a negative thing." (12) Naci is not happy about the teacher's approach to her difference:

> The explanation has not made me happy at all. On the contrary: now everybody knows that I am black, even those who maybe had not realized it, I thought. I have been betrayed, twice! Not only the teacher has not answered my question, but she has revealed my horrible defect to the whole class. I hate her, she does not understand anything. (13)

What the teacher does not understand is that by inscribing Naci's difference in language and publicly using her as a didactic object, she has essentialized Naci's identity as one of many black girls. Learning the power of language, Naci in turn decides to create an alternative white mother for herself. She tells her friends that her mother is blond and has blue eyes. She rewrites her mother as a new text that negates her blackness. She is, however, betrayed by her real mother who comes to meet Naci outside her school. One day, her friends realize that the blond mother with blue eyes does not exist. "For a week," writes Chohra, "I felt very much ashamed of my mother and of the color of her skin, and only now I know that I will never be able to feel ashamed long enough for having felt ashamed of her" (13). The mother becomes in Naci's imagination the woman who, once reinvented, can allow her to "pass," like Nella Larsen's mulatto characters, into the white world.

After deciding to "pass" into the white world, Naci discovers that her body betrays her. The body, which Judith Butler defines as "a region of cultural unruliness and disorder," becomes for Naci the mirror that reflects a black woman's limitations, that defines her as the reflection of her mother.[11] Torn between resembling the mother and wanting to be like Corinne and her white "perfect" dolls, Naci discovers that the confusion and disorder in her parallel the disorder and confusion in her reality, her house, her world. Her courtyard is compared to Corinne's: Naci's is untidy, the realm of confusion, and of the same imperfection that characterizes her identity. "Certain people," writes Sidonie Smith, "those positioned peripherally to the dominant group, those claiming and/or assigned marginalized identities, find themselves partitioned in their bodies."[12] Naci finds herself divided between her desire for whiteness and order and the feeling of being trapped in black disorder and imperfection. After discovering the unruliness of her courtyard, Naci feels the need to look at herself and finds a cracked mirror that, she says, "will do fine" for her (11). The superimposed and irremovable "imperfection" in the mirror confirms Naci's perception of herself as flawed and fragmented, but also motivates her in her future search for a different distribution of the fragments, for an alternative construction of her identity. The young Naci rejects the possibility of remaining the reflection of what she thinks is her mother's black body and of her black identity.

The maternal reaction to Naci's repudiation of her black identity is violent: the mother "spits in her [the daughter's] face" (15). The autobiography is created, says Chohra in the interview, in order to reinterpret her mother's strong but, according to Naci, incomprehensible reaction to a daughter's decision to "pass" into the white world. Chohra states that her book was written during a difficult pregnancy when she began to think about her mixed French-Algerian and Italian identity. The act of writing her life translated her desire to create a text that could prevent her child from being as ashamed of his dark-skinned mother as Naci had been of her black mother. The matrilinear link created in the autobiographical act connects Chohra to her mother's otherness and privileges the "sameness" between the two women. At the same time, Chohra also stresses the difference that separates her from her mother, whom she sees as the perpetuator of a patriarchal order and strict Muslim practice.

In the family, the mother is often the "woman who punishes" while the father has a more nurturing and less violent role in his children's education. Naci's punishments for her transgressions are always translated by her mother into the practice of torturing her sex:

> "Lie on the ground, without wearing your panties and with your legs open!" screamed my mother, holding in her hand a green pepper cut in the middle. I knew that punishment; I tried to escape, but my brothers immobilized me. Completely naked and with my legs open I looked like a chicken ready to be seasoned before going into the oven. The hot pepper, rubbed repeatedly on my sex, burned unbearably. It was like being on fire in my insides. I screamed with all my breath because of the pain and out of shame. (23)

The shame that the mother had refused to feel as a black person is reinscribed in the relationship with Naci, who learns to be ashamed as a woman. She is punished because she is female, and she is made aware of her biological identity through the pain inflicted by the mother with the collaboration of her brothers, who "keep her still." Naci's mother is, in their familial sphere, the instrument of patriarchy who teaches her daughter that the priority in her life is to "remain a virgin." (Among the Saharawi, "virginity is very important. If you lose it the punishment is ferocious: they stone you to death" [36].) Her castigations are, therefore, the mimicry of a threat, the loss of virginity. Naci's mother further chastises her daughter by cutting her braids, Naci's pride. "She cut them without pity," writes Chohra, "and I thought that it would have been better if she had amputated one of my arms" (15). This act, reminding Naci of an amputation (that is, castration), defines the maternal discourse on female subordination and obedience, which Naci cannot accept. Her reaction is to begin establishing her own politics of transgression and disobedience.

In Chohra's autobiography, Naci's noncompliance with the rules in her strict Muslim family reflects her desire to be the daughter of Algerian parents, but also her need to appropriate the culture of the Western country that she has known since birth. She represents a threat to the family and to its established hierarchical order. When she decides to become an actress, the mother accuses her of wanting to become a prostitute, of bringing shame to the family, of "castrating" the father's power: "Your father will have to cut his mustache in shame" (115). When she finds herself torn between choosing her mother or her dreams, she decides for her dreams (115).

Chohra's construction of her hybrid identity draws both from her familial past and traditions and from the Western culture that she partially appropriates. As a child her family takes her on a trip back to the Algerian Sahara, where she discovers how different she is from her Algerian relatives:

> [I thought] that they were savages and that I wanted to go back to France: it is not possible, these cannot be our relatives; they do not have chains to flush the toilet, instead of houses they live in tents like Indians, instead of light bulbs they use candles, of course, they do not have ceilings, where would they hang their chandeliers? They sleep in the middle of the road and my bed is not even soft, they do not have water taps, and, worst of all, they do not even have television sets! I cannot stay here any longer. Tomorrow I will go back to France. . . . I told my sister all this, hoping that she would agree, so that we could leave together, but she got angry instead. She even raised her voice, she, who is always calm. (34)

Naci behaves like an impatient European traveler who discovers that the "savages" do not measure up to European standards. Guilty of what Said calls "orientalism," Naci develops an essentializing approach to her relatives' culture as generically inferior: they are like all the "others," like Indians, for instance.[13] The sister's reaction to Naci's narrow-mindedness pushes Naci to spend more time exploring the novelty of these people's difference and she is soon drawn into her new familial life. She cannot, however, accept the subordinate role that women play. "According to the tradition," Chohra comments, "during the ceremony the [totally shaved] bride cannot move at all, nor can she raise her eyes from the ground. She is not even allowed to eat because she is not allowed to go to the bathroom" (39). Her practice of disobedience is inscribed within this new context as she refuses to accept the valued "feminine immobility" that appears as a recurring theme in the narrative. Naci is not allowed to be present at her brother's circumcision ceremony, but she disobeys: she spies on it and becomes afraid when her mother tells her that she will be circumcised as well. Her ceremony takes place without the music, food, and dances that followed her brother's circumcision. Her mother and grandmother take Naci to an oasis, where they keep her still while a local woman holding a razor makes five incisions on Naci's leg, above her right knee, and chants, "Nobody will succeed in penetrating you if he is not your husband. Nobody will abuse you and you will remain a virgin until you decide that you do not want to be a virgin any more" (43). The body emerges again as the focus of these familial practices: tradition is imprinted on her body, which now resembles the marked bodies of all the women in the tribe. However, these external signs that demonstrate Naci's identity as a member of her mother's family change in their meaning, as Naci still wants to go back to "her" country, France, where her tribal identity remains but a fragment in the complex creation of her hybrid self.

Learning about her familial past and traditions makes Naci forget about the highly missed television, but does not create a sense of community that allows her to "belong" in a metonymic relationship. Naci identifies herself, instead, with the hybrid community that inhabits the poor area of Marseilles where Naci's family lives. The crazy woman from Corsica, the Gypsies, the Sicilian family, and the old Arab man Aftari, who always talks about Allah, are the people that Naci knows (51). This community is chosen because it is varied. The members differ, and the links and similarities between its members are fewer than the differences. This community is not held together by shared traditions; it is arbitrarily viewed as a temporary "community" by Naci, who sees it as an alternative to her mother's community, strictly defined by a religious tradition. Difference is the rule, and sameness, Naci discovers, is ignorance. She has to face her teacher's irritation because she is dirty, as she does not wash her henna "stain" before coming to class. "She kept repeating," writes Chohra, "that whoever migrates and lives in another country must adapt to the habits and customs of that country" (57–58). The teacher becomes the champion of the ideology of immediate assimilation based on the superiority of white French traditions. Madame Cohen, the teacher, believes in the reductive assumption that living in one nation means to live in one culture. At the same time, because of her Jewish identity, she embodies the same difference that she tries to negate. Difference becomes a relative term, and Naci discovers the radically different "degrees" of otherness and its arbitrary interpretations by the power figures that she encounters in various communities and geographical contexts.

In her text, Chohra uses the verb *trasferirsi* (to move), which comes from the Latin verb *transferre* (to convey from one place to another). The past participle of this verb, *translatum,* becomes in English the verb "to translate." Diasporic cultures are based on the double meaning of the Latin verb and of its English appropriation. The physical movement to other countries becomes an act of translation of one's background into a new cultural context, and, in the case of literature, such movement between cultures becomes new hybrid texts.[14] Naci's translation of the familial culture is mediated through her parents' memories and her short trip to their motherland. Her education in the French system and the exposure to the mixed ethnic and cultural influences of the people in the Marseilles area where she lives create a text that eloquently mocks Madame Cohen's *reductio ad unum,* her idea of assimilation. Naci's hybrid identity lies at the intersection of several cultural influences that create a space between cultures. This space goes beyond any attempt to interweave the colonizer's culture (French culture, in this context, as Chohra's parents come from Algeria) with the colonized. The privileged position of the superior white culture is here weakened by the multiplication of influences. To such a plurality of influences Chohra's Italian experience is added. In her voluntary exile in Italy, Chohra chooses a new language in which she creates her retrospective narrative, her hybridity, and once more actively "translates" herself. The problematic relationship with the editor of her autobiographical text reveals Chohra's attempt to resist "being passively translated" into the new literary discourse and becoming the object of the discussion on difference.

The final chapter in Chohra's book was suggested by the editor. The initial manuscript contains the narrative in Italian of Naci's childhood in Marseilles, the trip to the Sahara, and her life in Paris, where she wanted to become an actress. The description of Naci's life in Italy appears in the last chapter and describes her arrival in a new country that she has always dreamed of seeing. For Italians she embodies a paradox: she is a black woman who travels in Italy as a tourist. Once more, Naci finds herself in a space in-between by destroying the stereotypes that define white people as tourists and black people as immigrants in Italy. Chohra, who calls herself a woman without a "homeland or a flag to revere" (131), witnesses racism and violence against the immigrants:

> I heard for the first time the term "vu' cumprà."[15] Some boys with a less than kind attitude were using it and laughing at a poor black boy, as black as ebony. He was selling eyeglasses and necklaces on a small colorful rug. They were saying it like an insult, in an arrogant tone of

voice. I did not understand then the meaning of those words, they disturbed my ecstasy as a tourist. I would not know why, but I instinctively compared my skin with the poor and unfortunate salesman's skin. He stood there with downcast eyes and a resigned expression. He must be Senegalese, I thought. They have this trade in their blood. I smiled at him, for solidarity, but he probably did not even see me. (132)

Chohra is a spectator to such events; the black identity shared by Naci and the Senegalese boy only underlines Naci's difference from the African vendor. She even supplies a biological explanation for this unknown man's trade, which tends to create a homogenizing definition of all Senegalese men. Her essentializing construction of other black identities underscores Chohra's privileged position in the new country. She falls in love with Rome and with a man and lives "in a world . . . that is a mixture of Algerian traditions and European dreams" (133). The Algerian past and the European future are represented in a hybrid present that allows Chohra to enter a public sphere, denied to other immigrant women.

Privileged female black voices have been made public through the publication of their life stories; this is definitely the case for both Nassera Chohra and, as I will later present, Maria Viarengo. Spivak defines the problem in talking about "representative" diasporic voices in the following terms: "Constructing the Other simply as an object of knowledge [means] leaving out the real Others because of the ones who are getting access into public places due to these waves of benevolence and so on" (63). Ignoring the problematic definition of "real Others," Spivak does expose the reality regarding emerging voices of women immigrants in Italy: the voices that have surfaced belong to a few privileged women who have succeeded in publishing their works.[16] Nassera Chohra moves from being a tourist to being a wife and a mother without sharing the experience of many other women immigrants who are domestic laborers and remain illegal immigrants. I do not attempt here to define degrees of "underprivilegedness," but rather to underline the impossibility of considering Nassera Chohra's life story as representative of women immigrants in Italy.

If on one hand the separation between Western and non-Western eyes becomes more difficult to define, on the other, issues of class have to be added to race and gender questions. Chohra, the tourist in Italy, acquires a position within the Italian middle class without going through intermediate stages, as do most other immigrants. The new community to which she relates in Italy is very different from the diasporic groups, founded by immigrants such as the Senegalese community or the Moroccan community, which link immigrants to their past and work as support groups in their present lives. Chohra narrates the uniqueness of her experience. Her European experience becomes the filter through which she reads her future and raises her son who is taught Arabic, French, and Italian (132). The autobiography concludes with a wish: "I wish that the future will show that white and black are nothing but gradations" (132). This utopian vision of the future is based on Chohra's privileged exile and on the representation of her "difference" from the "otherness" of both the people who have recently emigrated to Italy and the almost monocultural environment in the newly adopted land.[17]

Maria Viarengo's privileged position in the transnational space of italophone literature creates a parallel text to Chohra's narrative, as Viarengo's privileged condition is based on her socioeconomic and cultural status. Chohra's identity is defined through a kaleidoscopic fragmentation of cultural influences; Maria Viarengo's self is, instead, characterized by dichotomy: paternal and maternal, Western and non-Western. In her autobiographical text "Andiamo a spasso," Viarengo narrates her life story as the daughter of the only white man, the rich man, in an Ethiopian village, Ghidami. Born in 1949 in the former colony (Ethiopia was an Italian colony between 1936 and 1941), Viarengo tells her experience as the daughter of an Italian man and of an Ethiopian woman. Her bilingual education is based on the supremacy of Italian over Oromo. In fact, she was sent to an Italian school in Asmara (Eritrea) to be educated in Italian. The father's culture and language are privileged to the point that not only does she become fluent in Italian, but she also learns the paternal dialect, Piedmontese.

Viarengo constructs her autobiography as a collage that attempts to weaken the paternal influence by writing the memories of the mother she is "not supposed" to resemble. She translates her experience in a narrative made of autobiographical fragments that recount her childhoood between cultures and languages and her dramatic detachment from the motherland. Viarengo constructs her hybrid identity in Italian, Oromo, and Piedmontese. Her transnational narrative also acquires a new dimension as a transregional text. The issue of regionalism and regional identities is present in today's Italy, which has seen the rise in the past few years of the influence of regionalist parties such as the *Lega del Nord* (Northern League), a party that proclaims the financial and racial superiority of the north over the Italian south. Europe may be attempting to become a unified entity, but fragmentation, separation, and the subsequent attempts to create a hierarchical structure of racial and cultural identities undermine such a project. Viarengo begins her fragmented autobiographical piece from an elitist position: she is a woman who, thanks to her father's wealth, connections, and northern Italian origins, has "passed" into a white world and has had little in common with other migrant women's hard experience as domestic laborers. In the same autobiography, Viarengo, the woman who embodies both an African and a northern Italian identity, also creates a space of resistance against the public discourse on racial superiorities and inferiorities. Caren Kaplan argues that "resistance literature . . . breaks many of elite literature's laws: it is comparative but not always linked to a national language; it is overly political, sometimes anonymous, always pressuring the boundaries of established genres" (120). Resistance is played out in "Andiamo a spasso," as Viarengo resists her total "passing" into a world that she cannot accept as hers. In her autobiographical text she does not focus on her adult life in Italy, her marriage to an Italian man, or her two "white" daughters. The retrospective narrative deals with the story of both Maria and Abebù, of her "geographically" fragmented identity: Maria, the father's daughter, and Abebù, the mother's daughter. The fragmentation of her identity, which Viarengo privileges, is created as the opposite of the hierarchically arranged fragmentation of contemporary Italy and Europe.

Raised in Ethiopia, Asmara, and Karthoum, the protagonist, Maria/Abebù, is bewildered by Italy:

> In 1964 and 1966, Dad had brought us [Maria and her sister] to Italy. . . . Italy was the vacation land. . . . Italy, then, was our America.
>
> During our first stay in Rome, we were surprised by the relationship between white people and the professions that they practiced. At Fiumicino airport the porters were white, in bathrooms the attendants were white, in hotels the cleaning women, the waiters, the shoeshines, the street sweepers were white. How appalling! In Asmara every white lady had at least two black letté (maids). (74)

Maria, the *métisse,* looks at Italy through her African, but at the same time paternal Italian, eyes. Her hierarchically organized world collapses in her father's land, where she sees as a "white" person but is seen by Italians as black. Her social and economic status, which allows her to be a tourist and to buy an apartment in Turin, does not save her from embodying otherness for Italians. Viarengo perceives her difference through language:

I have heard people call me hanfez, klls, meticcia, mulatta, caffelatte, half-cast, ciuculatin, colored, armusch.

I have learned the art of looking like someone else, I always looked like whomever others wanted me to look like.

I have been Indian, Arab, Latin American, Sicilian. (74)

Outside of Ethiopia, her "Italian identity" loses the connotations that once had allowed Maria a privileged life in the former colony. Translated into her new land, Maria's identity acquires connotations of inferiority as she is renamed according to others' perception of her difference. It is a new act of geographical and linguistic translation that creates a space where racial and ethnic identities become arbitrarily modified.

Viarengo's rejection of the arbitrary translation of the title of her narrative parallels Chohra's refusal to become objectified. Only part of Viarengo's autobiographical act has been published. The journal *Linea d'ombra* (no. 54 [November 1990]) changed the title that Viarengo had kept in Oromo, her maternal language. "Scirscir n'demna" became "Andiamo a spasso" ("Let's go for a walk"), which is the "exact" translation, but not the same. Being "published" involves the act of "becoming public." In Viarengo's autobiographical act, her self is publicized in a superimposed translation that separates her from her mother and strengthens the link with her Italian father and, in the end, defeats Viarengo's initial act of resistance in which she had portrayed herself as that hybrid child that can never be totally "assimilated." This arbitrary use of the translation, therefore, colonizes Viarengo's voice in order to turn it into a "more" understandable text for Italian readers and modifies the core of Viarengo's agenda.

This movement toward the paternal land, culture, and language is based on separation and consequent isolation from the mother's land. At the beginning of her autobiographical text, Maria Viarengo reclaims her double self in order to be "two," both Maria and Abebù, the name given to Maria by her mother (74). She wants to reconstruct, after many years in Italy, a matrilinear link to her biological mother and the maternal land. Viarengo's autobiographical act acquires nostalgic undertones as the narration of the land, left behind when she was twenty years old, involves the definition of her desire to retrace her steps from the father's land and language to her mother's village and familial language. The danger in having privileged the father's heritage is to lose the hybrid self, to become one: "I was two. . . . Will I always be two?" (74). Hybridity becomes here a privileged space that must be preserved in order not to let the definition of otherness become a *reductio ad unum* and not to allow the *métisse* to turn into an essentialized object.

Maria Viarengo's life in Italy begins with her separation from the maternal community and the maternal language. In his book *Decolonising the Mind* (1986), Ngugi Wa Thiong'o asserts that adopting a new language involves a separation from the past "toward other worlds" (12). He refers to the colonizers' languages imposed over the African native languages. For Maria Viarengo, acquiring an education meant abandoning an African past in order to embrace the superiority of Western knowledge. As language is intended as both a "means of communication and a carrier of culture" (13), such a separation becomes a mutilation, an exile from a community. After leaving Ghidami, Maria Viarengo discovers that her double identity and her treasured multicultural self is considered by others as negative and inferior. The child Maria comes from an environment where her mother was Coptic, her maternal grandmother was Muslim, and her father was Catholic. As a child she is sent to a Catholic school, where she must change and conform. Like Chohra, Viarengo must reject her mixed past and mixed familial community in order to acquire *one* identity:

> In a big school the woman who spoke with my father asked him if I had been baptized; my father answered that we did what mother did in religious matters. The woman looked at me with a worried expression on her face and said, "She is the devil's daughter." I pressed against my father's leg, I started screaming that he was my father.
>
> What did these grown-ups want from me? Where was my mother? Why was father leaving us in this place? Did I have to change father? I was scared. (75)[18]

During the interview, Viarengo renarrated her experience in the religious school and summarized it by saying that the nuns tried to "cancel what she was in order to make her into what they wanted." As a child she was raised to learn Italian history, which, however, she in turn attempted to revise. One day, after learning about Cavour and Garibaldi, the nuns took the students to Adua (the site of the Italian defeat in a battle against the Ethiopians on March 1, 1896) and asked them to pray for the Italian soldiers killed. The child Maria protested and established her own politics of disobedience. Feeling both Italian and Ethiopian, she wanted to pray for the Ethiopian soldiers as well. She rebelled against the imposed separation from the maternal inheritance: her Ethiopian identity.

This first separation from the mother and the maternal land is repeated in Maria's life. As a child, she is brought to live with relatives in Khartoum, Sudan.

This movement involves a loss of the maternal language, as English, Italian, and Arabic "slowly . . . start to overwhelm Oromo" (75). Her sister Teru reacts by silencing herself; Teru only talks to Maria and creates a dialogue in Oromo in order to express her nostalgia for the "mother's warmth and softness" (75). Adopting the new languages (English, Arabic, and, mainly, Italian) over the maternal language involves a radical act of separation and mutilation against which Teru reacts by refusing the dominant languages imposed on her. She still has a voice in the maternal language, the private language shared with her sister, the link with the past (the Ethiopian identity) that she is forced to leave behind. Oromo is therefore enclosed in the private sphere and becomes unacceptable as a public language, as others are preferable in the hierarchical structure in which languages are inscribed.

The final separation from her African identity is decided by Maria's father. When he orders Maria to leave Africa, against her wish, Maria is twenty years old. Once in Italy, she immediately tries to buy a ticket to return "home," but her plans are hindered by the people her father asks to watch over her. Her father is protecting her from the village chief, whom, he is afraid, is planning to marry Maria. He wants her to continue her studies at the university. He also tells her that if she had been male she would have been allowed to stay in Ethiopia. Viarengo states in the interview that there have been times when she has "cursed" her female identity. She is punished for being a woman by being removed from her maternal land, her mother, her African hybridity. The father is attempting to protect her from the same patriarchal oppression that he embodies. He sees her future as the chief's wife, dedicated to serve the husband and have children. In this case, it is the father who does not want his daughter to be silenced. In her exile, which now, after twenty years, cannot be clearly defined as either voluntary or involuntary, she goes to school in Turin, marries, and has two children.

Her autobiographical act in Italian becomes the thread to connect the fragments that compose her hybrid identity, without privileging the paternal inheritance that has dominated her life. Viarengo describes her return to Ghidami:

> Ghidami is made of dirt, there is no word in Oromo to say asphalt. Turin has entered Ghidami with me and some postcards that I brought to grandmother.
> Mother was dead, she was thirty-six, leaving me with anger for a never-born dialogue when we would have been able to talk to each other like two women, and leaving me with impotence because of the forgotten language, Oromo Imbecu. (75)

Her text attempts to create a space where the chronological order is destroyed and past and present can be rewritten in a synchronic order. The sense of loss is, however, present, and some missing threads to her past leave the weaving of her story with wide gaps that cannot be filled. The discussion is brought back to the question asked at the beginning of her narrative, to the difficulty of remaining "double" without allowing one side to overwhelm the other.

Viarengo translates her interest in exploring her hybrid identity as an Ethiopian-Italian into the public discourse on the multicultural identity of Italy. In fact, in order to complement the issues of race, gender, and class discussed in her autobiographical text, Viarengo collaborates, by writing one chapter and various sections, in the creation of a book entitled *Uguali e diversi: Il mondo cultural, le reti di rapporti, i lavori degli immigratinon europei a Torino* (Equal and different: The cultural world, the system of relations, the work of the non-European immigrants in Turin, 1991). It is the first published research on the lives and problems of immigrants that relies on the collaboration of a group of non-Italian, non-European people to construct the text. Of the twenty-four collaborators, only six are Italian. The parts written by Maria Viarengo deal with marriage in Somalia and Morocco, immigrants' education, and their expectations. The texts are based on interviews and testimonies collected in Italy that attempt to define the cultural background of the immigrants in Italy. It is a text for Italian readers that aims to fight ignorance and prejudice against the immigrants. Viarengo works on a theoretical approach to ethnic, racial, and cultural identities and translates the problems discussed in her personal narrative into a discourse on other immigrations and hybrid identities.

Viarengo creates a discourse on hybridity and multicultural identities that involves the personal and the theoretical, the autobiographical narrative and public discussions of otherness. Now she is writing an autobiographical novel in order to expand on the already published text. Nassera Chohra was not very open in discussing her present and future literary work, but revealed that she will further explore her memories of her trip to the Algerian Sahara, this time without searching for a close collaboration with an Italian editor.

This critical essay, which has not done justice to Viarengo's and Chohra's literary voices, has considered their works in order to contribute to the discussion of a redefinition of the concept of Italian literature. In this redefinition of a literary space, both Viarengo and Chohra succeed in creating alternatives to a dichotomized portrayal of Western and non-Western cultures. They create a "more *dialogic* process that attempts to track the processes of displacement and realignment . . . , constructing something different and hybrid from the encounter: a third space that does not simply revise or invert the dualities [and binary oppositions], but revalues the ideological basis of division and difference."[19] They tried to create female identities that draw from the various cultural contexts that they have negotiated. In both cases, the mother figure becomes the center of their narratives: in Chohra's case she embodies the woman who does not understand the daughter's need to transgress and to create an independent identity that "betrays" the maternal expectations and obedience to tradition. In Viarengo's case, the mother is the protagonist of a nostalgic narrative in which the author attempts to connect with her African identity and her Ethiopian maternal inheritance.

In their separate, but parallel, projects, both authors create portrayals of themselves as women (Naci, Maria, Abebù) who struggle to connect and nurture the fragments of both their Western and non-Western identities. Viarengo and Chohra's interventions in Italian narrative and language create texts that defy the national as "natural" boundaries of literature: the transnational and multicultural contexts, which both Chohra and Viarengo create, aim to destroy linguistic and cultural dichotomies "in the act of revising and hybridizing the settled." Their Italian identities remain, however, privileged. These texts are written in Italian and address Italian readers. New "acts of translation" are needed to transfer these autobiographical acts into the linguistic and cultural non-Western contexts that the authors attempt to interweave.

Notes

1. I am aware of the problematic use of terms such as "Western" or "non-Western." I am not attempting to create clearly dichotomized portrayals. The complex term "non-Western cultures" does not indicate their complete separation from what is considered Western. I use such a term because, as Cheryl Johnson-Odim and Margaret Strobel state, "It seems less affirming to refer to people by a negative term denoting something they are not. Still, the terms 'non-Western' and 'Third World' can be useful for particular purposes if we remain aware of their limitations" (x).

2. I am here referring to a lecture given by Stanley Fish at Dartmouth College on July 23, 1993, entitled "Boutique Multi-Culturalism."

3. In his Italian collection of short stories entitled *Dove lo stato non c'è* (Where the state does not exist, 1991), the francophone writer Tahar Ben Jelloun tells the story of African immigrants who work in the tomato fields of southern Italy. His text, which narrates the inhuman lives of immigrants, also analyzes other centuries-old problems of the south (Ben Jelloun writes stories about the Mafia), problems that now become secondary to the solution of the immigration "emergency."

4. Homi Bhabha, "DissemiNation: Time, Narrative, and the Margins of the Modern Nation," 319–20.

5. Jaqueline Andall's essay is not yet published. I am grateful to her for allowing me to read her work. On migrant women, see also Jaqueline Andall, "Women Migrant Workers in Italy."

6. All interviews are still unpublished. I interviewed Maria Viarengo on December 28, 1992, and Nassera Chohra on June 8, 1993.

7. All translations are mine.

8. Carole Boyce Davies, "Collaboration and the Ordering Imperative in Life Story Production," 5.

9. I was given a copy of the manuscript of a few chapters without the editor's "corrections." The editor received the original manuscript in typed form. Nassera Chohra's husband, who was raised by Italian immigrants in Belgium and is therefore bilingual, helped Chohra type the text. Here are a couple of examples that show the difference between the original manuscript and the published form. The chapter entitled "Holiday in the Sahara" became "Sahara" in the published text. The chapter in the original manuscript began and continued in the present tense: "School is over and the vacation begins. This year, for the first time I will go on a vacation. A trip to Sahara has been planned by my parents." In the published form, this chapter was turned into the past tense: "Finally, school was over. This year, for the first time, we would go on vacation. My parents had planned a trip to Sahara." In the chapter "My best friend," the final changes are more evident. The order has been changed. In the manuscript the story begins with a description of the changes in the area where Naci lives: a new ethnic group moves in. In the published version Naci is introduced right away and the sequence of the paragraphs is changed. In the manuscript the chapter begins:

Another school year flies away.

In our area, the cayolle, all the houses are systematically emptied little by little and, they are occupied by a new (it is new for us) race of people: the Bagdad.

In the published version, the beginning is different:

The best friend of my teen age years was, without any doubt, Silvie. A girl from Corsica with a difficult personality, like mine. We were a steady couple of friends for, at least, three years. Then, our roads separated. She had become a woman too quickly and I, instead, remained a little girl for a lot longer.

I met Silvie after one of our many moves. I was twelve. New people had arrived at the Cayolle. They were called "Bagdad," they were Gypsies from the East, I think. (74)

10. The books in which an African author and an Italian writer appear as coauthors are Mario Fortunato and Salah Methnani, *Immigrato* (Immigrant), and P. A. Micheletti and Saidou Moussa Ba, *La promessa di Hamadi* (Hamadi's promise). The other texts edited by Italian writers are Pap Khouma, *Io, venditore di elefanti: Una vita per forza tra Dakar, Parigi e Milano* (I, an elephant salesman: A forced life between Dakar, Paris, and Milan), ed. Oreste Pivetta; Mohamed Bouchane, *Chiamatemi Alì,* (Call me Alì), ed. Carla de Girolamo and Daniele Miccione. Tahar Ben Jelloun's *Dove lo Stato non c'è: Racconti italiani (Where the State does not exist: Italian tales)* is presented as written "with the collaboration of Egi Volterrani," as stated on the cover right below the author's name. Moshen Melliti's *Pantanella: Canto lungo la strada (Pantanella: A song along the road)* was written in Arabic, but only published in the Italian translation made by Monica Ruotto. Renato Curcio is the editor of Hassan Itab's *La tana della iena (The hyena's den)*.

11. Judith Butler, "Variations on Sex and Gender: Beauvoir, Wittig and Foucault," 131.

12. Sidonie Smith, *Subjectivity, Identity, and the Body: Women's Autobiographical Practices in the Twentieth Century,* 10.

13. Edward Said, *Orientalism.*

14. Another element can be added to the repeated translations through different cultural contexts. It is the added element of my own translation of Chohra's and Viarengo's texts into English that draws, once more, my own identity into a discourse on other women's hybrid construction of their selves. The resulting connection between the private and the public, the theoretical and its translation into practice echoes both Chohra's and Viarengo's attempts to draw my own identity into the discussions taking place during the interviews.

15. The term "vu' cumprà" is used indiscriminately for all immigrants who sell objects in the streets. They are being ridiculed because they distort the Italian language and instead of offering their merchandise saying "vuole comprare" in correct Italian, they say something different (that is, they are stupid). They are reduced to being "funny," to being inferior and more acceptable in their identity as "vu' cumprà" because they are then not threatening and can easily be patronized.

16. It is, however, important to remember that this article was written in August 1993. The construction of immigrant women's identities is an ongoing process that is being redefined by the changing socioeconomic conditions of immigrants in Italy. My analysis does not attempt to define future works by women immigrants, but is limited to the present.

17. In *Razzismi, un vocabolario (Racisms, a dictionary)*, Laura Balbo and Luigi Manconi state: "Italian society must be described as a monocultural system. And monocolor: we are—more or less—white. Since the Unification of Italy, the fundamental political and cultural choice can be summarized in the following motto: 'facciamo gli italian' [let's be Italian]. Therefore, norms and practices that have had the aim of creating a culturally homogeneous national system have been in use" (37–38).

18. The first person plural is used because Maria Viarengo is also including her sister Teru, to whom the autobiographical text is dedicated.

19. Homi Bhabha, "Postcolonial Authority and Postmodern Guilt," 57.

Works Cited

Andall, Jaqueline. "Women Migrant Workers in Italy." *Women's Studies International Forum* 1 (1992): 41–48.

Balbo, Laura, and Luigi Manconi. *Razzismi, un vocabolario.* Milan: Feltrinelli, 1993.

Beverley, John. "The Margin at the Center: On *Testimonio* (Testimonial Narrative)." In *De/Colonizing the Subject: The Politics of Gender in Women's Autobiography,* edited by Sidonie Smith and Julia Watson, 91–114. Minneapolis: University of Minnesota Press, 1992.

Bhabha, Homi K. "DissemiNation: Time, Narrative, and the Margins of the Modern Nation." In *Nation and Narration,* edited by Homi K. Bhabha, 291–322. New York: Routledge, 1990.

———. "Postcolonial Authority and Postmodern Guilt." In *Cultural Studies,* edited by Lawrence Grossberg, Cary Nelson, and Paula Treichler, 56–66. New York: Routledge, 1992.

Boyce Davies, Carole. "Collaboration and the Ordering Imperative in Life Story Production." In *De/Colonizing the Subject: The Politics of Gender in Women's Autobiography,* edited by Sidonie Smith and Julia Watson, 3–19. Minneapolis: University of Minnesota Press, 1992.

Bouchane, Mohamed. *Chiamatemi Alì.* Edited by Carla de Girolamo and Daniele Miccione. Milan: Leonardo, 1990.

Braxton, Joanne M. *Black Women Writing Autobiography: A Tradition within a Tradition.* Philadelphia: Temple University Press, 1989.

Butler, Judith. "Variations on Sex and Gender: Beauvoir, Wittig and Foucault." In *Feminism as Critique: On the Politics of Gender,* edited by Seyla Denhabib and Drucilla Cornell. Minneapolis: University of Minnesota Press, 1987.

Chohra, Nassera. *Volevo diventare bianca.* Edited by Alessandra Atti di Sarro. Rome: E/O, 1993.

Crisantino, Amelia. *Ho trovato l'Occidente: Storie di donne immigrate a Palermo.* Palermo: La Luna, 1992.

Fortunato, Mario, and Salah Methnani. *Immigrato.* Rome and Naples: Theoria, 1990.

Ingram, Angela. "On the Contrary, Outside of It." In *Women's Writing in Exile,* edited by Mary Lynn Broe and Angela Ingram, 1–16. Chapel Hill: University of North Carolina Press, 1989.

Itab, Hassan. *La tana della iena.* Edited by Renato Curcio. Rome: Sensibili alle Foglie, 1991.

Jelloun, Tahar Ben. *Dove lo stato non c'è: Racconti italiani.* Edited by Egi Volterrani. Turin: Einaudi, 1991.

Johnson-Odim, Cheryl, and Margaret Strobel, eds. Introduction to *Expanding the Boundaries of Women's History: Essays on Women in the Third World.* Bloomington: Indiana University Press, 1992.

Kaplan, Caren. "Resisting Autobiography: Out-Law Genres and Transnational Feminist Subjects." In *De/Colonizing the Subject: The Politics of Gender in Women's Autobiography,* edited by Sidonie Smith and Julia Watson, 115–38. Minneapolis: University of Minnesota Press, 1992.

Khouma, Pap. *Io, venditore di elefanti: Una vita per forza tra Dakar, Parigi e Milano.* Edited by Oreste Pivetta. Milano: Garzanti, 1990.

Lionnet, Françoise. "Of Mangoes and Maroons: Language, History, and the Multicultural Subject of Michelle Cliff's Abeng." In *De/Colonizing the Subject: The Politics of Gender in Women's Autobiography,* edited by Sidonie Smith and Julia Watson, 321–45. Minneapolis: University of Minnesota Press, 1992.

Micheletti, P. A., and Saidou Moussa Ba. *La promessa di Hamadi.* Novara: DeAgostini, 1991.

Melliti, Moshen. *Pantanella: Canto lungo la strada.* Rome: Edizioni Lavoro, 1992.

Ngugi Wa Thiong'o. *Decolonising the Mind: The Politics of Language in African Literature.* Portsmouth, N.H.: Heinemann, 1986.

Passerini, Luisa. *Storia e soggettività: Le fonti orali, la memoria.* Florence: La Nuova Italia, 1988.

Said, Edward. *Orientalism.* New York: Pantheon Books, 1978.

Smith, Sidonie. *Subjectivity, Identity, and the Body: Women's Autobiographical Practices in the Twentieth Century.* Bloomington: Indiana University Press, 1993.

Spivak, Gayatri Chakravorty. *The Post-Colonial Critic: Interviews, Strategies, Dialogues.* Edited by Sarah Harasym. New York: Routledge, 1990.

Uguali e diversi: Il mondo culturale, le reti di rapporti, i lavori degli immigrati non europei a Torino. Turin: Rosenberg and Sellier, 1991.

Viarengo, Maria. "Andiamo a spasso?" *Linea d'ombra,* no. 54 (November 1990): 74–76.

6 / Exile in the Promised Land

Self-Decolonization and Bodily Re-Membering in Ken Bugul's The Abandoned Baobab

Julia Watson

> *To be exiled from the maternal continent is to be forever subjected to the rules of a foreign economy for which one also serves as a medium of exchange.*
> —Bella Brodzki

The Abandoned Baobab (originally published in French as *Le Baobab fou*, literally "the crazy baobab") is the autobiographical narrative of a Senegalese woman's experience of urban Brussels as a scholarship student in the late sixties and seventies.[1] Mariétou M'Baye, who adopted the pseudonym Ken Bugul in this, her first published work, rewrites the meaning of exile for an African woman. She revises her view of Europe from a space of liberation to a racist, neocolonial world in which she is lost, as a woman without a country, but "remembers" her multiple, conflicting narrative histories. As Elisabeth Mudimbe-Boyi has suggested, Ken Bugul's situatedness as a postcolonial African woman makes social identity at best a future-oriented and virtual possibility (212). To construct her identity as an agentified subject would require that she "decolonize" her inherited social position—as an exoticized and othered Muslim, sub-Saharan African woman in Europe—and renegotiate her African position as a marginal daughter abandoned by her mother, the fourth wife in a traditional polygamous Wolof family. The process of writing her autobiographical reflection, then, produces for Ken an understanding that she is exiled from both the traditional African and the modern European worlds, without a habitable social space. "Home" has a corporeal locus in the maternal body; but the mythic Africa of the past has died, and she is alienated from a real "home" both by her mother's and Mother Africa's ambivalence toward her and by the impossibility of assimilating to and being accepted in French-speaking Europe.

Autobiography and Ambivalence in Senegal

A reading of *The Abandoned Baobab* needs first to locate this narrative of intellectual emigration in its indigenous context. Ken Bugul's text is an ethnically, culturally, and generically specific perspective on the means and modes of writing identity for a postcolonial woman in French-speaking Europe. M'Baye's cultural alienation is literally encoded in the meaning of her pseudonym Ken Bugul.[2] In a 1984 interview with Bernard Magniér, M'Baye asserts that her French editor at Nouvelles Editions Africaines required her to take a pseudonym to protect her from scandal about her intimate revelations, and that she chose the name "Ken Bugul," a generic Wolof name rich with ambivalence (Magniér, 154). Given to children at birth in families where one or more children have died in infancy, it literally means "the person nobody wants." Although seemingly a term of universal rejection, "Ken Bugul" is in fact supposed to ward off jealous gods and permit the infant to survive. The name, then, resonates as a secret sign of the family's desire, beneath apparent indifference, to protect and claim the child. As a literary signature, this apparently self-negating pseudonym indicates M'Baye's consciousness of the ambiguities of social identity. Like her persona Ken Bugul, her text cannot be read unproblematically. Through it she both assigns herself a mark of cultural erasure and insists on her enduring significance within an African context. As Irène d'Almeida notes, "by naming herself Ken Bugul she ensures her survival as a writer born into a new name" (45).

The Abandoned Baobab is preeminently an autobiographical memoir of M'Baye's ambivalent status, although some critics have termed it a fictional narrative because of its fragmentary and recursive style, its multiple voices, and its contradictory tropings of exile.[3] But Ken's text bears witness autobiographically in insisting on her experience of the persistence of racism and class-based exclusion not only in postindependence Senegal but also in Europe.[4] M'Baye explicitly claimed her book's autobiographical dimensions in the interview with Magniér. She states of it, "The author and the character are the same person."

M'Baye stresses a significant difference between herself and her autobiographical persona, stating, "Me, I haven't finished living," and alluding to a radio re-
viewer who remarked of Ken Bugul, "That girl has nothing more to live for in
life. She should withdraw like a holy virgin, she has experienced everything"
(Magniér, 154).[5]

The Abandoned Baobab also indicates the status of an African woman as a
reader of Western culture on several levels.[6] Published in 1982 by Nouvelles
Editions Africaines, one of very few West African presses, in the series Lives of
Africa, it is among a small corpus of francophone African women's autobiographical writing published since independence and the first Senegalese
women's autobiography translated into English. The reception of Ken Bugul's
The Abandoned Baobab indicates the uneasy place it occupies within the Senegalese literary world and that world's ambivalence toward women's self-revela-
tion. While in 1984 it received a French prize for excellence, its reception was
less enthusiastic in Senegal, a nation that is nearly 90 percent Muslim. In a cultural context that officially demands a high moral standard of women, Ken
Bugul was criticized for her "scandalous" revelations of sexual laxity, drug ex-
perimentation, and moral decadence in Brussels. Although influential critic
and novelist Cheikh Aliou Ndao praised *The Abandoned Baobab* as "daring," he
also characterized the book's language as "too crude" and the author's comport-
ment as "unworthy of a woman."[7] Criticism of it was summed up by one Senegalese professor's remark to me: People felt that Ken Bugul had violated *kersa*, a
Wolof code of decorum and propriety that is one of three cardinal values incul-
cated in all children; the modesty and discretion of *kersa* are particularly valued
in young women.[8]

In a double-edged dismissal Ken Bugul was also criticized for not having
written a sufficiently political critique; her autobiography was denounced as a
form of personalized indulgence inadequate to the exploration of sociopolitical
relations (Bourjea, 194). Unlike the novels of Ousmane Sembene, with their
epic canvases delineating social interrelations under colonialism, or the implicitly dialogic address of Mariama Ba's *So Long a Letter*, *The Abandoned Baobab* is
an intensely monologic performance that interweaves several times of private
memory. Ken's presentation of African female subjectivity in Europe seemed to
resonate neither with the hundreds of thousands of Senegalese who study or
work abroad nor with readers in Senegal who aspire to European or American
immigration. Despite its translation into English, the original French text has
been out of print for years in Senegal. An overview such as Laurence Porter's

"Senegalese Literature Today" (1993) omits reference to Ken Bugul (women's writing is given only two paragraphs at the end of the essay). M'Baye left Senegal to work in family planning in Togo; the plays that she alluded to writing, in the Magniér interview, were not, to my knowledge, produced. She has recently published a novel in France, *Cendres et braises* (Ashes and embers).

The consequences for M'Baye of having published *The Abandoned Baobab* are evident: She went into literary, as well as political, exile from Senegal. This situation was particularly ironic because the project of writing the book refigured her European emigration as a form of cultural exile and an attempt to remember herself as an African female subject.

West African Contexts of *The Abandoned Baobab*

Ken Bugul's text is unusual among women's autobiographies. It marks not so much a declarative entrance into subjectivity, in a Western sense, as what novelist Norman Rush called, in his review of it, "spectacular ambivalence" about the desirability of occupying the literary space of women's autobiography and the social space of separate female identity (27). *The Abandoned Baobab* is set in a moment of the late sixties and seventies when no stable subject position is available to a young Senegalese woman from a traditional village who is dropped into urban Brussels. Indeed Ken assumes a dizzying repertoire of subject positions at various points in the narrative, from dutiful village daughter to proto-European cultural mimic to scorned third world outsider to exoticized black female body speculating on the "value" of her sexuality to world-weary wanderer without a country. Her ambivalence about female agency and her sense of inescapable exile need to be located within several contexts of West African literary history and social practice.

First, writing autobiography in Senegal is a relatively recent practice. Only a few autobiographical novels, all by men, were published before Senegalese independence in 1960.[9] Women enter into literature and written autobiography even more recently, in the postindependence period. Because of Senegal's low literacy rate (about 25 percent, with much lower literacy for women than men), written narrative is not a widespread means of organizing subjectivity.[10] Fictionalized narratives of the last two decades by writers such as Mariama Ba, Aminata Sow Fall, and Khady Fall have some strongly autobiographical features. The first explicitly autobiographical texts by women in Senegal were published in 1975: *Femme d'Afrique* (Woman of Africa), by Aoua Kéita from Mali, mixed an account of her sociopolitical struggle with fables, in a griot-like style. Nafissatou Diallo's *De Tilène au Plateau* (From Tilene to the Plateau, two regions of Dakar) is a memoir of growing up in and with the city of Dakar.[11] These autobiographies have been read generatively as the "birthing" (both Kéita and Diallo were midwives) of female literary subjectivity in Senegal, but they are above all tales of assimilation to the new urban world of postcolonial Dakar. Indeed, African women's written autobiography generally is a recent genre, and, as Mineke Schipper has proclaimed, Senegal "leads the way."[12] But, as Schipper also points out, the emphasis in most African autobiography is on authenticity and the narrative effects that reinforce that illusion (Schipper, " 'Who Am I?,' " 73). If Kéita and Diallo are first-generation women autobiographers documenting their locations, Ken Bugul occupies an uneasy place as an insubordinate second-generation writer whose narrative deliberately challenges tropes of realism and recounts a story of failure in assimilating either to European or, despite her quest, to African social identity. *The Abandoned Baobab* documents the difficulty of integration for an African woman between identities—rural and urban, oral and written, dutiful and assertive, Western and African.

Second, autobiography is written with a difference in francophone African literature and requires modified reading practices by Western readers. Although some critics have discussed it as an adaptation of the French *récit* to African landscapes, reading West African autobiography as a mimetic inscription of Western subjectivity is a form of "print colonialism" that both overreads and underreads the encoding and problematizing of colonial subjectivity (Miller, "Nationalism," 64). In his discussion of Laye Camara's *L'Enfant noir* (translated as *The Dark Child*), Christopher Miller has brilliantly argued that neither the inscription of an individualized self nor its recitation in French is unambiguous in a French colonial or recently postcolonial context.[13] Rather, Laye Camara's self-presentation subverts the hegemonic individualism that imperialistically overwrote his Mande specificity, even to inverting his name by perpetuating the colonial usage, "Camara Laye." Western critics misread *L'Enfant noir* in continuing to appropriate its African figuration of identity to Western norms of subjectivity. They deflect, by reductively inflecting, the hybrid francophone subjectivity it poses. Whether *L'Enfant noir* is read as a naive coming-of-age fable (as it usually is in Western readings) or, by some African critics (notably Mongo Beti), as a colonialist collaboration against the collective self-determination of Africans, its meaning as a performance of a specific Mande subjectivity is elided. As an orally oriented, ethnically specific, genealogically located, and covertly resistant subject, Laye Camara writes a multiply encoded autobiography. That difference needs to be heard by situating his narrative in the traditional Mande culture of what is now Guinea and weighing Laye Camara's complex reasons for his imposed self-exile, rather than reading his "deliverance" to or "assimilation" of French culture. As in *L'Enfant noir, The Abandoned Baobab's* narrator mixes mimicry and subversion of the norms of unified selfhood to figure her unstable subjectivity.

In her concept of the overlay of cultures as an act of *métissage,* the braiding of disparate voices in francophone autobiography, Françoise Lionnet has suggested an alternative reading practice that is enabling for many African texts, including Ken Bugul's. Ken makes a complex "braid" of colonialist critique and Western-fashioned self-authorization to make herself audible in European terms. Her narrative is not a simple story either of achieving unitary subjectivity or of returning to African origins unmarked by European selfhood.[14] Winifred Woodhull has also stressed how multiple, intertwined identities have a collective and not just an individual force. She points out that for much francophone writing, it is necessary to attend to "the hybrid, unstable identity not only of writers and intellectuals, but also of immigrants who continually negotiate between conflicting traditions"; and "to affirm the liberating aspects of the *gatherings* of dispersed identities, peoples, and histories" (8–9). Reading francophone African autobiographies of immigrants becomes a project of listening to effective speakers rather than speaking for them.

Third, Ken Bugul's narrative presents a range of African voices that are discursively at odds with those of Western autobiographical narratives. Mae Henderson has noted that multiple voices enunciate a complex subjectivity in black women's writing: "The black woman writer not only speaks familiarly in the discourse of the other(s), but as Other she is in contestorial dialogue with the hegemonic dominant and subdominant or 'ambiguously (non)hegemonic' discourses" (120). *The Abandoned Baobab* contains several dialogic voices that address or challenge one another. In its revelations about sexuality, it resembles less a literary memoir than the confessional narratives published as sensationalistic case studies in Senegalese tabloids. These accounts detail the effects on young village women of urban displacement, whether in Dakar, Paris, or Brussels, and moralize the loss of traditional values by focusing disapprovingly on the women's awakened sexual appetites, which threaten to destroy family ties.[15] Ken's confession both displays her sexuality and defies traditional values in a way that acknowledges their force. Other voices in the narrative have different resonances. Its first section, "The Prehistory of Ken," is narrated in the disembodied voice of a traditional elder speaking in the cadences of mythic, cyclical time. Another, Fanon-like voice enunciates a sometimes strident critique of European decadence and neocolonialism among postindependence middle-class Africans. At times a manifesto indicting European racism, at times a griot-like performance of African myth, at times a sociological witness to the harsh conditions experienced by women from developing countries in Western Europe, *The Abandoned Baobab's* dialogical voices defy containment in a unitary narrative frame and speak in many tongues.[16]

Fourth and finally, postcolonial writing relocates the genre of autobiography and refigures its definition outside a European frame of cultural reference. An autobiography of hybrid subjectivity such as Ken Bugul's challenges the imperialistic claim Georges Gusdorf has made about Western autobiography. Gusdorf claims that autobiography "expresses a concern peculiar to Western man"; if those of other cultures write an autobiography, "those men [*sic*] will thereby have been annexed by a sort of intellectual colonizing to a mentality that was not their own" (29).[17] In Gusdorf's terms, Ken's autobiography could only be a mimicry of logocentric Western selfhood; a Eurocentric model of autobiography must recontain other subjects through its model of individualism to conform to a Western norm of selfhood. But Ken's narrative reframes the terms of autobiography by imaging the birth of individual consciousness as a rupturing moment within collective life, a kind of cultural death even as it gives birth to individuated subjectivity. In recounting her efforts to assimilate as a scholarship student in Brussels and the subsequent exploitation of her exoticized status by European men, Ken reveals that her desire to mimic Europeans leads her to discover her own false consciousness modeled on a "decadent" European mentality and to subvert it by self-decolonization. She thus writes against Gusdorf's notion of autobiography as the West's means of making dutiful subjects inscribed in its cultural superiority.[18]

Ken's autobiographical performance is more productively read through Homi Bhabha's paradigm of the mimicry in which colonized subjects engage to underscore their lack of agency. As an "affect of hybridity" that both appropriates and resists, the colonial subject adopts a mask or camouflage that questions colonial authority (181).[19] Rather than remaking herself as a dutiful European subject in Gusdorf's terms, Ken adopts both the mimetic camouflage and the critique of European authority that appears liberatory but in fact compels assimilation. Ken's attempt to exorcise her own "intellectual colonizing" by parodic mimicry renegotiates the definition and uses of autobiography itelf, as the West has understood it, for an African audience.

Although Ken's autobiography indicts the Western recolonization of African female subjects through exclusionary educational and social practices that exoticize them as "black bodies," she also depends on autobiographical storytelling for her self-representation. If European representations doubly inscribe her as a mystified, exotic black woman and as an aberrant other whose blackness is a negative mirror to reflect Western superiority, Ken learns to both read and subvert her European encoding. Ken, then, uses European confessional autobiography to "decolonize" herself from European values and belief, but she is also and necessarily complicit in its writing practices.

If, as I argue, Ken redirects autobiography's premises to forge a narrative instrument of verbal exorcism for a non-Western narrative practice of bodily re-membering, she reworks it into a challenging and resistant text. Ken's metaphorics of dismemberment and re-membering frame her inescapable exile as an African woman in a European setting who counterposes her friends' claims of Europe's universal tolerance and enlightened rationality to their refusal to ascribe agency to the body of an African woman. Her autobiographical narrative traces her growing disillusionment with the discrepancy she discovers between what Europe claims to be and how it is experienced upon her body, specularly, sexually, and spiritually.

The Abandoned Baobab as a Narrative of Self-Imposed Exile

The performance of autobiographical re-membering in *The Abandoned Baobab* develops by critiquing Western claims to superior agency and rationality and evoking a lost, maternal, "African" origin. The quest for refigured subjectivity is expressed in its untranslatable epigraph: "Les êtres écrasés se remémorent." In the English translation this has been misleadingly rendered as "The obliterated shall be remembered."[20] But the impersonal plurals of the French phrase are self-reflexive, stressing that erased subjectivity is remembered in being embodied; the locus of acts of memory is corporeal, in and through the body. M'Baye's pluralizing and generalizing of the subject as "les êtres" stresses its "antiautobiographical" deindividuation and suggests that the "erased" ones are by extension the community of Africans outside Western, Cartesian history. Similarly, Ken's narrative of her extrication from Western defacements recognizes her condition of exile, in both Brussels and contemporary Dakar, as rooted in estrangement from bodies—the mother's body, the collective body of the village community, the bodies of Europeans she meets who do not acknowledge desire. She is also exiled *in* a body—because of her ambivalence about her own sexuality. Ken's epigraph announces a project of re-membering that must begin by discovering its dismemberment, its fragmented body.

Novelist Norman Rush, whose remarkable 1991 novel *Mating* is set in Africa, has proposed reading *The Abandoned Baobab* as a narrative of self-decolonization: "Ken is engaged in a heroic and wide-ranging process of self-decolonization conducted on three fronts—gender, color, and ethnicity. Ambivalence, spectacular ambivalence, reveals itself to be the central obstacle to her personal liberation" (27).[21]

Ken performs a decolonization by refiguring her emigration to Brussels as a self-imposed cultural exile. She employs non-European means, which she represents as a kind of autobiographical exorcism, to demystify Europe. While Rush ascribes Ken's ambivalence to the instability of how she views her African familial past and reads it as irresolvable within the narrative, Mildred Mortimer reads *The Abandoned Baobab* as Ken's journey toward awareness of her African subjectivity in a dialectical movement through possible formations of cultural identity in quest of liberation and incorporation into a social community. For Mortimer Ken is successful: in returning to Africa she can "assume the identity that she first sought to escape" and achieve "self-knowledge and perception," "self-affirmation and healing" through writing (176–77).[22] Irène d'Almeida concurs, noting, "What [Ken] discovers is both the multiplicity of selves and the depth of her cultural roots" in an autobiography that serves as public confession, exorcism, and therapeutic catharsis (54). But in an alternative reading, Elisabeth Mudimbe-Boyi argues that Ken's journey of "exile and errancy" is a negative bildungsroman in quest of a new, as yet virtual, cultural space that would provide a historical filiation for the complex multicultural identity she constructs. Although Ken is "deterritorialized," she can gesture literarily toward an unmarked territory that is both psychological and political. Clearly these readers differ on both the meaning and the resolution of Ken's European encounter. What does it mean to write African identity against the European grain? Ken's recoding of her European experience resituates her status as an African and "third world" woman immigrant in an urban French-speaking area and poses a repertoire of possible resolutions to her dilemma of self-imposed exile.

The narrative arrangement of *The Abandoned Baobab* employs three distinct modes and a spectrum of voices to narrate an inconsistent but compelling

story of Ken's othering in contemporary Brussels and her attempt to disen-
tangle herself from what, in Gusdorf's sense, is the imposition of Western autobiographical enchantments on her story. Ken attempts to write her way
through the uncoupling and relinking of her own textual body: She constructs
a progressively *dis*membered, *de*centered, "*de*cadent" self whose *dis*illusion-
ment enables her *dis*entanglement from what she perceives as European hegemony and her attempt to *re*member and *re*affiliate herself with all that Africa
signifies as a site and practice of an alternative, embodied identity.

The Abandoned Baobab's three parts correspond to three narrative modalities that map Ken's encounter with Europe: before the encounter, narrated in
the oral, griot style of a fable; the European experience as a "negative bildungsroman" told in several stages; and the attempt to exorcise her European
values and recover her African origins in baobab culture. This linear chronology is both counterpointed to, and driven by, the awakened voices of memory
that speak to her discontinuously and move her toward the reawakened memory of her mother as a source of an alternate African world, however remote
and unresponsive it remains. At every point this play of voices chants her narrative as a kind of call to a more immediate, less writerly world than the European
model of consciousness that has, in her colonial education, disciplined her.

The "African" voice of the first section, "The Prehistory of Ken," uses concrete images and homilies of the fable, a genealogical chain of ancestry, and a
dreamlike, mythic temporality to trace Ken's beginnings.[23] This tale of transgression and recuperation is, however, not a personal narrative. To recite an individual's story is to tell the history of several generations in the village of
Gouyé, in the savannah region of Ndoucoumane (south-central Senegal).
Characters are archetypal and enact fixed roles in a cyclic natural world where
there is no real death because the ancestors are reincarnated in succeeding generations. The cycle is, however, broken and time is introduced into the mythic
world of wholeness when an infant daughter, later identified as Ken, ruptures
the harmony with the force of individual consciousness. While sitting under a
baobab tree she thrusts an amber bead into her ear, emitting a cry that shatters
the communal wholeness and thereby transgresses the mother's domain. At this
point the voice of Ken Bugul emerges to narrate her journey of separation, voyage, exile, and quest for reintegration. Ken's preverbal howl of life enunciates a
discordant "I" in the "Prehistory" community anterior to and outside European time and consciousness.

Because of its idiosyncratic shapes, the baobab is a memorable landmark in the sun-seared Sahel. It is a lifeline for villagers in West Africa and is entwined with traditional life. Village elders sit in the shade of its enormous gnarled trunk to converse. Its long, pendulous fruit provides nourishment, medicine, and a delicious drink when mixed with milk, as well as bark for weaving baskets. Like the mother, the baobab connects the generations of a community and can stand as a marker long after it has died. In the "Prehistory" the baobab tree is a point of origin for the community and exists in a special metonymic relationship to Ken as a solitary marker of her own solitude. The baobab also provides the site of a potential return to all that Africa evokes metaphorically, locating Ken's embeddedness in Ndoucoumane. It frames her earliest memory of a maternal bond that she unwittingly transgressed in an Oedipal quest for self-assertion. Left standing in the village, the baobab stands in for Ken's realization of her inescapable double exile, both from and in her African home.[24]

Ken's entrance into individualized narration in the second section, "The History of Ken," counterpoints two stories: One is a linear journey of individuation and disillusionment through realization of how her Western socialization has schooled her to be an "object" of Europe's possession, materially and symbolically. Although she initially celebrates the growth of self-consciousness, discovering her culturally colonized status leads her to reinterpret her journey as a descent into the "inferno" of Western decadence and delusion. What she had conceived as the birth of liberated female selfhood in Europe is revealed to be a set of traps and constraints for an African woman. The second, counterpointed journey is recursive, toward her origins, as fragments of memory bring back her mother's voice in traces of her lost African self. This stream of memories emerges in and evokes images of her Senegalese village that are impressionistic, nonchronological, and obsessional. Gradually these memories are recollected and reordered as the basis for a hypothetical, alternative subjectivity enabled by, but in tension with, her European experience. Ken comes to articulate and interpret the childhood from which she was originally exiled in the village by her mother's departure, her schooling, and her forced sexual experience as a model of the colonial subject. Her narrative, far from being a sensationalistic confession, blends involuntary memory with the roles she scripts as European émigré in her multivoiced narrative.

Beginning her "History" by introducing the persona with "Ken Bugul remembers," Ken simultaneously enters European space and autobiographical utterance (23). Her narrative begins at the moment of her plane departure from Dakar, a symbolic birth of consciousness in which she feels she is tearing herself away from Mother Africa (25). Ken's initial naive conception is that she is going to the Western land of progress and enlightenment, "the North of dreams, the North of illusions . . . the Promised Land North" (23). She expects that her university scholarship in Brussels will create her as an ideal European self, but, with the logic of the negative bildungsroman, she gradually discovers that she has volunteered for greater cultural bondage.[25] In a series of emblematic incidents, she discovers herself as an object in Western eyes who will be used to confirm its superiority. Her situation is summed up in a prototypical statement of the postcolonial subject's dilemma: "I identified myself in them, they did not identify themselves in me" (53).

Ken's self-discovery of her social otherness in Europe is organized in several scenes of coming to autobiographical consciousness. They retrospectively form the stages of her self-decolonization and mark the moments of her discovery of how Europe in every sense frames her. I will discuss five of these.

1. *Self-mirroring as an inferior foreigner in European eyes.* In Brussels Ken initially experiences her own invisibility in her first residence, a Catholic girls' home for "foreigners." Her innocent African eyes are shocked by differences of the urban scene from West African village life. "Everybody walked too fast"; no one recognized her or issued greetings (34). Seeking to appear "western-normal" and behave as a consumer, Ken attempts to buy a long-haired European wig, but the clerk explains, using a mirror, that such wigs are for white women and she needs an Afro wig (37). For the first time Ken sees herself, in a shop window, as a racial other: "My eyes were bulging, my skin was shiny and black, the face terrifying" (37). Through a norm of European whiteness, she reads the *significance* of her black skin in a racist world as a marker of devalued difference, as d'Almeida suggests (55). She has no control of her own image, and both options, invisibility and marked foreignness, are intolerable.

2. *European containment of "foreign" women through controlling their sexuality and imposing a racist hierarchy.* In a subsequent scene of othering, Ken discovers how the discourse of eugenics is employed to racially mark and police women of color in Brussels. With Louis, her first Belgian boyfriend, she is rapidly disillusioned in romance as he fetishizes her Africanness and his own racial "transgression"; her realization is intensified by the discovery that she has exercised a parallel desire in dating French men in Senegal. Quickly becoming pregnant, she goes to a clinic to have an abortion, where she loses more of her innocence. Filled with women of "all colors" in similarly desperate situations, the clinic provides a moment of implicit solidarity, but one that drives home

the gendered basis of her oppression: "Women all women have the same destiny" (43). The racism exercised by the Belgian doctor she encounters is both subtler and sweeping. His attention to her in the back room seems at once condescending and prurient, like the laughter of a hyena and the terrorism of an executioner (44). Her African interpretive paradigm has not prepared her for the shock of his question about the racial identity of her fetus. On learning the father is white, he lectures her, as she lies naked on the table, on the evils of racial "mixing" and urges her to find her own "kind" (47). The humiliation of her bodily othering in the abortion paradoxically gives birth to a flood of involuntary memories of her family and her mother in the village of her childhood at a moment of sexual humiliation.[26]

3. *Collaboration as a willing accomplice in European exploitation of her symbolic value.* Ken's awakened sexuality is complex and fraught with ambivalence. She becomes attentive to race-based myths of "the Black man's supersexuality" and the corresponding myth of white females who seek them for liberation from their own repression. Frustrated that the white people whose company she enjoys and whom she has been socialized to study and serve do not reciprocate her identification, Ken becomes increasingly estranged from herself in "playing the Western game." She begins living with her "artistic" boyfriend, Jean Wermer, who introduces her to sexual licentiousness (57). Mystified at Jean's bisexuality, so unlike that in the village, Ken accepts his ménage à trois and engages in her own sexual and drug experiments in an effort to be accepted in the Brussels avant-garde (58). She contrasts the West's secularization of drugs and sexual rituals with the "sweet" African heritage that she begins recalling: "Ah! had I only known the sweet realities of my race and my people" (62). Increasingly conscious of how the discourse of savagery has been used by Europeans to control colonized peoples, Ken begins reversing the civilized-savage paradigm in noting of her European intimates: "These people would be true savages, if the stakes of their existence were limited only to these kinds of situations" (64). As her critique of European "savagery" develops, Ken increasingly regains her memory of the first loss, her mother, who left the family when Ken was a child of five. (Only late in the text do readers learn that the mother left only for a year and that the polygamous family provided her with several siblings and parental figures.) Psychically the loss is devastating, but it is also the key to formulating a quest for her African consciousness.

4. *Making self and other into objectified bodies.* As Ken descends into what she calls the underworld of Brussels, she becomes a sexual commodity to herself

and her intimates. Seeing herself and others only as bodies "removed from feeling and thought," she arranges nude photos of herself around her apartment as conscious self-mirrorings (70). Mocking White infatuation with Blackness, she conflates her own display with how Africa joined in exploiting itself in the wake of colonization: "once colonialism had displayed it, Africa had begun to show her backside and her skin across the world to command attention" (69). This denatured self-display makes her increasingly decentered, able to pose her identity only as questions: "Who was I? How was I? What game was I playing? I wasn't aware of anything" (71). She blames the process of neocolonialist guilt in contemporary Brussels for her self-loss and desire to become a display for others' eyes: "colonialism had created the distortion of the spirit necessary to enslave a race of people, leaving them no frame of reference" (71). Yet in the moment of experience, she cannot articulate Europe's individual and collective hold on Africans; rather she acts out her derangement in a "dream" of self-abandonment that is, her friend assures her, self-assertion Western-style. She dramatizes her sexuality by taking a job in a "sauna" that is in fact a brothel where her hands and her skin are commodities for others' pleasure. Increasingly she is objectified. Despite briefly returning to Senegal for her father's death, she returns to Brussels, in thrall to the chaos of her own life and seeking in the university cultural roots as her "umbilical cord" to the West (80).

As her consciousness and her alienation both increase, Ken starts consciously to parody the cultural role assigned to her. She mocks her Westernization as playing "the game of the color black: to be a Black woman who appeals to the white man" (82). She engages in what she considers fashionable lesbianism, contrasting its studied politics and jealousies with the village women, who "told each other their secrets, lived together" without "turn[ing] nature upside down" (84). She valorizes Africa as the site of a natural, spontaneous sexuality that emanates effortlessly from bodies in harmony with the world, while Europe can only be the space of exhausted poseurs. The rapid alternation of sexual conservatism and libertinism in her narration gives glimpses of a detached and even moralizing perspective on her past. In the momentum of her increasing alienation Ken asserts that she achieved trendy prominence, becoming a media socialite for others' amusement: "I based myself only on references . . . it wasn't me. They were stripping me, emptying me out, displaying me" (85). Lacking the coherent self that she believes Africa would give her, she sees herself victimized as a screen for European projections of the exotic. Relentlessly seeking possible alternate selves, Ken abandons the university for LSD, heroin, opium, alcohol, and hippie decadence, and bemusedly falls into an "abyss" of narco-tized sensuality (82). Without the community of her history, she claims, she cannot oppose the Promised Land's intoxicants.

Yet in her Augustine-like recollection of her degradation, Ken begins to transvalue her impression of a European view of African blackness as marginal-ized and exotic. She draws on the African Négritude movement that she en-counters in Brussels, both embracing its claims to the primacy of African culture and mistrusting it. Politicized, she can articulate her cultural position as a Black beauty eroticized by Europeans hungry for a mythic exoticism to coun-teract their own feeble, "pale" cultural exhaustion. At this stage of her self-de-colonization, she cannot resolve the complexities of her social position, but opposes the images projected upon her: "I wanted to look into the reflection of the mirror that had blinded me" (74). Seeking emancipation from her colo-nized status, Ken ironically performs as a mirrored history of blackness in Eu-ropean eyes.

5. *Self-speculation on her value as a prostitute.* As she comes to believe that European sexuality requires black female bodies to maintain its desire and that, therefore, she is implicated in maintaining the stereotypes that undermine her, Ken makes herself into a commodity for *self*-speculation. In a bid for cultural agency as an African woman, she begins to broker her sexual value, calculating and demanding its worth in social exchanges.[27] In this way she turns the confes-sion of her own "degeneracy" into an indictment of the West by reading its de-sire for her as a confession of weakness and inauthenticity in the service of its illusion of potent superiority. This critique ironically reframes the scenes of her own humiliation as her text "writes back" a countermyth of African superiority, exposing the West as a place of false consciousness: "Deep down, the Westerner is envious of the Black man's 'emotional wealth' " (88). Replacing colonialist ideology with an Afrocentrist conviction of the natural and emotional wealth of the essential self she has lost in the birth of her own consciousness, she is in-creasingly trapped in contradictory ideologies. Ken's contempt for the superfi-ciality of her European friends and her observation of the lack of community among Africans in Brussels fixes her in isolation.

As Ken becomes increasingly able to mimic and parody the exotic black other in which Europe has positioned her, she engages in calculated self-display. Performing as "African woman," she waits on her Western friends, serves them African food, gives them an intimate African fashion show: "The myth of Black eroticism was confirmed. . . . I was participating in the new vogue of organizing African, Asian, Peruvian evenings. I wanted to call the people of the West to witness" (92). Her jobs demand conspicuous self-display, as a model, a hat-check girl, a dancer-hostess. A specular commodity, she orchestrates the projection of her image in groups and manipulates it to cover the loss of her essential African self. Her bizarre behavior can be seen but not recognized by Europeans, who cannot read their own myths parodied. "The shock of colonization" she has experienced is perpetuated in their celebration of the exotic beauty of black women (96).

As bell hooks has argued, in charting issues of representation that black women encounter in Western culture, a black woman becomes an object of display to "civilized" Europeans in nineteenth-century France: "She is there to entertain guests with the naked image of Otherness. . . . Objectified in a manner similar to that of black female slaves . . . the black women whose naked bodies were displayed for whites at social functions had no presence" (62). Made into spectacle and scrutinized as a set of parts, the black woman has not yet been freed from racist objectification in late-twentieth-century American representational practices, despite her illusory autonomy. She continues to be positioned, in the conventional racist/sexist imagination, within only a few undermined subject positions, as "mammy or slut" or tragic mulatto, or a combination of these (74). Making an oppositional space in which "erotic recognition, desire, pleasure, and fulfillment" are at the center of black female subjectivity is, hooks argues, a necessary, as yet unrealized, project of self-decolonization if black women are to become active sexual subjects (76). *The Abandoned Baobab* employs a similar critique of racialized fantasies that are, for Ken, both product of and motive for the postcolonial European cultivation of the black female body in France and Belgium. Caught in a representational dilemma between the sexual licentiousness of the West, where she is acclaimed as the perfected exotic other, and the moral strictures of Islam in the village that exclude and "abandon" her, Ken finds no tenable space of subjectivity. She can remember herself as a daughter, but not re-member herself as a woman within any social community to which she has access.

From her self-objectification it is only a step to calculated prostitution, and Ken is easily engaged; she controls her value as a kind of exoticized sexual animal for Western eyes and organizes the scene of her own marketing. "Prostitution provided me with a moment of attention, a recognition different from the one that identified me daily with what I didn't want to be" (106). Arranging a rendezvous with a wealthy man she has picked up in a hotel bar, she demands an expensive mink cape as payment. In exchange she offers a specular reward, the view of her naked body arranged on animal fur. But the calculated use of herself as an exchange commodity on the sex market, although a form of revenge for what she sees as Western appropriation of black female bodies, leaves her trapped in mimicry as "the" black woman, without self-recognition.

Approaching absolute despair with how she has perfected an illusion of her desirability, at the cost of unreachable solitude, Ken turns to narrative as a means of undoing the sexual colonization in which she is complicit. In an extended reverie of her childhood as she lies naked on the mink cape in a Hilton hotel room after her "john's" departure, for the first time Ken recites her African history. Although her reverie makes her nearly suicidal about her foundationless life in Brussels, Ken has psychically found a means of extricating herself from the European dream that, she claims, has invaded, colonized, and dispossessed her. By reinstating the mother's voice that called her as a child, she rejects her power as a broker of white men's desire to consume her. Alienated from her body as the servant of others' desire but reinstalled in the body of memory, Ken plays out ambivalence with customers: "I could offer just my body, which I knew nothing about anymore. . . . The body was vibrant with truth, the body knew nothing about the problem of the undefined" (152). Finally stirred to rage in her quest for her childhood as an alternative to being "this black body, this color that took on every exploding form of alienating phenomena" and emptied of all consciousness, Ken tears herself away from Brussels as an alternative to suicide (153).

Bodily Re-Membering and African Space

In Ken's exhaustion a cry escapes her, "a piercing scream that broke the harmony," a voice from nothingness that echoes her "Prehistory" cry in the village under the baobab. Ken understands this cry narratively as the culmination of an African ritual of exorcism, declaring, "Black people needed to exorcise themselves, not to be enchanted" (130). At this moment she can perform a self-exorcism, by interpreting her past as a spell to be broken. Her exorcism has two phases: The first is dispossession of the false, colonized voice that has spoken through her. The force of that howl sends her literally back to Africa. The second phase of exorcism is subtler. After emptying one's heart, Ken recalls, one must sit down under the "tree of words" for the ancestral spirits to enter (130). Etymologically evocation, calling forth the voice one lacks, is the agent of her re-membering. Emptied with this cry that exorcises her European enchantment, Ken returns to Africa to recover the origin she remembers as her connective tissue.

As Ken's "Gallic" mind relinquishes its enchantment by Western philosophy and art, by whiteness itself, she is able to evoke the body of memory; that story, however, is insufficient for literal re-memberment in her African community. In her quest to remember, and therefore to have, a childhood, Ken seeks "the mother's" lost voice, for whom she can no longer use any possessive pronoun (such as "my").[28] Ken narratively evokes her mother's voice, lost at an early age when her mother left the family, as a source of African identity and connection. Her lament "Why has the mother gone?" is an unanswerable question, a lack of cultural ligature to connect herself to family and place.

In accomplishing her self-exorcism by evocation of the lost mother's voice, Ken's narrative discovers, near the end of the book, its beginning. She rejects the imposed European identity that others had hailed as her "self" and divests herself of it as a fiction: "I had no memories. I made them up and they were intense" (139). Near the end of the book she begins to affirm her origins with the three most conventional words in autobiography, "I was born": "I was born in Ndoucoumane" (139). Only in a backward movement to her village origin can her voice move from an echo of mimicry to the instrument of an "African" story fusing narrator and tradition. Her reinterpretation of her Western self as an exilic one empowers her effort to reclaim an African story.

But Ken's quest to return to and revivify her origins is as idealized as was her first quest for the Promised Land in Brussels, and it ends similarly, in the realization of her exile in her native land. In the book's final scene, as she stands before the baobab of her village childhood in silent reverie, she discovers that, in her absence, it has gone "mad" (*fou*) and died; it confronts her blankly. Just as the mother had abandoned her, she abandoned the baobab, although mythically claiming it as a site and means of re-memberment, a tree of life. Ken takes leave of the baobab as her "witness and accomplice" as she discovers and indicts a kind of autobiographical consciousness that both colonized and decolonized her, generating a narrative of both recovery and loss.

Ken's narrative is an effort not just to remember, but to *re*-member, her lost self through reinstating the erased voice of her mother as a guide. This framing of the synapses of memory as voice ties Ken to the deracinated baobab that, in a complex relationship, is metaphorically identified with her and also metonymically stands for her, nurturant yet "crazy." Ken's call to the mother is autobiographically resonant. As Bella Brodzki suggests in this chapter's epigraph, in women's autobiography the daughter-writer's search for maternal origins and the birth of language is a project in which desire can find no final resolution in a pre-Oedipal fusion. Ken is indeed "exiled from the maternal continent" and not only subjected to the rules of a European cultural economy in which her body is a medium of exchange; she is also exiled from her African village, even in her return to it. Without access to the social community of the "tree of words," she becomes little more than a static marker in exchanges in which she lacks value. Only in narrating her quest and loss can she claim an exilic subjectivity.

The ending of *The Abandoned Baobab* is open, unarticulated, in profound ambivalence between death and rebirth, loss and recovery, memory and experience, solitude and community, return and going forward. The mythic resonance of place, Ndoucoumane, is now only in story—a displaced verbal locus of ancestral connection. Self-decolonization from the spell of the European Promised Land cannot undo her exile through exorcism, although it evokes a narrative voice expressive of her loss. Ken re-members her story in the cultural space of an Africa of an irretrievable precolonial—as pre-Oedipal—past, but its locale is the narrative space of a virtual future. In revising the meaning of her intellectual emigration as a self-imposed exile from "authentic" identity, she articulates Africa as a set of oppositional possibilities in mythic space. Self-decolonization of her European values brings her into voice, but writing restores only longing, not the Africa that postcolonial Brussels has undermined and overwritten. The territory of *The Abandoned Baobab* is the embodied voice of story, an evocation in search of a reconnected community. The elusiveness of that community is in both its literary reputation and its geographic habitat, as her exiled text has been annexed to the Western institutions of autobiography and literary fame, at the cost of neglect in her home country.

Are other resolutions possible for West African women writers? Ghanaian novelist Ama Ata Aidoo, for example, is less ambivalently situated than Ken Bugul in both her cultural rejections and affirmations. In *Our Sister Killjoy,* Aidoo's autobiographical novel, Europe is a delusory world, "a cold strange land where dogs and cats eat better than many many children" (99).[29] She "demystifies" the invitation of African students to Europe as perpetual outsiders, marked by their blackness and unknown cultures. For Aidoo, as for Ken, the African woman is a foil on whom Europeans project their fantasies of dominance in order to validate and sustain a myth of Western superiority. But there are crucial differences in the ways that Aidoo and M'Baye resolve their protagonists' unease about Europe. Aidoo's protagonist Sissie returns to "Africa. Crazy old con-

tinent" at the end of the novel (133). In so doing, she asserts her sense of belonging and consolidates an identity. She is able unambivalently to forgive herself for her fantasies of desiring to become European—"We all fall
victim"—and denounces the West's cultural traps for Africans with a comic
view that tolerates the contradictions of contemporary Africa (90). Ken, a more
equivocal narrator, finds no validation of her sense of African belonging either
in the neocolonial setting of urban Dakar or in the displaced Africa of mythic
memory. Exiled to critical consciousness, she has no habitable subjectivity outside her text. The past is irretrievable, no matter where she is, without maternal
protection in either family or country. The self she has given birth to is still-
born, like the baobab that stands, marking an origin that no longer nourishes,
protects, or provides a livelihood.

What, then, does Ken's re-memory re-member if the experience of Europe
has dismembered her from both her community of origin and her ideal self? In
a sense the re-membering of her emigration to Brussels as exile rather than assimilation *is* Ken's textual body—fragmented, dislocated, held together by the
ligatures of memory but unable to affirm a coherent subjectivity. Hers is a "migratory subjectivity" with "multiple identities that do not always make for harmony" (Davies, *Black Women,* 36). Ken gestures toward French-speaking
Europe as a space of delusion and disenchantment, a disrupter of the embodied
integration that would enable her to become a social agent. And yet, Ken's denunciation of Europe as an intellectual and emotional exile for African women
depends on a European semiotics of difference and individuation, a metaphorics of specularity, and an autobiographical narrative for her performance of a
disrupted, inconclusive, yet innovative subjectification.

In her rereading of her education as exile, Ken uncovers, as Irène
d'Almeida suggests, what her valorization of Africa over Europe sought to resist: that the sacred tenets of an African ethos, the mother's "symbiosis" with the
child-centered family, are also "garbled" in a postcolonial world where cultural
identities formerly distinct as African and European now permeate and over-
write one another (54–55). For the migratory subject, exile becomes both a
condition of possibility and an informing horizon.

Notes

1. Ken Bugul (Mariétou M'Baye), *Le Baobab fou* (Dakar: Nouvelles Editions Africaines,
1982); published in English as *The Abandoned Baobab: The Autobiography of a Senegalese Woman,*

(Brooklyn: Lawrence Hill Books, 1991). All subsequent references are to the English translation, except where noted, and are in the text.

2. I will use M'Baye to refer to the author and Ken Bugul, or more briefly Ken, the Wolof word for "nobody," to refer to the narrative persona, as the author does. In French bibliographies she is indexed as Bugul, Ken, a Western appropriation.

3. See Servanne Woodward, who unproblematically describes *The Abandoned Baobab* as a novel, in "French-Language Fiction," in *A History of Twentieth-Century African Literature,* ed. Oyekan Owomoyela, 183. In the same volume Carole Boyce Davies and Elaine Savory Fido describe *The Abandoned Baobab* as "Bugul's novel—a kind of 'fictional biography' that some critics say is autobiographical" (322).

4. French remains the language of instruction and governmental bureaucracy in Senegal, despite independence in 1960. Senegal has long occupied a privileged place as a former colony of France that was the center of power of the vast French West African empire, with its capital in Saint Louis until the mid–nineteenth century, then in Dakar, still one of the chief cultural centers of West Africa.

5. In the discussion with Magniér her own "I" is fluid, at times acknowledging a distinction, as above; at other times conflating author and persona, for example, when speaking of her arrival in the West at age twenty-two as a scholarship student who first began to understand her blackness, "surrounded with all these Whites" (152). In the interview she states emphatically, "I don't know how to tell stories; my imagination is always nourished by things that are experienced, true, seen, felt, tasted, touched" (154).

6. As a Fulbright scholar in Senegal in 1992–93 who was neither a francophonist nor an Africanist, I was unprepared for the profound cultural differences we encountered and our own status as "toubabs," white foreigners, in everyday interactions. And I was often in search of a language to articulate what only became visible as one could describe it—in landscape, culture, family, sense of body, and place. *The Abandoned Baobab* was both enlightening and disturbing for its metaphorics of dislocation, its interplay of mythic and historical Africas, and its representation of travel as voluntary exile in an inescapably neocolonialist world.

7. Cheikh Aliou Ndao's review appeared in *Le Soleil,* Dakar, on November 11, 1982, and was quoted by Lucien Houdanou. The translation is mine.

8. I am grateful to Professor Oumar Ndongo, Department of English, Université Cheikh Anta Diop, Dakar, for this observation. Conversations with Gary Engelberg of the Baobab Center, Dakar; Professor Fatou Kandji, Ecole Normale Supérieure, Dakar; Fiona McLaughlin; and Babacar Kante, dean of the School of Law, Université de Saint Louis, were also enlightening about *kersa.* See Assane Sylla, *La philosophie morale des Wolof,* for an extensive discussion of the significance of *kersa* in Wolof culture. Sylla defines *kersa* as: "pudeur si respectueuse des convenances, qu'elle frise la timidité. Ainsi l'homme qui a du *kersa,* estimé pour sa délicatesse et sa retenue est souvent déclaré être *yiw*" (85).

9. See Anta Diouf Kéita, "L'Ecriture autobiographique dans le roman féminin sénégalais," for a discussion of the history of autobiographical novels, beginning in 1926 during the colonial period, and the explosion of autobiographical *récits* since 1975. Kéita observes that autobiographical writing is most pronounced in women's novels. This point is developed by Mary-Kay F. Miller, whose forthcoming essay "*L'Ex-Père de la nation:* Subversive Subtexts and the Return of the Maternal," argues that Aminata Sow Fall and other Senegalese women novelists redefine and rewrite autobiography as autobiographical fiction, disturbing the perception of women primarily as agents of reproduction and diluting autobiography's "power as a colonial tool for reproducing Western images of the self in a non-Western narrative." Professor Madior Diouf, in an unpublished dissertation, "Les formes du roman négro-africain de langue française, 1920–76," also discusses Senegalese autobiographical fiction.

10. Strong oral narrative traditions exist, some of them specific to women, and research is being done on oral Wolof narrative forms of self-presentation, including oral epic and song. Lisa McNee, a graduate student in comparative literature at Indiana University, is engaged in a dissertation research project in a northern Senegalese village on the use of *tassu,* a women's oral song form for reciting and memorializing their shared history.

11. Aoua Kéita, *Femme d'Afrique: La Vie d'Aoua Kéita racontée par elle-meme;* Nafissatou Diallo, *De Tilène au Plateau: Une enfance dakaroise.* Diallo's text is published in English as *A Dakar Childhood.*

12. Mineke Schipper, "Women and Literature"; quoted in Christopher Miller, *Theories of Africans,* 249.

13. See Christopher L. Miller, "*L'enfant noir,* Totemism, and Suspended Animism," in *Theories of Africans,* 114–80.

14. For an exploration of *métissage* as metaphor and cultural practice, see Françoise Lionnet, *Autobiographical Voices,* esp. 1–29.

15. There are book-length case studies of urban displacement. *Le Froid et le piment (Nous, travailleurs immigrés),* for example, is a group of interviews with disenfranchised and disheartened Senegalese expatriates in Paris conducted by writer Mame Seck Mbacké. Debra Boyd Buggs discusses one of the cases of tragic exile, the young girl Youmané from a strict Muslim family, who is seduced and abandoned by a white man and dies of grief.

16. For a suggestive discussion of the autobiographical manifesto in an American context, see Sidonie Smith, "Autobiographical Manifestos," in *Subjectivity, Identity, and the Body,* 154–82.

17. Georges Gusdorf's examples of non-Western autobiography include Gandhi's narrative and Westermann's collection of African autobiographies that "convey the shock of traditional civilizations on coming into contact with Europeans"; he does not acknowledge oral or traditional written forms of life writing (29).

18. Christopher Miller makes the important and provocative point that "exile, either voluntary or forced, has been an almost universal condition of [francophone West African] literature" ("Nationalism," 93). Most francophone writers have spent at least part of their lives elsewhere, and most often in French-speaking countries, as intellectual émigrés or colonial immigrants; some, such as Ousmane Sembene, could be described as "internal exiles" in their own countries.

19. Bhabha defines hybridity as a strategic mixing that intervenes in an authoritative discourse to subvert its authority: "Hybridity is a problematic of colonial representation and individuation that reverses the effects of the colonialist disavowal, so that other 'denied' knowledges enter upon the dominant discourse and estrange the basis of its authority—its rules of recognition" (175).

20. In the French text, p. v; in the English, p. iii.

21. Rush reads the autobiography's ambivalence acutely, noting: "But even as [Ken] counterposes the mythos of traditional Africa to the frantic, fragmented life of the white metropolis, her directly personal reminiscences of her family life yield a picture of coldness, arbitrariness and an entrenched and extreme patriarchalism . . . a dubious interpretive paradigm in which Africa represents warm spontaneity, even heedlessness, while the West stands for cold calculation and oppressive rationality. She alternately recoils from and embraces this paradigm" (28).

22. Mortimer stresses that "women's flight" to the "promised land" of Europe encounters "the dual constraints of colonialism and patriarchy" and can end in either "self-discovery or in illusory escape" (165). Memory provides a key to self-understanding, and writing offers a therapy for healing the threats of both the European encounter and the earlier abandonment by her mother in Ken's circular journey of self-integration. But this conclusion seems overly optimistic for what Mortimer has identified as Ken's dual alienation, as orphan in Africa and object in Europe (175). If Ken "attains lucidity and conquers solitude," it is beyond the space of a text in which discordant voices of abandonment and exile announce her disenchantment and efforts at self-decolonization (176).

23. My colleague Oumar Ndongo, at Université Cheikh Anta Diop in Dakar, has observed that this section, although narrated in French, uses Wolof locutions and syntax to evoke an oral, griot-like style. Not knowing Wolof, I cannot assess this, although the section is decidedly different and "un-French" in style. Clearly, the braiding of languages and styles contributes to the "hybrid" encoded subjectivity that Miller and Lionnet have commented on in other francophone texts, as well as the importance of multilingual reading if we are to "hear" the hybrid voices of texts.

24. Irène d'Almeida reads the baobab tree as representing *le repère*, the point of reference in people and place, that Ken seeks. It is a literal landmark in Gouyé; its protective human attributes symbolize the community she seeks; and, like her, it becomes a survivor, dead but upright (52–53). Mildred Mortimer reads the baobab's significance differently: "The baobab . . . functions as a metaphor for an African society that Bugul believes has also become an empty shell" (168).

25. Laura Sue Fuderer's study of the genre notes several variants of the negative bildungsroman in ethnic women's writing (3–5). She cites Sondra O'Neale's discussion, in "Race, Sex, and Self," of the themes of the negative bildungsroman specific to African American women writers— mature age, renunciation of assimilation into the black community as the price of growth, lack of mentors, and alienation from any possible "tribe"—and notes that they transvalue the traditional male form. To some extent all of the themes O'Neale identifies typify Ken's narrative, although they do not exhaust its repertoire.

26. Elisabeth Mudimbe-Boyi has rightly noted the negative-bildungsroman quality of the autobiography's scenes of attempts at social integration that keep mirroring to Ken her devalued otherness (203 n. 15).

27. I am indebted to Margit Stange's brilliant discussion of erotic self-speculation in Kate Chopin's *The Awakening* as a means of women's self-ownership, the owning of her sexual exchange value: "Her body is both what she owns and what she owns with" (205).

28. Irène d'Almeida comments on Ken Bugul's peculiar use of the the impersonal "the" with "mother" throughout her narrative. The personal pronoun "my" (*ma*) is used with "mother" only three times, each to express a desire for a mother—and childhood—that has been lost (48–49).

29. *Our Sister Killjoy* is subtitled, with self-conscious mockery, *or Reflections from a Black-eyed Squint.*

Works Cited

Aidoo, Ama Ata. *Our Sister Killjoy.* Harlow, England: Longman, 1977.

Bhabha, Homi K. "Signs Taken for Wonders: Questions of Ambivalence and Authority under a Tree outside Delhi, May 1817." In *"Race," Writing, and Difference,* edited by Henry Louis Gates Jr., 163–84. Chicago: University of Chicago Press, 1985.

Bourjea, Michelle. "Review of Ken Bugul, *Le Baobab fou.*" *Notre Librairie: La littérature sénégalaise* (Paris) 81 (October–December 1985): 193–94.

Brodzki, Bella. "Mothers, Displacement, and Language in the Autobiographies of Nathalie Sarraute and Christa Wolf." In *Life/Lines: Theorizing Women's Autobiography,* edited by Bella Brodzki and Celeste Schenck, 243–59. Ithaca, N.Y.: Cornell University Press, 1988.

Buggs, Debra Boyd. "Mouridism in Senegalese Fiction." In *Faces of Islam in African Literature,* edited by Kenneth W. Harrow, 201–14. Portsmouth, N.H.: Heinemann, 1991.

d'Almeida, Irène Assiba. *Francophone African Women Writers.* Gainesville: University Press of Florida, 1994.

Davies, Carole Boyce. *Black Women, Writing, and Identity: Migrations of the Subject.* New York: Routledge, 1994.

Davies, Carole Boyce, and Elaine Savory Fido. "African Women Writers: Toward a Literary History." In *A History of Twentieth-Century African Literature,* edited by Oyekan Owomoyela, 311–46. Lincoln: University of Nebraska Press, 1993.

Diallo, Nafissatou. *De Tilène au Plateau: Une enfance dakaroise.* Dakar: Les Nouvelles Editions Africaines, 1975. Published in English as *A Dakar Childhood.* Translated by Dorothy Blair. London: Longman Drumbeat, 1982.

Diouf, Madior. "Les formes du roman négro-africain de langue française, 1920–76." Unpublished dissertation, Université Cheikh Anta Diop, 1991.

Fuderer, Laura Sue. *The Female Bildungsroman in English.* New York: Modern Language Association, 1990.

Gusdorf, Georges. "Conditions and Limits of Autobiography." In *Autobiography: Essays Theoretical and Critical,* edited by James Olney, 28–48. Princeton, N.J.: Princeton University Press, 1980.

Henderson, Mae Gwendolyn. "Speaking in Tongues: Dialogics, Dialectics, and the Black Woman Writer's Literary Tradition." In *Reading Black, Reading Feminist,* edited by Henry Louis Gates Jr., 116–42. New York: Penguin Books, 1990.

hooks, bell. "Selling Hot Pussy: Representations of Black Female Sexuality in the Cultural Marketplace." In *Black Looks: Race and Representation,* 61–77. Boston: South End Press, 1992.

Houdanou, Lucien. "Islam et société dans la littérature feminine." *Nouvelles du sud* 7 (1987): 159–70.

Kéita, Anta Diouf. "L'Ecriture autobiographique dans le roman féminin sénégalais." In *Autobiographies et récits de vie en Afrique,* edited by Bernard Mouralis, 135–44. Paris: L'Harmattan, 1991.

Kéita, Aoua. *Femme d'Afrique.* Paris: Présence Africaine, 1975.

Ken Bugul (Mariétou M'Baye). *Le Baobab fou.* Dakar: Les Nouvelles Editions Africaines, 1982. Published in English as *The Abandoned Baobab: The Autobiography of a Senegalese Woman.* Translated by Marjolijn deJager. Brooklyn: Lawrence Hill, 1991.

———. *Cendres et braises.* Paris: L'Harmattan, 1994.

Lionnet, Françoise. *Autobiographical Voices.* Ithaca, N.Y.: Cornell University Press, 1989.

Magniér, Bernard. "Ken Bugul ou l'écriture thérapeutique: propos recueillis." *Notre Librairie: La littérature sénégalaise* (Paris): 81 (October–December 1985): 151–55.

Mbacké, Mame Seck. *Le Froid et le piment.* Dakar: Les Nouvelles Editions Africaines, 1983.

Miller, Christopher L. "Nationalism as Resistance and Resistance to Nationalism in the Literature of Francophone Africa." In *Post/Colonial Conditions: Exiles, Migrations, and Nomadisms,* edited by Françoise Lionnet and Ronnie Scharfman. *Yale French Studies,* no. 82 (1993): 62–100.

———. *Theories of Africans.* Chicago: University of Chicago Press, 1990.

Miller, Mary-Kay F. "*L'Ex-Père de la nation:* Subversive Subtexts and the Return of the Maternal." In *Postcolonial Subjects,* edited by Mary Jean Green et al. Minneapolis: University of Minnesota Press, 1996.

Mortimer, Mildred. "Women's Flight." In *Journeys through the French African Novel,* 165–77. Portsmouth, N.H.: Heinemann Books, 1990.

Mudimbe-Boyi, Elisabeth. "The Poetics of Exile and Errancy: Ken Bugul's *Le Baobab Fou* and Simone Schwarz-Bart's *Ti Jean L'Horizon.*" In *Post/Colonial Conditions: Exiles, Migrations, and Nomadisms,* edited by Françoise Lionnet and Ronnie Scharfman. *Yale French Studies,* no. 83 (1993): 194–212.

O'Neale, Sondra. "Race, Sex, and Self: Aspects of Bildung in Select Novels by Black American Women Novelists." *MELUS: The Journal of the Society for the Study of the Multi-ethnic Literature of the United States* 9, no. 4 (1982): 25–37.

Porter, Laurence M. "Senegalese Literature Today." *French Review* 66, no. 6 (May 1993): 887–99.

Rush, Norman. "The Woman in the Broken Mirror." Review of *The Abandoned Baobab. New York Times Book Review,* December 15, 1991, 1, 27–28.

Schipper, Mineke. "Le Je Africain: Pour une typologie des écrits à la premiere personne (fiction et non-fiction)." In *Autobiographies et récits de vie en Afrique,* edited by Bernard Mouralis, 7–22. Paris: L'Harmattan, 1991.

———. " 'Who Am I?' Fact and Fiction in African First-Person Narrative." *Research in African Literatures* 16, no. 1 (Spring 1985): 53–89.

Smith, Sidonie. *Subjectivity, Identity, and the Body.* Bloomington: Indiana University Press, 1993.

Stange, Margit A. "Personal Property: Exchange Value and the Female Self in *The Awakening.*" In *Case Studies in Contemporary Criticism: "The Awakening," Kate Chopin,* edited by Nancy A. Walker, 201–17. New York: St. Martin's Press, 1993.

Sylla, Assane. *La Philosophie morale des Wolof.* 2nd ed. Dakar: IFAN, 1994.

Woodhull, Winifred. "Exile." In *Post/Colonial Conditions: Exiles, Migrations, and Nomadisms,* edited by Françoise Lionnet and Ronnie Scharfman. *Yale French Studies,* no. 82 (1993): 7–24.

Woodward, Servanne. "French-Language Fiction." In *A History of Twentieth-Century African Literature,* edited by Oyekan Owomoyela, 173–97. Lincoln: University of Nebraska Press, 1993.

Part II

The New Europe and Its Old Margins

7 / Reclaiming Space

Jewish Women in Germany Today

Karen Remmler

Introduction

Fifty years after the end of World War II, the process of remembering the atrocities committed by German Nazis and their collaborators against the Jews is accompanied by heated debates in the German media and among scholars about the feasibility and effectiveness of symbolic acts of commemoration such as the erection of Holocaust memorials, the rebuilding of synagogues, and official ceremonies of commemoration.[1] Furthermore, the economic and social upheaval following German unification and the attempts to consolidate postwar histories of two German nations with different approaches to the Nazi past have complicated the constitution of a "unified" German national identity that is shaped by the present-day self-understanding and image of Germany both within its borders and the world at large.[2] As James Young recently remarked in an interview in the *Frankfurter Rundschau,* Germans are faced with the paradox of remembering a history they would rather forget and, at the same time, building a national identity based on the remembrance of a crime (Preisler). One way of establishing a nation is to ask those who were the victims of the crime committed in the name of that nation to acknowledge the public attempts to achieve reconciliation. This appears to be an impossible desire. For one, the majority of the victims are dead. Second, such "normalization" could obscure the fact that this history is part of the present and future of Germany.[3]

At the same time that Germany is integrating itself into the European Union while coping with the strain of unification, public representation of "intercultural cooperation" among Germans and "foreign fellow citizens" *(ausländische Mitbürger)* is common fare in the news media and in governmental publications.[4] One group of "fellow citizens" has a long and troubled history in Germany—"the" Jews. In order to allay fears about the trustworthiness of Germany as a European partner, Germany requires a public image that registers the pursuit of reconciliation with its Jewish citizens and residents—a reconciliation that some Jews find neither possible nor desirable (Jacoby, Schoppmann, and Lena-Henry; Seeligmann, "What Keeps the Jews in Germany Quiet?"). The public obsession (which by no means represents a collective consensus among Germans per se) with things Jewish is coupled with the concern about unification and about "coming to terms" with the Stasi legacy as well as the legacy of National Socialism in light of many Germans' need to remember their own experiences during and after the war.

Consequently, interest in Jewish-German relations and in Jewish culture in Germany has also become a central point of public and scholarly debate (Gilman and Remmler). Although studies on such topics as the so-called German-Jewish (negative) symbiosis abound, current writing on the relation between Jewish experiences and those of "other" Germans—those Germans who share citizenship with their white, predominantly Christian neighbors, but for whom ethnic background, skin color, or religion set them apart in the eyes of many "German" Germans—takes place, for the most part, outside of Germany or within minority circles in Germany.[5] In addition, discussions about multiculturalism are exacerbated by the varying connotations and official usages of the terms that distinguish different groups in Germany from one another. Words such as "minority," "foreigner," "immigrant," or "refugee" are often used interchangeably in public discourse, but have specific legal ramifications. The term *Ausländer* (foreigner or alien) designates anyone who is not German under constitutional law, whereas official ethnic minorities in Germany include the Sorbs and Danes, but not Roma or Sinti. Immigrants of Jewish background, religious, cultural, or both, are usually not included in statistics on foreigners living in Germany. Jewish immigrants from the former Soviet Union, for example, are categorized as *Kontingentflüchtlinge* (quota refugees), not as asylum seekers.[6]

Whereas American scholars have recognized the importance of distinguishing between the experiences of Jews and those of other cultural minorities who write about their experiences in German, little work exists in Germany and the United States on the present-day experience of Jewish women, both as Germans and as immigrants.[7] In order to question this lacuna and to consider how second-generation Jewish women view their Jewish experience within Germany in light of unification as well as in debates about the commemoration of the Shoah and German national identity, I turn to the self-definition and experiences of Jewish women who have immigrated to Germany or who are the daughters of Jewish immigrants who immigrated or returned to Germany after 1945. *Nach der Shoa geboren* (Born after the Shoah), edited by Jessica Jacoby, Claudia Schoppmann, and Wendy Zena-Henry, is a collection of interviews, interview summaries, and essays by Jewish women.[8] In reading the words of Jewish women, for whom Jewishness itself cannot be seen as a common denominator, since its meaning for each woman depends largely on other factors and experiences, I raise the following questions: How do Jewish women represent their Jewish experience in relation to other categories of identity, such as gender, class, sexuality, nationality, or ethnic affiliation? In what ways are they subjects within contemporary German culture and in what ways do they perceive the incorporation of their experience into the public narrative on German national identity? Why do they feel "disowned" (Jacoby, interview with author, January 16, 1995) or "instrumentalized" (Stern) as "living memorials" (Baader, *Nach der Shoa*, 17)? How does their heterogeneity counter a consolidated view of Jews as symbolic figures associated with the Shoah?

The collection *Nach der Shoa geboren* shakes up cultural and conceptual alignments between Jews and victims or Jews and women in order to show how other factors, such as sexuality, ethnic background, geographical place of origin, and class, affect the quality of Jewish life and its practice in Germany today. Drawing from their experience as Jewish women in Germany, the editors hoped that the collection would break taboos and expose stereotypes about Jewish female identity as well as bring attention to the detrimental effects of consolidating multiple subjectivities into monolithic categories. They dismiss notions of organic identity imposed upon them by the legacy of the destruction of the Jews and replace a fixed Jewish identity with one defined by a commitment to combating anti-Semitism, racism, sexism, and homophobia. According to many of the women in the collection, Jewish identity emerges in confrontation with events within German culture. As Esther Dischereit once put it, "I wake up in the morning and I am not a Jew. Then I hear the news on the radio that a synagogue in Lübeck has been fire bombed. Then I am very

Jewish" (conversation, January 7, 1995). The women who tell their stories in *Nach der Shoa geboren* refuse to represent *the* Jewish woman, but rather strive to redefine the meaning of Jewishness within German *and* Jewish culture.

Jewishness is only one factor in shaping the experience of the women who describe their lives in contemporary Germany. More often than not, ethnic background or previous nationality plays a large role in how the women define themselves vis-á-vis other Jews, Germans, and non-Jewish members of their ethnic origin in Germany. Thus the contributions of the women in *Nach der Shoa geboren* must be seen not only as a documentation of the immigrant experience as it is actually lived, but also as self-reflections about the meaning of Jewish identity for Jewish women for whom the postunification process of redefining Germanness within a German nation continues to transform their sense of Jewishness.

Postwar Jewish Immigration from 1945 to the Present

Compared with other cultural minorities, such as Turks, former Yugoslavians, Poles, Italians, Roma, and Sinti, Jews are much fewer in number.[9] Yet, they bear the largest symbolic significance for Germany's national identity today. Although approximately 40,000 Jews (the majority of whom are Eastern European, not German) were officially registered with the *Jüdische Gemeinde* (Jewish Community) as of 1994, unofficial estimates put the total number of Jews, including nonmembers or Germans with Jewish family background, between 50,000 and 70,000 (Bodemann, 49).

Immediately after the war, close to 200,000 Jewish survivors recovered in displaced person (DP) camps in Allied territory before moving on to Palestine and later Israel or the United States. Approximately 12,000 chose to remain in what later became the Federal Republic of Germany (FRG) or the German Democratic Republic (GDR) in 1949. Despite the criticism and dismay of many of their friends, Jews have been immigrating to the former FRG from its inception in 1949 to the present. Although a number of Jews immigrated to the GDR because of their political convictions, many left before the collapse of this German state in 1989. It wasn't until the 1980s, however, that Jews became more vocal in the public sphere of the FRG and that second-generation Jewish writers began writing about present-day Jewish experience in Germany (Seeligmann, "What Keeps the Jews in Germany Quiet?").

German Jews make up a small minority of the Jews officially registered with the *Jüdische Gemeinde*. In the early to middle seventies, in response to a rise in anti-Semitic incidents in the Soviet Union, Soviet Jews immigrated to the FRG and, after the fall of the Wall, to both former German states. In fact, former Soviet Jews make up close to two-thirds of the present Jewish population in cities such as Berlin and are crucial for maintaining Jewish presence in Germany.[10] More than half the Jews registered with the Jewish Community in Berlin today arrived in the last decade.[11] The more recent group of former Soviet Jews began coming to Berlin under a law that was passed by the short-lived post-Wall GDR parliament in 1990 before the two Germanys were unified. The law granted Soviet Jews the right to enter the territory of the former GDR under a special system that lifted previous quotas. After unification, the German federal government and the sixteen German federal states agreed on January 9, 1991, to accept Jews arriving directly from the former Soviet Union under the law of 1990, which allowed for the acceptance of refugees for humanitarian reasons. Soviet (not just Russian) Jews could apply for entry into Germany based solely on their Jewish ancestry and were granted immediate asylum.[12]

Most of the immigrants have little knowledge of Jewish culture, except for a vague attachment to Jewish holidays or Yiddish songs. Ironically, many are not considered Jewish under Jewish law. "In their homeland, they were 'branded' as Jews and faced discrimination, while in Germany they are excluded from the Jewish Community" (Miklis, 80). Thus, the immigrants are not only learning German and acclimating to German culture, but also learning to be Jews.

The situation of the former Soviet Jews differs from those Jews for whom Germany represents family ties or for those recent Jewish immigrants who may not plan to remain in Germany permanently. For the most part, the former face hardships common to the immigrant experience, such as language barriers, initial unemployment, and isolation, in addition to discrimination as "foreigners." The Jewish women represented in *Nach der Shoa geboren* fall, for the most part, into the latter two categories. Although individual life stories cannot be representative for any group, they serve as starting points from which to probe deeper into the relations between lived experience and the functionalization of this experience—in this case Jewishness in Germany after unification. As Frank Stern summarizes in his study on the attitudes toward Jews both as members of German society and as imaginary figures in the postwar German psyche, Germans tend to "instrumentalize" Jews for the purpose of cleansing their conscience and for keeping up a positive public image. On the one hand, the

Germans need the Jews to continue the process of *Vergangenheitsbewältigung* (working through the past) and to display their *Betroffenheit* (consternation or sadness). Yet the various events and actions commemorating the Jewish victims of the Nazis, although well intentioned and often cathartic for Germans, may only be compensatory acts that give Germans the opportunity to avoid dealing with live Jews and their differences. Jewish women and men are symbolically a central part of the German national identity, both as reminders for the nation's collective memory to take responsibility for the killing of millions of people and for the present nation striving for reconciliation and struggling with the negative consequences of unification. But the unification process itself and the ensuing debates about how to compensate the victims of the Stasi (the GDR secret police) have reminded Germans that there can be no resolution to the act of remembering. Just as both former German states avoided a direct confrontation with the Nazi past directly after the war, current debates about whether or not to give amnesty to former members of the Stasi demonstrate the complicated and painful truth about contemporary German society. Saturated with gestures of remembering the victims, it lacks the commitment to condemn those responsible and to take appropriate action against them.[13]

The Experience of Jewish Women in Germany Today

In present-day Germany "Jewishness" and "Germanness" are not diametrically opposed identities, but rather changing positions often dependent on the degree to which Germans are engaged with avoiding a confrontation with their German past by recovering a Jewish past. The various oral history projects, although well intentioned, often simplify Jewish experience. Jews living in Germany today are differently Jewish depending on gender, sexual preference, class, ethnic background, and individual circumstances. A Jewish woman immigrant from Iran living in a close-knit Iranian Jewish community in Hamburg has a different sense of her Jewishness than does a Russian Jewish woman attending the first Jewish service of her life in Berlin. As Jewish women construct their own sense of a Jewish self, they also commit to a social, cultural, and often political practice that distinguishes them from non-Jewish immigrants and from one another.

Issues of gender difference among Jews or the relation between gender and anti-Semitism have only recently been explored in any depth.[14] Although Jewish women writers such as Katja Behrens, Barbara Honigmann, or Esther Dischereit have addressed issues of female Jewish experience in their literary texts, the experience and heterogeneity of Jewish women immigrants has received little attention.[15] *Nach der Shoa geboren* is a first step toward filling a gap in the current plethora of oral history projects, museum exhibits, media projects, and cultural events dedicated to Jewish history, life, culture, or people, which rarely focus on gender. German feminists have, in the last decade, begun to draw on the work of American historians, such as Claudia Koonz, Renate Bridenthal, Atina Grossmann, and Marion Kaplan, in order to reexamine the role of women in National Socialism not only as victims of a patriarchal system but as perpetrators who made individual choices. Yet little work has been done by German feminists on the present-day role of anti-Semitism among women.[16] Ironically, it has been Jewish women such as Jessica Jacoby, Maria Baader, or Erica Fischer who have addressed this issue. The autobiographical accounts by female concentration camp survivors, such as Ruth Klüger, or by Jewish women who went into exile as adults, such as Herta Nathorff, or as children, such as Salomea Genin, have received notable attention. The remembrance of Jewish female experience in Berlin under Nazi rule, like that of Jewish culture in general, has begun to be acknowledged. For example, an oral history project to commemorate the work and life of the first (and last) female rabbi in Germany, Regina Jonas (killed in Auschwitz in 1944), will look at her life and work in Berlin (conversation with Iris Weiss, January 12, 1995). Accounts of Jewish women who attempted to survive the Nazi regime underground, such as Erica Fischer's *Aimée & Jaguar*—the depiction of the love relationship between an illegal Jewish woman and a German woman in Berlin in 1943, have also recently appeared. Nevertheless, information or public knowledge on the experience of Jewish women who have immigrated to Germany in recent years and the significance of Jewish and female identity for their relationship to present-day notions of German nationality remain sparse.

Although second-generation Jewish women have begun to write about their experiences in the form of poetry or short stories, much of their work is as yet unpublished. In their interviews for *Nach der Shoa geboren,* many women explore their relationship to Judaism by tracing their family's history and the meaning it and German history has had for their own lives within Germany. For most of the German Jewish women, the experiences of their parents as survivors of the Shoah in the camps or in exile cannot be separated from their own sense of themselves as outsiders in German society. Even as they participate actively in political debates about German national identity, they are themselves torn between their identities as Jews and Germans. Their relationship to Germany differs from other Jewish women of non-German descent who have immigrated to Germany and who have no previous family or emotional ties to Germany. Whereas in the former case, the women consider emigration out of Germany as a constant possibility, the latter group are more likely to experience the hardships of immigration facing non-Jewish women, such as the initial language barrier, alienation, homesickness, and poverty. Yet even they are faced with the "Jewish question" and find themselves making choices about how to publicly identify themselves in Germany. That is, their Jewish identity changes in character and degree according to how they perceive themselves to be perceived by Germans and to what extent they are willing to align themselves with the official Jewish Community or remain outside of it.

Jewish Women in the Former GDR

A number of the women represented in *Nach der Shoa geboren* grew up in the former GDR, the children of German Jewish immigrants for whom socialist politics eclipsed their Jewish background. Unification transformed the meaning of Jewish culture, particularly in Berlin, where the official Jewish Community of four hundred members in East Berlin was consolidated with the much larger Jewish Community in former West Berlin. Up until 1988, when the GDR head of state, Erich Honecker, announced plans to rebuild the New Synagogue in the Oranienburger Straße near the center of (East) Berlin, the GDR had emphasized the Communist affiliation of the victims of German fascism, rather than focusing on the Jewish heritage of the majority of the victims.[17] The former self-proclaimed antifascist state, within whose borders three major concentration camps—Buchenwald, Sachsenhausen, and Ravensbrück—were located, is now in the process of recovering the history of Jews within its territory.

Barbara Honigmann and Annette Leo are two women for whom the immigrant experience of their parents had a substantial impact on their life choices. Honigmann was born in 1949 in the former GDR. Her parents were Jews, for whom socialist political identity outweighed their attachment to their Jewish heritage.[18] In 1984 Honigmann left the GDR for Strasbourg in the hopes of finding a thriving Jewish community in which she could participate.

Honigmann's emigration from the GDR became a catalyst for writing about her Jewish identity in the former GDR. In a collection of short stories published in 1986, *Roman von einem Kinde,* Honigmann describes the process of emigration, an emigration leading to a chosen exile. Her memories of her life in the GDR are juxtaposed with the newfound experience of becoming a practicing Jew in France. In her short story, "Bonsoir, Madame Benhamou," the first-person narrator describes the sensation of being *fremd* (foreign, strange). While riding a bicycle on the way to an all-women Torah study group at the home of Madame Benhamou, she recalls the pain of leaving her former home and arriving in a foreign land: "This is where I have landed after a triple death jump without a safety net: from the East to the West, from Germany to France and out of assimilation into Torah Judaism" (111). Thus leaving the GDR in search of a Jewish community becomes a confrontation with other facets of her identity and personal history. Leaving the East behind means undoing the direction in which her parents embarked when they decided to leave their land of exile, England, to settle in the GDR. The narrator, as a German speaker in France, is also a German in a country for which the German language conjures up memories of the German occupation. In the painstaking process of becoming a religious Jew, the protagonist finds herself becoming more aware of her deep connections to East German culture. She describes the process of acclimation, made simpler by the beauty of Strasbourg, represented by the silhouette of the cathedral steeple at dusk. Even as she finds a community in which to immerse herself in Jewish tradition, the first encounters with the French language evoke a sense of alienation in the protagonist: "Now I finally know what it means to be foreign" (114). The sense of foreignness that she had felt in the back of her mind all along as the daughter of emigrants in the GDR rises to the surface in an environment in which her German accent reveals her foreignness.

Honigmann's essay in *Nach der Shoa geboren*, "Von den Legenden der Kindheit, dem Weggehen und der Wiederkehr" ("About the legends of childhood, the leaving and returning"), describes how the experience of exile shapes her construction of self, personal history, and relationship to Jewish German identity. Upon the death of her mother (her father died seven years previously), Honigmann notes how tightly her own life and that of other Jews in Germany whose parents survived the Shoah are intertwined. Even as Germans, their histories are irretrievably separate: "Others have heard other stories: from the Front, from Stalingrad, the flight from East Prussia and Silesia, from prisoner of war camps, and from the bombing of German cities" (35). Those Germans and Jews born after the war may share the same language and home, but the stories they heard as children about the plight of their parents during the war creates a gap. For Honigmann, her parents' stories about exile, about learning to cope with foreign languages and foreign customs while facing the bitter exclusion from a German culture in which they had forgotten their foreignness, have left their mark. Her parents' decision to settle in the GDR only secured their emigrant status and experience. Within the GDR, the emigrants, many of whom were German Jews, formed a community that also included their children.

Her father describes his choice as one of conviction that also clearly distinguishes his Jewishness from that of the religious Jew: "The Jews from the stetl were not 'our people,' rather the men who brought forth the Communist idea were. Furthermore, I am a German Jew, a Jewish German; they wanted to get me out of Germany, but I came back; that gives me a sense of satisfaction. I belong here, even when it leaves my heart cold and empty" (37). Honigmann sees her parents' disappointment as twofold. With the failure of socialism in the GDR, their life work as German socialists was for nought. They fall between the cracks, since they no longer belong to the Jews and have not become the Germans in the Germany they had hoped for. Consequently, Honigmann struggles to find her way out of this legacy. "In reality, I was searching for a minimum of Jewish identity in my life, for a regular year according to the Jewish, not the Christian, calendar and a dialogue about Judaism beyond the ever present discourse on anti-Semitism. A minimum . . . that was already too much for German circumstances" (38).

The dilemma of being Jewish and German, yet not belonging to the majority consensus of Germanness in Germany, places German Jewish women like Honigmann in a double bind. As a Jew, Honigmann's worldview is constantly adjusted according to the situation of other Jews. As a writer, she observes and records this experience, yet wonders about the accuracy of the label "Jewish" writer. "I left Germany as a Jewish woman, but in my work, in my very strong connection to the German language, I must return again and again" (40). Thus Honigmann remains a German, even as she becomes a Jew.

Like Honigmann, Annette Leo, who was born in 1948, grew up in the GDR and belongs to a generation of German Jews who are the children of the socialist cultural elite of the GDR. As Ostow has pointed out, Leo's search for Jewish roots is not simply a part of a worldwide movement among children of secular Jews to rediscover their Jewish heritage, but must also be seen within the specific context of the GDR. Once GDR socialism failed, many of its main proponents and their children were left without an identity to which they felt morally attached. Thus becoming Jewish was one way of distancing oneself from the disappointment of the GDR, but also of aligning oneself with a group within Germany that represented a culturally different German—the Jew.

Leo's writing focuses on her family history, their experience of exile under the Nazis, and the vicissitudes of remembering this legacy within the GDR. In her essay "Warum dieses Schweigen?" ("Why this silence?") she discusses her Jewish identity. Like Honigmann, Leo did not grow up with much exposure to Jewish tradition, culture, or religion. "If there had been no National Socialism and no murder of millions of Jews, then my parents' desire for assimilation would have been fulfilled. I would be a German today like everyone else" (*Nach der Shoa*, 96). Despite having a Communist father and growing up in the GDR with the knowledge that family members had been killed in the extermination camps, Leo's upbringing as a non-Jew kept her from exploring her own relationship to Jewish identity. It was not until she began to interview people of her parents' generation that her curiosity in her Jewish background grew.

Leo's work provides a valuable insight into the complicated situation in the GDR whereby official antifascism, the focus on the Communist legacy, and a refusal to recognize Israel as a legitimate state, couched in anti-imperialistic rhetoric, often hid the existence of anti-Semitism in the GDR. As one interviewee explains, many Jewish members of the Sozialistische Einheitspartei Deutschlands (SED) may have rejected their Jewish background in order to regain what had been brutally denied them by the Nazis—a German identity coupled with an antifascist ideology (98). And many held on to their ideals despite the contradictions between the humanitarian ideology of socialism and the outbreak of anti-Semitic campaigns in the early 1950s under the auspices of anti-Zionism.[19]

German Jewish Women Living in the FRG

For Maria Baader, born in 1959 in (West) Berlin, the daughter of a German Jewish father and non-Jewish German mother, November 9, 1989, was a decisive turning point in her life. November 9 not only marks the fall of the Wall, but also the November 9 Pogrom in 1938 in Nazi Germany, in which loosely organized bands of SA troops and other marauding Germans destroyed numerous Jewish stores and synagogues and imprisoned more than ten thousand Jews. Baader sees the events of the 1980s, such as the *Historikerstreit* (Historian's Debate) or the Bitburg affair, as attempts to relativize the crimes of National Socialism, a step that many Germans carried further by celebrating November 9, 1989, as a day that ended Germany's need to deal with its "dark" past (13). In the slogan "We are the people," exclaimed in rallies in the East, Baader sees the exclusion of Jews, immigrants, and Afro-Germans, for whom the rising antiforeigner propaganda from both legal and illegal right-wing, nationalist groups poses a serious threat. Finding herself in a "new" Germany, Baader began feeling like a foreigner. It was not her Jewishness that burdened her, but rather the constant reminder that even the most sincere rituals of remembrance do not make it possible for Jews who speak out against anti-Semitism to live a "normal" life in Germany. In her essay "Zweierlei Befreiung" (Two kinds of liberation), Baader describes the growing feeling of helplessness that she felt following German unification. Consequently, Baader left Germany and is currently living in New York City. She describes her pleasure at being in a city where Germanness and Jewishness are not in contradiction to one another, since being Jewish in the United States is not associated solely with victim status. "[To be the] subject of my history means the ability to leave Germany" (18). Although she cannot call Germany her home, by leaving Germany, Baader, like Honigmann, can also make peace with her Germanness.

Like other engaged Jewish women who tell their stories in *Nach der Shoa geboren*, such as Fischer or the political activist Jutta Oesterle-Schwerin, Baader wishes to see a transformation in the way that Germans and Jews talk with one another, a dialogue that does not exhaust itself in moralistic discussions about the symbolic meaning of memorials nor in attempts at reconciliation, but rather in a willingness to live with the contradictions and the discomfort of their shared history.

This dilemma is illustrated by Fischer in her essay "Zum ersten Mal öffentlich 'Ich bin eine Jüdin' sagen" (To say for the first time publicly "I am a Jewish woman").[20] Often Jewish women are invited to feminist conferences to represent the "Jewish" view, a practice Fischer finds irresponsible, since it ignores the multiple facets of Jewish identity and the differences among Jewish women. She describes an encounter between herself and a non-German feminist, who had hoped that Fischer and another Jewish woman would "help the German women establish their identity" (*Nach der Shoa*, 143). The workshop was designed to encourage the German participants to reach "a necessary better understanding of Jewish culture in order to understand [their] own" (143). Fischer's remark that she would prefer talking with Jewish women about her identity and that she would suggest that German women meet among themselves to discuss their identity as "descendants of the Nazis" was met with assurances that the German women had good intentions. Fischer objected to the German women's assumption that the grief over the losses caused by the war could be shared by Germans and Jews equally. As Nea Weissberg-Bob remarked to the German women, "Your loss is the impoverishment of German culture, mine is the loss of my grandparents" (*Nach der Shoa*, 143). Thus, like the different stories Germans and Jews hear about the past described by Honigmann, such attempts to have dialogue in the present lead again and again to an impasse.

Following the Waldheim affair and a growing marginalization of feminists in Austria, Fischer left Vienna and moved to Cologne. Fischer looks back at her nonengagement during the protests against Waldheim and against increasing anti-Semitism in Austria as a sign of her own fear of coming too close to a part of herself that she had long suppressed. Living in Germany gave her the distance she needed to begin to tackle the Jewish part of her identity. "And being foreign in exile seemed to me to be much more bearable than being foreign in the supposed 'Heimat' " (139). Fischer does not deny her privilege as a Jew with an English passport who comes from Austria. Thus she is protected from the discrimination directed toward other foreigners, whose skin color makes it impossible for them to pass as Germans. (She forgets that some of these "foreigners" are German.) Fischer remains critical of Germans, especially those Germans who seek out dialogue for the purpose of their own confrontation with their Germanness:

> Germans have a hard time accepting the fact when foreigners express their views in the offensive, without speaking about the Germans as the central theme. Jewish men and women are especially exploited by Germans for their confrontation with German culture, particularly because this culture was miserably mutilated by the disappearance of the Jews. (142)

In fact, she points out the contrast between the intellectual discussion about German nationalism that takes place in the media and the actions of skinheads on the streets. Whereas the first group talks in abstract terms, the latter group acts out their frustration and desire by attacking those they perceive to be non-Germans. Fischer implies that one can learn a lesson from the actions of the skinheads. Their disgruntlement with the current situation, the inundation of commemorative events and didactic posters put up by the Berlin senate, for example, may bring about the opposite of what such didactic measures set out to accomplish.

Fischer feels that the degree to which the Germans have incorporated the crimes of their ancestors into their present is directly related to the degree in which they work toward preventing anti-Semitism, racism, and the exclusion of those deemed other by a public consensus based on fear, arrogance, or prejudice. In the afterword to *Aimée & Jaguar,* Fischer ends with a provocative statement directed toward second-generation Germans:

> "Why didn't you do anything back then?" is the question that millions of young Germans and Austrians asked their parents with righteous indignation and [to which they] received no answer. The grown adults have no desire to ask themselves the same moral question. Otherwise they would have to bear the consequences. (292)

And bearing the consequences would not only mean taking in more refugees from Bosnia or elsewhere in the world, but also protesting against racist and/or anti-Semitic acts in Germany and taking stock of one's own history, not just that of the Jews or the Nazis "back then." It also means living with the knowledge that there can be no reconciliation, but only continued dialogue, genuine empathy for the other, and a willingness to acknowledge the effects of the destruction of European Jewish culture on German culture.

Like Fischer, other Jewish women of German heritage represented in *Nach der Shoa geboren* are directly involved in political projects or artistic endeavors that focus on the prevention of anti-Semitism, racism, and xenophobia. The statements by those women who were not born in Germany demonstrate that most came to Germany with an image of the German nation deeply imprinted in their consciousness. For many it was not a foreign land, but one that they had traversed many times in their nightmares.

Daniela Thau is one of the few women in the collection for whom Jewish religion plays a major role in her self-understanding as a Jew. She is a rabbi. She was born in 1952 in South Africa and came to Germany in 1958. After studying in Germany until 1976, she left to go to Israel and then to rabbinical school at the Leo Baeck College in London. Since 1983, she has been a practicing rabbi and has lived in Switzerland and Bangalore.

Thau's father came from an Orthodox Berlin family but broke with Orthodoxy upon his arrival in Palestine. Her mother came from a liberal Jewish family in southern Germany. Upon their return to Germany in 1958, Thau's father became a member of the Coblenz Jewish community for the simple reason that he knew Hebrew. After the family moved to Berlin in 1968, Thau joined a Jewish youth group and continued to inform herself about Jewish religion and thought. After completing work in Jewish studies, Thau decided she would become a rabbi. Faced with the impossibility of receiving rabbinical training as a woman under the auspices of the Jewish Community in Germany, Thau attended the Leo Baeck college in London. As an outsider in British society and a Jewish German married to a Jewish man whose family was anti-German, Thau was also confronted with her Germanness. She expresses her sadness at having less and less contact with Germany, yet feels as a woman rabbi that she no longer belongs to Germany. The Reform movement that had begun and flourished in Germany through 1933 has not been revived. Although more liberal members of the Jewish Community have supported the notion of having a female rabbi, more conservative members have vetoed the idea. Therefore Thau, for whom the struggle to be accepted as a rabbi in Berlin would have meant expending energy on an impossible task, decided not to return. "After five years of college I didn't have any strength left in 1983 to stand on my hind legs and to fight for a position in the Berlin community" (*Nach der Shoa*, 201).

Similarly, Thau's stance toward the unification of Germany is ambivalent. On the one hand, the fall of the Wall has recreated the spatial parameters of the Berlin her parents knew as young adults. The former center of Jewish life, the neighborhood surrounding the New Synagogue in the Oranienburger Straße near the center of what used to be East Berlin, is slowly regaining some of its Jewish flair. Yet the progressive branch of Judaism in Germany was destroyed along with Jewish culture by the Nazis. Thau regrets the lack of plurality in the present-day Jewish Community. "One must first teach the Jews living in Germany today that they live in the country that was once the center of the Reform movement; most of these Jews are not German Jews, they are Jews who have immigrated to Germany" (202). She doubts the possibility of Berlin having decentralized communities. Thus, even a rabbi is estranged from the current Jewish Community in Berlin, the city with the largest Jewish population in Germany today.

Non-German Jewish Women in Germany Today

Unlike German Jewish women, Jewish women of non-German ethnicity who have immigrated to or who have spent a considerable amount of time in Germany and have little relation to German culture are often seen as "foreigners" first and Jews second. The largest number of Jewish immigrants to Germany have come from the former Soviet Union. Many, like Anna Vinogradova, for whom "the entire Jewish cultural life is a blank page" (interview, 1), maintain strong cultural ties to their Russian heritage. "I would never say that I was not a Russian, I would never say that Russia is not my home, it is of course my home, not Israel" (interview, 2). Vinogradova left the Soviet Union in 1989 for personal reasons, yet recalls that increasing anti-Semitism in the mid-1980s had a strong influence on her decision: "I began to feel very bad and became conscious that I was a Jew" (5). Her family, like most Soviet Jewish families, had little contact with formal Jewish religion or tradition, despite Jewish family background. Her mother is Jewish, her father is not. At age sixteen, Vinogradova chose not to have her Jewish affiliation stamped in her passport, a choice she could make as the daughter of mixed marriage, but one more difficult for children of two Jewish parents. "What can one call the Jews who live there and feel attached? Jews or Russians, that is the question" (8). Vinogradova is careful to distinguish between the organized anti-Semitism in the former Soviet Union and the individual encounters with anti-Semitism in Germany, although she is often appalled by the anti-Semitic remarks of progressive Germans.

Whereas former Soviet Jews come to Germany with the intention of building new lives and have contributed by their sheer presence to a strengthening of the Jewish Community, other non-German Jews come to Germany without necessarily intending to stay. They are therefore not immigrants per se, but long-term residents. Vivet Alevi, for example, was born in Istanbul in 1952. She came to Berlin in 1972 to study graphic design. Alevi grew up in a middle-class Jewish milieu in Istanbul. Her family celebrated the major Jewish holidays, but was otherwise not particularly religious. According to Alevi, Jewish life in Turkey is marked by assimilation and integration. Alevi insists that there is a Jewish consciousness, even as many Jews choose not to openly identify themselves as Jews. Being Jewish in Turkey meant that she lived "always in the Diaspora" and that the nation Turkey was not her home, even as Istanbul fulfilled this function (*Nach der Shoa,* 68). Faced with what she considered to be the narrowness of her family's expectations, Alevi decided, after studying for a few years in Istanbul, to study in Cologne and then Berlin. Her relationship to the German past was one of only indirect concern. She did not hold the young Germans responsible for the deeds of their parents. At first she answered the questions that Germans asked her about her Turkish background, but began to notice that people did not ask further. "They had an image in their heads, and I did not fit this image" (71). She found that Germans expected her to be Turkish and were convinced that she had been in Germany for a long time, since she seemed so integrated. After living in Germany for six years, she began to seek out other Turks in order to inform herself about their situation. Her identity as a Turk and as a Jew became stronger once she understood herself as a member of a minority in Germany: "I grew up with the consciousness of being a white woman, until I got to know white Germans, who always degraded me to something or another, whether it was a member of an underdeveloped country, an underdeveloped culture, or because of my hair color" (72). She compares herself to Black women and empathizes with their situation, since her appearance sets her apart from "white" women in Germany.[21] In her interview, "Hier bin ich zur Türkin gemacht worden" (Here I was made into a Turk), Alevi describes how she began thinking about the meaning of identity when confronted by the situation of the Turkish minority in Germany and the tragic history of the Jews. "But in the German society I was confronted with [my Jewishness], until I at some point understood that it is apparently impossible here to be a citizen of the world" (65).

Like Alevi, Gila Wendt experienced the sensation of otherness based on her appearance, an experience she describes in her interview, "Manchmal lasse ich die Leute lieber in dem Glauben, ich sei aus Indien und nicht aus Israel" (Sometimes I let people think that I am from India and not from Israel). She is a Jew of non-German background for whom her Asian Indian background plays a decisive role in her self-identity. Wendt's family moved to a kibbutz in Israel from India in the 1950s. Her father, a Communist and a Jewish intellectual, was fascinated by the idea of a voluntary socialism as practiced in the kibbutz. Wendt was born in 1952 in Israel and came to Berlin in 1980 to study. In her interview, Wendt describes her encounters with Germans: "People see that I must come from somewhere else and they ask me quite rhetorically, where I come from" (*Nach der Shoa,* 31). In Germany, she often does not say she is from Israel, since she has no desire to become embroiled in undifferentiated discussions about Israel. In India she says she is from Germany for the same reason; to avoid the discussions about Israel. In Germany, she often experiences the same surprised glances that Alevi describes, since her appearance is "Western."

Conclusion

As the comments of the women in *Nach der Shoa geboren* indicate, German unification has not only transformed the actual living situation of Jews living in Germany, but also the meaning of Jewish culture in Germany. At the same time that Jewish culture is celebrated and "recovered," attacks against Turks, asylum seekers, and others perceived to be "foreigners" has risen. People whose appearance is perceived to be "Jewish" by individuals or groups in the radical right are also targeted. The increase in outward racism and anti-Semitism, although not solely a product of unification, runs parallel to the increased media and scholarly attention that Jewish culture and history is presently receiving. The current relations between German and Jews are marked by an "inability to become free of one another, since the Germans and the Jews became a pair in Auschwitz, whom even death cannot separate" (Honigmann, *Nach der Shoa,* 39).

Although one must be cautious in drawing conclusions from randomly collected interviews, *Nach der Shoa geboren* sheds light upon the meaning of Jewish identity in German society today and the ways in which this meaning is instrumentalized in debates not only about the public commemoration of the Jews killed by the Nazis, but also about the consequences of present-day anti-Semitism for German-Jewish relations. For example, one of the editors, Jacoby, distrusts the motives of non-Jewish Germans who show great enthusiasm for Jewish culture, learn Yiddish and Hebrew, play klezmer music, or act in plays based on Yiddish theater (interview with author, January 16, 1995). She traces this development not only to the controversial events of the mid-1980s, but also to a misunderstanding by Germans about the needs and feelings of Jews living in Germany today. The artificial revival of Jewish culture is a painful reminder of its destruction. "With all the appropriation of 'Jewish' space, I barely have any breathing space left" (Jacoby, interview with author, February 4, 1995).

The Germans' dedication to preserving or reviving European and Eastern European Jewish culture that was destroyed by their parents and grandparents is perhaps commendable, but the degree to which they expect their enthusiasm to absolve them from their responsibility to work through German history and, more recently, German-German history, makes their motives suspect. As Baader puts it in her essay, "Zweierlei Befreiung": "How can one, for everything in the whole world, live such a life that is a denial of one's own life, that legitimizes itself solely out of the past? Do the dead want us to live out our lives as living memorials?" (*Nach der Shoa,* 17). Consequently, like many of the other Jewish women who describe their experiences in the collection, Baader is at once the object of the German gaze and the forgotten subject of her own culture. Similarly, the presence of Jewish immigrants in Germany both legitimizes a national discourse about the "good" German and undermines the desire of some Germans to adhere to archaic notions of German citizenship. Jews in Germany are as much a part of the imaginary German nation as they are absent from it. They are often part of the imagined community of a multicultural German nation as "figures" rather than as living participants.

Issues of German nationality are a concern for many of the women, especially in relation to the anxiety of how their presence may be used by the proponents of an unburdened national German identity to legitimize Germany as a multicultural state. While some Germans would prefer to support nationalistic movements for the purpose of creating a Germany free of non-Germans or, at least, to establish a German identity free of the burden of the atrocities committed by their grandparents and parents, others strive to present Germany as an open society, a "foreigner friendly" rather than "foreigner unfriendly" community. A recent article entitled "The New Germans" in one of Germany's leading magazines, *Stern*, is a case in point. Color photos of seventeen young "foreign-looking" Germans, whose parents came to Germany as soldiers, guest workers, or refugees, accompany captions about their relations to Germany and to their German citizenship. A flag representing the country in which one or both parents were born also accompanies each photo, thus signaling that national ties other than German constitute the identity of those portrayed. Although the "new" Germans, for the most part, claim Germany as their home and feel proud to be German, they are often seen by Germans as non-Germans or are praised for their "good" German language skills by Germans who are surprised to hear a nonwhite person speak fluent German. Thus darker skin color is often seen by white Germans as a sign of non-Germanness. Interestingly, none of the seventeen young Germans is Jewish.

For the Jewish women represented in *Nach der Shoa geboren*, Jewishness is not necessarily a visible sign of difference. Jewish identity carries with it another sense of "foreignness" than that described by the non-Jewish "new" Germans depicted in the *Stern* article. And the experience of those Jewish women shows that unless they mention their Jewish identity, they can pass as non-Jewish Germans, as long as they are not perceived to be a member of a non-German ethnic group or do not speak German with an accent. The foreignness of Jews in Germany is then not physical per se, even though the metaphorical and anti-Semitic image of the Jew is represented as physical.[22] Rather, the present-day image with which Jews have to contend is a combination of anti-Semitic and philo-Semitic projections and the functionalization of Jewish culture in Germany's public sphere. They are also critical of the legal definition of German citizenship, which excludes those people without German lineage, in a country that represents itself officially as a multicultural society.

The contradictory nature of the marginalization experienced by Jewish women not only within German society, but also within groups or organizations with whom they would seem to have a "natural" alliance, such as the Jewish Community or the German women's movement, not only demonstrates the heterogeneity of Jewish female experience in Germany;[23] in addition, it confirms their determination to risk exposure as Jews in order to make their presence felt as active members of German society. The self-descriptions by Jewish women indicate that they are very much a part of the discourse on German national identity after unification—both as agents and as unwilling alibis for creating an image of reconciliation. As the experiences of the women show, "Jewishness" in present-day Germany is as much a representation honed by the national discourse among "Germans" as it is a self-definition by Jews living in Germany today. Consequently, the fall of the Wall has not put an end to discourses on Jewish identity in Germany, but rather has raised more questions than political and academic discourse can answer.

Notes

1. See Domansky, Preisler, and Seeligmann ("What Keeps the Jews in Germany Quiet?"). In addition to articles and newspaper reports, German television and radio programs have dedicated many of their talk and news shows to this topic. See, for example, "Denkmalstreit." This roundtable discussion with, among others, Lea Rosh, a major supporter of the building of a Holocaust memorial in the proximity of the bunker in which Hitler committed suicide, looked at the pros and cons of memorials for the process of commemoration. Consequently, the representation of the Third Reich and the experiences of the victims killed under Nazi rule has become the focus of remembrance. See also Friedlander, Hartman, and Young.

2. See Domansky for an in-depth analysis of the handling of the Nazi past in both the former GDR and the former FRG.

3. Michael Daxner, a critic of the current drive among Germans to achieve reconciliation, sees the "new love of Jews" to be a "backward hope of salvation." He says, "It is no virtue under the constant compulsion to remember, to act as though one were interested in Jewish culture for the sake of the Jews. What I criticize about the new love of Jews is that it is in reality a backward hope of salvation: if we show an interest in you now we can then be really concerned about what we have lost. Namely, we have lost your culture and now we have the right to be appalled but please, accept our gestures of reconciliation" ("Nur wer vergessen will"). All translations of German texts are my own, unless otherwise specified.

4. The monthly newsletter *Top. Berlin International* published by the Berlin Senate's Office for Social Affairs, for example, provides information about various initiatives to combat xenophobia and to promote intercultural cooperation. The number of private and public initiatives is astounding and would seem to contradict the general impression that Germans ignore xenophobia.

5. See Adelson and Suhr. Those works published in Germany on "other" others are often edited and written by Germans who fall into this category, many of whom are women. See Oguntoye, Opitz, and Schulz, and Hügel et al. Bade's work on the history and present situation of immigration in Germany is a notable exception.

6. For a discussion of the distinctions among terms that designate differences between Germans and non-Germans, see Bade. Another group for whom statistical information is difficult to access are Afro-Germans with German citizenship. They make up approximately one-third of the total Black population in Germany and may be perceived as foreigners on the street, but are not included in statistics on foreigner or immigrant populations (Campt). See Neudeck for a discussion on the relation between the German constitution and the actual practice of political asylum in light of debates on German citizenship.

7. Work on Jewish women has often been confined to the experiences of Jewish German women who survived the Shoah ("Frauen und Exil") or their history (Baader). One exception is Rapaport's study of the effects of sexism and anti-Semitism on the lives of Jewish women living in Germany today.

8. I would like to thank Jessica Jacoby for providing me with the original interviews that served as a basis for the book and for discussing not only the book's genesis, but also her experiences as a Jewish woman in Berlin. Quotations from the book are cited parenthetically in the text as *Nach der Shoa*, with the page number. Citations from the original interviews are cited as "interview," with the page number. The interviews were conducted by the editors of *Nach der Shoa geboren* for the most part in 1992. Unfortunately, because of space constraints, most of the interviews were not published in their entirety or were only summarized by the editors in the volume.

9. According to 1993 figures, 6.8 million foreigners make up 8.5 percent of the total population of Germany, 1.8 million of whom are Turkish. Approximately 1.5 million of those people counted as foreigners have refugee status ("Report," 16). One needs to view statistics on numbers of foreigners with caution. Given the time lag between the assessment of the actual numbers and publication; the various methods of counting people as foreigners, cultural minorities, or citizens; and the difficulty of ascertaining multiple identities, the figures must be seen as estimates. Immigrants from the former Soviet Union, many of whom are Jewish, are not generally listed as a separate group in the statistics provided by the German federal government.

10. Many Soviet Jews left their homeland as rising anti-Semitism in the former Soviet Union, brought on in part by the worsening economic and social conditions and the lack of external control previously provided by the central Soviet government, made their lives miserable at school, at the workplace, and on the street. Groups such as Pamjat (Memory) sponsor public rallies against the Jews, whom they blame for the "evils" of Soviet Communism, for taking away jobs, and even for the Stalinistic show trials. Jews living in the Soviet Republic and today in the Russian Federation are required to have the word "Jew" stamped in their passport, thus stigmatizing them publicly. See Burgauer, Miklis, and Duwidowitsch and Dietzel for historical overviews and personal accounts of the immigration of former Soviet Jews to Germany.

11. Although from the East, they cannot be equated with the Eastern European Jews who immigrated to Berlin at the turn of the century and through the 1920s. The latter were largely Orthodox Jews, and they settled in neighborhoods near the center of Berlin, such as the Spandauer Vorstadt or the Scheunenviertel, the very location where the first fifty Jewish families were permitted to live in Berlin under an edict proclaimed by Friedrich Wilhelm I for "protected" Jews in 1671 (Galliner, 20). Since 1989 more than 15,000 former Soviet Jews had immigrated to Germany, and, according to the Jewish Relief Organization in Berlin, the number continues to rise steadily (telephone conversation, March 14, 1995). Thus the official estimates of approximately 40,000 Jews registered with the Jewish community in Germany is in constant flux (Bubis, "Eine neue Ausreisewelle").

12. As of 1992 approximately 100,000 Russian Jews had applied for entry into Germany, despite the difficult process of obtaining and filling out countless forms, translating Russian documents into German, and confirming one's status as a Jew. The entire process can take up to a year, since the entry visa must also be accepted by the consulate in the former Soviet Union. After seven

years of residency the immigrants have the right to apply for German citizenship, under the condition that they give up their Russian passport, since double citizenship is (still) close to impossible in Germany (Miklis, 74).

13. For a polemical discussion about the shortcomings of the German justice system in adequately punishing perpetrators of right-wing violence, see Siegler, Tolmein, and Wiedemann. Although the majority of the neo-Nazi organizations have been declared illegal by the German government, they continue to operate underground, and their "leaders," although often on trial for illegal activities, rarely receive substantial prison sentences or fines (Annaun, 10). See also Bubis, " 'Ich kann nicht sagen.' "

14. More often, issues of "Jewishness" and gender are discussed in literary texts or as cultural metaphors. See Gilman and Remmler, Adelson, von Braun, and Jacoby, "Antisemitismus der Geschlechter."

15. See Leslie A. Adelson's essay in this volume (chapter 9) and her forthcoming article in *Yale Handbook of Jewish Writing in Germany.*

16. Compare Elaine Martin's collection of essays on fascism and German women writers.

17. A newspaper report in *Neues Deutschland,* the organ of the official party (SED) in the former GDR, summed up the project to rebuild the synagogue as follows: "[The plan to rebuild the synagogue] confirms that the ideals of antifascism in the GDR are part of its inevitable reality and that the socialist society is prepared to make the cultivation of Jewish culture and tradition its own" ("Symbolische Grundsteineinlegung für die Neue Synagoge Berlin").

18. Jeffrey Peck's film *Dies ist auch mein Land* addresses this issue. Many East German Jews chose not to identify as Jews, but rather as socialists or Communists. Many of their children, however, have returned to their Jewish roots, in part because of their dissatisfaction with the dysfunctional ideology of the GDR state. See also Genin, Ostow.

19. In 1953, following the Slansky trial in 1952, the SED removed Jews from leading positions in the party or demanded that Jews undergo humiliating processes of self-criticism (Leo, 99). More than five hundred Jews left the GDR, which only began to rehabilitate the Jews after Stalin's death by allowing Jewish organizations to reopen and reinstating Jewish members of the party. See Eschwege for more details on the complicated history of this period of the GDR.

20. Fischer, born in 1943 in England, came to Austria with her parents in 1948. Her mother, originally a Polish Jew, had come to Vienna at the age of seventeen to study applied art. She met Erica's father, a non-Jewish Austrian, in the Communist Union movement. In 1938 the couple emigrated to England, where Erica and her brother were born. Under protest by Erica's mother, the family returned to Vienna in 1948.

21. Other women of non-German ethnic background also consider themselves to be "Black," thus associating discrimination based on skin color with discrimination based on other signs of supposed non-Germanness, such as coming from a developing country or having a foreign accent (Bassiri, 24).

22. One thinks of the significance of circumcision for the identity and recognition of Jewish males, for example. See Gilman, *The Jew's Body.*

23. Jewish women who are not practicing Jews, who are lesbians, or who are insistent upon exposing sexist behavior within the Jewish Community often choose not to register with the Community. See "Die Busengrabscher in der Fasanenstraße." Furthermore, Jewish feminists feel misunderstood by non-Jewish German feminists, whose knowledge about the role of women in Jewish religion is minimal and is often reduced to statements such as "the Jewish religion is patriarchal," instead of a closer examination of the major role that women play within Jewish tradition. Some Jewish women seek alternative communities with women who are non-Jewish Germans, Afro-Germans, or Turks. The Shabbeskreis, a loosely organized group of women with German-Jewish, Kurdish, Turkish, and non-German Jewish backgrounds, was founded by Jacoby to provide an alternative space for women to practice Jewish spirituality and to exchange ideas and thoughts with

one another. Although it broke up one week before the fall of the Wall, the group created a space for Jewish women for whom the rigidity of the official Jewish Community was unacceptable (Jacoby, interview with author, January 16, 1995).

Works Cited

Adelson, Leslie. "There's No Place Like Home: Jeanette Lander and Ronnith Neumann's Utopian Quest for Jewish Identity in the Contemporary West German Context." *New German Critique* 50 (1990): 113–34.

Annaun, Wolf. "Die Braune-Armee-Fraktion." *Die Zeit,* January 13, 1995, 9–11.

Baader, Meike Sophia. "Grenzgängerinnen zwischen den Welten: Jüdische Frauen in Geschichte und Gegenwart." *Babylon* 13/14 (1994): 177–82.

Bade, Klaus J. *Ausländer Aussiedler Asyl: Ein Bestandsaufnahme.* Munich: Beck, 1994.

Bassiri, Nasrin. "Wir brauchen keine großen Schwestern: Die Schwierigkeit, eine 'schwarze' zu sein." *Zitty* 5 (1995): 24–26.

Behrens, Katja. *Die dreizehnte Fee.* Frankfurt am Main: Fischer, 1985.

Bodemann, Michal Y. "A Reemergence of German Jewry?" *Reemerging Jewish Culture in Germany: Life and Literature since 1989.* Edited by Sander G. Gilman and Karen Remmler, 46–61. New York: New York University Press, 1994.

Braun, Christina von. "Antisemitismus und Misogynie: Vom Zusammenhang zweier Erscheinungen." In *Von einer Welt in die andere: Jüdinnen im 19. und 20. Jahrhundert,* edited by Jutta Dick and Barbara Hahn, 179–96. Vienna: Christian Brandstätter, 1993.

Bridenthal, Renate, Atina Grossmann, and Marion Kaplan. *When Biology Became Destiny: Women in Weimar and Nazi Germany.* New York: Monthly Review Press, 1984.

Bubis, Ignatz. " 'Ich kann nicht sagen, ich bin ein cooler Typ.' " Interview. *Frankfurter Rundschau,* February 23, 1995, 7.

———. "Eine neue Ausreisewelle. Spiegel-Interview mit Ignatz Bubis, dem Vorsitzenden des Zentralrats der Juden, über jüdische Einwanderer." *Spiegel* 4 (January 1994): 54–55.

Burgauer, Erica. *Zwischen Erinnerung und Verdrängung—Juden in Deutschland nach 1945.* Reinbek bei Hamburg: Rowohlt, 1993.

"Die Busengrabscher in der Fasanenstraße." *Semittimes* 3, no. 4 (1992): 34.

Campt, Tina. "Afro-German Cultural Identity and the Politics of Positionality: Contests and Contexts in the Formation of a German Ethnic Identity." *New German Critique* 58 (Winter 1993): 109–26.

"Denkmalstreit." *Auslandsjournal.* January 23, 1995, B1.

Dick, Jutta, and Barbara Hahn, eds. *Von einer Welt in die andere: Jüdinnen im 19. und 20. Jahrhundert.* Vienna: Christian Brandstätter, 1993.

Dischereit, Esther. *Joëmis Tisch: Eine jüdische Geschichte.* Frankfurt am Main: Suhrkamp, 1988.

———. *Merryn.* Frankfurt am Main: Suhrkamp, 1992.

———. "No Exit from This Jewry." Translated by Michael Rohloff. In *Reemerging Jewish Culture in Germany: Life and Literature,* edited by Sander L. Gilman and Karen Remmler, 266–81. New York: New York University Press, 1994.

Domansky, Elisabeth. "Die gespaltene Erinnerung." In *Kunst und Literatur nach Auschwitz,* edited by Manuel Köppen, 178–96. Berlin: Erich Schmidt, 1994.

Duwidowitsch, Lyudmila, and Volker Dietzel, eds. *Russisch-jüdisches Roulette: Jüdische Emigranten erzählen ihr Leben.* Zurich: Assmann, 1993.

Eschwege, Helmut. "Die jüdische Bevölkerung der Jahre nach der Kapitulation Hitlerdeutschlands auf dem Gebiet der DDR bis zum Jahre 1953." In *Juden in der DDR: Geschichte— Probleme—Perspektiven,* edited by Siegfried Theodor Arndt et al., 63–100. Cologne: Brill, 1988.

Fischer, Erica. *Aimée & Jaguar: Eine Liebesgeschichte, Berlin 1943.* Cologne: Kiepenheuer & Witsch, 1994.

"Frauen und Exil: Zwischen Anpassung und Selbstbehauptung." *Exilforschung* 11 (1993).

Friedlander, Saul, ed. *Probing the Limits of Representation: Nazism and the "Final Solution."* Cambridge: Harvard University Press, 1992.

Galliner, Nicola, ed. *Wegweiser durch das jüdische Berlin: Geschichte und Gegenwart.* Berlin: Nicolai, 1987.

Genin, Salomea. *Scheindl und Salomea: Von Lemberg nach Berlin.* Frankfurt am Main: Fischer, 1992.

Gilman, Sander L. *The Jew's Body.* New York: Routledge, 1991.

Gilman, Sander L., and Karen Remmler, eds. *Reemerging Jewish Culture in Germany: Life and Literature since 1989.* New York: New York University Press, 1994.

Gilman, Sander L., and Jack Zipes. *Yale Handbook of Jewish Writing in Germany.* New Haven, Conn.: Yale University Press; forthcoming.

———. "Male Sexuality and Contemporary Jewish Literature in German: The Damaged Body as the Image of the Damaged Soul." In *Reemerging Jewish Culture in Germany: Life and Literature since 1989,* edited by Sander L. Gilman and Karen Remmler, 210–49. New York: New York University Press, 1994.

Hartman, Geoffrey H., ed. *Holocaust Remembrance: The Shapes of Memory.* Oxford: Blackwell, 1994.

Honigmann, Barbara. *Roman von einem Kinde.* Frankfurt am Main: Luchterhand, 1986.

Hügel, Ika, et al., eds. *Entfernte Verbindungen: Rassismus, Antisemitismus, Klassenunterdrückung.* Berlin: Orlando, 1993.

Jacoby, Jessica. "Antisemitismus der Geschlechter." In *Differenz Differenzen: Zur Auseinandersetzung mit dem Eigenen und dem Fremden im Kontext von Macht und Rassismus bei Frauen,* edited by Institut für Sozialpädagogische Forschung, 197–230. Mainz e.V. Bielefeld: Karin Böllert, 1994.

Jacoby, Jessica, Claudia Schoppmann, and Wendy Zena-Henry, eds. *Nach der Shoa geboren: Jüdische Frauen in Deutschland.* Berlin: Elefanten Press, 1994.

Klüger, Ruth. *Weiter leben: Eine Jugend.* Munich: dtv, 1994.

Koonz, Claudia. *Mothers in the Fatherland: Women, the Family and Nazi Politics.* New York: St. Martin's Press, 1986.

Leo, Annette. *Briefe zwischen Kommen und Gehen.* Berlin: Basisdruck, 1991.

Martin, Elaine, ed. *Gender Patriarchy and Fascism in the Third Reich: The Response of Women Writers.* Detroit, Mich.: Wayne State University Press, 1993.

Miklis, Monika. "Die Situation der jüdischen Emigranten aus der GUS in der Bundesrepublik Deutschland." In *Jüdisches Leben Heute in Deutschland,* edited by Uri R. Kaufmann, 71–84. Bonn: Inter Nationes, 1993.

Nathorff, Hertha. *Das Tagebuch der Hertha Nathorff: Berlin-New York Aufzeichnungen 1933–1945.* Edited by Wolfgang Benz. Frankfurt am Main: Fischer, 1988.

Neudeck, Rupert. *Asyl: Warum das Boot nicht voll ist.* Düsseldorf: Patmos, 1993.

"Nur wer vergessen will, darf sich erinnern: Ein WDR Funkhausgespräch." *Allgemeine Jüdische Wochenzeitung* 50, no. 3 (February 2, 1995): 15.

Oguntoye, Katharina, May Opitz, and Dagmar Schulz, eds. *Farbe bekennen: Afro-deutsche Frauen auf den Spuren ihrer Geschichte.* Berlin: Orlando, 1986.

Ostow, Robin. "Becoming Strangers: Jews in Germany's Five New Provinces." In *Reemerging Jewish Culture in Germany: Life and Literature since 1989,* edited by Sander L. Gilman and Karen Remmler, 62–76. New York: New York University Press, 1994.

Peck, Jeffrey. *Dies ist auch mein Land.* Film. 1992.

Preisler, Maximilian. "Die Erinnerung als Staatsgebrauch: Ein Gespräch mit dem Holocaust-Forscher James Young." *Frankfurter Rundschau,* January 21, 1995.

Rapaport, Lynn. "The Double Disadvantage—Being a Jewish Woman in Germany Today: Reflections on Jewish Aspects and Speculations on Gender Aspects of Disadvantage." In *Zur Geschichte der jüdischen Frau in Deutschland,* edited by Julius Carlebach, 219–36. Berlin: Metropol-Verlag, 1993.

Remmler, Karen. "En-gendering Bodies of Memory: Tracing the Genealogy of Identity in the Work of Esther Dischereit, Barbara Honigmann, and Irene Dische." In *Reemerging Jewish Culture in Germany: Life and Literature since 1989,* edited by Sander L. Gilman and Karen Remmler, 184–209. New York: New York University Press, 1994.

"Report by the Federal Government's Commissioner for Foreigners' Affairs on the Situation of Foreigners in the Federal Republic of Germany in 1993." Bonn, March 1994.

Seeligmann, Rafael. "Genug bemitleidet: Gegen ein deutsches Holocaust-Memorial." *Der Spiegel* 3 (1995): 162–63.

———. "What Keeps the Jews in Germany Quiet?" In *Reemerging Jewish Culture in Germany: Life and Literature since 1989,* edited by Sander L. Gilman and Karen Remmler, 173–83. New York: New York University Press, 1994.

———. "Wie der Judenschul'." *Der Spiegel* 10 (1995): 62–66.

Seitz, Christoph. "Die Neuen Deutschen." *Stern* 2 (1995): 12–19.

Siegler, Bernd, Oliver Tolmein, and Charlotte Wiedemann, eds. *Der Pakt: Die Rechten und der Staat.* Göttingen: Verlag der Werkstatt, 1993.

Stern, Frank. *The Whitewashing of the Yellow Badge: Antisemitism and Philosemitism in Postwar Germany.* Translated by William Templer. Oxford: Pergamon Press, 1992.

Suhr, Heidrun. "Minority Literature in the Federal Republic of Germany." *New German Critique* 46 (1989): 71–103.

"Symbolische Grundsteineinlegung für die Neue Synagoge Berlin." *Neues Deutschland,* November 11, 1988, 1,4.

Young, James. *The Texture of Memory: Holocaust Memorials and Meaning.* New Haven, Conn.: Yale University Press, 1993.

8 / Hidden Subjects, Secret Identities

Figuring Jews, Gypsies, and Gender
in 1990s Cinema of Eastern Europe

Catherine Portuges

*Where is that fragile line between different cultures, different religions, different
national or personal identities?*

—Agnieszka Holland[1]

In the post-Communist east-central European world of cultural migration and
renegotiated borders, the cultures of film and video occupy an interstitial representational space between politics and art. In a recent example of this positioning, the organizers of the twenty-fifth Hungarian Film Week in Budapest in
February 1994 arranged daily projections of footage produced by Bosnian cam-
eramen from the video collective, SA-Life, determined to bear daily witness to
interethnic violence. In the midst of a heavily programmed festival (twenty-five
features and more than one hundred documentaries), these shocking images
quickly took on an ethical dimension: how many fiction films, when confronted
by the Sarajevo footage, could measure up? In a period of diasporan migrations
that parallel those of World War II, when national and cultural boundaries are
contested and interethnic rivalries subvert dreams of unification, such interventions are important signs that visual culture plays a vital—if still undervalued—
role in cultural life, arguably no less important than the more frequently
discussed imperatives of political stability and economic recovery.[2]

From the privatization of formerly state-owned studios to redefinitions of the very subjects and meanings of cinema itself, few elements of audiovisual practice have remained untouched by what Homi Bhabha has called "the ethnographic minoritization of cultures."[3] That the shift to the market has given rise to painful losses as well as gains seems all too evident, and its effects upon the representation of ethnic, generational, and religious minorities are, I think, worth considering. Foregrounding such issues may, to be sure, be interpreted by some as tantamount to a betrayal of the process of democratization, even, for that matter, a reactionary gesture harking back to the "bad old days" of Communism, recent election results notwithstanding.[4] Yet it is in the deterritorialized terrain of the moving image, I wish to suggest, that the impact of the changes can perhaps most usefully be ascertained (see Portuges, "Seeing Subjects").

To that end, this essay endeavors to mark gender and ethnicity by foregrounding representations of Jews and Gypsies in east-central European— primarily Hungarian—cinema.[5] By exploring the inscription of these voices at the margin—outsiders for a thousand years who have nonetheless been able to sustain their cultural identities against seemingly insurmountable odds—we may also be in a better position to discover the ways in which the subjects of what was known as "the other Europe" negotiate the internal terrain of this difficult transitional moment. For while it has become a commonplace of official policy to assert that ethnic differences, erased or suppressed under Communism, have now reemerged with a vengeance (the "now that the lid is off" theory), closer examination of contemporary cinematic portrayals of Jews and Gypsies, and of the terms of their critical reception, are revelatory as well of the ambivalence and even anguish at the heart of evolving European identities.[6]

By listening to those voices from the margins most often silenced and thus enabling them to be heard, we take an important step toward reinscribing images of lives, communities, rituals, and observances long and conspicuously absent from public view in Eastern Europe, and hence bring them to the center of debate.[7] For in the words of Gyorgy Konrad:

> We are the needy relatives, we are the aborigines, we are the ones left behind—the backward, the stunted, the misshapen, the down-and-out, the moochers, parasites, conmen, suckers. Sentimental, old-fashioned, childish, uninformed, troubled, melodramatic, devious, unpredictable, negligent. The ones who don't answer letters, the ones who miss the great opportunity, the hard drinkers, the babblers, the porch-sitters, the deadline-missers, the promise-breakers, the brag-

garts, the immature, the monstrous, the undisciplined, the easily
offended, the ones who insult each other to death but cannot break
off relations. We are the maladjusted, the complainers intoxicated by
failure. . . . We are irritating, excessive, depressing, somehow unlucky.
People are accustomed to slight us. We are cheap labor; merchandise
may be had from us at a lower price; people bring us their old newspapers as a gift. Letters from us come sloppily typed, unnecessarily detailed. People smile at us pityingly, as long as we do not suddenly
become unpleasant. As long as we do not say anything strange, sharp;
as long as we do not stare at our nails and bare our teeth; as long as we
do not become wild and cynical. (*To Cave Explorers*)

This self-portrait by an "insider," long a dissident Hungarian writer and
president of PEN International, poses trenchantly the question of subject positioning, thereby implicating the Western artist or intellectual who—albeit un-
intentionally—may nonetheless reproduce the very "othering" from which
Jews and Gypsies have suffered for so long. How, then, do filmmakers, including those from Eastern Europe, address, avoid, or inscribe questions of gender,
age, and sexuality? What do their films have to say about national or "postnational" narratives that foreground ethnicity, religious conflict, and collective
memory? For as interrogation of the national has become a trope of postcolonial, post-Communist discourse in transitional and increasingly transnational
economies, the idea of national cinema itself is called into question, its essentializing definitional tendencies balancing uneasily with the porousness of current geopolitical and cultural remappings.[8]

An often ethnocentric Western media has been known to portray the former Eastern bloc as the "other" of the liberal, capitalist West—tribal, sensual,
lawless—a kind of "wild East" lacking historical or cultural specificity, not unlike the ways in which members of dominant East European communities at
times portray or imagine the Gypsies in their midst.[9] Five years into the post-
Communist transition, nationalism and interethnic conflict threaten to destabilize democratization, and a more insidious form of censorship—that of the
marketplace itself, replacing the state censorship apparatus—may yet compromise these efforts. As in Poland and Romania, a revitalized Socialist Party has
been returned to power in Hungary, in coalition with the Free Democrats, an
electoral response that is in part a sign of rising unemployment, poverty, and
inflation almost unknown in the ancien régime and in part a rejection of elements of nationalism in the former ruling party, the Magyar Democratic Forum. Among the most pressing items on the agenda of the new government are

the "media wars," a protracted battle over freedom of expression, defined by unrelenting parliamentary debates over a controversial media law and by the former ruling party's wholesale sackings of radio and television journalists critical of its policies in March 1994.[10] The development of post-Communist independent media—and, by extension, forms of visual expression—has in fact emerged as one of its more problematic and prominent areas of conflict, from issues of freedom of expression regarding questions of minority representation to privatization, fairness, and regulatory mechanisms.[11]

Nonetheless, in spite of a period of disarray within their own national cinemas, an impressive survey of outstanding films and videos from the region— from Bulgaria and Romania, Slovakia and Poland, and the Czech Republic and the former Yugoslavia, among others—could be undertaken here, but that is the topic of a larger project.[12] In any case, the active presence, visibility, participation, and leadership of younger (under forty) directors in this vital phase of cultural transformation endow their project with an even greater sense of purpose and urgency.[13] For some filmmakers who flourished, indeed prospered, under conditions of "inner emigration" fostered by state socialism, a period of grief and mourning followed the end of the cold war and the loss of familiar structures they had resisted by means of the cinematic apparatus. As the inequities, incongruities and disappointments of the post-Communist transformation continue to make themselves felt, new visual narratives—national and transnational, historical and contemporary, experimental and documentary— are being created to address them. The reception of films and videos screened at national and international festivals, from Budapest to Cannes, from Toronto to New York, leaves little doubt that, despite the very real difficulties faced by cinemas from smaller nations, often disparagingly referred to as "minor cinemas," a dynamic visual culture, unafraid of confronting minority social issues, has emerged in the "new Eastern Europe" of the 1990s, a necessarily multicultural, multilingual amalgam.

The interpreter of the moving image does well to note, however, that examination of concurrent representations of multiple cultures within the cinema of a single society (and, for that matter, within a film text or image) can be misleading. What is "multicultural" in one context, for instance, may well have a different resonance in another: multiculturalism in Hungarian debates on nationalism, for instance, is read otherwise than in the United States. For ethnic groups subordinate to a dominant culture, there is, of course, always a certain tension between the desire for integration or assimilation as opposed to separation or isolation. Whereas in the "mosaic" of coexisting groups in the United States a level of assimilation may, according to some, be maintained without necessarily sacrificing one's core ethnic identity, in Hungary the option of assimilation differs to such an extent that some would claim it difficult, if not impossible, to be at once Hungarian and an ethnic minority within Hungary (see Pera, "Imagining Multiculturalism").

By virtue of its extraordinary rendering of the interplay among ethnicity, class, gender, and generation, Ildiko Szabo's award-winning *Gyerekgyilkossagok* (Child murders, 1993),[14] her second feature and one of an increasing number of Hungarian films to be financed in international coproduction, epitomizes this "new wave" of younger-generation filmmaking.[15] One of the many Hungarian directors who write their own scripts, Szabo made several films as actress and costume designer before graduating in 1982 from the Budapest School of Dramatic Arts as a director, going on to make short subjects and documentaries with the famed Bela Balazs Studio. Szabo considers it especially difficult for a woman to be granted the opportunity to shoot a feature film: the Hungarian Motion Picture Foundation's panel of some seventy members, for example, which decides upon film projects to be supported, includes few women; moreover, in her view, individual applicants have a lesser probability of being granted funding in comparison with those who apply as a member of a studio, for under the decentralized, privatized system, studios are no longer directly responsible for the promotion and management of a film, a task that now falls in most cases to the individual director-filmmaker, whose role has inescapably become entrepreneurial.[16]

As the director asserts, "It is not a typically Hungarian film; it could happen anywhere,"[17] thereby raising the question of the national that so preoccupies filmmakers, a sign of the porousness of border crossings that characterize contemporary European and, for that matter, international cinema. Questions raised by critics, filmmakers, and foreign journalists at both the Twenty-fifth and Twenty-sixth Hungarian Film Weeks concerned criteria for defining a "Hungarian" film at a time when, for instance, directors of nearly one-fifth of the features in competition were not of Hungarian origin and when foreign capital made substantial contributions even to those pictures whose directors were Hungarian and interested in "Hungarian subjects." The film's title, *Child Murders*, suggests both the act of killing children and a child killer, its tragic veracity confirmed by the English case in early 1993 of two young children found guilty of having murdered another child, and by other recent internationally reported cases. A strikingly composed, black-and-white portrait of Zsolt, a twelve-year-old boy abandoned by his dissident mother and left to care for his bedridden, eccentric grandmother, herself once a famous prima donna and now a reclusive alcoholic in an impoverished area of Budapest, the film portrays him wandering aimless and alone among secret places along the Danube banks after the daily ritual of bathing and dressing his grandmother. Into his isolated world comes Juli, a young, pregnant Gypsy living in an abandoned railway car; befriending her earns Zsolt rejection and abuse from other children; when Juli miscarries, the two throw the infant into the Danube, and the young Gypsy hangs herself.

For centuries the pariahs of Europe and foreigners in every country, Gypsies (Sinti or Roma, known as Traveling People in Ireland) have been constituted as "the other," objects of fear, scorn, and even loathing, in many cases resisting assimilation, education, and conventional housing. Plagued by European xenophobia since the Middle Ages, both Gypsies and Jews—nonterritorial peoples who inhabited a vast range of the Continent—have been linked by a long history of persecution, culminating in their barbaric murder under the Third Reich. Although Communist rule in the Soviet Union and Eastern Europe officially silenced public expression of deeply rooted ethnic hatred, the recent revolutions in the former Eastern bloc no doubt contributed to the resurfacing of latent prejudices and resurgent nationalism.[18] These diverse Romany groups deploy their identities differently according to whether they are encountering Hungarians, Romanians, Saxons, Jews, Serbs, or Armenians. Now, however, the nature of Gypsy identity itself is undergoing reappraisal, and since the 1980s a pan-Gypsy nationalist movement has come into being, resulting in achievements such as a law passed in Hungary in 1993 that recognizes Gypsies as one of the country's thirteen nationalities. This new self-consciousness has come to mean that, no matter where they may live, Gypsies may see themselves as belonging to the same Romany nation, even though they may not be accorded such status by "host" countries.[19]

Convening in London in 1971, the first World Romany Congress condemned ethnic appellations traditionally applied to Gypsy groups, including *czigany, Gypsy, gitano,* and *zigeuner,* adopting instead "Roma" or "Rom" as a self-chosen ethnonym (see Kurti). Earlier Hungarian ethnographic films and documentaries have preserved the vanishing tradition of Hungarian peasantry, recording as well the experience of urban Gypsies: Pal Schiffer's *Fekete vonat* (Black train, 1970), *Gyuri,* and *Foldi paradicsom* (Earthly paradise, 1983) are now-classic visual anthropological texts on Gypsy life, while *Across the Tracks: Vlach Gypsies in Hungary* represents Gypsies in Northern Hungary as sharing features of Hungarian rural culture with other communities of that region—skill as horsetraders, resentment of the peasantry, and renown as accomplished dancers, singers, and musicians at frequent festive occasions.[20] Tony Gatlif's cinematic tribute to his people, *Latcho Drom* (Safe journey, 1994), suggests the contemporary celebratory spirit of evolving Gypsy identity in a panoramic musical tribute encompassing the variety of Roma music and dance in India, Egypt, Turkey, Romania, Hungary, Slovakia, France, and Spain. This remarkable film of the treasures of Gypsy heritage throughout the world documents the importance of music both as source of solace and as a means of recording history; using virtually no dialogue, the director thus laments the fact that, since the Roma peoples' flight from India a millenium ago, they have been ever-persecuted victims, first of Hitler's death camps and now as the target of increased racism in Eastern Europe. Each country's artists repeat, with variations, the theme of a typical dirge, "The whole world hates us," culminating in the song of a powerful flamenco singer whose words of remorse—"Why does your wicked mouth spit on me? . . . I envy the respect you give your dog"—are made ironic by the defiance of her gaze and voice.[21]

The fragile yet enduring role of cultural memory as another hallmark of Gypsy community is echoed in the Czech film *Elementary School* (Barrandov Studios, 1989), in a script based on the director's father's memoir (with the filmmaker playing the role of his own father), a cinematic autobiography in which a Gypsy boy, encouraged by his teacher, recounts an openly antifascist story of Gypsy bravery. Similarly, Julia Szederekenyi's *Paramicha, or Glonci the Rememberer,* the story of an old Gypsy woman whose power through memory remains undisputed, won first prize for best first feature in the 1993 Hungarian Film Week. Such documentations of the stories of elder Jews and Gypsies living the transition from Communism in Eastern Europe propose a link to contemporary generations often radically separated from the cultural, spiritual, and material lives of their elders. How an aging Gypsy woman sees herself—her daily rituals, family life, and the strategies she has developed to contend with life as a constant outsider—provides invaluable documentation of the survival of these communities for centuries, against the greatest odds.

In *Child Murders,* Ildiko Szabo likewise explores the ironic reversal of fortune that befell those Gypsies who were submitted first to forced collectivization and then privatization, causing unemployment as high as 50 percent in some Hungarian towns.[22] Thus the doubly marginalized status of a Gypsy woman is powerfully inscribed by the filmmaker in a mise-en-scène of brutal, beautifully photographed harshness, as the protagonist endures ultimate isolation as an impoverished social outcast in childbirth.[23] Based on an actual police investigation of a murder by a boy the same age as Zsolt, *Child Murders* creates an unflinching emotional universe of violent economic and social forces, a haunting, tragic narrative that earned the director selection by prestigious international festivals, as well as prizes for best first feature at the 1993 Cannes Film Festival and best director at the 1993 Budapest Hungarian Film Week.[24]

A timely intervention in current discourses of women's ambivalent relationship to the state and to the private sphere, Szabo's current, as yet unrealized, project concerns three divorcing women, based in part on her personal experience and that of her friends: "It's a woman's movie, not necessarily feminist, about what divorce looks like from our point of view," explained the director when I interviewed her in November 1993: "In Eastern Europe, marriage, like life in general, is more brutal than in the West; it's also funnier, more wicked. Hungary holds the record for divorce, and for suicide among young people; for female alcoholics, it is in second place worldwide. These statistics are, I think, serious enough to warrant making a movie about them."[25] Such experiences remain, for the most part, hidden in the secret recesses of personal and family life, resistant to institutional structures of social welfare, and articulated, if at all, primarily through interpretive modes—literature, cinema, and avant-garde art forms, which may well once again become the loci for oppositional strategies and positionings not unlike those they embodied under Communism.[26]

The "younger" generation to which Ildiko Szabo belongs can clearly no longer depend on support from a fully centralized economy organized to protect national film culture; indeed, the opportunity and the necessity of working under such turbulent conditions can be fraught with anxiety and uncertainty, as well as challenge and excitement. These filmmakers are compelled by the need to attract international audiences in an increasingly globalized film culture and at the same time are concerned not to abandon the specifically national concerns of a native audience all too eager to welcome nonnative cultural products. It should be remembered, however, that not all East European filmmakers are equally privileged: many in fact risked their professional reputations, even their lives, in order to make films that spoke out against totalitarian repression, as have so many others, in Bosnia as elsewhere. Still others, in particular those of the Prague Spring era, saw their completed projects shelved for years, some never to be released, or endured imprisonment and exile.[27]

In international festivals focusing on Eastern Europe and held in Moscow and Budapest, Karlovy Vary and Berlin, Toronto and San Francisco, filmmakers, journalists, critics, and other cultural workers have engaged in open debate and heated criticism of their own film industries—now that official censorship is past, they ask, what subjects are needed by our audiences? What paradigms of postnational cinematic practice can be of use? At the Twenty-fourth Budapest Film Week in February 1993, Zsolt Kezdi-Kovacs, director of Magyar Filmunio (the umbrella national film organization), introduced the festival by calling for a new attitude toward cinema: "Making films is not an easy business nowadays. (When has it been?) The general situation is also rather difficult. (When was it easy?) It is a time to appreciate those who have the courage to make films today. Who knows what sort of audience, what sort of world these films are made for? What kind of public will see those films? Who are those people, who still want to look at their own lives, pleasures, and pain, instead of a faraway universe tinted in rose and glamour? I think there must be such an audience. We filmmakers are a mirror to the world, and the mirror must be honest and true" (*XXIV Magyar Filmszemle*, introduction).

Despite their skepticism and, in some cases, private nostalgia for the "good old days" of dependable support for the arts even under Communist restriction, both established and younger filmmakers are confronting the post-Communist moment by taking up, if in some cases only tangentially, once-taboo subjects, and are thereby serving to focus public attention on such repressed, secret, or otherwise uncomfortable topics as the existence of Stalinist labor camps; the persecution of ethnic minorities, Gypsies, and Jews; the persistence of alcohol abuse and suicide; homelessness and the suffering of individuals and families dispersed and dislocated in the wake of war, conflict, and political and economic upheaval.[28]

As the texture of the transition from Communism grows more complex, cultural questions—in particular, those of the past, never far from Hungarian consciousness—begin to emerge, perhaps gradually taking their place alongside the urgent agendas of technology and market economy. As elsewhere in the "new Europe," such questions inevitably acquire a personal dimension, as East Europeans struggle to come to terms with their own complex ambivalence:

identities long suppressed or hidden now given shape, image, and voice by artists and writers intent on uncovering the secrets of a denied past, seeking answers to questions avoided for two generations. Judit Ember's video documentary *And Lead Us Not into Temptation* (*Es ne vigy minket kisertesbe*, Hungary, 1993) speaks eloquently to this search as the filmmaker returns to the provincial Hungarian village from which her family was deported, only to see traces of the home she knew in the silences, denials, and guilty glances of neighbors who knew the family all too well. Discreetly yet insistently, her knowing camera records the undeniable moments of complicity without accusation, filmed in peasant kitchens and village gardens, suggesting that even kind and affectionate people are capable of hatred and tempted beyond resistance by the opportunity to enrich themselves quickly at the expense of others' helplessness. Ember's investigation rewards the patient viewer, who may well conclude that genocide afflicts not only its direct victims but also those who are implicated in its relentless agenda.

It is thus perhaps not surprising that the history and culture of East European Jewry should occupy an increasingly visible place at the forefront of recent cinema in transition. One of the most commercially successful of recent Hungarian features, and Hungary's nominee for an Academy Award, was Robert Koltai's *Sose Halunk Meg* (We'll never die, 1992). Koltai both directs and stars in this autobiographical story of Gyuszi Bacsi, a lovable traveling salesman who frequents the racetrack, charms women of all ages, and manages to survive without worrying too much about money, all the while teaching his naive nephew the ways of the world. A low-budget, lighthearted farce, it outsold even American productions at the Hungarian box office, a prodigious feat in today's market.[29] Framed within the film is a telling scene of "hidden" Jews, in which a young Jewish boy, deprived of religious instruction by his assimilated family, is quickly taught by a young Catholic priest to say a prayer in Hebrew as his beloved uncle lies dying nearby. Although the film is set in the 1950s, the scene is readable as a comment on the renaissance of Judaism in a country whose Jewish community was decimated by the Holocaust, and where now members of a "third generation" of children and grandchildren of survivors, intent on recovering their lost and suppressed traditions, compete for coveted places in elite Jewish schools.[30]

The reference to a suppressed Jewish past in Koltai's 1992 film becomes, in films produced between 1993 and 1994, a more sustained investigation of Jewish history and culture—from ethnographic explorations of prewar village life to fictionalized reenactments of the experience of Hungarian Jews during the Holocaust.[31] One of the most important recent central European films to foreground hidden Jewish identity is *Why Wasn't He There?* (*Senkiföldje,* literally translated as "no man's land," 1993), directed by Andras Jeles, one of Hungary's most talented and original filmmakers, long a contestatory force in contemporary Hungarian cinema.[32] Based on the fictitious diary of a thirteen-year-old Jewish girl living in the countryside at the time of the persecution of Jews in Hungary, the summer of 1944, the film uses Auschwitz and the Gulag, fascism and dictatorship to interrogate human fate. Born in 1947, Jeles is tormented by "the immutability of the concentration camps. . . . We have not left Auschwitz behind, nor can we ever do so. We are in Auschwitz, it is impossible to extricate ourselves from it. This came as a revelation to me as I woke up one fine day. It was frightening to recognize that this is the real problem. It is this burden . . . that the period carries."[33]

Inviting comparison with *The Diary of Anne Frank,* the film portrays Eva's interior life and point of view to relate the slow disintegration of her family and home and the increasing hostility of the world outside. Intercutting newsreel footage and dream sequences—in which Eva imagines herself as the confidante of Dickens's David Copperfield, a fellow victim of humiliation and persecution—with episodes from her daily life, *Why Wasn't He There?* evokes the vitality and charm of a young girl's consciousness despite her apprehensions of the approaching disaster of extermination. The young protagonist observes the succession of unfolding horror: her uncles taken into forced labor, the growing food shortages, a bicycle confiscated, German soldiers filling the streets, the ubiquitous yellow star, and, inevitably, her own family forced into the Budapest ghetto, all rendered through the distorting lens of anxiety that shapes the daily life of this provincial petit bourgeois family.

Among the film's most memorable characters are that of the grandmother, whose gradual descent into madness from hatred and jealousy is a cinematic tour de force, and the mute servant girl, whose unearthly moan accompanies the family's transport to Auschwitz. Jeles's work is followed with devotion by Hungarians deeply appreciative of his ability to weave a complex mesh of Hungarian cultural, historical, and literary references. This contemplative cinematographic achievement is a fitting commemoration of the fiftieth anniversary of the destruction of Hungarian Jewry in which, between May and July 1944, more than four hundred thousand people were deported to perish in

Auschwitz.[34] *Why Wasn't He There?* is a courageous—if flawed—attempt to portray the unrepresentable, a cinematic endeavor that has proved daunting even to such extraordinary and experienced filmmakers as Krzystof Zanussi and Andrzey Wajda. Even Jeles's sensitively cadenced fictional sequences cannot match the power of documentary in its tyrannical objectivity.[35]

The dreamlike inscription of history, memory, and experience in Jewish Eastern Europe is, in fact, an important part of 1990s Hungarian and, for that matter, East European cinema: some eight hundred thousand Jews survived the war in Eastern Europe or returned afterward, not including the millions who lived in Stalin's Soviet Union (see *Jewish Heritage*). Under the Communist regimes, the story of the Jews was largely the story of their absence from cinema, for they had all but vanished from the Soviet screen even before World War II. Few Jewish characters appeared in films produced after the war by Hungary and Romania, the two other nations with the largest surviving Jewish minorities; in Poland, once home to three million Jews, Jewish characters occasionally played supporting roles in movies of wartime suffering. With Eastern Europe's largest and most assimilated Jewish population, outside of Russia, Hungary produced a few films with discreetly Jewish characters before the mid-1980s. Gyula Gazdag's masterful and influential *Package Tour* (*Tarsasutazas*), a 1984 documentary of Hungarian Jews revisiting the former concentration camps where they had been imprisoned, received little critical attention in Hungary following its release, indicating the extent of resistance to his uncompromising insistence on recovering the history of Hungarian Jewry a decade ago.[36] Even Imre Gyongyossy and Barna Kabay's *The Revolt of Job* (1983), the first Hungarian film to focus on the wartime deportation of the Jews, was only shown to foreign critics after the filmmakers themselves arranged a special screening. Most characteristic of the early 1980s was *Daniel Takes a Train,* directed by Pal Sandor, who, as a child, had lived through the liquidation of the Budapest ghetto.

Judit Elek's *Tutajosok* (Memoirs of a river, 1990), the first post-1989 Franco-Hungarian feature coproduction to explicitly denounce Hungarian anti-Semitism and the first to be made from an explicitly Jewish viewpoint, takes as its subject the first serious outburst of anti-Semitism in Hungarian history—the Tiszaeszlar trial (which had incidentally also formed the basis for *The Trial,* G. W. Pabst's "rehabilitation" film made in Austria in 1948). Waiting more than two decades, since her film student days, to tell this suppressed story of the presumed disappearance and ritual murder of a young Christian girl in the 1880s and the subsequent trial that anticipated the Dreyfus case, positioning liberals against anti-Semites, the director confesses that she "couldn't have done it [earlier] because . . . it was impossible then to speak openly about anti-Semitism. . . . We must know who we are, and what we can become; and that is impossible without digging down to the roots and uncovering our past."[37] The film was received with polite acknowledgment in Hungary, but, like Gazdag's *Package Tour,* it has since enjoyed a limited international afterlife in festivals and series.[38]

Like other films from Eastern Europe's celebrated cinematic tradition of historical allegory, *Memoirs of a River* draws unmistakable parallels between the case and the Stalin show trials of the late 1940s and 1950s and, thus, in some sense, utilizes the dream reconstruction strategies deployed by other filmmakers, as I have noted. Elek interrogates the Tisza River to uncover its buried memories, as does the Soviet documentary filmmaker Alexander Rodnjanski in a film on the fate of the legendary Raoul Wallenberg, the Swedish diplomat who saved the lives of tens of thousands of Hungarian Jews, only to disappear into Stalin's prison camps.[39] Perhaps the most lyrical example of hidden Jewish identities comes from Budapest-based filmmaker Peter Forgacs, who has refashioned home movies of the 1920s to 1940s, shot by citizens of the Hungarian capital, into *Privat Magyarorszag* (Private Hungary, 1989), a diary of elegiac portraits of the city drawn from film archive collections and a poetic ethnography that provides a riveting look at a culture about to vanish.

Among the memorable segments in this series is *Dusi es Jeno,* a moving portrayal of a Jewish couple whose carefully documented, ordinary lives punctuated by domestic rituals—meals taken on a terrace, regular promenades with a beloved dog—evoke the lives of thousands who perished and whose lives vanished without benefit of recorded images. Forgacs's *Notes of a Lady* (*Egy Urino notesza*), part 8 of this video diary edited from hundreds of hours of home movies, foregrounds sequences of a beautiful Jewish baroness's life in Hungary in the 1930s and 1940s both to signify and to mourn irrevocable personal, familial, and historical loss. It would seem that only now, after half a century of massive psychic denial and emotional "splitting," is the fate of East European Jews beginning to be more fully integrated through the mourning process and the grief work of cinematic representation.[40]

As the nations of Europe move toward a transnational European federation, both West and East struggle to reconcile issues of national, ethnic, and religious identity forgrounded in these and other contemporary documentary and feature films, in experimental and avant-garde video, and in the critical and theoretical discourse produced by print media devoted to culture and the arts. Yet cultural misreadings and archaic enmities further threaten to destabilize efforts toward intercultural progress in today's hybridized, globalized audiovisual era. Nonetheless, these films widen the space of discourse between East and West, while continuing to reassess the anxious effects of the post-Communist moment—isolation, alienation, and denigration—as well as the ethical, political, and artistic resistance to which these traumatic shifts have given expression.

As multivocal, multilingual texts, they speak equally as persuasively of strong national and historical traditions, of literary and artistic accomplishment, and of private concerns and personal stories, thereby refusing a strategy of containment. Voicing an emergent transnationality, the Gypsies, Jews, and other minorities on screen and behind the camera embody a new generation, one that is artistically, psychologically, and intellectually unafraid to confront the ghosts of the past and prepared to step forward into uncharted terrain. Most important, they deconstruct hegemonic readings "from the center," while attesting to the vitality of filmmakers' and videographers' role as intellectuals, as critics of existing systems, and as individuals in search of the personal, familial, and collective identity so long inaccessible to view. Visual artists capable of representing the fears and sufferings, anxieties and desires, losses and triumphs of their compatriots, these filmmakers and their subjects deserve encouragement and recognition for the persistence of vision and the unflagging commitment to a renewed cinema even in the face of threats to its very existence. These diasporic, haunted ethnoscapes, with their incomplete past and deceptively affluent present, call into question the meaning of borderlands: the mythical meanings of "elsewhere" are captured in films of refugees waiting with suspended steps in deterritorialized zones—Gypsies and Romanians, Turks and Croats, Albanians and Kurds awaiting permission to escape from an old nightmare, to make a new dream come true.

To revisit East European cinema today is to emerge with a deepened appreciation for the tenacity, perseverance, and sheer talent of its multigenerational practitioners, who are necessarily alert to the dangers of remarginalization, even effacement as a distinct cultural entity.[41] That they refigure private remembrance and public memory of once hidden subjects and secret identities in the 1990s gestures toward a vision of the future, transmuted and recreated in an apocalyptic, migratory moment marking the centenary of cinema itself, and one that might yet become the great subject of European cinema in the third millenium.

Notes

1. Agnieszka Holland, as quoted in the *San Francisco Chronicle,* July 5, 1991, in the context of the controversy over her 1991 film *Europa Europa,* when the Commission of German Film Functionaries declined to nominate any German film for an Academy Foreign Film Award in October of that year.

2. See Timothy Garton Ash, "Journey to the Post-Communist East." Situated at the crossroads between East and West, Hungary is no exception, as indicated by 1993 legislation on the entry, stay, and immigration of foreigners, as well as commitments undertaken in the United Nations Charter, the Universal Declaration of Human Rights, and the Closing Act of the Helsinki Conference. The spirit of these measures is perhaps well summed up in the phrase: "Adjust or else; welcome to [insert country's name]; now go home." For international debate on aspects of these problems, see *L'Evénement européen: Minorités—quelles chances pour l'Europe?* (Paris: Seuil, 1991), 16; and *Le Messager Européen,* no. 5 (Paris: Gallimard, 1991).

3. Homi Bhabha, "Anxious Nations, Nervous States," lecture given at the American Comparative Literature Association Conference "Borders/Exiles/Diasporas," Humanities Center, Claremont Graduate School, Claremont, Calif., March 1994.

4. For a provocative feminist critique of Communism, see Slavenka Drakulić's *How We Survived Communism and Even Laughed.* The author is a respected journalist and cultural commentator in Croatia whose work has appeared in the *Nation,* the *New York Times,* and the *New York Review of Books,* among other publications. She was a founding member of the executive committee of the first network of Eastern European women's groups and is on the advisory board of the Fourth International Interdisciplinary Congress of Women; her other books include *Holograms of Fear, Marble Skin,* and *The Balkan Express.*

5. Balancing a system of partial state support for cinema with privatized and restructured studios, Hungarian cinema has managed to maintain a consistent level of film and video production since 1989, when restructuring of its former centralized mechanism began. My qualification here is intentional, with due respect to those filmmakers from the region whose outlook on the future of their industries is far more pessimistic than mine. For a more detailed analysis of the post-Communist transition in the visual cultures of East Central Europe, see Catherine Portuges, "Border Crossings."

6. It is not insignificant that conflict within the audiovisual sphere in fact threatened to derail the GATT talks, resulting in exclusion of this area from the agreement negotiated in December 1993. At the same time, U.S. domination in the realm of the moving image, poses a potent threat to economies of the moving image as the proliferation of Hollywood movies far outstrips the drawing power of domestic European product, an audiovisual assault not limited to the former Eastern bloc: in France, long the strongest of European national film industries, the consequences of an American "hostile takeover" have prompted aggressive legislative measures, backed by the European Parliament, to protect French-language cinema as a "national" industry. Such responses to the Hollywood threat to the multicultural languages of cinema offer an instructive paradigm for post-Communist comparative film analysis. See Catherine Portuges, "Between Worlds."

7. For indispensable discussions of nationalism and ethnicity, see Anderson, Bhabha, Campeanu, Crowe and Kolsti, Featherstone, Fox, Gellner, and Hobsbawm.

8. According to a United Nations report, human migration has doubled since 1989, reaching crisis proportions greater than ever before in human history. Some one hundred million persons are living outside the country of their birth, and these numbers are said to be increasing on an unprecedented scale (broadcast on BBS World Service, July 6, 1993, WFCR Public Radio, Amherst, Mass.). Zygmunt Baumant defines the raison d'être of the national state as "designed primarily to deal with the problems of strangers, not enemies" (quoted in Featherstone, 153). The notion of "stranger" is a category of cultural significance introduced by the German sociologist Georg Simmel, yet where there is interethnic conflict, "stranger" becomes tantamount to "enemy" (see Laszlo

Kurti). Together with many of his colleagues, the distinguished director Rajko Grlic, from the former Yugoslavia, has found that the desire to continue making films in his native Croatian, or in multilingual coproductions, is faced with overwhelming obstacles, against the odds of dominant linguistic structures.

9. Here the Soviet Union long occupied the position of dominant colonialist superpower, the Orwellian "Big Brother" that served, albeit secondarily, to suppress questions of minority rights and ethnic antagonisms. Ostensibly in the service of international socialism, such suppression may undoubtedly be held to account in part, I suspect, for the relative absence of open civil conflict in the region until the 1980s. I acknowledge with gratitude the opportunities to present and explore some of these ideas through invitations from the following: "Dis-locations: Transnational Migration and Cultural Loss in East European Cinemas of the 1990s," American Association for the Advancement of Slavic Studies, Honolulu, November 1993; "National Cinemas Revisited: Hungarian Cinema in the 1990s," Ohio University, Athens, October 1993; "Cinema and Sexuality in Post-Communist Eastern Europe," the Humanities Center of the Claremont Graduate School, Claremont, California, November 1992; "Nationalism in Socialist and Post-Socialist Cinemas," Society for Cinema Studies, New Orleans, February 1993; "Ethnicity, Nationalism and Culture in East-Central European Cinema," Center for the Humanities, Wesleyan University, Middletown, Conn., May 1992; and "The Status of Hungarian Cinema," Art Gallery of Toronto Symposium: "Thirty-five Years of Hungarian Cinema," November 1991.

10. The First Annual Conference on Individual Rights versus the State, "The Development of Rights of Access to the Media," was held in Budapest under the auspices of the Central European University Institute for Constitutionalism and Legislative Policy, June 19–21, 1993. For a useful discussion of the proceedings, see Lauren Pera, "Access to the Media." The acrimonious firing of 129 employees of Hungarian Radio and Television precipitated the resignation of Dr. Elemer Hankiss, former president of Hungarian Radio and Television and now a professor at Georgetown University, Washington, D.C.

11. The extent to which Gyula Horn, prime minister of the Socialist Party, can address these questions and make credible the post-Communist Left remains to be seen. He has, to be sure, demonstrated an astonishing adaptive capacity, passing from the role of orthodox Communist to that of enlightened reformer. His father, a factory worker in Budapest's "red" district of Angyalfold, was a militant in the clandestine Communist Party against the authoritarian regime of Admiral Horthy in the 1930s; imprisoned, he was executed by the Nazis in 1944. Two of Gyula Horn's six brothers perished in diametrically opposite causes: one was killed by the Vietminh while serving in the Foreign Legion in Indochina; another, a dedicated Communist, was lynched by a crowd during the Hungarian insurrection of 1956 (cf. Yves-Michel Riols).

12. I am grateful to Katherine Cornell for inviting me to participate in "Cinema in Transition: Recent films from East and Central Europe," a festival/symposium presented by the New School for Social Research, New York City, April 1993. There I had the opportunity to view outstanding work and discuss issues with filmmakers from Hungary, Romania, Albania, Poland, Bulgaria, Slovakia, and the former Yugoslavia, including Dusan Makaveyev, Feliks Falk, Gyula Gazdag, Mircea Danieluc, Arpad Sopsits, Yvette Biro, Radu Nicoara, Robert Glinski, Rajko Grlic, and Srdjan Karanovic, among many others.

13. In 1993, for example, the Twenty-fourth Annual Hungarian Film Week awarded its top prizes to women directors for Best Picture and Best First Film, categories whose honors have traditionally been awarded to male colleagues.

14. *Child Murders* was written by Szabo, based on an idea by Zsuzsa Toth; the film has been screened at a number of international festivals, including Budapest, Toronto, Montreal, Thessaloniki, Munich, Puerto Rico, Taiwan, Sidney, Chicago, San Jose, Sundance, and the Directors' Fortnight, Cannes 1993. Szabo was awarded the Gene Moskowitz Prize for Best Film and Best Direction (Budapest), and, at the Cannes Festival, the Federation Internationale de la Presse Cine-

matographique (FIPRESCI) awarded the film its Prix de la Critique Internationale/FIPRESCI for "its uncompromising portrayal of contemporary social conflicts and for its pure and audacious style" (my translation).

15. The film was coproduced by Kulturelle Filmförderung, Nordrhein-Westfalen, Germany. Like other colleagues of her generation, Szabo fears that Eastern Europe may be surrendering its culture through indiscriminate joint ventures and media institution takeovers by foreign capital, yet at the same time acknowledges that it must look toward the West for vital support and assistance.

16. For selected further contextual and analytic studies of Hungarian and East European cinema, see Catherine Portuges (*Screen Memories*), Daniel J. Goulding, Istvan Nemeskurty, David Paul, and Graham Petrie.

17. These and subsequent citations are transcribed and translated from an interview I conducted with the director during the Eighteenth Toronto Festival of Festivals, Toronto, September 1993. I am indebted to Ildiko Szabo for sharing with me her insights on the status of women in Hungary and Eastern Europe, her own personal vision of the art of cinema, and her dynamic perspectives on culture and human relationships.

18. Overt hostility toward Jews and unrestrained persecution of Gypsies have erupted throughout the region, where new, democratically elected governments at times tolerated or even condoned such xenophobia. According to an April 1991 survey on democracy and economic reform in Eastern Europe, conducted for Freedom House and the American Jewish Committee, anti-Semitism persists in Hungary, Poland, the Czech Republic, and Slovakia, but "Jews are regarded less unfavorably in all these countries than several other groups studied, particularly Gypsies. . . . The strongest negative attitudes by far were expressed toward Gypsies." A Times Mirror poll found that "the one sentiment that unites Western and Eastern Europe is hatred of Gypsies" (see Toby F. Sonneman).

19. An association of Gypsy mothers, for instance, has been formed in Hungary, as have similar groupings of Gypsies throughout east-central Europe.

20. According to cultural anthropologist Laszlo Kurti, such treatments of Gypsy life fail to note "the profound and wide-ranging social issues of Gypsy life: emerging Gypsy consciousness and systematized formal history: the alarming drop-out rate in public schools; intensified Hungarian ethnocentrism and racism, with its concomitant marginalization; alcoholism; police brutality; unemployment, crime and prostitution in Gypsy communities."

21. *Latcho Drom* (Safe journey), color, 103 min., in Romany with English subtitles, New Yorker films.

22. Traditionally the last hired and first fired, Hungary's Gypsies, for example—estimated at 500,000 in a country of 10.5 million inhabitants—are said to have an unemployment rate as high as 40 to 45 percent, three times the national rate of nearly 14 percent (from *Budapest Business Journal,* November 1993).

23. See Eva Hoffman, *Exit into History,* 246. In this intimate narrative journey, the author of *Lost in Translation* returns to her Polish homeland and to five other countries—Hungary, Romania, Bulgaria, Slovakia, and the Czech Republic—in a vivid odyssey through landscapes in the midst of change. Her bicultural perspective is useful in probing and illuminating the complex politics and representations of the region. Here, the figure of the Gypsy may stand as well for Hungarians in general: a common joke has it that, at the end of the war, Hungarians used to say, "If the Germans conquered us, we were Jews; if the English, we were Hungarians; if the Russians, we were bourgeois"—in other words, female gender alone was not a requisite for the experience of discrimination.

24. In an interview with the director at the Toronto Film Festival, September 9, 1993, Ildiko Szabo emphasized the difficulty of finding a Western distributor for a film of such uncompromising solemnity; she was among the few East Europeans to be invited to the Sundance Film Festival in 1994. A number of East European filmmakers have since found distributors for their work, such as Mircea Dianieluc's *The Conjugal Bed* (Romania, 1992). Szabo's film was shot for 17 million

Hungarian forints (approximately U.S. $200,000), although the director was responsible for her own publicity, costume design, and scenery.

25. According to Szabo, five of her closest women friends between the ages of twenty-two and forty-five have committed suicide: "The reasons, of course, are very complicated, and I have my own theories as to why this happens. But the worst part is that it's not considered a particularly tragic event. Some see therapists but in Hungary that's not very common. I feel it's important to judge a country by how much it spends on education, health care, and the military. Now the changes are very sad; people are concerned in an unhealthy way with money, whereas under socialism money was a taboo topic—guilty, sinful, substituted by favors and privileges. Because of its history, the whole country has learned to steal, from spare parts to the black market. . . . Finally, it's easier just to collapse into it [*konnyebb megszakadni*]." The working title of her project is *Csajok* (Bitches). See Barbara Einhorn, *Cinderella Goes to Market,* one of the first book-length theoretical summaries of pre- and post-Communist developments through the perspective of gender.

26. An early post-Communist Hungarian documentary on the problem of suicide is *Hold Me Gently in Your Strong Arms* (1991), constructed of interviews with mental patients and their psychiatrists, allowing each to speak openly of their experiences and fears. Neither speculative nor explanatory, the film positions itself as a philosophical meditation on suicide as a long-accepted Hungarian "solution to the problems of life," and as such constitutes an intervention in the process of engaging issues forbidden under Communism.

27. For a more detailed analysis of the post-Communist transition in the visual cultures of east-central Europe, see Catherine Portuges, "Border Crossings."

28. Like war correspondents, film and video makers have sustained serious injury and even lost their lives while documenting revolution and other warfare (here I include those on the streets of Prague in spring 1966, in Budapest in 1956, and throughout the former Soviet Union and Eastern Europe in 1989 and thereafter).

29. The film's U.S. premiere took place in Santa Monica, California, in October 1993, and was sponsored by the association of Hungarian-American filmmakers, Cinergi.

30. Since 1989, two Jewish primary schools have been in operation once again in Hungary—The American Foundation School, with compulsory Jewish religious observance, and the Communal (Lauder) School, favoring a more modern religious approach. According to researchers Eva Kovas and Julia Vajda, "Perhaps the most important element [of contemporary Hungarian collective Jewish identity] . . . derives from the Shoah and from anti-Semitism. This new generation rediscovers or mobilizes its ethnic identity, returning to the symbols of its grandparents or creating new ones. The Hungarian Jewish renaissance can also be considered a third generation phenomenon. . . . Parents belonging to the second or third generation can once again send their children to Jewish schools, freely practise their religion and join Jewish cultural associations or Zionist organizations. Following the collective silence of the grandparents and their desire to assimilate, they can now own their Jewish identity or create pluralist forms of identity without precedent in 20th century Hungary" (89–90). Other researchers have corroborated the generational divide. Gene Lichtenstein writes in the *Jewish Journal of Greater Los Angeles:* "One man explained that he was puzzled by his grandchildren who had turned toward things Jewish. They were concerned about taking on a Jewish identity, seeking to learn more about the culture and the history. Where they get this from, I don't know, he said not quite approvingly"(33).

31. Since 1990, several Jewish film festivals have been held in Hungary, an important departure from the past.

32. Jeles is perhaps best known for his 1979 feature, *Kis Valentino,* a daring film about juvenile delinquency; his *Dream Brigade (Alombrigad*), a film of the early 1980s about the plight of Hungarian workers, was shelved in 1983 because of its daring portrayal of angry workers' unrest under socialism.

33. *Filmvilag,* May 1993, cited in Gergely Bikacsy.

214 / *Catherine Portuges*

34. Randolph L. Braham's prodigiously documented history, *The Politics of Genocide: The Holocaust in Hungary*, remains the authority of record on the subject. I wish to thank Michael Berenbaum, project director of the U.S. Holocaust Memorial Museum, for the opportunity to participate in a day-long symposium and commemoration on May 22, 1994, and especially Chana Michaeli and Paul Zador, Washington, D.C., for sharing with me their own experiences as Hungarian child survivors.

35. Such a documentary is *Chasing Shadows* (1994), a fifty-minute video production on the Jews of Beregova (in the Carpathian Mountains and now in the former Soviet Union), narrated in the first person by Rabbi Hugo Gryn, which juxtaposes rare archival documentary footage from Jewish prewar village life with sequences of Jews returning for the first time to their ancestral lands. The rabbi tells a well-known joke to illustrate the shifting political, cultural, and geographical boundaries with which his countrymen had to contend: "I was born in the Austro-Hungarian Empire, educated in Germany, trained in Hungary, worked in the USSR, and never left Beregova!" The interdependent, self-contained, and productive community of Beregova once boasted six synagogues where now there remains only one, for thirty-five Jewish communities. *Chasing Shadows* is distributed by the National Center for Jewish Film.

36. Personal communication with the director, Los Angeles, September 10, 1994. It should be noted that *Package Tour* has nonetheless received international distribution and favorable critical reviews at film festivals.

37. Judit Elek, *Tutajosok: filmforgatokonyv* (Budapest: Magveto Konyvkiado, 1990). The director graciously granted me an interview following the premiere of the film at the Budapest Film Week in February 1991, and again in February 1995, when she informed me of a forthcoming film project on the life of Elie Wiesel (in production).

38. A recent example is the January 1994 festival organized by the Jewish Museum and the Film Society of Lincoln Center, "Artists, Activists and Ordinary People: Jews in Twentieth-Century Europe."

39. The Jewish context of Elek's film recalls the Slovak-French coproduction by the Slovak director Juro Jakubisko, *Birds, Orphans, and Fools* (1969), shelved for twenty years and repremiered at the Karlovy Vary (in former Czechoslovakia) festival in 1990, as well as *Terezin Diary*, a 1989 U.S.-Czechoslovak coproduction directed by Don Weissman. Jakubisko's tragicomic love story concerns survivors of World War II in love with the same Jewish woman, a reference to the chaotic turn of events in Czechoslovakia after Soviet tanks suppressed the revolt of the Prague Spring in 1968. Weissman's films offer a tribute to the children who survived the Jewish ghetto of Terezin, interweaving their recollections and diaries into an autobiographical narrative, a Holocaust memorial.

40. Jewish film festivals and screenings have been organized to focus on the hidden history of East European Jews by the U.S. Holocaust Museum, Washington, D.C.; the Jewish Museum, New York City; and the Fourteenth Jewish Film Festival, San Francisco.

41. Gyula Gazdag, especially, provided the vital perspectives of an insider as a distinguished film director, former director of the Hungarian Film Academy, Budapest, and currently visiting professor of film at the University of California, Los Angeles.

Works Cited

Anderson, Benedict. *Imagined Communities*. London: Verso, 1983.

Ash, Timothy Garton. "Journey to the Post-Communist East." *New York Review of Books* 41, no. 12 (June 23, 1994): 13–20.

Bhabha, Homi K., ed. *Nation and Narration*. London: Routledge, 1990.

Bikacsy, Gergely. "Spectacle and Stammer." *Hungarian Quarterly* 34 (Winter 1993): 166–68.

Braham, Randolph L. *The Politics of Genocide: The Holocaust in Hungary*. Rev. and enl. ed. 2 vol.

New York: Rosenthal Institute for Holocaust Studies/Graduate Center, City University of New York; Boulder, Colo.: Social Science Monographs, 1994.

Drakulić, Slavenka. *How We Survived Communism and Even Laughed.* New York: Harper, 1993.

Campeanu, Pavel. *The Origins of Stalinism: From Leninist Revolution to Stalinist Society.* Translated by Michael Vale. Armonk, N.Y.: Sharpe, 1986.

Crowe, David, and John Kolsti, eds. *The Gypsies of Eastern Europe.* Armonk, N.Y.: Sharpe, 1991.

Einhorn, Barbara. *Cinderella Goes to Market: Citizenship, Gender and Women's Movements in East-Central Europe.* New York: Verso, 1993.

Featherstone, Mike, ed. *Global Culture: Nationalism, Globalization and Modernity.* London: Sage, 1990.

Fox, Richard G., ed. *Nationalist Ideologies and the Production of National Cultures.* Washington: American Anthropological Association, 1990.

Gellner, Ernest. *Nations and Nationalism.* Ithaca, N.Y.: Cornell University Press, 1983.

Goulding, Daniel J., ed. *Post New Wave Cinema in the Soviet Union and Eastern Europe.* Bloomington: Indiana University Press, 1989.

Hobsbawm, Eric J. *Nations and Nationalism since 1780: Program, Myth, Reality.* Cambridge: Cambridge University Press, 1990.

Hoffman, Eva. *Exit into History: A Journey through the New Eastern Europe.* New York: Viking, 1993.

XXIV Magyar Filmszemle. Budapest: Magyar Mozgokep Alapitvany, 1993.

Jewish Heritage in Central Europe. Published by Jewish Service. Vienna: Institute for the History of Jews in Austria, 1991.

Konrad, Gyorgy. *To Cave Explorers from the West.* New York: Penguin, 1987.

Kovas, Eva, and Julia Vajda. "Jewish Schools, Jewish Identity." *Budapest Review of Books* 3, no. 2 (Summer 1993): 89–90.

Kurti, Laszlo. "The Anthropology of Kazakhs, Tuvans and Gypsies: 'Disappearing' Socialism Visualized." *Budapest Review of Books* 4, no. 1 (Spring 1994): 7–15.

Lichtenstein, Gene. "Hungary: Forging a Jewish Identity." *Jewish Journal of Greater Los Angeles* 9, no. 28 (1994): 33.

Nemeskurty, Istvan. *Word and Image: History of the Hungarian Cinema.* Budapest: Corvina Kiado, 1985.

Paul, David., ed. *Politics, Art and Commitment in the East European Cinema.* New York: St. Martin's Press, 1983.

Pera, Lauren. "Access to the Media," *Budapest Review of Books* 3 (Spring 1993): 88–89.

———. "Imaging Multiculturalism," *Budapest Review of Books* 3 (Summer 1993): 84–85.

Petrie, Graham. *History Must Answer to Man: The Contemporary Hungarian Cinema.* Budapest: Corvina Kiado, 1978.

Portuges, Catherine. "Between Worlds: Re-Placing Hungarian Cinema." In *Before the Wall Came Down: Soviet and East European Filmmakers Working in the West,* edited by Graham Petrie and Ruth Dwyer, 63–70. New York: University Press of America, 1990.

———. "Border Crossings: Recent Trends in East and Central European Cinema." *Slavic Review* 51, no. 3 (Fall 1992): 531–35.

———. *Screen Memories: The Hungarian Cinema of Marta Meszaros.* Bloomington: Indiana University Press, 1993.

———. "Seeing Subjects: Women Directors and Cinematic Autobiography." In *Life/Lines: Theories of Women's Autobiography,* edited by Bella Brodzki and Celeste Schenk, 338–50. Ithaca, N.Y.: Cornell University Press, 1988.

Riols, Yves-Michel. "Les Deux Vies de Gyula Horn," *Le Monde,* June 1, 1994.

Sonneman, Toby F. "Old Hatreds in the New Europe: Roma after the Revolutions." *Tikkun* 7, no. 1 (1994): 49–50.

9 / Migrants' Literature or German Literature?

Torkan's Tufan:
Brief an einen islamischen Bruder

Leslie A. Adelson

What does it mean to assume, as I have reason to do, that many readers are completely unfamiliar with the name Torkan? Born in Iran in 1941, this West German citizen published three German novels between 1983 and 1987 alone.[1] Is this author's talent merely too new to have been fully discovered yet? Or does this blind spot in the eye of contemporary *Germanistik* (the conventional study of Germanic languages and literatures) point to certain epistemological problems in the ways in which West German literature of the 1980s is itself conceptualized? My discussion of Torkan's first German novel, *Tufan: Brief an einen islamischen Bruder* (Tufan: Letter to an Islamic brother, 1983), in the context of the so-called *Migrantenliteratur* (migrants' literature) seeks to prove the latter to be the case.

Anyone familiar with West Germany's *Ausländerbehörden* (the authorities responsible for dealing with foreigners) knows that peoples and persons from other countries are, first and foremost, categorized. These official categories in turn provide the criteria according to which the authorities determine the legal status of one's residence in the Federal Republic. Rather than merely alluding to

general background information on the tenuous situation of many foreign
writers on West German soil, the reference to German bureaucracy invokes a
structural analogy to what we as Germanists do when we quibble over the appropriate terminology with which to categorize literature written in German by
persons of "non-German" origin.[2] Are these texts *Gastarbeiterliteratur* (guest-
workers' literature)? *Gastliteratur* (guest literature)? *Ausländerliteratur* (foreigners' literature)? *Migrantenliteratur* (migrants' literature)? To what extent do we
consider them a "legitimate" part of the German literary landscape? While the
deliberations on the advantages and disadvantages of the terms commonly used
are numerous,[3] they are not necessarily all that varied. For they most often entail an effort to encapsulate the literature in question, to demarcate and regulate
the boundaries between it and a body of literature considered by implication to
be inherently German. This is true even for someone like Harald Weinrich,
who asks in his preface to one anthology whether there really is such a thing as
a German literature and who elsewhere pleads for "a German literature *from
outside*" (Ackermann, *Als Fremder in Deutschland,* 9, my emphasis).[4] Belying
this gesture of welcome is the problematic assumption that literature by foreigners living in the Federal Republic becomes German by virtue of the fact
that it teaches Germans something about the Germans themselves (Schaffernicht, 12; Weinrich, "Gastarbeiterliteratur," 12). This ethnocentric focus is reflected in the notions of "integration" and "enrichment" that circulate in the
debate on the so-called migrants' literature, as well as in the ways in which the
presence of particular themes is seen as sufficient to categorize a given text in
this manner.

When one claims that foreign writers have been successfully integrated
into German literature,[5] one sees this writing as an addendum, an appendage
that attests to cultural pluralism. What goes unchallenged are the epistemological and political implications of the notion that German literature has at its
center something distinctly German to which foreign elements can be added or
subtracted. As Heidrun Suhr contends, whether one rejects these elements or
embraces them, "dominant ideology is not threatened by this mere addition of
ethnic and cultural difference" (102). The same problem arises when we encounter the well-intentioned assertion that "migrants' literature" contributes to
the mutual "enrichment" of non-German writers and German readers (Ackermann, "Integrationsvorstellungen," 38; Heinze, 11; Özkan and Wörle, 8). In a
period of rising xenophobia one applauds the desire to treat authors of non-
German origins as equal partners in cultural exchange, but what if West Ger-

man society (as is the case) does not guarantee this premise of equality in real terms? The truth is that the notion of what is German in contemporary literature is as much contested on critical and scholarly terrain as is the designation of the Federal Republic as a *Vielvölkerstaat* (multiethnic state) in the public arena. The debate about what to call literature by non-Germans living in West Germany obscures the point that what is at stake is not the appropriate category for the foreign "addendum" but the fundamental need to reconceptualize our understanding of an identifiably German core of contemporary literature.

Even in the realm of intercultural *Germanistik,* an apparent openness to other cultures and a stated commitment to respecting difference are undermined by the belief that foreigners understand German literary texts in their respective hermeneutic frames of reference, while the *object* of their understanding remains German literature (see Wierlacher, 3–28). The need to question the constitutive premises of the literary phenomenon to be understood becomes immediately clear when we consider that the foreigners practicing intercultural *Germanistik* in their *Deutsch für Ausländer* (German for foreigners) classes also contribute on occasion to the production of German literature.[6] Not a mask to be tried on or put down at will, to be added to or subtracted from an allegedly essential body of German texts, difference is constitutive of contemporary West German writing.

Of course, the concept of difference was in the 1980s, and continues to be, highly contested. As noted, scholars and critics who argue that integration has taken place in the realm of German letters acknowledge cultural difference as something that "enriches" but does not in any fundamental way challenge what is "German." Self-appointed representatives of the *Gastarbeiterliteratur* downplayed their own diversity in favor of the unity of international worker solidarity,[7] while individual German and non-German authors alike have appealed to a human community in which specific differences are not seen as decisive. Günter Wallraff's *Ganz unten* (Down and out), for example, has been accused of generalizing the paradigms of oppression such that the historical specificity of race, culture, and politics is obfuscated (Teraoka, "Talking 'Turk,' " 119). Writers such as Aysel Özakin, Suleman Taufiq, and Jusuf Naoum (from Turkey, Syria, and Lebanon, respectively) have protested against having their authorship defined in terms of their national origins; they and others resent being reduced to stereotyped subjects of exotic interest for German readers and critics.[8] Reflected in this microcosm of West German culture of the last decade is a postmodernist tension between (white) Western intellectuals' desire to acknowledge third world difference and third world authors' resistance to having their differences homogenized for easy assimilation.[9] If what some have termed a "mendacious cultural 'pluralism' " can accommodate difference only as an enriching, exotic afterthought, then the political conditions of otherness in their social, historical, and cultural specificity can only be obscured and certainly not negotiated.[10]

One of the ways in which the embrace of German critics has disarmed otherness is to reduce all differences to something vaguely signified by a T-word. While it is true that the editors of the self-proclaimed "guest-worker literature" publication series asserted in 1983 that "we all become Turks" (Teraoka, "*Gastarbeiterliteratur,*" 89 n. 29; Heinze, 76),[11] this programmatic focus on the unifying transnational factor of economic oppression does not account for the widespread impression among writers of non-German background that their writings are taken seriously in the publishing world only if their otherness can be considered somehow "Turkish." For many writers, especially the non-Turkish ones, this means not being taken seriously at all; for Turkish writers it means being reduced to a national stereotype. As Torkan bitterly complained in a 1989 interview, foreigners' concerns are automatically assumed to be "Turkish" concerns.[12] By the same token foreigners' literature is assumed to be "Turkish" literature in Germany. A passage from Torkan's *Kaltland* (Cold country) highlights the proximity of this purportedly critical category to a racist erasure of difference among foreigners: "Ausland ist kein Land, aus dem alle Ausländer kommen. . . . Wir brauchen nur schwarze Haare zu haben und etwas dunklere Haut—schon sind wir alle Türken" ("A foreign country" is not a country that all foreigners come from. . . . All we need is black hair and slightly dark skin— already we're all Turks) (133). In Torkan's case her very name has led her to be mistaken for a Turkish writer.[13] I would argue that such "mistakes" are an attempt to render decipherable differences that many Germans read as "undecipherable hair": an ethnocentric response to the growing presence of racial, ethnic, and cultural others in West German society.[14] The dual gesture of welcoming difference with one hand and domesticating it with the other (by reducing all othernesses to a single signifier) can perhaps be seen as the humanist counterpart to the expressly racist denunciation of the Turkish population in West Germany.[15]

Although scholars may note that the "growing body of works by foreigners is difficult to categorize" (Suhr, 78), it remains to be emphasized that this difficulty arises when one posits difference as an aesthetic category rather than as a constitutive factor in the production and reception of contemporary German literature. For there can be no single category that could account adequately for the multiplicity of differences that clamor to be heard and read. Once we imagine difference to reside *outside* an alleged German center, as implied by the term *Migrantenliteratur* or any of the other contending terms, we preclude rigorous analysis of the construction of differences in their social, historical, political, and cultural specificity.[16] Even the categories of race, gender, and ethnicity are—as "fixed categories"—not especially helpful, since these phenomena, too, are constructed and imbricated in different ways for different groups at different times in different places.

This is the point at which I think it makes sense to discuss Torkan's novel *Tufan: Brief an einen islamischen Bruder* as representative not of "migrants' literature" in Germany but of West German literature of the 1980s. I propose this precisely because the author and the novel satisfy none of the standard criteria usually applied to literature written by foreigners living in the Federal Republic. Torkan was born and raised in Iran but is now a West German citizen. Although she emigrated in 1964, she did not enter Germany as a "guest worker," nor did she come from a country from which German capital ever recruited such labor; neither did she come seeking political asylum. Furthermore, unlike the authors most frequently associated with the so-called *Migrantenliteratur*, Torkan is a woman. Suhr is one of the few scholars to direct any substantive attention to non-German women writers in this area, but even most of her examples are Turkish authors (Suhr, 79, 92–96).[17] Of course, Turks do constitute the largest single national minority in the Federal Republic, and Suhr is appropriately critical of the "research on minority women" in which the "unquestioned standard of comparison is the white German woman" (92). The flip side of this standard, the difference on which it seeks to thrive (in this context), is the stereotype of the oppressed Muslim woman. And in the Western imagination Muslim women are, by definition, victims of oppression.[18]

Tufan challenges such expectations on all counts, expectations fostered by the very themes commonly ascribed to "migrants' literature": "Das Leiden am bundesdeutschen Alltag, das die Migrantenliteratur kennzeichnet, wird von der Suche nach Identität begleitet" (The search for identity accompanies the suffering experienced in everyday life in the Federal Republic; this suffering characterizes the migrants' literature) (Heinze, 51). At the crux of this statement is the characteristic supposition that *Migrantenliteratur* can be identified as such because it depicts displaced foreigners struggling with a loss of personal identity, cultural homeland, and political orientation in the face of German "coldness," hostility, and bureaucracy. When scholars, editors, and publishers stress this commonality in foreigners' experiencing themselves "between two cultures,"[19] they inadvertently reinforce the following ethnocentric premises: (1) Power emanates from a German "center" (however negatively assessed), and all "marginal" positions are structurally the same, such that any differences among or within these positions are not seen as making a difference worth recognizing as such. (2) Questions of personal identity, cultural homeland, and political orientation arise only once a foreigner enters Germany. The multidimensionality that has shaped such a person's development even prior to arriving in the Federal Republic is ignored or negated, as is the condition of nonsynchronicity that characterizes the lives of many of these authors and their characters. That is to say, while negotiating their encounters with West German society, they are also always negotiating—even if only in their consciousness— points of reference that lie outside Germany.[20] Obviously many German texts by foreign writers, including Torkan's second novel, *Kaltland,* do address themes seen as typical of *Migrantenliteratur.* My contention here is that a literary historical analysis that reduces non-German German literature to this type of thematic inventory relies on a myopic perspective. For one striking example, let us take the categorical obsession with the chilling absurdities and indignities of West German bureaucracy so often depicted in the so-called migrants' literature. Consider that German colonialists of the late nineteenth and early twentieth centuries read their extensive bureaucratic administration as a sign of German superiority over native peoples in Africa and the South Pacific (Castles et al., 99, 196). Literary depictions of foreigners' collisions with present-day bureaucracy are not merely about German "coldness" or postmodern alienation; they can and should be read as confrontations with a legacy of German racism and colonialism. Yet, if these non-German authors who deviate from the norms, themes, and attitudes established for them by critics and scholars of *Migrantenliteratur* are denied critical recognition as voices of German literature (or even *Migrantenliteratur*), then we are doomed to keep retracing the same tired steps in the hallways and waiting rooms of a bureaucratic scholarship that effectively administers literary phenomena when it could be engaging them.

The German-language novel that led me to these deliberations has fallen between the categorical cracks of literary criticism. For the autobiographical account of her traumatic childhood and adolescence in Iran and her adult attempts to grapple with the ghosts of this past, Torkan lends the first-person voice of the narrator to a female persona named Asar. Although Asar the woman and writer resides in West Germany, that country and its citizens are not objects of representation in *Tufan*. They are relegated to the periphery of the narrator's consciousness. By choosing to write about something other than Germans mistreating foreigners, by only tangentially touching on life in Germany, Torkan forces her readers to acknowledge at least one world that exists outside German daily life for some of those living in it. In this way the "foreigners" that people her text take on much more complex contours and histories than if they were reduced to the status of *Fremdkörper* (foreign bodies) in German culture, as is frequently the case in the so-called migrants' literature. Entitled "Remembrance" and "Return," the two halves of the novel vacillate between Asar's first-person narration of events recalled and an attempt at direct dialogue with Tufan, the younger brother of the title. The dialogue it hopes to enact can only be imagined and incomplete, since Asar began to write two months after learning of her brother's imprisonment by the Khomeini regime. Direct exchange is an impossibility: "Ich schreibe dir, stellvertretend für dich an mich" (I write to you, in your place, for you, to me) (5). By the time she learns of his execution, Tufan has already been dead for two months. Communications between brother and sister are marked by a jagged nonsynchronicity that Torkan does not try to erase; it is constitutive of their personal history and hence of Asar's narrative.

The brother characterized as "das ständige Opfer" (the perpetual victim) and "das ewige Opfer" (the eternal victim) at the novel's conclusion (161, 174) had been incarcerated and tortured by SAVAK, the notorious security organization of the shah. As an admirer of the Islamic modernist philosopher Ali Shari'ati (1933–77), however, he was appalled by the murderous excesses of the fundamentalist revolution in 1979. Accused of being an antirevolutionary by the people he had previously supported actively, Tufan was then imprisoned, tortured, and finally shot by the Khomeini government. No fundamentalist martyr for the revolutionary cause, Asar's brother seems to be a victim of the cruel twists of history.

All of this makes sense (in a senseless sort of way) unless we have read the first half of the novel. Here we see Tufan as anything but a victim. A religiously fanatic male child and adolescent in an educated, middle-class doctor's family, he torments his older sister with repeated brutal beatings and nearly constant surveillance. His control over her life (whether she may go to school, where she walks, whom she sees) is so extensive that she begins to internalize it. On one occasion, when she notices he is not behind her on a public street as she had thought, she screams out for him in desperation (100). In this section Asar is "das ständige Opfer" (11). Her "crime," which is preceded by her punishment and humiliation, is that she is a girl, destined to become a woman. The thinking that allows Tufan's parents to permit or encourage him to beat "the witch" (11) in his sister relies on the Muslim tenet that fathers, brothers, and husbands are responsible for safeguarding the moral and sexual integrity of their female relatives. Even though Asar's family is not especially religious (her father is a politically "enlightened" man), we can recognize in their treatment of her the view that a girl on the threshold of womanhood embodies *fitna* (chaos, disorder), which threatens to besmirch the honor *(namus)* of the men responsible for policing her virtue. As the author of *Beyond the Veil* notes, "The Muslim faces two threats: the infidel without and the woman within" (Mernissi, 43).

Yet, as recent scholarship on women in the diverse worlds of Islam details, there is no "uniform concept of female personhood in Muslim culture" or history (Waines, 653).[21] Whether women in Islam are seen as objects or subjects, as weak, inferior, and sinful or powerful, equal, and venerable depends greatly on how one interprets the sacred text of the Qur'an as well as on the historical vicissitude of Muslim societies. Torkan's own text enacts many of the conflicting positions held with regard to Muslim women. The author creates a narrator who bears witness to her own objectification and victimization as a female without becoming an object or remaining a victim of her brother's fanatic cruelty. Rejecting the role of the exotic other in both European and Iranian eyes,[22] Asar speaks as a subject, albeit one who does not yield to a false sense of assimilation or harmony. The experiences recounted in *Tufan* come close to coinciding with the last phase of the Pahlavi period, from 1953 to 1979, when women's rights and roles were especially hotly contested in Iran.[23] For the relatives who come to visit and judge Asar upon her first visit "home" in thirteen years, she is "eine gebrochene Frau" (a broken woman) (151), "broken" in their eyes because she does not satisfy the traditionalist image of Islamic woman. Yet, as the novel makes clear in ways too numerous to elaborate here, women's lives in late-twentieth-century Iran are characterized by the nonidentity of the actual and the ideal. Women live between these cracks.

Torkan's narrative takes these cracks as its foundation. It is not her German that is "broken" but the avenues of conscious memory and discourse. Weaving the stories that she does construct out of the "fragments" (44) available to her, Asar speaks of and through "Splitter der Erinnerung" (splinters of remembrance) (127). Although she is "des Erinnerns müde" (tired of remembering)

(158), the letter to Tufan attests to her determination not to be silent and not to forget. This is *Trauerarbeit* (labor of mourning), in which one woman tries to make sense of her traumatic experiences and her brother's tortured life without filling in the gaps with imagined information, wishful assumptions, or forced meaning. This female subject is the author of Torkan's narrative, not its master or mistress. Her stories are punctuated by questions of the past and the present. Asar ceases to be her brother's victim by telling her story, which is and always will be their story, as well.[24] However, there are no neatly knotted threads in this Persian-German tapestry. While the novel concludes with Asar's pronouncement that she will no longer judge her brother, she does not speak of forgiving, loving, or even knowing him.

This complex relationship between brother and sister, in which the roles of victim and victimizer are only seemingly transparent, has a number of implications for German literature. First of all, Asar is not represented as the victim of German bigotry. This automatically sets the novel apart from most of the so-called *Migrantenliteratur* and demands that we see this non-German woman with open eyes. Her "victimization" occurs in a completely different locale, which now enters our field of vision. And yet, Asar is not portrayed as a victim at all. Persecuted, humiliated, and brutalized as a girl and young woman, the narrator establishes herself as the subject of her personal history. Perhaps not so surprisingly, the only group of German readers to pay any real attention to *Tufan: Brief an einen islamischen Bruder* were West German feminists, who applauded the book because they thought it so clearly depicted Asar as a victim.[25] This is indicative of an ethnocentric bias that sees the novel only as an indictment of Islamic patriarchy, which Western feminists "know" to be oppressive to Muslim women; it is also indicative of an epistemological blind spot that has often prevented West German feminists from acknowledging women's historical role as anything other than pure victim.[26] With regard to modern German history in more general terms, one can also argue that an *Opfer/Täter* (victim/perpetrator) problematic has been central to much of West German literature since the demise of the Third Reich. This is certainly not to say that the way Torkan posits the relationship between victim and victimizer is *directly* applicable to literary representations of Nazis and their victims, but it does raise questions as to how we choose to understand, theorize, and narrate relations of power and oppression under changing historical and political circumstances. German literature by persons of non-German origins is one field in which such questions can and should be fruitfully discussed.

There is a poignant irony in Torkan's first novel when on two occasions German literature figures as a nonthreatening entity to the Pahlavi regime. Because of his anti-Shah activities, Tufan is not allowed to study engineering. The government considered a politically innocuous pursuit, such as *Germanistik,* more appropriate (68). Many years later, when Asar and her brother are together again in Tehran, the purchase of a banned book by Ali Schari'ati is made possible by a false cover bearing the alleged author's name: "Hinrich Bell" (152). The reference to Böll echoes in my mind as I read Asar's thoughts from 1977, when she returns to sites where she once witnessed acts of political oppression: "Diktatur? Unterdrückung? Menschenverachtung? Der Alltag ist kein Zeuge des Verbechens" (Dictatorship? Oppression? Disdain for humanity? Everyday life bears no witness to crime) (127). Are these not the sentiments of Alfred Schrella returning to Germany in 1958 in *Billard um halbzehn* (*Billiards at Half Past Nine*)? The refusal to engage the political implications of how we choose to understand *Migrantenliteratur* confines its role "in nonthreatening terms within the field of cultural pluralism."[27] The novel I have discussed here "threatens" us in the sense that reading it challenges us to rethink our perspectives on "otherness" in the interlocking realms of contemporary German aesthetics, culture, and politics.

Notes

This chapter first appeared in *German Quarterly* 63.3–4 (Summer–Fall 1990): 382–89. Reprinted by permission.

1. Torkan Daneshfar-Pätzoldt publishes under the single name Torkan. The Perspol-Verlag in Hamburg published all her novels from this period: *Tufan: Brief an einen islamischen Bruder* (1983); *Kaltland: Wah'schate Ssard* (1984); and *Allnacht: Roya und Alp-Traum* (1987). I would like to express my thanks to the Alexander von Humboldt Foundation and The Ohio State University for generously supporting the research on which this article is based.

2. Throughout this article I will be using the adjectives "German," "non-German," and "foreign," as well as the corresponding nouns. The reader is asked to imagine quotation marks around these terms at all times, as my purpose is to question any assumption of fixed definitions.

3. See, for example, the following articles in *LiLi: Zeitschrift für Literaturwissenschaft und Linguistik* 14 (1984): Kreuzer, "Gastarbeiter-Literatur, Ausländer-Literatur, Migranten-Literatur? Zur Einführung," 7–11; Weinrich, "Gastarbeiterliteratur in der Bundesrepublik Deutschland," 12–22; Ackermann, "Integrationsvorstellungen und Integrationsdarstellungen in der Ausländerliteratur," 23–39; and Seibert, "Zur 'Rettung der Zungen': Ausländerliteratur in ihren konzeptionellen Ansätzen," 40–61. Other relevant contributions include the main entries, prefaces, and afterwords to *Zu Hause in der Fremde,* ed. Schaffernicht; *Als Fremder in Deutschland,* ed. Ackermann; *In zwei Sprachen leben,* ed. Ackermann; *Türken deutscher Sprache,* ed. Ackermann; *Eine Fremde wie ich,* ed. Özkan and Wörle; *Eine nicht nur deutsche Literatur: Zur Standortbestimmung der "Ausländerliteratur,"* ed. Ackermann and Weinrich; *Chamissos Enkel,* ed. Friedrich; and *Über Grenzen,* ed. Esselborn. See as well Ackermann, " 'Gastarbeiter'literatur als Heraus-

forderung"; Weinrich, "Um eine deutsche Literatur von außen bittend"; Heinze, *Migrantenliteratur in der Bundesrepublik Deutschland: Bestandsaufnahme und Entwicklungstendenzen zu einer multikulturellen Literatursynthese;* and Reeg, *Schreiben in der Fremde: Literatur nationaler Minderheiten in der Bundesrepublik Deutschland.* Particularly helpful in sorting out the political implications of the various efforts to categorize literary texts by "non-German" writers are Teraoka's "*Gastarbeiterliteratur:* The Other Speaks Back" and "Talking 'Turk': On Narrative Strategies and Cultural Stereotypes"; as well as Suhr, "*Ausländerliteratur:* Minority Literature in the Federal Republic of Germany."

4. See also Weinrich, "Um eine deutsche Literatur von außen bittend." In "Gastarbeiterliteratur in der Bundesrepublik Deutschland" he even says that "German literature of the present is no longer produced by Germans alone" (12). In "*Gastarbeiterliteratur:* The Other Speaks Back" Teraoka discusses the "colonialist" implications of the Munich project to promote the writing of German literature by foreigners (see esp. 97–98). Both Weinrich and Ackermann have been extremely influential in this marketing endeavor.

5. See especially Ackermann, "Integrationsvorstellungen," 38. Even Ackermann acknowledges the discrepancy between levels of literary and social integration (32). For some more cogent thoughts on this discrepancy, see the Seibert article in the same volume.

6. The anthologies edited by Ackermann and Weinrich (see n. 3) came into being under the auspices of the Institut für Deutsch als Fremdsprache der Universität München.

7. See Teraoka's trenchant analysis of different approaches to *Gastarbeiterliteratur* in "*Gastarbeiterliteratur:* The Other Speaks Back." On this particular point see also Seibert, 44–45, and Suhr, 79–83.

8. Suhr (99) problematizes Özakin's extreme position. See Taufiq, "Natürlich: Kritik," in *Eine nicht nur deutsche Literatur,* ed. Ackermann and Weinrich, 75, and Naoum, "Aus dem Getto heraus," in ibid., 79.

9. Suhr takes a strong stand against this type of assimilation: " 'The Other' is not a homogeneous phenomenon and has definitely nothing in common with the sense of 'otherness' invoked by Western intellectuals struggling for identity" (98).

10. See JanMohamed and Lloyd's introductions to the two special issues of *Cultural Critique* on minority discourse: *Cultural Critique* 6 (1987): 5–12, esp. 9–10, and *Cultural Critique* 7 (1987): 5–17. For an insightful commentary on the epistemological implications of postmodernism, see Kumkum Sangari, "The Politics of the Possible," 157–86.

11. The editors cited here are Franco Biondi and Rafik Schami of the now defunct *Südwind Gastarbeiterdeutsch* series.

12. I conducted this interview with the author on October 13, 1989, in Hamburg.

13. This impression was explicitly conveyed to me in the 1989 interview.

14. The term "undecipherable hair" comes from an account by the Guatemalan journalist Julio Godoy of his experiences in West Germany over the last few years. See Godoy, "Nowhere at Home," 16.

15. Stephen Castles et al., in *Here for Good: Western Europe's New Ethnic Minorities* (100), notes that Turks bear the brunt of the growing racism in the Federal Republic. The obvious point to be made here is that the Turks themselves do not constitute a uniform other. On this topic see Ruth Mandel, "Turkish Headscarves and the 'Foreigner Problem': Constructing Difference through Emblems of Identity," and Czarina Wilpert, "Religion and Ethnicity: Orientations, Perceptions, and Strategies among Turkish Alevi and Sunni Migrants in Berlin."

16. Teraoka's work provides a refreshing example of just this type of analysis. Seibert refers to *Ausländerliteratur* as part (*Bestandteil*) of German literature (60), but we must clarify that it is an integral (albeit not necessarily integrated) part rather than a subcategory of something essentially German.

17. Weigel also includes comments on a few non-German women writers in *Die Stimme der Medusa*. See also Clausen, "Broken but Not Silent."

18. For an alternative view in the Iranian context, see Nashat, "Women in Pre-Revolutionary Iran: A Historical Overview."

19. See Heinze (40) and most of the articles in the *LiLi* volume cited in n. 3, especially those by Ackermann and Weinrich.

20. Interestingly, the only group of foreigners the stereotype credits with having significant identity problems before arriving in Germany are third world women. The assumption is that their crisis stems not from losing their identity in Europe, but from *finding* their "true" selves there (Westernized "emancipation"). One German-language publication by a non-German (in this case, Turkish) woman that makes it very difficult to overlook the kind of multidimensionality and nonsynchronicity to which I refer is Scheinhardt's *Drei Zypressen*.

21. For a variety of more detailed commentaries on this question, see the relevant articles in *Women and Revolution in Iran*, ed. Nashat; *Women in the Muslim World*, ed. Beck and Keddie; *Islam in the Contemporary World*, ed. Pullapilly; *Unspoken Worlds: Women's Religious Lives*, ed. Falk and Gross; *Women in Islamic Societies: Social Attitudes and Historical Perspectives*, ed. Utas; *Women in the World: A Comparative Study*, ed. Iglitzin and Ross; *Women and the Family in the Middle East: New Voices of Change*, ed. Fernea. See also Nashat, "Women in the Islamic Republic of Iran"; Higgins, "Women in the Islamic Republic of Iran: Legal, Social, and Ideological Changes"; Haeri, *Law of Desire: Temporary Marriage in Shi'i Iran*; El Saadawi, *The Hidden Face of Eve: Women in the Arab World*; and Mernissi, *Beyond the Veil*.

22. Coupled with her Persian physical appearance, Asar's European dress and behavior mark her as a prostitute when she returns to Iran in 1977 (Tufan, 128–31; 144).

23. Under Resa Shah the veil had been banned (1936–41) and education for women had been made compulsory. After Muhammed Resa Shah was put in power in 1953, the more Western-style attitudes and laws of the Pahlavi regime contended with the popular anti-Western precepts of Islamic social reform movements. In 1963 Iranian women were granted the right to vote; the Family Protection Laws of 1967 and 1975 gave them *somewhat* greater freedom in marriage and divorce. However, these concessions to Western concepts of legal rights did not serve to make the oppressive Pahlavi government very popular among Iranians of either sex. Asar's childhood and adolescence fall in the period *before* the major reforms in women's rights.

24. The last time she sees Tufan alive is "die letzte Nacht, bevor du für immer von mir gingst und mich seither nie mehr verlassen wirst" (the last night, before you left me forever and will never leave me again since) (180).

25. In my interview with Torkan she discussed the reception she received at various readings of this novel that she was invited to give.

26. For an especially polemical (and problematic) attack on this blind spot see Thürmer-Rohr, 22–36, as well as her essays in *Vagabundinnen: Feministische Essays*. I also think that the controversy over Koonz's book *Mothers in the Fatherland: Women, the Family, and Nazi Politics* and the West German reception of Duden's *Übergang* are relevant to this issue.

27. Suhr (97) is speaking here of the depoliticizing tendency to reduce foreigners' literature in Germany to its "literary aspects."

Works Cited

Ackermann, Irmgard. " 'Gastarbeiter'literatur als Herausforderung." *Frankfurter Hefte* 38 (1983): 56–64.

———. "Integrationsvorstellungen und Integrationsdarstellungen in der Ausländerliteratur. *LiLi: Zeitschrift für Literaturwissenschaft und Linguistik* 14 (1984): 23–39.

———, ed. *Als Fremder in Deutschland*. Munich: dtv, 1982.

————, ed. *In zwei Sprachen leben*. Munich: dtv, 1983.

————, ed. *Türken deutscher Sprache*. Munich: dtv, 1984.

Ackermann, Irmgard, and Harald Weinrich, eds. *Eine nicht nur deutsche Literatur: Zur Standortbestimmung der "Ausländerliteratur."* Munich: Piper, 1986.

Adelson, Leslie A. Interview with Torkan in Hamburg, October 13, 1989.

Beck, Lois, and Nikki Keddie, eds. *Women in the Muslim World*. Cambridge: Harvard University Press, 1978.

Castles, Stephen, Heather Booth, and Tina Wallace. *Here for Good: Western Europe's New Ethnic Minorities*. London: Pluto, 1984.

Clausen, Jeanette. "Broken but Not Silent: Language as Experience in Vera Kamenko's *Unter uns war Krieg*." In *Women in German Yearbook I*, edited by Marianne Burkhard and Edith Waldstein, 115-34. Lanham, New York: University Press of America, 1985.

Duden, Anne. *Übergang*. Berlin: Rotbuch, 1982.

El Saadawi, Nawal. *The Hidden Face of Eve: Women in the Arab World*. Translated by Sherif Hetata. Boston: Beacon, 1983.

Esselborn, Karl, ed. *Über Grenzen*. Munich: dtv, 1987.

Falk, Nancy Auer, and Rita M. Gross, eds. *Unspoken Worlds: Women's Religious Lives*. Belmont, Calif.: Wadsworth, 1989.

Fernea, Elizabeth Warnock, ed. *Women and the Family in the Middle East: New Voices of Change*. Austin: University of Texas Press, 1985.

Friedrich, Heinz, ed. *Chamissos Enkel*. Munich: dtv, 1986.

Godoy, Julio. "Nowhere at Home." *Mother Jones*, February/March 1990, 16.

Haeri, Shahla. *Law of Desire: Temporary Marriage in Shi'i Iran*. Syracuse: Syracuse University Press, 1989.

Heinze, Hartmut. *Migrantenliteratur in der Bundesrepublik Deutschland: Bestandsaufnahme und Entwicklungstendenzen zu einer multikulturellen Literatursynthese*. Berlin: Express, 1986.

Higgins, Patricia J. "Women in the Islamic Republic of Iran: Legal, Social, and Ideological Changes." *Signs* 10 (1985): 477–94.

Iglitzin, Lynne B., and Ruth Ross, eds. *Women in the World: A Comparative Study*. Santa Barbara, Calif., and Oxford: Clio, 1976.

JanMohamed, Abdul R., and David Lloyd. "Introduction." *Cultural Critique* 6 (1987): 5–12.

————. "Introduction." *Cultural Critique* 7 (1987): 5–17.

Koonz, Claudia. *Mothers in the Fatherland: Women, the Family, and Nazi Politics*. New York: St. Martin's Press, 1987.

Kreuzer, Helmut. "Gastarbeiter-Literatur, Ausländer-Literatur, Migranten-Literatur? Zur Einführung." *LiLi: Zeitschrift für Literaturwissenschaft und Linguistik* 14 (1984): 7–11.

Mandel, Ruth. "Turkish Headscarves and the 'Foreigner Problem': Constructing Difference through Emblems of Identity." *New German Critique* 46 (1989): 27–46.

Mernissi, Fatima. *Beyond the Veil: Male-Female Dynamics in Modern Muslim Society*. Rev. ed. Bloomington: Indiana University Press, 1987.

Nashat, Guity. "Women in Pre-Revolutionary Iran: A Historical Overview." In *Women and Revolution in Iran*, edited by Guity Nashat, 5–35. Boulder, Colo.: Westview, 1983.

————. "Women in the Islamic Republic of Iran." *Iranian Studies* 13 (1980): 165–96.

Özkan, Hülya, and Andrea Wörle, eds. *Eine Fremde wie ich*. Munich: dtv, 1985.

Pullapilly, Cyriac K., ed. *Islam in the Contemporary World*. Notre Dame: Cross Roads, 1980.

Reeg, Ulrike. *Schreiben in der Fremde: Literatur nationaler Minderheiten in der Bundesrepublik Deutschland*. Essen: Klartext, 1988.

Sangari, Kumkum. "The Politics of the Possible." *Cultural Critique* 7 (1987): 157–86.

Schaffernicht, Christian, ed. *Zu Hause in der Fremde*. Reinbek: Rowohlt, 1984.

Scheinhardt, Saliha. *Drei Zypressen.* Berlin: Express, 1984.

Seibert, Peter. "Zur 'Rettung der Zungen': Ausländerliteratur in ihren konzeptionellen Ansätzen." *LiLi: Zeitschrift für Literaturwissenschaft und Linguistik* 14 (1984): 40–61.

Suhr, Heidrun. *"Ausländerliteratur:* Minority Literature in the Federal Republic of Germany." *New German Critique* 46 (1989): 71–103.

Teraoka, Arlene Akiko. *"Gastarbeiterliteratur:* The Other Speaks Back." *Cultural Critique* 7 (1987): 77–101.

———. "Talking 'Turk': On Narrative Strategies and Cultural Stereotypes." *New German Critique* 46 (1989): 104–28.

Thürmer-Rohr, Christina. "Frauen in Gewaltverhältnissen: Zur Generalisierung des Opferbegriffs." In *Mittäterschaft und Entdeckungslust,* edited by Christina Thürmer-Rohr et al. Berlin: Orlanda Frauenverlag, 1989.

———. *Vagabundinnen: Feministische Essays.* Berlin: Orlanda Frauenverlag, 1987.

Torkan. *Allnacht: Roya und Alp-Traum.* Hamburg: Perspol-Verlag, 1987.

———. *Kaltland: Wah'schate Ssard.* Hamburg: Perspol-Verlag, 1984.

———. *Tufan: Brief an einen islamischen Bruder.* Hamburg: Perspol-Verlag, 1983.

Utas, Bo, ed. *Women in Islamic Societies: Social Attitudes and Historical Perspectives.* Brooklyn: Olive Branch, 1988.

Waines, David. "Through a Veil Darkly: The Study of Women in Muslim Societies. A Review Article." *Comparative Studies in Society and History* 24 (1982).

Weigel, Sigrid. *Die Stimme der Medusa: Schreibweisen in der Gegenwartsliteratur von Frauen.* Dülmen-Hiddengsel: tende, 1987.

Weinrich, Harald. "Gastarbeiterliteratur in der Bundesrepublik Deutschland." *LiLi: Zeitschrift für Literaturwissenschaft und Linguistik* 14 (1984): 12–22.

———. "Um eine deutsche Literatur von außen bittend." *Merkur* 37 (1983): 911–20.

Wierlacher, Alois. "Mit fremden Augen oder Fremdheit als Ferment: Uberlegungen zur Begründung einer interkulturellen Hermeneutik deutscher Literatur." In *Das Fremde und das Eigene: Prolegomena zu einer interkulturellen Germanistik,* edited by Alois Wierlacher, 3–28. Munich: iudicium, 1985.

Wilpert, Czarina. "Religion and Ethnicity: Orientations, Perceptions, and Strategies among Turkish Alevi and Sunni Migrants in Berlin." In *The New Islamic Presence in Western Europe,* edited by Tomas Gerholm and Yngve Georg Lithman, 88–106. London, New York: Mansell, 1988.

10 / Scheherazade's Daughters

The Thousand and One Tales of
Turkish-German Women Writers

Azade Seyhan

In a long poem titled "Piyer Lot," Turkish poet Nazim Hikmet parodies the clichéd images of the Orient produced by Western writers. Here, Hikmet's object of scorn and ridicule are portraits of an Orient of hashish, of resignation and fatalism, of women in golden cages in seraglios, of sultans dancing on silver trays.[1] This is the Orient of the best-selling books of French writer Pierre Loti and his contemporaries, an Orient that has found its way into European popular and literary imagination from the pages of *The Thousand and One Nights*. Yet, such an Orient never existed and does not exist now, intones Hikmet. These Occidental fictions of the Orient, he asserts, are invested in ideologies that perpetrate and perpetuate the economic and political rape and exploitation of large populations that inhabit the vast Asian continent.

Hikmet, one of the most widely read and translated modern Turkish poets, died in exile in Moscow in 1963. He was sixty-one. His poems serve as a steady source of inspiration to his compatriots living and writing in today's Germany. Hikmet had known marginalization, imprisonment, and exile in every form and turned his torturous life sentence into an immortal monument to human spirit in his poetry. An extremely prolific writer, who would continuously scribble on any scrap of paper he could find, Hikmet fought tirelessly in writing against all forms of torture, repression, and exploitation. Furthermore, as the poem "Piyer Loti" illustrates, he was a vocal critic of misrepresentations of non-Western cultures in the works of Western writers.

It is not a coincidence that Saliha Scheinhardt, a well-known Turkish woman writer writing in German, has called her second book *Drei Zypressen*. This is the German translation of one of Hikmet's famous poems, "Üç Selviler" (Three cypresses). The book, which portrays veiled lives of three Turkish women and their ordeals as foreigners in Germany, starts with the full text of Hikmet's "Drei Zypressen," as well as the text of his "Meine Landsleute" (My people). Hikmet's powerful poetry of exile, alienation, and critique often acts as an antidote to his compatriots' homesickness and sense of loss. His language is a source of strength and pride; it offers many Turkish writers in exile, separated by distance and history, a poetic shelter of cultural identity. "In this business," writes Hikmet in "Rubáiyat," meaning the business of the writer, "you need to be hard and a little conceited / not defeat, grief, or cruelty / but death alone / should see you surrender" (5: 44). His life and death confirmed this *rubá'i*.[2]

The literary discourse of Turkish women in Germany reflects the words and vision of the greatest revolutionary poet of the Turks. Doubly marginalized as unwanted foreign elements and as women, in that order, they have turned this double bind into a mode of sociocultural intervention. The collective writing of Turkish women in present-day Germany represents their historical and personal conflicts as ethnic and gendered subjects, their positioning between different traditions, and their agenda for the moral and cultural survival of their compatriots in a foreign discursive territory. As self-designated storytellers, they do this by continuously postponing the death of their language and cultural traditions in a world where advanced technology allows little or no time for leisurely spoken words, tales, and memories. Their endless search for the narratives of their history points, in a vein reminiscent of Scheherazade's tales in *The Thousand and One Nights,* to the desire for life and survival in a cramped cultural space.

Turkish women's writing in the context of a foreign culture provides productive lines of investigation for Turkish feminist studies in general. This mode of writing incorporates in a more emphatic way a critique of the oppressive practices women are subjected to in their native culture, as well as a critique of exclusionary practices directed at ethnic minorities and other marginalized groups in Eurocentric societies. It presents a more sharpened vision of what acts of marginalizing entail. Turkish women writing in Germany provide us with multicultural texts of critically transformative power. They draw on the literary culture of writing by and about women in their native country, they question the ideologies implicated in certain representations of women both in their own cultural traditions and in the popular culture of their host country, and, finally, they subvert, fragment, and reconfigure these images in liberating ways. Their writing becomes a site of social intervention in the oppressive practices against women in their home and host cultures.

These texts, furthermore, reflect on the broader implications of differences in race, power, and gender relations that come into focus at the intersection of personal and historical destinies. They interrogate the legitimacy of the representations of otherness often dictated by the dominant ideologies of the host(ile) culture. Aysel Özakin, Saliha Scheinhardt, Alev Tekinay, Zehra Çirak, Emine Sevgi Özdamar, and others challenge and question the image of Turkish women depicted by many German writers and social scientists as remnants of a medieval culture, as unassimilated foreign objects in a modern society, literally as eyesores, with covered heads, bundled or bound bodies, cattlelike, bought and sold.[3] In her well-presented summary of the literary production of foreign women writers in Germany, Heidrun Suhr points out the lack of critical reception of their works. Anthologies presenting their writings, Suhr states, offer no critical insight, and editors treat them as the homogeneous category of "Ausländerinnenliteratur" (Literature by foreign women writers). Suhr, furthermore, criticizes the lack of cultural sensitivity displayed in the research on minority women, which often defines "the unquestioned standard of comparison" as "the white German woman; the 'other' woman is obviously different and as such inferior." She argues that demeaning references to these women as " 'indigestible foreign objects' " undermine a true understanding of their condition (92). This is the double burden of the Turkish woman writer in Germany: to challenge her lowly status in her own culture and the negative images of her womanhood and ethnic identity in the host culture. Her writing is at once a poetic fragmentation and a reconstruction of fossilized misrepresentations in the form of pervasive images; it is critical combat with oppressive practices on both fronts. Her language is no longer the overly modest and self-doubting language of properly brought up Turkish women, often marked by conciliatory prefaces and qualifiers. Neither is it a language of final statements. Rather it is a dialogue with her history, geography, and cultural mythology. This dialogue needs to be heard in its proper context.

Unfortunately, most studies of these "Türkinnen deutscher Sprache" (German-speaking Turkish women) represent appropriative translations of a cultural discourse that resists easy understanding, for it is already marked by conflicts and contestations rooted in its recent history. A critically rigorous and historically informed investigation of these texts needs to situate them in frameworks of contiguity linking them to their larger sociocultural context. To read them in the absence of their history risks complicity in their misrepresentation. This study is an attempt to understand Turkish women's writing in Germany in the context of representations of women in modern Turkish literary history and in terms of the writers' personal and collective histories of immigration and assimilation into a foreign idiom. This will enable us to see to what extent the writing of the Turkish woman writer in exile is a continuation of the native cultural traditions and to what extent that writing transforms or subverts those traditions.

Reşat Nuri Güntekin's *Çalikuşu* (The wren), although first published more than seventy years ago in 1922, is a novel every young Turkish woman has read and reread. Its enduring popularity is evident in the feature movies and television miniseries it still generates. In terms of starting an unprecedented trend among young readers, *Çalikuşu* may be compared, albeit in a much more positive light, to Goethe's *Sorrows of Young Werther*. As is well known, this is the tragi-ironic story of a young man who is silently, painfully, and hopelessly in love with a married woman, a sorry state that leads to his suicide. The story triggered a great wave of suicides among despondent lovers who were fished out of rivers with copies of the book in their pockets. On a much more positive note, Güntekin's novel touched an idealistic nerve in scores of educated young women and led them to escape the confines of their homes and seek teaching jobs in remote corners of Anatolia.

"Çalikuşu" is the nickname of a spunky orphaned girl, Feride, who, left to the care of an aunt, has been sent off to a French convent school, Notre Dame de Sion, in Istanbul. Very much a tomboy and troublemaker at the boarding school, Feride, nevertheless, gets an excellent education, graduates, falls in love with her cousin Kamran, and runs away from home the day before her wedding to Kamran, after she meets another woman who tells her that she was Kamran's lover when he was studying in Switzerland. After her disappearance on the eve of her wedding, Feride applies to the Ministry of Education for a teaching job. The schools she is assigned to are in the remotest and most desolate corners of Anatolia, and her life in these backward schools, which are mostly Qur'an schools, is enough to break the will of the toughest and most idealistic young person. Unable to survive for long in any one place, she transfers from one school to the other. Feride is portrayed as a very daring, likable, and admirable young woman. Yet her story and her life as a teacher are almost exclusively governed by the dictates of her sexuality. She ventures out of her comfortable life initially not out of a sense of idealism, but because she feels betrayed by a man she loves and is motivated by the desire to punish him with her disappearance. She never stops loving him—in the most soap-operatic way. She is pursued by unwanted suitors everywhere she goes. She attracts attention not by what she is doing—teaching—but by her womanhood and sensuality. She adopts a beautiful child abandoned by a weak father and mean stepmother in one of the villages. From then on, rumors and propositions from all kinds of men follow her. In order to protect herself from would-be seducers lurking at every corner, she agrees to marry an old doctor who serves as the shield to protect her virtue, virginity, and virginality. The good doctor takes her and her adopted daughter in. Theirs is a marriage in name only, and the book makes it very explicit that the doctor never touches her. Somewhat conveniently the adopted child dies, and the doctor gets cancer. Knowing he has very little time left, the doctor finds and contacts Kamran and makes him promise that he will marry Feride after his death, all this without her knowledge. After the doctor's death, Feride and Kamran are reunited and live happily ever after. End of the teaching career, before it really ever began.

As can be seen from this very brief summary, Güntekin's novel gives a sympathetic but confusing portrayal of an "emancipated" woman. Feride dares to be different in a moment of anger and despondency. Many an idealistic and rebellious young woman found a very likable role model in her. However, after her stint as a teacher in Anatolian schools, a career burdened by becoming an object of desire against her wishes, she assumes the role of wife and future biological mother. It is interesting that the child she saves from apathetic and mean parents is not allowed to live, thus leaving her free to marry the man she has all along loved and to bear his children.

In spite of its somewhat simplistic portrayal of the heroine and its overly sentimental tone, the book became a modern classic of Turkish literature and was instrumental in legitimizing the actual emancipation of young Turkish women, at least in a professional sense. Turkish women had been granted equal rights in all aspects of life under the law through the reforms, in the twenties and thirties, of Kemal Atatürk, founder and first president of the Turkish republic. Although legally equal to men, traditionally women remain the property of men among the more conservative communities. A strong sense of duality was introduced into Turkish society in the nineteenth century with the onset of what is known as the Westernization movement. Since then, a minority of educated, often Western-trained urban elites and the majority of Anatolians, schooled only in the Qur'anic tradition, have lived as virtual foreigners to one another in the same land. Güntekin's novel, in a sense, is a social document that very clearly represents this foreignness of the Anatolian land to an Istanbul intellectual. Feride walks into a foreign territory where customs, rituals, traditions, and everyday practices of life, heavily influenced by strict Islamic tenets, subject her to real culture shock. In one of the most desolate villages of Anatolia, Zeyniler Köyü, the head teacher tells Feride that she cannot teach in the single-classroom school without completely covering herself, because there are men in the class, boys as old as eleven years of age.

Written in the form of a diary kept by Feride, except for the last chapter, which is recounted by the narrator, *Çalıkuşu* was instrumental in the voluntary mobilization of a women's army of educators. Inspired by Feride and the widespread popularity of the novel, they left their homes to take up teaching posts in remote corners of Anatolia. Like the modern Peace Corps volunteers, these women went to "foreign" countries in a very real sense. Many were resented by the religious communities in conservative villages and small towns where they taught. Often they were driven away by hostility and harassment. An anecdote tells the story of a young teacher who approached Güntekin, while he was visiting a village as superintendent of schools, to tell him that he was responsible for her misery in that hellhole. However, in spite of the misery and hardship, many persevered and succeeded in their mission. The romanticism attached to teaching as well as leaving home, going to the *yaban orel* (Turkish has many words corresponding to the German notion of *Fremde,* a foreign place, which has no satisfactory English translation), remains strong among young and educated Turkish women. Many women who went to Germany in the sixties as "guest workers" were teachers and teachers' aides. In fact, Aysel Özakin, one of the most prominent Turkish women writers in Germany, was, like Feride, a French teacher in the Anatolian provinces before settling in Istanbul and then moving on to Germany as a political asylum seeker.

Another book that has played a controversial and powerful role in modern Turkish literary history is *Sinekli Bakkal* (Sinekli Bakkal Street) by Halide Edip Adivar, a freedom fighter alongside Atatürk during the Turkish War of Independence, a politician and a star orator, and one of the most visible of emancipated women of her time. Originally published in English in England a year before its Turkish version appeared in 1936, this novel is an attempt to represent, in the story of its female protagonist Rabia, the contestation and reconciliation of differing world views and politics, Islamic mysticism and Western art, and Oriental despotism and the progressive ideals of the Young Turks. Rabia, daughter of a famed puppeteer, is an accomplished artist, a woman with an unusually beautiful voice who is reputed to have opened a new era in Eastern music. She is a *hafiz* (a Qur'an reciter) who turns the performance of Qur'anic recitation into an art form of the highest sublimity. She and her mother were separated from her enlightened and politically progressive father by the mother's father, a reactionary imam. When her father, Tevfik, returns from political exile, Rabia leaves her grandfather to live with her father. Although the story is Rabia's story, a story literally about her voice, her talent is fully realized only when complemented by that of her husband, the Italian pianist Peregrini. Once again, at the heart of the novel, there is a love story, and, whatever the merits of the novel, the centrality of the female protagonist's artistic brilliance is relativized, if not eclipsed, by a man's talent. Nevertheless, the novel showed that even within Islamic constraints, a woman could achieve artistic status, reconcile her Islamic upbringing with Western traditions, and even marry a Westerner—although he had to convert to Islam to marry her.

More recently, writers such as Adalet Agaoglu, Furüzan, Pinar Kür, and Sevgi Asena have used various genres—novel, drama, short story, criticism—to portray the joyless, loveless, repressed lives of modern Turkish women. Agaoglu's celebrated *Evcilik Oyunu* (Marriage game) of 1964 is a haunting, expressionistic play about unhappy arranged marriages, obsession with an unmarried woman's virginity and married women's virtue, the emptiness of marriages that are sham unions, loveless families, and spiritless, forced friendships informed by jealousy, boredom, and mindless and vicious gossip. Agaoglu is a vocal and powerful critic of Turkish urban women's imprisonment in the so-called Western-style monogamous marriage.

Some of the recent writing about women in Turkey has tended to be derivative, often drawing amply on books by European authors. In varying degrees, works in Turkish women's studies incorporate ideas of Western feminisms. Furthermore, the depiction, in recent Turkish literary discourse, of women in very strong sexual terms, as predominantly sexual identities—lustful, sexually repressed and frustrated, defined in terms of her men (father, brother, husband)—although intended as critical correction, is not necessarily empowering to women. The writing of Turkish women in Germany, on the other hand, has gone beyond predictable formulas and concern with sexual identities. These writings challenge both the logic of their own cultural history as well as the myth of Western notions and practices of women's liberation. What are some of the distinguishing features of this discourse? I would like to briefly look at two paradigmatic models developed within a relatively short chronological span. These models represent not necessarily a progressive development but rather different stages of formation beyond the narrow ethnic concerns that informed the first experiments in immigrant writing. The first stage presents strong influences of the sociopolitical history of the homeland, as these affect personal and collective destinies in the land of immigration. Confessional and political in tone, this writing finds its most sophisticated expression in Aysel Özakin's work. The second phase reflects an aesthetically provocative attempt at negotiating different literary traditions, venturing into a symbolically dense experimental field that resists easy access. Metafictional in character, this phase, exemplified most impressively in the work of Alev Tekinay and Emine Sevgi Özdamar, presents a heteroglot writing space informed by different languages, those of dream and waking, myth and fact, madness and reason, "East" and "West."

The early works of Turkish women in Germany were to a great extent autobiographical or biographical. This is significant, because autobiography was a rare literary commodity in women's writing in Turkey as recently as twenty years ago. Writing the self is an act of symbolic unveiling. In many repressive, patriarchal societies, the female body constitutes a site of both terror and fascination and is covered. Similarly, the female voice can be considered a source and an instrument of seduction and evil. Therein lies for me the significance of Adivar's novel, where the female voice becomes an instrument of God's language, the Qur'an, which is considered God's direct speech in Islam. When the body is covered and the voice silenced, the woman is effectively absented from public space. Writing is participation in public discourse; writing the self is the imposition of the private on the public, appropriation of the public debate. The predominance of autobiographical elements in Turkish women's writing, most notably in the groundbreaking work of Aysel Özakin, constitutes a statement of self-assertion and public intervention. By remembering fragments of personal and collective histories, the female ethnic subject invents a linguistic and cultural space that is liberating, for it enables new dialogues with her past and present contexts.

It is interesting to note that a great majority of Turkish women who immigrated on their own to West Germany in the early sixties were, unlike the men, not unskilled and illiterate workers but teachers, civil servants, craftswomen, and seamstresses. When West Germany started importing foreign labor, many women who were trapped in low-paying teaching jobs actually enlisted as factory workers to escape the confines of their dead-end lives, family circle, and work. Most picked up German with relative speed and ease. And many started writing soon afterward. Doubly marginalized in a hostile society, often alienated from their own cultural milieu and compatriots, writing became the proverbial therapy. Özakin's work shows how empowering and redeeming the language of the self can be. Her autobiographical selves are reinvented time and again in words that precipitate deeds. Without this means of expression, alienation and frustration can turn into destructive rage. Özakin analyzes with a keen eye for detail such fury and impotence among her compatriots.

Özakin's writing belongs to the stage where the confessional is inevitably embedded in the political. In her collection of short stories, *Soll ich hier alt werden?* (Should I grow old here?), which are brief autobiographical narratives, Özakin rewrites her life as a political activist through sketches of her terror-torn country in the late seventies and through the histories of her compatriots and expatriates who suffered persecution, torture, and exile. The short story cycle lends itself ideally to a more politicized vision. It gives the writer the space and the latitude to present various configurations of events without the restraints of a linear narrative that requires sustained coherence. Özakin's accounts are critical and self-reflexive engagements with the social dictates governing individual fates both in Turkey and in Germany.

Soll ich hier alt werden? is a carefully crafted collection of tales that cover a wide range of social and cultural problems enacted in various landscapes of the two countries. Özakin is an extremely visual writer, which accounts for the powerful translatability of her work. In "Die dunkelhaarigen Kinder von Berlin" (The dark-haired children of Berlin) and "Stille Solidarität" (Silent solidarity), she portrays the tragic lot of young Turkish girls in Berlin and in a small Anatolian village, respectively. The first is the story of a little girl deprived of her childhood. Her small and frail body is practically crippled by being covered from head to toe like an old woman's. The narrator observes this child of a Turkish worker trying to mix in with the other children playing in the park. But her ridiculous attire and timidity paralyze the fun. Her "vielfältige und unübersichtliche Welt" (many-layered and invisible world) (5) becomes the object of the narrator's curiosity. She tries but fails to coax this withdrawn and silent child into a conversation with her. "Ein altes, ein einsames Kind" (an old, lonely child) (6), the girl is silenced by absent parents who make their presence known in the image of her constricted body and by an environment that pushes her away from itself. Both the body and the language of this female child are erased from public space. "Stille Solidarität" is the story of another form of exploitation of female children, one very much in evidence in Turkey. It is an unsentimental yet grippingly told account of a form of adoption that, in effect, involves selecting an able-bodied female child of eleven or twelve, taking her from poor parents who can ill afford to feed her, and having her serve as a maid and nanny in the home of the "adoptive parents" until the biological children are grown up. These girls are called *evlatlik* (roughly translated as substitute or foster child); their status is that of slaves. The adoption is not legal, the child-maids have no rights, and the biological parents often never see them again. In most cases, these girls live with the adoptive families all their lives, never marry, and take care of old or ailing "parents" until these die. Then they are left all alone, often in middle age, with no money, no education, and no family. Most families treat their *evlatlik* fairly and try to provide for her modestly in their wills. Especially when their own children leave, they cherish the companionship of the *evlatlik*. But, on the whole, this is a terribly exploitative practice and, surprisingly enough, not much criticized. Özakin's sketch renders the stark brutality of tearing a reluctant child away from a despondent mother somewhere in the provinces. The child boards the bus with a fur-clad woman from Istanbul who is irritated by her tears and ignores her during the trip. A poor migrant worker going to Istanbul to look for work witnesses, with great sympathy for the child, this cruel episode, and the name of the story refers to the "silent solidarity" that develops between these two Anatolians on their way to a life of labor in Istanbul.

Other stories in this collection sketch with unsparing candor the varying experiental structures of social marginalization of Turks both at home and in Germany. The Turkish landscapes are marked and marred by social inequities, absence of laws or enforcement of existing laws for protecting the innocent, and the sharp dualities that separate the urbanites from the villagers, the secular from the religious, and tradition from modernity. The German scenes are characterized by an absence of affect, warmth, and human communication. In *Die Leidenschaft der Anderen* (Passion of the others, or Passion of the other woman), a cycle of autobiographical sketches marking the stations of the writer's voluntary exile in Germany, Özakin's accounts become recreations of an occluded political history, reenactments of suppressed accounts of torture and of a culture of horror that victimized many friends she left behind. These nameless victims, men and women, are redeemed in her writing and restored in symbolic naming to their historical role. In one of the last episodes of *Die Leidenschaft der Anderen,* Özakin tells, in a language of impassioned mourning, of her decision to seek political asylum in Germany. Traveling with a group of Turkish writers whose leader is not embarrassed to praise the military junta, Özakin feels indignant and silently mocks his misrepresentation of facts. In the midst of this false spectacle, she asks for a Turkish newspaper and glances at the picture of a hanged man whom she immediately recognizes as Erhan. In anguish she recalls how Erhan was wrongly accused of shooting a soldier during a demonstration. A journalist friend of Özakin's had asked her before her trip whether she could do anything to bring Erhan's case to the attention of human rights advocates in the West. Staring in horror at the dead man's picture, Özakin feels she can no longer tolerate the lies her group leader manufactures to present a positive image of the junta and Turkish politics. Right there and then, she decides to leave all behind, her country, family, friends, and successful writing career, and seek political asylum in Germany. At this point Özakin's narrative of memory becomes a fond speculation about the particulars of Erhan's life. He is, in effect, restored as the symbolic marker of the writer's empowerment and the agent for the transmission of the tales of unsung heroes like himself. Özakin's tales inform her own ethnopolitical subjectivity through the exiled lives of her compatriots. Her language, like that of many other Turkish women writers in Germany, is not monologic but dialogic, in the Bakhtinian sense. In *The Dialogic Imagination,* Mikhail Bakhtin defines the novel by its generic tendency to orchestrate

> all its themes . . . by means of the social diversity of speech types [*raznorečie*] and by the differing individual voices that flourish under such conditions. Authorial speech, the speeches of the narrators, inserted genres, the speech of characters are merely those fundamental compositional features with whose help heteroglossia [*raznorečie*] can enter the novel; each of them permits a multiplicity of social voices and a wide variety of their links and interrelationships [always more or less dialogized]. These distinctive links and interrelationships between utterances and languages, this movement of the theme through different languages and speech types, its dispersion into the rivulets and droplets of social heteroglossia, its dialogization—this is the basic distinguishing feature of the stylistics of the novel. (263)

Turkish women writers' narratives of affiliation and disaffiliation are multi-voiced, echoing the necessarily differing positions of their people, who embody the sharply separated social contexts and rituals of their homeland. This is not the simple alterity of being other. Here, alterity assumes a dynamic alteration that rejects polarizing notions of identity and culture. Speech is recorded in a wide variety of social registers, as in the Bakhtinian definition of the novel. These records are given equal representation, thus acknowledging the contestations among symbolic and social codes employed by different narrators. In Alev Tekinay's work, for example, a sense for the carnivalesque, in which various forms of folkloristic, ritualistic, and parodistic languages playfully clash and harmonize, sets the narrative tone. Dialogues between dream, myth, memory, and lived fact create a more empowering field of interaction for the speaking subject.

Alev Tekinay's work represents a phase where the ties to the sociopolitical culture of the homeland no longer occupy a central place. In her work, the characters are hyphenated; they are Turkish-Germans, moving in and out of shifting topographies between dream and reality, memory and existence, and Turkish and German. She also employs the story form, albeit stripped of its overtly biographical and political dimensions. Her stories may be seen as syntheses of Occidental and Oriental worlds, as a blurb on the jacket of her story collection, *Ein Feuer brennt in mir* (A fire burns in me), states. However, they represent much more complex strategies of literary narration. She combines metanarrative devices known to Western readers from the work of Luigi Pirandello, Italo Calvino, Vladimir Nabakov, and others with similar devices used by Turkish storytellers, who present oral rather than written performances of their tales. Often she transplants Turkish idioms directly into German soil, as the title of her collection shows. "Ein Feuer brennt in mir" is an approximate translation of two similar expressions in Turkish, which, however, differ greatly in meaning. *İçim yanıyor* (it is burning inside me) signifies a state of regret, longing, or emotional pain. *İçimdeki ateş* or *içimde bir ateş var* (the fire in me, or there is a fire in me) implies a powerful desire, a will to action capable of producing fireproof results. Like the union of opposite expressions in her title, Tekinay's tales are extended metaphors and allegories that effortlessly move between contrasting visions, idioms, geographies, and histories. She often uses variations on the doppelgänger motif, as in the story of Yakup and Jacob in *Ein Feuer*, who meet each other in a student dormitory room, knowing nothing of each others' languages, lives, or tastes. Initially, they are merely amazing look-alikes. In time, as each learns the other's language and can mimic each other's respective dialects perfectly, they exchange places and assume one another's identity. The German Jacob becomes Yakup and moves to Anatolia to live with Yakup's family, who believes he is Yakup, and Yakup becomes Jacob and gets a teaching position in a German school.

An almost flawless example of metafictional narrative is Tekinay's story "Achterbahn" (The roller coaster). The roller-coaster ride is itself the perfect metaphor for unannounced and seamless crossovers between fact and imagination, dream and waking, and instantaneous journeys in time and space. The story opens with the writer-narrator stating that the Oktoberfest festivities in Munich created such a strong urge in her to write a story that she could not wait to get to her desk. She decides that a certain young countryman she spots in the crowd will be the hero of her story. As she begins writing, the hero comes to life and chides her for creating yet another stereotypical story about a Turkish migrant peasant suffering from alienation: "Über die Einsamkeit in der Fremde, Magenkrankheit, Heimweh, Sehnsucht, Kälte usw. Das alles kennen wir ja schon" (Loneliness in the foreign country, ulcers, homesickness, longing, coldness, and so on. We already know all that) (89). This reflection on the status of Turkish fiction as a metafictional device works well, because it is not a mere stylistic exercise. Rather it is an allegory of a recent period in Turkish literary history that not only played out its destiny in Turkish literature but also traveled with Turkish migrants to claim a major role in their literature in Germany. The hero tells the author that he does not want to be a peasant or guest worker called Ali or Mustafa but a student from a well-educated urban family. He claims the more fashionable and sexier name Tamer. He will not be a player in yet another version of the overworked "Dorfromantik" (village romanticism): "Diese klicheehafte Dorfromantik mit den immer gleichen Beschreibungen in Rückblenden: Die goldgelben Weizenfelder wehten leise im Hitzedunst, und so weiter und so fort" (This cliché village romanticism with always the same descriptions in flashback: the golden fields of corn blowing gently in the haze, and so forth and so on) (89–90).

The reference here is twofold. On the one hand, this is an ironic reflection on an earlier phase of immigrant literature, marked by excessive longings for the Anatolian homeland left behind. Romanticized and glorified in memory, these desolate lands become a permanent landscape of escape in earlier migrant literature. On the other hand, this genre of village romanticism is an extended version of a dominant literary trend of the fifties and sixties in Turkey. Mahmut Makal, a writer and a graduate of the now defunct village institutes, published a novel called *Bizim Köy* (Our village) in 1950. The literature of modern Turkey up to that point had confined its focus to urban life, Westernization, effects of the latter on the former, and, at the most, fleeting impressions of life in the provinces seen through the eyes of an urban protagonist. The popularity of *Bizim Köy*, written by a village teacher and recounting in realistic detail the life in this "other country," ushered in a period known as *Köy Edebiyati* (village literature). For almost two decades, the poverty and hardships suffered by Turkish peasants, their ruthless exploitation in the hands of landowners, and their deception by politicians who used religious propaganda as a tool to perpetuate the oppression of this class were portrayed in grim naturalistic detail in an endless series of novels, a good number of which were actually very well written. Many of these works also glorified a simpler way of life closer to the earth and nature in a place not yet touched by corruption born of material greed. By the time the Turkish reading public had tired of village literature, its themes were picked up by migrant writers. This is understandable, since most guest workers or immigrants in the fifties and sixties were themselves children of Anatolian villages. In most cases, they had migrated first to Istanbul or Ankara and then to Germany. The burdens of this double immigration sharpened their sense of longing for the poorer but simpler life, which seemed happier in retrospect. Understandably, they carried over the themes of a literary tradition they were most familiar with into their first writing experiments in the foreign context. However, as in Turkey, the experiment outlived its historical necessity.

Tekinay's hero will have none of this village romanticism and also refuses her plot outline. Then he gets on the roller coaster. Here, in vividly described scenes reminiscent of the television show *The Twilight Zone,* Tamer finds himself in his hometown, Izmir, without papers and money. This episode, recounted in the mode of a dream language, floats between subconscious images and conscious self-dialogues, and the falling in and jumping out of consciousness implicitly mimics the roller-coaster ride. This indeterminacy of place, experience, and meaning so unnerves the hero that when he spots the author in an open air pub in Izmir, he implores for forgiveness and begs her to write an end to this story. "Zwinge deine Phantasie und tu etwas" (Force your imagination and do something) (104). She replies that imagination cannot be forced, that he chose to write his own story anyway, and that stories need not have endings (104). Although at the end of the story, Tamer is at the end of the ride and finds himself at the amusement park back in Munich, the story is suspended in the twilight zone of meaning. Tamer catches a glimpse of the author in the park. She seems familiar, but he cannot remember where he knows her from. In the final analysis, as the author of the story within the story states, "das Ende kann man auch dem Leser überlassen" (the ending can also be left to the reader) (104). At the end, like the reader looking for meaning, Tamer wanders "von Karussell zu Karussell, ohne daß er sich entscheiden konnte, was er mit diesem Abend anfangen sollte" (from carousel to carousel, without being able to figure out what this evening was all about) (107). And he freezes in the chilly October weather of Munich, still wearing the thin summer shirt his brother in Izmir had lent him. Tekinay's self-conscious narrative moves lightly between places, images, languages, and metaphors. But it is not merely an experiment in ironic allegorization. She tells a story and history through tropes that negotiate and dialogize literary traditions of different lands, linguistic and cultural differences, and zones separated in time and space.

Emine Sevgi Özdamar's work carries the metafictional tradition and magical realism that informs Tekinay's work even further. Both writers have been awarded coveted literary prizes and have traveled far beyond the confines of an ethnic aesthetic. In 1990, Tekinay received the Chamisso Prize and Özdamar the Ingeborg Bachmann Prize. Özdamar's writing is about language in all its forms and manifestations, as speech and script, as language game and everyday practice, as ritual and performance, and as survival and mastery. Born in the Eastern province of Malatya in 1946, Özdamar first came to Germany at the age of nineteen. After an early stint as a factory worker, she studied drama in Berlin and performed in numerous plays as well as feature films. Her dramatic training is evident in the way she directs language in performance. In *Mutterzunge* (Mother tongue), her collection of stories tinged with hues of magical realism, Özdamar presents the reader with a series of narratives that unfold in verbal images resembling a surrealistic film.

The first two stories of *Mutterzunge,* "Mutterzunge" and "Großvaterzunge" (Grandfather tongue), are about how language determines the reality of our experience, time (and history), space, and relationships. "In meiner Sprache heißt Zunge: Sprache" (in my language "tongue" means "language"),[4] begins "Mutterzunge." "Zunge hat keine Knochen, wohin man sie dreht, dreht sie sich dorthin" (the tongue has no bones; it turns wherever you turn it) (7). In her very first sentences, Özdamar underlines the latitude given to language, its acrobatic skill of expression, and its infinite possibilities of articulation and transaction. "Zunge drehen" (turning the tongue) is the translation of a Turkish idiom, *dili dönmek,* often used in the negative as *dilim dönmüyor,* meaning I can't pronounce or articulate something. The narrator then refers to herself as one with "gedrehten Zunge" (turned tongue) (7), someone capable of articulation. She highlights the expressive playing field of language games by directly translating highly metaphorical Turkish expressions into German and explaining how they constitute the structure where interaction, transaction, contestation, combat, reconciliation, healing, and just about every form of human activity takes place. After her long sojourn in Germany, the narrator declares that when she thinks of "mother sentences" spoken by her mother in her mother tongue, they would sound like a foreign language she learned well (6). In order to come back to her mother tongue, she needs a detour through the grandfather tongue. Before 1928, Turkish was written in Arabic script. In the framework of Atatürk's Westernization reforms, the Latin script was adopted. The narrator cannot read the Arabic script, and her grandfather cannot read the Latin script. She wonders what would happen if both she and her grandfather would go deaf and not be able to communicate. So she decides to find the famous Arabic teacher Ibni Abdullah in West Berlin in order to take Arabic lessons from him.

This is a love story told in German but framed by conversations between the old and the new, the religious and the secular (and carnal), and Arabic and Turkish. It is also a story of being in love with language(s). This story is, furthermore, a celebration of Arabic calligraphy, which is a picture alphabet. Since Islam forbade the representation of images, calligraphy became the dominant visual art form in Arabic and Ottoman culture. The narrator often recites visual poetry of Arabic letters. During the lessons at Ibni Abdullah's house, her Turkish and Arabic words, Qur'an recitations by other students of Ibni Abdullah, and Turkish lyrics are in performance clashing and harmonizing all at once. Many Turkish words have Arabic roots, and by going to the roots, the narrator can trace branches of lyric, lore, and legend intertwined in the two linguistic cultures. The common language of all students in Ibni Abdullah's house is ironically German. How can the narrator express passion in Turkish to her Arabic lover? Only in German translation. Her own self and idiom are respectively enriched by love and the exchange and simultaneous presence of three languages.

In the final analysis, such a story is more than a metalinguistic commentary. It also tells a veiled political history. Atatürk has been criticized by both leftist and rightist groups for erasing all traces of the Islamic Ottoman culture, thus creating a vacuum where modern Turks struggle to define a cultural identity. Learning Arabic or using Arabic loanwords in Turkish is often construed as a politically reactionary act. Modern Turkish intellectuals make a concerted

effort to speak and write *öz Türkçe* (authentic Turkish). The movement to reclaim and recreate an earlier, "purer" form of Turkish free of the strong influence of Ottoman (a hybrid court language made up of some Turkish and
mostly Arabic and Persian loanwords) was launched by Atatürk when he established the Türk Dil Kurumu (Turkish Language Association). This association
publishes a great number of books, professional journals, and dictionaries
aimed at freeing Turkish from its bondage to Arabic and Persian (and, more recently, foreign languages such as English and French) and expanding its lexical
possibilities through derivations of new words from root forms of old Turkic
languages. The ideology of a "pure" Turkish has also met with the kind of criticism directed at practices of denying one's cultural heritage. Özdamar implicitly maintains that she can have much easier and unproblematic access to the
knowledge of Arabic in Germany than in Turkey, where such interest could be
seen as a fundamentalist religious gesture.

Özdamar's narrative strategies often defy translatability, although she does
literally translate Turkish expressions into German. The reader is expected to
engage in a more informed way with another discursive practice. This requires
learning another system of cultural signification, a sense for the experiences of
people whose reality is determined by different language acts. Although written
in grammatically flawless and visually enticing German, this writing requires
translation at many levels—historical, political, social, and cultural. Multicultural citizenship requires the admission of not knowing the other and willingness to learn about the other. Following Özdamar, let me recall a Turkish
proverb that illustrates this statement better than any critical musing I can offer:
Bilmemek degil, ögrenmemek ayip (It is not a shame not to know but a shame not
to learn).

The lesson of this proverb is embedded in the tales of the Turkish storytellers in Germany. In the narrative transmission of their complex cultural heritage, they ask their readers to make an effort to educate themselves in and
through other idioms, traditions, and histories. They celebrate in their dialo-
gized stories linguistic, cultural, and geographical difference. Tekinay and Özdamar take us on a roller-coaster ride between reality and fantasy, the literal and
the figural, allegory and irony, and polyglot borders. They endow their past and
present with alternative meanings. This confrontation with the indetermina-
cies of language, meaning, and so-called reality poses the reader a critical challenge. In an article in *Die Zeit,* where Özdamar tells the story of staging her play
"Karagöz in Alamania"[5] with a cast of actors from many countries and a star

donkey, she mentions with some sarcasm that the theater management, without consulting her, distributed leaflets to the audience before the opening night of the play. These were intended to prepare theatergoers for the confusion that would arise from the fantastic elements and the nonlogical ordering of the sequences in the play. Insisting on the universality of so-called logic, linearity, and order undermines the understanding of the infinite diversity of patterns that govern social and cultural lives.

The multiperspectival writing of Turkish women in Germany also serves as a warning to avoid homogenizing diversity into blandness and seeing and recreating all in our image. This involves a critical look at our understanding of otherness, constructions of otherness, and the brainwashing power of representations in condemning otherness. The voices of Özakin, Tekinay, Özdamar, and other storytellers entertain, instruct, and guide their German readers to cross the border into their own cultural domain. As immigrants and representatives of a non-Western culture, they were all along expected to learn another language, cultural practice, history, and way of life. They had to undertake the labor of self-transformation, sparing their Western hosts the same. Their writing is a challenge for the reader to engage in a genuine conversation of cultural bilingualism, an effort to reverse the one-sided perceptions of other lesser-known, often misunderstood and misrepresented cultures. "One of the benefits of being a writer displaced from your own country is that you can construct a literary tradition for yourself," states Salman Rushdie in an interview, "you can build your own family really, which obviously does draw partly on your own old cultural roots. But you can also take them from wherever you want" (25). Many Turkish writers in Germany create their literary traditions from their cultural roots but also from literary communities they enter. This practice of writing liberates cultural production from the confines of a ghettoized ethnic aesthetic. In the stories of modern Turkish Scheherazades, the semantic implication of the title *The Thousand and One Nights*—as infinity and one more—takes on concrete form as the boundless mobility and resilience of languages in dialogue.

Notes

1. Hikmet, *Şiirler*, 1:165–66. This poem is an irate articulation of Hikmet's anger at French writer Pierre Loti's alleged negative representation of Turks. (Hikmet deliberately spells Pierre as "Piyer," the Turkish spelling, which is fully phonetic.) Loti (real name, Julian Viaud, 1850–1923) is the author of *Aziyade*, a novel about a young Turkish woman he loved and abandoned. Hikmet's an-

ger was fueled by the rumor that Loti, supposedly a great Turcophile, was in fact serving as a navy officer in an Allied Powers warship that bombarded the Dardanelles in World War I.

2. A *rubá'i* is a quatrain in iambic pentameter, patterned after those of the *Rubáiyát of Omar Khayyám. Rubáiyat* is the plural form of *rubá'i.* All translations from the original Turkish and German are mine.

3. A case in point is an apparently sympathetic but, in fact, extremely unflattering portrayal of Turkish women in Germany in an article, "Knüppel im Kreuz, Kind im Bauch" (Cudgel on the back, child in the belly), in *Der Spiegel,* October 29, 1990, 98–117. This article in a highly respected weekly, which reports the murder of a young Turkish woman by her brother, misreads an act of domestic violence as a universal cultural code without substantiating this claim by proper documentation or any understanding of so-called Turkish cultural codes. Through the use of lengthy personal observations by German female sociologists and psychologists, the condition of Turkish women in Germany is described as "ein Stück Mittelalter mitten in Deutschland" (a piece of the Middle Ages in the middle of Germany).

4. Although in English, as in Turkish, tongue and language can be synonyms, this is not the case with the German *Zunge* and *Sprache.*

5. Karagöz is the name of a character in the famous traditional Turkish shadow puppet theater. "Alamania," or rather "Alamanya" in Turkish spelling, is how Anatolian peasants often pronounce the Turkish word "Almanya" (Germany). In her article, Özdamar translates Karagöz literally as "Schwarzauge" (Blackeye).

Works Cited

Adivar, Halide Edip. *Sinekli Bakkal.* 27th ed. Istanbul: Atlas, 1969.
Bakhtin, M. M. *The Dialogic Imagination.* Translated by Caryl Emerson and Michael Holquist.
    Edited by Michael Holquist. Austin: University of Texas Press, 1981.
Güntekin, Reşat Nuri. *Çalikuşu.* 20th ed. Istanbul: Inkilap and Aka, 1975.
Hikmet, Nazim. *Siirler.* Istanbul: Cem Yayinevi, 1978.
Özakin, Aysel. *Soll ich hier alt werden? Türkin in Deutschland.* Translated by H. A. Schmiede.
    Hamburg: Goldmann, 1987.
Özdamar, Emine Sevgi. *Mutterzunge.* Berlin: Rotbuch, 1990.
Rushdie, Salman. Interview, "Dialogue with History." *South: The Third World Magazine* 27
    (1983): 24–25.
Suhr, Heidrun. *"Ausländerliteratur:* Minority Literature in the Federal Republic of Germany."
    New German Critique 46 (1989): 71–103.
Tekinay, Alev. *Es brennt ein Feuer in mir.* Frankfurt am Main: Brandes & Apsel, 1990.

11 / "Life from Its Very Beginning at Its End"[1]

The Unhomely Boundaries in the Works of Bulgarian Author Blaga Dimitrova

Hannelore Scholz

"Our daily bread. Dried-up fear."
—Blaga Dimitrova, *Fenster zur Hoffnung* (Window on hope)

During the first demonstration of the democratic revolution in November 1989 in Sofia, the capital of Bulgaria, two books were carried like placards: *Fascism* by Zhelyu Zhelev and *The Face* by Blaga Dimitrova. Zhelyu Zhelev became president of Bulgaria (until 1994) and Blaga Dimitrova became vice president.

It is difficult to introduce an author who found herself in the promising yet difficult position of recording times of upheaval. The poet-politician wanted to take part in Bulgaria's democratization process; her many political essays demonstrate her struggle with this task. At the same time, interpretations of her literary works were published, which led to a virulent campaign against her, sparked by the illegal publication of her early collection of poems, *Verses,* by the agency Sofia Press. Because her early published work had included poems praising Stalin, she found herself, like Christa Wolf,[2] at the center of a public debate. The cultural and political discourse at that time indicated that a political power shift was on its way, and the controversy surrounding Blaga Dimitrova's early poems was a convenient way to hasten the dissolution of the transitional government in Bulgaria's continuing process of democratization.[3] She was turned out of office in the summer of 1993.

The collapse of the Eastern bloc also meant the end of the illusion that it was possible to create a social and moral world order. Blaga Dimitrova's work can be characterized within the framework of the value system derived from that world order, for she had criticized the "utopia" of socialism very early on. As early as 1945, she became a member of the writers' association, but she refused to take political office. As a non-Party member she was persecuted in various ways and was considered to be a "dissident." Dimitrova was aware of her position as the "moralische Instanz" (moral example) of the Balkans (see Bogdal). She saw this as a heavy responsibility. What is fascinating about her literary and political activities is that from the very beginning she always looked beyond the narrow national borders of Bulgaria.

Considering the embattled history of the autonomous state of Bulgaria, the position Dimitrova took is notable in that this small Balkan country was ruled by Turkey from 1396 until 1878; only through tremendous struggles was it able to preserve its national identity. Numerous uprisings (in 1598, 1686, and 1688) fought against the so-called Turkish yoke; they were supported by Bulgarian culture with its pronounced national elements. The Bulgarian monasteries played a special role by preserving Old Bulgarian literary traditions that bear witness to resistance against ethnic assimilation.

New Bulgarian literature (from the mid–eighteenth century to the present) arose amid the struggle against Turkish feudal rule and the spiritual patronage of the Greek clergy. In the nineteenth century Bulgarian literature smacked decidedly of self-promotion as it played its part in the efforts to develop a Bulgarian national consciousness, a Bulgarian national culture, a Bulgarian school system, and a literary language, and in the creation of a Bulgarian national church. The development of a Bulgarian national literature, the tradition that Blaga Dimitrova is part of, was thus closely connected with the fight for national liberation from the start. The liberation of Bulgaria as a result of the Russo-Turkish war of 1877–78 introduced a new phase of literary development. "National rebirth" became the dominant theme of Bulgarian literature. At the same time, with the patriotic pathos and the nationalistic program of the time, ideological battle lines were drawn against the high proportion of "ethnic minorities."[4] Around one-sixth of Bulgaria's population belong not to Bulgaria's Southern Slavic ethnic majority, but to one of the country's numerous ethnic minorities or ethnic-religious groups (Troebst, 474).

Dimitrova recognized the consequences of the mass expulsions following the second Balkan War of 1913 as having been the systematic goal of politics and war strategies.[5] Nationalism, the "European disease," resulted in a population transfer in the Balkans, with a treaty between Bulgaria and Turkey that led to the "voluntary" resettlement of fifty thousand people (see Glotz). In her essays, Dimitrova thematized the contradiction inherent in the fact that Bulgaria was, on the one hand, all for union with European peoples in a multicultural program but, on the other hand, was attempting to assimilate the minorities in its own country with brutality and force. She arrived at this insight by way of her specific socialization.

Dimitrova was born in Bjala Slatina on January 2, 1922. In 1941 she graduated from a high school in Sofia that emphasized the humanities. Up until 1945 she studied at the Kliment-Ochridski University in Sofia, and then studied at the Gorky Institute in Moscow, where she wrote her dissertation on the theme "Majakovski and Bulgarian poetry." From 1950 to 1958 she worked for the periodical *September* and in 1962 worked at the publishing house Bulgarian Writer. From 1963, she worked as an editor at the publishing house People Culture. From 1952 to 1954, working as a journalist, she lived in the Rhodope Mountains in southern Bulgaria, where a large percentage of the population was Muslim. She could watch social changes more or less as they happened. These impressions made their mark on her early lyric poetry. The same could be said of her travel journal *Judgment Day* (1969) and her journal *Underground Sky* (1972).[6] Both works result from her struggle to come to terms with the Vietnam War. She went to Vietnam five times, took part in international conferences, and adopted a Vietnamese child whose parents had been killed in the war.

Lyric poetry became the dominant genre of her early creative period. In Bulgaria, this genre had a strong tradition of women writers. Ellisaveta Bagrjana and Dora Gabe were women who made their mark on Bulgarian literature. Dimitrova coauthored a book with Jordan Vassilev on the noted lyric poet Bagrjana, consciously placing herself within this literary tradition. Dimitrova herself published about ten volumes of poetry, individual cycles of which were translated into more than twenty-five languages.[7] In addition, she wrote novels, dramas, translations, and satirical-ironic essays. Her prose works include *Journey to Oneself* (1965), translated into five languages; *Love in a Roundabout Way*

(1967), translated into a dozen languages; *The Avalanche* (1971), translated into four languages; and *The Face*.

Her last novel, *The Face* was written in 1981 (although it could not be published completely until 1990). It is a wide-ranging social novel, in which the following themes are discussed: the "patriotic war," the liberation from fascism, large-scale building projects in the Rhodope Mountains, the repressive system of socialism in Bulgaria, xenophobia and intolerance, and the deficiency syndromes that result from repression and alienation. Without a doubt, Dimitrova had already anticipated the collapse of socialism. Her main theme in this novel is the victim/perpetrator dynamic issue, embedded within social, psychological, and cultural aspects of Bulgarian society. The novel convincingly documents the biographical and ideological turning points of people of various social classes, presenting them as identity crises. By criticizing the social model of Bulgaria, she blasted the ideology represented by the state and the Party. When the novel was first published, with cuts, in 1982 (censors had stamped the backs of the pages seven hundred times), there were grave consequences. The editor of the publishing house was fired; copies that had already been sold were recalled and taken to a prison for books that actually existed in Plovdiv (Dimitrova, "Mysteries," 4ff.; *Challenges,* 119ff.). Bulgaria's cultural policymakers, who were accountable to the state and the Party, affirmed their national and patriotic evaluation: "This novel was written according to the dictates of enemy agents outside the borders of the homeland" ("Mysteries," 4ff.).

Dimitrova expressed the problems she had with her own identity as a Bulgarian in her early lyric poetry. For example, her themes include problematic national patriotism, the lost utopia, totalitarian forms of nationalism, exile from home, and homelessness. Moreover, her female characters make demands as to how they want to live their lives. These demands were read as a criticism of Bulgarian socialist patriarchy. Her poetry shows difference between the sexes as social difference, and expresses national differences with the Turkish population and other minorities. But that was a taboo in socialist Bulgaria. To bring the inhuman treatment of minorities into the public eye meant censorship, surveillance, and the loss of publishing opportunities.

Against the backdrop of the bloody events in connection with "Bulgarianization," Dimitrova took sides definitively. She formulated the idea of a new consciousness for the intellectual with a European orientation, the blossoming of a new "identity," as opposed to supporting the notion of narrow Bulgarian, nationalistic norms that had led people to develop a hatred against everything foreign in the country. For Dimitrova this nationalistic ideology is still in effect. Statements of fact about minority politics in Bulgaria are problematical because there very little factual information has been examined (Troebst, 476f.).

In contrast to neighboring Balkan states, Bulgaria's constitution of May 16, 1971, contained no collective concept of minorities. The ethnic groups in question were granted a single concession to minority rights: "the right to learn their own language in addition to the obligatory learning of the Bulgarian language." But against this was the fact that there had not been any schools for minorities since the 1970s. The reason is found in the history of ethnic minorities and ethnic-religious groups in the Bulgarian state, which was founded in 1878 and united with Eastern Rumelia in 1885. It is a story of diminishment, concentration, and assimilation, step by step. Not only the concentration of strong minorities, primarily of Islamic faith, but also the politics of the state and people's attitudes to this problem must be seen in the context of the complex heritage of the Ottoman Empire. The majority of Bulgaria's ethnic problems come from traditional Islamic groups' answer to state "socialist" calls for modernization, developed from 1878 onward as an ideology. Key events include the following: 1934, the establishment of an authoritative corporate regime with the goal of assimilation; 1958, the beginning of the assimilatory phase of the ethnic policies of the postwar period; 1984, the beginning of massive pressure for assimilation, using force if necessary, on the Turks, among others (Troebst, 478). These measures have become known as "Bulgarianization." This is the background against which Blaga Dimitrova the politician made a commitment to Bulgarian national and international policies that needed to be changed.

Her intensive production of essays after 1989 provides plenty of evidence that she connects identity problems of a national nature with international ways of formulating the questions. Hence in what follows I will take a look at her collection of political essays, *Challenges,* and her story "Elmaz," in which she thematizes the problem of "Bulgarianization." Using this selection, I will investigate the presentation of female subjectivity; that is, I will analyze the main characters/female narrators in terms of their becoming subjects and in terms of the social and sexual consciousness expressed by their perceptions, memories, and experiences.

I see feminist discussion about various subject models as part of a tradition of a series of models from the history of philosophy, as well as theoretical models, particularly those of European Romanticism and German classicism. Here I will mention the work of Jessica Benjamin, for whom becoming a female subject is a process of balancing between identity and difference, in such a way that the other/the foreign is not assimilated as one searches for one's identity. For Benjamin, the self's broad differentiation process is based on a dialogical or polyphonic structure, which mediates between what is one's own and what is foreign in such a way that the foreign can continue to exist within the self.

Benjamin's criticism of the traditional subject model keeps open one particular dimension: becoming a female subject offers the opportunity to enter into an exchange with other subjects and with the world, without defining the existence of the foreign/other as part of the self and thus neutralizing its difference. A subject model that would be socially relevant and gender specific has to show how differences can be defined. Blaga Dimitrova has this to say: "Who am I, really? A witness? Participant? Victim? Nailed to the cross between what I was and what I am, split into numerous beings, I am whole like never before" ("Elmaz," 276).

A wall defined the ridge of fear.
—Blaga Dimitrova, *Fenster zur Hoffnung*

Blaga Dimitrova's artistic career began very early. The daughter of a lawyer and a teacher, she grew up in Veliko Tirnovo, Bulgaria, and published her first poetic efforts in school and student newspapers.

She belonged to a generation that had experienced the war. In an interview with me she spoke of an "antifascist way of life" that was directed against a "ladylike mentality."[8] Jews and antifascists hid at her house, and she fought with other Bulgarian intellectuals against the transportation of Jews to concentration camps.[9] According to her own statements, these experiences were integral to her search for a "new image of women." When she was delegated to Moscow in 1946 as a scholar destined to teach at a university, she was appalled by the image of women that prevailed there, so that she fought, with all the means at her disposal, against discrimination against women. Literature became her medium, lyric poetry her principal genre. Her disillusionment about the true nature of Stalinism would come later.

In her lyric poetry, one poetic method became dominant. She put the lyric voice in tension with reality. Thus she was able to connect her newfound moral-ethical aspects to the self. The female lyric voice could gain its own distance from the ideal through the elucidation of its inner spiritual-emotional world and could thematize friction with the outside world.

By the late fifties, it seemed to Dimitrova that limiting one's range of vision to a single viewpoint was too confining to allow her to give aesthetic expression to the new social inconsistencies. Prose offered a wider field. Her first novel, *Journey to Oneself* (1965), with its strongly autobiographical features, explores a new way of writing. It contains notes written in the form of a journal with purposeful diversions, essayistic fragments, and a provoking disregard for the chronological sequence of events. This prose work combines documentary segments and general statements with a subjective point of view. It is mainly concerned with moral purity and honesty, with a subjective truth arrived at through experience.

Her second novel, *Love in a Roundabout Way*, has an epic structure defined by multiple levels of narration. Notably, this came at the same time as Christa Wolf's development of "subjective authenticity" (*Lesen und Schreiben*, 212) as a writing method in the novel *Nachdenken über Christa T.* (In my opinion, this says something about the level of social and individual developmental problems in both countries.)

Both in her first novel and in *The Avalanche* (1971), the male and female characters are shown in their contradictory social and sexual consciousnesses. The focus of narration stays with the female main characters, as is the case in Christa Wolf's novels, but the narratives are polyphonic in both speech and reflection. There are no unequivocal subjective identities, and consequently nothing can be attributed to them. The I/you/we positions change constantly, giving rise to a specific kind of irony and satire with a dimension that I would like to call subjective/female/moral analysis. In his essay "What Is an Author?" Michel Foucault connected two different series of questions with the two questions "Who speaks?" and "Who cares who speaks?" The ambiguity of many places in Blaga Dimitrova's lyric poetry and prose delays the answers to these questions. If a sentence or a statement can originate from several voices, then a new kind of depth develops, different from the "depths within oneself." It becomes apparent, then, that the problem of the authenticity of one's identity and of nationality is as yet unsolved. The boundaries are not definable. What is more, Dimitrova does not pursue Foucault's second line of questioning; rather she poses her own series of questions. But questions themselves become questionable, because one can't always find *one* answer. Thus in Dimitrova's writings, the depiction and characterization of identities is ambivalent; transitions between voices are border crossings.

The characters of the novels cannot be analyzed here in detail.[10] To summarize: In the novels *Love in a Roundabout Way* and *The Avalanche*, the male and female characters are constructed dualistically. Bojan is the representative of the totalitarian state and Party apparatus of Bulgaria. He seems to be oriented one-dimensionally, by reason. Bojan and Neda have already been involved in conflicts when they were younger, conflicts that are more noticeable when they meet in the middle of their lives. Their differences encompass their choices of profession. (He is an economist and she an archaeologist.) Similar conflicts exist also between Dara and Assen in *The Avalanche*. But there is a new departure in her novel *The Face*. Dimitrova combines ideological criticism with criticism of language in this grand-scale social novel. The ensemble of characters, no matter how different their social, cultural, and political circumstances, are situated in a country (Bulgaria) that allows life only within a "room with closed doors." Within it, the communication systems are interfered with.

She reprises this theme in her essay, "The New Alienation in the Mirror of Posttotalitarian Language." She writes, "My generation in Bulgaria lived their lives without freedom. But every word, the hint of truth found an echo in our room with closed doors. Today's turn to complete freedom of expression irritates us like a leap from one planet to another. Words lose their meaning, their integrity melts like snow in springtime" (*Challenges,* 216).[11]

After 1989, the understanding of the function of literature changed and so the circumstances of communication changed also. Dimitrova describes these changes as a laborious search for a new "face."[12] This is characterized by unresolved old contradictions and by new united European contradictions, which are experienced as social and cultural East-West conflicts. East-West contradictions are shown most clearly in Dimitrova's reworking of the "Sisyphus myth" (see Staitscheva, 153f.). She uses the story of Sisyphus to create a parable of her own situation and that of Bulgarian women. His rock is "solidified history." "That is not a stone at all, but a fragment of solidified history, a conglomeration of humiliations, struggles, and suffering, tears turned into marble, blood, and sweat, a people's fate petrified" (Staitscheva, 47).

The Bulgarian people's hope of shedding this petrified existence grows, as do their fears that they will not find a place of their own in the European Union. In her essay "On the Threshold of the Common European House," she describes the fears that accompanied seeing the fall of the Berlin Wall: "The Berlin Wall does not come all the way down, however. We still have to tear it down, stone by stone, inside ourselves. It is still standing, deaf and monstrous, in our souls, in our consciousness, and in our subconscious. It continues to divide us with its prejudices and its lack of trust. The legacy of the mania for espionage is tremendous. It will cost us plenty of effort, will, and time, before we can overcome it" (quoted in Staitscheva, 158).

Dimitrova recognized the difficulties caused for everyone by the ideological and biographical breaks with the past. She put all her hope in the women who represented the cultures of the new nations, in people's tolerance when dealing with foreign cultures, and in humanity, which allows one's own culture to exist in what is foreign and what is foreign to exist in one's own. Her house of Europe is based on the acceptance of a balance between nationality and internationality.

In these democratization processes, literature has an important educational task, alongside its function of creating identities. It must penetrate the past aesthetically, characterize what has happened, and at the same time be the basis for what is to come. Taking part in the project of an integrated free Europe includes, for Dimitrova, breaking with limited national traditions. Even before 1989, she stated: "Of course, I am not concerned with the well-known forms of poetics of so-called engaged literature. What I imagine is the new land that contemporary poets must open up for themselves, with the help of almighty tradition, that is, they must break with tradition over and over again. Today, since you have realized that politics can become a hell (and what a hell!), since you can no longer be certain who will benefit from your efforts, since our former self-deception about our utopias has vanished in the light of the future, but nevertheless you can't avoid following your internal promptings and joining in. In spite of all your fears that joining in could make you partly responsible for new mistakes" (*Challenges,* 66). She describes the conflict between artistic and political work as a compromise full of contradictions. "An intellectual cannot convince by screaming. . . . A writer cannot talk in terms of black and white. He must bring to light the truth, full of contradictions, about the world and about himself. But the present moment demands one-track thinking. That estranges me from myself" (*Challenges,* 216).

In a series of essays, Dimitrova describes with subtle irony her tendencies to feel estrangement. She describes being spied on, the code of signals she and her husband used, their "phone secrets" that ensured that information could not be saved by the listening devices installed in the apartment and in their telephone. She feels that the extensive activities of the Stasi, which were degrading and frightening and which barred creativity and self-determination, are still having aftereffects. On a visit to Berlin on December 18, 1989, she wrote that only when "espionage mania" has been overcome will free thinking become possible. Individuals must become free of fears and self-censorship, "so that people can breathe freely. Without looking round and listening in. Worthy of a free Europe" (*Challenges,* 27).

Dimitrova's image of Europe has utopian characteristics. Europe functions as a counterpart to the Balkans, becoming a symbol for the freedom and dignity of the individual. Hence, she constructs forms of encounter between women from Eastern and Western European cultures. Central to her views is the avoidance of polarities, of imposed national boundaries, in favor of a recognition of individual peoples and cultures. Dimitrova's image of a multicultural Europe is part of her political program, and it leads to changes in aesthetic representation.

In her story *Was bleibt* (What remains), Christa Wolf uses similar themes of surveillance, rigidity, and lack of creativity in totalitarian systems. Like the Bulgarian author, she highlights the problems of our relationship with language as a flawed system of communication. Both authors anticipate a new language, for "every social and political change engenders its own typical language and its own style" (*Challenges,* 6). While for Christa Wolf the critique of language ends with the search for the new real language, Blaga Dimitrova criticizes the new rules of posttotalitarian language, as did Orwell: "The grandiloquence of the soapbox. Truth from the highest authority. Aggressiveness. Invalidation of other views. Judgments in black and white, with no shades of gray. Demagogy. Repetitions. Clichés. Only the humor in it, often fairly coarse, but refreshing, has a slightly reviving effect. We are in a linguistic vicious circle" (*Challenges,* 6).

This summing-up defines a divergence from Christa Wolf's expressed views. The "Westernization" of everyday East German culture has conservative aspects, according to Christa Wolf, and the metamorphosis of language into a "new language," which has yet to be discovered, remains a utopian moment. To Blaga Dimitrova the use of old and new superlatives has within it the Bulgarian Communists' strategy of justifying themselves through language, and in her opinion these people need new hate objects, and to depict them verbally (extremists, neofascists, neo-Stalinists, terrorists). She describes tendencies to self-estrangement, even within the realm of language.

Dimitrova describes a further problem of Eastern European adaptation to Western Europe in her text "Women in Power" (*Challenges*). She calls for forms of power for women; otherwise the new power system will become established, with women once again excluded. She treats the issue of women as a social one, following the Communist and social democratic tradition, and consequently as an issue subordinate to the patriarchal society as a whole. For this reason, she hardly ever deals explicitly with issues about the sexes. In her texts, "If—The Question Mark" and "Europe, Where Did We Meet?" (both in *Challenges*), she describes her fears with regard to the possibility of new ethnic conflicts flaring up. She describes the city of her youth, Veliko Tirnovo, with its artists from all over the world, as a multicultural center of the twenties and thirties and has made it into a utopian model for European intercultural exchange. Here the differences between the various cultures were productive and allowed a collective consciousness of European artistry to develop.

Being able to be other and to recognize the foreign becomes the most important value in interpersonal relations. This paradigm requires the absence of fear and hatred. The freedom that has just been achieved is still very vulnerable, according to Dimitrova, since it will not automatically lead to self-determination for the Bulgarian nation, for "the latest image of our country—it has no face, it needs an imported image" (*Challenges*, 15).

As much as Dimitrova would like, on the one hand, to bring to her small country the possibility of multicultural "European" community, she backs, on the other hand, the development of national specialties of Bulgaria, which do, however include things foreign, other, things not home-grown in the Balkans. Her subjective experiences with "Bulgarianization" have an important part to play in this. In July 1989, according to Emilia Staitscheva,[13] the nationalistic campaign against the Turkish population reached its climax. The author took the side of her Turkish compatriots. From then on she was followed and watched by the Bulgarian secret service. A Turkish crescent moon, with a star in the middle, was daubed on the front door of Dimitrova's apartment with oily gray paint. When it became known that an American journalist was coming to the apartment for an interview, these symbols were painted over. Her text "The Door" is based on real events. She ends the essay with this wish: "My united European house! I hope your doors will be made of a resistant, waterlike crystalline material that can't be affected by tar, stars of David, swastikas, crescent moons, skulls and crossbones, and other stigmas" (*Challenges*, 15).

Bulgaria did not free itself from the so-called Ottoman yoke until 1876. Those five hundred years of foreign rule by the Turks were later used brutally and relentlessly in the ideology, were used to fight against minorities in the name of national rebirth. For example, at the time of the so-called process of rebirth, tremendous outrages were committed against ethnic minorities—the Roma, Sinti, and Turks. The name changing ordered by the police seemed to Dimitrova like the obliteration of identity. In her essay "The Name" (*Challenges*), she sensitively thematizes the psychological problems that accompany this kind of repression. In her story "Elmaz" she points out the massive amount of force that was used: "Tanks rattled through the peaceful villages. Hordes of armed men forced their way into their Turkish compatriots' houses and forced them at gunpoint to change their names. Anyone who resisted was knocked unconscious and thrown into prison. Finally, three hundred thousand people were driven en masse on a 'trip' to Turkey" ("Elmaz," 265). For Dimitrova these outrages were human rights violations, and she condemned them with conviction.

The creative inspiration in her story "Elmaz" is informative with respect to our theme. The first-person narrator (a woman and a poet) receives a letter from a young Turkish woman whose name was Elmaz and who now wishes to call herself Blaga, because she hopes this name may help her to escape further discrimination. Thereupon the narrator decides to change her name to Elmaz: "I called myself Elmaz." And there was a secret baptism "in a chapel at the crossroads of fear and conscience. A pocket mirror served as a font. Looking to see my face, I became absorbed in its cool, shiny depths" ("Elmaz," 264). The autobiographical features of this story are obvious. The letter described above is the moment that gives the narrator the impetus to seek her own roots and take stock of her life by seeking "signs of identity." In contrast to Elmaz, who is young, the narrator (like the author) is over seventy years old. And the name change is chosen freely by Blaga.

On her first birthday after the name change, Blaga/Elmaz makes the definitive discovery that without any images of an enemy, she has lost her identity. With the new, foreign name she has no biography, and thus no past. In order to gain a past she must denounce herself. "Elmaz is a false name, behind which an elderly, well-known author is hiding, who would like to extricate herself from her sins. What kind of sins? Any other time would scarcely recognize this phenomenon: a poet is ashamed of his poems, and longs to destroy them. Instead of immortality, they burden her with a lifelong stigma. Why? Because in her fiery, youthful fervor, she was naive enough to extol a utopia. And so, morally, she was one of the participants in the crime" ("Elmaz," 269).

The motivation for her name change is to set herself apart from her earlier poems, to understand their production as a historical mistake. Only by becoming Elmaz, by taking the position of the other, can she analyze the motivation for her own writing in the Rhodope Mountains and account to herself for what she had done and for what she had left undone. She draws a picture of herself as Blaga/Elmaz, as a guilty innocent confronting fateful consequences.

Along with her political and politicocultural self-criticism, the narrator explores her constant lovesickness in a fictional dialogue with Elmaz. The voice of lovesickness—embodied by Elmaz—as the other of the socialist society can be experienced as the "inexplicable." In Blaga's painful process of becoming a subject as Elmaz, she must get rid of pathos and sentimentality. The new concept of herself as the other was at first, in effect, a political working through of female experience and perception.

In the text, with its strongly autobiographical structure, liberation from one's accustomed life situation is described above all as liberation from one's own imposed self-control: "I free myself from myself, as a wolf in a trap bites its paw off to free itself from the iron. Only to get caught in the bigger trap of the woods, the wild, the world" ("Elmaz," 278).

The individualization process is described with all its inconsistencies. Freeing oneself is pointless if the external framework remains too rigid, but also if the new setting cannot be experienced as liberating. Only in a dream—where one's self-control and the control of the secret services end—can the narrator gain confidence in herself and a new feeling of self-worth as a woman. "I'm coming, Mother," is phrased as a certainty, although in the last part of the text, "Signs of Identity," it is also interpreted as a dream.

In the text, the moments of authenticity are not given an unequivocal meaning. The boundaries between Elmaz and Blaga keep shifting; unequivocal boundaries are not needed, since many experiences within the same social context are also multigenerational. The boundaries are unhomely/uncanny, undefinable.

Becoming certain of oneself as a process of finding oneself allows for a critique of ideology that leads to changed positions. The newly gained reality is an important orientation. Only as the foreigner, the other, only with this perspective on her past and future life, can the narrator as a woman gain a perspective for her work as a writer: "The more fanatical the degradation of my person, the greater my self-awareness and stubbornness. I will hold on; they won't break me. I exist—that's the sign of my identity" ("Elmaz," 283).

Translated by Elizabeth Naylor Endres

Notes

Where possible, Hannelore Scholz used German translations of Blaga Dimitrova's works; most of them have not yet been translated into English. Hence, for clarity, my own translations of the titles and of quotations from German translations are used throughout this essay, and page numbers are from the German translations, which appear in the list of works cited, their titles followed in parentheses by my translation into English as used in the text. Works that have not yet been translated into German are listed in the Works Cited section in English translation, and again this English title is used in the text. The collection *Challenges* was made available to the author in the form of as yet unpublished translations into German by Barbara Müller, and where the author gives quotations from Müller I have translated them from German into English; page citations in the text are those of the Bulgarian text.   Trans.

1. Dimitrova, "Elmaz," 265.
2. On the so-called "Deutsch-deutsche Literaturstreit," see Deiritz and Krauss.
3. On this new change in the government, see "Bulgarien—Land in Sicht. Kurs klar," *Frankfurter Allgemeine Zeitung*, "Blick durch die Wirtschaft," December 8, 1994.
4. On this controversial concept, see Troebst.
5. Bulgaria had to take in 120,000 refugees of Bulgarian heritage. See Glotz.
6. *Judgment Day* has been translated into seven languages.
7. These facts are taken from Staitscheva's essay.
8. Interview with Hannelore Scholz, June 5, 1985.
9. During the time of fascism no concentration camps for Jews were built in Bulgaria. Bulgarian Jews were transported to other countries.
10. For a more detailed description, see Scholz.
11. I am grateful to Emilia Staitscheva for giving me the essays translated into German by Barbara Müller. The original essays are from the volume *Challenges*, which I cite after Müller.
12. In Bulgarian "face" means individuality, originality, and an unchangeable profile.
13. Emilia Staitscheva teaches modern German literature at the University of Sofia.

Works Cited

Benjamin, Jessica. "A Desire of One's Own: Psychoanalytic Feminism and Intersubjective Space." In *Feminist Studies/Critical Studies*, edited by Teresa de Lauretis, 78–101. Bloomington: Indiana University Press, 1987.
———, ed. *Unbestimmte Grenzen: Beiträge zur Psychoanalyse der Geschlechter.* Frankfurt am Main: Fischer, 1995.
Bogdal, Klaus-Michael. "Wer darf sprechen? Schriftsteller als moralische Instanz: Überlegungen zu einem Ende und einem Anfang." In *Der Deutsch-deutsche Literaturstreit*, ed. Karl Deiritz and Hannes Krauss, 40–49. Hamburg: Luchterhand Literaturverlag, 1991.
Deiritz, Karl, and Hannes Krauss, eds. *Der Deutsch-deutsche Literaturstreit, oder, "Freunde, es spricht sich schlecht mit gebundener Zunge."* Hamburg: Luchterhand Literaturverlag, 1991.
Dimitrova, Blaga. *Challenges: Political Etudes.* Sofia: Institute of Culture, 1991.
———. "Elmaz." In *Das Buch der Ränder*, edited by Karl-Markus Gauß, 264–83. Klagenfurt and Salzburg, 1992.
———. *The Face: Novel.* 2nd rev. ed. Sofia: Bulgarian Writer, 1990.
———. *Fenster zur Hoffnung* (Window on hope). Edited and translated into German by Wolfgang Köppe. 1st ed. Berlin: Volk und Welt, 1986.
———. *Journey to Oneself.* Translated into English by Radost Pridham. London: Cassell, 1969.
———. *Judgment Day: Travel Diary Novel.* Plovdiv: Danov, 1969.
———. *Die Lawine* (The avalanche). Translated into German by Egon Hartmann. 1st ed. Berlin: Volk und Welt, 1981.
———. *Liebe auf Umwegen* (Love in a roundabout way). Translated into German by Barbara Sparing. Berlin: Volk und Welt, 1969.

————. "Mysteries about the Novel *Face.*" *Every Sunday* 16 (1991).

————. *Underground Sky: The Vietnamese Diary.* Sofia: Partizdat, 1972.

————. *Verses for the Chief.* Sofia: Bulgarian Writer, 1950.

Foucault, Michel. "Was ist ein Autor?" In *Schriften zur Literatur,* 7–31. Frankfurt am Main: Fischer, 1978.

Glotz, Peter. "Die Krankheit Nationalismus." *Die Zeit,* no. 12 (March 17, 1995).

Scholz, Hannelore. "Sie haben begonnen, den Gipfel Menschen zu besteigen: Weltanschaulich-moralische Umrisse von Frauengestalten bei Blaga Dimitrova und Christa Wolf." *Archiv für bulgarische Philologie* (Sofia) 1 (1988): 174–88.

Staitscheva, Emilia. "Herausforderungen an Sisyphus oder: die bulgarische Dichterin Blaga Dimitrova in der Wende zur Demokratie." In *Ich will meine Trauer nicht leugnen und nicht meine Hoffnung: Veränderungen kultureller Selbstwahrnehmungen von ostdeutschen und osteuropäischen Frauen nach 1989,* edited by Helga Grubitzsch, Eva Kaufmann, and Hannelore Scholz. Bochum: Dr. Winkler, 1994.

Troebst, Stefan. "Nationale Minderheiten." In *Südosteuropahandbuch: Band VI, Bulgarien,* edited by Klaus-Detlev von Grothusen, 474–89. Göttingen: Vandenhoeck & Ruprecht, 1990.

Wolf, Christa. *Lesen und Schreiben.* Darmstadt: Luchterhand, 1985.

————. *Nachdenken über Christa T.* Halle: Mitteldeutscher, 1968. Published in English as *The Quest for Christa T.* New York: Farrar, Straus and Giroux, 1979.

————. *Was bleibt: Erzählung.* Frankfurt am Main: Luchterhand, 1990. Published in English as *What Remains and Other Stories.* New York: Farrar, Straus and Giroux, 1979.

Zhelev, Zhelyu. *Fascism.* Sofia: Narodna Kultura, n.d.

12 / Exile, Immigrant, Re/Unified

Writing (East) Postunification Identity in Germany

Gisela Brinker-Gabler

Dis/re/located in Germany

In his essay "DissemiNation: Time, Narrative, and the Margins of the Modern Nation," Homi Bhabha writes that nowadays the *modern* nation is being rewritten by those who live at its margins. These include, according to Bhabha, "the colonized" and "the women," as well as "migrants" and "immigrants." It is from the margins that the idea of a nation as a harmonious community is being questioned most radically today. Division, multiplicity, and ambivalence are taking the place of unity and community. In this essay, I will assume that Bhabha's observation may be applied to the analysis and interpretation of Germany's postunification situation and cultural production. Germany's unification in 1990 was an important and far-reaching event not only for the "two Germanys" but also for the European Community, struggling with political and economical integration, international economic pressures, and waves of refugees and immigrants. Although German unification has often been represented as a "family reunion,"[1] in practical terms it has been a very complicated process involving a wide range of political, economic, social, and legal factors, against the backdrop of Germany's difficult historical legacy.

To be "unified" means a great many different things in places as different as East and West Germany, and therefore the search for a new identity and legitimacy has become very different for East and West German subjects. When the East German state "acceded to the Federal Republic and ceased to exist," as Jürgen Kocka puts it (176), East Germans were at the same time insider and outsider, familiar and foreign, central and marginal—participating in *one* (West) German nation-state but deprived of the history and traditions of their former nation-state. They experienced a specific form of displacement that I would like to term dis/re/location; this involves a rupture of the collective East German subject and the individual subject—which is also a rupture of language—and a re-placement in a reunited Germany with new conditions of experience. Whereas large numbers of the population supported German unification, especially at the beginning, its actual effect was to relegate various groups to the very margins of society. Among them were people who had not been involved with the revolutionary movement at all, as well as those who took part in the East German Revolution but were not in favor of national unification because they "held fast to the idea of a Third Way: Socialism with a human face," to use Katie Hafner's phrase,[2] and those who supported unification under a new constitution, "which would have offered the opportunity to bring elements from both the West and the East together into a new and better solution" (Kocka, 177).

Various forms of displacement, and their representation in narratives and the visual arts, have become the focus of theory and interpretation in recent years.[3] I myself am a border crosser, having relocated three times for professional reasons across the borderline called the Atlantic; I also have painful early childhood memories of coming to West Germany as a refugee from the eastern provinces. My own experiences of loss and gain prevent me from embracing "authentic identities" and from welcoming "happy nomadism" in any abstract sense, and have awakened my interest in the negotiation of boundaries, as well as making me aware of the possibilities and constraints of border positions. In this essay, I will discuss various forms of displacement to see how they might relate to postunification displacement. Then I will take a look at recent works by two East German writers, Christa Wolf and Helga Königsdorf,[4] who offer different perspectives on how to develop a shared sociopolitical space. Exploring the ways in which postunification displacement inscribes itself in their texts, I will look into the processes of differentiation, examining the underlying subject positions and perspectives that might produce an ideological bloc—an "us-against-them" mind-set—or perhaps allow instead for other, more complex positionings.

Thinking about Borders and Displacement

The postunification situation as experienced by former citizens of the German Democratic Republic (GDR) brings to mind a range of displaced positions, which, although they are not specific to this particular situation, allow us to think it through from different perspectives. I have in mind the terms "exile," "immigrant," and "borderline intellectual," representing three situations or types of personality created by displacement. One must bear in mind the wide range of situations for which terms of displacement are being used today. On the one hand they are used to address acute political, social, economic, and racial inequalities, while on the other hand we find many different metaphorical uses of these terms within postmodern theories that define the situation of subjects, for example, the intellectual, the cultural outsider, or social and political outlaw. Accordingly, when I speak of postunification displacement, I do not necessarily mean a *geographical* displacement, although geographical displacements took place en masse both before and after unification. As I use the term, it refers to the *spiritual* or *psychic* displacement that came with the change from GDR to German citizenship. I could discuss the use of this terminology in relation to West German left-wing intellectuals or the generation of '68, who have been blamed for having failed to play their part in the events around unification. But for now I will focus on the situation of East Germans in general.

People who are displaced, exiles or émigrés, migrants or immigrants, for example, all confront what Benedict Anderson describes as the experience of multiple styles of community, clashes of different cultures and histories. There can be a positive or a negative stance toward new cultural, social, and national communities. As JanMohamed argues, an *immigrant's* stance toward the new host culture is positive, because it has been deliberately chosen as a new home. The *exile's* stance, in contrast, is negative, because of "an involuntary or enforced rupture between the collective subject of the original culture and the individual subject" (101). Although I think there will always most likely be mixed feelings, sooner or later we might at first think of former East Germans as "exiles" or "immigrants" in the new project called "unified Germany." Despite staying "at home," East German subjects have faced a dislocation from their history and culture, as well as from the systems that regulated their public and private lives. Not only have they experienced a "spiritual" displacement, but their social, economic, political, and juridical circumstances have also changed. Some might argue that the word "exile" is too strong to describe the kind of change involved. It is true that the situation of East Germans is a far cry from an exile that follows the horrifying reality of suffering, death, and destruction. Yet it is not just a metaphorical exile; it represents a real loss. Based on the new conditions of experience and the rupture between the collective GDR subject and the individual subject, which is also a rupture of language, I find the use of this term legitimate. Christa Wolf, for example, talks about *Entfremdung* (*Auf dem Weg nach Tabou,* 46), a term that describes both estrangement (*fremd werden*) and alienation (*zum Fremden werden*).

As JanMohamed explains, it is the *immigrant* who "is often eager to discard with deliberate speed the formative influences of his or her own culture and to take on the values of the new culture," whereas the nostalgia associated with *exile* often makes the individual indifferent to the values and characteristics of the host culture (101). Todorov defines an exile as "a being who has lost his country without thereby acquiring another, who lives in double exteriority" (249). Edward Said, in his essay "Intellectual Exile: Expatriates and Marginals," uses exile as a trope for any dislocation and migration. As he points out, different kinds of exile (becoming an expatriate, migrant, or immigrant, for example) are based on differing relations to one's homeland. But how can you describe someone's relations to a "homeland" that has ceased to exist, like the former Yugoslavia or the former GDR? However, all exiles share the same relation with their host country; they are all foreigners. This definition allows Said to move from exile as an actual condition to exile in its metaphorical sense. He suggests that we think of intellectuals as exiles, and cites as an exemplary case Adorno, "the intellectual as a permanent exile" (119). Intellectuals, however, can also be collaborators, and since Germany's unification there have been many discussions for and against East German intellectuals' alleged complicity in the "Unrechtssystem" (injustice system). Said thinks of intellectuals as exiles who can never fully arrive, who are at odds with their society, and who have a double perspective, never seeing things in isolation. Virginia Woolf's famous phrase on women's exile in a patriarchal culture also comes to mind: "If one is a woman one is often surprised by a sudden splitting off of consciousness, say in walking down Whitehall, when from being the natural inheritor of that civilisation, she becomes, on the contrary, outside of it, alien and critical" (101). As Louise Yelin describes, here exile is "on one hand, to be displaced by that culture ('outside' or exiled from); on the other to be engaged in transforming/displacing it ('alien and critical')" (396). This paradigm of exile as a positionality involving both being displaced and displacing echoes Homi Bhabha's project of a rewriting of nations by those on the margins. It applies equally well to JanMohamed's definition of interstitial space in terms of the "border intellectual," of which there are two types, "based on the *intentionality of their intellectual orientation*" (97). Whereas the "syncretic" intellectual, more "at home" in both cultures, is able to combine elements of the two cultures "in order to articulate new syncretic forms and experiences," the "specular" border intellectual, finding himself or herself unable or unwilling to be "at home" in both cultures, "subjects the cultures to analytic scrutiny rather than combining them; he or she utilizes his or her interstitial cultural space as a vantage point from which to define, implicitly or unexplicitly, other, utopian possibilities of group formation" (97).

I find these reflections on exile, immigrant, and borderline intellectual personalities quite illuminating for this discussion of postunification cultural production (literature from all sides and from in between) because they show us new ways to think about borders and the effects of crossing them. I will address the specifics of the postunification situation for East German subjects by using the term "re/unified," which I spell with a slash to denote the experience of the split between East and West and the struggle to overcome it. I will discuss texts by Christa Wolf and Helga Königsdorf that describe the German/German struggle from the shifting perspectives of the "exile" and "immigrant," the "resistant" and "ambivalent re/unified" intellectual. Christa Wolf can be seen as an exile, in her case a *triple* exteriority (to rewrite Todorov's phrase): the loss of a country and at the same time the loss of the envisioned "Third Way" (an alternative democratic socialist state), *without* having really acquired a new "home" in the "new" Germany. She is "auf dem Weg" (on her way), and as a resistant re/unified intellectual, she uses her interstitial space to define new possibilities. This stance is strongly connected with the need to recollect and rearticulate the past and with the struggle not to forget it. In contrast, Helga Königsdorf's stance toward the new community is rather that of an immigrant, whose situation is not quite "deliberately chosen," but is soon accepted as an indisputable political reality. Her writings express an ambivalent re/unified positioning, an attempt to cross existing bridges between diverse communities and to build new ones.

Envisioning a New Commonality: A Project of Critical Memory

Christa Wolf's *Auf dem Weg nach Tabou* is a "hybrid" book, made up of various textual components such as essays, letters by Wolf and by others, sections addressed to specific people and others that read like journal entries, factual accounts, prose, poetry, with some of the texts subjective, others encoded, symbolic. It is a book about loss, displacement, and the search for a new place. What kind of place? Tabou. In *A Model Childhood* "Glitzerwörter" (glitter words) function as taboos limiting the expressible: "One shouldn't try to call everything by its name, so as to give purity, awe, and reverence a chance to survive in the realm of the unspoken" (123). In her essay "Auf dem Weg nach Tabou: Versuch über Paul Parin," which was actually a speech given by Wolf at the awards ceremony where Parin received the Erich Fried prize in 1992, she wrote: "Tabou, ein Ort, den es nicht gibt, dessen Name immer wieder aufleuchtet, lockend, verführend, bis sie sich aufmachen," and here Wolf is talking about a book by Parin, "bis sie sich aufmachen müssen, ihn zu suchen, ein Ort, den man, wie billig, nur unter äußerster Anstrengung aller körperlichen und geistigen Kräfte erreichen kann. Den man 'vergessen' muß, damit er einem endlich entgegenkommt" (Tabou, a place that does not exist, whose name keeps beckoning, seductively, until they must set out to find it, a place that can only be reached through the utmost exertion of one's physical and spiritual resources—as is only right. A place one must "forget" in order for it to finally come toward you) (186).

Tabou, with its unusual spelling "ou" (this is also the French spelling of "taboo"), suggests a taboo word for 'u-topia," which comes from the Greek *u* (not) and *topos* (place). Another of Christa Wolf's books also alludes to utopia in its title: *No Place on Earth,* the story of a fictitious meeting between the Romantic poets Karoline Günderrode and Heinrich Kleist. This time, by choosing the title *Auf dem Weg nach Tabou,* Wolf positions herself as someone who does not inhabit a fixed place, and also someone who does not have to arrive somewhere. On the other hand there is a place, a "home," which is the irreducible first condition of the writer's subject position, a place to which she always returns from her various travels, as the reader learns, with excitement: Berlin. Berlin is both a geopolitical and metaphorical location: a town separated by a wall that made it a metaphor for the cold war, representing the polarities of East versus West, capitalism versus socialism. The Wall and the polarities it represented still have an impact upon identification and imaginary identities. As McKenzie Wark suggests, "The wall not only partitions one set of people from another, it interpellates those individuals, it structures their sense of who they are, particularly in the east" (35). Identities have been shaped around polarities that cannot easily be discarded; imaginary walls are sturdier than concrete ones.

With the meeting of East and West at the Wall a masked ball began, indeed, as McKenzie Wark suggests, a ball where both East and West looked at each other and took off their masks, only to realize that they were strangers to each other, only masquerading as East and West, respectively. In the final section of her book, written in 1994, Christa Wolf still calls for people (on both sides) to dismiss the phantoms that represent not only the other country but also their own country. It might be even more disturbing if, at the the masked ball, the faces under the masks turned out to be only more masks.

The writing self (which I would call the first-person narrator if this were a narrative) of *Auf dem Weg nach Tabou* speaks from an irreducible first condition, as all of us write from the perspective of a particular place and time, from a history and culture specific to ourselves. The specific historical conjuncture of this book is indicated by the subtitle *1990–1994;* each year also functions as a chapter heading. Marking this period as a time of "unity," but only an abstract, unrepresentable unity, the texts in *Tabou* mediate the split that divides historical subjects by redrawing the boundaries between the "nation us" and the "aliens outside." However, they also differentiate the "aliens within" and transgress real and imaginary boundaries because of other interests of cultural importance. "Outside" there are the "unwissenden oder übelwollenden Sieger" (ignorant or malicious conquerers) or, ironically, "die von Herkunft her Gerechten" (those whose backgrounds make them right) (81) as opposed to the "gutgläubigen" (gullible) GDR citizens, "zu Monster dämonisiert" (demonized as monsters) by West Germany and its media. Clearly the effect of the assymetries of power in a time of "absorption," these simplistic polarities overlook complex identities and preclude the emergence of different meanings and possibilities. But, as cultural and political identity is always constructed by a process of othering, outside *and* within, the others "within" are also presented in a kind of simplistic fashion: "die kleinen Geister, Arschkriecher, die Aufsteiger, and [s]olche, die sich niemals und nirgends wehren" (small minds, grovelers, social climbers, and the kind of people who never, ever put up a fight). More significant in terms of the alienation of the writing self, there are those named "die Anderen" (others), of whom it is said that they have not been "others" from the beginning. With regard to the controversial Stasi episode of 1960,[5] Wolf writes that at that time "ich habe sie noch nicht als DIE ANDEREN gesehen" (I did not yet see them as the others) (274). This suggests that in the past there was an idea (or indoctrinated idea) of a shared culture and community that has undergone a continuous process of change caused by the recognition of significant differences, either latent or apparent. Community therefore divides, multiplies, and fragments before the reader's eyes until in the end, in one of the last sections of the book, Wolf writes: " 'Wir' sage ich und meine eine kleine Gruppe von Freunden" (I say "we" and I mean a small group of friends) (294). Previously Wolf used "we" to refer to intellectuals, while acknowledging differences among them that mark important shifts in affiliations and solidarities: she mentions the differences between the artistic and scientific intelligentsia, which have to do with their social position and thus their dependence on the system. Elsewhere she talks about the intelligentsia in Brechtian terms, as "Tuis," which means "gekauft vom System" (bought by the system) as opposed to those intellectuals who, Wolf says, remained there and tolerated the contradictions, "der Teil der Intelligenz, der nach geistigen Alternativen zum Konsumdenken und zur Entfremdungspraxis des Kapitalismus sucht" (those among the intelligentsia who are looking for spiritual alternatives to capitalism's consumerism and practice of alienation) (75), or "wir, die Mitglieder der Akademie [der Künste]" (we, the members of the Academy [of Arts]) (72).

By following the processes of differentiation of this "we," wherein community shrinks to "we, a small group of friends," Wolf allows herself to become a resistant re/unified subject. Caught between the East's and the West's cultures and various groups, none of which are deemed sufficiently enabling or productive, she is not interested in combining them but instead looks for other possibilities. This is corroborated by the fact that in the eighties, Wolf turned her back on the current debate about contemporary GDR society, focusing instead on the threat of Western rationality and technology, which now appears to be the worse evil. This came at the same time as her decision to divide her life between the walled city of Berlin and a place in the country.

Diversity has transformed not only community and solidarity but also, unavoidably, the self. The self, no longer an autonomous identity, has become the decentered "multiple self," which Christa Wolf talks about in the story *Was bleibt* (What remains) and also in her response to a letter by Efim Etkind, who mentions that narrative.[6] The opportunity for boundaries to shift and for solidarities to change was made possible only by a fragmentation of the sovereignty of the self. But all this happened within a power struggle and an involved discourse that changed as of 1990. Now the I who writes orients herself not toward the West in general, nor toward the Federal Republic of Germany, which now represents the united Germany, but a third space, elsewhere, Tabou. What can take you to this space? The "principle of home," for example. On page 169, exactly in the middle of the 339-page book, following an essay entitled "Nagel-probe" (Experiment/Test with nails), which tells various "Nagelgeschichten" (stories about nails),[7] and before the essay "Auf dem Weg nach Tabou" (On the way to Tabou), we find the poem "Prinzip Hoffnung," the title of which alludes to Ernst Bloch's classic study, *The Principle Hope:*

Prinzip Hoffnung

Genagelt
ans Kreuz Vergangenheit
Jede Bewegung
treibt
die Nägel
ins Fleisch.

The Principle of Hope

Nailed
to the cross of the past
Every movement
drives
the nails
into the flesh.

How should we read the principle of hope? Ernst Bloch, in *Das Prinzip Hoffnung,* is the forward-looking thinker, while here the I, an I in exile, is nailed to the past, wounded and in pain. As for Benjamin's angel, fixation on the past brings torment. But the poem suggests that suffering itself is the principle of hope. Out of "suffering history" come imagination, desire, and thought. There must be a painful struggle of memory against forgetting. A voice, a future, can emerge only from this process. As we read in *Cassandra:* "Who will find a voice again, and when? It will be one whose skull is split by pain" (8).

The experience of "losing one's voice" is described in the prose section "Be-fund" (Findings), which follows the text of "Auf dem Weg nach Tabou." In an almost Kafkaesque manner the text describes how someone has a feeling, a "Gesträuch" (thicket) develops in the throat, up to the jaws, so that the voice cannot get through, or at least not in its full strength. The loss of words, specific words like "truth," "loyalty," "love," and "betrayal," indicates that the old system of values and the old language structure have been lost, without new ones being there to replace them. No longer positioned within her own culture, history, and language, the I, an I in exile, is silenced. If one has no voice, who will speak for you, instead of you? "Wohin wird die Geschichte dieser vierzig Jahre geraten, die ja kein Phantom ist, aber bei ihrem Verschwinden Phantomschmerz hinterlassen wird. . . . Die Literatur wird leisten müssen, was sie immer und überall leisten muß, wird die blinden Flecken in unserer Vergangenheit erkunden müssen und die Menschen in die neuen Verhältnisse begleiten" (Where will the history of these forty years go, which is not a phantom, but will leave behind phantom pains when it disappears. . . . Literature will have to do what it must always do everywhere: it will have to investigate the blind spots in our past and accompany people on their way to their new circumstances) (21). As in the past, literary anamnesis must prevent cultural amnesia. The past is not merely a phantom, but it is also not a given to which one can return easily. As Stuart Hall reminds us, "There is a past to be learned about, but the past is now seen, and it has to be grasped as a history, as something that has to be told" ("Cultural Identity," 226). It must be constructed by the use of memory, fantasy, and narrative. To use Julia Watson's phrase, recollection is "inevitably the memory of memories" (78). Writing history is a political issue, since it illuminates not only the past but also the present, which means transforming it.

Auf dem Weg nach Tabou marks the early stage in the production of a "history." As Wolf mentions, this production will marginalize the writer; also, this history can *only* be produced from the margins. For many East Germans, German unification means that their past has been taken away from them, appropriated and devalued by the West, undermining the East's self-worth. Those on the margins, such as those from the East, must not only produce a history of their own, but must also survive while actively resisting cultural attempts at homogenization on the one hand (77) and total rejection on the other (81). To be homogenized means to be neutralized, to be disconnected from one's history; yet to be rejected by culture, as a citizen of an "Unrechtsstaat" (a play on the words "Rechtsstaat," constitutionally governed state, and "unrecht," unjust), for example, allows the rejecting (West) culture to remain intact. Writing, in contrast, means remembering, that is resisting. In spite of the difficulties of their position, re/unified intellectuals from the East have the advantage of having access to more than one discourse and history, which allows for ambivalence and also the ability to transcend division by imagining and constructing new possibilities.

Writing *Auf dem Weg nach Tabou*, between "here" and "there" becomes an endeavor of a new mode of production, shifting from the "most subjective" to the "most objective," from the writing subject to the passive mediator. In "Selbstanzeige" (Announcement about myself), right at the beginning of *Auf dem Weg nach Tabou,* Wolf describes her "Schreibideal" (ideal writing style): "Eine Art Mit-Schrift. . . . Ein Griffel folgte möglichst genau der Lebensspur, die Hand, die ihn führte, wäre meine Hand und auch nicht meine Hand, viele und vieles schriebe mit, das Subjektivste und das Objektivste verschränkten sich unauflösbar, wie im Leben" (A kind of participatory writing. . . . A pen followed the traces of life as closely as possible, the hand that held it might be my hand or might not be my hand; many people and many things might be writing with me; the most subjective and the most objective clasped one another inextricably, as in life) (9). Moving back and forth, the author/mediator presents an interconnection of diverse voices, from the past or present, from the East or West—voices of friends, acquaintances, colleagues, intellectuals, as well as people with whom one comes into contact in everyday life, such as a taxi driver, a child, a shop assistant, a physiotherapist. There are also subjective and analytical passages that often take the form of a dialogue or have an addressee. A textual web that allows for multiple voicing—one's own voices, voices of difference, voices of subjects rendered mute—has replaced the viewpoint of the "all-knowing" subject.

With her texts Christa Wolf manages to be "unterwegs" (underway) both in a literal sense, on trips to and from Berlin, Vienna, Zurich, and Santa Monica, and in a metaphorical sense, in the "encounters" with artists and intellectuals both living and dead who are her "Weggefährten" (fellow travelers), providing orientation, perspectives, and self-questioning (Max Frisch, Heinrich Böll, Anna Seghers, Paul Parin, Ilse Aichinger, Efim Etkin, Grace Paley, Jürgen Habermas, Friederike Mayröcker, Günter Grass, Volker and Anna Braun, and Nuria Quevedo). A multiply linked subjectivity emerges, as Ernst Bloch might have had in mind: "Ein Mensch nimmt mit sich, wenn er wandert" (People take things along when they go wandering) (49). Bloch and even Benjamin are brought to mind by Wolf's attentive and critical eye for ordinary utilitarian things, "die kleinen Dinge," like a table, a loaf of bread, and, in a nostalgic vein (a mark of exile), trash cans made of ebonite and wooden clothespins she buys, and images she collects, like "das leicht verwahrloste Haus" (the slightly dilapidated house) and a "kurzes Stück Kopfsteinpflaster" (some feet of cobblestone pavement), images she saves as "eine Art Wegzehrung für schlechtere Tage" (like provisions for a rainy day) (99).

The new community that emerges from the structure and style of the book allows for differentiation, as we see, for example, in Wolf's response to Habermas's letter, which details her discrimination between the Western intellectual as being exclusively oriented toward the West and the Eastern intellectual as having entry to both East *and* West. Also, this new community allows for affiliation, as shown in the essay "Die Wahrheit unserer Zungen" (The truth of our tongues), about the American writer Grace Paley, whose works have, according to Wolf, a "weibliche Form" (female form) (85) and display what children mean for a woman writer; or the essay about Nuria Quevedo, the bicultural painter, who says, "Jeder muß die Bilder lesen, wie er es braucht" (Everyone must read the pictures the way he needs to) (306). And this new community also allows for identification, as shown by the unique "Gespräch unter Deutschen" (Conversation among Germans), a conversation with Inge and Otl Aicher. *Auf dem Weg nach Tabou* is a rejection of abstract calls for national integration, "gesamtdeutsche Identität" (unified German identity). By writing her own narrative(s) through the narrative of others, Wolf creates an alternative community (*Gemeinschaft*), and with it an identity for herself, a history she can identify with, which legitimizes her experience of being not "national" but local and translocal at the same time.

But what about the reality of the "new Germany," the question of national integration and "unified German identity"? This acute reality is addressed in the last section of the book under the subheading "1994," which lists only one contribution: "Abschied von Phantomen—Zur Sache: Deutschland" (Saying goodbye to phantoms: About Germany), a talk given in February 1994 in Dresden. Wolf describes an experience she had in May 1993 when talking to some Americans (as a fellow of the Getty Foundation, she lived in the United States during 1992 and 1993). For the first time ever, she was confronted with the fact that she was liable to be called to account for crimes happening in the "neuen, großen, vereinigten Deutschland" (new, big, united Germany). "Von einer Sekunde zur anderen hatte ich jetzt die Verantwortung zu übernehmen für die Untaten in Rostock *und* für die in Mölln" (From one moment to the next, I now had to take responsibility for the atrocities in Rostock *and* those in Mölln) (327). From that moment she began to see Germany in a new light: "Was ich sah, war ein in innere Widersprüche und Kämpfe verwickeltes Land, über dem sich, wie ein Regenbogen, erklärend die Losung DEUTSCHE EINHEIT wölbte" (What I saw was a country enmeshed in inner contradictions and conflicts, with the slogan GERMAN UNITY spanning it like a rainbow) (327–28).

"O Deutschland, wie bist du zerrissen/Und nicht mit dir allein" (O Germany, how torn apart you are. And not by yourself)—Brecht's "Deutschland-

Gedicht" from 1952 is placed at the beginning of this final section of *Auf dem Weg nach Tabou* below the heading "1994." Bitterness and hurt can still be felt because of the lack of social integration and because a new process of othering has emerged over the last four years: the Western "temporalizing" of the Eastern others, as being "auf einer niederigen Zivilationsstufe" (at a lower level of civilization) and "ungeschliffen, plebejisch, proletenhaft" (uncouth, plebeian, proletarian), altogether "Brüder and Schwester aus einer sehr fremden Familie" (brothers and sisters from a family who are very much strangers) (329), whose past is presented as a "Skandalchronik" (chronicle of scandals) like her own. Looking for the right word to describe her feelings, Wolf uses the term "unheimlich" (whose literal meaning is "uncanny," but in order to include the connotations of the word "Heim" [home], I will translate it as "un-homely"): "Da wurde mir unheimlich. . . . Unheimlich vor dem Verschwinden der Realität" (I felt un-homely. . . . Un-homely about the disappearance of reality) (330). "Unhomely" here, I suggest, finally means the true realization of the loss of the national "home." This opens up a thinking of overcoming it. Wolf calls for a bilateral effort of facing up to the *one* united German issue, the shared responsibility for the Nazi atrocities; this issue, says Wolf, leads to three further questions: "Was war? Was ist? Was bleibt?" (What was? What is? What remains?) The future of the new nation demands coming to terms with "der deutschen Wirklichkeit" (German reality): "Tätst Du Dir selbst vertrauen/wär alles Kinderspiel" (If you trusted yourself/everything would be child's play) (311). Just as the last lines of Brecht's poems refer to an earlier time, yet also a time that is still anticipated, that is "heimatlich" (homely), the last paragraph of this final section of the book evokes the intimate circle of a community collected around a single table, sharing bread and wine, as a trope for a new nation:

> Brot als archaisches Symbol . . . [d]as regt, zusammen mit Wein, zum Gespräch an, zur Vertrautheit, Freundschaft, Gastfreundschaft. Das würde mir gefallen, und auch das gibt es ja: Deutsche aus verschiedenen Himmelsrichtungen, die miteinander arbeiten, Projekte entwickeln, die sich dann um den Tisch setzen, miteinander reden, auch streiten, essen, gemeinsam die Suppe auslöffeln, die sie sich eingebrockt haben. Das Brot auf den Tisch legen, das sie aus ihren verschiedenen Landschaften mitgebracht haben, es einander zu kosten geben und es gerne und großzügig mit anderen teilen. (339)

> [Bread as an archaic symbol . . . that, together with wine, invites conversation, intimacy, friendship, hospitality. I would like that, and it

does happen: Germans from different directions, who work together and develop projects, who then sit at the table, talk to one another, and also argue, eat, and together consume the soup into which they have broken their bread. To put bread on the table that they have brought from their different regions, to give it to one another to taste, and to share it gladly and generously with one another"]

(What is lost in this translation is the allusion to the German saying, "Die Suppe, die man sich eingebrockt hat, muß man selber auslöffeln"—"The soup into which you've broken your bread you must eat yourself"; in other words, "You've made your bed, now lie in it.") This is an appealing, "homely" vision, suffused with the tempting odor of German bread as a force for bringing together a community (a vision that I personally must admit to being attracted to because of my own love for German bread). To be sure, the "homely," as we are aware, always has its own restrictive attachments. Christa Wolf's view of "coming into unity" follows the Latin *communitatem,* fellowship. Mutual support arises from continual conversation and sharing, from the feast, as Hölderlin writes, "das bereitet ist . . . zum Abend der Zeit und zur Verheißung der kommenden" (that is prepared . . . for the evening of time and as a promise for the time to come).[8] Community has as its core a "Gruppe Gleichgesinnter, Gleichberechtigter" (group of like-minded equals). This is, according to Wolf—in her speech on Paul Parin, "Auf dem Weg nach Tabou"—at the core of his (and her) utopia. Community conveys the utopia of early Romanticism that openly looks toward the future and a socialist vision of fully liberated and supportive humanity. But is this concept really compatible with multiple differences and contradictions, particularly the multicultural nature of the new Germany and the new Europe? Does the process of becoming a nation depend only on the relationship of German nationals with one another and not also with national others? Taking Wolf's "bread as an archaic symbol" literally, will people from all directions be able to participate in the feast if they bring not German bread, but instead pita bread, challah, or *lahvash*?

In a speech at the West German university at Hildesheim in January 1990, before the unification in October, Wolf expressed hope for the possibility "alte Fremdheiten allmählich aufzulösen und keine neuen entstehen zu lassen" (to gradually dissolve old enmities and not allow any new ones to arise) (22). We might have to ask ourselves whether this hope does not already point toward an exclusive notion of community—a nation that, as time goes on, precludes the need to deal with the the "foreign" within and without, with the contradictions and specificities of a heterogeneous community. Superseding the ideology of borders means overcoming restrictive dualities by opening oneself up for a *continuous* process of differentiation, for an *ongoing* negotiation that destabilizes fixed collective identities. It seems to me that Christa Wolf's utopian unity has yet to become a " 'unities'-in-difference," to use Stuart Hall's term (*Minimal Selves*, 45). How can this next step become a reality? How much sense of community is necessary? And what kind of national identity, if not a "natural" one, do we want to promote? I will continue to address these questions as I turn to the works of Helga Königsdorf.

Envisioning a New Commonality: Building New Alliances

Helga Königsdorf has been writing critical commentary on German/German events since what is known as the "Wende" (turning point, that is, the events of 1989), and her writings have been published in several collections. I will be concentrating mainly on two of her collections, *Aus dem Dilemma eine Chance machen* (Making an opportunity out of a dilemma, 1990) and *Von der unverzüglichen Rettung der Welt* (On saving the world without delay, 1994), which take the events of 1990 to 1994 as their theme. Königsdorf's earlier volume *1989 oder Ein Moment Schönheit* (1989 or a moment of beauty), an example of what I would like to term "witness literature" about the "turning point," expresses a strong commitment to deal with the realities of the present: "Nicht Nostalgie, nicht Illusion, sondern schnelles Einstellen auf die neuen Bedingungen ist das Gebot der Stunde" (The need of the moment is neither nostalgia, nor illusions, but rapid adaptation to the new circumstances) (*Ein Moment,* 146). *Ein Moment* presents the fast-paced events of that year, with a love story, among other things, interwoven into the plot. The immediacy and authenticity of the experience are the main emphases. Like Wolf's *Auf dem Weg nach Tabou, Ein Moment* is a hybrid text, a collage made up of different kinds of texts, in this case speeches, letters (some of them addressed to numbers), poems, newspaper articles, and passages printed in Courier type that detail important political events. The author switches back and forth between presenting information and offering subjective private or political opinions, between the style of a news reporter and a laconic, often very casual style of critical analysis, expressed in candid language. The book's introduction emphasizes the uniqueness of the events that were happening, and the combination of personal and political themes creates an "Effekt der Monumentalisierung" (monumentalizing effect), to borrow Sabine Wilke's phrase (486), which also affects the writing self: "Nach diesem Jahr werden Gedichte unmöglich sein. Nach diesem Jahr wird es keine Liebe und keine Revolution mehr geben. Wenn ich könnte, würde ich den Frühling verbieten" (After this year poetry will be impossible. After this year there will be no more love and no more revolutions. If I could, I would prevent spring from coming) (n.p.).

One of the most notable insights in *Ein Moment*, which is developed further in the books she published in 1991 und 1994, is about the *impossibility* of utopia, that is, the impossibility of a consensual ideology (and so, unlike Wolf, Königsdorf is really entitled to talk about a rupture): "Der allgemein verordnete Konsens ist zu Ende" (The statutory general consensus is at an end). "Wir werden in der Zukunft Meinungsvielfalt, Interessenkonflikte, Streit ertragen müssen, vor allem lernen müssen, daß es auch hierin eine Kultur gibt" (In the future we will have to put up with plurality of opinions, conflicts of interest, and controversy, and above all we will have to learn that all of this represents a culture, too) (*Ein Moment*, 146).

Following her radical avowal of heterogeneity, Helga Königsdorf launches a critical analysis of the past, socialism, the Party, and the "Weltverbesserer" (people who [think they] are improving the world), and also attempts to create a new sense of place, such as through her reflections on "Heimat" (homeland), "Europa" (Europe), and the possibilities of "linker Politik" (left-wing politics). But this recognition of heterogeneity does not yet mean giving up a project of collective identity and collective rhetoric. Königsdorf does, however, make a categorical statement at the beginning of *Dilemma*: "Wenn ich also von uns spreche, so meine ich durchweg mich" (So when I talk about us, I always mean myself). However in Königsdorf's writings, "us" or "we" can by no means be reduced to "I" in all cases, as in the statement, "Wir, die wir uns später die Basis nannten" (We who later called ourselves the basis) (16). Yet her statement succinctly describes the new situation. While *Ein Moment* begins with a section entitled "Von der Schwierigkeit 'ich' zu sagen" (The difficulty of saying "I"), which was a paper presented by Königsdorf at the Tenth Writers' Conference of the GDR in 1987, at the beginning of *Dilemma* she states very pointedly that saying "I" has now become unavoidable: "Denn von den Intellektuellen, von den Andersdenkenden also, denkt per Definition ein jeder anders als der andere. Wenn ich also von uns spreche, so meine ich durchweg mich" (For by definition, every one of the intellectuals, that is, the dissidents, has a different way of thinking. So when I talk about us, I always mean myself)

(*Dilemma*, 7). But when does one actually begin to speak as "I"? A section of *Dilemma* written in 1990 states:

> Im Herbst der Moment Schönheit, in dem die Utopie zum Greifen nahe schien. Ein falscher Schein. Ein Irrtum. In Wahrheit ist sie nie so fern gewesen wie in diesem Augenblick. Wir, die wir dafür gestritten hatten, die wir so lange gehofft hatten, man kann uns bornierte Träumer nennen oder was auch immer, wir waren einen Moment närrisch vor Glück, daß wir unser Metier verließen und die Wirklichkeit zu unserem Kunstwerk machen wollten.
>
> Sicher ist das alles ein bißchen vereinfachend, wie alles, was gesagt werden wird, und trifft auf den einzelnen in sehr unterschiedlichem Maße zu. Auch das Maß der Mitschuld, das jeder empfindet, wird sehr verschieden sein, und es ist sicher auch verschieden. Und das ist dann der Punkt, wo das Ich-Sagen notwendig wird. (35)

[In the fall, the moment of beauty, in which utopia seemed within our grasp. A deception. An error. In reality, it has never been so far away as it is at this moment. We who fought for it, who had hoped for so long, could be called slow-witted dreamers or whatever, for a moment we were so foolish with happiness that we left our métier and wanted to make reality into our work of art.

Of course that's all a bit of a simplification, like everything anybody says, and it applies to each individual to a very different degree. The degree of complicity everyone feels will also be very different, and really is very different. And that is the point where saying "I" becomes necessary.]

The events of the revolution are still a time of "we," while afterward "we" becomes fragmented by different levels of complicity in the past. But also "Schmerz" (pain) und "Verlustgefühl" (a sense of loss) serve to differentiate between those who feel these things and others, who as Königsdorf writes, "schon immer Gesamtdeutsche waren" (have been united Germans all along) (*Dilemma*, 31). Of course, this division comes from further back in the history of the GDR, but only now can it be openly confronted and articulated (as Christa Wolf would agree). Königsdorf talks about people "die entweder von Anfang an durch ihre Erfahrung nicht an eine Reformierbarkeit von innen her glaubten. Und diejenigen, die ihre ganze Hoffnung auf Reformen setzten. Über diejenigen, die alles gut finden wollten, spreche ich hier nicht" (who either right from the start, due to experience, did not believe in the possibility of reform. And those who placed all their hope in reforms. I'm not talking about the people who always thought everything was fine) (*Dilemma*, 8). Of course, this is an oversimplification, given the manifold effects of oppression and exclusion, as well as the various possibilities of inclusion and participation in a totalitarian state. Königsdorf positions herself among the reformers, and this is *one* of the groups she includes among "us." But "we" also unabashedly stands for the intellectuals or for GDR citizens in general. The continued use of "us" and "we" throughout, with few exceptions, could be held to demonstrate the difficulty of always including the idea of diversity in one's reflections about a past that claimed that there was *one* community, but in fact suppressed diversity and hushed it up. But who are "we" really? This is a question posed by Königsdorf herself shortly before the middle of the book in a section called " 'Einig Europa' oder die Idee von der 'deutschen Tüchtigkeit' " ("United Europe" or the idea of "German efficiency"), a paper presented in Frankfurt in 1990. Here Königsdorf suddenly starts talking about "us" as "Germans." The "we" of GDR citizens, intellectuals, or reformers has become a united German "we" for the first time. Königsdorf's latest publication shows an even more significant change. In *Über die unverzügliche Rettung der Welt,* "we" sometimes refers to GDR citizens and sometimes to united Germans, or citizens of the industrialized nations, environmentalists, or Berliners. Clearly, Königsdorf's faith in diversity is not an avowal of particularity but a declaration of loyalty to various group identities, which constructs her as a new postunification subject. "We" now allows for the crossing of boundaries, is open to various political interventions and alliances, and moves back and forth between margins and centers.

This "we" that can speak for both same and other has a problematical side to it that should not be overlooked: Königsdorf empowers herself by appropriating the authority to speak for the groups with which she identifies, at the cost of diversity. Her earlier cautious remark, "So when I talk about us, I always mean myself," does not quite make up for the problem, although it clearly indicates her awareness of it. Yet, taking into account the loss of the *one* (illusional) community and the psychological impact of this loss, Königsdorf's "we" rhetoric seems to me to be a strategy to enable the East German subject to speak out and to come into agency. One aspect of the postunification situation is very relevant in this regard, in that the dissolution of the GDR and what many people felt to be its "annexation" to West Germany (or "colonization") were offensive to many former GDR citizens, for within a short period of time all their efforts to create a socialist society were made null and void and all the values of their society had become worthless, as though East Germany, the so-called "Unrechtsstaat," had no positive contributions to offer the "new Germany." But for Königsdorf, as well as for many other East Germans, the ability to talk about "us" is something that Western societies lack, and so represents something positive that could be contributed by the East German side: "Das 'Wir', das ich noch immer gebrauchte, war längst nicht mehr. Es löste sich in die vielen Ichs auf. Aber wir brachten die Erfahrung mit, daß "Wir" möglich ist. Wir hatten uns immer für das Ganze verantwortlich gefühlt" (The "we" I was still using ceased to exist a long time ago. It dissolved into many "I's." But we brought with us the experience that "we" is possible. We had always felt responsible for the whole) (*Rettung*, 45). The old totalizing "we" has dissolved; the multiple "I" allows for multiple alliances. Thus, the "we" rhetoric has become a strategy to evoke political responsibility here and now.

Königsdorf's recognition that there can be multiple alliances came from a thorough evaluation of the ambivalence of a community, such as the Party or the homeland in general. The Party represented community in romantic, religious, and family senses, Königsdorf writes. Its authority rested in the utopia written on its banners, the utopia of socialism, and in people's unquestioning belief in it, along with their desire for security: "Nichts fürchteten wir so sehr wie den Liebesentzug der Gemeinschaft" (There was nothing we feared so much as the community's withdrawal of its love) (*Dilemma*, 13). The expectation of love makes people prisoners and leads to concealment and self-censorship. When Königsdorf states baldly, "Der Sozialismus ist tot" (Socialism is dead), she renounces not only socialism, but also utopia in general and its inherent hegemonization, "weil fälschlicherweise der Konsens eines 'Endzustandes' postuliert und nicht die Realität mit ihren Interessengegensätzen als Tatsache anerkannt wird" (because erroneously the consensus of a "final condition" is postulated, and reality with its conflicts of interest is not recognized as fact) (*Dilemma*, 71). The "Third Way," democratic socialism, is indeed conceivable, but for Königsdorf this possibility is unrealistic because it is "viel weniger effektiv als das andere System" (much less effective than the other system) (*Dilemma*, 7). However, the renunciation of consensus—the basis of every utopia—and the embracing of dissension *do* seem realistic to Königsdorf, since such a perspective allows a recognition of social diversity, as opposed to the old view that saw everyone as essentially the same.

Distancing oneself from socialism does not inevitably mean embracing capitalism, however. Königsdorf is concerned that one should take a critical view of capitalism, otherwise known as the market economy. This would require a thorough study of political and economic legalities. As Rosi Braidotti reminds us: "We simply need new forms of literacy in order to decode today's world" (109). In Königsdorf's texts political-economic and scientific discourse are often juxtaposed, in accordance with her definition of poets as "Aufklärer" (educators). But is the loss of community and utopia really bearable? Does the longing for a time when utopia will once more be possible still linger in Königsdorf's mind, as it does in Wolf's?

Königsdorf's texts call for a new politics of location. Dismantling old communities and undermining new incorporations, she becomes what I call the "ambivalent re/unified" subject. "Dismissed" from the old community, one must seek out new possibilities to find a space, locally, nationally, and globally. Let us turn to Königsdorf's reflections about "Heimat" (one's homeland) and her development of what I would like to term "critical regionalism" in *Aus dem Dilemma eine Chance machen*. The "new" reunified Germany does not at first offer something one can identify with, but it offers the remembrance of something that was forgotten, a situated meaning and emotional belonging that were erased by the socialist state. In an essay that Königsdorf originally wrote for the book *Thüringen* published by Merian, she states: "Nichts schien mich mehr mit dieser Gegend zu verbinden. Und nun ist da plötzlich so etwas wie ein Heimatgefühl. Es ist viel leichter, mich wieder an Thüringen zu gewöhnen, als an das große Deutschland. Plötzlich weiß ich, daß es wichtig ist, irgendwo Gräber zu haben. . . . Aber es sind nicht Gräber allein. Es ist die Gegend, die voller Überlieferungen und Legenden war. . . . Trotzdem war nichts mehr in mir als eine heimliche Sehnsucht nach Heimat. Diese gefährliche Sehnsucht" (Nothing seemed to connect me with this region any longer. And now, suddenly, there's a feeling of something like a homeland. It's much easier to get used to Thuringia than it is to get used to the whole of Germany. Suddenly I realize it's important to have graves somewhere. . . . But it's not just graves. It's the region that was full of traditions and legends. Suddenly I was filled with a secret longing for a homeland. That dangerous longing) (*Dilemma*, 36). A sense of homeland is rooted in the personal and collective memory connected to a region. The loss of the "larger" community and "homeland," the loss of the Party, leads *at first* to a retreat into regional security, which seems so well ordered. The longing for a homeland is openly expressed, not simply repressed or hushed up, but at the same time it is evaluated critically. Königsdorf is aware of the preconditions of a homeland: its provincialism and parochialism, its marginalization and exclusion of others. She describes, for example, meeting one of her old acquaintances in the village of her birth: "Es kommen jetzt so viele Türken, sagt Frau Sch. Sagt es aber nicht sehr überzeugt, eher verlegen. Aber in einem halben Jahr, vielleicht auch früher, wird sie an ihre Türkengeschichte glauben" (There are so many Turks coming in now, says Mrs. Sch. But she doesn't say it with conviction; she seems embarrassed. But give her another six months, maybe even less, and she'll believe in her story about the Turks) (*Dilemma,* 38). Königsdorf exposes the illusion of "Heimat," its promises of familiarity and timelessness, by weaving into her text the reality that the familiar and the unfamiliar go together, and that the time factor is unescapable: "Vertraut und zugleich fremd. Immer wieder beginnt etwas Neues" (Familiar and unfamiliar at the same time. Something new is always happening (*Dilemma,* 43).

Whereas "local community" is seen as filling in for something lost, the transnational community of the "New Europe" is called into question. The reason seems to be, as Werner Creutziger puts it, the East German experience that "immer höhere Zentralisation, die Große Kompetenz nichts bringt" (ever greater centralization, the Great Competence brings nothing) (175). I think, too, that this new community is "unheimlich" (un-homely) for those from the East, because for them it is too much of a *Western* project, which for forty years was engaged *against* the East. Making the idea of a Europe that includes West *and* East into a reality is necessary, Königsdorf believes, although difficult to classify: "Sie kann nicht verordnet werden. Sie muß langsam wachsen, indem auch zwischen Ost und West demokratische Strukturen geschaffen werden, in denen Widersprüche ausgetragen werden können" (It cannot be decreed. It must grow slowly, while democratic structures are created between East and West where contradictions can be argued out) (*Dilemma,* 48). Despite her approval for this idea, certain reservations about the idea of Europe are still evident in Königsdorf's writings. Europe by no means replaces the lost utopia.

Thinking about a new beginning makes it imperative for Königsdorf to deal with the question of the Party. She strongly criticizes "the Left"—not only "the Left" in its narrower sense, meaning the PDS (Partei Demokratischer Sozialismus, the Party of Democratic Socialism), successor to the SED (Sozialistische Einheitspartei Deutschlands, the Socialist Unity Party of Germany), but also the electoral alliance prior to the Bundestag elections of 1990, formed by the PDS and various groups of left-wingers from the West and independent left-wingers from the East. Königsdorf believes the Left to be "so, wie sie sich heute darstellt, ziemlich überflüssig" (fairly superfluous, the way it is today) (*Dilemma,* 64). The Left is not in a position to meet the radical challenge of the present, which for Königsdorf means "den Grenzen der Welt" (the boundaries of the world). By "Grenzen," which means "limits" as well as "boundaries," she means limits in terms of growth and resources, the worldwide population explosion, and science and technology's destructive potential. The old worldview with its neat division between Left and Right seems completely obsolete to Königsdorf in view of the new realities; it has become "superfluous." Furthermore, dualistic worldviews in general begin to break down for Königsdorf, like the one based on gender, when she writes, for example: "Die Frauen bei den Linken sind vielleicht überhaupt das Erstaunlichste. Sie kämpfen immer noch gegen das Patriarchat und haben längst die Macht" (The most astonishing thing is possibly the left-wing women. They are still fighting against the patriarchy although they have held power for some time) (*Dilemma*, 58). Writing postunification identity becomes a project of letting go of old boundaries by realizing the new "boundaries of the world." Königsdorf sees a new vision taking the place of the lost utopia, a new responsibility that is just as grave as the old one: instead of "Weltverbesserung" (improving the world), there is the need for "Weltrettung" (saving the world). What has really changed? Königsdorf feels that socialism, which was supposed to *improve* the world, failed because it was based on a false understanding of human nature; *saving* the world, on the other hand, is a shared task necessary for our collective and personal survival and is anchored in the here and now: "Der Versuch, Endgültiges zu konzipieren, mußte scheitern, weil er in sich entwicklungsfeindlich war. Es kann nur ein adaptiver Vorgang sein, bei dem Ziel und Strategien nach jedem Schritt neu durchdacht werden. Es gibt keinen festen Punkt" (The attempt to conceive something final was destined to fail, because it was hostile to new developments. There can only be an adaptive process, in which one's goal and strategies are reconsidered after every step of the way. There is no fixed point) (*Rettung*, 109). There can also be no fixed image of human nature. As different as the two processes are, *improving* and *saving* the world have this in common: both are critical of capitalism or the market economy. Not that Königsdorf thinks this system can be replaced, but it must be "ökologisch und sozial verträglich gestaltet werden" (set up so as to be ecologically and socially acceptable) (*Rettung*, 118).

In contrast to Wolf, Königsdorf hopes to find a foundation for the national not through a common project of "Vergangenheitsbewältigung" (coming to terms with the past), which Wolf believes is the only thing that will make the future possible, but through a "gemeinsamen Neuanfang" (new start together). From her "ambivalent" re/unified position the transnational gains priority.

Without question this view must also be seen in relation to a tendency already present in early socialism, that is, considering nations as only temporary phenomena, and this is also true for her visionary thinking. In *Ein Moment* Königsdorf begins to talk about the need for a "neue Vision" (new vision), and she develops this idea further in *Dilemma* and *Rettung*. In the last chapter of *Rettung*, whose title is almost identical to that of the book itself, "Von der unverzüglichen Rettung der Welt," Königsdorf not only uses her typical scientific and economic language but also speaks in the voice of a mystic or prophetess. The chapter is introduced by a quotation from her earlier book *Respektloser Umgang*, in which she questions the ethics of science: "Ich habe eine Botschaft empfangen. Sie mir zu eigen gemacht. Einmalig, unverwechselbar, weil jeder Mensch etwas Einmaliges ist. Ich gebe sie weiter. Hinterlasse in den Menschen um mich eine Spur, die vereint mit anderen Spuren erneut Botschaft wird, auch wenn mein Name längst vergessen ist. Unsterblich sind wir, so lange diesem Leben Kontinuität beschieden ist" (I have received a message. I have made it my own. One of a kind, unmistakable, because every person is one of a kind. I pass the message on. I leave a trace among the people around me, which, combined with other traces, becomes a message again, even if my name has long been forgotten. We are immortal, so long as this life is granted continuity) (*Rettung*, 107). Beginning with a macrocosmic image of an earth in labor giving premature birth to humankind, which finally reaches a position where it can "mit einem Handstreich alle Voraussetzungen für das Leben zu zerstören" (destroy in one fell swoop all prerequisites for life) (*Rettung*, 109), Königsdorf considers political, ethical, economic, and social questions. Finally she calls for a new vision: "Die neue Vision wird eine sehr komplizierte Aufgabe sein. Meine Vision ist eine demokratische Weltordnung. Eine Demokratie, in der die kulturelle Identität als Wert anerkannt wird und die zivilisierte Lösung von Konflikten Gebot ist. . . . Eine Demokratie, in der integriert wird, soweit die Probleme es erfordern. Aber keinesfalls ein Weltstaat mit Welthoheitsrechten" (The new vision will be a very complicated project. My vision is a democratic world order. A democracy, in which one's cultural identity is recognized as a positive value, and the resolution of conflicts in a civilized manner is a requirement. . . . A democracy in which there is integration, insofar as problems may demand it. But by no means will it be a world state with sovereignty over the world) (*Rettung*, 121–22). The new vision, according to Königsdorf, is an open-ended project to be constructed: "Aber wir sind ohne Karte und Kompaß. Wir kennen den Weg nicht" (But we don't have a map or a compass. We don't know the way) (*Rettung*, 68).

The central question, then, is how to construct a way. Königsdorf invites us to think about the mobilization of "social energies": "Die soziale Energie, die einem System innewohnt, könnte man sich, in Entsprechung zur Mechanik, zusammengesetzt denken aus der Energie, die durch die laufenden gesellschaftlichen Prozesse schon als Bewegungsenergie realisiert ist, und aus der Energie, die sich in den unaufgelösten Interessengegensätzen aufspeichert" (By analogy with mechanics, one could imagine the social energy inherent within a system to be made up of the energy already realized as kinetic energy through ongoing social processes, and of the energy stored up within unresolved conflicts of interest) (*Rettung*, 111). This latter kind of energy might be discharged violently, in wars and revolutions. For Königsdorf, the energy stored in unresolved conflicts of interest can be consciously released, to have an impact on the underlying social structure. She sees this as an adaptive process, where one must reconsider one's goal and strategies after each step forward. The prerequisite is a specific figuration of the collective and the personal: "In der Fähigkeit Ich zu sagen, es mit Wir zu konfrontieren, es in das Wir einzubringen, Wir zu verändern, auf neue Weise Ich zu sagen" (In the ability to say I, to confront it with we, to bring it into the we, to change the we, to say I in a new way) (*Rettung*, 110). The personal is constituted by collectivity and vice versa. The fluidity of the I allows for the exchange of views, and permits common interests to be discovered and mobile coalitions to form. Königsdorf calls for us to live up to our politicoeconomic, technological, and ecological present and to approach the future creatively. The discursive production of a consciousness of the economic, technological, and ecological challenges of the present rearranges geographical spaces and makes it obsolete to think in terms of boundaries, those of the nation or of Europe, in view of what she calls "die Grenzen der Welt" (the boundaries of the world). But Königsdorf is not talking about eliminating the concept of nations. Nations are important to Königsdorf for the organizational structure they provide, as is the new united German nation, and she considers it essential to deal with the past. Of course, there must be a change in priorities; instead of focusing on the problem of "Deutsch sein" (being German), it is necessary to envision an innovative site of collaboration and contestation vis-à-vis a global world, which Königsdorf, as a scientist, sees as viable but extremely endangered considering the ecological, political, and sociological possibilities.

"Ganz normal Deutsch sein" (to just be a normal German) (*Rettung*, 120): is that possible? On the one hand, this might be read as a strategy to subvert old collective ideas, "imagining," to use Homi Bhabha's phrase, "the possibility of other contending and liberating forms of cultural identification." (311).⁹ Considering the reality of two different political and economic systems, each with its own goals and value judgments, and considering the effects that meritocracies and socialism have on people, it really does seem as though the simplest way to achieve community is by a new beginning. On the other hand, this can be read as disregarding the specifics of history and responsibility, effacing the pre- and postwar East and West German subject, the Nazi atrocities, and the divided culture. Also, we have to ask whether "normal German" can mean at the same time being Jewish, being an immigrant, a refugee, or a guest worker. While Königsdorf problematizes consensual ideology in her search for a reassuring postnational discourse based on being a "normal German," she marginalizes inequalities in citizenship, opportunities, and histories.

Filiation versus Affiliation

Said, in his reflections on exile, distinguishes between different positions of displacement by suggesting that there are several different relations to the homeland but only one relation to the host country: all exiles are foreigners. JanMohamed takes this one step further by differentiating the relation to the host country in separating exile and immigrant, and by opening up the interstitial space of the border intellectual, where new experiences of nationality and community can be negotiated. Whereas JanMohamed's "syncretic" and "specular" border intellectuals are faced with a separation between "home" and "host" cultures, postunification subjects from the East are faced with a dissolved nation-state and a re/unified home/host culture, a union dominated by the West (host) incorporating the East (home). This union is creating various kinds of location and identity politics, which I have attempted to throw some light on through my study of the texts discussed above. More specific and detailed studies are called for in the future.

As there are different points of departure, there are also various ways of struggling with the im/possibility of unification and envisioning a new commonality that could emerge from the coming together of East and West. Negotiating rupture, marginalization, and differing communities destabilizes subject positions and creates various new shifting sites: the exile and the immigrant, the resistant re/unified subject who transcends the new unity by creating an alternative community, and the ambivalent re/unified subject who constantly crosses borders, traversing boundaries. In addition, East-West unity creates both (to use Deleuze and Guattari's terminology) "re-territorialization," that is, the following of a utopian impulse to search for a common ground and the valorizing of *filiation,* and "de-territorialization," a search for a common beginning by taking on global responsibility and valorizing *affiliation.*

In Christa Wolf's case, what was and what could *potentially* have been cannot easily be discarded and must be recalled, recollected in an intertextual web of voices in resistance to official amnesia. Nourishment or "home" does not come from the new reality (which actually is resisted), but from an alternative community, discursively constructed across borders. In Königsdorf's texts, on the other hand, the postunification subject is struggling to make sense of the new reality. Faced with the new options of differing locations, she both resists fixation on the past and rejects an uncritical participation in the new "unified" culture. To work on unity from this position means focusing on a new beginning and a vision. The energy released by the confrontations that come from dualistic thinking "among Germans" should be diverted into productive exchanges of views that go beyond strictly national concerns. Wolf, when she is finally able to confront the reality of postunification Germany, finds it "unheimlich" (un-homely), marked by a deep division between East and West, with a continued stigmatization of the East and a past that must not be forgotten. Yet, coming to terms with this "brutal" reality can create a new avenue for integration, and perhaps prepare a common ground for a united nation.

Christa Wolf's utopia is, in Eileen and Stephen Yeo's terms, a "community from below," emphasizing ethical relationships based on family and friendship, made *by* people *for* themselves, not defined by an already existing (German) state (231). (A similar concept was developed in the eighteenth century, one associated with Herder and the Romantics.) In contrast to this there is the "community from above," the modern state, with its abstract relationships, that is, its abstract calls for a social contract. Julia Kristeva mentions this with reference to Montesquieu in her recent collection of texts, *Nation without Nationalism.*[10] Wolf's utopia of a *romantic* unified Germany, hoping for and demanding a consensus, a coming to terms with the realities that have been suppressed, is at odds with Königsdorf's vision of a *modern* unity, characterized by contradictions and dissension but held together by a sense of inter/national responsibility. As the emergence of new forms of racism, anti-Semitism, and right-wing nationalism in Europe, dredging up old mythical "differences," have resulted in violent, murderous acts in East and West and especially in the united Germany, as the integration of Europe threatens to make it a fortress, armed against the so-called third world, the search for (un)common grounds is now indispensable.

Translated by Elizabeth Naylor Endres

Notes

1. John Borneman points out that there has been an inflationary use of familiar clichés and kinship metaphors to describe the process of unification. I agree partly with his criticism but don't share his following judgment: "East and West Germans are not kin reuniting, but two separate peoples, each with its own set of dispositions, who are suddenly, in one of those accidental moments in history, thrown together in a national whole" (114). In my opinion, East and West Germans are separate and not separate peoples, both/and. They share one history and culture before 1945, of which, of course, they made different use after the post–World War II separation.

2. I thank Helen L. Cafferty for bringing my attention to Katie Hafner's article.

3. See, for example, the essay collection *Displacements: Cultural Identities in Question,* edited by Angelika Bammer. Bammer calls displacement "the separation of people from their native culture either through physical dislocation as refugees, immigrants, migrants, exiles, or expatriates or the colonizing imposition of a foreign culture" (xi). See also Carole Boyce Davies, *Black Women, Writing, and Identity: Migrations of the Subject.*

4. Christa Wolf, born in 1929, is the best-known East German writer, both nationally and internationally. A writer mainly of novels and essays, she gained her reputation in the United States primarily with her autobiographical novel *A Model Childhood* (1976, trans. 1980) and the novel *Cassandra* (1983, trans. 1984). Her earlier works include *The Divided Heaven* (1963, trans. 1981), *Quest for Christa T.* (1968, trans. 1979), *No Place on Earth* (1979, trans. 1982), *Accident: A Day's News* (1987, trans. 1989), and *Author's Dimension* (1986, trans. 1993). Helga Königsdorf, born in 1938, is a mathematician and writer. She made her debut with a prose collection in 1978 entitled *Meine ungehörigen Träume,* in which she writes about alienated life in a socialist society, with a feminist focus on women that is unusual for that time. Her later prose works include *Mit Klitschmann im Regen* (1983), *Lichtverhältnisse* (1988), *Respektloser Umgang* (1986), and *Ungelegener Befund* (1990). So far none of her works has been translated into English. See Sigrid Lange, "Topographische Irritationen: Frauenliteratur nach dem Ende der DDR," for a discussion of recent literature of younger women authors.

5. In early 1993 it was published that in the late 1950s and early 1960s Christa Wolf had worked for the Stasi (Staatsicherheitsdienst, or Secret Service). In a letter to Günter Grass, published in *Tabou,* Wolf writes about her file, which mentions three meetings in 1959 with two men in Berlin, "wo ich hätte wissen und mich erinnern müssen, daß es sich um Mitarbeit handelte" (when I should have known and remembered that it had something to do with collaboration); three meetings in 1960 with a Stasi man in Halle, "der uns über den Charakter dieser Kontakte im unklaren ließ" (who left us unsure about the nature of these contacts); and a final meeting in 1962, after which the file was closed: "Ich hätte nicht die 'richtige Liebe zur Sache' gezeigt, heißt es da unter anderem. Die entscheidenden Erinnerungen, nämlich daß ich einen Decknamen hatte, daß ich mich in Berlin einmal in einer konspirativen Wohnung mit ihnen getroffen habe und daß ich einen handschriftlichen Bericht verfaßt habe—Dinge, die ich mir schwer verzeihen kann—sind nicht wiederaufgetaucht" (It says among other things that I was not really "into this job." The most important memory, that is, the fact that I had an alias, that I once met with them in a top secret apartment in Berlin, and that I composed a handwritten report—things, I find it hard to forgive myself for—did not come up again) (*Tabou,* 259).

6. In 1990 Wolf published *Was bleibt* (What remains), a novella based on her own experience of Stasi surveillance in the late 1970s. Shortly after publication of this novella, written a decade beforehand, she was attacked for not having published it earlier, before the fall of the Wall. While she was claiming to be a victim, she was accused of being a collaborator or "Staatsdichterin" (state poet). In the controversy about Wolf's relations to the socialist regime, she and her work often stand for other GDR writers who were criticized as having been much too loyal to the GDR leadership. A debate known as the "Literaturstreit" developed in which the whole of East and West

German postwar literature was dismissed as a product of "Gesinnungsästhetik." For more information on the "Literaturstreit," see Thomas Anz, ed., *"Es geht nicht um Christa Wolf,"* and Daglind Sonolet, "Towards a New Aesthetic."

7. On "Nagelprobe," which was first published in a catalog on the "Nagelkünstler" ("nailartist") Guenther Uecker, see Claire Baldwin, " 'Nagelprobe': On German Trials."

8. Bread and wine refer of course to the Last Supper. However, the ideas in many of Christa Wolf's texts seems closer to the utopia of the early Romantics, who, as Manfred Frank correctly emphasizes, did not think in Christian terms, strictly speaking (Frank, 338). The quotation is taken from Friedrich Hölderlin's *Friedensfeier* (Frank, 339).

9. Homi Bhabha discusses here Ernest Renan's "will to nation," which requires forgetting: "Yet every French citizen has to have forgotten [is obliged to have forgotten] Saint Bartholomew's Night's Massacre, or the massacres that took place in the Midi in the thirteenth century" (Renan, "What Is a Nation," in *Nation and Narration,* ed. Bhabha, 8–22; 11). Bhabha comments, "Being obliged to forget becomes the basis for remembering the nation, peopling it anew, imagining the possibility of other contending and liberating forms of cultural identification" (311).

10. See Gisela Brinker-Gabler, "Thinking through Cosmopolitanism and Nationalism: Julia Kristeva, Montesquieu, and Herder," paper presented at the 1994 Modern Language Association convention (in print).

Works Cited

Anderson, Benedict. *Imagined Communities: Reflections on the Origin and Spread of Nationalism.* London: Verso, 1991.

Anz, Thomas, ed. *"Es geht nicht um Christa Wolf": Der Literaturstreit im vereinten Deutschland.* Munich: Edition Spangenberg, 1991.

Baldwin, Claire. " 'Nagelprobe': On German Trials." *Colloquia Germanica* 27, no. 3 (1994): 1–11.

Bammer, Angelika, ed. *Displacements: Cultural Identities in Question.* Bloomington: Indiana University Press, 1994.

Bhabha, Homi K. "DissemiNation: Time, Narrative, and the Margins of the Modern Nation." In *Nation and Narration,* edited by Homi K. Bhabha, 291–322. London: Routledge, 1990.

Bloch, Ernst. *Tübinger Einleitungen in die Philosophie.* vol. 13. Frankfurt am Main: Suhrkamp, 1970.

Borneman, John. "Time-Space Compression and the Continental Divide in German Subjectivity." *New Formations* 21 (Winter 1993): 102–18.

Braidotti, Rosi. *Nomadic Thought.* London: Routledge, 1994.

Brinker-Gabler, Gisela. "Thinking through Cosmopolitanism and Nationalism: Julia Kristeva, Montesquieu, and Herder." Paper presented at the Modern Language Assocation convention, 1994.

Creuzinger, Werner. "Flucht aus der Nation." *neue deutsche literatur* 42 no. 6 (November/December 1994): 173–80.

Davies, Carole Boyce. *Black Women, Writing and Identity: Migrations of the Subject.* London: Routledge, 1994.

Frank, Manfred. *Der kommende Gott: Vorlesungen über die neue Mythologie.* Frankfurt am Main: Suhrkamp, 1982.

Hafner, Katie. "A Nation of Readers Dumps Its Writers." *New York Times Magazine,* January 10, 1993, sec. 6.

Hall, Stuart. "Cultural Identity and Diaspora." In *Identity: Community, Culture, Difference,* edited by John Rutherford, 222–37. London: Lawrence and Wishart, 1990.

———. "Minimal Selves." In *Identity,* edited by Lisa Appignanesi, 44–46. London: ICA Document 6, 1987.

JanMohamed, Abdul R. "Worldliness-without-World, Homelessness-as-Home: Toward a Definition of the Specular Border Intellectual." In *Edward Said: A Critical Reader,* edited by Michael Sprinker, 96–120. Oxford: Blackwell, 1992.

Kocka, Jürgen. "Crisis of Unification: How Germany Changes." Translated by Lieselotte Anderson. *Daedalus* 123 (Winter 1994): 173–209.

Königsdorf, Helga. *Aus dem Dilemma eine Chance machen: Aufsätze und Reden.* Hamburg: Luchterhand, 1990.

———. *1989 oder ein Moment Schönheit: Eine Collage aus Briefen, Gedichten, Texten.* Berlin: Aufbau, 1990.

———. *Über die unverzügliche Rettung der Welt: Essays.* Berlin: Aufbau, 1994.

Kristeva, Julia. *Nations without Nationalism.* Translated by Leon S. Roudicz. New York: Columbia University Press, 1993.

Lange, Sigrid. "Topographische Irritationen: Frauenliteratur nach dem Ende der DDR." *Colloquia Germanica* 27, no. 3 (1994): 255–74.

Said, Edward. "Intellectual Exile: Expatriates and Marginals." *Grand Street* 12, no. 3 (Fall 1993): 113–25.

Sonolet, Daglind. "Towards a New Aesthetic." *New Formations* 16 (Spring 1992): 119–35.

Todorov, Tzvetan. *The Conquest of America.* New York: Harper, 1987.

Wark, McKenzie. "Europe's Masked Ball: East Meets West at the Wall." *New Formations* 12 (Winter 1990): 33–42.

Watson, Julia. "Toward an Anti-Metaphysics of Autobiography." *The Culture of Autobiography: Constructions of Self-Representation,* edited by Robert Folkenflik, 57–79. Stanford: Stanford University Press, 1993.

Wilke, Sabine. "Was kommt? Eine erste exemplarische Annäherung an die Literatur der Wende." *German Studies Review* 16, no. 3 (October 1993): 483–514.

Wolf, Christa. *Auf dem Weg nach Tabou: Texte 1990–1994.* Cologne: Kiepenheuer & Witsch, 1994.

———. *Cassandra. A Novel and Four Essays.* Translated by Jan van Heurck. New York: Farrar, Straus and Giroux, 1984.

———. *A Model Childhood.* Translated by Ursule Molinaro and Hedwig Rappolt. New York: Farrar, Straus and Giroux, 1980.

———. *What Remains and Other Stories.* Translated by Heike Schwarzbauer and Rick Takvorian. New York: Farrar, Straus and Giroux, 1992.

Woolf, Virginia. *A Room of One's Own.* New York: Harcourt, Brace and World, 1929.

Yelin, Louise. "Exiled in and Exiled From: The Politics and Poetics of *Burger's Daughter.*" In *Women Writing in Exile,* edited by Mary Lynn Broe and Angela Ingram, 395–411. Chapel Hill: University of North Carolina Press, 1989.

Yeo, Eileen, and Stephen Yeo. "On the Uses of 'Community': From Owenism to the Present." In *New Views of Co-operation,* edited by Stephen Yeo, 229–58. London: Routledge, 1988.

Part III

Nationalisms, Gender, and Sexualities

13 / EU-phoria?

Irish National Identity, European Union, and The Crying Game

Katrina Irving

Such are the contradictions of Irish modernization that we have prematurely entered the post-modern era. We are experiencing . . . in politics a "new right" without an old left, "post-nationalism" with the national question materially unresolved; at the social level, a return to "family values" without the advances of feminism; at the cultural level the nostalgia and historicist pastiche of "post-modernism" without the astringent purgative of modernism. We are entering the future . . . walking backwards.

—Desmond Bell[1]

To some Irish advocates of the Maastricht Treaty, not the least negligible of the potential benefits to be obtained from closer links with the members of the European Union is a solution to the "Northern Question." Over the past few decades, historians, social commentators, and an occasional politician have critiqued the construction and maintenance, within nationalist ideology, of a sectarian version of "Irishness" that, among its manifold violences, militates against the possibility of national reunification. The need to refashion Irish national identity in a more pluralist direction has become increasingly evident: the breakdown of peace talks with the British, following the Irish Republican Army's abandonment of the cease-fire in February 1996, underscores the urgency of this project. This refashioning may, perhaps, be facilitated by the emergence of the New Europe. As Richard Kearney has surmised, the need to make common cause as economically disadvantaged units against the more powerful and developed member states within the institutions of the European Union (EU), may tend to soften the calcified divide between North and South. The concept of a "Europe of the Regions" floated by certain Irish and British intellectuals and politicians opens up the possibility of a dissolution of national borders within the larger EU entity and a subsequent recoalescence of boundaries around the smaller unit of the "region."[2] Taking their places as small regional units with a patchwork of regions, both North and South will, this argument runs, embrace a more pluralist perspective, and the struggle for reunification will grow increasingly irrelevant.[3]

In this essay, I want to demonstrate that many of the most enlightened critiques of nationalist identity, including those elicited by the prospect of Maastricht, continue to write out internal difference even as they claim, in good faith, the necessity for a pluralist refashioning of "Irishness." Critiques of nationalist discourse in the Irish context reproduce, in other words, the logic of that discourse, which, characteristically, elides indigenous difference in order to promulgate the myth of the "pure," undivided internal nation space.[4] My discussion centers on an analysis of Neil Jordan's *The Crying Game,* released in 1992. As a filmic variant of this nationalist critique, Jordan's text simultaneously argues the need for a more inclusive definition of "Irishness" as the key to the solution of the Northern Question and, paradoxically, remains complicitous in nationalist ideology's most damaging effect: the repression of those differences of class, gender, and sexuality that fracture the country along axes besides that of religion.

The film contains what, at first viewing, would appear to be two distinct narrative strands. A narrative dealing with Irish Republican Army (IRA) terrorists at work in contemporary Ireland and Britain is interwoven with a romance between a black, British, male cross-dresser (Dil) and one of those terrorists, a white, Northern Irish "provisional" (Fergus). Fergus's involvement in terrorist activities is counterpointed with a personal crisis, which is precipitated when he discovers that Dil, with whom he has fallen in love, believing her to be a woman, in fact is a cross-dressed man. The film's denouement occurs when the ostensibly "public" narrative of political violence meshes, uncontrollably, with the "private."

How does the theme of violent insurrection against colonial rule illumine and relate to Fergus's personal crisis, as provoked by the figure of Dil? Or, to frame the question somewhat differently, what function does the theme of cross-dressing serve in the narrative? Marjorie Garber has argued that "the presence of the transvestite, in a text, in a culture, signals a category crisis elsewhere" ("Occidental Tourist," 125). The transvestite, as a signifier of "gender undecidability" (the "third sex"), provokes crisis in other binarisms operative within a culture or text, indeed, undermines the very process of categorization ("Occidental Tourist," 125).[5] Hence, we could say that Fergus's imbroglio with the liminal figure Dil serves as a displacement of the film's primary preoccupation: the need to deconstruct *national* identities as the latter have traditionally been constituted. Thus, for example, the film's doubling of the character of Jody—the black British soldier taken hostage by the IRA—with his captor, Fergus, throws into question normative constructions of "Irishness" as the latter are constructed in opposition to "Englishness."[6] Critiquing the constructed nature of such formulations, Jordan also indicts the futility of the IRA violence that erupts continually into the film's narrative, and that is premised precisely on essentialist nationalist ideology. The latter is seen to be all the more obsolete in an increasingly hybrid global context. In this reading, then, the film's problematization of normative sex/gender relations emerges as a displacement of the text's major preoccupation: the need to overcome essentialist formulations of "national identity."

The binarism that most interests me here, however, and that is most effectively critiqued in *The Crying Game,* is that instantiated by the film's two narrative registers. Jordan is not concerned merely to posit a homologous relationship between the struggle for national liberation and Fergus's personal crisis. On the contrary, the film insists that we read the latter, and its putative resolution, not solely as a displacement of the national conflict, but *at a literal level, too:* as a specific and pragmatic means of resolving "The Troubles." If, as R. Radhakrishnan, along with other critics of nationalist discourse, has argued, the nationalist agenda typically suspends questions of indigenous individual rights in order to prioritize the struggle against the enemy outside,[7] Jordan's film, as I shall show, suggests that the Irish question may be resolved, not through violent insurrection, but through an augmentation of personal freedoms for that nation's citizens. Thus the question posed during the latter part of the film—will Fergus manage to maintain an intimate relationship with Dil, despite her challenge to traditional sex/gender equations—speaks, in the specific context of the "Irish Question," to the issue of the national struggle. The latter's resolution will be accomplished, paradoxically, through a pressuring of the politics of liberal individualism.

In his essay "National Identity and Conflict in Northern Ireland," Brian Girvin argues that "the question of identity is at the heart of any understanding" of the Northern Question (107).[8] The conflict, coalescing as an antagonism between two sets of identities (the Catholic minority versus the Protestant majority), emerged as a result of British imperialist policy in both North and South. However, the calcification of the opposition between these two sets of identities has also been inflected by the construction of a particular version of Irish nationality in the South—itself also formed partly in reaction to British colonial policy. Drawing on the work of Bell and Gallagher, Girvin argues specifically that, for the Northern minority and the Southern majority, the Catholic religion has been key "in the emergence and cohesion of modern Irish nationalism" (109). Continuing, he asserts that "it is possible to characterize Irish nationalism as a specifically Catholic phenomenon" (109). The historic roots of this articulation between religion and nationality have been traced to "the confiscation of Ireland and the passage of the anti-Catholic Penal Laws from 1695 to 1709" (Moran, 17). This "secured the position of the Protestant Ascendancy [and] . . . guaranteed the identification of Catholicism with Irish nationalism" (17). Terence Brown has argued that Catholicity and Irish identity became imbricated for the populace during the latter half of the nineteenth century:

> The church with her formally regularized rites and practices offered to most Irishmen and women in the period a way to be Irish which set them apart from the rest of the inhabitants of the British Isles, meeting the needs thereby of a nascent Irish nationalism at a time when the Irish language and the Gaelic culture of the past were enduring a protracted decline. (23)

After formal partition in 1921, this association continued apace. Irish national identity, forged in opposition to that of the Protestant former colonizer specifically and to the forces of modernity in general, was centrally organized around issues of Catholic morality.[9] After independence, the consolidation of a particular version of "Irishness" over and against the perceived sexual/social degeneracy of a modernizing Britain contributed to the ever more rigid division between North and South.[10] Even as Ireland itself began to modernize, the construction of Ireland as a communal, traditional culture devoted to "family" values grew into a nationalist orthodoxy. Under the premiership of Eamonn deValera, especially, this identification of Irish identity with a specifically Catholic version of morality was institutionalized (Brown, 116): the republic's constitution of 1937 recognized the special place of the Catholic Church in the new state.

The extent to which the sectarian construction of Irish identity exacerbated the Northern problem was recognized in the 1970s by Prime Minister Garret Fitzgerald, who, accordingly, inaugurated a "constitutional crusade" that aimed to conciliate Northern Protestants by making the constitution less sectarian in nature (the clause linking the Catholic Church with the destiny of the Irish people was removed).[11] However, as Terence Brown indicates wryly, the subsequent referenda on abortion (1983) and divorce (1987), as well as the attempt to decriminalize homosexuality, all of which issued in defeats for the effort to remove the hegemony of Catholic morality within the culture, could not have been very reassuring to the Northern majority (264).

It is within the context of this recent reassessment of the effect of the articulation of Irishness and the Catholic faith on the Northern Question that we need to read the politics of *The Crying Game.* A Southern Irish Catholic, Jordan addresses in this text the need to reconfigure the essentialist, sectarian versions of Irishness to which both the Southern majority and the Northern minority remain largely wedded. Explicitly linking the Northern Question with the issue of identity, Jordan has argued that "the Irish question is—how to get rid of it. There are more interesting questions than the crippling one about 'Irish identity' " (Kearney, *Across the Frontiers,* 197). Crucially, and this is my main point here, it is within this context that *The Crying Game*'s deconstruction of the opposition between a politics concerned with the implementation of civil rights and a politics directed toward the goal of national liberation must be read. If the construction of an Irish identity grounded in Catholic notions of morality has inflected the Northern issue, then the corollary of this observation is that, in the South, debates over individual freedoms are always inevitably implicated in the question of reunification. Issues of morality and "arguments in favour of internal social change have become inextricabl[y] bound up with or subsumed in the larger debate on the relations between the two parts of the country, between the different traditions" (G. O'Tuathaigh, quoted in Bew and Patterson, 83). As *The Crying Game* demonstrates, the politics of liberal individualism is not, for Ireland, merely an internal matter: to augment personal freedoms is also, to a degree, to mitigate the divide between North and South.

The opening sequences of *The Crying Game* take place in Ireland and depict an IRA "cell" taking as hostage a black British soldier, Jody, who is serving out his tour of duty in the North. The unfolding relationship between Jody and Fergus, who is assigned to guard the prisoner, provides Jordan with an opportunity to broach the issue of national and racial stereotyping. Jody complains of the racism to which he has been subject in the North, a racism that assumes the noncommensurability of "black" and "British":[12]

> I got sent to the only place in the world they call you nigger to your face. . . . (He imitates a Belfast accent): "Go back to your banana tree, Nigger." No use telling them I came from Tottenham. (191)

But Jody is not devoid of racist presuppositions either. Hence his initial reaction to being held hostage:

JODY: You're going to kill me . . . you're all tough undeluded motherfuckers. . . . It's not in your nature to let me go.

FERGUS: What the hell do you know about my nature? (189)

Predictably, each individual's presuppositions about the national and racial "character" of the other is undermined by their burgeoning relationship, and Jordan wrings a weak irony from his device of having Jody originate from Antigua: the agent of British imperialism in Ireland is originally a subject of a former colony. The film intimates that the bond that grows between the two men is premised on their positions as, respectively, subject and former subject of a colonized or formerly colonized state, as well as on their mutual marginalization within their own cultures. They are both economically disadvantaged (they are working class) and members of minority communities (Fergus as a Catholic in Northern Ireland and Jody as a black in Britain).

What concerns me here, however, is not Jordan's rather trite point that, once beyond national and racial stereotypes, there remain essentially good and essentially bad people, a point conveyed in this scene by Jody's parable of the frog and the scorpion and echoed by Fergus in the film's closing shot, as he retells the fable to Dil. What interests me is his exploration of the constituents of Irish nationalist identity, both exemplified and satirized in the interplay between the three core members of this particular IRA "cell": Peter, the leader; Fergus; and Jude, Fergus's girlfriend. The location in which Jody is held is an abandoned farmhouse: interactions with the political prisoner, who is being held in a dilapidated greenhouse, are intercut with scenes of Jude distributing tea and sandwiches in the main house, while Peter reads a newspaper in front of a fire burning in the hearth. Perched on the mantelpiece are the traditional icons of devout Catholicism—the bleeding heart and the statue of the Virgin. Peter, the leader of the cell, alternates between militaristic and patriarchal language, and the extent to which the latter role predominates in the minds of the others becomes evident in Jude's response to Jody's request to remove his blindfold: "I'll have to ask *himself*" (Jordan, 186; my emphasis). This linguistic formulation is a way of referring to the husband, or head of the household, in Irish colloquial speech. Both Partha Chatterjee and R. Radhakrishnan have pointed out that, within the colonial and postcolonial context, the construction of national identity is customarily erected athwart a particular fault line:[13] the division between "outer" and "inner" spaces (Radhakrishnan, 83–85; Chatterjee 237–52). Radhakrishnan, for example, elaborating on the work of Chatterjee, argues that "the nationalist subject,"

> forced by colonialism to negotiate with Western blueprints of reason, progress and enlightenment . . . straddles two regions or spaces, internalizing Western epistemological modes at the outer or the purely pragmatic level, and at the inner level maintaining a traditional identity. . . . The locus of the true self, the inner/traditional/spiritual sense of place, is exiled from processes of history while the locus of historical knowledge fails to speak for the true identity of the nationalist subject. (85)

Inevitably, the figure of Woman is positioned as the inner repository of the nation's essence, situated outside the processes of change and progress (Chatterjee, 238–39, 243). Irish nationalist ideology, which typically "idealiz[es] . . . rural life" and is "often centered on female icons of ideal domesticity, especially mother-figures who are associated with unmediated naturalness" (Coughlan, 90) is hardly exempt from this nostalgia, and the opening scenes of *The Crying Game* are centrally concerned to deconstruct this dichotomization of the "inner," feminized, rural, familial space and the "outer," historicized, masculine realm of political engagement (Chatterjee, 238–39, 243). The division collapses as the IRA cell members play out a version of the familial rural idyll, even as they engage in revolutionary struggle.

In this long opening section, Jordan also indicates the extent to which Oedipal heterosexuality, decisively inflected by a particular interpretation of Catholic dogma, organizes and underwrites the nationalist impulse in the Irish context. The Oedipal subtext of Irish nationalist discourse achieved its most famous manifestation in Yeats's 1910 play, *Kathleen ni Houlihan:* Ireland is figured forth as both mother and beloved. The Sean Bhean Bhoct, or poor old woman, for whom her sons sacrifice themselves, is transformed via this sacrifice into the beloved, a beautiful young girl, Kathleen ni Houlihan (Keane, 16–17 and passim). Closely linked to this myth of the nation as mother/beloved is the role ordained for women in Irish nationalist ideology, that of the good mother, "static . . . sitting by the fire . . . fixed in her domestic sphere, . . . iconized by her connection with spirituality into a secular Irish Madonna" (Hywel, 25). And it is this discourse, too, that sets in place the dichotomy between individual and national liberation that Jordan is concerned to deconstruct. The nationalist depiction of Ireland as Mother Eire poses to the Irish male subject a choice between "serving narrow, personal, ends, or self-sacrifice on behalf of the Mother/Nation" (Cairns and Richards, 129).

The Oedipal constituents of Irish nationalism are explored in *The Crying Game* chiefly through Jude and Fergus's relationship. Although he is Jude's lover during this section of the film, Fergus's subordinate military relationship to both Peter and her, as well as his conversations with Jody, which consist of storytelling and discussions of the relative merits of the game of cricket over that of hurling, serve to infantilize him during the opening scenes. Equally, the nationalist construction of the mother as a figure of "unmediated naturalness" is satirically undercut in the figure of Jude, who, despite her maternal ministrations in matters of nutrition, is presented as pathologically violent. Her vicious and unprovoked assaults on the bound and helpless Jody are a parodic inversion of the deification of the passive mother common in nationalist ideology,[14] while the biblical resonances of her name bespeak the extent to which the nationalist myth is a siren call.

Ultimately, Jody is not killed by his captors, but by members of his own "side." Escaping from Fergus, who has orders from Peter to shoot him, he is run over by state armored vehicles, as the hideout is discovered and firebombed by British military forces. Fergus, thus violently wrenched from his "family," needs to go underground in Britain for a while, or as he puts it, he needs "to lose himself awhile" (206). His attempt to forge a new life there, apart from Jude, the IRA (which he is now anxious to quit), and country, is presented as a maturation process: his final conversations with Jody prefigure this separation and depict it as a process of parturition: "When I was a child . . . I thought as a child. But when I became a man I put away childish things" (202). His attempt to leave behind the entrammeling past and "become a man" is symbolized in his assumption of a new name, "Jimmy."

However, the extent to which he can truly remake himself is tested when he, in accordance with a prior agreement with Jody, seeks out the latter's girlfriend, Dil. Fergus finds himself drawn into a sexual relationship with her, until the revelation that she is biologically male interrupts that unfolding intimacy. Fergus's reaction to this fact is acute and visceral: he strikes Dil and then vomits copiously into the bathtub. Simultaneously (the next night), Jude returns to Fergus's life and attempts to reassert her sexual claims on him:

> She lies down on the bed beside him, takes off a black leather glove and puts her hand on his crotch.
>
> JUDE: Fuck me, Fergus.
>
> He takes her hand away.
>
> JUDE: Am I to take it that's a no?

Jude stands here as a figure for Fergus's rapid regression to Oedipal heterosexuality in the face of Dil's startling revelation that she is a cross-dressed man, while Fergus's rejection of her attempt to renew their sexual relationship prompts Jude to refer to him as "boy," intermittently, for the remainder of the film.

But Jude's attempted seduction of Fergus in this scene forces him to negotiate more than two different sexual object choices. For Jude has sought him out chiefly to recruit him for further terrorist activity in Britain:

> JUDE: We've got some plans here. And we'll need a Mr. Nobody to execute them.
>
> FERGUS: No way, Jude. I'm out.
>
> JUDE: You're never out, Fergus. . . .
>
> JODY: Maybe you don't care whether you die or not. But consider the girl, Fergus. The wee black chick. (239–40)

Jude is a figure for the inexorable claims of nationalism on Fergus, while her role as IRA activist, her power to force Fergus to carry out further terrorist violence (*Dil:* Does she own you? *Fergus:* I'm afraid so), combined with her sexual coerciveness in this scene, underscores the extent to which Irish nationalism is underwritten by, and premised on, Oedipal heterosexuality. Equally, Jude's return the very night that Dil has revealed herself to Fergus exemplifies Garber's point that transvestite presence unsettles conceptual dichotomies above and beyond that of gender. Hence Dil's revelation provokes, not solely a crisis in Fergus's sexual orientation, but a crisis in his interpellation as a national subject, too. The question arises as to whether Fergus will be prompted to return to the comforting, rigid binaries of nationalist ideology that he has so recently left behind: the crisis in sexuality serves as a displacement of the issue of national identity. Thus when Jude informs Fergus that "you're never out," the choice of language implies, in the light of Fergus's prior encounter with Dil, the extent to which his sexual identity and his nationalist identity are imbricated. What we assume that he needs to get free of is not solely the IRA but the Oedipal sexuality that underwrites that version of nationalism.

The facility with which the figure of the cross-dressed homosexual upsets the stable categories of nationalist binaries is elucidated by Garber's use of Lacanian psychoanalytic theory to discuss the textual and cultural function of transvestism. She argues that the latter "is a space of possibility structuring and confounding culture" (*Vested Interests,* 17). Like the Symbolic order, transvestism puts into crisis binary thinking (11). If "the Imaginary is a dimension in which the human subject's relation to himself, and to other people, is structured like, and by, his relation to his mirror image: a dyadic, symmetrical complementarity . . . based on the fiction of a stable identity" (12), then the Symbolic, or "third category," intervenes in that dyad. Both the Symbolic and the transvestite provoke a crisis: "three puts in question the idea of one: of identity, of self-sufficiency, self-knowledge" (11). Fergus's supercession of the Imaginary is figured in his rejection of the maternal, violently nationalist Jude and in his attempt to negotiate a relationship with Dil. As Jude leaves Fergus at the end of the scene in which she has attempted to seduce him back into the IRA, and her own bed, she admonishes him to "keep the faith," a phrase whose multiple allusions again both condense and bring into play all the levels of identity formation that have been operative in the film. At one level, the phrase is a parody of a farewell between two lovers, and takes on added resonance given Fergus's rejection of Jude. "The faith" is also, at its most literal, a reference to Catholicism. Traditionally, however, it is a colloquialism for militant republicanism: the engagement in violent anti-imperialist struggle. Once again, it underscores the extent to which the figure of Jude condenses and enforces conformity to the Catholic, heterosexual Oedipal identity that constitutes the Irish nationalist subject position.

Were we to leave our reading of the relation between the sexual and national identity politics in *The Crying Game* as solely one of displacement, Jordan's latest film could be indicted, as his earlier films have been, for its insufficient attention to the "political and cultural complexity" of the Northern Question that it ostensibly addresses (Hill, 184).[15] However, as I have been suggesting all along, we need to read Fergus's sexual conflict as more than merely analogous to his crisis in national identity. The way in which he will resolve the former serves as a potential solution to the national struggle. If the film's momentum is partially generated by the question of whether Dil and Fergus will continue their relationship, this is not merely because it is employing the conventional narrative dynamics of the popular film. Rather, Fergus's grappling with Dil's transvestism constitutes that attempt to accommodate difference which is, as my brief recounting of recent critiques of Irish nationalist discourse has shown, seen by many thinkers as crucial in moving toward a solution of the Northern Question. Such an accommodation is also demonstrated, albeit all too briefly, to be dependent on Fergus's recognition of his own split and shifting subjectivity.

I cited earlier Radhakrishnan's point that the postcolonial state forges its national identity athwart a schism. This instability enables Radhakrishnan to explain why nationalist ideology and politics fail to recognize and deal with the nation's multiplicity of internal differences. Such ideology constructs, instead, a "pure" undivided internal national identity outside the trammels of history, change, and progress, a construction that inevitably serves to repress, indeed oppress, those "others" who would negate this national integrity. In the Irish context, the imperative to retain the image of a pristine Catholic nation has led to the expulsion of all those issues and subjects who would mar this putative purity. Hence, we might adduce the instance of Ireland's notorious exportation to Britain of its abortion problem. It is this sectarianism, too, that has militated against a peaceful solution to the Northern Question and produced multiple calls for a pluralistic identity politics, one less in thrall to the dictates of Catholic orthodoxy.[16] A notorious and eloquent example of these pluralistic pleas was the public shredding of Pope John Paul II's photograph by popular Irish singer Sinead O'Connor on the American television show, *Saturday Night Live,* in 1992.

It is within this historically specific context that Fergus's acceptance of Dil becomes charged with a significance containing national implications. Their continued relationship stands for the possibility of developing a genuinely pluralistic and inclusive conception of Irish identity, with the latter reconstituted to encompass sexual, racial, and ethnic minorities. Correspondingly, his rejection of Jude, more definitively accomplished in the film, figures as a rejection of the fiction of a stable, unitary identity underpinning the intolerant binarisms of republican nationalism. Tellingly, once Dil becomes an IRA target herself, the only way Fergus can protect her from them is to physically erase the signs of her difference and to normalize her into masculinity: he crops her hair and dresses her in cricket whites. Only by erasing the signs of her transvestism and concealing her challenge to gender boundaries can a cross-dresser exist in a world controlled by nationalist ideologues wedded to the violence of the binary.

If a voluntary return to Jude, and all that she stands for, is never posited as a genuine option for Fergus in the film (and Dil's violent annihilation of her in the penultimate scene in the film redoubles that impossibility), the film doesn't provide a definitive resolution to Fergus's identity problems. It remains unclear at the end of the film whether Fergus will take over Jody's role thoroughly and become Dil's partner. True, the film closes the distance between Jody and Fergus by having the latter end the film in the same situation as the former (in captivity) and by fading out to the sounds of Fergus reciting Jody's tale of the scorpion and the frog to Dil, who has come to visit him in prison. However, the type of relationship Fergus envisions with Dil remains uncertain. He remains uneasy with her attempt to construct their relationship as a romantic and domesticated one:

DIL: Got you the multivitamins and the iron tablets, hon—

FERGUS: Don't call me that. (266)

Further, the method by which he attempts to negotiate his relationship to her after the revelation bodes ill for any true acceptance of her:

FERGUS: I should have known, shouldn't I. . . . Kind of wish I didn't.

DIL: You can always pretend.

FERGUS: That's true . . . won't quite be the same though, will it?

DIL: Are you pretending yet?

FERGUS: I'm working on it.

Garber has discussed the use in narrative structures of what she calls "the cultural habit of translating, or looking through the transvestite" (*Vested Interests,* 202). Translation, in the case of the cross-dressed man, would be to view her as, "in actuality," a man: "looking through" is to ignore the presence of the transvestite as such and to read her as a woman, which is what Fergus aspires to in this scene. Both strategies serve to elide the profoundly unsettling position of the transvestite as "neither one, nor the other," the "third" position. Hence his reactions here remain circumscribed by nationalist strategies: the disavowal of difference in order to retain the illusion of exemplary unity. The narrative attains only a tentative closure, deferring what is, in the context of the current Irish political-cultural context, unanswerable.

But the narrative itself, no less than Fergus, is ambiguous, finally, in its treatment of difference and its relationship to the traditional construct of "Irishness" as a homogeneous entity. If to encounter alterity "confronts us with the possibility of being an other" (Julia Kristeva, quoted in Burgin, 63), then it is clear that Dil's revelation midway through the film provokes just such a confrontation for Fergus. His reaction illustrates the momentary evisceration of his hitherto stable identity, and what seems to be intimated, at least in this scene, is that pluralism in the Irish context is not "a matter of our aptitude for accepting the other; but of being in his or her place, which amounts to thinking of oneself and making oneself other than oneself" (Kristeva, quoted in Burgin, 62). However, despite this momentary intimation that Fergus's repulsion stems from disavowal of his own alterity, the narrative, as it progresses, tends to repress this crucial insight. Fergus's struggle is increasingly presented as a matter of accepting and comprehending Dil, rather than a struggle to accept his own nonhomogeneous identity. The progressive "othering" of Dil in the penultimate scenes of the film, as her representation increasingly draws on stereotypes of the doomed homosexual (her alcoholism, violence, and mental instability are stressed), not only underscores the increasing separation between the two protagonists, but also serves to align the audience with Fergus's normative position.

Jordan's film emerges, then, as symptomatic, rather than critical of, the homogenizing imperative of nationalist rhetoric. But nowhere does the film's reproduction of nationalism's monologic narrative of identity appear more clearly than in its treatment of Jude, the female IRA member. As the most recent incarnation of the "Mother Eire" figure of nationalist mythology, Jude bears the burden of the text's antinationalist animus. As Patrick Keane has pointed out, antinationalist discourse often inverts the traditional representation of Kathleen ni Houlihan, and in the work of Yeats and Joyce, the latter is transmuted into the Devouring Mother:

> When one's nation is personified as beloved, mother, and Muse— Dana, Eire, Fotla, Banba, Dark Rosaleen, the Shan Van Vocht, Cathleen ni Houlihan—she is a necessarily ambiguous figure: a Triple Goddess at once creative and destructive, benevolent and malign, nurturing and devouring. (7)

In more recent Irish writing, this deconstruction and parody of the Mother Eire figure continues apace, with the Sean Bhean Bhocht, for example, translated in the work of contemporary poet Paul Muldoon into the figure of "Anorexia" (Cairns and Richards, 132).

Jody early warns Fergus that women in general, and Jude in particular, are "dangerous." It is Jude who seduces Jody and thus facilitates his capture: in the latter part of the film Jude, typically garbed in green, is gratuitously and pathologically violent. Her ability to coerce Fergus into carrying out IRA terrorist acts further demonizes her, while her attempt to seduce him conflates female sexuality, murderous violence, and nationalist zeal. Her bloody annihilation at the hands of Dil—several bullets hit her full frontally at point-blank range—is meant to be read as an uncompromising rejection of that nationalist mythology that continues to fuel the North-South conflict. Of course, only the most obtuse viewer could miss the misogyny operative here. The film, despite its postnationalist pretensions, rejoins nationalist discourse in evading the issue of Ireland's marginal populations by denying their existence.

Were Jordan's film unique in its complicity with nationalist ideology, the fact would not warrant such extended comment. Nor would it elicit in me, as an expatriate Irish lesbian, such mingled anger and sadness. Unfortunately this complicity is reproduced across a range of contemporary Irish historical and critical texts. Jordan's film is similar to many current discussions of the "Irish Question," including those called forth by the prospect of the New Europe, which, under the sign of pluralism, redouble the traditional effacing of our marginal populations (women, homosexuals, the unemployed and working classes, the traveling people).[17] Indeed, it's tempting to read Jude's violent and bloody extermination at the hands of Dil as an inadvertent allegory of that process whereby "postnational" critics, invoking the putative pluralism that firmer EU links will bring, deny indigenous difference.

Terence Brown's *Ireland: A Social and Cultural History* (revised American edition published in 1985) is an important and insightful assessment of the deleterious effects that defining Irish national identity in narrowly sectarian terms has had. His thesis, broadly stated, is that the stagnation and general "lack of cultural and social innovation" (16) in Ireland in the decades following independence cannot simply be attributed to the financial difficulties faced by the newly independent nation. Rather, he attributes the "social and cultural conservatism of the new state" (16) to "the social homogeneity of the twenty-six counties" (17). Such homogeneity, accomplished in one fell swoop by partition, meant that those "imaginatively comprehensive visions" of a future Ireland, which had been called forth, indeed necessitated, by prepartition diversity, would no longer be required (17). The necessary elements for a dialectical, dynamic political process were simply lacking in the newly independent Ireland. Brown doubts that this diversity will emerge in the near future, especially since, given current demographic trends, "the Protestant population may disappear in the republic at the beginning of the next century. Pluralism as a concept will by then . . . have little more than academic significance in the twenty-six counties of Southern Ireland" (236). To make the obvious point, it is Brown's debilitatingly narrow definition of pluralism, along with his confident homogenization of the republic's subjects on the basis of their common religion, that yields this pessimistic conclusion. Even as he argues the need to "recreate Irish national identity after a new image," Brown, fixated on the religious element in the constitution of Irish culture, remains blind to the rich heterogeneity of Irish society, which is made up of multiple differences of class, gender, sexuality, and generation (237).

In a similar vein, he argues that "one has only to ponder on the possible fate of the Irish language to realize how little Irish diversity there may be to accommodate in any future Irish redefinition of identity[!]" (236). Such comments from one of our most insightful cultural critics, with their utter erasure of our materially oppressed minority groups, is symptomatic of a larger and continuing blindness among our writers and thinkers. The possibility that these minority groups might provide an oppositional force is unthinkable in Brown's account, because these elements are not acknowledged as part of the social scene. His lament for the culture's lack of diversity ultimately colludes with that which he critiques: the nationalist definition of Ireland as a homogeneous entity.

What is desperately needed in the Irish context is frank acknowledgment of those peoples who have been repressed by stiflingly rigid conceptions of Irish identity. It might have been hoped that discussions elicited by the prospect of Maastricht concerning the impact of the "new Europe" on sectarian versions of Irish identity might, at last, produce such an acknowledgment. Unfortunately these are still not forthcoming. Indeed, in the writings of one of the most prolific and sophisticated of such critics, Richard Kearney, a characteristic sleight-of-hand is performed whereby such subaltern elements are both simultaneously invoked and repressed.

In two edited volumes, *Visions of Europe* (1992) and *Across the Frontiers: Ireland in the 1990s* (1988), Kearney and his contributers discuss the cultural and sociopolitical implications of closer European union on the continent as a whole, and on Ireland and traditional conceptions of Irish identity.[18] With regard to the latter, Kearney argues that what is needed in contemporary Ireland is "a transition from traditional nationalism to a postnationalism" ("Postmodernity and Nationalism," 586). Ireland, newly repositioned within the larger constellation of European nations, will, after Maastricht, perforce define itself within and against that larger entity, as opposed to its former colonial masters. In addition, Kearney argues that the concept of nation-state will be largely redundant within this new entity, to be replaced by a productive tension between the demands of federalism and that of regionalism. The prospect of a Europe defined in terms of regions rather than that of discrete nation-states holds out the possibility of forging an Irish identity that could transcend the sectarianism of the past. Writes Kearney:

> What we are talking about then is not the liquidation of nations but their supercession (*aufhebung*) into a post-nationalist network of communities where national identities may live on where they belong—in languages, sports, arts, customs, memories and myths—while simultaneously fostering the expression of minority and regional cultures within each nation. (*Across the Frontiers,* 17)

What is troubling about this reformulation is not only the embracing of the union as a new deus ex machina that will force us, despite ourselves, to embrace pluralism, but also Kearney's persistent conceptualization of difference as a matter of "regional cultures" defined by linguistic and ethnic specifics. Hence, immediately after the above statement, he continues, "In Western Europe there are over twenty minority languages, in addition to immigrant ones, involving over seventy million speakers" (17–18). For Ireland, of course, the problem is not that of redefining Irishness in a way that could accommodate diasporic/refugee populations but the much more mundane task of acknowledging and extending equal citizenship and opportunities to our indigenous minorities.

The dangers of what Eagleton has called "bad utopianism," the belief that we could simply jettison rather than work through our national identities in some EU-phoric moment, are manifested clearly in the volume *Across the Frontiers* (Eagleton, 25). Included in this collection, along with scholarly essays on the implications of European Community unity for traditional concepts of Irish identity, are transcripts of informal discussions between Kearney and, respectively, Bono (of the rock group U2), Robert Ballagh (the artist), Paul Durcan (the poet), and Neil Jordan himself. Grouped to form a unit entitled "migrant minds," Kearney's introduction to the section runs thus:

> Disillusioned with the "hard ideologies" which have defined us according to a single unadulterated "identity" . . . this new generation of

Irish artists affirms the positive value of confusion, uncertainty, home-lessness, migrancy, questioning, questing for "another place." (186)

All four attest to a discomfort and unease with normative constructs of "Irishness." Typical is Bono's statement that "the idea of an incomplete, questioning, even abandoned identity is very attractive to me" (190). Bono continues thus: "I was called a 'White Nigger' once by a black musician, and I took it as he meant it, as a compliment. The Irish, like the blacks, feel like outsiders" (190). Durcan, too, argues for the arbitrary nature of that construct dubbed "Irish identity" and states: "I find . . . attractive . . . Bono's idea of the Irish black-man" (195). Here, antiessentialist theories of identity are grasped eagerly as all four book a ride in the "post-modern carnival."[19] However, in a section that lays claim to the exuberant joys of "difference," there seems to have been no imperative to include discussions with those peoples who have been and continue to be materially oppressed by virtue of their culturally constructed and minimally negotiable identities; women, gays, traveling people, and so on. Under the sign of pluralism Ireland's subalterns are again effaced.

Jordan's film, along with postnationalist social critique, colludes in, even as it attempts to problematize, contemporary Irish culture's relentlessly homogenizing imperative. Pluralism in the Irish context will be achieved, not through the intercession of some deus ex machina, whether figured in the guise of the EU, as in the writings of contemporary social and political commentators, or a black, transvestite homosexual, as in Jordan's film. Nor will it be achieved by embracing poststructuralist insights about the constructed nature of identity per se. A pluralist politics in the Irish context must engage in a double movement. It must recognize the split and shifting nature of subjectivity while simultaneously acknowledging our indigenous minorities who have been, and continue to be, marginalized in Irish society by virtue of their very categorization.[20]

Notes

1. Desmond Bell, "Ireland without Frontiers? The Challenge of the Communications Revolution," 229.

2. See Kearney's discussion with Neal Ascherson in *Visions of Europe* ("Nations and Regions," 13–22). See also John Hume's and T. J. Barrington's respective essays—"Europe of the Regions" and "Frontiers of the Mind"—both in *Across the Frontiers,* ed. Richard Kearney. Northern Irish politician Hume argues that: "Regionalism . . . is the real 'new republicanism.' . . . Rather than being any reversal of the national destiny, this will allow us better to fulfil our potential as a people; . . . to rediscover the cultural interaction between Ireland and Europe; to reinvolve ourselves in political relationships with those on the continental mainland and to enjoy properly the

inchoate European outlook and vision which was lost in our oppressive and obsessive relationship with Britain" (56).

3. For an extended presentation of this argument, see Kearney's "Introduction: Thinking Otherwise," in *Across the Frontiers,* ed. Kearney, esp. 10–12.

4. See R. Radhakrishnan's essay in *Nationalisms and Sexualities,* ed. Parker et al., in which he outlines succinctly this exclusionary tendency of nationalist discourse.

5. See also Marjorie Garber's *Vested Interests,* esp. 10–16.

6. For discussions of "Irishness" as a category constructed in opposition to "Englishness" and vice versa, see Jones and Stallybrass's "Dismantling Irena," in which the authors argue that "from the early sixteenth century, in common with colonialist discourse in the New World as well as the old, English writers figured Ireland as a virgin inviting penetration by virile explorers" (164). See also Brian Girvin, "National Identity and Conflict in Northern Ireland," and Terence Brown, *Ireland: A Social and Cultural History, 1992 to the Present.*

7. See Partha Chatterjee's essay in *Recasting Women* as well as Radhakrishnan's piece in *Nationalisms and Sexualities.* The latter draws from and elaborates on the issues raised by Chatterjee. For discussion of the IRA's subordination of feminist concerns and goals to the national struggle, see Catherine Shannon's essay.

8. David Lloyd also makes this point in his *Anomalous States:* "What may need emphasis . . . is the role which a politics of identity has played in producing the form of the current civil war in Ireland" (19).

9. For a contrary argument, however, see Luke Gibbons's article in *Across the Frontiers,* ed. Kearney. He holds that the construction of Irishness as a composite of traditional, communal, and familial values was coeval with the impact of modernity, rather than momentarily supplanted by it. Discourses of traditionalism provided the Irish with a way to cope with the onslaught of industrialization and modernity. For more on this issue, see also Brown, *Ireland,* 25, 169.

10. I draw on Brown's *Ireland* and Theodore Hoppen's *Ireland since 1800* in this and the next paragraph.

11. See Bew and Patterson's "Ireland in the 1990s," esp. 85–87.

12. See Paul Gilroy's *There Ain't No Black in the Union Jack* for a sophisticated discussion of how "Blackness" and "Britishness" were constructed as mutually exclusive identities in Britain during the Thatcher years.

13. I am indebted to Partha Chatterjee's essay, "The Nationalist Resolution of the Women's Question," which discusses the nationalist handling of the "Women's Question" in the Indian colonial context during the late nineteenth century. The essay also points to the continuing failure of the contemporary Indian nation-state "to effectively include within its body the whole of the demographic mass which it claimed to represent" (251), an exclusion directly related to the earlier construction of woman within nationalist ideology. This work has been extremely helpful in my attempt to limn the contours of nationalist ideology in the Irish context and has revealed the link between the former and the ongoing occlusions of Irish identity as hegemonically formulated.

14. See the essays in *Gender and Irish Writing,* edited by Toni O'Brien Johnson and David Cairns, for a discussion of this—ongoing—deification.

15. John Hill, speaking of Jordan's earlier treatments of the Northern Question, has argued, "Both *Angel* and *Cal* have proved unequal to the challenge of their subject-matter and, as a result, have obscured, as much as they have illuminated, the issues with which they have dealt" (184). For Hill these films are similar to earlier British filmic treatments of the IRA and the Northern Question in that they are unable to "respond intelligently to history" and are unwilling "to engage with economic, political and cultural complexity" (184).

16. Bew and Patterson articulate the necessity for this shift thus: "Without a fundamental reassessment of the continuing power of the Catholic and Nationalist components in the political

culture of the Republic, there will continue to be a deep and bitter division in popular culture and attitudes" (90).

17. The term "traveling people" is used to describe Ireland's nomadic Gypsy population, dubbed more often, and pejoratively, "tinkers."

18. For a succinct presentation of Kearney's position vis-à-vis Ireland's cultural and social prospects after the implementation of Maastricht, see his recent essay in *Modern Fiction Studies,* "Post Modernity and Nationalism: A European Perspective."

19. The term is Douglas Kellner's. See his *Jean Baudrillard: From Marxism to Postmodernism and Beyond.*

20. I'm indebted here to Terry Eagleton's essay "Nationalism: Irony and Commitment." His warning about the dangers of a "bad Utopianism" that would, precisely, seek to immediately transcend the oppressive identity constructs of the past, rather than go "all the way through . . . and out the other side," is salutary and timely (23).

Works Cited

Bell, Desmond. "Ireland without Frontiers? The Challenge of the Communications Revolution." In *Across the Frontiers,* edited by Richard Kearney, 219–230. Dublin: Wolfhound Press, 1988.

Bell, G. *The British in Ireland.* London: Pluto Press, 1984.

Bew, Paul, and Henry Patterson. "Ireland in the 1990s—North and South." In *Across the Frontiers,* edited by Richard Kearney, 78–90. Dublin: Wolfhound Press, 1988.

Boyce, D. George. *Nationalism in Ireland.* 2nd ed. London: Routledge 1991.

Brown, Terence. *Ireland: A Social and Cultural History, 1922 to the Present.* Ithaca, N.Y.: Cornell University Press, 1985.

Buckley, Suzann, and Pamela Lonergan. "Women and the Troubles, 1969–1980." In *Terrorism In Ireland,* edited by Yonah Alexander and Alan O'Day, 75–87. London: Croom Helm, 1984.

Burgin, Victor. "Paranoiac Space." *New Formations* 61–75.

Cairns, David, and Shaun Richards. "Tropes and Traps: Aspects of 'Woman' and Nationality in Twentieth Century Irish Drama." In *Gender in Irish Writing,* edited by Toni O'Brien Johnson and David Cairns, 128–37. Milton Keynes, England: Open University Press, 1991. 128–137.

Chatterjee, Partha. "The Nationalist Resolution of the Women's Question." In *Recasting Women: Essays in Indian Colonial History,* edited by Kumkum Sangari and Sudesh Vaid, 233–53. New Brunswick, N.J.: Rutgers University Press, 1990.

Coughlan, Patricia. " 'Bog Queens': The Representation of Women in the Poetry of John Montague and Seamus Heaney." In *Gender in Irish Writing,* edited by Toni O'Brien Johnson and David Cairns, 88–111. Milton Keynes, England: Open University Press, 1991.

Eagleton, Terry. "Nationalism: Irony and Commitment." In Terry Eagleton, Fredric Jameson, and Edward W. Said, *Nationalism, Colonialism, and Literature,* 23–42. Minneapolis: University of Minnesota Press, 1990.

Eagleton, Terry, Fredric Jameson, and Edward W. Said. *Nationalism, Colonialism, and Literature.* Minneapolis: University of Minnesota Press, 1990.

Gallagher, F. *The Invisible Island.* London: Gollanz, 1957.

Garber, Marjorie. "The Occidental Tourist: M. Butterfly and the Scandal of Transvestism." In *Nationalisms and Sexualities,* edited by Andrew Parker, Mary Russo, Doris Sommer, and Patricia Yaeger, 121–46. New York: Routledge, 1992.

———. *Vested Interests: Cross-Dressing and Cultural Anxiety.* New York: Routledge, 1992.

Gilroy, Paul. *There Ain't No Black in the Union Jack: The Cultural Politics of Race and Nation.* London: Hutchinson, 1987.

Girvin, Brian. "National Identity and Conflict in Northern Ireland." In *Politics and Society in Contemporary Ireland,* edited by Brian Girvin and Roland Sturm, 105–34. Aldershot: Gower, 1986.

Hill, John. "Images of Violence." In *Cinema and Ireland,* edited by Kevin Rockett, Luke Gibbons, and John Hill, 147–93. London: Croom Helm, 1987.

Hoppen, K. Theodore. *Ireland since 1800: Conflict and Conformity.* London: Longman, 1989.

Hywel, Elin Ap. "Elise and the Great Queens of Ireland: 'Femininity' as constructed by Sinn Fein and the Abbey Theatre, 1901–1907." In *Gender in Irish Writing,* edited by Toni O'Brien Johnson and David Cairns, 23–39. Milton Keynes, England: Open University Press, 1991.

Jones, Ann R., and Peter Stallybrass. "Dismantling Irena: The Sexualizing of Ireland in Early Modern England." In *Nationalisms and Sexualities,* edited by Andrew Parker et al., 157–71. New York: Routledge, 1992.

Jordan, Neil. "*The Crying Game:* The Original Screenplay." In *A Neil Jordan Reader,* 177–266. New York: Vintage, 1993.

Keane, Patrick J. *Yeats, Joyce, Ireland, and the Myth of the Devouring Female.* Columbia: University of Missouri Press, 1988.

Kearney, Richard. *Across the Frontiers: Ireland in the 1990s.* Dublin: Wolfhound Press, 1988.

———. "Postmodernity and Nationalism: A European Perspective." *Modern Fiction Studies* 38, no. 3 (1992): 581–93.

———. *Visions of Europe: Conversations on the Legacy and Future of Europe.* Dublin: Wolfhound Press, 1992.

Kellner, Douglas. *Jean Baudrillard: From Marxism to Postmodernism and Beyond.* Cambridge: Polity Press, 1989.

Lloyd, David. *Anomalous States: Irish Writing and the Post-Colonial Moment.* Durham, N.C.: Duke University Press, 1993.

Moran, Sean Farrell. "Patrick Pearse and Patriotic Soteriology: The Irish Republican Tradition and the Sanctification of Political Self-Immolation." In *The Irish Terrorism Experience,* edited by Yonah Alexander and Alan O'Day, 9–28. Aldershot: Dartmouth, 1991.

Radhakrishnan, R. "Nationalism, Gender, and the Narrative of Identity." In *Nationalisms and Sexualities,* edited by Andrew Parker et al., 77–95. New York: Routledge, 1992.

Rockett, Kevin, Luke Gibbons, and John Hill, *Cinema and Ireland.* London, Croom Helm, 1987.

Shannon, Catherine. "Catholic Women and the Northern Irish Troubles." In *Ireland's Terrorist Trauma: Interdisciplinary Perspectives,* 234–48, edited by Yonah Alexander and Alan O'Day. New York: St. Martin's Press, 1989.

14 / Maternal Abject, Fascist Apocalypse, and Daughter Separation in Contemporary Swedish Novels

Ebba Witt-Brattström

How do we reach knowledge about the Other? How can we engender empathy, how be stricken by compassion, how create that capacity for identification that will counteract racism's bloody separation between "them" and "us"? How do we explain the attraction of that fascination that begins in love and ends in hate? How can we realize that the potentialities of "victim/executioner which characterize each identity, each subject, each sex" are constantly at work within all of us?[1] In this essay I investigate the way that the increasing immigration to Sweden after World Wars I and II provided a metaphor for writers of exile within patriarchal society, a metaphor that has now become the generic means through which contemporary Swedish women writers explore issues of nationalism and multiculturalism. The essay opens with a discussion of the theory of abjection introduced by Julia Kristeva (herself a Bulgarian immigrant living in Paris) and goes on to apply the concept of abjection to two Swedish women authors of different generations.

Psychoanalysis explains the origin of xenophobia and racism as an ambivalent desire for the Other. Located at a time and a place beyond the subject, the desire for the maternal preobject enacts its drama, a drama centered around rejection. This repressed "truth" about our civilization can be captured by literature, if only in glimpses.

Humanity's innate fear of its own prehistory is a cultural heritage that resounds in the modern literary text as well. The genre of nausea is well represented by male authors (Céline, Bataille, Sartre, and so on); few female authors, however, cultivate the theme of abjection, possibly because it is harder for the female subject to keep the distance from the body of the archaic mother. In contrast to the male subject, she is herself part of the same chaos by virtue of her sex, her maternity, or her identification with the mother. Woman, says Julia Kristeva, pays a higher price to become a speaking subject.[2] She has gained access to the symbolic order through rejecting the mother and identifying with the law of the Father; she has thereby censored herself as a female body. Part of her remains in the preverbal state that the embryonic subject has to reject in order to develop. But as birthgiver and mother she also *is* this maternal abject, not least for her children. Woman, says Kristeva, is the speaking animal—both cultural being and link in the biological chain of the species.[3] Maybe it is this paradoxical location that enables the female writing subject to articulate the fundamental conditions of humanity with a deeper insight, being both body and consciousness, sex and intellect, homo sapiens and subject. And maybe it comes more naturally for women to experience this doubleness as a threat.

In the work of two Swedish authors of different generations I detect a preoccupation with the subject's split between body and speech, its basis in a scenario where the I and the Other form a part of the genetic program of humanity. By focusing on the problem of boundaries and characterizing it as unknown, abject, Birgitta Trotzig and Mare Kandre approach an analysis of how the potential for victim or torturer characterizes each subject. Inscribing themselves in a tradition little explored by female authors—that of apocalypse, nausea, grotesque—they capture a deeply repressed truth about our civilization. Two novels by Trotzig—*The Disease* (1972) and *The Mud King's Daughter* (1984)—describe, in terms of developmental psychology, the conditions of one man and one woman from the poorest sections of the Swedish proletariat in the twentieth century. The younger author, Kandre (born in 1962), further develops this analysis in *Bübin's Brat* (1987), in which she describes the creation of boundaries within a pubescent girl. Strongly ritualistic, these texts are written against the backdrop of the fascism and racism of the Second World War. Mare Kandre is of Estonian extraction and her text reverberates with Baltic wartime trauma. The instinctual origin of racism and xenophobia is located in the separation between mother and child, where identity is established; a bloody event that can only be conveyed in metaphors of destruction. Trotzig's *The Disease* strives to connect the subject's experience of threat from the archaic mother with a sustained critique of civilization; the instinctual basis of fascism is revealed. The novel also polemicizes against the apocalyptic, biblical heritage and reveals its androcentric assumptions. I will therefore discuss it more exhaustively than the other novels of my essay.

Governed by the Absence of the Mother

Sär—och sönderfallet: är om det som alltihop handlar—vart tog hon vägen? varför kom hon aldrig tillbaka? kanske det var i henne som det hela höll ihop? men det är så dags nu.[4]

[Disintegration, decay: is what it's all about—where did she go? why did she never come back? maybe it was in her that it all held together? but it's too late now.]

In *The Disease* (1972), the protagonist is Elje Jesaja (he who cometh in the name of the Lord) Ström, a legally incapacitated farmhand from Skåne, Sweden's southernmost county. Born in 1914 and deceased in 1947, his short life encompasses two world wars. He is a product of the dregs of civilization, an Oedipus of the rural proletariat.

Motherless at an early age, Elje is brought up by his father, the farmworker Albin Ström, to deny his mother, a Galician guest worker who disappeared when he was six months old, and to venerate his father's belief in a divine avenging justice as depicted by Jehovah's Witnesses. The transformation that Elje's personality will undergo is anticipated in the presentation of the characters of Elje and Albin. Through an ambiguous use of the third person *he,* they fluctuate in and out of each other, their lines become vague and their experiences similar. The main thread of the novel, Elje's discourse, thus includes his father's story, which in itself contains the suggestion for a modern proletarian novel. Albin's life seems to him a "veil of fake order imperfectly drawn over arching darknesses of disorder." This is the darkness that speaks in him when, seized with blind desire, he rapes the Galician guest worker who becomes Elje's mother. After her disappearance (partly caused by Albin's brutality), he turns to Judge Rutherford's interminable writings about how to prepare for the extinction of sin and the end of the world.

His son becomes his life and his work, to be kept unpolluted, at a distance from what is "impure" (such as sex, woman, Galician). But the son does not develop into an apostle of purity. "The boy—he was like nobody. He was wrong."

He resists, not only in his incorrigible affinity with his mother and his poor understanding, but also in establishing a "hollow" reality against that of his father and of order.

Elje's early sense of being split, divided, and governed by the absence of his mother makes him increasingly schizophrenic. Albin clings to the order of authority; Elje dwells in chaos. This is the starting point. All through the novel, these two guiding principles exist side by side, and when they clash, the result is destruction.

Elje's discourse includes Albin's story, but writes it in accordance with Elje's possibilities and history. The overall movement is a search for *her,* for "the split, the forgotten scorch of fire, the trace." It is a desperate struggle for confirmation, for becoming *somebody.* Only once does he come close to the goal of his dreams, and that is when he falls in love. On his knees in the row of beets he spots the most insignificant of the workers apart from himself, a Galician woman. Suddenly the void is filled and Elje's curiosity is raised. What lies at the bottom of those dark holes that are the end point of his fantasies about her? From where comes her strange smell? To find the answer to his questions he defies his fears of the terrible "birthing machine" he knows that she is carrying with her, hidden under her gray skirt, and runs away to Gdynia, Poland, to find her. It is April 1939 and the woman he finds, after wandering terror-stricken around the poor quarters with their well-known smell of unwashed bodies, turns out to be a prostitute. The father-part in him takes over. Albin "had been right: evil are the sex and the advances."

Elje spends the major part of World War II crouched upon his bed in the lunatic asylum, watching the battles of cloud formations in the sky. He dies after committing a sex murder on a Galician refugee woman, an assistant nurse at the hospital.

Elje's inner reality is marked by his paradoxical experience of existence as simultaneously formed by the absence of his mother and ruled by her presence. The world is the body of a woman who makes herself known only in fragments, an imaginary mother by whom Elje is safely enclosed or claustrophobically abandoned. The outside world is also covered by a kind of fetal membrane: the ground, the twilight, the surface of the water, even the houses have skin. In contrast with this living and warm earth-mother stands Elje's own body, "smooth and gray like the cold fields. When he touched it, it might just as well be made of wood." He spends an entire winter rolled up in his blanket like a butterfly in its cocoon; only after this recreation of the fetal position does he dare to run away from his father. When he falls in love, fetal movements spread in his language. What he seeks in the meeting with woman—who always (also) represents his mother, she who disappeared—is regeneration. As a child he keeps (from his father) the secret of this intense longing for his mother; as a grown-up he tries to hide the facts of sexual maturation and insistent sexual drive. Longing and masturbation go together and are both part of the forbidden. Elje seeks a refuge in the forest, where he finds an excuse to go as often as he dares. He fills a pit with decomposed leaves and furrows himself down. Here, in the smell of "the dampness of life and the juices of death," the experience of the mother can be arranged. Covered with earth and old leaves, overwhelmed by sensations of smell and taste, he is a body with no border against the external world, at one with Mother Earth. (In this pit he also dies.)

> Han ser moder och gräs Han ser henne inte
>> Vem gråter gråter? Som jorden själv grät
>> I jord under linklädnad som under en brudklänning De brustna ögonen svarta insjunkenheten i jorden
>> Höga moder och låga lätt tung som kyrktornet med innanmätet av mörker krypande med jord i munnen krälande som mask och rötter utan kropp gränslinjer upplöst spottad på jämrande ylande hynda i största förnedring förlorade förlorade
>> Ensam berövad allt ända till namnet
>> Nattmoder släckta förstörda ansikte du lysande
>> —som fläderbuskens läppar svagt fränt doftande rör sig fram och åter över hålan skuggansiktet det insjunkna avlånga hålformen i jorden som gräset tecknar där någon legat och åter rest sig och gått sin väg (112)

> [He sees mother and grass He does not see her
>> Who is crying crying? As if the earth itself cried
>> In earth under linen raiment as under a wedding dress. The darkened eyes black the sinking down into the earth
>> Mother high and low light heavy as the church tower darkness inside crawling dirt in the mouth crawling as worms and roots without body boundaries dissolved spat on wailing howling bitch in utter degradation lost lost
>> Alone deprived of everything even down to the name
>> Night mother extinguished ruined face you shining
>> —like the lips of the elder bush softly sharply fragrantly moving back and forth over the hollow the shadow face the sunken oval hollow shape in the earth which the grass draws where somebody has lain and risen again and gone away]

This is a key passage. The compressed sentence fragments point us back to the memory trace—the (dead?) mother—and forward to the novel's denouement in the ritual murder on the (holy) fertile female body, the black madonna, the "night mother."

With the use of a schizophrenic discourse Birgitta Trotzig approaches a more corporeal layer of language. According to Gilles Deleuze, the schizophreniac experiences no surface and cannot, as the case is in normal speech, differentiate sounds and signs from body and corporality.[5] The surface is a sieve, the body split and disconnected. Words are emptied of their meaning, losing their power to express phenomena that are distinct from the body's actions and passions. All words become physical. The schizophrenic discourse in *The Disease* makes it possible to express the instinctual basis of the subject's (in this case Elje's/Albin's) existence. Words acquire an infantile materiality; they deliver, as in the birth and fetus metaphors, or obstruct, as in the Judge's language. Body parts have their own lives, especially Elje's fumbling hands, an inheritance from his father. The same goes for feet, lips, feeling, hearing: Elje exists as a collection of scattered parts.

The Emperor, Elje's alter ego, is thus also a part of his body, namely, his penis. Born during Elje's secret masturbation sessions, the Emperor materializes out of the special blend that arises in Elje's combined longing for symbiosis and attraction for the "order" of authority. Elje's own experiences of the "evil pudenda" and Judge Rutherford's apocalyptic language later supply the fixed formulas for the novel's movement from desperate search to persecution and destruction.

In the language of the Emperor, with its penchant for the low and the sexual, we recognize the stylistic devices of the grotesque. This overall principle, which is the right arm of the law and death, gets its revenge when the story of Elje's individual psychosis is expanded to include one of the cruel massacres of contemporary history. For Elje enters the service of the Emperor at the same time as World War II breaks out. The confused fantasies of the mental patient Ström differ only marginally from the description of the Nazi devastation of a city called Brnsk in Poland. It was in Brnsk that Elje was seized after his defeat with the prostitute, and it was in Brnsk that the Emperor finally took over. When Germany declares war on Poland, Elje interprets this as divine justice coming at last.

In the act of extermination all living things are to be annihilated—not only human life but the principle of life, represented by female fertility. The description of how the Emperor becomes the law of the psychotic Elje becomes a critique of Western civilization's denial and fear of a prelinguistic chaos close to the body of the mother.

The Disease takes place in an apocalyptic genre, an ancient form traceable to the Greek oracles, but probably even older (Egypt or Persia); it is most clearly represented by the Hebrew prophets. It is no coincidence that the Revelation of Saint John is an intertext in the novel. The characteristic of this genre is above all its fear of the feminine, of the demonic, of sexuality. In her book *Powers of Horror,* Julia Kristeva claims that the apocalyptic vision is grounded in primal fantasies that arise from a very early narcissistic wound. She also finds apocalyptic overtones in the modern literature engaged with horror and nausea. This is a theory that fits well into my subsequent reading of *The Disease.*

The starting point of *Powers of Horror* is the nothingness that brings forth the human subject: the rejection of the vegetative state close to the mother's body. In the corporal world "mother-and-me" one is at the mercy of what is felt as a pulling, threatening nothingness. The embryonic individual wants to advance; it divines an existence beyond this "nothingness"—an "order." In this border state there is neither subject nor object, only *abject* (*l'abjet* = the repulsive; from *ab-jectio* = repulsion, really casting away.) The movement up and away opens the way for the acquisition of language, which comes later. In this rejection of "maternal love" the ego is born.

According to Kristeva this precarious foundation of identity lives within us as a latent position, in the future emerging as feelings of repugnance and horror for everything that seems to threaten order, identity, system. But these feelings are ambivalent, as we simultaneously carry the memory of the loss of something good, the primal state (the good breast, vegetating in the warmth, the glitter in our mother's eye, and so on). The fascination with instances of disgust becomes easily understandable: these are at once a threat and a promise of a forgotten existence before the birth of the ego.

The memory trace, the pull downward and backward, is still present in writing, especially modern writing, says Kristeva. Hidden under the phallic system's naive conceptualization (the belief that only that which can be named exists) lies an imagined mother, who is the original "site" of language.

The ambivalence toward this prehistory is present not only in every subject, but also in the history of humankind. In *Powers of Horror* Kristeva enumerates various ritual attempts at formulating the anxiety and tempering it through taboos. As the very first of these, fundamental for all civilization, she sees the incest taboo. "Incest prohibition throws a veil over primary narcissism and the always ambivalent threats with which it menaces subjective identity. It cuts short the temptation to return, with abjection and jouissance, to that passivity status within the symbolic function, where the subject, fluctuating between inside and outside, pleasure and pain, word and deed, would find death, along with nirvana."[6] The function of religious rites would then be to parry the subject's fear and longing for an irrevocable sinking back into the great mother. In primitive societies without writing, the rites are a kind of real language. They are not only symbols, but carry a material, translinguistic, magical significance as well. Purification rites identify and exclude the unclean object, which thereby becomes a distinguishable nonobject. In primitive societies the purification rite is followed by a separation of the sexes, a separation that almost always entails men gaining privileges over women. It seems that the demonic potential of femininity has to be checked in order not to threaten the proper and pure "I." The rite ensures the separation from the archaic mother; it becomes a real boundary against impurity. What is impure? Female sexuality (menstrual blood, birthgiving) and decay (food, disease, death).

These magical boundaries are carried over into the culture of writing. In the Old Testament the symbolic identity is formed with the logic of separation, "that ye may put difference between holy and unholy, and between unclean and clean," as says Leviticus.[7] Extensive regulations are established to help the male keep unstained. The menstruating female body is especially threatening: "And if a man shall lie with a woman having her sickness, and shall uncover her nakedness; he hath discovered her fountain, and she hath uncovered the fountain of her blood: and both of them shall be cut off from among their people."[8]

The Disease polemicizes against the apocalyptic heritage. The writing of loathing and disgust is turned into a writing of resistance.

How is the female abject described in *The Disease*? Let us start with the mother. She is typical of Trotzig's women: nameless, gray, clumsy, of feeble intellect, without language, foreign, and scared. She is seen almost exclusively through the eyes of the male, Albin, and appears as an animal with gray reptilian skin, a flayed ewe, or a birthing sow. She does not belong to the order of Being but abides in the cyclic chronology of birth and death: "But also this not-being, *was*. And had time. And had even caused such circumstances which more than most others have time—which is counted in months and now approached the last month." Elje's mother, like the other women in the novel (all similar to the point of confusion), is a helpless victim of her sexuality, her great birthing machine. The birthing machine is the instinctual counterpart of the apparatus-that-knows-better, that is, the power, the Law. Its principal representative is the Emperor, who is clean and proper, exemplary: "He has no sex (but he knows of a thing that can be raised and lowered, enlarged and shrunk)." To him sexuality is an instrument of power, a tool to master (and destroy) people. Fear is the breath of life for him. When Elje is taken out for a walk by the assistant nurse he is soon to kill, her clumsy soft hand stirs the memories of those women in his life who have disappeared or betrayed him. In the touch he is close to reconciliation. But as soon as he feels her frightened smell he is transformed into the Emperor who avidly breathes this "smell of the one who has been sullied and polluted and humiliated by force and chased."

The absent and nameless mother, the blurry beet gatherer, the ugly gray prostitute in Gdynia, all exist in the inner reality of the two men, as a kind of (negative) opposite, as threatening and distorted mirror images of whatever is fluid and bottomless in themselves.

But the novel also contains a counterdiscourse which does not submit to this polarity. It exists from the beginning, at first only suggested, but growing in the course of the novel, increasingly questioning and threatening the parallel Elje/Emperor discourse. Neither realistic nor psychotic, this discourse is rather sadly lyrical, with a religious undertone. Here the female sex, the "Impurity," speaks a discourse of living.

The counterdiscourse begins in the few lines allotted to Elje's mother as a person. She is there given a vaguely indicated individuality: we are told that she worships the Black Madonna, Chestoschowa, and that she abandons her baby because she feels inadequate and scared.

When the abject acquires a history it stops being abject and becomes a person, a destiny. Gone are the coarse words, left is a gloomy narrative about the biological and social curse. The tentative information given about the mother constitutes a prelude to the main part of the counterdiscourse, the swinekeeper's tale. Through this female destiny the counterdiscourse grows in strength and becomes a force to count on. The novel's structure becomes more dynamic, and the struggle between the principles of life and death comes to the forefront. It must be remembered, however, that the counterdiscourse is no alternative power; it thematizes powerlessness. It speaks in the gaps in the dominating threefold (father, son, emperor) discourse, and becomes visible only in the last third of *The Disease*.

We meet the swinekeeper in a twenty-five-page section as a counterpart to

Elje; her destiny is told quietly, realistically, chronologically. Her fate could be the fate of the mother or the beet gatherer or the prostitute. But instead the story points forward. She is that woman, the assistant nurse, whom Elje finds at the end of the novel, in the nonmeeting that ends in the death of both of them.

The swinekeeper comes from a forest but is sent down to the plains at five years of age to tend the animals. At the lowest rung of the social ladder of the village, she herself is treated worse than an animal. Nobody sees her, except as a working creature and later also as sex; no one speaks to her, so she forgets words. She is reduced to living through her body, which becomes her bleeding heart, expressing her longing (desire) and her pains. The body *answers* to the actual repression she is subjected to, and the "biological curse" receives its social explanation. To compensate for the misery of her lot she cultivates a growing paranoia. She fantasizes that she is of royal blood, a fantasy based on her one experience of human community, her confirmation. For a single day her stinking rags are exchanged for a white dress. The swinekeeper becomes the bride of Christ just as Elje becomes the Emperor. But the psychotic discourse is here grounded in a social context: even the birth metaphors describe a real condition, since the swinekeeper soon becomes pregnant. The swinekeeper's story is the story of how woman is made into abject. Her sexual degradation is systematic and is even explicitly placed within the larger context in which the novel will culminate. Her fate will be completed as a victim, as an object for the men of the village who see her as

> ett ting som fanns till hands att släcka det grövsta med. Sedan steg man upp och knäppte byxorna och lämnade visslande svinhuskammaren—eller inte sällan en fördjupning i lä ute på markerna, omgivna av grishjorden—och tänkte inte mer på saken: den hade varit för hastig och fruktansvärd för att den alls skulle kunna hanteras av minnet, den sjönk rakt igenom och var borta—vissa saker är på det viset för tunga och går omedelbart till botten och är borta. Ända till dess någon domens dag, icke uttalbar dröm eller en till döden gående sjukdom blottar detta bottenlager som under livets gång har samlat sig och bildat ett eller annat mönster—ett eller annat—. (164)

[a thing that was there to quench the most acute desire. Then you got up and buttoned your trousers and left the swine barn—or often a hollow in the grounds sheltered from the wind, surrounded by the herd of swine—whistling, and thought no more about the matter: it had been too quick and horrible to be dealt with by memory, it sank right through and was gone—some things are like that, too heavy, and sink to the bottom at once and are gone. Until a day of judgment, an unspeakable dream or a deadly illness reveals this bottom layer that has accreted in the course of a lifetime and created some pattern or another—one or another—.]

These men employ the sexuality of the Emperor, the sexuality that wields control with a device that can be raised or lowered. The Emperor is a thing (a penis), and the swinekeeper is to him (and to the village men) an object to use. What comes of this contamination? Death. She gives birth to a dead baby boy with darkened face and buries him at the shrine of Chestoschowa, where she flees after having been expelled from all human society. After this we lose trace of her for a while. She disappears "as if she were no one, just no one," but will turn up again at the mental hospital of Brnsk.

But first the text returns to Elje, who is now preparing for the last great battle. After having read on the news bills that Germany has declared war on Poland, he has a fit of joy because "the war against Poland and impurity was begun." When he is taken to the mental hospital, crammed with psychopharmacological drugs, he has a vision that clearly explains what is to be erased from the face of the earth:

> en kvinna som knäböjande och hopvriden grät och grät. Han såg henne snett neråt genom trapphuset som genom en i genomskärning öppen bur: lår, grova lårknotor, könet skälver som ett födslovått djurkön, den grova halsen med utstående starkt böjda senor och det våldsamt tillbakakastade huvudet, liksom ut ur alla lemmar pressar sig tårarna brännande fram. Hon sitter där fastlåst i en orörlighet sådan som godset i kaolinbrännugnens tvåtusengradiga hetta: brinnande sten: ett ämne förvandlas till ett annat, ämne stiger till ämne: allt låst i vartannat till en sådan grad av värmeutveckling, det ena förtär det andra, att denna världen och flera andra lätteligen skulle kunna flyga i stoft av det. Hon gråter. Kroppen och allting i henne gråter. Hela jorden och jordens själva inälvor gråter.
>   Så går det den som sätter sig upp mot kejsaren. (184)

[a woman, kneeling and twisted, who cried and cried. He saw her obliquely down the stairwell as through a cage open in cross section: thighs, coarse bones, the sex vibrating like the wet sex of an animal in birth, the thick throat with protruding, strongly curved sinews and the head violently thrown back, the burning tears press forth as if they came from all her limbs. She sits there locked in immobility like the material in the two-thousand-degree heat of a kaolin furnace: burning stone: a substance is transformed into another, substance rises into substance: everything interlocked at such a degree of heat, one thing consuming the other, that this world and several others easily could turn into ashes from it. She is crying. Her body and everything in her are crying. The whole earth and its very bowels are crying.

This is what happens to the one who rebels against the Emperor.]

This is what the female abject looks like, encircled and confined by the Emperor. The description awakens associations to the gas chambers and their extinction of "impure" peoples. We are in September of 1939, and Judgment Day is near.

The destruction of Brnsk shines through in the text fragments like a modern altar triptych of Judgment Day. On the left altar-piece the weeping Mother Earth is sitting, as we have seen her above, with her sex uncovered and her head thrown back. It could be at the moment of delivery, in the violent bearing down of the expulsion stage. Or is it the trance of torture and confinement? The middle piece is the fragment that opens the description of the massacre. Brnsk is aflame like a body on a "sacrificial pyre."

The body of the city burns like a witch at the stake. A terrible face hangs in the sky and darkens the horizon. Is it the face of Mother Earth? Or of God? In the center of the picture, in the town square, the crucifixion takes place. There is a gallows:

> Högst upp i denna träställning hängde ännu kvar en stelfrusen kvinnokropp, brösten var avskurna och de stora mörka sårgroparna var överdragna med rimfrost som med mögel. Där högt uppe i rymden högt över staden med bara tvärbjälken över sig svängde hon runt i de uppåtstigande värmeluftströmmarna som kläppen i en klocka. (200)

> [At the top of this wooden construction the frozen body of a woman still hung, her breasts had been cut off and the large dark wounds were covered with hoarfrost as with mold. There high up in the sky high above the city with only the crossbeam above her she was swinging around in the rising streams of hot air like the tongue of a bell.]

The holy maternal body is murdered and the lifegiving breasts are cut off, an act of meaningless torture but symbolically significant.

And so for the right-hand side of the altarpiece. There the Queen of Poland walks at the head of "a stumbling dancing wailing population." The lunatics are taken out of the city to be executed in the marshes, and "first went the Queen of Poland with her blouse torn open and her chest naked, an immovable mute face shining with grease, from which the small empty eyes were gazing straight and without blinking at death-in-life, the endless . . . "

The swinekeeper, because it is she, on this day of judgment reveals who she is: the Queen of Poland, Mother Earth, with uncovered breast on her way to be destroyed by the power of the Emperor.

But she escapes.

Let us pause for a moment and investigate the basis of the counterdiscourse. There is in *The Disease* a kind of maternal form in language: a "chora" in Kristeva's sense,[9] a maternal container and preform to all signification, a hollow center that in the course of the novel gathers the scattered metaphors (life of the fetus, tree of life, and so on). A shadowy preform gives meaning to the discourse of the female body, that which tries to name the depth beyond the alluvia. Resistance arises when suddenly, in the passage about the massacre at Brnsk, this preform is filled and can be placed in opposition to the automatically registering writing of abjection. These metaphors have deep root systems; they come from below. But the complete body, the maternal body, is gone, as if it had been exploded, hanging with its face toward the earth, striving downward to totality and completion. It is only indicated in the hollow forms that Elje is so obsessed with. In his pit it exists as a longing: "like the lips of the elder bush softly sharply fragrantly moving back and forth over the hollow the shadow face the sunken oval hollow shape in the earth that the grass draws where somebody has lain and risen again and gone away." What it takes to fill this hollow is first hinted at in the story of the swinekeeper. She is the one who will finally symbolize what Elje seeks.

The disease comes and the bottom layer is revealed: it is a body on the pyre, a maimed and humiliated dead woman. That is what the vanished pattern looks like.

The name of the disease is indifference, an indifference unto death. What happened in the hollow in the grounds, surrounded by the herd of swine, must be forgotten, in order for the terrible not to happen: that you feel *compassion,* and thereby through identification become the equal of this woman.

When at last the impure is symbolized, the maternal abject, the raped and desecrated Mother Earth, is allowed to speak. The novel offers resistance; the text insists and returns to this female body hanging like the tongue without its church bell in the town of Brnsk, which has to be set on fire again to eliminate the traces of massacre. She becomes a symbol of struggle: the fire does not reach her; this massacre of everything living will not let itself be erased from memory.

She is still dangling triumphantly, visible, as a reminder of what cannot ultimately be repressed.

The disease cannot be limited to single repulsive actions in wartime; the story tells us when Elje kills *her* (the woman-mother) for whom he has been longing and searching all his life. The ritual overtones of the deed become clear when he asks the holy body, now his home and refuge, for forgiveness. She is the Black Madonna, the Queen of the earth, and he is no longer the Emperor. The counterdiscourse gets the last word in *The Disease.*

Describing the History of the Abject

If the abject, as in Trotzig, is the repellent, heavy bottom layer of memory, and literature in condensed moments its memory, then abjection is the signified of lack. Admittedly, there is a realist aspect of Birgitta Trotzig's writing that faces the golden age of modern Swedish literature, the autodidacts of the 1930s like Harry Martinson, Vilhelm Moberg, and Ivar Lo Johansson. But into their world of rejection and outsidership Trotzig introduces woman, the unknown, the foreign. All her women are bearers of an animal side, an evasive dimension that is reinforced and revealed in pregnancy.

The Mud King's Daughter is an attempt at going further, at describing the history of the abject from within its own position. It deals with a farm girl who gets pregnant by a vagrant in the 1930s and her illegitimate daughter, who repeats her fate in the 1950s. The critique is leveled at the creation of the Swedish welfare state, founded on the exclusion of those who deviate in terms of race, class, and gender, those who were hidden away in the workers' quarters.

The universal apocalypse does not take place, since the perspective is adapted to the limited horizon of Trotzig's women characters. Through the intertext, Hans Christian Andersen's fairy tale "The Mud King's Daughter," Trotzig can describe the abjectal mechanisms in terms of a postpartum depression. Andersen tells the story of an Egyptian princess of the twelfth century, who flies to Denmark in the guise of a swan in order to find a special moss flower that will cure her dying father. When she kneels beside the Danish marsh she is pulled down into the mud by the Mud King and forced to become his wife. The result of this union is a child who in the daytime looks like her mother but has her father's wild and bloodthirsty temperament. In the nighttime she resembles her father and takes the shape of a toad, but her mother's mild and sad disposition shines through her eyes. After many vicissitudes, when the girl has been saved by Christianity, mother and daughter are united, and they return to Egypt and the grandfather.

In Trotzig's novel mud is linked to waste, blood, fetal movements, instinct, and death. Here the protagonist, Mojan, finds her pleasure when she sleeps with the unemployed and dirty vagrant who becomes the father of her baby girl. The girl has a particularly cheerful temper; she is the kind who makes everybody laugh. Markedly physical, as a child she plays the clown in order to be accepted by her playmates. But all too early she also becomes something else: she is sexually abused, and feels her ability to give the boys an orgasm as her only, but magic, power. Her mother works day and night, partly as a textile worker, partly as a charwoman. She puts a curtain ring on her left ring finger, holds moral sermons on the stairs, and struggles to uphold the appearance of a respectability seen through by all her neighbors. But the girl escapes her; she belongs to the same rootless kind as her father, the Gypsy she longs for. As in the case of Elje, her longing for a father and her strong instinctual life melt together into a governing principle that takes the position of a superego. The girl becomes pregnant at the age of fourteen and gives birth to a son, the image of his grandfather the vagrant. The boy is placed in a foster home and the young mother follows the path of the abject when she becomes a prostitute, and eventually drowns herself when she realizes that her son is lost to her forever. A few years later, Mojan connects with the grandson, now a hardened juvenile delinquent and mass murderer, who is finally shot to death by the police in the sixties.

Could this be the history of the Swedish female abject? One misses the European apocalypse that colored the fate of the swinekeeper in *The Disease*. Trotzig is checked by her own image of the female abject as a speechless object rather than a subject, which is why the intricate discursivity that made *The Disease* into a masterpiece is missing. The brilliant sections are in the descriptions of Mojan's and her daughter's experiences of their bodies as sexual machines.

But *The Mud King's Daughter* is an attempt at going further in the description of the most forbidden to explore the boundaries of abjection, an alluring and forbidden "elsewhere." In the portrayal of the constant threat from within against the invisible borders between mother and daughter there is a tension that leads to an absolutely scandalous view of the child as abject. Note how closely Trotzig places the mother's feeling of disgusted distance to what we normally call mother love in its most banal form:

Inne i mörkret låg kungadottern nyfödd och såg på henne med mörka levande dyögon. Ur dyn hade ett under fötts och vilade nu skimrande på sin bladstängel över vattendjupen.

Men plötsligt låg ett främmande djur där. Det trevade omkring sig med svaga lemmar. Moderns kropp hävdes av ett vidrigt illamående. Djuret rörde sakta som ett vått kräldjur på sina ofullständiga lemmar. De liknade sega blommor av kött. Ögonen var hinnhöljda, slemhöljda. Det var ett sugdjur, sugdjuret måste äta, äta sönder henne. Det sög, hon löstes upp. Nu kunde hon inte känna vad som var hon själv längre, gränsen mellan henne själv och allt annat hade lösts upp, allt hade blivit sönderfallande våt hud. Det främmande djuret ville dra ner henne under vattenytan, suga ner henne i det glidande, ta henne, sönderdela henne, äta henne.

Nu kände hon hur också hennes ansikte flöt isär. Hon skulle inte kunnat känna igen sig själv i den som visade sig där. Hade hon sett sig i en spegel skulle det ha varit en annan som visade sig där.

Men så vaknade hon till igen:

Flickan måste ha en vinterkappa.[10]

[In the dark lay the royal daughter, newborn, and gazed at her with dark mud eyes. Out of the mud a miracle had been born and was now resting, shimmering on its leaf stem above the depths of water.

But suddenly an unknown animal was lying there. It was groping about with weak limbs. The mother's body heaved with repulsive nausea. The animal slowly moved like a wet reptile on its imperfect limbs. They resembled leathery flowers of flesh. Its eyes were covered with film, covered with slime. It was a sucking-animal, the sucking-animal had to eat, eat her through. It sucked, she dissolved. Now she could no longer feel where she began and ended, the border between herself and everything else had dissolved, everything had become disintegrating wet skin. The unknown animal wanted to drag her down beneath the surface of the water, pull her down into the slippery stuff, take her, divide her, eat her.

Now she felt her face flowing apart, too. She would not have been able to recognize herself in the one who appeared there. If she had looked in a mirror it would have been another who had shown herself there.

But then she came to again:

The girl must have a winter coat.]

"There Is Nothing like the Abjection of Self"

With *The Mud King's Daughter* Birgitta Trotzig has forced the abject out into the borderland where Mare Kandre can step in. Kandre's texts constantly explore the conflict between fascism and Communism within the Baltic states through images of biological womanhood as trauma. Deeply influenced by Trotzig, Kandre in her novel *Bübin's Brat* takes her starting point in the insight formulated by Trotzig's novel: "For the sex is the child in the life of man: devouring, furious, formative." Kandre's *Bübin's Brat* locates the existential split in a girl's transformation into woman. The site is a rotting garden in the shadow of war, and the chronology is cyclic, in a hot month where a drama is enacted between women in different phases of life. "No one gets out of here, whole and unchanged."

Mare Kandre uses the technique employed by Trotzig in the swinekeeper's tale in *The Disease*. Like Trotzig, Kandre locates the existential pain in the body as the site of abjection but changes it by showing that it is also—ultimately— the site of psychic growth. The paranoia helps the young woman to get rid of her girl-self. If the swinekeeper's tale is the story of how woman comes to symbolize the abject through her bodily functions, the woman in *Bübin's Brat* points to identity's inner condition.

"There is nothing like the abjection of self to show that all abjection is in fact recognition of the *want* on which every being, meaning, language, or desire is founded," Kristeva writes.[11] This is less a question of identity than of place, she claims, polemicizing against Freud. "Where" am I, rather than "who" am I. We are at the threshold of original repression, before the unconscious in the Freudian sense begins to function, before the creation of the ego, its objects and its ideas. The abject comes before the symbolic, and is thus observable primarily as a symptom. It has only one of the properties of the object, that of being the opposite of an ego. "Where am I?"—this can be said to be the question for Mare Kandre in *Bübin's Brat*. "Who is she? This big, terrible girl of flesh—In the way of everything."

Mare Kandre's book covers the time of a menstrual cycle and describes a puberty rite in strongly symbolic language. Everything has ceased to function in the village; people are half-starved and uncertain about the future. The protagonist lives without words, in a world of smells and weariness, together with her strict and deeply religious guardians, the mother figure Bübin and the blind uncle. In a state of growing panic she feels her body change beyond her control. "Nothing can help me now. My body is incomprehensible and heavy, I can feel the blood concentrate in the white bone cradle of my pelvis, and my great, black weight of fear." In her helpless state her increasingly diffuse identity is invaded by loathsome feelings from without. "I step in dung and feces and the smell makes me dizzy and delirious, I have to fill my mouth with hair and chew." The only distinct thing is the transformed body. "But I have to do everything myself. I carefully lift my shift over my head, I cannot get away now: the breasts are heavy and small, the sex is on the outside, and whatever way you see it: dark and grown out."

When the blood starts coming the ugly, clumsy, and moronically persistent Brat or Kid turns up, a rival for Bübin's caring, with clear traits of a younger sister and at the same time an image of the protagonist as a girl: "But the kid is distinct. Nothing has happened to her, she still has shiny, white hair and tiny hands." These two, who bear the same name (the protagonist is called Kindchen), immediately develop a hatred for each other. "I think, what does she want from me? I do not understand. She is weak and pale, feeble-minded and frail, her hair thick with light and her body so underfed and thin that it makes me furious. She is not someone I have to spare." The Brat symbolizes that yoke of infantility that the protagonist has to cast off. When they are left alone, orphaned and hungry, they are driven to duel, but also to involuntary identification. Before Kindchen can stage her brutal resurrection as a woman, she has to approach "the sour, pungent evaporations of the Brat"; she must let herself be loosened up and become "soft and swelled of face, as if I had lain dead overnight." The voyage away from this similarity and corpselikeness to the formation of a separate subject becomes a struggle of life and death.

The transformation also involves a denial of the mother figure within: "Bübin, Bübin's place, is empty, and you can see the world displaced, memories worn down, but everything else big and exaggerated." As the infant in the abjectal phase of primary narcissism rejects the memory of the good side of symbiosis, and simultaneously with deadly automatism incorporates the rejecting movement in the foundation of its own identity, so the protagonist in Kandre's novel realizes that she has to take care of, that is, kill, the Brat, who represents the impossible return to Bübin's caring: "All through the days now I sit in Bübin's room and watch the Brat in her bed, enthralled. I cannot move for loathing—I feel more and more encumbered. More and more depressed."

The ritualistic trait is obvious: the protagonist feels a holiness, a stillness in her task, even if the murder itself appears like a burst of fury in self-defense against the attacks of the abject—or like a vanquishing of compassion. When she has heaved the body down into the well, the berries have ripened and it is time to "bleed again, but this time as a relief, a kind of opening."

In *Bübin's Brat,* Mare Kandre appears as a direct heiress of Birgitta Trotzig. The melancholy and soiled environment and the view of biological difference as a destiny similar to the galley slave's resemble that closeness to the corporal, loathsome, and apocalyptic that ever since *The Exposed* (1957) has been the literary attitude of Birgitta Trotzig. But Kandre represents a displacement in this genre that may be a sign of the times. Where Trotzig uses a technique that lets the empathy trickle into the dismissive male gaze on the formless, bleeding, and disgusting female abjects (who in Trotzig's texts are typically nameless and described in the third person), Kandre fearlessly steps in and speaks in the first person. Her (former) ego is primarily an abject in her own eyes, and the male gaze is not present at all in *Bübin's Brat.* In fact, the cold father figure called Uncle is blind. But he has power over the Book from which Kindchen is forced to read aloud. In this daily act, a demonstration of the oppressive effect of words on the secretly menstruating girl, I see a specification of Trotzig's demonstration in *The Disease* of how the boy Elje is psychologically wrecked by the Old Testament God's right to "put difference between holy and unholy, and between unclean and clean."[12] According to the Old Testament, the condition for keeping pure and unpolluted, that is, "holy" and separate, is to keep away from menstruation, birth, decay—in short, the reproductive female body and death. That these two go together in Kindchen's imagination we understand from the horror with which she watches a little black coffin being taken away or notes in terror that the pregnant elder sister of a playmate has died in childbirth. But unlike Trotzig's boy, who incorporates the Judge's words within his psyche, Kandre's teenage girl opposes Uncle's Book and feels both rage and boredom. She hears how "everything becomes difficult and separate—inside, outside— how the grass parts its dense blades and the leaves fall off. Then I open the book and start to read in a low, toneless voice."

Bübin's Brat balances on an edge; the text is both symbolic and realistic. The author is of Estonian immigrant extraction, and the description of the background could be taken from a land in dissolution, for example, the Estonian countryside during the final stage of the German or the first Soviet invasion; a time when people were in need and did not unnecessarily talk to each other for fear of informers or deserted "forest brothers" in the vicinity. But above all the piercing metaphoric and phobic prose gives a symbolic image of the black and painful passage from girl to woman, a dark land pointed out by Edith Södergran in 1918 as the place where "girls, growing to women, were imprisoned, suffering like animals."[13]

In Mare Kandre's dark land the terrified young woman is reduced to a shamefully swelling womb: "I disappear here in this wild growing! It forces me up into the middle of the skull, to a point behind the forehead, more and more silent, and I know that I am this now: none." Forehead and cranium, the brain is emptied of thoughts when the uterus is emptied of blood. In the dawn the protagonist creeps out to bury her bloody rags and in her excited state imagines how the trees and the forest "wince" and lose their color in her presence. She squats and buries her bloody bundle in the earth.

When the brain tissue is placed on an equality with menstrual blood, the brain, the site of spirituality, is drained and becomes an empty womb: "When everything is done I feel the blood come away from the inside of my head and all that is left is an empty white spot."

The positionality of the Kandrean sex in the 1980s has a counterpart in the late 1880s. The desperately bleeding Kindchen could have spoken the same words as Victoria Benedictsson's resigned character Nina in the short story "Out of the Darkness": "My brain had its sick spot, and all the material that life gave me went to nourish this one point." The point, the spot, is the biological destiny; it is Nina's degrading opinion of woman as the pariah of culture: "Everything is shame in a woman because she is nothing in herself, she is only part of her sex." In the Swedish novelistic tradition there is a recurring discussion around the location of sex in culture in the twentieth century, too. Prominent representatives of this discussion are Agnes von Krusenstjerna, Moa Martinson, Ulla Isaksson, and Birgitta Trotzig. In the latter's debut, *The Lives of Lovers* (1951), the young Aimée's disgust with her body and her sex ("a furry dark parasitic animal [which] had clung to her pudenda and swelled with her blood") resembles Kindchen's to the point of confusion.

In *Bübin's Brat* Kandre paints the picture of the female body as a dark continent characterized by rivalry and cruelty in the interaction between the women—the older Bübin, the young Kindchen, and the girl called the Kid or the Brat. In the last sentence of the novel an opening is discernible, which, however, does not partake of the atmosphere of concentration-camp hell characteristic of this novel. Kindchen, who is now a murderer (if the novel is read realistically), but whole and separate from her disgusting part (if read symbolically), washes herself, walks out the gate, and hears, "A girl is laughing in the village. A boy is calling. I am clean and warm—Anxious and alert."

In this perspective, *Bübin's Brat* may seem a return to the feminine mystique, but I claim that it rather wants to modify the conception of female corporeality. Kandre drastically changes the place of the "female animal" Kindchen and the Brat are no Nice Girls who behave well; the enormous strength possessed by the girl in her changing cocoon has an explosive power. When, increasingly furious and desperate, the sex speaks, it can move the mountains, or at least change the reader's conception of reality.

In an earlier book, the collection of poems *The Annunciation* (1986), Kandre places herself in "the humid cell of the monthly autism." This positioning is efficient and immediately creates clearsightedness: the protagonist sees love "come off" the "brave face" of her lover when he treads "the open grounds of reality." Left to her own destiny, she is enveloped in the reality of the body: "The blood berries curdle from the border of the membrane and the dark organ of the womb roars, the pain flares up in the glands of the breasts." But this truth of the sex breeds a wrath that gives the ego a face, at the same time as "the world" outside is dissolved. Not until the woman in a love scene takes her lover and invades his "reality" with her sex as a weapon can the world be reestablished and can she escape from her biological cell life: "I have lowered myself over you, planted my open sex in your naked breast, emptied the lung's bellows of instinct, milked the semen from your clean scrotum / I do not ask, because nothing is right." Paradoxically, Kandre's women remain in the reader's memory as very strong characters, although it is their "animal side" that has mostly spoken.

The historical context charges these strongly symbolic texts about the relation to the other, to the unknown. A progression from female object to female subject can be observed, new points of departure in the continuing process of acquiring knowledge, which women's literary tradition can be seen as.

Trotzig begins in empathy with the nameless, sexually abused emigrant woman, but can only picture defeat, showing how woman's difference severs her from human communities. Kandre picks up the thread here by entering into the actual process of splitting the core of identity, and succeeds in indicating an escape through a bloody separation. The girl—understood as the prehistory of the subject—is dead, but the woman is alive.

Translated by Rachel Åkerstedt

Notes

1. Julia Kristeva, "Women's Time," 459.
2. Julia Kristeva, *About Chinese Women*, 43.
3. Ibid., 17–24.
4. Birgitta Trotzig, *Sjukdomen* (The disease), 156. Further page references will be given parenthetically in the text.
5. Gilles Deleuze, "The Schizophrenic and Language," 324–340.
6. Julia Kristeva, *Powers of Horror*, 63.
7. Leviticus 10.10.
8. Leviticus 20.18.
9. "In this way the drives, which are 'energy' charges as well as 'psychical' marks, articulate what we call a chora: a nonexpressive totality formed by the drives and their stases in a motility that is as full of movement as it is regulated" (Julia Kristeva, *Revolution in Poetic Language*, 25). For a further explication of the function of the chora, see ibid., 25–30.
10. Birgitta Trotzig, *Dykungens dotter* (The Mud King's daughter), 76.
11. Kristeva, *Powers of Horror*, 5.
12. Leviticus 10.10.
13. Edith Södergran (1892–1923), "Landet som icke är."

Works Cited

Andersen, Hans Christian. *Eventyr og historier* (Fairy tales). Copenhagen: Gyldendahl, 1835–72.
Benedictsson, Victoria [Ernst Ahlgren, pseud.]. "Ur mörkret" (Out of the darkness). In *Samlade skrifter I–VII*. Stockholm: Bonniers, 1918–20.
Deleuze, Gilles. "The Schizophrenic and Language: Surface and Depth in Lewis Carroll and Antonin Artaud." In *Literature and Psychoanalysis,* edited by Edith Kurzweil and William Phillips. New York: Columbia University Press, 1983.
Kandre, Mare. *Bebådelsen* (The annunciation). Stockholm: Bonniers, 1986.
———. *Bübins unge* (Bübin's brat). Stockholm: Bonniers, 1987.
Kristeva, Julia. *About Chinese Women*. London: Boyars, 1977.
———. *Powers of Horror: An Essay on Abjection.* New York: Columbia University Press, 1982.
———. *Revolution in Poetic Language.* New York: Columbia University Press, 1984.
———. "Women's Time." In *Feminisms: An Anthology of Literary Theory and Criticism,* edited by Robyn R. Warhol and Diane Price Herndl. New Brunswick, N.J.: Rutgers University Press, 1991.
Södergran, Edith. *Landet som icke är* (The land which is not). Helsinki: Schildts, 1925.
Trotzig, Birgitta. *Dykungens dotter* (The Mud King's daughter). Stockholm: Bonniers, 1985.
———. *Sjukdomen* (The disease). Stockholm: Bonniers, 1972.

15 / *Ona*

The New Elle-*Literacy*
and the Post-Soviet Woman

Greta N. Slobin

Debates about various aspects of the woman's question, submerged since the 1920s, have recaptured the attention of Russian media from the beginning of perestroika. The remarkable public interest in problems of sexuality represents a sharp departure from the attitudes of the decidedly puritanical socialist state. Discussions concerning the role and status of women, feminism and femininity, and especially the previously taboo subject of prostitution reflect the enormity of social change in the former Soviet Union.[1] New conditions have found immediate reflection in the representation of women in popular culture, especially film, as well as in beauty contests and advertisements.[2] The late perestroika period was a time of relative optimism when many new publishing ventures attempted to gain the attention of a possible audience and find a market before the new stringent laws and high costs of publishing went into effect.[3] One such publication is the 1990 issue of an expensive glossy magazine, *Ona* (She), the new Russian *Elle,* a remarkable document that takes upon itself the task of charting possibilities for the emerging identity of the new Russian woman. Ideas contained within its sleek covers proffer much more than the expected frivolity, entertainment, and escape of its Western counterparts or the erotic titillation of *Andrei,* the Russian *Playboy.* Serious editorial statements and

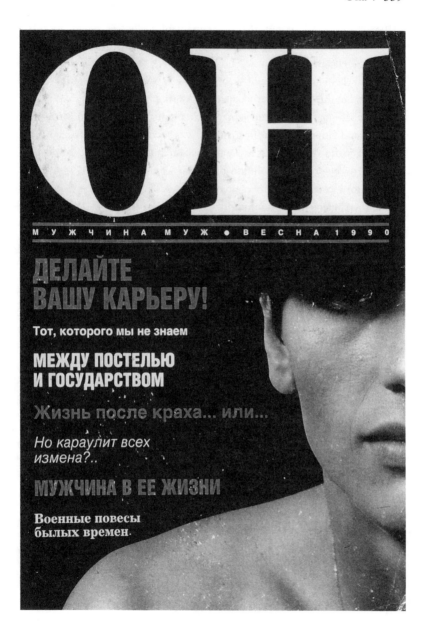

ОН

МУЖЧИНА МУЖ ● ВЕСНА 1990

ДЕЛАЙТЕ ВАШУ КАРЬЕРУ!

Тот, которого мы не знаем

МЕЖДУ ПОСТЕЛЬЮ И ГОСУДАРСТВОМ

Жизнь после краха... или...

Но караулит всех измена?..

МУЖЧИНА В ЕЕ ЖИЗНИ

Военные повесы былых времен.

essays by major writers known in the high-culture literary sphere are interspersed with the usual features of a popular woman's magazine, such as advertisements, recipes, beauty advice, and the horoscope. The issue goes beyond the change in the representation of woman from "worker-producer to plaything-consumer" in the early perestroika period (McAndrew, 87).

The baffling mix of options, pragmatic and fey, liberating and patriarchal, fantastic and visionary, in the first issue of *Ona* represents a microcosm of a nation at a crossroads. It reflects the main social trends of the late perestroika period shortly before the dissolution of the Soviet Union in 1991, trends that account for a continued sense of anarchy today. The two decisive factors that define the change—the beginning of the fall of the empire in 1989 and the move from a socialist system toward a democracy and a market economy on the Western capitalist model—hold the promise of new freedom in the indefinable future, while their immediate impact is felt in the hardship and anxiety of daily life. The concurrent resurgence of nationalism in the Soviet Union and the regained independence of the former Warsaw Pact countries of Eastern Europe demonstrate the defeat of "the Marxist theoretical assimilation of the national question within an internationalist communism" (Parker et al., 3). Marxism failed in yet another sphere—the promise of sexual equality. The conjunction of gender and national redefinition, revealed in contemporary debates in the media about sexuality in Russia, finds striking expression in *Ona*.

The multiplicity of voices and the influx of new information and divergent opinions in the media fill a power vacuum in the public sphere of a country long ruled by Party decree. A look at the magazine's sponsors confirms its serious intent of socialization and outreach: the National Commission of Television and Radio of the USSR, the National Commission of Publishing of the USSR, the Ministry of Forest Industry, and the State Commission of Light Industry at Gosplan. The collaboration of powerful media and publishing institutions and industry, including the Forest Industry, points to an effort at regrouping in a radically altered situation. The new venture is introduced with an opening statement about the magazine's goals written by Vasily Bogdanov, who is the president of the association called New Style (Novyi stil'), one of the magazine's sponsors. Its title "To Ascend the Red Hillock" ("Podniatsia na Krasnuiu Gorku") implies an ascent toward a dream or an ideal. Despite its eclectic material, ranging from high culture to lowbrow offerings, it is apparent that *Ona* is aimed primarily at an audience of ambitious, professional, educated female readers who want change. Although Bogdanov's call for "reaching for the impossible" would no doubt remind these readers of a Soviet ideological cliché, he applies the old precept to very pragmatic goals: it propagates yuppie consumerism, a definite move away from socialist egalitarianism to individual fulfillment in the post-Communist state.

The magazine's broad reformist thrust as a media channel for social correctives is a tactical move to occupy the space created by the retreat of the dominant Communist system of values, with its proclaimed social and sexual equality. As the reading of *Ona* will demonstrate, its positioning in relation to Russia's socialist past, as well as to the West, reveals a great deal about the country's efforts to envision a future. The predicament is first visible from the cover portrait of a female face split in half. The visual construction is meant to and does elicit an immediate response: why the split, where is the other half and what might it be? There are actually two possible matching halves: one on the magazine's back cover, the other on the counterpart men's magazine *On* (He), with a similarly split male face. At first glance, the sexuality of the split faces appears somewhat ambiguous. The editors explain that the separation of sexes or the emphasis on difference is a necessary one at present, although they claim that the union of the two is to be postponed only temporarily, arguing that "a separation must precede a firm union" (10).

The split performs several functions. It calls immediate attention to the fragmentation of the self and the problem of sexual identity in a period of social and national redefinition. At the same time, the split face on the sleek Western-style cover also fragments and reconfigures the notion of market and the West.[4] *Ona* attempts to create a new language of desire, a new division of the public and private sphere as commodity fetishism slowly and painfully enters the stage, more a phantasm than a reality. People on the street who cannot afford to buy *Ona,* for example, can pay to skim through it and similar expensive new publications at newspaper stands.[5] But who is the woman the magazine seeks to construct and to serve?

In my reading of the magazine I will demonstrate how *Ona* maps out several venues for creating a new feminine consciousness, or an *Elle*-literacy, that promises a departure from the traditional image of the *Soviet Woman* (the popular magazine about women in the Soviet Union): recovery of ideologies suppressed in socialist society, formation of an entrepreneurial class, woman as consumer, and woman as symbol of the new nation. Although the sense of "departure" is clear, the identity of the "new" woman remains contested within the covers of this sleek magazine.

Editorial statements concerning problems of sexuality in the former Soviet Union and the options offered here confirm that gender plays a crucial role in the transition process. The variety of ways to imagine the identity of the post-Soviet woman is inseparable from Russia's struggle to reinvent itself as a nation. And as Benedict Anderson notes in the chapter "Memory and Forgetting" in *Imagined Communities,* this requires an understanding of "what a person is being asked to forget/remember or to forget to remember for creation of national identity" (Anderson, 205). As we will see, despite the plurality of voices *Ona* is strikingly specific about what the post-Soviet woman is urged to forget and what she is asked to remember.

Utopian Mythology

In his short introduction to the magazine Bogdanov claims that this new publication will help readers, bringing them "advice, help, solace" so that they can become "more open, generous; help them achieve success in life and realize themselves more fully." The new *Ona* intends to foster optimism at a time when anxiety dominates everyday life, which has become "complex, tense, filled to the brim with struggle, conflicts." He points to the endemic "irritating lack" (*defitsit*) of consumer goods that has long been a way of life for Soviet citizens, but in this context the linkage implies new desire to be filled by capitalist models of commodification and Western individualism: "We, its creators, wish not only to help the person to dress well, succeed in a career, and attain reciprocity in love" ("My, ikh sozdatelli, pytaemsia ne prosto pomoch cheloveku krasivo odevatsia, delat' kar'eru, dobitsia vzaimnosti u liubimogo ili liubimoi" [2]).

But this publication intends to reach beyond the surface image of a successful reader that wishes to create. The editors hope that the journal will become "a source of support [*oplot*] in personal life and the life of the soul, the support of that which is most precious, to which one would want to return to recharge with new strength." Indeed, the aims of the new magazine have a broad reformist and pedagogical thrust: "We wish to help readers to get rid of egalitarian psychology or leveling [*uravnilovka*], poverty, to remind them that they are not a mass marching single file, that nature created each one to be unique" ("ne sherenga, ne massa, chto priroda sozdala kazhdogo nepovtorimym i edinstvennym" [2]). In a decisive departure from the ethos of socialism, *Ona* not only will teach readers how to become successful consumers, but will also offer new sources of moral support to replace the old ideology now considered bankrupt.

For this purpose Bogdanov draws on a personal legend of his childhood as topos, but this is not a story of a Communist whose social consciousness stems from early memories of social injustice. It comes from the author's memory of his grandmother, with whom he grew up in the village Kekhta, in the Arkhangel'sk region of old Northern Russia, on the banks of the Dvina River.

Across from the Red Hillock there was another village settled by the Old Believers, the "hardworking, talented people" who used to fascinate the young boy. Although life was "more fun" (*veselee*) in his village, their life was "somehow cleaner, wiser, more significant" ("chishche, chto li, mudree, znachitel'nee"). There was an old unmarried woman, Baba Pavla (she had taken "vows of maidenhood" at sixteen so that her brothers and father might come back from World War I alive), who baked "the best pies." He muses about how, in the old days, people built their villages on hills for ecological and aesthetic reasons, how they understood "human ecology" (*ekologiia cheloveka*), the ecology of the personality (*lichnost'*) that strove to raise itself, to "safeguard itself spiritually" ("sberech' sebia dukhovno").

As a grown man he returns to his grandmother's village with his daughter, thereby creating an "invented tradition" now that Communism is no longer a dominant ideology.[6] The transmission of "tradition" proceeds from grandmother (using the "authentic" old-world wisdom, from which society has been severed), via the son who now seeks an alternative way of life, to the granddaughter who will presumably become part of the new mythology. Note that although the old tradition appears matrilineal, the Soviet mother has been lost in the shuffle, and it is the granddaughter's generation growing up in the post-Soviet world who is charged with the tradition.

Bogdanov's message is rife with internal contradictions. The whole notion of *ascending* "the Red Hillock" is paradoxical. Although it contains symbols of "striving" and "going beyond the limits," familiar from Soviet ideological discourse, they now carry new meaning. Thus "ascent" acquires the old spiritual connotations; and "red," the archaic meaning of "beautiful." The ascent signifies here the striving toward a goal that will require a great effort of acting "beyond your strength and look[ing] with optimism at the world around you" ("sdelat' nechto bol'shee, chem v tvoikh silakh" [2]). The goal is also radically different: it is the creation of a new mythology that involves a return to ancient roots, more specifically to a notion of spiritual purity lost in the seventeenth-century religious schism and again in 1917.

The utopian return to origin is a conservative, patriarchal tactic. As one of the main ideologies in the magazine, it represents a form of posttotalitarian nostalgia. It is part of a larger phenomenon described by Larissa Lissyutkina, in "Soviet Women at the Crossroads of Perestroika," as a desire "for any form of cultural integration . . . intensified in times of disintegration of all cultural norms and values" (277). At the same time, the attempt to return to a premodern past ruptured by the Revolution expresses a need for "a narrative of continuity . . . for identity for nations as for persons" (Anderson, 205). As *Ona* demonstrates, women figure prominently in this evolving narrative of post-Communism.

The first introductory statement of editorial intent definitely presents a tall order for a magazine. Its social function is no less ambitious than a reeducation or psychological reorientation of its readers in the transition from egalitarian to individual social psychology, Western style. But the proposition of a simultaneous cultural assimilation of both native and Western models is couched in a peculiarly familiar Soviet idiom that is frankly didactic and moralistic. The fact that the new message is wrapped in verbal clichés constitutes the nexus of the present predicament, where ideologies from different cultural and historical spheres are at loggerheads in the struggle for the country's future.

The Patriarchal/Nationalist Model

It is not surprising that the most consistent and unified vision of the post-Soviet woman is proposed by a prominent male writer, Valentin Rasputin, a leading member of the nationalist Pamyat group, who seeks a native Russian solution to the problem of gender. His essay in *Ona* counteracts its pointedly ironic title, the French saying "Cherchez la femme." While dismissing any notion of possible Western models, Rasputin suggests that the new Russian woman can be found where she had been left at the time of the revolution, that is, just where her natural destiny had placed her—at home. Rasputin refers to an ancient name for woman *mirotkushchaia,* "world weaver," or the creator of the cosmic hearth (compare *bereginia,* "the guardian of the hearth")—then delineates the traditional character of the Russian woman as sacrificial and self-denying.

Rasputin considers emancipation the beginning of the evil that has befallen woman. He then goes on to attribute all social upheavals in modern times to "the desire to demand and take by force," when society seems "infected by madness" (127). And to strengthen his argument about the evil of modernity,

Rasputin refers to a book of essays titled *Traits of a Contemporary Woman,* written at the turn of the century by a woman, N. A. Lukhmanova. He feels the book is applicable to the current situation and ought to be reprinted. In describing the losses incurred by the modern woman, the author states that the "soul, calm, and thought have disappeared from a woman's face, as has the spiritual charm that creates real female beauty" (122). Women are said to suffer from excessive neurosis, nerves, and hysteria bordering on psychopathology. Rasputin bolsters his argument further by referring to the prerevolutionary writer of patriarchal bent, Vasily Rozanov, who claims that while in old photographs women look beautiful, now there is hardly "a pretty face" in a crowd, now one could only refer to some "cute mug" (*khoroshenkie mordochki*). Rasputin refers to other contemporary writers of his conservative school, known as "country prose," Shukshin and Belov, who describe "the tragic laceration in woman that hit her heart." He concludes that, having escaped "family slavery," woman fell into a no less oppressive "slavery of society" (128).

Similar arguments holding sovietization responsible for "denaturing women" are used by nationalist groups in Eastern Europe, such as the Smallholders Party in Hungary.[7] While Rasputin admits that there is no turning back, because the whole human society has changed, he addresses the call "cherchez la femme" to the woman herself, presumably because the object of the quest for the immutable female essence is within her. Rasputin presents a typical antifeminist argument demonstrating the "historical inevitability of patriarchy" (Butler, 35). It is easy to extend his argument to the nationalist desire for the reconstruction of the old Russian monarchy that was destroyed by the Revolution. Both Rasputin and Bogdanov create a regressive genealogy of gender that harks back to a distant historical past or a utopian moment that intends to provide narrative continuity for a new Russian national and feminine identity.

Leveling/Egalitarianism versus Difference

A considerably more pragmatic approach to the quest for the new woman emerges in the magazine's lengthy interview with the two journalists Larisa Vasilyeva and Svetlana Stepunina, who discuss the conception of *Ona* during the planning stage. It was agreed that two magazines *Ona* and *On* should be considered at the same time. In arguing for sexual difference, the editors admit the difficulties encountered in the decision-making process and conclude that the separation is necessary at present. As we will see, this separation is conditioned by the construction of gender in Soviet society and its legacy in the present.

Stepunina sheds new light on the process of gender identity in her proposal that the emphasis on sexual difference is only temporary. Like Bogdanov, she explains the decision in terms of an analogy with Soviet political and social strategies, arguing that *leveling* of class and other social distinctions is responsible for the underlying social malaise: "We steadily directed our efforts toward erasing boundaries: between city and village, between physical and intellectual labor. . . . Did we not erase too many boundaries between man and woman?" ("My mnogo i nastoichivo stirali grani: mezhdu gorodom i derevnei, mezhdu trudom fizicheskim i umstvennym. . . . Ne slishkom li mnogo granei sterli my mezhdu muzhchinoi i zhenshchinoi?" [10]) She argues for reestablishing *difference* through the traditional notions of woman as wife, mother, daughter, and sister, and of man as brother, son, husband, and father. These separate roles represent the familiar, established dual trope of nation as a nurturing motherland and a stern, ideological fatherland. Establishing "difference" in this case does not yet entail a new equality that might be different from Soviet-style "leveling."

In the nature/culture argument proposed here, "culture" refers to the Soviet ideology of *leveling* that had dominated all areas of the social as well as personal lives of the citizens. The term "nature" refers to *human ecology*, which had been ignored in Soviet society, with dire results. According to the editors, the main ecological problem in society today is "the disturbance of human nature" ("narushenie liudskogo estestva" [12]). One of them remembers the conservative 1970s, when the highest praise for a woman was an archaic Slavonic feminine noun *bereginia*, "guardian of the hearth." According to the sociological statistics of the 1980s, when the slowdown of the economy became a problem for the reformers, 60 percent of women said they wouldn't quit a job even if there were enough money in the family.[8] The author claims that despite the statistics, more and more women choose to stay home to ensure that "the children are healthy, and the husband happy" ("i deti zdorovy, i muzh ne obizhen" [34]). She concludes with the following statement: "I think that it is our strongest women that return to the family, because they sense the trouble hovering over the home with their essential being."

It is not accidental that, as the promise of reform was accompanied by the downfall of the economy, the rapidly growing unemployment of women was greeted with the call for their return to the hearth. The call came from Gorbachev himself: "Women no longer have enough time to perform their duties at home—housework, the upbringing of children, and the creation of a good family atmosphere. . . . We are holding heated debates . . . to put the question of what we shall do to make it possible for women to return to their purely womanly mission."[9]

Vasilyeva asserts that the "essential" nature of woman as nurturer is beginning to find new expression: "In our time, the woman must finally reveal her essence, finding solutions to problems in her domain" ("zhenshchina v nashe vremia dolzhna nakonets proiavit svoe estestvo, reshaia problemy, ei podvlastnye" [10]). She specifies that these problems may be twofold: (1) *ethical*—only the woman can direct the strengthening, development, and nurturing of the family and its morality, honor, dignity, and charity—and (2) *ecological*—only the woman guards the family cleanliness and order.

The presumption that women would do things better is familiar from the second wave of American feminism. The *ecological* argument applies to society at large—if women were in charge, they would not allow the barbarous destruction of forests and the pollution of rivers and air. The *ethical* argument assumes that a woman is neighborly and would not want her son to go to war; thus the war in Afghanistan could have been avoided and so, too, the Armenian-Azerbaijan conflict. Finally, an economics argument joins familial and national management—since woman is in charge of family *economics,* she could do the same for the state. The editors express envy of Margaret Thatcher and of England in general, because two women are in charge of it, Thatcher and Queen Elizabeth. The skewed perspective of an essentialist argument becomes problematic when sexual difference is universalized and female superiority becomes simply the other side of the patriarchal coin.

As we observe public debates about sexual difference, we must note specific forms of opposition in posttotalitarian society, often hard to understand from a contemporary Western feminist viewpoint. In the aforementioned essay, "Soviet Women at the Crossroads of Perestroika," Lissyutkina points out that the "depoliticized cultural opposition oriented to women's roles in the home, the feminine esthetic, and the symbolism of chivalry, rather than a political women's movement, expresses an opposition to a totalitarian system built on force and the denial of individual differences, including the differences between men and women" (277). A Russian social anthropologist, Irina Popova, perceives the irony in this trend toward domesticity: "So, now it is considered liberation to be a sex symbol, get married early and stay home with the kids." But in comparing this conservative turn in the present Russian society to 1950s

America, Popova notes the difference between them, confirming Lissyutkina's observation that this is an oppositional move: "Because of a rebellion against the state-decreed sexual puritanism of the Soviet era, the ideal Russian woman is more sex kitten than homecoming queen" (Shogren, A17).

However oppositional the new women's culture may be, the editors' essentialist argument about the sexes is not so different from that of traditional Soviet literature, which is dominated by three social categories: the patriarchal, the economic, and the demographic. In her study of *Sex-Role Socialization in the USSR,* Lynne Attwood finds that in the totalitarian system "the dominant theme is that women should 'choose' between work or family" (207). She concludes that "while feminists and social learning theorists in the West have used an understanding of personality development to challenge these [sexual] stereotypes, Soviet pedagogical writers call for a better understanding of the process in order to more successfully develop them" (205).

It is interesting to note that "leveling" is seen as a basic social problem facing post-Communist society everywhere. In *How We Survived Communism and Even Laughed,* Slavenka Drakulić writes: "In socialism, we are not used to thinking of ourselves as poor; the communist principle of *uravnilovka* (leveling) made us all live more or less under the same conditions" (121). For Lissyutkina, the effects of leveling recall stock images of the "sexless figures in boots as road workers, construction workers, vegetable farmers, etc. The ideal of woman-comrade . . . " She also notes the warping of relations between the sexes: "deritualization of sexual behavior, destruction of its semantics (courtship, wedding norms, norms of intimacy and monogamy)" in Soviet society (277). This is another form of posttotalitarian nostalgia for traditional codes of sexual behavior in Western societies.

In their thinking about the process of change, the editors of *Ona* first of all attack the effects of socialist egalitarianism or leveling on sexual identity as a key factor. They also propose a move away from secular ideology toward new mythology and the "invention of tradition," which requires the revival of premodern as well as of prerevolutionary Russian culture, endowed with spiritual significance. It is impossible not to note that this utopian nostalgia for the premodern Russian past counteracts the role that the West plays in the process of change as it inspires the desire for commodities, provides models of success and consumption, but also sends threatening ideologies, such as feminism, to Russia. Raymond Williams's triad of social forces—dominant, residual, and emergent in a new cultural formation—is useful in understanding the post-Soviet situation. As the range of choices contained between the covers of *Ona* amply demonstrates, the former Soviet Union remains poised in a state of "pre-emergence, active and pressing, but not yet fully articulated" (126).

This returns us to the split, illustrated by the two magazine covers. This acknowledgment of sexual difference as proposed here would subsume equality only temporarily, until a possible future unity that would somehow be different from socialist egalitarianism. Both editors agree, however, that more needs to be known about men. The main problem or the worst *defitsit* (lack) in society is "the lack of understanding" ("defitsit ponimaniia" [51]) between the sexes. The slogan for the day is "to understand all about one another" ("Vse drug o druge poniat' "). The editors suggest that there is insufficient understanding of men, who need to acknowledge their own capacity for nurturing. The restitution of maleness is regarded as a problem shared by other postsocialist societies, including Czechoslovakia (Havelkova, 70–71).

How the sexual difference figured here might promote a future understanding between the sexes remains unclear. One could argue, however, that the split is not so much a choice as a symptom of social change. It is a necessary prerequisite for creating a new class of consumers as part of the economic reform and transition to market capitalism. It is also a symbol of political change marked by the dissolution of the empire. Indeed, the relations between new national entities within the former Soviet Union and their alliances with Russia are constantly reconfigured as conflict flares up in various areas of the region.

Models of Femininity: Native and Western

The magazine, striking in its eclecticism, represents current efforts to create a new language and culture of desire, foreign in a socialist context, through a range of means that include prerevolutionary Russian culture as well as contemporary Western capitalist and media models. The magazine reprints a document from the prerevolutionary period that, ironically enough, would be as unacceptable to Rasputin as it would have been to the Soviet censor. This is Nikolai Berdyaev's "Letter to His Future Wife, L. Iu. Rapp," taken from his book *Eros and Personality* (*Eros i ilichnost'*), published in 1904. In this letter the philosopher shares his innermost thoughts, reveals the importance of sexuality for him as a man and the anxiety about sexual degeneration (*vyrozhdenie pola*) typical of the decadent period, and tries to convince his bride-to-be that their relations have to go beyond the platonic, childlike stage. He writes about sexuality as part of a religious, mystical life, of sexual duality as a "fundamental law of life, and maybe of the world" (53). At the end of the letter he entreats his future wife to consider this, because, as he puts it, his greatest failure would be not awakening a woman in her, because sexual relations ought not to be mechanistic: "Remember that we can be husband and wife in the highest sense only if each one of us has sex, if as polar opposites we strive to flow as one. Otherwise it cannot be justified" ("Pomni, chto muzhem i zhenoi v nastoiashchem i samom vysokom smysle my mozhem byt' esli u kazhdogo iz nas est' pol, esli kak poliarnye protivopolozhnosti my stremimsia slitsia v odno. Inache eto ne mozhet byt' opravdano" [53]). He asks her "to forgive him for these underground thoughts and feelings." While conscious of the gender difference ("polar opposites"), Berdyaev nevertheless envisions what a unity might represent.

It appears that the sexual revolution at the turn of the century, curtailed along with many experimental ideas at the end of the twenties, is still capable of awakening interest in the contemporary Russian mind. Berdyaev takes for granted sexual separation as a precondition for future harmony. The importance of sexuality is confirmed by another feature in the magazine, the story of Lili Brik, Mayakovsky's great love. Written by an established scholar, Vasily Katanian, this is a tale about an unconventional woman involved in a celebrated ménage à trois of the twenties, a time of considerable sexual freedom.

There are several miscellaneous fragments under the heading "Retro" citing various tidbits from prerevolutionary Russian sources. From the magazine *A Woman's Life,* for example, one piece elaborates the distinction between a coquette and a flirt; another considers hands (firm or wet, for example) and character; and a fragment on women's labor describes how it is devalued in society and calls for "equal pay" in the future. The essay on the "Beauty of the Eyes" from *The New Journal of Foreign Literature, Art, and Science (Novyi zhurnal inostrannoi literatury, iskusstva i nauki,* vol. 3, [August 1903]) is illustrated with images of different types of women from the Victorian period and quotes John Ruskin as a great aesthete and an authority on the subject.

It is interesting to note that the two exceptional contemporary Russian women featured in the magazine are both performers: a television star and a film and theater actress. Although by no means ordinary women, they nevertheless affirm their longing for conventional feminine aspects of life—home, kitchen, husband, children. One of them, Tatyana Vasilyeva, makes a feminist statement about her notion of an ideal woman: "independent of age, this is always the woman who has a center or axis [*sterzhen'*] and that center is her life's work" (50). Both women agree that no matter what they have achieved, a woman must be true to her nature—nurturing, feminine, seductive, attuned to the mysteries of life and of men in her life. Another model is provided in the profile of the only ethnically non-Russian woman featured in the magazine, an outstanding young organist from Abkhazia, Liudmila Galustian, who overcame a childhood spinal injury and succeeded in a brilliant musical career. Despite her busy performance schedule, she finds time for a series of concerts for young audiences. She speaks to the children about "how to live most vividly, how to realize yourself in it, how to be a success" ("o tom, kak iarche prozhit' zhizn', kak sbyt'sia v nei, kak voplotitsia, kak dostich' uspekha" [37]). She also tells them that "one can't live without music, without art." The exceptional women present enticing possibilities, while at the same time they represent a traditional Soviet image of a successful, educated woman.

Examples of unconventional sexuality from the prerevolutionary period and the early 1920s, as well as of contemporary professional women who seem "to have it all," suggest to the reader that a range of choices is now possible. However, the magazine's attempt to reach out to Western consumer culture and its effort to create a new language of desire, both foreign to the Soviet ethos, are not realistically applicable to a majority of women in the Russia of the 1990s, whose basic economic security is now under threat. In catering to nascent commodity fetishism in Russia, *Ona* presents two glamorized American models of successful women. One of them is Estée Lauder and her multi-million-dollar family dynasty, with the stress on the strong family bonds. Her story may perhaps have some interest for Russia's nouveau riches who engage in conspicuous consumption.[10] But for the majority of readers the moral of her success is clear: it is inseparable from family life. Another famous Western woman is the film star Jane Fonda (before her marriage to Ted Turner), who insists that she values and wants to retain her independence. No more realistic than the ideal of a Communist woman, such examples point to the rise of the phantasm of success and consumption in the economically underdeveloped post-Communist state.

The range of choices presented in *Ona* appears baffling at first, as the contested views of premodern and modern prerevolutionary past are conjured to appear side by side with the present. While women are asked to forget the immediate socialist past, the distant past that they are asked to remember instead is either that of a mythical, utopian, indigenous Russia or of the complex prerevolutionary Russian culture. The present remains curiously vague in the unreal models of success from Western media and popular culture. The ambivalence in the search for direction is strikingly apparent in the style of the magazine's iconography. The magazine is not really commercial—there are no ads here, and consumer literacy has not reached Russia yet. But the iconography betrays the cultural confusion of the present. There are awkwardly posed photographs of clothing worn by overly made-up models who look like men in drag, yet whose hairstyles appear either excessively stiff from hair spray or naively romantic and old-fashioned. The current Western image of the "free" or "casual" or "liberated" woman has not reached Russia yet. One image appears especially striking. Titled "A Costume for Joy," it portrays a nubile but sweet-looking model scantily covered by two printed scarves with beads draped over shoulders and wrist. The caption is a quotation from Lidia Orlova, chief editor of *Fashion Magazine:* "Women are becoming overly business oriented, even when it is not necessary. Fashion tries to return them to femininity even in the correct working clothes. But it is important to preserve that 'tiny bit' that distinguishes good taste from bad" (96). Whether the caption promotes or condones the image remains curiously ambiguous, but it clearly asserts a new separation between the public sphere and the new private sphere as part of the transition to a capitalist economy.

It is hardly surprising that *Ona* is equally ambiguous about its goals: the "pleasure" principle of Western magazines had not yet reached Russian media by 1990. In her book *Inside Women's Magazines,* Janice Winship suggests that pleasure "depends on being familiar with the cultural codes of what is meant to be pleasurable, and on occupying the appropriate social spaces."[11] As our reading of *Ona* demonstrates, the cultural codes and the appropriate social spaces of work, leisure, and the market are in the process of redefinition. The presence of explicit ideologies in *Ona* far outweighs the pleasure of the magazine's sleek format. The pleasure is now marketed by the publication of a Russian version of *Cosmopolitan* in 1994, complete with ads, American and Russian models, and ideas for the nouveau riches—an excellent example of the phantasmagoria of consumption.

Conclusion

Although *Ona* is ambivalent about its own identity as a high culture or a popular magazine, there is much that connects it with the latter. Perhaps some answers in the ongoing debate about gender can be found in the newly emerging popular culture, which seeks to assert the primacy of consumer-based pluralist society. In his study *Understanding Popular Culture,* John Fiske defines its space as located "at the interface between the cultural resources provided by capitalism and everyday life" (129). He underscores "relevance" as a central criterion and notes that "popular culture is always formed within a structure of dominance" (133). It is also characterized by repetitiousness and circulation of texts.

As the first issue of *Ona* shows, all of these conditions are nascent in Russia at this stage of a fully articulated "preemergence." However, in a recent book, *Russian Popular Culture,* which is especially about music, Richard Stites strikes a hopeful note in his view of popular culture, which despite its uneven development at the height of glasnost reflects "many polarities and emotional values. But it also indicated spontaneity, freedom, competition, individualism—a market place of ideas and feelings" (203). Ideas included in *Ona* present a clearly delimited range of voices, which along with many others continue to reach the public through a variety of new publications for women, as, for example, *Delovaia zhenshchina* (Business woman), *Natali* (a snobbish French form of the Russian name), *Sudarushka* (Little lady, a prerevolutionary form of address), and others. Despite the pluralism of voices in post-Communist Russia, the sexual split illustrated on the cover of *Ona* remains in force, and the prospect of reconciliation appears unrealistic in the sexual, as well as in the national, arena. The West, with its phantasmagoric images of consumer heaven, advertised in public spaces and on television, frustrates and angers many Russians. Moreover, Russian women have lost ground and have gained little from the reforms so far, either economically or politically. According to the Russian journalist, Nadezhda Azhgikhina, "the media majority peddle two images—housewife and beauty-pageant contestant. The common working woman is considered a 'second-rate' creature compared not only with a man but with a geisha" (5).

It is premature to look for a feminist image of the post-Soviet woman in this stage of preemergence. Although the Czech scholar Hana Havelkova argues that "the feminist view is necessary," she insists on the particularity of her country's situation and offers "a *plaidoyer* in favor of the necessity of prefeminist reflection on the postsocial experience if a potential feminist view is not to have, right from the beginning, distorted optics, failing to discriminate what is the problem of women and what is a problem for all" (71–72). The editors of *Ona* appear to be engaged in a prefeminist reflection at this time. Similar concerns have contributed to the formation of various grassroots groups that have appeared during perestroika and the emergent "male democracy." In her essay

"New Women's Organisations," the Russian feminist Olga Lipovskaia acknowledges that "there is no sisterhood yet," attributing this to a lack of a "civil society" in the country (78). However, she predicts that feminist activity and ideas will remain confined to the family: "There will be much less emphasis than in the West on separatism and division between the sexes, much more desire to find compromises in the realm of family life" (80). Lipovskaia concurs with the editors of *Ona* in stressing the importance of women in the family and the "ecology" of the nation, even though the editors predict that the separation symbolized by the split-image cover will be short-lived.

However, neither the recognition of sexual difference nor the hope for an eventual reconciliation of the sexes addresses the "gender blind spot" that the American feminist scholar Helena Goscilo finds justifiably striking in a society where "the majority of Russians, including those trained in deciphering the values and political allegiances attaching to ostensibly innocuous discourse, seem impervious to sexist language or strategies" (242). The Russian feminist Lissyutkina confirms this: "In Soviet society there are few studies about the real character of this conflict (man/woman) and its reflection in the consciousness of both men and women. . . . There are no studies of how both sides survive, accept and interpret the conflict" (278).

It is important to remember in this context that the word "gender" is foreign to the Russian vocabulary. In her essay "Genre and Gender," Lidia Curti points to the common Latin–Greek–Old French root (*gen* = to produce) of the two related terms, which in English differ by one letter only. The author notes further that "gender" refers to the grammatical category, first marking the difference and "only within the difference does it then recognize wholes."[12] This relationship between the two words is not evident in Russian. The Moscow Center for Gender Studies, established in 1988, ushered in the beginning of such work, placing the term in limited circulation as one of a multitude of new Western words and concepts recently adopted in Russian. However, in Russian the *g* in the word "gender" is pronounced as in "gander," losing the important connection with the root *gen-* and with "genre." Thus the etymological gap in Russian makes the term not only foreign, but incomprehensible, so that its broader circulation in the language is doubtful at present.

As a media and social experiment of a society in transition, the first issue of *Ona* allows the reader to observe one version of the complex process of formation of the "technology of gender," which Teresa de Lauretis defines as "a symbolic system or systems of meaning that correlates sex to cultural concerns according to social values and hierarchies." Furthermore, she notes that "although the meanings vary with each culture, a sex-gender system is always intimately connected with political and economic factors in each society" (de Lauretis, 5).

For a conscious observer of political change in the former Soviet Union, it is clear that the gender "blind spot" cannot be separated from the national struggle for redefinition in Russia. The emphases on biological sex differences link national and sexual identity, implying that clearly defined sexuality will have a positive effect on the new state. The previously suppressed differences between the sexes, like those between Russia and the former republics, now independent states, require a necessary separation to affirm their identity or difference. Russia's identity as a nation is typical of a postcolonial situation, characterized by uneasy, often conflictual relations with the new independent states at its borders. In the article titled "Nationalism Explodes: Russia Confronts Its 'Near Abroad,' " Robert Cullen describes the belief formed after the putsch of 1991 that "Russia and the former republics would reassemble in some sort of voluntary confederation, not unlike the European Community, with Russia as the senior partner." He reports that so far "the dissolution of the old union has produced little but pain, humiliation and bloodshed" as Russia seeks a new role to play in areas of nationalist conflict within the former Soviet borders.[13] The magazine's continued emphasis on women's role in returning to Russia's national past and the almost complete absence of ethnic subjects, who have moved from former marginalization to a position beyond peripheral vision, confirm Russia's troubled relations with neighboring states. In the extended situation of political and economic uncertainty, with alarming statistics on disease and lower life expectancy, Russia's women are called upon, once again, to bear the burdens of transition.

Notes

1. For an early essay on the subject that surveys the media across the former Soviet Union, see Elizabeth Waters, "Restructuring the 'Woman's Question': Perestroika and Prostitution."

2. See Lynne Attwood, "Sex and the Cinema," and Elizabeth Waters, "Soviet Beauty Contests."

3. For an extensive overview of the economic shift and its effect on culture, see Nancy Condee and Vadim Padunov, "Pair-A-Dice Lost: The Socialist Gamble, Market Determinism, and Compulsory Postmodernism."

4. I would like to thank Herman Gray for this and other suggestions. I would also like to thank Rebecca Connor and Maya Slobin for their insightful reading of the cover.

5. Mikhail Yampolsky, personal communication.

6. On the creation of a "national culture" in Wales and Scotland in the modern period, see *The Invention of Tradition,* edited by Eric Hobsbawm and Terence Ranger.

7. See Francine Molyneux, "The 'Woman's Question,' " 76 n. 26.

8. In this context it is interesting to note how the Czech scholar Hana Havelkova addresses the right to work, maternity leave policy, and so on: "first, for most women their jobs and work outside the household have become a personal value" (71).

9. Quoted in Chanie Rosenberg, *Women and Perestroika: Present, Past, and Future for Women in Russia,* 100.

10. For the extravagant habits of this group, see Celestine Bohlen's report, "Russia's New Rich on a Buying Spree," *New York Times,* July 31, 1993.

11. See the chapter titled "Work and Leisure: Feminine Pleasures," in Janice Winship, *Inside Women's Magazines,* 52.

12. Lidia Curti, "Genre and Gender," 152.

13. *Nation,* September 20, 1993, 274. Russia's "new role" has extended to an armed conflict in the war in Chechnya, after the former republic proclaimed independence.

Works Cited

Anderson, Benedict. *Imagined Communities: Reflections on the Origin and Spread of Nationalism.* Rev. ed. London: Verso, 1991.

Attwood, Lynne. *The New Soviet Man and Woman: Sex-Role Socialization in the USSR.* Bloomington: Indiana University Press, 1990.

———. "Sex and the Cinema." In *Sex and Russian Society,* edited by Igor Kon and James Riordan, 64–88. Bloomington: Indiana University Press, 1993.

Azhgikhina, Nadezhda. "Believing the Impossible." *Women's Review of Books,* July, 1993.

Butler, Judith. *Gender Trouble.* London: Routledge, 1992.

Condee, Nancy, and Vadim Padunov. "Pair-A-Dice Lost: The Socialist Gamble, Market Determinism, and Compulsory Postmodernism." In *Postcommunism: Rethinking the Second World,* edited by Greta Slobin. Special issue of *New Formations,* no. 22 (Spring 1994): 72–94.

Curti, Lidia. "Genre and Gender." *Cultural Studies* 2, no. 2 (May 1988).

de Lauretis, Teresa. *Technologies of Gender: Essays on Theory, Film, and Fiction.* Bloomington: Indiana University Press, 1987.

Drakulić, Svetlana. *How We Survived Communism and Even Laughed.* New York: HarperPerennial, 1991.

Fiske, John. *Understanding Popular Culture.* Boston: Unwin Hyman, 1989.

Goscilo, Helena. *Late Soviet Culture: From Perestroika to Novostroika.* London: Duke University Press, 1993.

Havelkova, Hana. "A Few Prefeminist Thoughts." In *Gender Politics and Post-Communism: Reflections from Eastern Europe and the Former Soviet Union,* edited by Nanette Funk and Magda Mueller, 62–73. New York and London: Routledge, 1993.

Eric Hobsbawm and Terence Ranger, eds. *The Invention of Tradition.* Cambridge: Cambridge University Press, 1984.

Lipovskaia, Olga. "New Women's Organisations." In *Perestroika and Soviet Women,* edited by Mary Buckley, 72–81. Cambridge: Cambridge University Press, 1992.

Lissyutkina, Larissa. "Soviet Women at the Crossroads of Perestroika." In *Gender Politics and Post-Communism: Reflections from Eastern Europe and the Former Soviet Union,* edited by Nanette Funk and Magda Mueller. New York: Routledge, 1993.

McAndrew, Maggie. "Soviet Women's Magazines." In *Soviet Sisterhood: British Feminists on Women in the USSR,* edited by Barbara Holland. London: Fourth Estate, 1985.

Molyneux, Francine. "The 'Woman's Question.'" In *After the Fall,* edited by Robin Blackburn. London: Verso, 1991.

Ona 1 (1990).

Parker, Andrew, Mary Russo, Doris Sommer, and Patricia Yaeger, eds. *Nationalisms and Sexualities.* London: Routledge, 1992.

Rosenberg, Chanie. *Women and Perestroika: Present, Past, and Future for Women in Russia.* London: Bookmarks, 1990.

Shogren, Elizabeth. "Russian Women Lose Ground in Post-USSR Era." *San Jose Mercury News,* February 13, 1993.

Stites, Richard. *Russian Popular Culture: Entertainment and Society since 1900.* Cambridge: Cambridge University Press, 1992.

Waters, Elizabeth. "Restructuring the 'Woman's Question': Perestroika and Prostitution." *Feminist Review,* no. 33 (Autumn 1989): 4–19.

———. "Soviet Beauty Contests." In *Sex and Russian Society,* edited by Igor Kon and James Riordan, 116–34. Bloomington: Indiana University Press, 1993.

Williams, Raymond. *Literature and Marxism.* Oxford: Oxford University Press, 1988.

Winship, Janice. *Inside Women's Magazines.* London: Pandora Press, 1987.

16 / What Are Women Made Of?

Inventing Women in the Yugoslav Area

Svetlana Slapšak

This essay is an attempt at linking contemporary "inventions" of women in the Yugoslav area with those of the Balkan tradition—mythological or other constructs that bear signs of both repression and traumatization, both presence and absence of women in male-dominated Balkan societies. My frame of interpretation will primarily be the invention of women in the prevailing male-ruled public discourse; women's response to that (if any); and, finally, the way the invention of women influenced the cultural disaster we are facing in what used to be a multicultural society in Yugoslavia. Recent tragic developments and their impact on women clearly call for further reflection. I do not want to underestimate the novelty of separate national, and often nationalist, inventions of women in the new independent or still warring states; indeed, it is important to see what immediate changes have been produced, what traumatic points have been touched upon, and which new inventories match the old ones. The "transition," which in former Yugoslavia has all the characteristics of violent social revolution, means new ideology and new narratives, and there is always a *text* that depends largely on local popular tradition, be it media, mass culture, or oral tradition; in the case of many central and south European cultures, academia participates in this text to a larger extent than should perhaps be expected.

Beginning with the striking example of the catalog by the ancient Greek poet Simonides of women types, each described as a different animal species

and classified according to her usefulness and degree of submissiveness to a potential husband (the "bodiless" working bee actually being, according to the author, the only recommendable kind), ancient texts about women offer a vast
range of inventions, from mythological narratives (Loraux 1981, 1989) and
sometimes fantastic medical speculations on the female body (Sissa) to full political projects and feminist utopias (Auger). For regional studies in Balkan humanities, ancient sources and their modern interpretations are important, and
ancient women's studies are inevitable in any conceptualization of Balkan
women's studies.

Not surprisingly, my use of "invention" of collective women refers to the
usage adopted by the French anthropological school of ancient studies, represented by works of Vidal-Naquet, Vernant, and Detienne, which I find highly
relevant for the discussion on Balkan phenomena in diachrony. Further key
works of similar orientation, dealing with imagining the other, colonizing the
other, or presenting the other in the Balkan area, include, besides the seminal
work by Nicole Loraux on the invention of Athenian democracy, that by Michael Herzfeld on the invention of modern Greece and of Edward Said on the
European invention of the Orient. The discussions on social construct and history of sexuality point to the importance of text analysis, but also of new narratives as experiments in social construct. My intention here is to explore the texts
pertinent to the invention of women in the Balkan and Yugoslav area. The
question in the title refers to the elements *constructive* of these texts, to the inventive *material,* and also to possible linking of these inventions to creation
myths in different sources. Narratives on secondary creation of woman (from
mud, rib, animal species, and so on) develop to more complex inventions in
which women are conceived as a dangerous tribe (Amazons) or even race, as Loraux has demonstrated. All of these elements of construction can be recognized
in inventions of Balkan and Yugoslav women, and all of them are marked by repressive strategies of controlling the unpredictable collective other. The more
the other—women—are secluded and controlled, the more the trauma of their
absence is important and affects the male *self,* as Froma Zeitlin has demonstrated in her study on women in ancient Greek drama.

I would argue that the basic text on inventing women in the Balkan area is
still the text of the oral tradition, along with the complying texts of the cultured
literature and of stereotype-producing media. The oral tradition of the Yugoslav
space, backbone of all national constructs here since the beginning of the nineteenth century, backed by romanticist Western inventors of the Balkans and

eventually defined in both local and international academic research, firmly remains the panoply of the patriarchal social values and ideals. Vuk Karadžić, founder of Serbian laic philology and linguistic revolutionary, defined, in his very first editions of oral poetry, two main gender-genres: heroic poems and women's poetry; the latter included everything else—lyrics, ballads, work songs, ritual songs, lullabies, mournings, riddles, and so on. Vuk Karadžić found a number of women singers who were blind (some of them known today only by this denomination, *slepica*), and who performed epic (heroic) poems as well, but this did not affect his classification. In terms of our discussion it is interesting to note, however, that recently one of the most productive creators of nationalist Serbian stereotypes based on epic tradition, the poet Matija Bećković, found it necessary to declare that blind women singers actually "did not understand what they were singing about" (Bećković, 50). Most of the repressive models for women's behavior, ranging from submissiveness to silence in front of men, not to mention division of labor, come from epic examples.

Opposed to that, there was in former Yugoslavia the text of the egalitarian Communist ideology. With the full establishment of the "new class" in the 1950s, however, Communist discourse ceased to be relevant to the wider public; its jargon became restricted to communication among elites within political institutions and was increasingly incomprehensible to the majority. The "idealists" who would take the Party discourse seriously were often ridiculed by their Party comembers, and many Party members, especially cultured people and academic populations, invested much in relativizing privately what they were forced to say publicly. In many ways, the Yugoslav system was a typical Mediterranean protocol structure, transparently cynical in its dual morality. Those who publicly opposed the system would be characterized privately as "stubborn" and "naive," while the Party structure and media would use a choice of labels, ranging from "well-known elements" to "anarcho-liberals," "Western mercenaries," "KGB/CIA agents," and so on. The dissidents could very easily be accused even of being "leftists"! This situation prevented any serious discussion on class, and with the legal system providing all the basic rights for women, even some privileges and positive segregation, inventing women as "class" would have been unrealistic. In fact, the initial investment in women by the Communist Party during and immediately after World War II was stopped shortly after the war, when women's numbers and creativity were no longer needed in assuring military success and the cleaning of the ruins. It is clear that there was a kind of anesthetic effect of the Communist Party on the strong movement of women, and as early as the 1950s, most women's organizations in former Yugoslavia were transformed into sterile transmittors of Party politics. Women who adhered to ideas of equality, civil rights, women's welfare, and protection, naturally embedded in discourse that was strongly antipatriarchal, discovered that they had been seduced and manipulated. The same ideologists who had been accused by the bourgeois media before World War II of promoting the fearful "free love" and who, after the war, banned the veil (on Muslim women) by law and produced propaganda movies against dangerous abortions without medical assistance, adopted silently the patriarchal patterns at hand. The final result was that the ideological text concerning women was abandoned both by the ruling party and by the dissidents, which perceived feminism as marginal and as blurring the central issue of transition of power.

The concept of the society traumatized by the absence of women's voices and intervention can therefore be applied successfully to traditional Balkan societies and recognized in modern texts. In a number of texts, from medieval times on, women's intervention, be it subversive or submissive, is "readable." I will discuss three such examples: the first one is women's lamentation, which presents a vigorous continuity, documented since antiquity at least in most Balkan and Mediterranean cultures, and which has recently been "recycled" within the peace movement; the second is a subversion inside the corpus of oral poetry on the Battle of Kosovo, which is the basic text of invention of Serbian nationalism; and the third is a case of subversion within a very specific genre that developed in dissident circles in the countries under Communist rule, namely the memoirs of gulag, lager, or prison, or any form of repression and suffering under the Communist regime, for that matter. In this very specific Yugoslav space of inventing the male self as the victim of Stalinism and Communist repression, there was also a women's subversion.

With these three examples as paradigms, I would like to prove that women's subversion covers the crucial points of any male self-invention, and that in a war of genders in Balkan cultures and texts, women's guerrilla activity was quite efficient and creative.

Among areas of women's intervention that have a long cultural, ritual, and social history, women's power over death, discussed lately by Gail Holst-Warhaft can be traced back to ancient Balkan rituals, and it has not lost much of its meaning in the power struggle between sexes today. In almost all traditional Balkan cultures, Slavic or non-Slavic, women still have exclusive power over the rituals concerning the body of the deceased (heroes), and Holst-

Warhaft documents clearly both the attempts by the state at different moments in the past to reduce this power and the circumstances in which the power would be restored to women. Although her material relates to the Greek situation, much of her discussion applies to any area of the Balkans, regardless of religious and cultural diversity. Like childbirth, attending to the dead is miasma, pollution that must be avoided by the male: the period in which both the mother and the newborn child are "impure" and avoided by men can be compared to the period in which the house of the dead is considered polluted.

At the beginning of this war in Yugoslavia, women in the rural districts of Croatia, both Serbian and Croat, appeared dressed in black around the coffins of the first victims, images that were widely publicized on television. The viewer could see how they touched the body and communicated with the dead, while men stood around, exempt from this kind of communication. Women, not necessarily relatives of the deceased, some of them hired professionals, would also do the traditional mourning, using formulas from oral poetry, both lamentations and epics. The genre of lamentations covers the domain of real women's power. It has often been repressed by the ruling male discourse, either by diminishing its professional scope or by proclaiming lamentations and their performers "primitive" and socially inadequate. But the lamentation could also be manipulated into representing the collective, the national—to symbolize the collective victim, the suffering *ours,* to invoke the revenge, to provoke martial enthusiasm. And that is exactly how the women in black appearing by the coffins of the first victims of the Yugoslav war and performing lamentations were used. They were there to represent the patriarchal community that would be dishonored in case revenge were to be denied; they pointed to the "failure" of the legal system and stressed the power of traditional, unwritten, inherited justice, which would most likely take the form of straightforward lynching.

For urban women, watching these scenes on television and perceiving them as part of the heavy nationalist propaganda under way in all Yugoslav republics and as an obvious introduction to the war, this was a touching testimony of a once-in-a-lifetime public appearance by rural women, manipulated and yet sincere in expressing their bitterness. This, along with the knowledge of other contemporary uses of lamentations and mourning clothes (in Israel and Lebanon), inspired feminists in several Yugoslav cities to perform an urban ritual of "women in black." It was an ingenious answer to the manipulation of rural women, and was followed by many women's groups in Europe and in the United States. The women's message, the narrative, evokes women as victims:

they appear in public spaces wearing black, voiceless but holding banners with texts. They play with the power of death, wearing the black ritual costume of the Balkan cultures, but they are pleading for peace and negotiation, for compromise and dialogue. At the same time, the message invokes the ritual hero's fears and man's subconscious apprehensions. No wonder these women were attacked by Serbian fascists and paramilitary troops on several occasions (see Women in Black). Their further activities were clearly defined, especially during the times of army draft: women, who could move through the city without risk, ensured cover for the conscientious objectors and deserters-to-be and secured their leaving the country. For more than two years, the peace movement in Serbia (and particularily in the capital, Belgrade) relied practically on women alone. As in the two world wars before, women gained new power; in this war they knew how to use traditional patterns and rituals (such as lamentations) to express and pursue their politics of peace.

If one of the inventions of nationalism is the collective women's body (and quite obviously so when we come to the topic of rape), then women have at least the possibility of interrupting the message and recoding it using the same stereotyped images and symbols. If women are made of *black* and *fear,* they can use their supposed "body material" to form new narratives that will be easily recognized, but the resulting message will be entirely different. If the nationalist invention of the world and of women is a collage of elements made readable even by the illiterate, the antinationalist and antiwar invention could perhaps reorganize the same elements to form a new collage. The weak point of any nationalist invention is structure. Therefore, the main tools of women's response must be knowledge of the local culture, of genres of public discourse, and of communication systems and media practices. Never before, at least not in the Balkan area, has the urgent need to act politically been so linked to intellectual activity and to the humanities. And never before have the humanities been so linked to nationalist ideologies or the academics so active in providing the new political forces with nationalist discourse. Gender division is clearly visible here. Since women represent the main body of the peace movement, they need to have their own academic institutions in which to explore and research new discourses, new narratives, and new tools of interpretation. Parallel Centers for Women's Studies in Zagreb (Croatia) and Belgrade (Serbia), which already cooperate, represent models of such new orientation.

The basic text for Serbian nationalist invention is the epic poetry centered on Kosovo; it is a set of heroic poems about the fight against Turks and the famous Battle of Kosovo (1389), the heroes' dilemmas and decisions facing the battle, and the heroic deeds performed during the battle. Chronologically, poems that form this epic cycle range from the fifteenth to the eighteenth centuries. According to the Kosovo myth, the king-saint Lazar decides to choose "the kingdom of Heaven," meaning heroic death, instead of humiliating negotiations with Turks.

Three women appear in the story: the king's spouse, Queen Milica; the heroic mother of nine sons, Mother of Yugovići (otherwise nameless); and the Maiden of Kosovo, spouse-to-be, whose suitors take part in the battle. The Queen tries to stop her husband and brothers from going to the battle; the Mother dies of sorrow when a raven brings her the hand of her youngest son; and the Maiden, after reviewing the knights before the battle, cares for the wounded afterward, only to find out that all the eligible died heroically. At first sight, and in most readings until now, these women have been interpreted as symbols of the collective unconscious, the people, *the nation.* They symbolize suffering, loss, lack of future, impending sterility, and slavery. Although the battle was never recorded as a Serbian defeat in historical sources and although, according to all historical sources, the queen married her daughter to the son of the Turkish sultan (killed by the Serbian hero during the battle) and the queen's son became an ally of the Turks, the stereotyped image linked to the sanctification of King Lazar has remained highly productive in the invention of the Serbian national text: defeat, revenge, and the choice of heroism, however hopeless.

And yet a different set of values and ideas is preserved in the corpus of oral poetry, defined as "women's poetry" by its first editor Vuk Karadžić as early as the beginning of the nineteenth century—lyrical genres performed and created by women and for a female public. The examples I am referring to probably date from before the seventeenth century. In one short poem from the corpus of women's poetry, two *multicolored* birds (not the usual black ravens) come to Queen Milica and, after giving her a detailed description of her husband's heroic image (a classical *blason*), ask her if she would wish to see him. Her answer is dry and ironic: she prefers him to stay "there"; she managed, without him being around, to marry off her daughters and her sons, and they all live happily (Karadžić, 213–14). The quality of everyday life is here opposed to heroic life-wasting. The subversive women's intervention is quite obvious, and it can be identified as the carnival procedure, the reversal of "high" ideas, and the opposition between colors (life) and heroic solidity (death).

Following Roland Barthes's analysis in *S/Z* (120–21), the use of *blason* should by itself imply dismemberment of the body, a cannibalistic attitude toward the other in the text. Barthes used this medieval troubadour poetry device to develop his ideas on the other in a text. *Blason,* also a heraldic term, is in fact a highly schematized description (of a lady), listing different parts that form a catalog of (her) body. *Blason* as a decentered description is in fact a destructive/deconstructive technique in which the sense of unity is imperatively avoided. This interpretation seems perfectly applicable to Serbian oral poetry on medieval topics.

Following Barthes's thinking, we can trace in both epic (male) and women's poetry examples of this device featuring powerful narrative and ideological constructs. In the epic, the Maiden of Kosovo first reviews the knights as they come to the church for the blessing before the battle, using on them the *blason* technique to help her choose the one she wants, and then she reviews them again at the battlefield, this time literally dismembered. At the beginning of the poem, the three knights are described in the form of a body catalog, including the feather on the helmet, the chest armor, the sword, and the scarf. The Kosovo Maiden chooses the youngest and the fairest (who also happens to be the richest), and the other two suitors promise to be the groom's godbrothers. In the second part of the poem, the Kosovo Maiden attends to the wounded after the battle, and while talking to a dismembered and almost dying knight, she learns about her suitors and how they died. Her final words, which are the final words of the entire poem, are a curse against the destiny that leaves her without husband and without offspring. Understandably enough, this finale was usually interpreted as a cry of the collective (the Serbs), with the woman voicing the universal national feeling. We would argue, however, that the Kosovo Maiden, by using *blason* to depict her heroic men, accuses them for choosing war. Barthes's idea of cannibalistic impulses, of symbolic dismemberment of the other's body, bears here a different set of signs: used against the male body, *blason* points to the superficiality of heroic decorum, to the emptiness of associated values, to death winning over life. For the Kosovo Maiden, *blason* is symbolic of future sterility.

In another epic poem, the Mother of Yugovići dies of a symbolic *blason,* as the raven brings her the hand of her youngest son. In one of the versions of the poem, her heart "explodes" at the sight. The fragmentation of the body is real, and it means the end of life, the death of a mother. Again, literary criticism invested in patriotic interpretation and did not notice women's voices and stylistic devices revealing women's ideology.

However, in the poem classified as women's poetry—created by women and for the use of women—Queen Milica openly and merrily rejects *blason* as the code of perception, as the multicolored birds depict her husband in armor, with helmet, feathers, sword, and the rest of the apparatus, and clearly opposes therewith the whole heroic tradition. This example would also testify to the range of freedom obtained in seclusion: women who live and work together and have their set of oral genres to amuse themselves perfect their narrative skills, indulge in criticism of the male oppressor, and express themselves in the typical—if not the only possible—form of woman's resistance, joke and carnivalization. In the cases of epic poems about the Kosovo Maiden and the Mother of Yugovići, woman's voice transgresses the genre limitations and built-in ideology. In the case of the short poem on Queen Milica and the multicolored birds, however, it is a self-conscious and ironical woman author who addresses her supportive public in a marginal and oppressed but self-confident group, which has its strategies, its codes of communications, and its unity of goals.

If, according to Roland Barthes, the woman in medieval texts was made (invented) of nonstructured body parts that do not denote *her* whole, but do denote *his* destructiveness, then the response by woman's voice in Serbian epic and women's poetry offers an inverse but parallel invention of the male body, a carnivalesque procedure that points to the ideological differences between the nation of men and the nation of women. The life of widowed Queen Milica as told by Serbian historians, her contemporaries, was oriented toward a different politics of her nation: not only did she establish family bonds with Turks through the marriage of her daughter, but she also had at least two successful diplomatic missions to Constantinople. She traveled with another widowed noblewoman and nun, Euphemia, the first Serbian woman author and the originator of the cult of King-Saint Lazar, to bring to Trnovo (today's Bulgaria) the remnants of Saint Friday (Paraskevi in Greek tradition, Petka in Serbian), the strongest Balkan female saint. We could say that this was clearly a feminist mission—namely, to establish an important women's cult and therewith protection, and to ensure peace with the other, even the conqueror. Distancing themselves radically from the ideology and heroic values of their dead husbands and rulers, the two women worked to define a new national identity, based on women's needs. Their newly invented woman was made of entirely new ideological elements and new narratives—survival, negotiation, mixing the cultures, solidarity, new iconology, and new cults, all of this responding to the new upcoming modes of repression.

The use of women in mass movements during and after World War II can be studied as yet another instance of invention. The partisan resistance movement explored the texts of equality of the sexes in order to use the immense power of women. Women were needed to fight, to attend to the wounded, and to feed the warriors. The Communist text was perfectly suitable there, both for exploring the "liberating" stereotype and for honoring the traditional patriarchal values (patriotism, heroism, women's sacrifice). The invention was a real success, so that a massive women's pro-Communist movement was formed, and a huge number of women, whether interested in ideology or not, invested in the general idea of working and fighting for something new and justified, honest and progressive, respectful and efficient.

The Antifascist Women's Front, organized by the Party, activated large numbers of women of all ages and social groups and played an important role shortly after the war, especially in educating women, abolishing superstitions about women, participating in public works, rebuilding the country, and forming a new attitude of independent Yugoslav women. As early as the beginning of the 1950s, however, this movement was abolished by the Communist leadership, arguably because of its immense political potential, which they may have perceived as threatening.

During the important student uprising in 1968, attempts to revive the women's movement were rejected as "Western fashion" in the circles that unsuccessfully tried to confront the Communist discourse by using the "more Communist" argumentation concerning the state and the future of the country. Also in the years following the students' movement, when groups of dissidents gradually enlarged the space of public dialogue, feminism and women's issues were considered, among the dissidents themselves, to be a minor and distracting political investment.

In socialist Yugoslavia shortly before and during the decade after Tito's death, the passion of revealing hidden and obscured sides of the country's recent history produced an important output of texts, personal memoirs, life stories, and documentary material. This genre had actually been present in Yugoslavia for some time: it was typical of the kind of liberalism promoted by the regime that anything coming from or bearing any sign or trademark of dissidence toward the Soviet bloc, be it testimony, memoirs, or literary texts, would be immediately translated into Yugoslav languages. Often such works would be first published in Yugoslavia and only later in the West. Naturally, the regime was much more sensitive to texts referring to the Yugoslav past, so that only in the 1980s, after Tito's death, was there a real boom of such testimonies. Those of Yugoslav Communists who were put in prison or concentration camps on isolated islands, because they did not react promptly to the political changes in 1948, were first to appear, revealing thus the ugly domestic face, a real Stalinist turn on Tito's resistance to Stalin. Most of the memoirs and life stories from this period were written by men: they follow a certain phantom dissident Eastern and central European genre, in which description of sufferings is mixed with philosophy and political theory. There is one book, however, written by a woman. Shortly before his untimely death, Danilo Kiš (probably the best-known Yugoslav writer after Nobel Prize winner Ivo Andric), having a special interest in Stalinist psychology, visited Israel and met the woman who exiled from Yugoslavia after spending several years in camps and prisons. Kiš interviewed her for Yugoslav television and convinced her to tell her story. This Jewish woman, Ženi Lebl, was sentenced to several years in jail for telling a joke about Tito. When she was close to being released, she could not stop laughing in front of the investigators, so she was convicted again. The whole text is a woman's subversion of dissidents' seriousness and dull politics, and praise of women's weapons to fight injustice and fear: irony, laughter, vital force, and life values (Lebl). Among the dissident writers such values were certainly not high on the agenda. A good example of the basically male vision of dissidents' suffering is found in Solzhenitsyn's descriptions from Siberian concentration camps, in which female camps, their morale, and the attitudes of women are clearly denigrated. They are considered "worse" than male camps uniquely by gender presence.

In Serbia, the women's movement became instrumental only within the peace movement against Milošević's regime: since the male members of the peace movement had to hide during the period of the army draft, only women were able to move freely, organizing rallies and civil disobedience actions and, not least, hiding the disobedient recruits. The result was spectacular: feminists have obtained a long-denied public voice, and women's groups, even those that are openly lesbian, have their legitimate place within the diversified "opposition of the opposition" in Belgrade now. If "women made of women" have been used and manipulated by the ruling ideology, a similar context has enabled the women's movement to use the same inventive narrative and to explore—not without irony—another stereotype, which women subverted.

The social divisions in the former Yugoslav society also had their gender dimension: women had a large presence in academia; they were even more numerous than men in certain fields and disciplines (art history, languages, and literature), but could advance only to a certain level and would be drastically underrepresented among emeriti or members of the academy. On the level of discourse and narrative production, one of the most notable divisions was the one linked to the Communist model of state-controlled professional associations. Thus, the Translators' Association in all the federal republics consisted predominantly of women, and the Writers' Associations consisted predominantly of men. Yugoslav society was a multiethnic society and, according to the constitution, the equality of all the spoken languages was guaranteed. The federal parliament, which obviously did not have much to do with democracy, was at least very efficient in respecting language rights: it had an enormous apparatus of translators, most of whom were women. The stereotype of women being more capable as communicators found its pragmatic and dogmatic parallel in this state invention. In fact, this multicultural and multilingual tradition was entirely neglected in Yugoslav literatures, even in modern times, and it is perhaps not by chance that women authors explored in particular women's language invention.

The Serbian writer Jelena Dimitrijević, almost forgotten by Serbian and Yugoslav literary criticism, is a case in point: this Western-educated poet of patriotic rhymes found herself with her husband, a Serbian administrator, in the newly liberated parts of southern Serbia (town of Niš) by the end of the nineteenth century. Instead of investing in patriotism and traditional values, she examined the Turkish families who had not left with the Turkish army and administrators, obviously believing in the state system that they supposed would not care about ethnicity—as was the case when the Turks ruled territories. Dimitrijević entered the world of secluded women, the harems, not necessarily luscious places packed with yearning seminude women, but family groups consisting of a spouse, an aunt, daughters, a grandmother, and maybe an unmarried sister. She started to write about these women, and eventually her language became heavily impregnated with Turkish, Gypsy, Arabic, and other words, to the point that, today, it is not possible to read her text without a dictionary. She later wrote a novel about the first Turkish liberated women and their tragic destinies (Dimitrijević 1912). It is a fiction with documentary details, like the fact that these women, who could not leave their homes without a male companion, could communicate in an impressive number of languages: Turkish, as their mother tongue; Arabic, to read the Qu'ran; Persian, to read classical literature; Greek, Ladino Jewish, Armenian, and Serbo-Croatian in order to communicate with the merchants and at the market; Roma and Albanian to communicate with the musicians and dancers; and German, English, and French to communicate with their governesses from Europe.

The invention of women in the language, of translation as basically a matter of women's language mastery, has been used by women authors later, and among the generation that was finally dissipated by the current war, several names have to be mentioned: Hana Dalipi, who wrote prose in which Albanian and Serbo-Croatian are mixed in women's language spoken in an ethnically mixed family; Dubravka Ugrešić, who played with women's languages in highly ironical prose, now available in English; and Rada Iveković, whose essays echo her philosophical works on multilingualism as a feature of women's writing.

To conclude this tentative catalog of some prominent inventions of women, mainly by women, let us review some of men's inventions of women, especially in the domain of writing: What is women's writing made of? The invention of women's writing in Yugoslav literatures starts with the invention of national literature itself: according to Yugoslav criticism of the modern era, men write with their heads and women, curiously enough, with their hearts and hands. How a woman should be oriented in literary matters can be illustrated by two cruel examples: Sima Milutinović Sarajlija, an early nineteenth-century poet with Byronic attitudes in life and writing, had a spouse who was known by the nickname Punktatorka (the one who puts periods). A Romantic poet would write in a passionate inspiration, and the woman would correct the spelling and other mistakes. In a second example of inventing women, a young Serbian writer, Isidora Sekulić, started her career at the beginning of the twentieth century by writing intimate lyrical prose, self-analytical and introverted. The leading critic of the epoch, Jovan Skerlić, author of a rationalist national program—very much progressive in his time—scolded the young woman for writing about her headaches at the moment when "our boys" are being killed in war. Sekulić left her writing, engaged in criticism, and became the prototype of the severe and ludicrous male critic, obtaining power over writers that could be compared to that of Skerlić himself. He died before World War I was over; she lived until after World War II, desperately fighting to preserve her authority and power as a critic.

The history of Yugoslav literatures, at least in the decade or two before this war, features clear division between women's and men's writing, offering a striking gender-genre opposition parallel to the situation in modern world literatures. Men predominantly wrote prose, novels, and criticism; women predominantly wrote poetry, nonrealistic and genre-innovative novels, and less appreciated genres like sketches, diaries, letters, experimental prose, and so on. This is a very schematic picture: there was a strong genre-experimental movement in Croatian literature; there was an obvious response to the leading realistic prose writing in Serbia by younger and more educated writers; and much of the poetry was written by men. Several critics, women critics, invested much of their knowledge in determining and analyzing women's writing. However, the invention was so strong that several women authors felt an urge to deny their women's investment in writing "serious" genres. The current war, which has already demonstrated many possibilities for women to change the inventive discourses and to be changed by them, has also offered feminists and women writers new narratives, new politics of writing and publishing, and new patterns of self-definition. Two famous Croatian writers, both denounced lately by Croatian state-controlled media as "witches," Dubravka Ugrešić and Slavenka Drakulić, changed their writing in new directions. Drakulić, who started with a "my story" genre in *Holograms of Fear,* describing her fight with kidney disease and an eventual transplant that saved her life, continued with a sometimes oversimplifying and stereotyped description of women in Eastern countries (Drakulić 1993). Finally, her newest book, *Balkan Express* (Drakulić 1994), not only confirms the acquired stereotypes about the war in Yugoslavia, but also openly flirts with the official discourse of Croatia (the issue of who destroyed the famous historic bridge in Mostar), which puts her journalist's credibility in question. Ugrešić left her highly complicated postmodernist playfulness around genres and started writing essays and comments about life in warring Croatia and life in exile. Her newest book, *Have a Nice Day,* which is a witty and not quite merciful account of her view of the United States, was simply not acceptable for the already established power division of the regional studies specialists. In an incredibly insensitive review of her book, the author of *Balkan Ghosts,* Robert D. Kaplan, explains: *"Have a Nice Day: From the Balkan War to the American Dream* is a cynical and ironic description of the United States, written from the point of view of a foreigner whose society the United States has failed to defend." Kaplan's own book is far from being a complete, inspired, and critically oriented work, but this is not the point. What really brings out the fatal misunderstanding between the two cultures—one of them living only in the memory of its participants—is exactly the memory of what the standards of criticism and text analysis used to be back in the Yugoslav culture, even when published in weeklies and dailies. If these differences are not made known, described, and explained, the context might disappear along with the variety of testimonies denied, and only a privileged few might be allowed access to sources of knowledge and information. This kind of loss, originating from the understandable wish to simplify, today threatens academic research on the area. But I do believe that in the intellectual climate in which nothing, from new theories to new political issues, can pass without being scrutinized and discussed from all possible points of view, the confusing complexity and paradoxes, the nuances and controversies, and the complicated answers to simple questions on this faraway small culture, being destroyed as we write, should not be difficult to accept for the academic community.

Notes

In the course of discussing this article, the editors pointed out to me the article "National Identity and Socialist Majority" by Renata Salecl, which also appeared in her book *Spoils of Freedom*. To my understanding, this text shows nicely the limitations of one model of interpretation by one academic group and the pitfalls of one line of interpretation being accepted in an environment as sufficient without being confronted with other views. Salecl seeks to explain the Yugoslav catastrophe with the help of Lacanian theory, a rather risky business when applied to a complicated social and political situation, where the most popular local collective self-explanation is historical. One possible strategy there is to analyze such narratives and demonstrate their manipulative dimension. Salecl certainly touches upon several of them, but while some are criticized (for example, the Serbian Kosovo myth or Serbian attitudes to the bones of their ancestors), others are just accepted (the Albanian myth of origin), and most are not dealt with at all (for example, new or revived myths of origin of other nations or of Croats or Slovenes). Indeed, the Lacanian approach does not help Salecl avoid some of the blatant stereotypes about Eastern Europe, such as that of nationalisms in the former socialist countries being a reaction to the rule of the Communist Party, responsible for the destruction of most traditional points of social identification. The mere consideration of parallel developments in Greece should suffice to throw doubt on this admittedly quite popular nonexplanation.

Salecl defines two forms of nationalism within the former Yugoslav space: that practiced in Croatia and Slovenia, typified by its attitude toward women (concern about the "future of the nation," stigmatization of women without children, and so on), and on the other side the type of nationalism as practiced in Serbia, with its authoritarian populism and with other nations viewed as "enemy." Very strong common features that blur this picture are not dealt with: the symbolic vocabulary of the nationalist discourse, mainly invented by intellectuals in the late 1980s, include many identical terms, expressions, and stylistic figures on all warring sides, and parallelisms between Croatian and Serbian nationalist discourses are often stunning; rituals with bones, although by far most spectacular in Serbia, are popular enough in Slovenia and Croatia (for example, the idea of "national appeasement" over the bones of victims from all sides involved in the conflicts of World War II); on the other hand, the Orthodox Church and some outspoken nationalist-fascists in Serbia have launched action against women who refuse to give birth to future Serb warriors, and recently a law was proposed that would seriously limit women's right to choose.

The most evident flaw, however, of Salecl's book, which, according to its subtitle, is about feminism after all, is that it fails to mention any feminism, or feminists for that matter, within the

Yugoslav space (with the notable exception of the author herself). Not only is no feminist author quoted or any feminine reference from former Yugoslavia included in her bibliography, other than the journalist and author Slavenka Drakulić; she denies openly any feminism in the space of Yugoslavia, past or present. The difficulties of starting feminist discussion in former Warsaw Pact countries are simply copied into the situation in the former Yugoslav space, hiding therewith what the book should be expected to be discussing—the feminist tradition, the strong movement within academia in Croatia in the 1970s, feminist and lesbian movements in Slovenia in the 1980s, and, most notably, the growth of feminism and women's activism shortly before and during this war, including Serbia. So while some of her psychoanalytical discussion may be interesting and innovative, as an analysis of developments in Yugoslavia her book is deceiving, and as a source of information about feminism there it is unusable.

Works Cited

Auger, D. "Le théatre d'Aristophanes: Le mythe, l'utopie et les femmes." In *Aristophane: Les femmes et la cité,* edited by P. Vidal-Naquet, M. Rosellini, S. Said, and D. Auger, 71–101. Fontenay aux Roses: Les cahiers de Fontenay, 1979.

Barthes, Roland. *S/Z.* Paris: Seuil, 1970.

Bećković, Matija. *Sluzba* (The liturgy). Belgrade: SKZ, 1990.

Dalipi, Hana. *Vikend u Materini* (A weekend in Mother's womb). Belgrade: Prosveta, 1986.

Dimitrijević, Jelena. *Nove* (The new ones). Belgrade: SKZ, 1912.

———. *Pisma iz niških harema* (Letters from harems in Niš). Reprint, Belgrade: Narodna Biblioteka Srbije, 1986.

Drakulić, Slavenka. *Balkan Express.* London: Vintage Books, 1994.

———. *How We Survived Communism and Even Laughed.* London: Vintage Books, 1993.

Herzfeld, Michael. *Ours Once More: Folklore, Ideology and the Making of Modern Greece.* Austin: University of Texas Press, 1982.

Holst-Warhaft, Gail. *Dangerous Voices: Women's Laments and Greek Literature.* New York: Routledge, 1992.

Iveković, Rada. *Benares.* Zagreb: GZH, 1989.

Kaplan, Robert D. *Balkan Ghosts: A Journey through History.* New York: St. Martin's Press, 1993.

Karadžić, Vuk. *Srpske narodne pjesme iz neobjavljenih rukopisa Vuka Stef. Karadžića* (Serbian oral poetry from the unpublished manuscripts of Vuk Karadžić). Belgrade: SANU, 1973.

Lebl, Ženi. *Ljubičica bela* (A white violet). Belgrade: IDM, 1988.

Loraux, Nicole. *Les enfants d'Athéna: Idées atheniennes sur la citoyennété et la division des sexes.* Paris: Maspéro, 1981.

Said, Susanne. "L'Assemblée des femmes: Les femmes, l'économie et la politique." In *Aristophane: Les femmes et la cité,* edited by P. Vidal-Naquet et al., 33–69. Fontenay aux Roses: Les cahiers de Fontenay, 1979.

Salecl, Renata. *Spoils of Freedom: Psychoanalysis and Feminism after the Fall of Socialism.* New York: Routledge, 1994.

Sissa, Giulia. *Greek Virginity.* Cambridge, Mass.: Harvard University Press, 1990.

Ugrešić, Dubravka. *Fording the Stream of Consciousness.* Evanston, Ill.: Northwestern University Press, 1993.

———. *Have a Nice Day: From the Balkans to the American Dream.* London: Viking, 1995.

Women in Black. *Women for Peace.* Edited by Staša Zajević. Belgrade, 1994.

Zeitlin, Froma. "Playing the Other: Theater, Theatricality, and the Feminine in Greek Drama," *Representations* 11 (1985): 63–94.

Contributors

Leslie A. Adelson is professor of German studies at Cornell University. She is the author of *Crisis of Subjectivity: Botho Strauß's Challenge to West German Prose of the 1970s* and *Making Bodies, Making History: Feminism and German Identity,* as well as numerous articles on contemporary German literature, feminist cultural theory, minority discourse in the German context, and interdisciplinary German cultural studies. For *Making Bodies, Making History* she was awarded the Modern Language Association's first Aldo and Jeanne Scaglione Prize for an Outstanding Scholarly Study in the field of Germanic Languages and Literatures.

Gisela Brinker-Gabler is professor and graduate program director in the Department of Comparative Literature at the State University of New York at Binghamton. She has published *Poetisch-Wissenschaftliche Mittelalter-Rezeption; Deutsche Dichterinnen vom 16. Jahrhundert bis zur Gegenwart; Lexikon deutschsprachiger Schriftstellerinnen, 1800–1945;* and two volumes of critical writing on women authors of German-speaking Europe, *Deutsche Literatur von Frauen.* She started and edited the book series *Die Frau in der Gesellschaft* for Fischer Taschenbuch Verlag, Frankfurt. She also has published several women's autobiographies and anthologies of women's theoretical and political writings: *Zur Psychologie der Frau; Frauen und Beruf; Frauen gegen den Krieg; Fanny Lewald: Meine Lebensgeschichte; Toni Sender: Autobiographie einer deutschen Rebellin;* and *Kämpferin für den Frieden: Bertha von Suttner.* She recently edited *Encountering the Other(s): Studies in Literature, History and Culture.*

Carole Boyce Davies is a professor in the Departments of English, African Studies, and Comparative Literature at the State University of New York, Binghamton. She has coedited the following critical texts: *Ngambika: Studies of Women in African Literature; Out of the Kumbla: Caribbean Women and Literature;* and a two-volume collection of critical and creative writing, *Moving be-*

yond Boundaries, vol. 1, *International Dimensions of Black Women's Writing,* and vol. 2, *Black Women's Diaspora.* In addition to numerous scholarly articles, she is the author of *Black Women, Writing, and Identity: Migrations of the Subject.*

Katrina Irving is assistant professor of English at George Mason University. She writes and teaches in the areas of cultural studies and American literature. Previous publications include articles in *Journal of Film and Video, Modern Fiction Studies, Popular Music,* and *College Literature.*

Françoise Lionnet teaches French and comparative literature at Northwestern University. She is the author of *Autobiographical Voices: Race, Gender, Self-Portraiture* and *Postcolonial Representations: Women, Literature, Identity* and is coeditor of a double volume of *Yale French Studies* titled *Post/Colonial Conditions: Exiles, Migrations, Nomadisms* and of a special issue of *Signs,* "Postcolonial, Emergent, and Indigenous Feminisms." She has written extensively on francophone and French literature and culture and on anglophone, African, and African American literature.

Graziella Parati is the author of *Public History, Private Stories: Italian Women's Autobiography* and of articles on Italian women writers, African Italian literature, and italophone studies. She teaches in the Department of French and Italian at Dartmouth College. She has edited a special issue of the journal *Italian Studies in Southern Africa* devoted to contemporary African Italian texts.

Catherine Portuges is professor and graduate program director in the Department of Comparative Literature at the University of Massachusetts, Amherst, where she also serves as director of the Interdepartmental Program in Film Studies. She is coeditor of *Gendered Subjects: The Dynamics of Feminist Pedagogy* and author of articles on East European and French cinema, culture, and gender published in *Yale French Studies, Discourse, Genders,* and *Slavic Review* and in *Life/Lines: Theorizing Women's Autobiography,* edited by Bella Brodzki and Celeste Schenk. Her most recent book is *Screen Memories: The Hungarian Cinema of Marta Meszaros.* Her current project is a book on post-Communist cinemas in transition.

Gita Rajan teaches Victorian literature and postcolonial and cultural studies at Fairfield University and has published in all three areas. She is coeditor of *A Cultural Studies Reader: History, Theory, Practice; English Postcoloniality: Literatures from around the World;* and *Postcolonial Discourse and Changing Cultural Contexts.* She has also been a fellow at the Yale Center for British Art and an Andrew Mellon Foundation fellow, researching the enunciation of anOther, feminist aesthetic within the Indo-British construct.

Karen Remmler teaches German at Mount Holyoke College. Her research includes articles on the relationship between postmodernist discourse and the representation of the body in torture, body politics in the former German Democratic Republic, and the remembrance of the Shoah. She is currently engaged in a research project on Jewish cultural identities and memory sites in Berlin, and has recently completed a book on the structures of remembrance in Ingeborg Bachmann's *Todesarten.*

Hannelore Scholz has taught at Humboldt-Universität zu Berlin since 1976. In 1993 she was a visiting professor at Brown University in Providence, Rhode Island. Her publications include work on literature of the eighteenth and twentieth centuries, recent German literature, gender studies, and women's studies.

Azade Seyhan teaches German and comparative literature at Bryn Mawr College. She has published extensively on literary history and theory, German romanticism, modernity, and cultural criticism. She has coedited a special issue of the *New German Critique,* "Minorities in German Culture," and is the author of *Representation and Its Discontents: The Critical Legacy of German Romanticism.* She is completing a book titled *Geographies of Memory: Women's Narratives on the Modern Diaspora.*

Svetlana Slapšak teaches Balkanology and women's writing in the Department of Sociology at the University of Ljubljana. She also has taught courses in ancient drama, Balkan women, modern Greek language and literature, gender studies, and ancient anthropology. In 1994, Slapšak founded the feminist periodical *ProFemina* (published in Serbo-Croatian and English), and she is preparing for publication books on nationalism and the adventure novel and on Balkan feminisms, as well as an anthology of *rembetika.* Slapšak has long been active in peace and women's groups and has helped organize aid and educational assistance for Bosnian and other refugees in Slovenia. She received the American PEN Freedom to Write Award in 1993.

Greta N. Slobin is associate professor of Russian literature at the University of California, Santa Cruz. Her research interests include the Silver Age in Russian culture, the early revolutionary and Soviet period, literary theory, film, gender, and postcommunist culture in Russia and east-central Europe. Her book *Remizov's Fictions: 1900–1921* is to be published in Russian translation in Saint Petersburg. She edited a special issue of the British journal *New Formations* titled *Postcommunism: Rethinking the Second World.* Her publications include "Revolution Must Come First: Reading Aksenov's *Island of Crimea*," in *Nationalisms and Sexualities,* edited by Andrew Parker et al.; "A Forgotten Melody and Remembered Popular Tradition," in *The Spirit of Soviet Film Satire: Laughter with a Lash,* edited by Andrew Horton; and "Marina Tsvetaeva: Story of an Inscription," in *To S. K.: In Celebration of the Life and Career of Simon Karlinsky,* edited by M. S. Flier and R. P. Hughes.

Sidonie Smith is the author of *Where I'm Bound: Patterns of Slavery and Freedom in Black American Autobiography; A Poetics of Women's Autobiography: Marginality and the Fictions of Self-Representation;* and *Subjectivity, Identity, and the Body: Women's Autobiographical Practices in the Twentieth Century,* as well as numerous articles, and is coeditor with Julia Watson of *De/Colonizing the Subject: The Politics of Gender in Women's Autobiography* and *Getting a Life: The Everyday Uses of Autobiography* (both University of Minnesota Press).

Julia Watson is professor of liberal studies and director of women's studies at the University of Montana. She is coeditor with Sidonie Smith of *De/Colonizing the Subject: The Politics of Gender in Women's Autobiography; Getting a Life: The Everyday Uses of Autobiography* (both University of Minnesota Press); and *Theorizing Women's Autobiography: A Reader.* Her essays on women's autobiography, autobiographical theory, western women's life writing, and Montaigne have appeared in collections. She is currently at work on a comparative study of women's autobiography.

Ebba Witt-Brattström is assistant professor of comparative literature at the University of Stockholm, Sweden. She is a well-known feminist in the Nordic countries, in addition to being a scholar and the mother of three sons. She has published several books, mostly on women writers, and is the Swedish editor of a Nordic women's literary history in five parts. Forthcoming is a study of the Swedish-Finnish poet Edith Södergran, *"I Am Law unto Myself": Edith Södergran and the New Woman of the North.*

Winifred Woodhull is associate professor of French at the University of California, San Diego. Her publications include articles on French writers and theorists, as well as on literary representations of colonial and postcolonial relations between France and the Maghreb, including *Transfigurations of the Maghreb: Feminism, Decolonization, and Literatures* (University of Minnesota Press). She is currently studying French colonial cinema of the 1930s.

Index

Compiled by Suzanne Sherman Aboulfadl

Abandoned Baobab, The (Ken Bugul), 143–67; bodily re-membering and African space in, 159–62; dialogic voices in, 148; narrative modalities in, 152; as narrative of self-imposed exile, 150–59; self-decolonization in, 151–57; Senegalese critics on, 145; West African contexts of, 146–50

Abjection: in *Bübin's Brat*, 331–35; concept of, 315–16; in *The Disease*, 322–26; in *The Mud King's Daughter*, 328–31

"Achterbahn," 242

Across the Frontiers: Ireland in the 1990s (Kearney), 309

Across the Tracks: Vlach Gypsies in Hungary (film), 202

Adelson, Leslie A., 21

Adivar, Halide Edip, 235–36

Affiliation: vs. filiation, 288–89

African Americans: Beurs and, 49–51

Africans: sub-Saharan, stigmatization of, 32

Agaoglu, Adalet, 236

Aidoo, Ama Ata, 161

Aimée & Jaguar (Fischer), 177, 184

Alevi, Vivet, 186

Algeria: Beur women in, 35–36

Algerian women: in Chohra's *Volvevo diventare bianca*, 119–33

Allen, Paula Gunn, 110

Alterity: in Turkish-German women's writing, 241

American Indian, 50; in Belghoul's *Georgette!*, 56–57

Amos, Valerie, 100, 102

Amrita (Jhabvala), 87

Andall, Jaqueline, 119, 139n

Andersen, Hans Christian, 328

Anderson, Benedict, 2, 12, 25n, 82–83, 97n, 266, 342

And Lead Us Not into Temptation (Ember), 205

Annunciation, The (Kandre), 335

Anti-Semitism: in Austria, 183; in Eastern Europe, 212n; in France, 8; in GDR, 181; in Germany, 188; in Hungary, 207–8; in Soviet Union, 186, 191n; among women, 177

Anzaldúa, Gloria, 92, 109

Appadurai, Arjun, 80–81

Arabic language: Turkish and, 245–46

Arabs: in France, 70 (*see also* Beurs); stigmatization of, 32

Aronowitz, Stanley, 92

As a Blackwoman (Sullivan), 112

Asena, Sevgi, 236

Asian Americans: stigmatization of, 32

Assimilation: in France, 41–42; irresolvable issues in, 9–10

Asylum: legal restrictions on, 7

Atatürk, Kemal, 234, 245

Athenian democracy, 359

Attwood, Lynne, 348

Auf dem Weg nach Tabou (Wolf), 268–78; community in, 270–71, 274–75, 277–78; multiple voicing in, 274

Auschwitz, 206

Aus dem Dilemma eine Chance machen (Königsdorf), 278

Austen, Jane, 87

Authentic Lie, The (Namjoshi), 90

Autobiography: editor intervention in, 122–24, 140n; in francophone literature, 147–48; immigrant, 122; postcolonial, characteristics of, 146–50;

Senegalese, 144–46, 146–47; by Turk-
ish-German women, 237–38; Western,
Gusdorf's critique of, 149
Avalanche, The (Dimitrova), 255–56

Ba, Mariama, 145, 146
Baader, Maria, 177, 181–82, 188
Backward Place, A (Jhabvala), 87, 93
Bagrjana, Ellisaveta, 251
Bakhtin, Mikhail, 240
Balbo, Laura, 141n
Balibar, Etienne, 10, 18, 33, 40–41
Balkan area: humanism's link to political inter-
vention in, 363; invention of women in,
by men, 370–71; memoirs of repression
under Communism in, 361; multilin-
gual women in, 369–70; oral poetry on
Battle of Kosovo in, 361; women's
lamentation genre in, 361, 362; women's
power over death rituals in, 361–62. *See
also* Yugoslav area
Balkan Express (Drakulić), 371
Balkan Ghosts (Kaplan), 371
Balkan society: invention of women in, 359;
male domination in, 358
Ballagh, Robert, 310–11
Bammer, Angelika, 25n, 290n
Barthes, Roland, 62, 364–66
Battle of Kosovo: oral poetry on, 361; as text
for Serbian nationalist invention,
363–66
Baumant, Zygmunt, 210n
Because of India (Namjoshi), 90, 94–95
Beckett, Samuel, 65
Bećković, Matija, 360
Behrens, Katja, 176
Belghoul, Farida, 18, 33, 45, 51–69
Bell, Desmond, 295
Benaïssa, Aïcha, 33–38
Benedictsson, Victoria, 334
Benjamin, Jessica, 253–54
Ben Jelloun, Tahar, 139n, 140n
Berbers: stigmatization of, 32
Berdyaev, Nikolai, 349
Beregova, 214n
Berlin Wall: fall of, 256–57; metaphorical sig-
nificance of, 269–70
Bernabé, Jean, 62
Beti, Mongo, 147

Beur literature: *Beur's Story*, 38–40, 51, 52,
62n; binarism in, 45–46; critics' treatment of, 44–45; ethnic group relations
in, 49; *Georgette!*, 51–59
Beurs, 18; Algerian law and, 35–36; ambivalent identity of, 32, 38–40, 44, 52–53;
derivation of term, 59n; dress of, as sign
of ethnic ambivalence, 72–73; French
law and, 37–38; French vs. Algerian
identity of, 34–40; relation to African
Americans, 49–51; relation to Islam, 46;
writings of, 32
Beur's Story (Kessas), 38–40, 51, 52, 60n
Beverley, John, 123
Beyala, Calixthe, 48
"Beyond the Culture Wars: Identities in Dia-
logue" (Gates), 81
Beyond the Veil (Mernissi), 223
Bhabha, Homi K., 17, 78, 92, 149, 164n, 197,
264, 267–68, 287–88, 291n
Binarism, 44; in Beur literature, 33, 45–46; in
The Crying Game, 297
"Birth Certificate," 108
Bitburg affair, 181
Bizim Köy, 243
Black British, White British (Hiro), 103
Black Teacher (Gilroy), 104
Black Train (Schiffer), 201
Black women, 19; in Britain, 100–17; debate
about designation of, 114n;—, historical
background of, 102–3;—, police brutal-
ity and, 103;—, unbelongingness as
theme of literature by, 105–10;—, upris-
ing textualities of, 111–14; in Chohra's
Volevo diventare bianca, 125–28; mean-
ings of home for, 101; in postcolonial
Europe, 151–67
Black Women: Bringing It All Back Home
(Prescod), 103
Black Women Writing Autobiography (Braxton),
120
Blanchot, Maurice, 65
Blason: in Serbian oral poetry, 364–65
Bloch, Ernst, 272, 274
Bluest Eye, The (Morrison), 126
Bogdanov, Vasily, 340, 342, 343
Bona, Dominique, 60n
Bono, 310–11
"Bonsoir, Madame Benhamou," 179

Border intellectuals, 79–81, 266–68; identity politics and, 91–95; JanMohamed on, 91–92, 268; R. P. Jhabvala, 87; Kamala Markandaya, 84–86; Suniti Namjoshi, 89–91; syncretic, 91; syncretic vs. specular, 80, 268, 288

Born after the Shoah, 17

Borneman, John, 290n

Bouchane, Mohamed, 119, 140n

Boukhedenna, Sakinna, 32

Bousquet, Gisèle, 46

Boyce Davies, Carole, 19, 122

Boy-Sandwich (Gilroy), 108

Braham, Randolph L., 214n

Braidotti, Rosi, 283

Braxton, J. M., 120

Brecht, Bertholt, 275–76

Bridenthal, Renate, 177

Bridglal, Sindamani, 108

Brinker-Gabler, Gisela, 22

Brodzki, Bella, 143, 160–61

Brontë, Charlotte, 85

Brown, Terence, 299, 308–9

Brown, Wendy, 14

Bryan, Beverley, 103

Bübin's Brat (Kandre): female body in, 334–35; theme of abjection in, 331–35

Bugul, Ken. *See* Ken Bugul; M'Baye, Mariétou

Bulgaria: democratization in, 249; ethnic minorities in, 250–51, 253, 259–60; historical perspective on, 250; Jews in, 254; Turks in, 21–22

Bulgarian literature, 249–63; after 1989, 256; in nineteenth century, 250–51. *See also* Dimitrova, Blaga

Burford, Barbara, 113

Butler, Judith, 127

Çalikuşu (Güntekin), 233–35

Camara, Laye, 147–48

Capitalism: Königsdorf's view of, 282–83; print, 2–3

Carnets de Shérazade, Les, 62–77. *See also* Sebbar, Leïla

Castles, Stephen, 226n

Catholicism: Irish identity and, 298–99, 305

Challenge (Dimitrova), 253, 259

Chamoiseau, Patrick, 62

Charting the Journey, 101

Chasing Shadows (video), 214n

Chatterjee, Partha, 25n, 301, 312n

Chechnya, 5

Child Murders (Szabo), 200–1, 202–3, 211–12n

Chohra, Nassera, 119–20, 121–33, 138; dialogic process in writings of, 138–39

Chopin, Kate, 165n

Chowdhry, Maya, 108

Cinema, Eastern European, 196–215; GATT agreement and, 210n; post-Communist, 199–205; representations of Jews and Gypsies in, 197–215; repression of creators of, 203–4

Çirak, Zehra, 232

Citizenship: based on residence vs. nationality, 44; of immigrants, 9; for white male, 14

Class: ethnicization of, 33; as factor in immigrant experience, 132–33

Coffer Dams, The (Markandaya), 84

Cold Country (Torkan), 219

Collins, Merle, 109

Colonial Legacy in Caribbean Literature, The (Saakana), 102

Colonialism: of modern France, 41–42

Communism: feminist critique of, 210n; in Yugoslav area, 360–61, 367

Community: ambivalence of, 282; imagined, 82; local vs. transnational, 284–85; and politics of location, 283–84; transnational, 1, 4 (*see also* Internationalism; Transnationalism); vernacular, 3; in Wolf's *Auf dem Weg nach Tabou*, 270–71, 274–75, 277–78

Condé, Maryse, 72

Confiant, Raphael, 62

Conjugal Bed, The (Dianieluc), 212n

Constructionism: defined, 83–84; vs. essentialism, 81–84; stereotypes of, 96

Conversations of Cow, The (Namjoshi), 90, 95

Crane, Ralph, 88

Creutziger, Werner, 284

Crisantino, Amelia, 121

Critical regionalism, 283–84

Croatia: nationalism in, 372n; women's power over death rituals in, 362; women's writing in, 371

Croatian literature: genre-experimental movement in, 371

Crying Game, The (Jordan), 296–314; misogyny in, 308; Oedipal constituents of, 302–4; transvestism in, 296–97, 304–6
Cullen, Robert, 355
Curti, Lidia, 354
Curtius, Ernst Robert, 16
Czechoslovakia, 4–5
Czech Republic: film portrayal of Gypsies in, 202

Dabydeen, David, 102
Dadzie, Stella, 103
Dakar: autobiographical writing from, 147
Dalipi, Hana, 370
d'Almeida, Irène, 144, 151, 154, 162, 165n
Dancing the Tightrope (Burford), 113
Daneshfar-Pätzoldt, Torkan. See Torkan
Daniel Takes a Train (Sandor), 207
Das Prinzip Hoffnung (Bloch), 272
Davies, Carole Boyce, 122
Daxner, Michael, 190n
Death rituals: Balkan women's power over, 361–62
de Certeau, Michel, 74
Decolonising the Mind (Ngugi Wa Thiong'o), 136
de Lauretis, Teresa, 354
Deleuze, Gilles, 320
Democracy, Athenian, 359
Democratic socialism, 282
Derrida, Jacques, 65
Deterritorialization, 289
deValera, Eamonn, 298
Dhingra, L., 109
Diallo, Nafissatou, 147
Dialogic Imagination, The (Bakhtin), 240
Dialogic language: in Turkish-German women's writing, 240
Dianieluc, Mircea, 212n
Diary of Anne Frank, The, 206
"Diary of Home," 108
Diaspora: identities of, in Chohra's writings, 125–26; vs. trajectories of border intellectuals, 80–81. See also Immigration; Migration
Die Leidenschaft der Anderen (Özakin), 239–40
Dimitrijević, Jelena: writings on Turkish women, 369–70

Dimitrova, Blaga, 21, 249–63; biography of, 251; critique of socialism by, 250; image of Europe of, 258; in political office, 249–50; and theme of Bulgarianization, 253–54
Di Sarro, Alessandra Atti, 122–24
Dischereit, Esther, 173–74, 176–77
Disease, The (Trotzig), 316–29, 333; abjection in, 322–26; genre of, 321; as polemic against apocalyptic heritage, 322–23; subject governed by absence of mother in, 317–28; victim/executioner dichotomy in, 323
Displacement: after German unification, 266–68; Said's discussion of, 288
"DissemiNation: Time, Narrative, and the Margins of the Modern Nation" (Bhabha), 264
Djebar, Assia, 66
Doppelgänger motif, 241
Down and Out (Wallraff), 218
Drakulić, Slavenka, 348, 371
Drei Zypressen (Scheinhardt), 231
Durcan, Paul, 310–11
Dusi es Jeno (Forgacs), 208
Dyer, Richard, 55

Earthly Paradise (Schiffer), 201
Eastern Europe: attitudes toward Gypsies and Jews in, 212n; 1990s cinema of, 196–215 (see also Cinema, Eastern European); separatist movements in, 4–5; Western media portrayal of, 198–99
East Germans: displacement of, 22; as exiles or immigrants, 266–67; postunification displacement of, 265; postunification identity of, 279–83
East Germany. See German Democratic Republic
Eco, Umberto, 6
Economics: in construction of federated Europe, 82
Egy Urino notesza (Forgacs), 208
Elek, Judit, 20, 207, 208, 214n
Elementary School (film), 202
Eliot, George, 85
Elle-literacy, 341. See also Ona
"Elmaz," 253, 260
Ember, Judit, 205

Emecheta, Buchi, 113
Emma (Austen), 87
Eritrea: immigrants from, 118
Erkkila, Betsy, 13
Eros and Personality (Berdyaev), 349
Esmond in India (Jhabvala), 87, 93
Esquivel, Laura, 90
Essentialism: vs. constructionism, 79, 81–84;
    defined, 83–84; stereotypes of, 96
Essentially Speaking (Fuss), 83
Ethiopia: Italians in, 133–35. *See also*
    Viarengo, Maria
"Ethnic Monitoring, or a Geography Lesson,"
    108
Ethnicity: fictive, 41, 51, 56; in France, 31–
    61 (*see also* Beurs; Maghrebian immi-
    grants); nationalism and, 3; in poly-
    ethnic state, 4
Etkin, Efim, 271
Europe: federated, 79; federated, controversy
    over, 5–6;—, essentialist/constructionist
    model of, 81–84;—, market forces in
    creation of, 82;—, racial and cultural
    identities as impediments to, 134; immi-
    gration limitations in, 7; immigration to,
    6–7; political change in, 1; resident for-
    eign nationals in, 7; transnational com-
    munity of, 284; United States of, 5. *See
    also* Eastern Europe
European Community: political and economic
    implications of, 25n
European Union: dissolution of borders in,
    296; Ireland and, 295–314; Northern
    Question and, 295
Evclik Oyunu (Agaoglu), 236
Exile(s): attitude toward new culture, 266; in-
    tellectuals as, 267; Said's discussion of,
    267, 288; self-imposed, in writing of
    Ken Bulgul, 150–59
Exit into History (Hoffman), 212n
Experience of India, An (Jhabvala), 87
Exposed, The (Trotzig), 333
Ezekiel, Nissim, 88, 98n

Face, The (Dimitrova), 249, 252, 256
Family: as trope for nation, 12–13
Fanon, Frantz, 85
Fascism (Zhelev), 249
Fat Black Woman's Poems (Nichols), 112

Federal Republic of Germany: classification of
    foreigners by, 216–17; guest workers in,
    25n; Jewish women in, 181–85; multi-
    culturalism in, 219; struggle for identity
    in, 220–21
Fekete vonat (Schiffer), 200
Femininity: constructions of, nationalism and,
    11
Feminist Fables (Namjoshi), 90, 95
Femme d'Afrique (Kéita), 146
Feuer brennt in mir, Ein (A fire burns in me)
    (Tekinay), 241
Filiation: vs. affiliation, 288–89
Finding a Voice: Asian Women in Britain (Wil-
    son), 103–4
Fischer, Erica, 177, 182–85, 192n
Fish, Stanley, 118
Fiske, John, 353
Fitzgerald, Garret, 299
Flesh and Paper (Namjoshi), 90
Fonda, Jane, 351
Forgacs, Peter, 208
Forster, E. M., 78, 87, 94
Fortunate, Mario, 140n
Foucault, Michel, 64–65, 71, 255
Fox, Richard G., 96
France: Americanization of, 50; Arabs in, 70
    (*see also* Beurs); attempted Europeaniza-
    tion of, 33; Beur women in, 33–38; eth-
    nic groups in, 31–61, 48–51 (*see also*
    Beurs; Maghrebian immigrants; Viet-
    namese); Europeanization of, 43–44;
    historic and contemporary colonialism
    of, 41–42; immigrant groups in, 32; im-
    migration to, 18; myth of assimilation
    in, 41–42; provincial, heterogeneity of,
    72; Vietnamese in, 46–47; violence to-
    ward immigrants in, 8
Francophone literature, 63–64; autobiography
    in, 147–48; Mariétou M'Baye, 143–67;
    "opposition" to French literature, 66
Francophone writers: hybridity in, 148
French, European: as ethnic group, 51
French Code of Nationality: article 23 of,
    42–43
French literature: francophone literature and,
    63–64
From the Bedside Book of Nightmares
    (Namjoshi), 90

Fuderer, Laura Sue, 165n
Fuller, Vernella, 19, 107
Furüzan, 236
Fuss, Diana, 83–84, 89

Gabe, Dora, 251
Galustian, Ludmila, 351
Gandhi, Mohandas, 25n
Ganguly, Keya, 17
Ganz unten (Wallraff), 218
Garber, Marjorie, 297, 304, 306
Gastarbeiterliteratur, 217–29
Gates, Henry Louis, Jr., 79, 81, 86, 98n
Gatlif, Tony, 202
Gazdag, Gyula, 20, 207, 208
Gender: development of stereotypes of, 11; na-
    tionalism and, 11–16; and public vs. pri-
    vate sphere, 13–14
General Agreement on Tariffs and Trade
    (GATT): film industry and, 210n
Genin, Salomea, 177
George, Stephanie, 111
Georgette! (Belghoul), 33, 45, 51–59
German Democratic Republic: Jewish women
    in, 178–81; Jews in, 192n; postunifica-
    tion experience of, 266–68. *See also* Ger-
    many, unification of
German-Jewish relations, 188
German literature: classification of, 217–29;
    Literaturstreit debate, 290–91n;
    victim/perpetrator problematic in, 224
Germans: vs. non-Germans, 191n; "normal,"
    287–88
Germany: anti-Semitism in, 188; demand-ori-
    ented recruitment of immigrants in, 9;
    foreign population of, 191n; foreign
    writers in, 217–29; Gypsies in, 25n; Jew-
    ish population of, 191n; Jewish women
    in, 171–95; migrant identity problems
    in, 227n; neo-Nazis in, 192n; "new"
    Germans in, 189; non-German Jewish
    women in, 185–87; unification of, 22,
    273 (*see also 1989 oder Ein Moment
    Schönheit*); unification of, and ap-
    proaches to Nazi past, 171;—, common
    history and culture and, 290n;—, com-
    munity and, 270–71;—, critical region-
    alism and, 283–84;—, displacement
    and, 266–68;—, identity and, 20,

264–92, 275–77;—, im/possibility of,
    288;—, and Jews living in Germany,
    187–88;—, reterritorialization and de-
    territorialization and, 288–89;—, vio-
    lence toward immigrants in, 8;
    xenophobia in, 190n. *See also* Federal
    Republic of Germany; German Democ-
    ratic Republic
Get Ready for Battle (Jhabvala), 87
Ghetto: French minorities in, 50
Gibbon, Luke, 312n
Gilroy, Beryl, 104, 108
Gilroy, Paul, 102
Giroux, Henry, 92
Girvin, Brian, 298
Güntekin, Resat Nuri, 233–35
Goethe, Johann Wolfgang, 233
Going Back Home (Fuller), 107–8
Golden Honeycomb, The (Markandaya), 84,
    92–93
Gorbachev, Mikhail, 346–47
Goscilo, Helena, 354
Grewal, Shabnam, 101
Grossmann, Atina, 177
Gryn, Rabbi Hugo, 214n
Gusdorf, Georges, 149, 164n
Gyerekgyilkossagok (Szabo), 200
Gyongyossy, Imre, 207
Gypsies: attitudes toward, in Eastern Europe,
    212n; in Eastern European cinema,
    197–215; in Germany, 25n; in Ireland,
    313n; legal recognition of, 201; and pan-
    Gypsy nationalist movement, 201–2;
    women, 20
Gyuri (Schiffer), 201

Hall, Stuart, 110, 273
Handful of Rice, A (Markandaya), 84, 85
Hanscombe, Gillian, 90
Hardy, Thomas, 85
Hargreaves, Alec, 34
Have a Nice Day (Ugrešić), 371
Havelkova, Hana, 353
*Heart of the Race: Black Women's Lives in
    Britain, The*, 103
Heat and Dust (Jhabvala), 87, 94
Heath, Stephen, 89
Heckmann, Friedrich, 3
Heimat: illusions of, 283–84

Henderson, Mae, 148
Herzfeld, Michael, 359
Hierarchy: legitimation of, 12
Hikmet, Nazim, 230–31
Hikmet, Sürler, 247–48n
Hill, John, 312n
Hiro, Dilip, 103
Historikerstreit, 181
Hoffman, Eva, 212n
Hold Me Gently in Your Strong Arms (film),
    213n
Holland, Agnieszka, 210n
Holocaust memorial: in Germany, 190n
Holograms of Fear (Drakulić), 371
Holst-Warhaft, Gail, 361–62
Homeland: illusions of, 283–84
Honecker, Erich, 178
Honigmann, Barbara, 176, 178–79
hooks, bell, 158
Horn, Gyula, 211n
Houari, Leïla, 59n
Householder, The (Jhabvala), 87
*How We Survived Communism and Even
    Laughed* (Drakulić), 348
Howards End (Forster), 78
Hungary: anti-Semitism in, 207–8; cinema in,
    200–8, 210n (*see also* Cinema, Eastern
    European); Gypsies in, 201, 212n;
    Gypsy and Jewish women in, 20; Holo-
    caust in, 214n; Jews in, 205–6, 206–8,
    213n; multiculuralism in, 199–200; So-
    cialist Party in, 198–99; suicide in, 213n
Huston, Nancy, 67
Hutcheon, Linda, 66
Hybridity: in francophone writers, 148; in
    italophone writers, 135–36, 138

Identity: bicultural, 18–19; changing Euro-
    pean concepts of, 1; (con)figuring,
    78–99; corporate, women's questioning
    of, 17; cultural, 286, 288; of diaspora vs.
    border intellectual, 80–81; diasporic,
    125–26, 132; of East Germans, 279–83;
    French, racism and, 43; German, after
    unification, 20, 275–77 (*see also* Ger-
    many, unification of); of German immi-
    grants, 227n; home and, 105–10; Irish,
    22–23, 304–5, 309 (*see also* Irishness); in
    Königsdorf's *Ein Moment*, 287; lesbian,

98n; in migrants' literature, 220–21;
    multicultural, Viarengo on, 138; na-
    tional, 9, 13, 16–17, 41; nationalism
    and, 3; and Northern Question, 298;
    postcolonial, 17; post-Soviet, 342 (*see
    also Ona*); sexual, in Turkish literature,
    236–37; victim/executioner dichotomy
    within, 315. *See also* Subject
Identity politics: border intellectuals and,
    91–95
I Is a Long Memoried Woman (Nichols),
    112
Imagined Communities (Anderson), 82–83,
    342
Immigrant women, 15–16; Italian narratives
    of, 118–42
Immigrants: assimilation of, 9–10; attitude to-
    ward new culture, 266; autobiographies
    of, 122; class of, 132–33; demand-ori-
    ented recruitment of, 9; female (*see* Im-
    migrant women); JanMohamed's
    discussion of, 288; in Turin, Italy, 138;
    violence against, 7–8
Immigration, 1–2, 315; French use of term,
    32; laws, 7, 119; nationalism and, 6–10;
    as term that stigmatizes minority groups,
    31–32. *See also* Diaspora; Migration
Imperialism: and feminist theory and practice,
    102; U.S., 110–11
India: constructed identity of, 83; decoloniza-
    tion of, 84; Indian writing in English vs.
    Anglo-Indian writing about, 88–89; as
    pre-British federation, 83
Indian, American, 50; in Belghoul's *Georgette!*,
    56–57
Indian women, 18–19
Indian writing (in English), 84–86
Indo-British literature, 78–99
Indo-British relations, 84–86
"Intellectual Exile: Expatriates and Marginals"
    (Said), 267
Intellectuals, border. *See* Border intellectuals
Internationalism: history of, 4–5
Interviewing: hierarchical nature of, 121–22;
    reciprocal relations in, 140n
In the Ditch (Emecheta), 113
Iran: Muslim women in, 222–24, 227n
Ireland: and national identity, 22–23,
    295–314

Ireland: A Social and Cultural History (Brown), 308–9
Irish Republican Army, 295, 296
Irishness, 307, 309, 312n; inclusivity of, and Northern Question, 296. *See also* Nationalism, Irish
Irving, Katrina, 22
Isaksson, Ulla, 334
Islam: Maghrebians' and Beurs' relation to, 46; women in, 223. *See also* Muslim women
Ismay, Maureen, 106
Italians: in Ethiopia, 133–35
Italophone literature, 120, 122; Nassera Chohra, 119–33; common themes in, 125; editor intervention in, 122–24, 140n; hybridity of writers of, 135–36, 138; migration in, 125; Maria Viarengo, 132–39
Italy: colonial experience of, 118–19; immigrants in, 19, 118–20; immigration law in, 119; regionalism in, 133–34
Iveković, Rada, 370

Jacoby, Jessica, 173, 177, 188, 191n, 192n
James, Selma, 103
Jameson, Fredric, 85
Janjua, Shahida, 109
JanMohamed, Abdul, 18–19, 22, 266, 267, 268; on border intellectuals, 80–81, 91–92; on exiles vs. immigrants, 288
Jeles, Andras, 206, 213n
Jewish cinema: in Hungary, 213n
Jewish-German relations, 172
Jewish women: in Germany, 20, 171–95; identities of, 173–74, 174–75, 180; interaction with non-Jewish Germans, 182–83; Jewish law and, 175; non-German, 185–87; postwar immigration of, 174–76; women's anti-Semitism toward, 177
Jews: in Bulgaria, 254; in Eastern European cinema, 197–215; in GDR, 192n; in Germany, 172, 175–76, 187–88, 190n; in Hungary, 205–6, 206–8; Russian, in Germany, 185–86; Soviet, immigration to Germany, 175, 191–92n; in Turkey, 186–87
Jhabvala, Ruth Prawer, 18–19, 78, 80, 83, 87–89, 97n

Jin, Meiling, 109
Johansson, Ivar Lo, 328
John Paul II, 305
Johnson-Odim, Cheryl, 139n
Jonas, Regina, 177
Jordan, June, 101
Jordan, Neil, 22, 296–314. *See also Crying Game, The*
Journey to Oneself (Dimitrova), 255
Joyce, James, 307
Jude the Obscure (Hardy), 85

Kabay, Barna, 207
Kaltland (Torkan), 219, 221
Kandre, Mare, 23, 316, 331–35. *See also Bübin's Brat*
Kaplan, Caren, 124, 134
Kaplan, Marion, 177
Kaplan, Robert D., 371
Karadžić, Vuk, 360, 364
Katanian, Vasily, 350
Kathleen ni Houlihan (Yeats), 301–2, 307
Katrak, K. H., 25–26n
Kay, Jackie, 101
Keane, Patrick, 307
Kearney, Richard, 295–96, 309–10, 311–12n
Kéita, Anta Diouf, 163n
Kéita, Aoua, 146–47
Ken Bugul, 19, 143–67; significance of name, 144. *See also* M'baye, Mariétou
Kessas, Ferrudja, 33, 38–40, 52
Kezdi-Kovacs, Zsolt, 204
Khatibi, Abdelkebir, 63, 65, 68
Khouma, Pap, 125, 140n
Kipling, Rudyard, 87
Kirby, Vicky, 98n
Klüger, Ruth, 177
Kocka, Jürgen, 265
Koltai, Robert, 20, 205
Königsdorf, Helga, 22, 265, 268, 289; on turning point of 1989, 278–88. *See also 1989 oder Ein Moment Schönheit*
Konrad, Gyorgy, 197–98
Koonz, Claudia, 177
Kosovo, Battle of. *See* Battle of Kosovo
Kovas, Eva, 213n
Kür, Pinar, 236

Kristeva, Julia, 23, 25n, 289, 315–16, 321–22, 327
Kurti, Laszlo, 212n

Lamentation genre: of Balkan women, 361, 362; Serbian women's political use of, 362–63
Landor, Liliane, 101
Language: adoption of, 136–37; dialogic, in Turkish-German women's writing, 240; as mother tongue, 12
Laronde, Michel, 66
Larsen, Nella, 127
Latcho Drom (Gatlif), 200
Latinos: stigmatization of, 32
Lauder, Estée, 351
Lazy Thoughts of a Lazy Woman (Nichols), 112
Lebl, Ženi, 368
Left politics: Königsdorf's critique of, 284–85
Le Huu Khoa, 46–48
L'Enfant noir (Laye Camara), 147–48
Leo, Annette, 178, 180–81
Lesbians: Black, uprising textualities of, 112–13; identity, 98n; subject, 89–91
Let It Be Told: Black Women Writers in Britain (Ngcobo), 104–5
Lewis, Gail, 101
Life stories: of immigrants, 122
Like Water for Chocolate (Esquivel), 90
Lionnet, Françoise, 18, 148
Lipovskaia, Olga, 354
Lissyutkina, Larissa, 347, 354
Literature: national vs. transnational, 16–17; resistance, 134; third world, critical views of, 85. *See also under specific ethnic or national types*
Lives of Lovers, The (Trotzig), 334
Lloyd, David, 312n
Loraux, Nicole, 359
Lorde, Audre, 112
Lost in Translation (Hoffman), 212n
Loti, Pierre, 230–31
Love in a Roundabout Way (Dimitrova), 255–56
Love in Two Languages (Khatibi), 63
Lukhmanova, N. A., 345

Maastricht Treaty, 5–6, 10, 295, 296; Ireland after, 310

Maghrebian immigrants, 18, 32, 46
Maghrebian literature, 44–45; Leïla Sebbar, 66
Magical realism: in Özdamar's writings, 244–46
Magniér, Bernard, 144, 163n
Makal, Mahmut, 242–43
Mali: autobiographical writing from, 146–47
Malika (Bona), 60n
Maman a un amant (Beyala), 48–49
Mancon, Luigi, 141n
Mani, Lata, 25–26n
Manon Lescaut (Prévost), 63, 65, 74
"Margin at the Center: On *Testimonio*," (Beverley), 123
Marginalization, social: in Turkish-German women's writing, 239–40
Markandaya, Kamala, 18–19, 78, 80, 83, 84–86, 94, 96–97n
Marriage Game (Agaoglu), 236
Martelli Law, 7
Martinson, Harry, 328
Martinson, Moa, 334
Marxism: failures of, 340
Masculinity: nationalism and constructions of, 11
Mating (Rush), 151
Mbacké, Mame Seck, 164n
M'Baye, Mariétou, 19–20, 143–67. *See also* Ken Bugul
McClintock, Anne, 11
Media: in Eastern Europe, 198–99
Mehta, Gita, 79
"Meine Landsleute" (Hikmet), 231
Melliti, Moshen, 140n
Memmi, Albert, 85
Memoirs of a River (Elek), 207–8
Men: citizenship of, 14
Metafictional narratives: in Turkish-German women's writings, 237, 242
Methani, Salah, 119, 140n
Micheletti, P. A., 140n
Middle Easterners: stigmatization of, 32. *See also specific ethnic or national groups*
Middlemarch (Eliot), 85
Migrantenliteratur: themes of, 221; *Tufan* as, 220–25. *See also Gastarbeiterliteratur*; Torkan; Turkish-German women writers

Migration: by italophone writers, 125; since 1989, 210–11n; and sense of unbelonging, 105–10. *See also* Diaspora; Immigration

Miller, Christopher, 164n

Millett, Kate, 90

Minorities: stigmatization of, 31–32

Mirza, Heidi Safia, 103

Moberg, Vilhelm, 328

Model Childhood, A (Wolf), 269

Montagu, Ashley, 81

Montaigne, 64

Morokvasic, Mirjana, 15–16

Morrison, Toni, 66, 126

Mortimer, Mildred, 151, 164n

Mosse, George L., 11, 14

Mothers of Maya Dilip, The (Namjoshi), 90

Mouffe, Chantal, 24

Métissage, 134–35, 148

Mudimbe-Boyi, Elisabeth, 143, 151, 165n

Mud King's Daughter, The (Trotzig): theme of abjection in, 328–31

Muldoon, Paul, 307

Multiculturalism: in Germany, 219; in Hungary vs. U.S., 199–200

Muslims: violence against, 8

Muslim women, 8; in Brussels, 143–67; in Chohra's *Volvevo diventare bianca*, 119–33; in Iran, 227n; oppression of, 21; stereotyping of, 220; in Torkan's *Tufan*, 222–24; Western feminist attitudes toward, 224

Nach der Shoa geboren, 21, 173–74, 175–77

Naipaul, V. S., 65, 79

Namjoshi, Suniti, 18–19, 78–99, 89–91; as border intellectual, 94–95

Naoum, Jusuf, 218

Nathorff, Herta, 177

Nation: demotic-unitarian, 3–4; family as trope for, 12–13; as female, 11, 301–2; as rewritten by marginal members of, 264

"National Identity and Conflict in Northern Ireland" (Girvin), 298

Nationalism: and attitudes toward immigration and multiculturalism, 8–9; in Balkan area, 363; "clean" vs. "dirty," 41; coerced polyethnic, 4, 10; and concept of literature, 16–17; ethnic, 3; gender and, 11–16; history of, 2–6; identity content of, 3; immigration and, 6–10; institutions fostering, 41; Irish (*see also The Crying Game*), 301, 310; Irish Catholicism and, 298–99, 305; polyethnic, 4–5, 10; racism and, 10, 40–41; in Slovenia and Croatia, 372n; in Soviet Union, 340; during wartime, 15

Nationalist subject, 301. *See also* Identity, national

Nation without Nationalism (Kristeva), 289

Native American. *See* Indian, American

Nature of Passion, The (Jhabvala), 87

Ndao, Cheikh Aliou, 145

Ndongo, Oumar, 163n, 165n

N'Dour, Youssou, 118

Nectar in a Sieve (Markandaya), 84

Nederveen Pieterse, Jan, 7

Née en France (Benaïssa), 33–38

Neo-Nazis: German government and, 192n

1989 oder Ein Moment Schönheit (Königsdorf), 278; personal/collective identity in, 287; politics of location in, 283–84; transnational vision in, 285–86; utopia in, 279–80

New Dominion, A (Jhabvala), 87, 93

Ngcobo, Lauretta, 104–5

Ngugi Wa Thiong'o, 136

Nichols, Grace, 111–12

"No Dialects Please," 109–10

No Place on Earth (Wolf), 269

Northern Ireland: and question of identity, 298

Notes of a Lady (Forgacs), 208

"Notes towards Home," 101

Nowhere Man, The (Markandaya), 84, 92–93

O'Connor, Sinead, 305

Oesterle-Schwerin, Jutta, 182

Ona: audience for, 340; goals of, 352; leveling/egalitarianism vs. difference in, 345–49; models of femininity in, 349–52; new feminine consciousness in, 341–42; patriarchal/nationalist model in, 344–45; as reflection of late perestroika, 340; reformist thrust of, 341; utopian nostalgia in, 342–44, 348–49, 351

O'Neale, Sondra, 165n
Oppression: uprisings against, 111–14
Oral narrative traditions: in Senegal, 164n
Orientalism, 129, 230; European, 66; India
    and, 96; in Markandaya's novels, 93;
    Said's work on, 359; women and, 69–74
Orlova, Lidia, 352
Other: in psychoanalytic theory, 315; in Turk-
    ish-German women's writing, 241
Our Sister Killjoy (Aidoo), 161, 165n
Our Village (Makal), 243
"Out of the Darkness," 334
Özakin, Aysel, 218, 232, 235, 237–40
Özdamar, Emine Sevgi, 232, 237; magical re-
    alism of, 244–46

Pabst, G. W., 207
Package Tour (Gazdag), 207, 208
Paley, Grace, 275
Paramicha, or Glonci the Rememberer (Szed-
    erekenyi), 202
Parati, Graziella, 19
Parin, Paul, 277
Parmar, Pratibha, 100, 101, 102
Parry, Benita, 94
Partei Demokratischer Sozialismus (Party of
    Democratic Socialism): Königsdorf's cri-
    tique of, 284–85
Passage to India, A (Forster), 87, 94
Passerini, Luisa, 121–22
Passion: Discourses on Blackwomen's Creativity
    (Sulter), 112
*Passion of the Other*s (Özakin), 239
Patriotism: vs. nationalism, 41; and vocabulary
    of kinship, 12–13
Peck, Jeffrey, 192n
Perestroika: Russian women during, 337, 340
Petit prince de Belleville, Le (Beyala), 48
"Piyer Lot," 230
Pleasure City (Markandaya), 84, 92–93
Policing against Black People (Institute of Race
    Relations), 103
*Politics of Genocide: The Holocaust in Hungary,
    The* (Braham), 214n
Politics of location, 283–84
"Politics of the Possible, The" (Sangari), 110
Ponchelet, Sophie, 33–34
Popova, Irina, 347–48
Porter, Lawrence, 145–46

Portuges, Catherine, 20
Portuguese: in France, 32
Possession (Markandaya), 84, 92–93
Postcolonial autobiography: characteristics of,
    146–50
Post-Colonial Critic, The (Spivak), 120, 124
Postcoloniality: uprisings and, 110–12
Powers of Horror (Kristeva), 321–22
Prescod, Marsha, 103
Prévost, Abbé, 63
Pride and Prejudice (Austen), 87
Print capitalism, 2–3
Privat Magyarorszag (Private Hungary) (For-
    gacs), 208
Public and private spheres, 13–14
Pynchon, Thomas, 65

Quevedo, Nuria, 275

Race: ethical definition of, 79
Racism: as American problem, 51; in France,
    33, 43; nationalism and, 10, 40–41; psy-
    choanalytic theories of, 315
Radhakrishnan, R., 297, 301, 305
Rajan, Gita, 18
Raj Quartet, The (Scott), 87, 93
Rasputin, Valentin, 344–45
Regionalism, 133–34, 283–84
Remmler, Karen, 20
Renan, Ernest, 291n
Reproduction: by immigrant women, 16
Resistance literature, 134
Reterritorialization, 288–89
Revolt of Job, The (film), 207
Rich, Adrienne, 90, 94
Riley, Joan, 19, 105, 107
Road to Renewal, The (Hall), 110
Robbins, Bruce, 92
Rodnjanski, Alexander, 208
"Roller Coaster, The," 242
Roma, 20. *See also* Gypsies
Roman von einem Kinde (Honigmann), 178
Room with a View, A (Forster), 78
Rooney, Ellen, 89
Rosh, Lea, 190n
Rostock riots, 6
Rotten Pomerack (Collins), 109
Rozanov, Vasily, 345
Rubá'i, 231, 248n

Rush, Norman, 146, 151, 164n
Rushdie, Salman, 66, 79, 94
Ruskin, John, 350
Russia: gender and national redefinition in, 23–24
Russian women, 337–57; in Bogdanov's utopian mythology, 342–44; feminist image of, 353–54; and native and Western models of femininity, 349–52; and nature/culture argument, 346–47; patriarchal/nationalist model of, 344–45; in popular culture, 337

Saakana, Amon Saba, 102
Sacred Hoop, The (Allen), 110
Safe Journey (Gatlif), 202
Saharawi, 128
Said, Edward, 22, 80, 129, 267, 359; on displacement, 288
Saidou Moussa Ba, 140n
Saket, Lesley, 108–9
Salecl, Renata, 372–73n
SA-Life, 196
Sandor, Pal, 207
Sangari, Kumkum, 110
Sarajevo: film coverage of, 196
Sarajlija, Sima Milutinović, 370
Scafe, Suzanne, 103
Scheinhardt, Saliha, 231, 232
Schiffer, Pal, 201
Schipper, Mineke, 147
Scholz, Hannelore, 21
Schoppmann, Claudia, 173
Schwarz, Bill, 2
Scott, Paul, 87, 93
Sebbar, Leïla, 18, 44, 62–77; and deconstruction of European history, 74–75; in francophone vs. French classification, 66; Maghrebian critics of, 66–67
Second Class Citizen (Emecheta), 113
Sekulić, Isadora, 370
Self-decolonization: *The Abandoned Baobab* as narrative of, 151–57
Seligman, Adam, 25n
Sembene, Ousmane, 145
Senegal: autobiographical writing in, 144–46, 146–48; immigrants from, 19–20; oral narrative traditions in, 164n
Senegalese literature, 143. *See also* Ken Bugul

Senegalese women: in Europe, 143–67
Senkifoldje (Jeles), 206
Sense and Sensibility (Austen), 87
Serbia: peace movement strategies in, 363; women's movement in, 368
Serres, Michel, 74
Sex-Role Socialization in the USSR (Attwood), 348
Sexuality: nationalism and constructions of, 11
Seyhan, Azade, 21
Shari'ati, Ali, 222
"Sheep and the Goats, The," 109
Shérazade trilogy (Sebbar), 62–77
Silence of Desire, A (Markandaya), 84, 85
Silverman, Maxim, 18, 33, 42–43, 50, 59
Simmel, Georg, 210n
Simonides: cataloging of women by, 358–59
Sinekli Bakkal (Adivar), 235
Sinti. *See* Gypsies
Skerlić, Jovan, 370
Skinheads, 183
Slapšak, Svetlana, 24
Slobin, Greta, 23–24
Slovenia: nationalism in, 372n
Smith, Anthony D., 24–25n
Smith, Sidonie, 98n, 127
Socialism: and coerced polyethnic state, 4; democratic, 282; in Hungary, 198–99; state, collapse of, 2
Social marginalization: in Turkish-German women's writing, 239–40
Södergran, Edith, 334
Soll ich hier alt werden? (Should I grow old here?) (Özakin), 238–39
Solomon, F. A., 112
So Long a Letter (Ba), 145
Some Inner Fury (Markandaya), 84, 85
Sorrows of Young Werther (Goethe), 233
Sose Halunk Meg (Koltai), 205
Soviet literature, traditional, 348
Soviet Union: anti-Semitism in, 191n; as coerced polyethnic state, 4; Jews in, 175, 186, 191–92n; resurgence of nationalism in, 340; women in, after 1989 (*see* Ona; Russian women)
Spivak, Gayatri, 89, 110, 120–21, 124, 132
Staitscheva, Emilia, 259
Stalin, Josef: show trials of, 208

Stange, Margit, 165n
Stepunina, Svetlana, 345–49
Stern, Frank, 175
Stites, Richard, 353
Strangers and Sisters: Women, Race, and Immigration (James), 103
Strobel, Margaret, 139n
Subject: ambivalent re/unified, 283; diasporic, 80–81; lesbian, 89–91; nationalist, 301; white male, as citizen, 14. *See also* Identity
Subjective authenticity, 255
Subjectivity: and construction and deconstruction of national identity, 17; new forms of, 16–17
Suhr, Heidrun, 217, 220, 232
Suicide: in Hungary, 213n
Sulter, Maud, 112
Sweden: immigration to, 23, 315
Swedish novels, 315–36. *See also* Kandre, Mare; Trotzig, Birgitta
Switzerland: as polyethnic state, 4, 10
Szabo, Ildiko, 20, 200–1, 202–3, 211–13n
Szederekenyi, Julia, 202

Tagoe, Nana Wilson, 102
Tarasutazas (Gazdag), 207
Taufiq, Suleman, 218
Tekinay, Alev, 232, 237, 241–44
Terezin: survivors of, 214n
Testimonial narratives: as collaboration, 123–24
Tharoor, Shashi, 79
Thau, Daniela, 184–85
There Ain't No Black in the Union Jack (Gilroy), 102
Thousand and One Nights, The, 74, 230, 231
Three Cypresses (Scheinhardt), 231
Threshing Floor, The (Burford), 113
Thurow, Lester, 5
Tiszaeszlar trial, 207
Todorov, Tzvetan, 66, 267, 268
Torkan, 216–29
Toubon, Jacques, 41
To Whom She Will (Jhabvala), 87
Traits of a Contemporary Woman (Lukhmanova), 345
Transnationalism: and concept of literature, 16–17; East German experience and,

284–85; in Königsdorf's *Ein Moment*, 285–86; national interests and, 5–6
Transvestism: in *The Crying Game*, 296–97, 304–6
Travelers (Jhabvala), 87
Traversée de la mangrove (Condé), 72
Trial, The (Kafka), 207
Trotzig, Birgitta, 23, 316, 320, 333. *See also* *The Disease; The Mud King's Daughter*
Tufan: Brief an einen islamischen Bruder (Torkan), 216–29
Tunde, Carmen, 113
Turkey: Jews in, 186–87; Westernization movement in, 235
Turkish language: Arabic and, 245–46
Turkish women: German depictions of, 232; Dimitrijević's writings about, 369–70; oppression of, 231–32
Turkish-German women, 21, 232–33, 248n
Turkish-German women writers, 230–48; autobiography by, 237–38; dialogic language of, 240; feminist studies of, 231–32; metafictional narratives of, 237, 242; and theme of social marginalization, 239–40
Turks: in Bulgaria, 21–22, 259; in Federal Republic of Germany, 226n; as guest workers in Germany, 9; stigmatization of, 32
Turning point: Königsdorf's commentary on, 278–88; witness literature about, 278
Tutajosok (Elek), 207
Tu t'appelleras Tanga (Beyala), 60n
Two Virgins (Markandaya), 84, 86

Ugrešić, Dubravka, 370, 371
Unbelonging, The (Riley), 105
Understanding Popular Culture (Fiske), 353
United States: imperialism of, 110–11; multiculturalism in, 199–200; race relations in, 50
United States of Europe, 5
Uprising textualities: of Black women writing in England, 111–14; as resistance to imperialism, 110–14
Utopia: in Königsdorf's *Ein Moment*, 279–80, 285; loss of, 283; as posttotalitarian nostalgia, in *Ona*, 342–44; in Wolf's writings, 269, 289, 291n

Vajda, Julia, 213n
Vasilyeva, Larisa, 345–49
Vasilyeva, Tatyana, 350
Vassilev, Jordan, 251
Vernacular community, 3
Viarengo, Maria, 119–21, 124–25, 132–39
Vietnamese: in France, heterogeneity of, 46–47
Village literature, 243
Vinogradova, Anna, 185–86
Visions of Europe (Kearney), 309, 311–12n
Vogel, Ursula, 14
Volevo diventare bianca (Chohra), 125–26
Von der unverzüglichen Rettung der Welt (Königsdorf), 278
von Krusenstjerna, Agnes, 334

Waiting in the Twilight (Riley), 107
Wajda, Andrzey, 207
Waldheim affair, 183
Wallenberg, Raoul, 208
Wallraff, Günter, 218
War: nationalism during, 15
Wark, McKenzie, 269–70
"Warum dieses Schweigen?" (Leo), 181
Was bleibt (What remains) (Wolf), 258
Watson, Julia, 20, 273
Weinrich, Harald, 217
Weissberg-Bob, Nea, 183
We'll Never Die (Koltai), 205
Wende. See Turning point
Wendt, Gila, 187
West Germany. See Federal Republic of Germany
Why Wasn't He There? (film), 206
Wilke, Sabine, 279
Williams, Claudette, 107–8
Williams, Raymond, 348
"Will You," 109
Wilson, Amrit, 103
Winship, Janice, 352
Witt-Brattström, Ebba, 23
Wolf, Christa, 22, 249, 255, 258, 265, 267, 268–78, 289; Stasi association of, 290n; utopia in writings of, 291n; works of, 290n. See also Auf dem Weg nach Tabou

Wolof culture, 143–45, 164n
Women: immigrant, 15–16; in Orientalist discourse, 69–74; Simonides' cataloging of, 358–59; in struggles of national liberation, 25n; work of, 14. See also Muslim women; Yugoslav area, inventing women in
Woodhull, Winifred, 18, 148
Woolf, Virginia, 267
"Worldliness-without-World, Homelessness-as-Home" (JanMohamed), 80
World Romany Congress, 201
Wren, The (Güntekin), 233–35
Wuthering Heights (Brontë), 85

Xenophobia, 7–8, 190n; psychoanalytic theories of, 315

Yeats, William Butler, 301–2, 307
Yelin, Louise, 267
Yeo, Eileen, 289
Yeo, Stephen, 289
Young, James, 171
Young, Female, and Black (Mirza), 103
Yugoslav area: dissident testimonials in, 367–68; egalitarian Communist ideology in, 360–61; inventing women in, 358–73; male-dominated society in, 358; social divisions in, gender dimension of, 368–69; after Tito's death, 368; values of epic heroic poetry vs. "women's poetry" in, 364, 366. See also Balkan area
Yugoslavia: as coerced polyethnic state, 4; discourses of gender in, 24
Yugoslav literature: women's vs. men's, 370–71
Yugoslav women; as collective other, 359; oral poetry by, 360

Zahno, Kamila, 108
Zanussi, Krzystof, 207
Zeida de nulle part (Houari), 59n
Zeitlin, Froma, 359
Zena-Henry, Wendy, 173
Zhelev, Zhelyu, 249
"Zweierlei Befreiung" (Baader), 182